Rethinking Architecture

Rethinking Architecture brings together for the first time the principal writings on architecture by many of the key philosophers and cultural theorists of the twentieth century.

These essays contain some of the most insightful observations on contemporary architecture, and offer refreshingly original perspectives on the subject. Together they constitute a body of material which prompts the rethinking of many accepted tenets of architectural theory from a broader cultural perspective.

The editor, Neil Leach, has grouped writings covering common themes and approaches into well-defined sections, and has written helpful introductions for each section and for each author.

Neil Leach is director of the MA in Architecture and Critical Theory at the University of Nottingham.

Rethinking Architecture

A reader in cultural theory

Edited by Neil Leach

London and New York

First published 1997
by Routledge
11 New Fetter Lane, London EC4P 4EE

Simultaneously published in the USA and Canada
by Routledge
29 West 35th Street, New York, NY 10001

Reprinted 1997

Typeset in Sabon by Solidus (Bristol) Limited
Printed and bound in Great Britain by T.J.
International Ltd, Padstow, Cornwall

British Library Cataloguing in Publication Data
A catalogue record for this book is available from
the British Library

*Library of Congress Cataloging in Publication
Data*
Leach, Neil,
  Rethinking architecture: a reader in cultural
theory/Neil Leach.
  Includes bibliographical reference and index.
  1. Architecture – Philosophy.   I. Title.
NA2500.L47   1996
721 '.1–dc20   96–19406

ISBN 0–415–12826–9

CONTENTS

PREFACE

The discipline of architecture has gone through something of a metamorphosis in recent years. There is evidence of a clear shift both in the nature of debates within architecture and in its relationship with other academic disciplines. Not only are architects and architectural theorists becoming more and more receptive to the whole domain of cultural theory, but cultural theorists, philosophers, sociologists and many others are now to be found increasingly engaged with questions of architecture and the built environment. This volume was born of a desire to support this development, and to reinforce these links. It attempts to situate architecture within a broader cultural context, and to consider not only how debates from cultural theory, philosophy and so on might begin to inform a discussion about architecture, but also how architecture and the built environment might offer a potentially rich field for analysis for cultural studies and other disciplines.

This volume was spawned largely by the MA in Architecture and Critical Theory at the University of Nottingham, a course that was set up initially to fill what was perceived as being a gap in standard architectural education, but which has since attracted students from many other disciplines. Much of the material contained in this volume was uncovered during preparation for seminars and lectures on the course, and already existed as a collection of unbound, well-thumbed photocopies long before the book was conceived. I am grateful to all those who have contributed to the MA, both to those who have taught on the course and to those who supported its establishment, especially Peter Fawcett and Bernard McGuirk. Likewise I am grateful to the remarkable group of students who have been on the course. Their enthusiasm and spirit of enquiry have been a constant source of inspiration and delight, and many of the questions that they have raised have fed into this volume.

I would like to record a vote of thanks to all those who have offered help and often indispensable advice in the actual preparation of *Rethinking Architecture*. In particular, I am indebted to Andrew Ballantyne, Geoffrey Bennington, Andrew Bowie, Peter Carl, Sarah Chaplin, Matt Connell, Neal Curtis, David Frisby, Graeme Gilloch,

Jonathan Hale, Vaughan Hart, Nick Heffernen, Paul Hegarty, Eric Holding, Bill Hutson, Susan Marks, Giles Peaker, Doina Petrescu, Jane Rendell, Ioana Sandi, Ingrid Scheibler, Adam Sharman, Yvonne Sherratt, Jon Simons, Simon Tormey and Christina Ujma.

I am also grateful for the advice and assistance of the authors themselves, especially Andrew Benjamin, Hélène Cixous, Jacques Derrida, Jürgen Habermas and Fredric Jameson, and to all those who have given permission to reprint the articles.

I must also thank Tristan Palmer for his insight and enthusiasm in setting up this project, and Sarah Lloyd, Michael Leiser and Diana Wallwork at Routledge for their support in seeing it through to completion.

Finally, I must express my indebtedness to Dalibor Vesely and Joseph Rykwert. I was privileged to have been taught by them whilst a student at the University of Cambridge, and it was their charismatic and influential teaching which was the ultimate source of inspiration for this volume.

Neil Leach
Nottingham, 1996

ACKNOWLEDGMENTS

The editor and publishers gratefully acknowledge the following for permission to reproduce material in this book:

Academy Editions: Gianni Vattimo, 'The End of Modernity, The End of The Project?', trans. David Webb.

Anyone Corporation: Fredric Jameson, 'Is Space Political?', in Cynthia Davidson (ed.), *Anyplace*.

Architectural Association and Bernard Tschumi: Jacques Derrida, 'Point de Folie – maintenant l'architecture', trans. Kate Linker.

Blackwell Publishers: Henri Lefebvre, *The Production of Space* (extracts), trans. David Nicholson-Smith; Gianni Vattimo, 'Ornament/Monument,' *The End of Modernity*, trans. Jon Snyder (UK and Commonwealth English language rights). Jean-François Lyotard, '*Domus* and the Megalopolis', *The Inhuman*, trans. Geoffrey Bennington and Rachel Bowlby (UK and Commonwealth English language rights).

Hélène Cixous: Hélène Cixous, 'Attacks of the Castle', trans. Eric Prenowitz.

Columbia University Press: Fredric Jameson, 'The Constraints of Postmodernism' (extract), *The Seeds of Time*; Gilles Deleuze, 'Postscript on the Societies of Control'.

Jacques Derrida: Jacques Derrida, 'Architecture Where the Desire May Live', interview with Eva Meyer.

Duke University Press: Fredric Jameson, 'The Cultural Logic of Late Capitalism' (extracts), *Postmodernism, or the Cultural Logic of Late Capitalism*.

Farrar, Straus and Giroux: Roland Barthes, 'The Eiffel Tower,' *The Eiffel Tower and Other Mythologies*, trans. Richard Howard.

David Frisby: Siegfried Kracauer, 'On Employment Exchanges: The Construction of a Space', trans. David Frisby.

Jürgen Habermas: Jürgen Habermas, 'Modern and Postmodern Architecture', trans. Helen Tsoskounglou.

Harcourt, Brace & Company: Walter Benjamin, 'Paris, Capital of the Nineteenth Century', *Reflections*, trans. Edmund Jephcott; 'On Some Motifs in Baudelaire', *Illuminations*, trans. Harry Zohn (this work is to be included in the forthcoming collected works of Walter Benjamin to be published by Harvard University Press); Umberto Eco, 'How an Exposition Exposes Itself', *Travels in Hyperreality*, trans. William Weaver.

Harper Collins Publishers: Martin Heidegger, 'Building, Dwelling, Thinking', '. . . Poetically Man Dwells . . .', 'The Origin of the Work of Art' (extracts), *Poetry, Language, Thought*, trans. Albert Hofstadter.

Harvard University Press: Siegfried Kracauer, 'The Hotel Lobby' (extract), *Mass Ornament*, trans. Thomas Levin.

Paul Hegarty: Georges Bataille, 'Architecture', 'Slaughterhouse', 'Museum', trans. Paul Hegarty.

Johns Hopkins University Press: Gianni Vattimo, 'Ornament/Monument,' *The End of Modernity*, trans. Jon Snyder (American rights); Michel Foucault, 'Space, Knowledge, Power', interview with Paul Rabinow, trans. Christian Hubert.

Institute of Architecture and Urban Studies: Theodor Adorno, 'Functionalism Today', trans. Jane Newman and John Smith; Ernst Bloch, 'Formative Education, Engineering Form, Ornament', trans. Jane Newman and John Smith; Michel Foucault, 'Other Spaces: The Principles of Heterotopia'.

Kluwer Academic Publishers: Martin Heidegger, 'Art and Space', trans. Charles Siebert.

Penguin Books, UK: Michel Foucault, 'Panopticism' (extract), *Discipline and Punish*, trans. Alan Sheridan.

Penguin Books, USA: Gaston Bachelard, *Poetics of Space* (extract), trans. Maria Jolas.

Routledge: Andrew Benjamin, 'Eisenman and the Housing of Tradition', *Art, Mimesis and the Avant-Garde*.

Sage Publications: Georg Simmel, 'Bridge and Door', trans. Mark Ritter.

Semiotext(e): Paul Virilio, 'The Overexposed City', *Lost Dimension*, trans. Daniel Moshenberg.

Sheed and Ward: Hans-Georg Gadamer, 'The Ontological Foundation of the Occasional and the Decorative', *Truth and Method*.

Suhrkamp Verlag: Siegfried Kracauer, 'Über Arbeitsnachsweise'.

University of Chicago Press: Georg Simmel, 'The Metropolis and Mental Life', trans. Edward Shils.

University of Michigan Press: Jean Baudrillard, *Simulacra and Simulations*, (extracts), trans. Sheila Faria Glaser.

University of Minnesota Press: Gilles Deleuze, 'City/State' (with Félix Guattari), trans. Brian Massumi.

Verso: Jean Baudrillard, *America* (extracts), trans. Chris Turner.

9H Publications: Jürgen Habermas, 'Modern and Post-Modern Architecture', trans. Helen Tsoskounglou.

Considerable effort has been made to trace and contact copyright holders and to secure replies prior to publication. However, this has not always been possible. The editor and publishers apologize for any errors and omissions. If notified, the publisher will endeavour to correct these at the earliest opportunity.

INTRODUCTION

This volume brings together for the first time a series of well-known essays on architecture by key thinkers of the twentieth century supported by a number of hitherto lesser known pieces, some of which have not previously appeared in English. In so doing the volume attempts to show that there is a consistent body of critical thought on architecture that exists outside of mainstream architectural discourse; such a body, it is argued, offers an effective means of rethinking architectural theory.

It is perhaps no coincidence that this volume appears at the end of the twentieth century, a period that seems to be marked by a moment of recuperation. Whereas the twentieth century began on a note of optimism with visions of a futuristic utopia, it ends on a note of reflection. Whereas it opened with slogans such as 'Towards a New Architecture', it closes with a 'rethinking' of architecture. This is in line with a general tendency that Fredric Jameson has detected within culture at large which he has described as an 'inverted millenarianism'.[1] Premonitions of the future, typical of traditional millenarianism, have been replaced by analysis of the past, and by reflection, in particular, on the collapse of various concepts on which contemporary society has been grounded. In this 'inverted millenarianism' attention is directed not forwards, but backwards. It is as though the very foundations of contemporary culture have themselves been undermined. Culture is going through a crisis – 'a crisis', as Jürgen Habermas describes it, 'of legitimation' – a crisis that might loosely be termed 'postmodernity'.

This situation is particularly evident in architecture. One of the themes that has dominated recent discussion about architecture at the end of the twentieth century and that informs many of the essays in this collection is the collapse of confidence in the Modern Movement. Modernism has been called into question. The 'soulless container architecture' of much contemporary construction is universally despised, yet not all would agree as to what should be the alternative. Habermas detects two broad strains that appear as polar opposites but that share a common platform in their opposition to modernism as it has evolved. On the one hand, as Habermas notes, there are those who champion a historical revivalism, a Neo-Historicism, which claims to reject outright all tenets of modernism; similarly there are those who espouse a postmodern stage-set architecture, which likewise rejects modernism while nonetheless remaining within its orbit. On the other hand, there are those who seek to rework and reinvigorate the Modern Movement, and who would support a critical continuation of modernism. Hal Foster has described the two radically different strains of this curious alliance as a 'postmodernism of reaction' and a 'postmodernism of resistance'.[2] The former, according to Foster, 'repudiates' modernism and seeks refuge in the forms of the past. The latter remains committed to the project of modernism and seeks to rework it through a process of critical re-evaluation.

Within the realm of music, Theodor Adorno has noted, 'Logically, the ageing of modern music should not drive composers back to obsolete forms, but should lead them to an insistent self-criticism.'[3] These sentiments could easily be readdressed to the context of architecture. As such they would reflect the premise of this volume. The ageing of modern *architecture*, one might argue, should not drive *architects* back to the escapism of 'obsolete forms', but should lead them instead to an 'insistent self-criticism'. In other words, a critical reappraisal might show architecture a way forward. Yet such a suggestion immediately raises two fundamental questions. How might architecture enact this 'insistent self-criticism'? How might architecture acquire the tools to perform this self-criticism?

Clearly this self-criticism must come from the domain of theory, since theory, as Gilles Deleuze has observed, 'is exactly like a box of tools'.[4] Yet, arguably, architectural theory has been deficient in the very tools of self-criticism. As the contents of this volume reveal, once caught in the full glare of external critique, architectural theory is exposed for all its shortcomings. These external critiques employ precisely the tools that architecture itself needs. By testing itself against a broader cultural debate, architecture might hope to acquire these tools of self-criticism. By engaging with the theoretical debates traditionally perceived as being 'outside' its domain, architecture might therefore become more rigorous in its own self-criticism.

For architecture to open up to impulses from other disciplines need not be thought of as an indulgence. On the contrary, the indulgence may lie in architecture's failure in the past to engage substantively with other disciplines. Architecture is not the autonomous art it is often held out to be. Buildings are designed and constructed within a complex web of social and political concerns. To ignore the conditions under which architecture is practised is to fail to understand the full social import of architecture. Furthermore, only an extreme positivist would claim that our reception of the built environment is not mediated by consciousness. The refusal to address the ways in which this mediation takes place is a refusal to address the full question of architecture.

Traditionally, architectural discourse has been largely a discourse of form. In general it has been dominated by debates that revolve around questions of style. These debates have tended to be grounded on little more than moralistic arguments that seek their authority in terms such as 'sincerity' and 'appropriateness'. Such debates have been trapped within the realm of symptoms. Invariably they have failed to probe any further, and to investigate the underlying causes. Architectural discourse, in other words, has operated largely at a superficial level. The extracts selected here, however, seek to transcend the limitations of such an approach. They offer a variety of depth models that explore the way in which architecture might be perceived, and that attempt to expose the forces by which the built environment is generated. Architectural form can be seen to be the result of deeper concerns, as Siegfried Kracauer acknowledges:

> Spatial images are the dreams of society. Wherever the hieroglyphics of any
> spatial image are deciphered, there the basis of social reality presents itself.[5]

Architecture is the product of a way of thinking. If the problems of architecture are to be traced to their roots, then attention needs to be focused on the thinking and considerations that inform its production. Material included in this volume has been selected to address these questions. The contents have been divided into five sections – *Modernism*; *Phenomenology*; *Structuralism*; *Postmodernism*; and *Poststructuralism*. Although these categories do not cover all the key movements in twentieth-century Western critical thought – indeed some areas such as feminism remain sadly underrepresented – they have been adopted as a convenient means of dividing up the available material.

Each section addresses the question of architecture from a different perspective. The extracts included under modernism, for example, deal largely with the problems of the sudden onslaught of modernisation. Architecture reflects the social conditions of the new age. There is at the core of contemporary existence a transcendental homelessness which Kracauer evokes so lucidly in his description of the hotel lobby, the quintessential space of modernity. These new conditions have engendered a new response in the modern blasé individual of Georg Simmel's metropolis, or the *flâneur* of Walter Benjamin's arcades. The response to this new condition can be understood in psychoanalytic terms, whereby consciousness acts as a buffer against the continual shocks that constitute the experience of modernity.

The extracts included under phenomenology, meanwhile, address humankind's situatedness in the world, and focus on the depthlessness of modern existence. Phenomenology offers a model to probe below the surface and to enquire about the fundamental basis of the human condition. It is precisely by exposing the impoverished mechanisms by which space has been perceived traditionally that the extracts point the way forward to an approach that seeks to transcend these limitations. Space is never empty space, but, as Foucault observes, it is always 'saturated with qualities.'[6] Nor is the eye of the architect, as Lefebvre reminds us, ever innocent.[7] The world of blueprints remains a reduced, abstracted world. Once the full ontological potential of space is understood, architects might begin to incorporate such considerations into their design processes.

Structuralism, through the study of semiology, offers a further model for understanding architecture. The semiological approach addresses how architecture can be read semantically. In so doing it opens up a domain often either not fully appreciated by architects, or overlooked entirely. Indeed architects have tended to stress the functional aspects of architecture to the detriment of any semantic dimension. Yet, as Barthes observes, humankind has the capacity to attach meaning to even the most technological of artefacts.

The question of how architecture might be understood semantically is further elaborated by the poststructuralist contributions. Here the emphasis shifts increasingly away from a discussion of form towards one of content. Indeed in the work of Michel Foucault, Gilles Deleuze and Paul Virilio, the authority of architectural form is called into question. Their work serves as a necessary corrective to the often inflated claims ascribed to architectural form by architects themselves. The primacy of the physical can be seen to be eroded by new ways of thinking that are themselves engendered by advances in technology and tools of representation.

Likewise on the question of postmodernism, the premise of the articles selected is that, far from being a question of mere architectural style, postmodernism is necessarily related to the conditions of late capitalism. Thus Fredric Jameson attempts to go beyond a descriptive understanding of architecture that pigeon-holes it according to stylistic categories, to analyse the conditions that have given rise to it. Architectural forms can be seen to constitute the epiphenomena of broader underlying social forces. An understanding of the conditions under which these forms have been generated lifts the debate beyond the level of a discussion of symptoms. In so doing it exposes the shortcomings of Jencks's appropriation of the term 'postmodernism' to refer in the main to a select group of often commercial office buildings characterized by the use of historicist motifs.

The extracts selected for this volume therefore open up the possibilities of how architecture might be understood beyond the narrow focus of traditional architectural discourse. They present a range of methodologies – a set of tools – for addressing the question of architecture and for understanding it within a broader cultural context. Although some of the material is well known within architectural circles, and has been absorbed into mainstream architectural education, much of the material will be new to an architectural audience. By introducing this material to an architectural domain, the nature of that domain will have been altered.

The essays have all been written by thinkers from 'outside' architecture. With the exception of Kracauer, none of the contributors has undertaken any recognized training in architecture, and even Kracauer had abandoned the profession by the time he wrote the essays included here. At first sight this may seem an impediment. The absence of any background training, it could be argued, would automatically prevent any useful contribution to the discourse of architectural theory. The content of these essays, however, provides sufficient evidence to suggest otherwise. Indeed, as Theodor Adorno observes, a certain professional distance might be precisely what is required in order to maintain the necessary critical distance.

> It seems to me, however, not unrealistic that at times – in latent crisis situations – it may help to remove oneself farther from phenomena than the spirit of technical competence would usually allow. The principle of 'fittingness to the material' rests on the foundation of the division of labour. Nevertheless, it is advisable even for experts to occasionally take into account the extent to which their expertise may suffer from just that division of labour, as the artistic naïvité underlying it can impose its own limitations.[8]

Thus a certain tension is allowed to develop between a way of thinking that belongs specifically to the world of architects and one that is generated 'outside' that world.

The essays in this volume therefore stand in opposition to the mainstream body of accepted architectural theory. Indeed, on occasions they offer a direct critique of specific works of architectural theory. For example, Theodor Adorno's essay, 'Functionalism today', can profitably be set against Adolf Loos's seminal piece, 'Ornament and crime', while the section included from Fredric Jameson's *Seeds of Time*, 'The Constraints of Postmodernism', is a direct response to Kenneth Frampton's equally seminal essay, 'Towards a critical regionalism'.[9] The reason for including pieces critical of such canonical works of architectural theory is not to undermine their authority, but rather to reinforce their lines of thought by exposing the weaknesses in their argument. The essays contained in this volume offer a number of strategies for *rethinking* architectural theory, strategies whose aims are broadly in line with Jacques Derrida's own project:

> To go after [architecture]: not in order to attack, destroy or deroute it, to criticise or disqualify it. Rather, in order to *think* it in fact, to detach itself sufficiently to apprehend it in a thought which goes beyond the theorem – and becomes a work in its turn.[10]

The authors of these essays are all key thinkers who have made substantial contributions to twentieth-century Western thought. Yet they come from a range of backgrounds. While many have worked within the specific discipline of philosophy, others have less clearly defined affiliations. Often inter-disciplinary in their approach, they demonstrate the value of transgressing 'professional' boundaries in their approach to architecture no less than to other disciplines. Such transgressions remain potentially problematic, a point that Derrida acknowledges. On the one hand, Derrida supports the need to 'contaminate' architecture, 'to put architecture in communication with other media, other arts'.[11] On the other hand, he is very suspicious of the 'over-easy mixing of discourses'. It is necessary to acknowledge 'multiplicity' and 'heterogeneity' – the 'specificity of discourses' – in order to avoid a general homogenization.[12] One must remain alert, as Derrida advises, to the special conditions of architecture, the 'consistency' of architecture, 'the duration, hardness, the monumental, mineral or ligneous subsistence, the hyletics of tradition'.[13] The materiality on which architecture is founded cannot be ignored.

At the same time it could be argued that the processes of universalization and differentiation are dialectically related, and that the one anticipates the other in a mechanism of reciprocal presupposition. In other words, the very immersion of architecture in the seemingly homogenizing morass of inter-disciplinarity is precisely what guarantees and augments its own individuality. Far from denying the specificity of architecture, it actually promotes it.

Transgression remains an important characteristic of the works included in this volume. The works are *necessarily* transgressive, in that they have been written by authors whose disciplines – according to the traditional view – lie 'outside' architecture. This is not to say, however, that the limits or boundaries of architecture are to be ignored, and that any sense of specificity or difference is to be erased. Transgression does not deny the principle of limit. Indeed transgression can be defined only in relation to a limit, and likewise a limit is not a limit unless it can be transgressed. As Foucault observes:

> The limit and transgression depend on each other for whatever density of being they possess: a limit could not exist if it were absolutely uncrossable and, reciprocally, transgression would be pointless if it merely crossed a limit composed of illusions and shadows.[14]

According to Foucault, transgression is precisely that which exposes the limit as limit. The moment of transgression is that which illuminates the limit in a lightning-like flash.

> Transgression is an action which involves the limit, that narrow zone of a line where it displays the flash of its passage, but perhaps also its entire trajectory, even its origin.[15]

Likewise, transgression does not deny specificity or difference. Rather it highlights and celebrates it. It reveals the difference between what is before and beyond the limit. Yet transgression does establish the principle that the limit may be transgressed, and challenges the condition of openness and exclusion.

Transgression, then, can help to expose how architecture could be otherwise. Indeed, if this volume is to have the impact intended, the understanding of architecture as a hermetic self-contained discourse will have been revised. Not only must traditional thinking about architecture be radically rethought, but the very boundaries by which it has been 'delimited' as a separate area of endeavour must themselves be redefined.

The question of tradition lies at the heart of this problem. The premise of this volume is that in order for architecture to rethink itself it must not be constrained by the limitations of tradition. To accept uncritically what has been handed down would be to subscribe in Andrew Benjamin's terms to 'the recuperative and nihilistic unfolding of tradition.'[16] Even the attempt to recuperate is misguided if, as Foucault comments, there can be no 'return'.[17] Yet equally, to follow Andrew Benjamin's argument, an absolute break with tradition is impossible, in that the break must be defined against tradition, thereby maintaining a relationship with tradition. If it is impossible to escape tradition entirely, we might understand rethinking as a form of reworking, which refuses to be limited by tradition. This reworking addresses not just the practices and thinking that have been sanctioned by tradition, but also the definitions that have been inherited. The very identity of architecture has to be readdressed so that what rethinking entails is a 'refusal to take over the answer to the question of identity'.[18]

This refusal to be limited by tradition – this insistence that the identity of architecture must be called into question – necessarily implies that the very notion of definition must be interrogated. In other words, the nature of the boundary that defines architecture needs to be reconsidered, and the relationship between what is 'inside' and 'outside' needs to be readdressed. Terms such as 'inside' and 'outside' imply a strong demarcation between self and other. Traditionally, architecture's relationship to other disciplines has been premised on a marked sense of alterity and exclusivity. Architecture has been given clearly defined boundaries. Architecture, for example, is architecture because it is not painting or sculpture. The nature of these boundaries therefore needs to be interrogated in a way that does not deny the specificity of the discipline of architecture, but rather in a way that attempts to redefine its relationship to other disciplines. What this volume seeks is a new understanding of boundary, based not on exclusivity or opposition, but on an openness to other disciplines. By revising the very concept of boundary, architecture's own position – its defensiveness against outside discourses – will be renegotiated. Architecture will be opened up to the potentially fruitful and provocative methodologies that other 'disciplines' have already embraced.

Franz Kafka tells a tale about a door in his well-known short story, 'Before the Law'. It is a parable about access and denial in the context of the law.

> Before the law stands a doorkeeper. To this doorkeeper there comes a man from the country and prays for admittance to the law. But the doorkeeper says that he cannot grant admittance at the moment.[19]

Years pass and the man still waits, growing old and increasingly blind. As he is approaching death, the man eventually asks the doorkeeper a question he has yet to ask. Why has no one else attempted to gain admittance through the door? The doorkeeper answers, 'No one else could ever be admitted here, since this gate was made only for you. I am now going to shut it.'[20]

The parable of the door before the law has provoked numerous interpretations. Hélène Cixous, for example, presents it as an allegory for female exclusion under patriarchy.[21] The man remains convinced of his own exclusion, even though the door has been left open only for him, just as women have remained convinced of their own exclusion under the law of patriarchy. Exclusion, then, may merely be a question of *perceived* exclusion. This allegory may be reread within the context of the demarcation of architecture. The door is the door to the other. Architecture has likewise remained convinced of its own exclusion from other discourses. Architecture has not dared to cross the threshold of the door, even though that door has remained open.

In a further story, 'The Great Wall of China', Kafka tells the tale of a wall.[22] It is a wall that is built on mythical foundations. Not only is its effectiveness as a wall debatable, in that – amongst other considerations – it is rumoured to have gaps, but its very justification could also be called into question. The wall is justified as protection against the 'other', in this case the supposedly barbarian hordes to the north, who are depicted in popular imagery as savages 'with great pointed teeth'. In fact the peoples to the south have no real understanding of those to the north. Furthermore, if these supposed savages had been intent on invasion, the vast distance separating the two peoples would have been defence in itself. The wall, then, in Kafka's terms, is a wall built on suspicion, whose role, while purportedly being to keep out the 'other', is in fact to bond those 'protected' by it, and to fan allegiance to the emperor. Indeed the very building of the wall unites the people into 'a ring of brothers, a current of blood no longer confined within the narrow circulation of one body, but sweetly rolling and yet ever returning throughout the endless leagues of China'.[23]

The wall, then, may act as a physical manifestation of a social order, serving to reinforce that condition. The wall may lend a sense of identity to what is enclosed within its boundaries, while engendering a sense of alterity towards what is outside. The wall creates a sense of exclusion that is both social and physical. While Kafka's tale of the door might be taken as a parable about perceived *exclusion*, his tale about the wall might be taken as one about perceived *alterity*.

The door, by breaching the wall, and by opening up to the 'other', can expose the wall for what it is, and reveal the underlying social constructs on which it is founded. The act of breaching is in effect the moment of transgression. The opening of the door reveals the wall as wall, just as, in illuminating the limit, transgression exposes the limit as limit. The door, therefore, serves as the key for understanding the whole question of limit and transgression, of openness and exclusion.

The theme of openness and exclusion is pursued in several essays in this volume. Georg Simmel uses the bridge and the door in his discussion of these two conceptual categories. 'The bridge', he observes, 'indicates how humankind unifies the separatedness of merely natural being, and the door how it separates the uniform, continuous unity of natural being.'[24] Of the two, according to Simmel, the door has 'the richer and livelier significance'. Not only does it not dictate direction and movement, but it 'represents in a more decisive manner how separating and connecting are only two sides of precisely the same act'. Moreover, the door through its very form, 'transcends the separation between the inner and the outer'. The door becomes emblematic of a more flexible attitude towards the boundary. It allows for a 'permanent interchange between the bounded and the boundaryless'. The door does not deny the concept of boundary. Indeed it is precisely part of that boundary. Rather it exposes how that boundary might be treated as potentially more permeable. Andrew Benjamin likewise evokes the emblem of the door in arguing against the foreclosure of function, teleology or the aesthetics of form. 'Works with open doors,' he concludes, 'must be what is henceforth demanded by philosophy and architecture.'[25]

The door as architectural member becomes a tool of conceptual thought that must itself be returned to architecture. Architecture has long inhabited philosophy as metaphor, as we are informed by Jacques Derrida and Andrew Benjamin. In returning to architecture such a metaphor, architecture is reminded of its own metaphoricity, of its very dependence on the realm of the conceptual. Philosophy inhabits architecture, no less than architecture inhabits philosophy.

Such then is the project of this volume. It is a project that builds upon its own erasure. Once the very conditions under which architecture has situated itself in relation to its 'outside', once the question of not only what is 'outside' but also the very nature of exclusion has been recast, and once it has been shown that architecture could be otherwise, this work will have cancelled itself out. The question of what is relevant to architecture will have been reconsidered, and the very definition of architecture will have been revised. Architecture will have been rethought.

NOTES

1   Fredric Jameson, 'The Cultural Logic of Late Capitalism', p. 238.
2   Hal Foster, preface to Hal Foster (ed.), *Postmodern Culture*, London and Concord, Mass.: Pluto Press, 1985, pp. ix–x.
3   Adorno, 'Reconciliation Under Duress' in *Aesthetics and Politics*, London and New York: Verso, 1980, p. 167.
4   Gilles Deleuze and Michel Foucault, 'Intellectuals and Power' in Donald Bouchard (ed.), *Language, Counter-Memory, Practice*, Donald Bouchard and Sherry Simon (trans.), Ithaca, New York: Cornell University Press, 1977, p. 206.
5   Siegfried Kracauer, 'On Employment Agencies: The Construction of a Space', p. 60.
6   Michel Foucault, 'Of Other Spaces: Utopias and Heterotopias', p. 349.
7   Henri Lefebvre, p. 143.

8 Adorno, 'Functionalism Today', p. 6.
9 Kenneth Frampton, 'Towards a Critical Regionalism: Six Points for an Architecture of Resistance' in Hal Foster (ed.), *Postmodern Culture*, London and Concord, Mass.: Pluto Press, 1985, pp. 16–30.
10 Jacques Derrida, 'Point de Folie', p. 326.
11 Jacques Derrida in discussion with Christopher Norris, *Deconstruction Omnibus*, A. Papadakis, C. Cooke, A. Benjamin (eds), London: Academy Editions, 1988, p. 72.
12 Ibid., p. 75.
13 Derrida, 'Point de Folie', p. 326.
14 Michel Foucault, 'Preface to Transgression' in Donald Bouchard (ed.), *Language, Counter-Memory, Practice*, Donald Bouchard and Sherry Simon (trans.), Ithaca, New York: Cornell University Press, 1977, p. 34.
15 Foucault, 'Preface to Transgression', pp. 33–4.
16 Andrew Benjamin, 'Eisenman and the Housing of Tradition', p. 298.
17 Michel Foucault, p. 372.
18 Andrew Benjamin, p. 290.
19 Franz Kafka, *The Penguin Complete Stories of Franz Kafka*, Nahum N. Glatzer (ed.), London: Penguin, 1983, p. 3.
20 Ibid., p. 4.
21 On this see Morag Schiach, *Hélène Cixous: A Politics of Writing*, London: Routledge, 1991, p. 11.
22 Kafka op. cit., pp. 235–48.
23 Kafka op. cit., p. 238.
24 Simmel, 'Bridge and Door', p. 69.
25 Andrew Benjamin, 'Eisenman and the Housing of Tradition', p. 298.

PART I

MODERNISM

MODERNISM

Modernism is the aesthetic practice of modernity, a period which is almost impossible to define. For some modernity began with Descartes, and can therefore be identified with the Enlightenment. For others it owes its origins to Charles Baudelaire and Gustave Flaubert, and the bloody suppression of the revolutions of 1848. For others still modernity is an essentially twentieth-century condition. Likewise, modernism itself resists easy definition. Indeed the provisionality of modernism, its fragmentary nature and constant search for progress and new forms, would seem to preclude any totalizing definition. Whatever its precise definition, 'modernism' has been adopted here as a term of convenience to group together the work of certain thinkers who have a broadly modernist outlook, and who focus on the social problems and the aesthetic practices of modernity. Many of the extracts are underpinned by a Marxist understanding of aesthetics as the embodiment of underlying social and political forces. Yet they go beyond a traditional Marxist view to see aesthetics as having an important cultural role.

The extracts were written in the early part of the twentieth century, a period of great social change, exposed to the sudden onslaught of modernization. A central theme that emerges is the shock of the new. The writings mark a moment of reflection in the very face of this shock. They capture with an astonishing lucidity the very essence of modernity. Georg Simmel's essay, 'The Metropolis and Mental Life', offers a penetrating insight into the modernist metropolis. The 'intensification of emotional life' resulting from the overstimulation of the senses produces the blasé individual who, like the *flâneur* of Benjamin's arcades, can be seen as both the product of and a resistance against the modernist condition. Kracauer's 'Hotel Lobby', like Edward Hopper's hauntingly vacant interiors, evokes the transcendental homelessness of contemporary existence. Modernity can be seen to be two-edged, and these writings serve as a necessary check to the utopianism of much of modernist culture, not least in architectural discourse.

It is towards the potential impoverishment of the Modern Movement in architecture that Adorno turns his attention. Indeed his essay, a powerful critique of Adolf Loos's architectural writings, exposes the paradoxes at the very heart of the modernist project. Architecture in its commitment to functionalism – a functionalism that is ultimately little more than a style – must not overlook its social 'function'. In a similar manner, Ernst Bloch notes the impoverishment of the 'railway-station character' of a culture whose architecture has lost the caresses of the muse. He calls instead for an architecture with wings, an architecture that might offer a glimpse of some utopian world of the future.

At first sight Georges Bataille's writings sit uncomfortably in this category. Often he has been categorized ahead of his time as a poststructuralist. Yet in his critique of modernity, Bataille has much in common with other theorists included here. From this point of view the essays can be seen as a form of postmodernism *avant la lettre*. Indeed we might even go so far as to suggest that postmodernism already existed within modernism as a critical strain of resistance. Modernism's demise could be attributed perhaps to its failure to heed these very cogent internal critiques.

THEODOR W. ADORNO

German philosopher and musicologist Theodor Adorno (1903–1969) was a *Theodor W. Adorno* leading member of the Frankfurt Institute for Social Research. He was appointed its director in 1959. Adorno's thought is informed by a range of German thinkers, and his work could be described as a heterodox Marxism with a strong Freudian influence. Thus commodity fetishism and the role of the unconscious form a crucial part of his thinking. From Hegel, Adorno inherited the notion of the dialectic, but appropriated it in its negative form. He opposed the Hegelian notion of 'identity' thinking, and championed instead a way of seeking to 'describe' an object negatively, by what it could not be, seeking to arrive at an approximation of the 'truth' through a 'constellation' of such negative critiques.

In his aesthetic theory, Adorno recognized the emancipatory potential of art. Through its autonomy, art offered a vision of an alternative world. It negated reified consciousness and rejected the dominant order. However, only autonomous art – art that required the engagement of the viewer – could offer this resistance. Adorno therefore distinguished between art and the products of the culture industry whose purpose was largely that of distraction and amusement.

In the essay 'Functionalism Today', Adorno addresses the question of architecture and exposes the paradoxes within Adolf Loos's treatment of functionalism and ornament. The purposive and the purpose-free arts, according to Adorno, can never be absolutely separated. They are held in a dialectical relationship. Purpose-free arts often have a social function, while there can be no 'chemically pure' purposefulness. Thus functionalism in architecture can never be pure functionalism. 'The absolute rejection of style', Adorno concludes famously, 'becomes itself a form of style.' In his championing of functionalism, Loos had dismissed ornament as the decadent product of erotic symbolism. Yet, as Adorno argues, even the functional may attract the symbolic. Symbols are born of the need to identify with one's surroundings, and humans attach symbolic significance to even the most technical of objects, such as the airplane or the car.

The essay is an attack on the meanness of postwar German reconstruction. Against the 'false' objectivity of *Neue Sachlichkeit*, Adorno argues for an architecture of sustained aesthetic reflection, an architecture 'innervated' by the imagination. Above all, he calls for an architecture of generosity, which 'thinks more of men than they actually are'.

Although criticized for his elitist treatment of art and for his deeply pessimistic approach to the Enlightenment, Adorno remains a figure of enduring appeal. In particular his early and incisive critique of the culture industry has exerted a marked influence on theorists of postmodernity such as Fredric Jameson.

Adorno   FUNCTIONALISM TODAY

I would first like to express my gratitude for the confidence shown me by Adolf
Arndt in his invitation to speak here today. At the same time, I must also
express my serious doubts as to whether I really have the right to speak before
you. *Métier,* expertise in both matters of handicraft and of technique, counts in
your circle for a great deal. And rightly so. If there is one idea of lasting influence which has developed out of the Werkbund movement, it is precisely this
emphasis on concrete competence as opposed to an aesthetics removed and
isolated from material questions. I am familiar with this dictum from my own
métier, music. There it became a fundamental theorem, thanks to a school
which cultivated close personal relationships with both Adolf Loos and the
Bauhaus, and which was therefore fully aware of its intellectual ties to
objectivity (*Sachlichkeit*)[1] in the arts. Nevertheless, I can make no claim to
competence in matters of architecture. And yet, I do not resist the temptation,
and knowingly face the danger that you may briefly tolerate me as a dilettante
and then cast me aside. I do this firstly because of my pleasure in presenting
some of my reflections in public, and to you in particular; and secondly,
because of Adolf Loos's comment that while an artwork need not appeal to
anyone, a house is responsible to each and everyone.[2] I am not yet sure whether
this statement is in fact valid, but in the meantime, I need not be holier than the
pope.

I find that the style of German reconstruction fills me with a disturbing
discontent, one which many of you may certainly share. Since I no less than the
specialists must constantly face this feeling, I feel justified in examining its
foundations. Common elements between music and architecture have been discussed repeatedly, almost to the point of ennui. In uniting that which I see in
architecture with that which I understand about the difficulties in music, I may
not be transgressing the law of the division of labour as much as it may seem.
But to accomplish this union, I must stand at a greater distance from these
subjects than you may justifiably expect. It seems to me, however, not
unrealistic that at times – in latent crisis situations – it may help to remove
oneself farther from phenomena than the spirit of technical competence would
usually allow. The principle of 'fittingness to the material' (*Material-
gerechtigkeit*)[3] rests on the foundation of the division of labour. Nevertheless, it
is advisable even for experts to occasionally take into account the extent to
which their expertise may suffer from just that division of labour, as the artistic
naiveté underlying it can impose its own limitations.

Let me begin with the fact that the anti-ornamental movement has affected
the 'purpose-free' arts (*zweckfreie Künste*)[4] as well. It lies in the nature of
artworks to inquire after the essential and necessary in them and to react
against all superfluous elements. After the critical tradition declined to offer the
arts a canon of right and wrong, the responsibility to take such considerations
into account was placed on each individual work; each had to test itself against
its own immanent logic, regardless of whether or not it was motivated by some
external purpose. This was by no means a new position. Mozart, though clearly
still standard-bearer and critical representative of the great tradition, responded
in the following way to the minor objection of a member of the royal family

– 'But so many notes, my dear Mozart' – after the premier of his 'Abduction'   *Adorno*
with 'Not one note more, Your Majesty, than was necessary.' In his *Critique of
Judgment*, Kant grounded this norm philosophically in the formula of 'purposiveness without a purpose' (*Zweckmässigkeit ohne Zweck*). The formula
reflects an essential impulse in the judgment of taste. And yet it does not
account for the historical dynamic. Based on a language stemming from the
realm of materials, what this language defines as necessary can later become
superfluous, even terribly ornamental, as soon as it can no longer be legitimated in a second kind of language, which is commonly called style. What was
functional yesterday can therefore become the opposite tomorrow. Loos was
thoroughly aware of this historical dynamic contained in the concept of
ornament. Even representative, luxurious, pompous and, in a certain sense,
burlesque elements may appear in certain forms of art as necessary, and not at
all burlesque. To criticise the Baroque for this reason would be philistine.
Criticism of ornament means no more than criticism of that which has lost its
functional and symbolic signification. Ornament becomes then a mere decaying
and poisonous organic vestige. The new art is opposed to this, for it represents
the fictitiousness of a depraved romanticism, an ornamentation embarrassingly
trapped in its own impotence. Modern music and architecture, by concentrating strictly on expression and construction, both strive together with equal
rigour to efface all such ornament. Schönberg's compositional innovations,
Karl Kraus's literary struggle against journalistic clichés and Loos's
denunciation of ornament are not vague analogies in intellectual history; they
reflect precisely the same intention. This insight necessitates a correction of
Loos's thesis, which he, in his open-mindedness, would probably not have
rejected: the question of functionalism does not coincide with the question of
practical function. The purpose-free (*zweckfrei*) and the purposeful (*zweck-
gebunden*) arts do not form the radical opposition which he imputed. The
difference between the necessary and the superfluous is inherent in a work, and
is not defined by the work's relationship – or the lack of it – to something
outside itself.

In Loos's thought and in the early period of functionalism, purposeful and
aesthetically autonomous products were separated from one another by
absolute fact. This separation, which is in fact the object of our reflection, arose
from the contemporary polemic against the applied arts and crafts (*Kunstgewerbe*).[5] Although they determined the period of Loos's development, he soon
escaped from them. Loos was thus situated historically between Peter
Altenberg and Le Corbusier. The movement of applied art had its beginnings in
Ruskin and Morris. Revolting against the shapelessness of mass-produced,
pseudo-individualized forms, it rallied around such new concepts as 'will to
style', 'stylization' and 'shaping', and around the idea that one should apply
art, reintroduce it into life in order to restore life to it. Their slogans were
numerous and had a powerful effect. Nevertheless, Loos noticed quite early the
implausibility of such endeavours: articles for use lose meaning as soon as they
are displaced or disengaged in such a way that their use is no longer required.
Art, with its definitive protest against the dominance of purpose over human
life, suffers once it is reduced to that practical level to which it objects, in
Hölderlin's words: 'For never from now on/Shall the sacred serve mere use.'
Loos found the artificial art of practical objects repulsive. Similarly, he felt that

Adorno the practical reorientation of purpose-free art would eventually subordinate it
to the destructive autocracy of profit, which even arts and crafts, at least in
their beginnings, had once opposed. Contrary to these efforts, Loos preached
for the return to an honest handicraft[6] which would place itself in the service of
technical innovations without having to borrow forms from art. His claims
suffer from too simple an antithesis. Their restorative element, not unlike that
of the individualization of crafts, has since become equally clear. To this day,
they are still bound to discussions of objectivity.

In any given product, freedom from purpose and purposefulness can never
be absolutely separated from one another. The two notions are historically
interconnected. The ornaments, after all, which Loos expulsed with a
vehemence quite out of character, are often actually vestiges of outmoded
means of production. And conversely, numerous purposes, like sociability,
dance and entertainment, have filtered into purpose-free art; they have been
generally incorporated into its formal and generic laws. Purposefulness without
purpose is thus really the sublimation of purpose. Nothing exists as an aesthetic
object in itself, but only within the field of tension of such sublimation. Therefore there is no chemically pure purposefulness set up as the opposite of the
purpose-free aesthetic. Even the most pure forms of purpose are nourished by
ideas – like formal transparency and graspability – which in fact are derived
from artistic experience. No form can be said to be determined exhaustively by
its purpose. This can be seen even in one of Schönberg's revolutionary works,
the First Chamber Symphony, about which Loos wrote some of his most
insightful words. Ironically, an ornamental theme appears, with a double beat
recalling at once a central motif from Wagner's 'Götterdämmerung' and the
theme from the First Movement of Bruckner's Seventh Symphony. The ornament is the sustaining invention, if you will, objective in its own right. Precisely
this transitional theme becomes the model of a canonical exposition in the
fourfold counterpoint, and thereby the model of the first extreme constructivist
complex in modern music. Schönberg's belief in such material was appropriated from the *Kunstgewerbe* religion, which worshipped the supposed
nobility of matter; it still continues to provide inspiration even in autonomous
art. He combined with this belief the ideas of a construction fitting to the
material. To it corresponds an undialectical concept of beauty, which encompasses autonomous art like a nature preserve. That art aspires to autonomy
does not mean that it unconditionally purges itself of ornamental elements; the
very existence of art, judged by the criteria of the practical, is ornamental. If
Loos's aversion to ornament had been rigidly consistent, he would have had to
extend it to all of art. To his credit, he stopped before reaching this conclusion.
In this circumspection, by the way, he is similar to the positivists. On the one
hand, they would expunge from the realm of philosophy anything which they
deem poetic. On the other, they sense no infringement by poetry itself on their
kind of positivism. Thus, they tolerate poetry if it remains in a special realm,
neutralized and unchallenged, since they have already relaxed the notion of
objective truth.

The belief that a substance bears within itself its own adequate form
presumes that it is already invested with meaning. Such a doctrine made the
symbolist aesthetic possible. The resistance to the excesses of the applied arts
pertained not just to hidden forms, but also to the cult of materials. It created

an aura of essentiality about them. Loos expressed precisely this notion in his *Adorno* critique of batik. Meanwhile, the invention of artificial products – materials originating in industry – no longer permitted the archaic faith in an innate beauty, the foundation of a magic connected with precious elements. Furthermore, the crisis arising from the latest developments of autonomous art demonstrated how little meaningful organization could depend on the material itself. Whenever organizational principles rely too heavily on material, the result approaches mere patchwork. The idea of fittingness to the materials in purposeful art cannot remain indifferent to such criticisms. Indeed, the illusion of purposefulness as its own purpose cannot stand up to the simplest social reality. Something would be purposeful here and now only if it were so in terms of the present society. Yet, certain irrationalities – Marx's term for them was *faux frais* – are essential to society; the social process always proceeds, in spite of all particular planning, by its own inner nature, aimlessly and irrationally. Such irrationality leaves its mark on all ends and purposes, and thereby also on the rationality of the means devised to achieve those ends. Thus, a self-mocking contradiction emerges in the omnipresence of advertisements: they are intended to be purposeful for profit. And yet all purposefulness is technically defined by its measure of material appropriateness. If an advertisement were strictly functional, without ornamental surplus, it would no longer fulfil its purpose as advertisement. Of course, the fear of technology is largely stuffy and old-fashioned, even reactionary. And yet it does have its validity, for it reflects the anxiety felt in the face of the violence which an irrational society can impose on its members, indeed on everything which is forced to exist within its confines. This anxiety reflects a common childhood experience, with which Loos seems unfamiliar, even though he is otherwise strongly influenced by the circumstances of his youth: the longing for castles with long chambers and silk tapestries, the utopia of escapism. Something of this utopia lives on in the modern aversion to the escalator, to Loos's celebrated kitchen, to the factory smokestack, to the shabby side of an antagonistic society. It is heightened by outward appearances. Deconstruction of these appearances, however, has little power over the completely denigrated sphere, where praxis continues as always. One might attack the pinnacles of the bogus castles of the moderns (which Thorstein Veblen despised), the ornaments, for example, pasted onto shoes; but where this is possible, it merely aggravates an already horrifying situation. The process has implications for the world of pictures as well. Positivist art, a culture of the existing, has been exchanged for aesthetic truth. One envisions the prospect of a new *Ackerstrasse*.[7]

The limits of functionalism to date have been the limits of the bourgeoisie in its practical sense. Even in Loos, the sworn enemy of Viennese kitsch, one finds some remarkably bourgeois traces. Since the bourgeois structure had already permeated so many feudalistic and absolutist forms in his city, Loos believed he could use its rigorous principles to free himself from traditional formulas. His writings, for example, contain attacks on awkward Viennese formality. Furthermore, his polemics are coloured by a unique strain of puritanism, which nears obsession. Loos's thought, like so much bourgeois criticism of culture, is an intersection of two fundamental directions. On the one hand, he realized that this culture was actually not at all cultural. This informed above all his relationship to his native environment. On the other, he felt a deep animosity

Adorno toward culture in general, which called for the prohibition not only of superficial veneer, but also of all soft and smooth touches. In this he disregarded the
fact that culture is not the place for untamed nature, nor for a merciless
domination over nature. The future of *Sachlichkeit* could be a liberating one
only if it shed its barbarous traits. It could no longer inflict on men – whom it
supposedly upheld as its only measure – the sadistic blows of sharp edges, bare
calculated rooms, stairways, and the like. Virtually every consumer had probably felt all too painfully the impracticability of the mercilessly practical. Hence
our bitter suspicion is formulated: the absolute rejection of style becomes style.
Loos traces ornament back to erotic symbols. In turn, his rigid rejection of
ornamentation is coupled with his disgust with erotic symbolism. He finds
uncurbed nature both regressive and embarrassing. The tone of his condem-
nations of ornament echoes an often openly expressed rage against moral
delinquency: 'But the man of our time who, out of inner compulsion, smears
walls with erotic symbols is a criminal and a degenerate.'[8] The insult
'degenerate' connects Loos to movements of which he certainly would not have
approved. 'One can', he says, 'measure the culture of a country by the amount
of graffiti on the bathroom walls.'[9] But in southern countries, in Mediterranean
countries in general, one finds a great deal. In fact, the Surrealists made much
use of such unreflected expressions. Loos would certainly have hesitated before
imputing a lack of culture to these areas. His hatred of ornament can best be
understood by examining a psychological argument.[10] He seems to see in ornament the mimetic impulse, which runs contrary to rational objectification; he
sees in it an expression which, even in sadness and lament, is related to the
pleasure principle. Arguing from this principle, one must accept that there is a
factor of expression in every object. Any special relegation of this factor to art
alone would be an oversimplification. It cannot be separated from objects of
use. Thus, even when these objects lack expression, they must pay tribute to it
by attempting to avoid it. Hence all obsolete objects of use eventually become
an expression, a collective picture of the epoch. There is barely a practical form
which, along with its appropriateness for use, would not therefore also be a
symbol. Psychoanalysis too has demonstrated this principle on the basis of
unconscious images, among which the house figures prominently. According to
Freud, symbolic intention quickly allies itself to technical forms, like the airplane, and according to contemporary American research in mass psychology,
often to the car. Thus, purposeful forms are the language of their own purposes.
By means of the mimetic impulse, the living being equates himself with objects
in his surroundings. This occurs long before artists initiate conscious imitation.
What begins as symbol becomes ornament, and finally appears superfluous; it
had its origins, nevertheless, in natural shapes, to which men adapted themselves through their artifacts. The inner image which is expressed in that
impulse was once something external, something coercively objective. This
argument explains the fact, known since Loos, that ornament, indeed artistic
form in general, cannot be invented. The achievement of all artists, and not just
those interested in specific ends, is reduced to something incomparably more
modest than the art-religion of the nineteenth and early twentieth centuries
would have been willing to accept. The psychological basis of ornament hence
undercuts aesthetic principles and aims. However, the question is by no means
settled how art would be possible in any form if ornamentation were no longer

a substantial element, if art itself could no longer invent any true ornaments.   *Adorno*

This last difficulty, which *Sachlichkeit* unavoidably encounters, is not a mere error. It cannot be arbitrarily corrected. It follows directly from the historical character of the subject. Use – or consumption – is much more closely related to the pleasure principle than an object of artistic representation responsible only to its own formal laws; it means the 'using up of', the denial of the object, that it ought not to be. Pleasure appears, according to the bourgeois work ethic, as wasted energy. Loos's formulation makes clear how much as an early cultural critic he was fundamentally attached to that order whose manifestations he chastised wherever they failed to follow their own principles: 'Ornament is wasted work energy and thereby wasted health. It has always been so. But today it also means wasted material, and both mean wasted capital.'[11] Two irreconcilable motifs coincide in this statement: economy, for where else, if not in the norms of profitability, is it stated that nothing should be wasted; and the dream of the totally technological world, free from the shame of work. The second motif points beyond the commercial world. For Loos it takes the form of the realization that the widely lamented impotency to create ornament and the so-called extinction of stylizing energy (which he exposed as an invention of art historians) imply an advance in the arts. He realized in addition that those aspects of an industrialized society, which by bourgeois standards are negative, actually represent its positive side:

Style used to mean ornament. So I said: don't lament! Don't you see? Precisely this makes our age great, that it is incapable of producing new ornament. We have conquered ornament, we have struggled to the stage of non-ornamentation. Watch, the time is near. Fulfilment awaits us. Soon the streets of the cities will shine like white walls. Like Zion, the sacred city, heaven's capital. Then salvation will be ours.[12]

In this conception, the state free of ornament would be a utopia of concretely fulfilled presence, no longer in need of symbols. Objective truth, all the belief in things, would cling to this utopia. This utopia remains hidden for Loos by his crucial experience with *Jugendstil*:

Individual man is incapable of creating form; therefore, so is the architect. The architect, however, attempts the impossible again and again – and always in vain. Form, or ornament, is the result of the unconscious cooperation of men belonging to a whole cultural sphere. Everything else is art. Art is the self-imposed will of the genius. God gave him his mission.[13]

This axiom, that the artist fulfils a divine mission, no longer holds. A general demystification, which began in the commercial realm, has encroached upon art. With it, the absolute difference between inflexible purposefulness and autonomous freedom has been reduced as well. But here we face another contradiction. On the one hand, the purely purpose-oriented forms have been revealed as insufficient, monotonous, deficient and narrow-mindedly practical. At times, of course, individual masterpieces do stand out; but then, one tends to attribute the success to the creator's 'genius', and not to something objective within the achievement itself. On the other, the attempt to bring into the work

Adorno   the external element of imagination as a corrective, to help the matter out with this element which stems from outside of it, is equally pointless; it serves only to mistakenly resurrect decoration, which has been justifiably criticized by modern architecture. The results are extremely disheartening. A critical analysis of the mediocre modernity of the style of German reconstruction by a true expert would be extremely relevant. My suspicion in the *Minima Moralia* that the world is no longer habitable has already been confirmed; the heavy shadow of instability bears upon built form, the shadow of mass migrations, which had their preludes in the years of Hitler and his war. This contradiction must be consciously grasped in all its necessity. But we cannot stop there. If we do, we give in to a continually threatening catastrophe. The most recent catastrophe, the air raids, have already led architecture into a condition from which it cannot escape.

The poles of the contradiction are revealed in two concepts, which seem mutually exclusive: handicraft and imagination. Loos expressly rejected the latter in the context of the world of use:

> Pure and clean construction has had to replace the imaginative
> forms of past centuries and the flourishing ornamentation of past
> ages. Straight lines; sharp, straight edges: the craftsman works only
> with these. He has nothing but a purpose in mind and nothing but
> materials and tools in front of him.[14]

Le Corbusier, however, sanctioned imagination in his theoretical writings, at least in a somewhat general sense: 'The task of the architect: knowledge of men, creative imagination, beauty. Freedom of choice (spiritual man).'[15] We may safely assume that in general the more advanced architects tend to prefer handicraft, while more backward and unimaginative architects all too gladly praise imagination. We must be wary, however, of simply accepting the concepts of handicraft and imagination in the loose sense in which they have been tossed back and forth in the ongoing polemic. Only then can we hope to reach an alternative. The word 'handicraft', which immediately gains consent, covers something qualitatively different. Only unreasonable dilettantism and blatant idealism would attempt to deny that each authentic and, in the broadest sense, artistic activity requires a precise understanding of the materials and techniques at the artist's disposal, and to be sure, at the most advanced level.

Only the artist who has never subjected himself to the discipline of creating a picture, who believes in the intuitive origins of painting, fears that closeness to materials and technical understanding will destroy his originality. He has never learned what is historically available, and can never make use of it. And so he conjures up out of the supposed depths of his own interiority that which is merely the residue of outmoded forms. The word 'handicraft' appeals to such a simple truth. But quite different chords resonate unavoidably along with it. The syllable 'hand' exposes a past means of production; it recalls a simple economy of wares. These means of production have since disappeared. Ever since the proposals of the English precursors of 'modern style' they have been reduced to a masquerade. One associates the notion of handicraft with the apron of a Hans Sachs, or possibly the great world chronicle. At times, I cannot suppress the suspicion that such an archaic 'shirt sleeves' ethos survives even among the younger proponents of 'handcraftiness'; they are despisers of art. If some feel themselves superior to art, then it is only because they have never experienced it as Loos did. For Loos, appreciation of both art and its applied form led to a bitter emotional conflict. In the area of music, I know of one advocate of handicraft who spoke with plainly romantic anti-romanticism of the 'hut mentality'. I once caught him thinking of handicrafts as stereotypical formulas, practices as he called them, which were supposed to spare the energies of the composer; it never dawned on him that nowadays the uniqueness of each concrete task excludes such formalization. Thanks to attitudes such as his, handicraft is transformed into that which it wants to repudiate: the same lifeless, reified repetition which ornament had propagated. I dare not judge whether a similar kind of perversity is at work in the concept of form-making when viewed as a detached operation, independent from the immanent demands and laws of the object to be formed. In any case, I would imagine that the retrospective infatuation with the aura of the socially doomed craftsman is quite compatible with the disdainfully trumped-up attitude of his successor, the expert. Proud of his expertise and as unpolished as his tables and chairs, the expert disregards those reflections needed in this age which no longer possesses anything to grasp on to. It is impossible to do without the expert; it is impossible in this age of commercial means of production to recreate that state before the division of labour which society has irretrievably obliterated. But likewise, it is impossible to raise the expert to the measure of all things. His disillusioned modernity, which claims to have shed all ideologies, is easily appropriated into the mask of the petty bourgeois routine. Handicraft becomes handcraftiness. Good handicraft means the fittingness of means to an end. The ends are certainly not independent of the means. The means have their own logic, a logic which points beyond them. If the fittingness of the means becomes an end in itself, it becomes fetishized. The handworker mentality begins to produce the opposite effect from its original intention, when it was used to fight the silk smoking jacket and the beret. It hinders the objective reason behind productive forces instead of allowing it to unfold. Whenever handicraft is established as a norm today, one must closely examine the intention. The concept of handicraft stands in close relationship to function. Its functions, however, are by no means necessarily enlightened or advanced.

The concept of imagination, like that of handicraft, must not be adopted without critical analysis. Psychological triviality – imagination as nothing but the image of something not yet present – is clearly insufficient. As an interpretation, it explains merely what is determined by imagination in artistic processes, and, I presume, also in the purposeful arts. Walter Benjamin once defined imagination as the ability to interpolate in minutest detail. Undeniably, such a definition accomplishes much more than current views which tend either to elevate the concept into an immaterial heaven or to condemn it on objective grounds. Imagination in the production of a work of representational art is not pleasure in free invention, in creation *ex nihilo*. There is no such thing in any art, even in autonomous art, the realm to which Loos restricted imagination. Any penetrating analysis of the autonomous work of art concludes that the additions invented by the artist above and beyond the given state of materials and forms are *miniscule* and of limited value. On the other hand, the reduction of imagination to an anticipatory adaptation to material ends is equally inadequate; it transforms imagination into an eternal sameness. It is impossible to

Adorno   ascribe Le Corbusier's powerful imaginative feats completely to the relationship between architecture and the human body, as he does in his own writings. Clearly there exists, perhaps imperceptible in the materials and forms which the artist acquires and develops something more than material and forms. Imagination means to *innervate* this something. This is not as absurd a notion as it may sound. For the forms, even the materials, are by no means merely given by nature, as an unreflective artist might easily presume. History has accumulated in them, and spirit permeates them. What they contain is not a positive law; and yet, their content emerges as a sharply outlined figure of the problem. Artistic imagination awakens these accumulated elements by becoming aware of the innate problematic of the material. The minimal progress of imagination responds to the wordless question posed to it by the materials and forms in their quiet and elemental language. Separate impulses, even purpose and immanent formal laws, are thereby fused together. An interaction takes place between purpose, space and material. None of these facets makes up any one Ur-phenomenon to which all the others can be reduced. It is here that the insight furnished by philosophy that no thought can lead to an absolute beginning – that such absolutes are the products of abstraction – exerts its influence on aesthetics. Hence music, which had so long emphasized the supposed primacy of the individual tone, had to discover finally the more complex relationships of its components. The tone receives meaning only within the functional structure of the system, without which it would be a merely physical entity. Superstition alone can hope to extract from it a latent aesthetic structure. One speaks, with good reason, of a sense of space (*Raumgefühl*) in architecture. But this sense of space is not a pure, abstract essence, not a sense of spatiality itself, since space is only conceivable as concrete space, within specific dimensions. A sense of space is closely connected with purposes. Even when architecture attempts to elevate this sense beyond the realm of purposefulness, it is still simultaneously immanent in the purpose. The success of such a synthesis is the principal criterion for great architecture. Architecture inquires: how can a certain purpose become space; through which forms, which materials? All factors relate reciprocally to one another. Architectonic imagination is, according to this conception of it, the ability to articulate space purposefully. It permits purposes to become space. It constructs forms according to purposes. Conversely, space and the sense of space can become more than impoverished purpose only when imagination impregnates them with purposefulness. Imagination breaks out of the immanent connections of purpose, to which it owes its very existence.

I am fully conscious of the ease with which concepts like a sense of space can degenerate into clichés, in the end even be applied to arts and crafts. Here I feel the limits of the non-expert who is unable to render these concepts sufficiently precise although they have been so enlightening in modern architecture. And yet, I permit myself a certain degree of speculation: the sense of space, in contradistinction to the abstract idea of space, corresponds in the visual realm to musicality in the acoustical. Musicality cannot be reduced to an abstract conception of time – for example, the ability, however beneficial, to conceive of the time units of a metronome without having to listen to one. Similarly, the sense of space is not limited to spatial images, even though these are probably a prerequisite for every architect if he is to read his outlines and blueprints the

way a musician reads his score. A sense of space seems to demand more, namely   *Adorno*
that something can occur to the artist out of space itself; this cannot be something arbitrary in space and indifferent toward space. Analogously, the
musician invents his melodies, indeed all his musical structures, out of time
itself, out of the need to organize time. Mere time relationships do not suffice,
since they are indifferent toward the concrete musical event; nor does the
invention of individual musical passages or complexes, since their time structures and time relationships are not conceived along with them. In the
productive sense of space, purpose takes over to a large extent the role of
content, as opposed to the formal constituents which the architect creates out
of space. The tension between form and content which makes all artistic
creation possible communicates itself through purpose especially in the
purpose-oriented arts. The new 'objective' asceticism does contain therefore an
element of truth; unmediated subjective expression would indeed be inadequate
for architecture. Where only such expression is striven for, the result is not
architecture, but filmsets, at times, as in the old Golem film, even good ones.
The position of subjective expression, then, is occupied in architecture by the
function for the subject. Architecture would thus attain a higher standard the
more intensely it reciprocally mediated the two extremes – formal construction
and function.

The subject's function, however, is not determined by some generalized
person of an unchanging physical nature but by concrete social norms.
Functional architecture represents the rational character as opposed to the
suppressed instincts of empirical subjects, who, in the present society, still seek
their fortunes in all conceivable nooks and crannies. It calls upon a human
potential which is grasped in principle by our advanced consciousness, but
which is suffocated in most men, who have been kept spiritually impotent.
Architecture worthy of human beings thinks better of men than they actually
are. It views them in the way they could be according to the status of their own
productive energies as embodied in technology. Architecture contradicts the
needs of the here and now as soon as it proceeds to serve those needs – without
simultaneously representing any absolute or lasting ideology. Architecture still
remains, as Loos's book title complained seventy years ago, a cry into emptiness. The fact that the great architects from Loos to Le Corbusier and Scharoun
were able to realize only a small portion of their work in stone and concrete
cannot be explained solely by the reactions of unreasonable contractors and
administrators (although that explanation must not be underestimated). This
fact is conditioned by a social antagonism over which the greatest architecture
has no power: the same society which developed human productive energies to
unimaginable proportions has chained them to conditions of production
imposed upon them; thus the people who in reality constitute the productive
energies become deformed according to the measure of their working
conditions. This fundamental contradiction is most clearly visible in architecture. It is just as difficult for architecture to rid itself of the tensions which
this contradiction produces as it is for the consumer. Things are not universally
correct in architecture and universally incorrect in men. Men suffer enough
injustice, for their consciousness and unconsciousness are trapped in a state of
minority; they have not, so to speak, come of age. This nonage hinders their
identification with their own concerns. Because architecture is in fact both

Adorno autonomous and purpose-oriented, it cannot simply negate men as they are. And yet it must do precisely that if it is to remain autonomous. If it would bypass mankind *tel quel,* then it would be accommodating itself to what would be a questionable anthropology and even ontology. It was not merely by chance that Le Corbusier envisioned human prototypes. Living men, even the most backward and conventionally naive, have the right to the fulfilment of their needs, even though those needs may be false ones. Once thought supersedes without consideration the subjective desires for the sake of truly objective needs, it is transformed into brutal oppression. So it is with the *volonté générale* against the *volonté de tous.* Even in the false needs of a human being there lives a bit of freedom. It is expressed in what economic theory once called the 'use value' as opposed to the 'exchange value.' Hence there are those to whom legitimate architecture appears as an enemy; it withholds from them that which they, by their very nature, want and even need.

Beyond the phenomenon of the 'cultural lag', this antinomy may have its origin in the development of the concept of art. Art, in order to be art according to its own formal laws, must be crystallized in autonomous form. This constitutes its truth content; otherwise, it would be subservient to that which it negates by its very existence. And yet, as a human product, it is never completely removed from humanity. It contains as a constitutive element something of that which it necessarily resists. Where art obliterates its own memory, forgetting that it is only there for others, it becomes a fetish, a self-conscious and thereby relativized absolute. Such was the dream of *Jugendstil* beauty. But art is also compelled to strive for pure self-immanence if it is not to become sacrificed to fraudulence. The result is a *quid pro quo.* An activity which envisions as its subject a liberated, emancipated humanity, possible only in a transformed society, appears in the present state as an adaptation to a technology which has degenerated into an end in itself, into a self-purpose. Such an apotheosis of objectification is the irreconcilable opponent of art. The result, moreover, is not mere appearance. The more consistently both autonomous and so-called applied art reject their own magical and mythical origins and follow their own formal laws, the greater the danger of such an adaptation becomes. Art possesses no sure means to counter such a danger. Thorstein Veblen's *aporia* is thus repeated: before 1900, he demanded that men think purely technologically, causally, mechanistically in order to overcome the living deceit of their world of images. He thereby sanctioned the objective categories of that economy which he criticized; in a free state, men would no longer be subservient to a technology which, in fact, existed only for them; it would be there to serve them. However, in the present epoch men have been absorbed into technology and have left only their empty shells behind, as if they had passed into it their better half. Their own consciousness has been objectified in the face of technology, as if objective technology had in some sense the right to criticize consciousness. Technology is there for men: this is a plausible proposition, but it has been degraded to the vulgar ideology of regressionism. This is evident in the fact that one need only invoke it to be rewarded from all sides with enthusiastic understanding. The whole situation is somehow false; nothing in it can smooth over the contradiction. On the one hand, an imagined utopia, free from the binding purposes of the existing order, would become powerless, a detached ornament, since it must take its elements and structure

from that very order. On the other, any attempt to ban the utopian factor, like a *Adorno*
prohibition of images, immediately falls victim to the spell of the prevailing
order.

The concern of functionalism is a subordination to usefulness. What is not
useful is assailed without question because developments in the arts have
brought its inherent aesthetic insufficiency into the open. The merely useful,
however, is interwoven with relationships of guilt, the means to the devastation
of the world, a hopelessness which denies all but deceptive consolations to
mankind. But even if this contradiction can never be ultimately eliminated, one
must take a first step in trying to grasp it; in bourgeois society, usefulness has its
own dialectic. The useful object would be the highest achievement, an anthro-
pomorphized 'thing', the reconciliation with objects which are no longer closed
off from humanity and which no longer suffer humiliation at the hands of men.
Childhood perception of technical things promises such a state; they appear as
images of a near and helpful spirit, cleansed of profit motivation. Such a
conception was not unfamiliar to the theorists of social utopias. It provides a
pleasant refuge from true development, and allows a vision of useful things
which have lost their coldness. Mankind would no longer suffer from the
'thingly' character of the world,[16] and likewise 'things' would come into their
own. Once redeemed from their own 'thingliness', 'things' would find their
purpose. But in present society all usefulness is displaced, bewitched. Society
deceives us when it says that it allows things to appear as if they are there by
mankind's will. In fact, they are produced for profit's sake; they satisfy human
needs only incidentally. They call forth new needs and maintain them according
to the profit motive. Since what is useful and beneficial to man, cleansed of
human domination and exploitation, would be correct, nothing is more
aesthetically unbearable than the present shape of things, subjugated and
internally deformed into their opposite. The *raison d'être* of all autonomous art
since the dawning of the bourgeois era is that only useless objects testify to that
which may have at one point been useful; it represents correct and fortunate
use, a contact with things beyond the antithesis between use and uselessness.
This conception implies that men who desire betterment must rise up against
practicability. If they overvalue it and react to it, they join the camp of the
enemy. It is said that work does not defile. Like most proverbial expressions,
this covers up the converse truth; exchange defiles useful work. The curse of
exchange has overtaken autonomous art as well. In autonomous art, the useless
is contained within its limited and particular form; it is thus helplessly exposed
to the criticism waged by its opposite, the useful. Conversely in the useful, that
which is now the case is closed off to its possibilities. The obscure secret of art
is the fetishistic character of goods and wares. Functionalism would like to
break out of this entanglement; and yet, it can only rattle its chains in vain as
long as it remains trapped in an entangled society.

I have tried to make you aware of certain contradictions whose solution
cannot be delineated by a non-expert. It is indeed doubtful whether they can be
solved today at all. To this extent, I could expect you to criticize me for the
uselessness of my argumentation. My defence is implicit in my thesis that the
concepts of useful and useless cannot be accepted without due consideration.
The time is over when we can isolate ourselves in our respective tasks. The
object at hand demands the kind of reflection which objectivity (*Sachlichkeit*)

Adorno generally rebuked in a clearly non-objective manner. By demanding immediate legitimation of a thought, by demanding to know what good that thought is now, the thought is usually brought to a standstill at a point where it can offer insights which one day might even improve praxis in an unpredictable way. Thought has its own coercive impulse, like the one you are familiar with in your work with your material. The work of an artist, whether or not it is directed toward a particular purpose, can no longer proceed naively on a prescribed path. It manifests a crisis which demands that the expert – regardless of his prideful craftsmanship – go beyond his craft in order to satisfy it. He must do this in two ways. First, with regard to social things; he must account for the position of his work in society and for the social limits which he encounters on all sides. This consideration becomes crucial in problems concerning city planning, even beyond the tasks of reconstruction, where architectonic questions collide with social questions such as the existence or non-existence of a collective social subject. It hardly needs mentioning that city planning is insufficient so long as it centres on particular instead of collective social ends. The merely immediate, practical principles of city planning do not coincide with those of a truly rational conception free from social irrationalities; they lack that collective social subject which must be the prime concern of city planning. Herein lies one reason why city planning threatens either to degenerate into chaos or to hinder the productive architectonic achievement of individuals.

Second, and I would like to emphasize this aspect to you, architecture, indeed every purposeful art, demands constant *aesthetic* reflection. I know how suspect the word 'aesthetic' must sound to you. You think perhaps of professors who, with their eyes raised to heaven, spew forth formalistic laws of eternal and everlasting beauty, which are no more than recipes for the production of ephemeral, classicist kitsch. In fact, the opposite must be the case in true aesthetics. It must absorb precisely those objections which it once raised in principle against all artists. Aesthetics would condemn itself if it continued unreflectively, speculatively, without relentless self-criticism. Aesthetics as an integral facet of philosophy awaits a new impulse which must come from reflective efforts. Hence recent artistic praxis has turned to aesthetics. Aesthetics becomes a practical necessity once it becomes clear that concepts like usefulness and uselessness in art, like the separation of autonomous and purpose-oriented art, imagination and ornament, must once again be discussed before the artist can act positively or negatively according to such categories. Whether you like it or not, you are being pushed daily to considerations, aesthetic considerations, which transcend your immediate tasks. Your experience calls Molière's Monsieur Jourdain to mind, who discovers to his amazement in studying rhetoric that he has been speaking prose for his entire life. Once your activity compels you to aesthetic considerations, you deliver yourself up to its power. You can no longer break off and conjure up ideas arbitrarily in the name of pure and thorough expertise. The artist who does not pursue aesthetic thought energetically tends to lapse into dilettantish hypothesis and groping justifications for the sake of defending his own intellectual construct. In music, Pierre Boulez, one of the most technically competent contemporary composers, extended constructivism to its extreme in some of his compositions; subsequently, however, he emphatically announced

the necessity of aesthetics. Such an aesthetics would not presume to herald *Adorno*
principles which establish the key to beauty or ugliness itself. This discretion
alone would place the problem of ornament in a new light. Beauty today can
have no other measure except the depth to which a work resolves contradictions. A work must cut through the contradictions and overcome them, not
by covering them up, but by pursuing them. Mere formal beauty, whatever that
might be, is empty and meaningless; the beauty of its content is lost in the pre-
artistic sensual pleasure of the observer. Beauty is either the resultant of force
vectors or it is nothing at all. A modified aesthetics would outline its own object
with increasing clarity as it would begin to feel more intensely the need to
investigate it. Unlike traditional aesthetics, it would not necessarily view the
concept of art as its given correlate. Aesthetic thought today must surpass art
by thinking art. It would thereby surpass the current opposition of purposeful
and purpose-free, under which the producer must suffer as much as the
observer.

NOTES

1   The *Neue Sachlichkeit* movement, one of the main post-expressionist trends in German art, is
    commonly translated as 'New Objectivity'. The word *sachlich*, however, carries a series of
    connotations. Along with its emphasis on the 'thing' (*Sache*) it implies a frame of mind of
    being 'matter of fact', 'down to earth'.
2   See Adolf Loos, *Sämtliche Schriften, I*, Franz Glück (ed.), Vienna/Munich, 1962, p. 314 ff.
3   *Gerechtigkeit* implies not just 'fittingness' or 'appropriateness', but even a stronger legal or
    moral 'justice'.
4   The word *Zweck* appears throughout Adorno's speech, both alone and in various
    combinations. It permeates the tradition of German aesthetics since Kant. While it basically
    means 'purpose', it must sometimes be rendered in English as 'goal' or 'end' (as in 'means and
    end', *Mittel und Zweck*). Hence there is a certain consistency in Adorno's use of the word
    which cannot always be maintained in English.
5   *Kunstgewerbe* carries perhaps more seriousness than 'arts and crafts'. It covers the range of
    the applied arts.
6   The word *Handwerk* in German means both 'handwork' and 'craftsmanship' or 'skill'.
    Because Adorno later emphasizes the 'hand' aspect, we have decided on 'handicraft'.
7   The reference here is unclear. It means literally 'Field (or Acre) Street'. Perhaps he is referring
    to a real street, a movement, or a historical place or event. We have not been able to trace it.
8   Adolf Loos, op. cit., p. 277.
9   Ibid.
10 It is unclear in the original text to what extent the following argument is Adorno's or Loos's.
    We have tried, to some extent, to maintain the ambiguity.
11 Adolf Loos, op. cit., p. 282 ff.
12 Ibid., p. 278.
13 Ibid., p. 393.
14 Ibid., p. 345.
15 Le Corbusier, *Mein Werk*, Stuttgart, 1960, p. 306.
16 The word *Ding* ('thing') is also attached to numerous traditions in German thought and
    therefore has a certain philosophical or poetical importance (hence the 'thingliness of things').
    Heidegger and Rilke, for example, both tried to elevate the notion of *Ding* to a new essential
    and existential status.

GEORGES BATAILLE

Georges Bataille French writer and critic Georges Bataille (1897–1962) remains a controversial figure within French intellectual life. While he exerted an undoubted influence on many later thinkers, such as Jean Baudrillard, his often disturbing prose has led many to question his sanity. Yet the images of horror and obscenity in Bataille's writing play a crucial role as strategies of transgression within a world dominated by social norms and established hierarchies. Bataille seeks to untie such hierarchies and to expose them as fictions. He indulges in a form of counter-intuitive writing, which attempts to move beyond our inherited understanding of the world. Thus in his famous example of the 'solar-anus', Bataille presents an image of the sun *excreting* light. The sun and excrement *both* stand for creation and creativity. Too much sun only blinds the viewer.

Architecture enters Bataille's field of interest at both a metaphoric and a literal level. Architecture for Bataille allows for the possibility of metaphor, and forms such as the pyramid and the labyrinth are employed as metaphors for social structuration. On a second level, the hierarchies and interconnections of society can be seen to be encoded within the built environment. Architecture therefore serves as a literal manifestation of social structuration which cements the existing order. Bataille, as a theorist of transgression intent on overturning accepted norms, would have been opposed to whatever might propagate these norms. Bataille can therefore be read as a theorist *against* architecture.

In 'Architecture', one of three entries for the incomplete *Documents* dictionary, Bataille echoes some of the themes of an early essay, 'Notre-Dame de Rheims', where he had described the physical fabric of the cathedral as the embodiment of Christian values. In addition to being a manifestation of social values, architecture may condition social behaviour. Not only is architecture 'the expression of the very soul of societies', but it also has 'the authority to command and prohibit'.

'The Slaughterhouse' and 'The Museum' are the two further entries by Bataille. They give a more representative sample of the main body of his work. The slaughterhouse is the site of exclusion and the museum is the site of attraction. Yet for Bataille they are related. The slaughterhouse is 'cursed and quarantined like a boat with cholera aboard', but this is only because humans have lost touch with the notion of sacrifice. The museum is linked to the slaughterhouse, in that the palace of the Louvre was only turned into a museum after the slaughter of the French royalty. 'The origin of the modern museum,' Bataille observes, 'would thus be linked to the development of the guillotine.'

ARCHITECTURE   *Bataille*

Architecture is the expression of the very being of societies, in the same way that human physiognomy is the expression of the being of individuals. However, it is more to the physiognomies of official characters (prelates, magistrates, admirals) that this comparison must be referred. In practice, only the ideal being of society, that which orders and prohibits with authority, expresses itself in what are architectural compositions in the strict sense of the term. Thus, the great monuments are raised up like dams, pitting the logic of majesty and authority against all the shady elements: it is in the form of cathedrals and palaces that Church and State speak and impose silence on the multitudes. It is obvious, actually, that monuments inspire socially acceptable behaviour, and often a very real fear. The storming of the Bastille is symbolic of this state of affairs: it is difficult to explain this impulse of the mob other than by the animosity the people hold against the monuments which are their true masters.

Moreover, every time that architectural composition turns up somewhere other than in monuments, whether it is in physiognomy, costume, magic or painting, the predominant taste for authority, whether human or divine, can be inferred. The great compositions of certain painters express the will to restrict spirit to an official ideal. The disappearance of academic construction in painting, on the other hand, leaves the way open for expression (even going as far as exaltation) of psychological processes that are most incompatible with social stability. It is this, for the most part, that explains the intense reactions provoked in the last half century by the progressive transformation of painting, which had, until then, been characterized by a sort of concealed architectural skeleton.

It is clear, furthermore, that the mathematical regulation set in stone is nothing other than the culmination of an evolution of earthly forms, whose direction is given, in the biological order, by the transition from simian to human form, with this last presenting all the components of architecture. Men seem to represent only an intermediary stage in the morphological process that goes from apes to great edifices. Forms have become ever more static, ever more dominant. Moreover, the human order is bound up from the start with the architectural order, which is nothing but a development of the former. Such that if you attack architecture, whose monumental productions are now the true masters all across the land, gathering the servile multitudes in their shadow, enforcing admiration and astonishment, order and constraint, you are in some ways attacking man. A whole worldly activity, without doubt the most brilliant in the intellectual order, currently tends in this direction, denouncing the inadequacy of human predominance: thus, strange though it may seem, when it is a question of a creature as elegant as the human being, a way opens – as indicated by the painters – towards a bestial monstrousness; as if there were no other possibility for escape from the architectural galley.

Bataille

SLAUGHTERHOUSE

The slaughterhouse emerges from religion insofar as the temples of times past (not to mention the Hindu temples of today) had a dual purpose, being used for both supplication and slaughter. From this, without doubt (and this much can be adjudged from the chaotic appearance of the abattoirs of today), comes the startling coincidence of mythological mysteries with the lugubrious grandeur that characterizes the places where blood flows. It is curious to see an aching regret being expressed in America: W. B. Seabrook finds that current customs are insipid, remarking that the blood of sacrifice is not mixed in with cocktails.[1] Meanwhile, today, the slaughterhouse is cursed and quarantined like a boat carrying cholera. In fact, the victims of this curse are not butchers or animals, but the good people themselves, who, through this, are only able to bear their own ugliness, an ugliness that is effectively an answer to an unhealthy need for cleanliness, for a bilious small-mindedness and for boredom. The curse (which terrifies only those who utter it) leads them to vegetate as far as possible from the slaughterhouses. They exile themselves, by way of antidote, in an amorphous world, where there is no longer anything terrible, and where, enduring the ineradicable obsession with ignominy, they are reduced to eating cheese.

NOTE

1   W. B. Seabrook, *The Magic Island*, London: Marlowe & Co., 1989.

MUSEUM

According to the *Grande Encyclopédie*, the first museum in the modern sense of the word (that is, the first public collection) would have been founded in France by the Convention, on 27 July 1793. The origin of the modern museum would thus be linked to the development of the guillotine. However, Oxford's Ashmolean Museum, belonging to the University, and founded at the end of the seventeenth century, was already a public collection.

Museums have clearly developed beyond even the most optimistic hopes of the founders. It is not just that the museums of the world, as a whole, today represent a colossal accumulation of riches, but that all those who visit the museums of the world represent without doubt the most grandiose spectacle of a humanity freed from material concerns, and devoted to contemplation.

It should be taken into account that the rooms and art objects form only the container, the content of which is formed by the visitors. It is this content that distinguishes a museum from a private collection. A museum is like the lungs of a city – every Sunday the crowds flow through the museum like blood, coming out purified and fresh. The paintings are only dead surfaces, and the play, the flashes, the streams of light described by authorized critics occur within the crowd. On Sunday, at five o clock, at the exit of the Louvre, it is interesting to admire the stream of visitors, who are visibly animated by the desire to be totally like the heavenly apparition with which their eyes are still enraptured.

Grandville has schematized the container's connections with the content in   *Bataille*
museums, through an exaggeration (superficially at least) of the links formed
provisionally between visitors and visited. Similarly, when a native of the Ivory
Coast places some polished stone axes from the neolithic period into a receptacle full of water, bathes in the receptacle, and offers fowl to what he believes
to be 'thunderstones' (fallen from the sky in a crack of thunder), he merely
prefigures the attitude of enthusiasm and of profound communion with the
objects that characterizes the visitor of the modern museum.

The museum is the colossal mirror in which man finally contemplates himself in every aspect, finds himself literally admirable, and abandons himself to
the ecstasy expressed in all the art reviews.

WALTER BENJAMIN

Walter Benjamin   German literary theorist and critic Walter Benjamin (1892–1940) was a key theorist of modernity. He was above all a theorist of modernity as *urban* modernity. For Benjamin, it was through the jostling crowds of the city, and the decaying fabric of its buildings as they passed into obsolescence that one could understand modernity.

During the course of his life Benjamin became increasingly obsessed with the city. Following a series of inspired portraits of cities such as Berlin, Moscow, Marseilles and Naples, Benjamin devoted himself to a lengthy and sprawling study of the Parisian arcades, the *Passagenwerk*, or 'Arcades Project', a study which sadly remained incomplete, when he committed suicide on the Spanish border while fleeing the Nazis. An extract of the fragmentary remains of this work, 'On Some Motifs in Baudelaire', is included here. The figure whom Benjamin associates most with the arcades is the *flâneur*, who, feigning disinterest, is generated in opposition to – yet equally spawned by – the anonymity of modern existence. Unlike Simmel's blasé individual, the *flâneur* is not so much a creature of the crowd as someone who remains aloof from the crowd, and observes it from afar. Yet the *flâneur* is also to some extent blasé. The nerves of the modern metropolitan individual are constantly being bombarded with stimuli. Drawing on Freud, Benjamin explains how consciousness acts as a buffer, inducing an anaesthetizing defence against the fragmentary, alienating nature of modernity.

Benjamin offers a novel insight into the modern metropolis. Benjamin's metropolis is one entwined with myth, a seemingly paradoxical position in that, for many, modernity is seen as the obviation of myth, the disenchantment of the world. For Benjamin the metropolis is a form of dreamworld, the intoxicating site of the phantasmagoric, the kaleidoscopic and the cacophonous. The metropolis is *enslaved* by myth, a myth that adopts new guises in the supposedly progressive, fashionable world of the commodity. For Benjamin it is precisely the fetishization of the commodity, the repetition of the 'nothing-new' within the fashion industry, and the 'deception' of progress which constitutes and fuels the 'myth' of the metropolis.

Benjamin's work has much in common with that of Georg Simmel and Siegfried Kracauer. However, his position is markedly different to that of Heidegger, especially in relation to the work of art. The significance of Benjamin's thought should not be underestimated. Benjamin sowed the seeds of a critical engagement with the image which has influenced the work of Jean Baudrillard and many other subsequent theorists.

ON SOME MOTIFS IN BAUDELAIRE   *Benjamin*

The crowd – no subject was more entitled to the attention of nineteenth-century writers. It was getting ready to take shape as a public in broad strata who had acquired facility in reading. It became a customer; it wished to find itself portrayed in the contemporary novel, as the patrons did in the paintings of the Middle Ages. The most successful author of the century met this demand out of inner necessity. To him, crowd meant almost in the ancient sense – the crowd of the clients, the public. Victor Hugo was the first to address the crowd in his titles: *Les Misérables, Les Travailleurs de la Mer*. In France, Hugo was the only writer able to compete with the serial novel. As is generally known, Eugène Sue was the master of this genre, which began to be the source of revelation for the man in the street. In 1850 an overwhelming majority elected him to Parliament as representative of the city of Paris. It is no accident that the young Marx chose Sue's *Les Mystères de Paris* for an attack. He early recognized it as his task to forge the amorphous mass, which was then being wooed by an aesthetic socialism, into the iron of the proletariat. Engels' description of these masses in his early writings may be regarded as a prelude, however modest, to one of Marx's themes. In his book The *Condition of the Working Class in England*, Engels writes:

> A city like London, where one can roam about for hours without reaching the beginning of an end, without seeing the slightest indication that open country is nearby, is really something very special. This colossal centralization, this agglomeration of three and a half million people on a single spot has multiplied the strength of these three and a half million inhabitants a hundredfold ... But the price that has been paid is not discovered until later. Only when one has tramped the pavements of the main streets for a few days does one notice that these Londoners have had to sacrifice what is best in human nature in order to create all the wonders of civilization with which their city teems, that a hundred creative faculties that lay dormant in them remained inactive and were suppressed ... There is something distasteful about the very bustle of the streets, something that is abhorrent to human nature itself. Hundreds of thousands of people of all classes and ranks of society jostle past one another; are they not all human beings with the same characteristics and potentialities, equally interested in the pursuit of happiness? ... And yet they rush past one another as if they had nothing in common or were in no way associated with one another. Their only agreement is a tacit one: that everyone should keep to the right of the pavement, so as not to impede the stream of people moving in the opposite direction. No one even bothers to spare a glance for the others. The greater the number of people that are packed into a tiny space, the more repulsive and offensive becomes the brutal indifference, the unfeeling concentration of each person on his private affairs.

This description differs markedly from those to be found in minor French masters, such as Gozlan, Delvau, or Lurine. It lacks the skill and ease with

Benjamin which the *flâneur* moves among the crowd and which the journalist eagerly
learns from him. Engels is dismayed by the crowd; he responds with a moral
reaction, and an aesthetic one as well; the speed with which people rush past
one another unsettles him. The charm of his description lies in the intersecting
of unshakeable critical integrity with an old-fashioned attitude. The writer
came from a Germany that was still provincial; he may never have faced the
temptation to lose himself in a stream of people. When Hegel went to Paris
for the first time, not long before his death, he wrote to his wife: 'When I walk
through the streets, people look just as they do in Berlin; they wear the same
clothes and the faces are about the same – the same aspect, but in a large
crowd.' To move in this crowd was natural for a Parisian. No matter how
great the distance which an individual cared to keep from it, he still was
coloured by it and, unlike Engels, was not able to view it from without. As
regards Baudelaire, the masses were anything but external to him; indeed, it is
easy to trace in his works his defensive reaction to their attraction and allure.

The masses had become so much a part of Baudelaire that it is rare to find a
description of them in his works. His most important subjects are hardly ever
encountered in descriptive form. As Dujardin so aptly put it, he was 'more
concerned with implanting the image in the memory than with adorning and
elaborating it'. It is futile to search in *Les Fleurs du Mal* or in *Spleen de Paris* for
any counterpart to the portrayals of the city which Victor Hugo did with such
mastery. Baudelaire describes neither the Parisians nor their city. Forgoing such
descriptions enables him to invoke the ones in the form of the other. His crowd
is always the crowd of a big city, his Paris is invariably overpopulated. It is this
that makes him so superior to Barbier, whose descriptive method caused a rift
between the masses and the city.[1] In *Tableaux Parisiens* the secret presence of a
crowd is demonstrable almost everywhere. When Baudelaire takes the dawn as
his theme, the deserted streets emanate something of that 'silence of a throng'
which Hugo senses in nocturnal Paris. As Baudelaire looks at the plates in the
anatomical works for sale on the dusty banks of the Seine, the mass of the
departed takes the place of the singular skeletons on these pages. In the figures
of the *danse macabre,* he sees a compact mass on the move. The heroism of the
wizened old women whom the cycle 'Les petites vieilles' follows on their
rounds, consists in their standing apart from the crowd, unable to keep its pace,
no longer participating with their thoughts in the present. The mass was the
agitated veil; through it Baudelaire saw Paris. The presence of the mass determines one of the most famous components of *Les Fleurs du Mal.*

In the sonnet '*À une passante*' the crowd is nowhere named in either word or
phrase. And yet the whole happening hinges on it, just as the progress of a
sailboat depends on the wind.

> *La rue assourdissante autour de moi hurlait.*
> *Longue, mince, en grand deuil, douleur majestueuse,*
> *Une femme passa, d'une main fastueuse*
> *Soulevant, balancant le feston et l'ourlet;*
>
> *Agile et noble, avec sa jambe de statue.*
> *Moi, je buvais, crispé comme un extravagant,*
> *Dans son oeil, ciel livide où germe l'outragan,*
> *La douceur qui fascine et le plaisir qui tue.*

Benjamin

Un éclair . . . puis la nuit! – Fugitive beauté
Dont le regard m'a fait soudainement renaître,
Ne te verraije plus que dans l'éternité?

Ailleurs, bien loin d'ici! Trop tard! Jamais peut-être!
Car j'ignore où tu fuis, tu ne sais où je vais,
O toi que j'eusse aimée, ô toi qui le savais!

The deafening street was screaming all around me.
Tall, slender, in deep mourning – majestic grief –
A woman made her way, with fastidious hand
Raising and swaying festoon and hem;

Agile and noble, with her statue's limbs.
And there was I, who drank, contorted like a madman,
Within her eyes, that livid sky where hurricane is born
Gentleness that fascinates, pleasure that kills.

A lightning-flash . . . then night! – O fleeting beauty
Whose glance all of a sudden gave me new birth,
Shall I see you again only in eternity?

Far, far from here! Too late! or maybe, *never?*
For I know not where you flee, you know not where I go,
O you I would have loved (o you who knew it too!)

In a widow's veil, mysteriously and mutely borne along by the crowd, an unknown woman comes into the poet's field of vision. What this sonnet communicates is simply this: far from experiencing the crowd as an opposed, antagonistic element, this very crowd brings to the city dweller the figure that fascinates. The delight of the urban poet is love – not at first sight, but at last sight. It is a farewell forever which coincides in the poem with the moment of enchantment. Thus the sonnet supplies the figure of shock, indeed of catastrophe. But the nature of the poet's emotions has been affected as well. What makes his body contract in a tremor – *crispé comme un extravagant*, Baudelaire says – is not the rapture of a man whose every fibre is suffused with *eros*; it is, rather, like the kind of sexual shock that can beset a lonely man. The fact that 'these verses could only have been written in a big city', as Thibaudet put it, is not very meaningful. They reveal the stigmata which life in a metropolis inflicts upon love. Proust read the sonnet in this light, and that is why he gave his later echo of the woman in mourning, which appeared to him one day in the form of Albertine, the evocative caption 'La Parisienne'.

> When Albertine came into my room again, she wore a black satin dress. It made her pale, and she resembled the type of the fiery and yet pale Parisian woman, the woman who is not used to fresh air and has been affected by living among the masses and possibly in an atmosphere of vice, the kind that can be recognized by a certain glance which seems unsteady if there is no rouge on her cheeks.

This is the look – even as late as Proust – of the object of a love which only a city dweller experiences, which Baudelaire captured for poetry, and of which one might not infrequently say that it was spared, rather than denied, fulfilment.[2]

. story by Poe which Baudelaire translated may be regarded as the classic xample among the older versions of the motif of the crowd. It is marked by :ertain peculiarities which, upon closer inspection, reveal aspects of social forces of such power and hidden depth that we may count them among those which alone are capable of exerting both a subtle and a profound effect upon artistic production. The story is entitled 'The Man of the Crowd'. Set in London, its narrator is a man who, after a long illness, ventures out again for the first time into the hustle and bustle of the city. In the late afternoon hours of an autumn day he installs himself behind a window in a big London coffee-house. He looks over the other guests, pores over advertisements in the paper, but his main focus of interest is the throng of people surging past his window in the street.

> The latter is one of the principal thoroughfares of the city, and had been very much crowded during the whole day. But, as the darkness came on, the throng momently increased; and by the time the lamps were well lighted, two dense and continuous tides of population were rushing past the door. At this particular period of the evening I had never before been in a similar situation, and the tumultuous sea of human heads filled me, therefore, with a delicious novelty of emotion. I gave up, at length, all care of things within the hotel, and became absorbed in contemplation of the scene without.

Important as it is, let us disregard the narrative to which this is the prelude and examine the setting.

The appearance of the London crowd as Poe describes it is as gloomy and fitful as the light of the gas lamps overhead. This applies not only to the riffraff that is 'brought forth from its den' as night falls. The employees of higher rank, 'the upper clerks of staunch firms', Poe describes as follows:

> They had all slightly bald heads, from which the right ears, long used to pen-holding, had an odd habit of standing off on end. I observed that they always removed or settled their hats with both hands, and wore watches, with short gold chains of a substantial and ancient pattern.

Even more striking is his description of the crowd's movements.

> By far the greater number of those who went by had a satisfied business-like demeanour, and seemed to be thinking only of making their way through the press. Their brows were knit, and their eyes rolled quickly; when pushed against by fellow-wayfarers they evinced no symptom of impatience, but adjusted their clothes and hurried on. Others, still a numerous class, were restless in their movements, had flushed faces, and talked and gesticulated to them-selves, as if feeling in solitude on account of the very denseness of the company around. When impeded in their progress, these people suddenly ceased muttering, but redoubled their gesticulations, and awaited, with an absent and overdone smile upon the lips, the course of the persons impeding them. If jostled, they bowed pro-fusely to the jostlers, and appeared overwhelmed with confusion.[3]

One might think he was speaking of half-drunken wretches. Actually, they were 'noblemen, merchants, attorneys, tradesmen, stockjobbers'.[4]

Poe's manner of presentation cannot be called realism. It shows a purposely distorting imagination at work, one that removes the text far from what is commonly advocated as the model of social realism. Barbier, perhaps one of the best examples of this type of realism that come to mind, describes things in a less eccentric way. Moreover, he chose a more transparent subject: the oppressed masses. Poe is not concerned with these; he deals with 'people' pure and simple. For him, as for Engels, there was something menacing in the spectacle they presented. It is precisely this image of big-city crowds that became decisive for Baudelaire. If he succumbed to the force by which he was drawn to them and, as a *flâneur*, was made one of them, he was nevertheless unable to rid himself of a sense of their essentially inhuman make-up. He becomes their accomplice even as he dissociates himself from them. He becomes deeply involved with them, only to relegate them to oblivion with a single glance of contempt. There is something compelling about this ambivalence where he cautiously admits to it. Perhaps the charm of his '*Crépuscule du soir*,' so difficult to account for, is bound up with this.

Baudelaire saw fit to equate the man of the crowd, whom Poe's narrator follows throughout the length and breadth of nocturnal London, with the *flâneur*. It is hard to accept this view. The man of the crowd is no *flâneur*. In him, composure has given way to manic behaviour. Hence he exemplifies, rather, what had to become of the *flâneur* once he was deprived of the milieu to which he belonged. If London ever provided it for him, it was certainly not the setting described by Poe. In comparison, Baudelaire's Paris preserved some features that dated back to the happy old days. Ferries were still crossing the Seine at points that would later be spanned by the arch of a bridge. In the year of Baudelaire's death it was still possible for some entrepreneur to cater to the comfort of the well-to-do with a fleet of five hundred sedan chairs circulating about the city. Arcades where the *flâneur* would not be exposed to the sight of carriages that did not recognize pedestrians as rivals were enjoying undiminished popularity.[5] There was the pedestrian who would let himself be jostled by the crowd, but there was also the *flâneur* who demanded elbow room and was unwilling to forgo the life of a gentleman of leisure. Let the many attend to their daily affairs; the man of leisure can indulge in the perambulations of the *flâneur* only if as such he is already out of place. He is as much out of place in an atmosphere of complete leisure as in the feverish turmoil of the city. London has its man of the crowd. His counterpart, as it were, is the boy Nante (Ferdinand), of the street corner, a popular figure in Berlin before the March Revolution of 1848; the Parisian *flâneur* might be said to stand midway between them.[6]

How the man of leisure looks upon the crowd is revealed in a short piece by E. T. A. Hoffmann, the last that he wrote, entitled 'The Cousin's Corner Window'. It antedates Poe's story by fifteen years and is probably one of the earliest attempts to capture the street scene of a large city. The differences between the two pieces are worth noting. Poe's narrator observes from behind the window of a public coffeehouse, whereas the cousin is installed at home. Poe's observer succumbs to the fascination of the scene, which finally lures him outside into the whirl of the crowd. Hoffmann's cousin, looking out from his corner window, is immobilized as a paralytic; he would not be able to follow the crowd even if he were in the midst of it. His attitude toward the crowd is, rather, one of superiority, inspired as it is by his observation post at the window of an apartment building. From this vantage point he scrutinizes the throng; it is market day, and they all feel in their element. His opera glasses enable him to pick out individual genre scenes. The employment of this instrument is thoroughly in keeping with the inner disposition of its user. He would like, as he admits, to initiate his visitor into the 'principles of the art of seeing'.[7] This consists of an ability to enjoy *tableaux vivants* – a favourite pursuit of the Biedermeier period. Edifying sayings provide the interpretation.[8] One can look upon the narrative as an attempt which was then due to be made. But it is obvious that the conditions under which it was made in Berlin prevented it from being a complete success. If Hoffmann had ever set foot in Paris or London, or if he had been intent upon depicting the masses as such, he would not have focused on a market place; he would not have portrayed the scene as being dominated by women; he would perhaps have seized on the motifs that Poe derives from the swarming crowds under the gas lamps. Actually, there would have been no need for these motifs in order to bring out the uncanny elements that other students of the physiognomy of the big city have felt. A thoughtful observation by Heine is relevant here: 'Heine's eyesight,' wrote a correspondent in a letter to Varnhagen in 1838,

> caused him acute trouble in the spring. On the last such occasion I was walking down one of the boulevards with him. The magnificence, the life of this in its way unique thoroughfare roused me to boundless admiration, something that prompted Heine this time to make a significant point in stressing the horror with which this centre of the world was tinged.

Fear, revulsion and horror were the emotions which the big-city crowd aroused in those who first observed it. For Poe it has something barbaric; discipline just barely manages to tame it. Later, James Ensor tirelessly confronted its discipline with its wildness; he liked to put military groups in his carnival mobs, and both got along splendidly – as the prototype of totalitarian states, in which the police make common cause with the looters. Valéry, who had a fine eye for the cluster of symptoms called 'civilization', has characterized one of the pertinent facts.

> The inhabitant of the great urban centres reverts to a state of savagery – that is, of isolation. The feeling of being dependent on others, which used to be kept alive by need, is gradually blunted in the smooth functioning of the social mechanism. Any improvement of this mechanism eliminates certain modes of behaviour and emotions.

Comfort isolates; on the other hand, it brings those enjoying it closer to mechanization. The invention of the match around the middle of the nineteenth century brought forth a number of innovations which have one thing in common: one abrupt movement of the hand triggers a process of many steps. This development is taking place in many areas. One case in point is the telephone, where the lifting of a receiver has taken the place of the steady movement that used to be required to crank the older models. Of the countless movements of switching, inserting, pressing and the like, the 'snapping' of the photographer has had the greatest consequences. A touch of the finger now sufficed to fix an event for an unlimited period of time. The camera gave the moment a posthumous shock, as it were. Haptic experiences of this kind were joined by optic ones, such as are supplied by the advertising pages of a newspaper or the traffic of a big city. Moving through this traffic involves the individual in a series of shocks and collisions. At dangerous intersections, nervous impulses flow through him in rapid succession, like the energy from a battery. Baudelaire speaks of a man who plunges into the crowd as into a reservoir of electric energy. Circumscribing the experience of the shock, he calls this man 'a *kaleidoscope* equipped with consciousness'. Whereas Poe's passers-by cast glances in all directions which still appeared to be aimless, today's pedestrians are obliged to do so in order to keep abreast of traffic signals. Thus technology has subjected the human sensorium to a complex kind of training. There came a day when a new and urgent need for stimuli was met by the film. In a film, perception in the form of shocks was established as a formal principle. That which determines the rhythm of production on a conveyor belt is the basis of the rhythm of reception in the film.

Marx had good reason to stress the great fluidity of the connection between segments in manual labour. This connection appears to the factory worker on an assembly line in an independent, objectified form. Independently of the worker's volition, the article being worked on comes within his range of action and moves away from him just as arbitrarily. 'It is a common characteristic of all capitalist production . . . ,' wrote Marx, 'that the worker does not make use of the working conditions. The working conditions make use of the worker; but it takes machinery to give this reversal a technically concrete form.' In working with machines, workers learn to co-ordinate 'their own movements with the uniformly constant movements of an automaton'. These words shed a peculiar light on the absurd kind of uniformity with which Poe wants to saddle the crowd – uniformities of attire and behaviour, but also a uniformity of facial expression. Those smiles provide food for thought. They are probably the familiar kind, as expressed in the phrase 'keep smiling'; in that context they function as a mimetic shock absorber. 'All machine work,' it is said in the above context, 'requires early drilling of the worker.' This drill must be differentiated from practice. Practice, which was the sole determinant in craftsmanship, still had a function in manufacturing. With it as the basis, 'each particular area of production finds its appropriate technical form in *experience* and *slowly* perfects it'. To be sure, it quickly crystallizes it, 'as soon as a certain degree of maturity has been attained'. On the other hand, this same manufacturing produces

> in every handicraft it seizes a class of so-called unskilled labourers which the handicraft system strictly excluded. In developing the greatly simplified specialty to the point of virtuosity at the cost of the work capacity as a whole, it starts turning the lack of any development into a specialty. In addition to ranks we get the simple division of workers into the skilled and the unskilled.

The unskilled worker is the one most deeply degraded by the drill of the machines. His work has been sealed off from experience; practice counts for

Benjamin nothing there.[9] What the Fun Fair achieves with its dodgem cars and other
similar amusements is nothing but a taste of the drill to which the unskilled
labourer is subjected in the factory – a sample which at times was for him the
entire menu; for the art of being off centre, in which the little man could acquire
training in places like the fun fair, flourished concomitantly with unemployment. Poe's text makes us understand the true connection between wildness
and discipline. His pedestrians act as if they had adapted themselves to the
machines and could express themselves only automatically. Their behaviour is
a reaction to shocks. 'If jostled, they bowed profusely to the jostlers.'

NOTES

1   Characteristic of Barbier's method is his poem 'Londres' which in 24 lines describes the city,
    awkwardly closing with the following verses:

> *Enfin, dans un amas de choses, sombre, immense,*
> *Un peuple noir, vivant et mourant en silence.*
> *Des êtres par milliers, suivant l'instinct fatal,*
> *Et courant après l'or par le bien et le mal.*
> (Auguste Barbier, *Iambes et poèmes*. Paris, 1841.)

> Finally, within a huge and sombre mass of things,
> A blackened people, who live and die in silence.
> Thousands of beings, who follow a fatal instinct,
> Pursuing gold with good and evil means.

Barbier's tendentious poems, particularly the London cycle, *Lazare*, influenced Baudelaire
more profoundly than people have been willing to admit. Baudelaire's 'Crépuscule du soir'
concludes as follows:

> *. . . ils finissent*
> Leur destinée et vont vers le gouffre commun;
> L'hôpital se remplit de leurs soupirs. – Plus d'un
> Ne viendra plus chercher la soupe parfumée,
> *Au coin du feu, le soir, auprès d'une âme aimée.*

> . . . their fate
> Accomplished, they approach the common pit;
> Their sighings fill the ward. – More than one
> Will come no more to get his fragrant soup,
> At night, by the fireside, next to a beloved one.

Compare this with the end of the eighth stanza of Barbier's 'Mineurs de Newcastle':

> *Et plus d'un qui rêvait, dans le fond de son âme*
> *Aux douceurs du logis, à l'oeil bleu de sa femme,*
> *Trouve au ventre du gouffre un éternel tombeau.*

> And more than one who in his heart of hearts had dreams
> Of home, sweet home, and of his wife's blue eyes,
> Finds, within the belly of the pit, an everlasting tomb.

With a little masterful retouching Baudelaire turns a 'miner's fate' into the commonplace end
of big-city dwellers.

2   The motif of love for a woman passing by occurs in an early poem by Stefan George. The poet
    has missed the important thing: the stream in which the woman moves past, borne along by
    the crowd. The result is a self-conscious elegy. The poet's glances – so he must confess to his
    lady – have 'moved away, moist with longing/before they dared mingle with yours' ('*feucht
    vor sehnen fortgezogen/eh sie in deine sich zu tauchen trauten*'. Stefan George, *Hymnen.
    Pilgerfahrten. Algabal.* Berlin, 1922). Baudelaire leaves no doubt that *he* looked deep into the
    eyes of the passer-by.

3   This passage has a parallel in 'Un Jour de pluie'. Even though it bears another name, this poem
    must be ascribed to Baudelaire. The last verse, which gives the poem its extraordinarily sombre
    quality, has an exact counterpart in 'The Man of the Crowd'. Poe writes: 'The rays of the gas
    lamps, feeble at first in their struggle with the dying day, had now at length gained ascendancy, and

threw over everything a fitful and garish lustre. All was dark yet splendid – as that ebony to which *Benjamin*
has been likened the style of Tertullian.' This coincidence is all the more astonishing here as the
following verses were written in 1843 at the latest, a period when Baudelaire did not know Poe.

> *Chacun, nous coudoyant sur le trottoir glissant,*
> *Egoïste et brutal, passe et nous éclabousse,*
> *Ou, pour courir plus vite, en s'éloignant nous pousse.*
> *Partout fange, déluge, obscurité du ciel.*
> *Noir tableau qu'eût rêvé le noir Ezéchiel.*

> Each one, elbowing us upon the slippery sidewalk,
> Selfish and savage goes by and splashes us,
> Or, to run the faster, gives us a push as he makes off.
> Mud everywhere, deluge, darkness in the sky.
> A sombre scene that Ezekiel the sombre might have dreamed.

4   There is something demonic about Poe's businessmen. One is reminded of Marx, who blamed
the 'feverishly youthful pace of material production' in the United States for the lack of 'either
time or opportunity ... to abolish the old world of the spirit'. As darkness descends,
Baudelaire has 'the harmful demons' awaken in the air 'sluggish as a bunch of businessmen'.
This passage in '*Crépuscule du soir*' may have been inspired by Poe's text.

5   A pedestrian knew how to display his nonchalance provocatively on certain occasions.
Around 1840 it was briefly fashionable to take turtles for a walk in the arcades. The *flâneurs*
liked to have the turtles set the pace for them. If they had had their way, progress would have
been obliged to accommodate itself to this pace. But this attitude did not prevail; Taylor, who
popularized the watchword 'Down with dawdling!', carried the day.

6   In Glassbrenner's character the man of leisure appears as a paltry scion of the *citoyen*. Nante,
Berlin's street-corner boy, has no reason to bestir himself. He makes himself at home on the
street, which naturally does not lead him anywhere, and is as comfortable as the philistine is in
his four walls.

7   What leads up to this confession is remarkable. The visitor says that the cousin watches the
bustle down below only because he enjoys the changing play of the colours; in the long run, he
says, this must be tiring. In a similar vein, and probably not much later, Gogol wrote of a fair
in the Ukraine: 'So many people were on their way there that it made one's eyes swim.' The
daily sight of a lively crowd may once have constituted a spectacle to which one's eyes had to
adapt first. On the basis of this supposition, one may assume that once the eyes had mastered
this task they welcomed opportunities to test their newly acquired faculties. This would mean
that the technique of Impressionist painting, whereby the picture is garnered in a riot of dabs
of colour, would be a reflection of experiences with which the eyes of a big-city dweller have
become familiar. A picture like Monet's 'Cathedral of Chartres', which is like an ant-heap of
stone, would be an illustration of this hypothesis.

8   In his story E. T. A. Hoffmann devotes edifying reflections, for instance, to the blind man who
lifts his head toward the sky. In the last line of 'Les Aveugles', Baudelaire, who knew this story,
modifies Hoffmann's reflections in such a way as to disprove their edifying quality: '*Que
cherchent-ils au Ciel, tous ces aveugles?*' [What are all those blind people looking for in the sky?]

9   The shorter the training period of an industrial worker is, the longer that of a military man
becomes. It may be part of society's preparation for total war that training is shifting from the
practice of production to the practice of destruction.

PARIS, CAPITAL OF THE NINETEENTH CENTURY

The waters are blue and the vegetation pink;
The evening sweet to behold;
People are out walking. Great ladies promenade;
    and behind them walk the small ladies.
                    Nguyen-Trong-Hiep: *Paris, Capital of France* (1897)

1. Fourier, or The Arcades

De ces palais les colonnes magiques
A l'amateur montrent de toutes parts

Benjamin   Dans les objets qu'étalent leurs portiques
              Que l'industrie est rivale aux arts.
                                                    Nouveaux tableaux de Paris (1828)

Most of the Paris arcades are built in the decade and a half after 1822. The first
condition for this new fashion is the boom in the textile trade. The *magasins de
nouveauté,* the first establishments to keep large stocks of goods on their
premises, begin to appear, precursors of the department stores. It is the time of
which Balzac wrote, 'The great poem of display chants its many-coloured
strophes from the Madeleine to the Porte-Saint-Denis.' The arcades are a centre
of trade in luxury goods. In their fittings art is brought in to the service of
commerce. Contemporaries never tire of admiring them. They long remain a
centre of attraction for foreigners. An *Illustrated Guide to Paris* said:

> These arcades, a recent invention of industrial luxury, are glass-
> roofed, marble-walled passages cut through whole blocks of
> houses, whose owners have combined in this speculation. On either
> side of the passages, which draw their light from above, run the
> most elegant shops, so that an arcade of this kind is a city, indeed, a
> world in miniature.

The arcades are the scene of the first gas lighting.

The second condition for the construction of the arcades is the advent of
building in iron. The Empire saw in this technique an aid to a renewal of
architecture in the ancient Greek manner. The architectural theorist Bötticher
expresses a general conviction when he says, 'with regard to the artistic form of
the new system, the formal principle of the Hellenic style' should be introduced.
Empire is the style of revolutionary heroism for which the state is an end in
itself. Just as Napoleon failed to recognize the functional nature of the state as
an instrument of domination by the bourgeois class, neither did the master
builders of his time perceive the functional nature of iron, through which the
constructive principle began its domination of architecture. These builders
model their pillars on Pompeian columns, their factories on houses, as later the
first railway stations are to resemble chalets. 'Construction fills the role of the
unconscious.' Nevertheless the idea of the engineer, originating in the revolutionary wars, begins to assert itself, and battle is joined between constructor
and decorator, Ecole Polytechnique and Ecole des Beaux-Arts.

In iron, an artificial building material makes its appearance for the first time
in the history of architecture. It undergoes a development that accelerates in the
course of the century. The decisive breakthrough comes when it emerges that
the locomotive, with which experiments had been made since the end of the
1820s, could only be used on iron rails. The rail becomes the first prefabricated
iron component, the forerunner of the girder. Iron is avoided in residential
buildings and used in arcades, exhibition halls, stations – buildings serving
transitory purposes. Simultaneously, the architectonic scope for the application
of glass expands. The social conditions for its intensified use as a building
material do not arrive, however, until a hundred years later. Even in
Scheerbart's 'glass architecture' (1914) it appears in utopian contexts.

Chaque époque rêve la suivante.

                                                    Michelet, *Avenir! Avenir!*

Corresponding in the collective consciousness to the forms of the new means of   *Benjamin*
production, which at first were still dominated by the old (Marx), are images in
which the new is intermingled with the old. These images are wishful fantasies,
and in them the collective seeks both to preserve and to transfigure the
inchoateness of the social product and the deficiencies in the social system of
production. In addition, these wish-fulfilling images manifest an emphatic
striving for dissociation with the outmoded – which means, however, with the
most recent past. These tendencies direct the visual imagination, which has
been activated by the new, back to the primaeval past. In the dream in which,
before the eyes of each epoch, that which is to follow appears in images, the
latter appears wedded to elements from prehistory, that is, of a classless society.
Intimations of this, deposited in the unconscious of the collective, mingle with
the new to produce the utopia that has left its traces in thousands of configurations of life, from permanent buildings to fleeting fashions.

This state of affairs is discernible in Fourier's utopia. Its chief impetus comes
from the advent of machines. But this is not directly expressed in his accounts
of it; these have their origin in the morality of trade and the false morality
propagated in its service. His phalanstery is supposed to lead men back to
conditions in which virtue is superfluous. Its highly complicated organization is
like a piece of machinery. The meshing of passions, the intricate interaction of
the *passions mécanistes* with the *passion cabaliste,* are primitive analogies to
machinery in the material of psychology. This human machinery produces the
land of milk and honey, the primaeval wish symbol that Fourier's utopia filled
with new life.

In the arcades, Fourier saw the architectonic canon of the phalanstery. His
reactionary modification of them is characteristic: whereas they originally serve
commercial purposes, he makes them into dwelling places. The phalanstery
becomes a city of arcades. Fourier installs in the austere, formal world of the
Empire the colourful idyll of Biedermeier. Its radiance lasts, though paled, till
Zola. He takes up Fourier's ideas in *Travail,* as he takes leave of the arcades in
Thérèse Raquin. Marx defends Fourier to Carl Grun, emphasizing his 'colossal
vision of man'. He also draws attention to Fourier's humour. And in fact Jean
Paul in *Levana is* as closely related to Fourier the pedagogue as Scheerbart in
his 'glass architecture' is to Fourier the utopian.

LOUIS-PHILIPPE, OR THE INTERIOR

Une tête, sur la table de nuit, repose
Comme un renoncule.

Baudelaire, 'Un martyre'

Under Louis-Philippe the private citizen enters the stage of history. The
extension of the democratic apparatus through a new franchise coincides with
the parliamentary corruption organized by Guihot. Under its protection the
ruling class makes history by pursuing its business interests. It promotes railway construction to improve its share holdings. It favours Louis-Philippe as a
private citizen at the head of affairs. By the time of the July Revolution, the
bourgeoisie has realized the aims of 1789 (Marx).

For the private person, living space becomes, for the first time, antithetical to

Benjamin   the place of work. The former is constituted by the interior; the office is its complement. The private person who squares his accounts with reality in his office demands that the interior be maintained in his illusions. This need is all the more pressing since he has no intention of extending his commercial considerations into social ones. In shaping his private environment he represses both. From this spring the phantasmagorias of the interior. For the private individual the private environment represents the universe. In it he gathers remote places and the past. His drawing room is a box in the world theatre.

Excursus on art nouveau. About the turn of the century, the interior is shaken by art nouveau. Admittedly the latter, through its ideology, seems to bring with it the consummation of the interior – the transfiguration of the solitary soul appears its goal. Individualism is its theory. In Vandervelde the house appears as the expression of personality. Ornament is to this house what the signature is to a painting. The real meaning of art nouveau is not expressed in this ideology. It represents art's last attempt to escape from its ivory tower, which is besieged by technology. Art nouveau mobilizes all the reserves of inwardness. They find their expression in mediumistic line-language, in the flower as the symbol of naked, vegetal nature confronting a technically armed environment. The new elements of iron building, girder forms, preoccupy art nouveau. In ornamentation it strives to win back these forms for art. Concrete offers it the prospect of new plastic possibilities in architecture. About this time the real centre of gravity of living space is transferred to the office. The de-realized individual creates a place for himself in the private home. Art nouveau is summed up by *The Master Builder* – the attempt by the individual to do battle with technology on the basis of his inwardness leads to his downfall.

Je crois . . . à mon âme: la Chose.

Léon Deubel, *Oeuvres* (Paris 1929)

The interior is the retreat of art. The collector is a true inmate of the interior. He makes the transfiguration of things his business. To him falls the Sisyphean task of obliterating the commodity-like character of things through his ownership of them. But he merely confers connoisseur value on them, instead of intrinsic value. The collector dreams that he is not only in a distant or past world but also, at the same time, in a better one, in which, although men are as unprovided with what they need as in the everyday world, things are free of the drudgery of being useful.

The interior is not only the universe but also the *etui* of the private person. To live means to leave traces. In the interior these are emphasized. An abundance of covers and protectors, liners and cases is devised, on which the traces of objects of everyday use are imprinted. The traces of the occupant also leave their impression on the interior. The detective story that follows these traces comes into being. His 'philosophy of furniture', along with his detective novellas, shows Poe to be the first physiognomist of the interior. The criminals of the first detective novels are neither gentlemen nor apaches, but private members of the bourgeoisie.

BAUDELAIRE, OR THE STREETS OF PARIS

Tout pour moi devient Allégorie.

Baudelaire, 'Le cygne'

Baudelaire's genius, which is fed on melancholy, is an allegorical genius. In   *Benjamin*
Baudelaire Paris becomes for the first time a subject of lyric poetry. This poetry
is not regional art; rather, the gaze of the allegorist that falls on the city is
estranged. It is the gaze of the *flâneur,* whose mode of life still surrounds the
approaching desolation of city life with a propitiatory lustre. The *flâneur* is still
on the threshold, of the city as of the bourgeois class. Neither has yet engulfed
him; in neither is he at home. He seeks refuge in the crowd. Early contributions
to a physiognomics of the crowd are to be found in Engels and Poe. The crowd
is the veil through which the familiar city lures the *flâneur* like a phantasmagoria. In it the city is now a landscape, now a room. Both, then, constitute
the department store that puts even *flânerie* to use for commodity circulation.
The department store is the *flâneur*'s last practical joke.

In the *flâneur* the intelligentsia pays a visit to the marketplace, ostensibly to
look around, yet in reality to find a buyer. In this intermediate phase, in which
it still has patrons but is already beginning to familiarize itself with the market,
it appears as bohemianism. The uncertainty of its political function corresponds to the uncertainty of its economic position. This is most strikingly
expressed in the professional conspirators, who are certainly a part of Bohemia.
Their first field of activity is the army; later it becomes the petit bourgeoisie,
occasionally the proletariat. Yet this stratum sees its opponents in the real
leaders of the latter. The *Communist Manifesto* puts an end to their political
existence. Baudelaire's poetry draws its strength from the rebellious emotion-
alism of this group. He throws his lot in with the asocial. His only sexual
communion is realized with a whore.

> Facilis descensus Averni
>
>   Virgil, *Aeneid*

What is unique in Baudelaire's poetry is that the images of women and death
are permeated by a third, that of Paris. The Paris of his poems is a submerged
city, more submarine than subterranean. The chthonic elements of the city – its
topo-graphical formation, the old deserted bed of the Seine – doubtless left their
impression on his work. Yet what is decisive in Baudelaire's 'deathly idyll' of the
city is a social, modern substratum. Modernity is a main accent in his poetry.
He shatters the ideal as spleen (*Spleen et Idéal*). But it is precisely modernity
that is always quoting primaeval history. This happens here through the
ambiguity attending the social relationships and products of this epoch.
Ambiguity is the pictorial image of dialectics, the law of dialectics seen at a
standstill. This standstill is utopia and the dialectic image therefore a dream
image. Such an image is presented by the pure commodity: as fetish. Such an
image are the arcades, which are both house and stars. Such an image is the
prostitute, who is saleswoman and wares in one.

> Le voyage pour découvrir ma géographie
>   Note of a madman (Paris 1907)

The last poem of the *Flowers of Evil*, 'The Journey': 'Oh death, old captain, it is
time, let us weigh anchor.' The last journey of the *flâneur*: death. Its destination:
the new. 'To the depths of the unknown, there to find something new.' Novelty
is a quality independent of the intrinsic value of the commodity. It is the origin
of the illusion inseverable from the images produced by the collective

unconscious. It is the quintessence of false consciousness, whose indefatigable agent is fashion. The illusion of novelty is reflected, like one mirror in another, in the illusion of perpetual sameness. The product of this reflection is the phantasmagoria of 'cultural history', in which the bourgeoisie savours its false consciousness to the last. The art that begins to doubt its task and ceases to be 'inseparable from utility' (Baudelaire) must make novelty its highest value. The snob becomes its *arbiter novarum rerum*. He is to art what the dandy is to fashion. As in the seventeenth century the canon of dialectical imagery came to be allegory, in the nineteenth it is novelty. The *magasins de nouveauté* are joined by the newspapers. The press organizes the market in intellectual values, in which prices at first soar. Nonconformists rebel against the handing over of art to the market. They gather around the banner of '*l'art pour l'art*'. This slogan springs from the conception of the total artwork, which attempts to isolate art from the development of technology. The solemnity with which it is celebrated is the corollary to the frivolity that glorifies the commodity. Both abstract from the social existence of man. Baudelaire succumbs to the infatuation of Wagner.

HAUSSMANN, OR THE BARRICADES

> J'ai le culte du Beau, du Bien, des grandes choses,
> De la belle nature inspirant le grand art,
> Qu'il enchante l'oreille ou charme le regard;
> J'ai l'amour du printemps en fleurs: femmes et roses.
> > Baron Haussmann, *Confession d'un lion devenu vieux*

> The blossomy realm of decoration,
> Landscape and architecture's charm
> And all effects of scenery repose
> Upon perspective's law alone.
> > Franz Böhle, *Theatrical Catechism*

Haussmann's urban ideal was of long perspectives of streets and thoroughfares. This corresponds to the inclination, noticeable again and again in the nineteenth century, to ennoble technical necessities by artistic aims. The institutions of the secular and clerical dominance of the bourgeoisie were to find their apotheosis in a framework of streets. Streets, before their completion, were draped in canvas and unveiled like monuments. Haussmann's efficiency is integrated with Napoleonic idealism. The latter favours finance capital. Paris experiences a flowering of speculation. Playing the Stock Exchange displaces the game of chance in the forms that had come down from feudal society. To the phantasmagorias of space to which the *flâneur* abandons himself, correspond the phantasmagorias of time indulged in by the gambler. Gambling converts time into a narcotic. Lafargue declares gaming an imitation in miniature of the mysteries of economic prosperity. The expropriations by Haussmann call into being a fraudulent speculation. The arbitration of the Court of Cassation, inspired by the bourgeois and Orleanist opposition, increases the financial risk of Haussmannization. Haussmann attempts to strengthen his dictatorship and to place Paris under an emergency regime. In 1864 he gives expression in a parliamentary speech to his hatred of the rootless population of big cities. The

latter is constantly increased by his enterprises. The rise in rents drives the *Benjamin*
proletariat into the suburbs. The *quartiers* of Paris thus lose their individual
physiognomies. The red belt is formed. Haussmann gave himself the name of
'artist in demolition'. He felt himself called to his work and stresses this in his
memoirs. Meanwhile, he estranges Parisians from their city. They begin to be
conscious of its inhuman character. Maxime du Camp's monumental work
Paris has its origin in this consciousness. The *Jérémiades d'un Haussmannisé*
give it the form of a biblical lament.

The true purpose of Haussmann's work was to secure the city against civil
war. He wanted to make the erection of barricades in Paris impossible for all
time. With such intent Louis-Philippe had already introduced wooden paving.
Yet the barricades played a part in the February Revolution. Engels studies the
technique of barricade fighting. Haussmann seeks to prevent barricades in two
ways. The breadth of the streets is intended to make their erection impossible,
and new thoroughfares are to open the shortest route between the barracks and
the working-class districts. Contemporaries christen the enterprise 'strategic
embellishment'.

> Fais voir, en déjouant la ruse,
> O République, à ces pervers
> Ta grande face de Méduse
> Au milieu de rouges éclairs.
>
> Workers' song (about 1850)

The barricade is resurrected in the Commune. It is stronger and better secured
than ever. It stretches across the great boulevards, often reaching the height of
the first floor, and covers the trenches behind it. Just as the *Communist
Manifesto* ends the epoch of the professional conspirator, the Commune puts
an end to the phantasmagoria that dominates the freedom of the proletariat. It
dispels the illusion that the task of the proletarian revolution is to complete the
work of 1789 hand in hand with the bourgeoisie. This illusion prevailed from
1831 to 1871, from the Lyons uprising to the Commune. The bourgeoisie never
shared this error. The struggle of the bourgeoisie against the social rights of the
proletariat has already begun in the Great Revolution and coincides with the
philanthropic movement that conceals it, attaining its fullest development
under Napoleon III. Under him is written the monumental work of this political
tendency: Le Play's *European Workers*. Besides the covert position of philan-
thropy, the bourgeoisie was always ready to take up the overt position of class
struggle. As early as 1831 it recognizes, in the *Journal des Débats*, 'Every
industrialist lives in his factory like the plantation owners among their slaves.'
If, on the one hand, the lack of a guiding theory of revolution was the undoing
of the old workers' uprisings, it was also, on the other, the condition for the
immediate energy and enthusiasm with which they set about establishing a new
society. This enthusiasm, which reached its climax in the Commune, for a time
won over to the workers the best elements of the bourgeoisie, but in the end led
them to succumb to their worst. Rimbaud and Courbet declare their support
for the Commune. The Paris fire is the fitting conclusion to Haussmann's work
of destruction.

> My good father had been in Paris.
>
> Karl Gutzkow, *Letters from Paris* (1842)

Benjamin   Balzac was the first to speak of the ruins of the bourgeoisie. But only
Surrealism exposed them to view. The development of the forces of production
reduced the wish symbols of the previous century to rubble even before the
monuments representing them had crumbled. In the nineteenth century this
development emancipated constructive forms from art, as the sciences freed
themselves from philosophy in the sixteenth century. Architecture makes a
start as constructional engineering. The reproduction of nature in photography follows. Fantasy creation prepares itself to become practical as
commercial art. Literature is subjected to montage in the *feuilleton*. All these
products are on the point of going to market as wares. But they hesitate on the
brink. From this epoch stem the arcades and interiors, the exhibitions and
panoramas. They are residues of a dream world. The realization of dream
elements in waking is the textbook example of dialectical thinking. For this
reason dialectical thinking is the organ of historical awakening. Each epoch
not only dreams the next, but also, in dreaming, strives toward the moment of
waking. It bears its end in itself and unfolds it – as Hegel already saw – with
ruse. In the convulsions of the commodity economy we begin to recognize the
monuments of the bourgeoisie as ruins even before they have crumbled.

ERNST BLOCH

German philosopher Ernst Bloch (1885–1977) was a theorist of the avant-garde *Ernst Bloch*
and a philosopher of expressionism. With Georg Lukacs he had studied under
Georg Simmel, and was also influenced by Hegel and Schelling. Bloch was part of
the Max Weber circle, and subsequently became a close associate of Walter
Benjamin and Siegfried Kracauer. Politically Bloch remained a controversial figure.
An outspoken critic of various political regimes, including the United States which
he accused of fascism and imperialism, Bloch nonetheless supported Stalinist
Russia, a gesture that effectively isolated him from many of his academic col-
leagues. Although he developed into a committed Marxist, Bloch's politics
remained suffused with bourgeois humanism. Likewise his intellectual position was
an ideosyncratic one, embodying traces of Jewish mysticism.

Bloch was a deeply utopian aesthetic theorist who looked to art and literature as
means of illuminating a better future. Art, literature and other everyday phenomena offered a means of criticizing existing social conditions, and provided a glimpse
of a world where there would no longer be any exploitation of humans by fellow
humans. 'More than anything else, Bloch placed great faith in art and literature to
raise the not yet conscious to a point where it could grasp the direction humankind
would have to take to bring about the fulfilment of those needs, wants and wishes
that he saw scattered in dreams and daydreams.'[1] Thus aesthetic formulations
exposed what was missing in contemporary life and revealed what might still come
in a utopian world of the future.

Bloch's interest in architecture stemmed from his work in aesthetics, and was
reinforced by his subsequent marriage to the architect Karola Piotrowski. He
established himself as a defender of ornament, and a champion of expressionism.
Contemporary architecture for Bloch was impoverished. It had lost 'the caresses of
the Muse'. Functionalism had paralysed architecture and stripped it of all imagination. If architecture was to fulfil its utopian function in line with art and
literature, and provide a more intuitive means for experiencing the world – as had
the Gothic cathedral – it needed to be more humane. Architecture should learn the
lesson of art and sculpture, and free itself from the harsh shackles of enlightenment
rationality. For Bloch, Hans Scharoun's Philharmonic Hall in Berlin offered an
example of the way forward, an architecture with 'wings' which would confront
the alienation of the 'railway-station character of our existence'.

Bloch's criticism of functionalism as a manifestation of the shortcomings of
enlightenment rationality has clear parallels in Adorno's article 'Functionalism
Today', included in this volume. Comparisons can also be made with the work of
Simmel, Benjamin and Kracauer.

Bloch

NOTE

1   Jack Zipes, introduction to Ernst Bloch, *The Utopian Function of Art and Literature*, Jack Zipes and Frank Mecklenburg (trans.), Cambridge, Mass.: MIT Press, 1988.

FORMATIVE EDUCATION, ENGINEERING FORM, ORNAMENT

Bloch

PART ONE

We also take on the form of our surroundings. Not only does the man make his world, but the world makes the man. *Homo faber* and also *homo fabricatus*[1] – both are equally true; they are dialectically interrelated. The very way in which a chair causes us to sit has – at least at times – an effect on our general posture. And as for the arrangement of the furniture in a room, as telling as it can be of the arranger, at the same time it clearly contains him and his guests in its form. So, for example, the more approachable and gregarious personality is expressed in the abundance of seats offered in his rooms. On the other hand, even more telling is the room which lacks ample chairs but whose walls are richly decorated with elevated *objets d'art*. Hence the manner in which objects fill a space generally reflects the manners of those who are served by them.

PART TWO

Of course, these manners never depend solely on the taste of the individual, of Mr. Jones or Mr Doe. They are never as individual as the name on the door, notwithstanding any so-called personal touches. The most appropriate posture in the chair, as well as that of the chair itself, is determined by the social *habitus* of an entire era, i.e. by its fashion-determining class and, not least, by the petty bourgeoisie's imitation of the taste of the ruling class, by the latter perhaps most revealingly. This relationship is most visible in the visible, in exterior and interior architecture, both of which dominate by imposing the forms of those who dominate. This relationship, then, is what is called style. Up until the first half of the last century, there existed a relatively genuine architectonic style, i.e. one without the deceptions of a class which set the fashion and its false creations. However, especially in the realm of home decoration and construction, the appearance of the *nouveau riche* bourgeoisie brought with it a decline in craftsmanship, enduring mediocrity, and the swindle of mechanical reproduction. This trend served that entire counterfeit enterprise which can be called the *Gründerzeit*[2] of art history.

We are a direct result of this period even though it is barely past as a social era. Through its products, it became clear how our so-called artistic taste *should not taste*; in it we saw bad taste. Nothing should be as it was then, when the *parvenu* wore a false mask, when there were coverings everywhere, stuffed Renaissance furniture, overly high plaster ceilings, and plaster busts of Goethe and Schiller around. Enough of all this; unless of course such abominable kitsch – the petty bourgeoisie tapestry circa 1880, the halberd with a tiny thermometer on its plush post – was to be taken surrealistically, as a harmless caricature. Of course, à la Werkbund-Bauhaus, such things were and are not even under consideration; those movements strove to liberate themselves from such unmitigated kitsch, not only aesthetically, but also morally, out of honesty. And so, around the turn of the century and into the following decades, there

Bloch arose an asceticism, partially indebted to socialism, against swindle and extravagance, and absolutely anti-ornament. It was intended to educate to pure purposive-functional form,[3] and thereby to make the pure table, for example, sharp against, as Adolf Loos said, the scabrous and cancerous ornament. Indeed, every ornament became suspect, was condemned for being scabrous and cancerous. This bolstered a general disgust with the epigonal nature and decadence of the *Gründerzeit*, an aversion to its attachment to long since faded, indiscriminately mimicked styles that had lost their validity. But it never confronted the question of whether the social *habitus*, which had posited the decayed charm of the *Gründerzeit*, in the meantime had itself become any more honest. Or whether the ornament-free honesty of pure functionalism[4] might not itself be transformed into a fig leaf which concealed the not quite so great honesty of the conditions behind it. In any case, from this time on, knightly castles no longer served as buffets, and entrances to railway stations à la Palladio were no longer built to mask ticket windows and train tracks within.

PART THREE

Of course, since there was suddenly a demand for more reality than appearance, we were forced to give up our most prized souvenirs. The reason, according to pure purpose, was that after all this time a smooth spoon or some other implement would be easier to handle than a senselessly decorated one. The small devices were there precisely to be useful, effort-saving; they and their own clear form made the break with embellishments. Naturally, 'honest' clarity was praised above all in such desertions, and ranged from naked stainless steel chairs to interior walls of unplastered rough tiles. Yet it is still striking that such thoroughly ornamental decorations as Oriental carpets are foregrounded with particular delight against the background of such clarity. The 'honest' was the trump ever since the earlier Werkbund, even if its bareness called attention to itself and required Kilims, Kirmans, and Kazaks to disguise it. And yet, even granting that this asceticism and deliberate purity without false appearances are self-consistent, the question persists: what could this kind of honesty or even 'new objectivity'[5] mean in real terms? That is, in terms of a less clear, perhaps even consciously opaque social life? The obscurity was maintained even as a new *clarté* was being created outside of the realm of the technical arts with their fig leaves and shadow-casting light. Claudel once sang of the new *clarté*, 'Into the waves of the divine light/the building master places planfully/a stone framework like a filter/and grants the whole construct the water of a pearl.' Even then, no, precisely then, the inhabitants though beautifully illuminated in this transparency, could not yet discover their new humanity, indeed nor even their old one. For especially in the built, exterior space of architecture, the pre-existing life-forms clouded the water of the pearl, not only in a narrow, social sense, but also technologically. The accelerating pace, the desire to break all records, and the restless annihilation of human interaction, all these introduced an unprecedented problematization into the emphatic *clarté* of the Lichtstadt (radiant city) itself. So much greenery, free space, hygiene, overview, serenity, visible dignity had been projected. But time and again, the conditions within its confines and those outside did not conform to

the same ideals, and the architecture could not establish alone a small enclave
of realized inhabitability. The pace of work and its traffic, the objectification of
the means precisely by disassociating them from any purpose, end, meaning
and humane use, have largely transformed our cities into a dangerous nightmare. In our transformed cityscapes, man has remained – or more accurately
has become – at best peripheral to the measure of things. Contradictions are
deeply embedded. No humanitarian planning or just regulation of work has yet
been able to manage even the chaos of the traffic, not to mention the termite
existence in box houses. A modern urban planner, Doxiadis, no romantic
reactionary, bears witness in his book *Architecture in Transition*: monstrous,
schematically rigid skyscrapers project out of a raging sea of lacquered tin.
This life and its built space are clearly and painfully distant from the humanitarian *clarté* of the kind Le Corbusier had once intended for his 'new
Attica' constructed in steel, glass and light. And time and again, in a realm of
general alienation, where clarity is merely an ideology of monotonous vacuity,
precisely the purposively pursued form[6] of implements and buildings
increasingly forfeits all differentiation involved in differing formations of
purpose.[7] Forms are no longer differentiated humanely, true to purpose:
bungalow, airport (minus runway), theatre, university, slaughter house – all are
rendered uniform in the domineering form of the glass box. An unquestionably
high price has been paid by this kind of clarity for its dissociation from the
patchwork of decorative kitsch of the *Gründerzeit;* geometrical monotony,
alienated from purpose, together with an undernourishment of the imagination
and extreme self-alienation, all represented by this coldness, this vacuous non-
aura.

PART FOUR

From this arises another position, another posture; other ideas begin to come to
mind. It was implied above that the *Gründerzeit* has not yet been superseded if
it still serves as a necessary foil, if it is still allowed to dictate the poverty of any
richness, to force the hypocritical reaction of total bareness. But this is no
longer the architectural task, as it was for Loos, when an urgent *medicina
mentis* was needed against the raging scabs and cancers.

So it was too, and probably remains, a necessary remedy in other places
against a Red *Gründerzeit* and its corresponding Stalinist style. And yet, something else, the sentence published forty years ago in *The Spirit of Utopia* is still
valid: 'Birth forceps must be smooth, but by no means sugar tongs.'[8] This is
valid, that is, for all birth forceps. The strictly functional[9] implement serves and
emancipates us best, indeed only when it is free of decoration. Art in general,
furthermore, is not there for decoration: it is in principle too good for that. And
so it is correct that art has been liberated from this merely luxurious employment of decoration. However, this assertion has nothing in common with the
application to all interior and exterior architecture of forceps purity, which
serves only to elevate the depravity of ornamental imagination so as to justify
the egg cartons or glass boxes. And we must be reminded and warned, objectively, again and again: circumstances do not allow a general extension and
maintenance of the sanitary purity of pure functionalism.[10] Sociologically, such
purity, an ideological kind of clarity, is and remains a distracting, deceptive

Bloch

smokescreen. It is not without reason that it occasionally joined forces with other arts outside of architecture which also strove for the smoothness of neoclassicism, as if the latter's external regularity once and for all excused a lack of imagination. It is true, of course, that genuine classicism, ever since the nobler times of simplicity and peaceful grandeur,[11] had no special fecundity when it came to ornaments. Yet now it plays a different role, accompanying the supposedly pure geometrization arising in a void together with the artificially advanced death of ornament. 'Duke, this Mortimer happened to die conveniently,' is the line from *Maria Stuart;* the same is true, *mutatis mutandis,* of the exultation upon ornament's death and the synthetically manufactured lack of imagination. And so, enough said on the ornamental wasteland, unique in spite of everything, especially when compared to the precision enchanted forest of the primitive, of East Asian, Islamic, Gothic or Baroque art.

But will the limbs of this seriously paralysed body ever be revived? Is the laming seizure not even more shocking and extraordinary since it has struck the once blooming and comprehensive art of architecture? The problem is as serious as it is urgent: perhaps it can be taken as a slight sign of improvement that the superstitious ornament taboo no longer wields such absolute power. At least not in the way it did in Loos's day when it was in full strength and was employed, albeit exaggeratedly, as a *medicina mentis.* Increasingly architects may no longer conceive of themselves as joyfully excused from the demands of ornamental architectural imagination. The formations of their figures may finally indulge in the suspect wave and sunflower contours of art nouveau, in which van de Velde had his origins. The limbs, artificially paralysed for so long, are slowly reviving in the wave-like interior stairways of Scharoun's Berlin Philharmonic Hall; the movement began even earlier, in a completely different way, in the exterior contours of Frank Lloyd Wright's buildings. In these examples, the constraints of the late-capitalist rat-race and alienation are confronted with something significantly new and different, namely the transition beyond the overall railway-station character[12] of our existence. These are mere beginnings, certainly, and they are constantly threatened; they too often become calcified forms; a temporary return of identity takes hold and architecture becomes for the first time merely a faceless screen, an antiflower. But now – and this is truly amazing – how is it possible that at the same time, in the formation of the same space, five steps from the pale glass box, contemporaneous painting and sculpture wander off on an entirely different path, become exorbitant?[13] It is not a question here of their special calibre – which in some cases was extremely high – but of the astonishing contrast *vis à vis* the undernourished architectural imagination, of the boldness, of the imaginative extravagance of these entire genres. Even a quick pursuit of the high and low points[14] of the movement leads unavoidably into an open, unmarked, and therefore yet uncritical and uncriticized voyage for the imagination. A journey from the days of the 'Blauer Reiter' (1912), from both before and then after, from Kandinsky, Franz Marc, de Chirico, Picasso, Chagall, Klee, Max Ernst, from Archipenko, Boccioni, today Henry Moore, Giacometti – to name but a few contrasts. They retrieved exotic flora from their journey, ornamental imagination. These artists avoided above all the danger of a damnably perspicacious talent, which had only produced a monotony of form. In any case, the synchrony is peculiar: an architecture which needed wings, and *Bloch* pictorial and plastic arts which, if anything, could have done with some ballast, given the emphatic repulsive force that has always pushed them up and away from those ever-present fixtures, the leaden commercial buildings (even in Expressionism they had shown signs, surrealistic traits, of their flight away into upper, alternate and underworlds.) And so, the revealed skeletons of our architecture share space with the literal extravagance of the other fine, but still formative, arts.[15]

PART FIVE

But now: is this temporal coincidence of ice and fire mere chance? In general, after all, there does exist a connection between sober purification and the place made free by it for something quite different, not unlike the relationship between emancipation from the inessential made possible by technological automatization and the leisure achieved thereby for the essential. And yet, if we look more closely at the case at hand, it seems that the split between mere dwelling cubicles[16] and that which had once allowed those buildings to participate in the fine arts (those which form the essential)[17] is a split out of context, without connection. But is, or better, does the split *remain* unmediated if we take into account those signs which could be grouped under the heading 'march separately, but toward a united front' (even if those signs were often undesired and certainly unused, above all, still unused architecturally)?[18] This could form a possible, certainly not yet conscious conspiracy which makes the temporal coincidence of the dwelling machine and the excessive plastic and pictorial arts in the end essentially more than mere chance. 'Railway-station character' already disappeared as a slogan; but the more internal transition, namely of the unity of the fine arts as a whole, is still buried and obscure, another contributing factor to the ornamental bareness of architecture. But Klee, of all people – yet not really of all people – was at the Bauhaus; Lenbach could certainly never have been there. Or, as another sign of *rapprochement*, a Chagall painting hangs inappropriately, although not as an absolutely foreign body, in the glass foyer of the new Frankfurt theatre; this is possibly a more authentic home for it than in the epigonal rigidity of an old Kaiser Wilhelm memorial church. And above all, an especially remarkable simultaneity: in the midst of the first functionalist[19] buildings the Folkwang Museum was opened in Essen; it was stuffed full of displays of expressionisms – only, of course, in the company of primitive and atavistic art, apart from any kind of metallurgic new world functions and forms. To make up for this, however, purely technological forms, especially metals, are extending increasingly further into contemporary sculpture; we need only think of the perforated hollow bronze statues by Henry Moore, or the stylized fine mechanics of even as 'literary' a sculptor as Zadkin. To no less a degree, as Hans Curjel has correctly emphasized, the rebellion in form by Picasso, Kandinsky, Boccioni, Kirchner, *et al.* has exerted an influence back on its origins, on Werkbund and Bauhaus, on pure architecture that focused only on the technical. However, the effect has been limited to frame construction and can hardly be said to have aroused a renaissance of ornament, except in a few cases, here and there, where mere evolutionary reform produced revolutionary reversals. This even took place

1 through the channel of literature; for example, Scheerbart's influence on Bruno Taut. At least this new frame painting did engender an inclination for what we might call qualitative, as opposed to quantitative, construction – to such an extent that, although the effort was never pursued and in fact was even eradicated, veritable living creatures intervened in and emerged from the lines on the drawing board, from a geometry which did not want to remain inorganic. There were a few hopeful signs – but, as can be seen clearly in the conventional figures of the high-rise and the newest of new Brasilia, they have still never retrieved what was lost: the caresses of a Muse. The juxtaposition of pure technology in architecture and the Chagallian in the isolated remaining fine arts[20] never overcame the mere contiguity of the latter's ability to facilitate and emancipate on the one hand and the former's power of essence on the other.[21]

PART SIX

Must it remain thus? Will disassociated formation[22] never again become allied? Must architecture alone stop being an art, stop blossoming, indeed stop being as it once was? That it has achieved marvellous feats of engineering technology there is no doubt; but formative imagination is something else. This form of imagination is protean; its ever-changing ornamental features are experiments with us, not just with the skeleton within a building, or even with the building as such. The present dichotomy, with mechanical emancipation and its extension into architecture on the one hand, and expressive abundance liberated in the realms of painting and sculpture on the other, must therefore not be made absolute, functionless, insurmountable. 'March separately, but toward a united front': in the era of transition, in our truly formative,[23] i.e. progressive productions, this should not degenerate into a mere hardening of differences. The very simultaneous appearance of engineering and expressive forms points to a *tertium*, to a more fundamental unity underlying this unfinished epoch. Its railway-station character proves to be both tempting and open in terms of productive possibility, both directing and experimental for each of the two factions of the fine arts[24] created by it – whereby architecture never wants to forget that it is a fine art. This Exodus character,[25] as such able to unite only via a processive utopian common denominator, offers a set of by no means tranquil, least of all classicistic forms, to budding ornamentation. But even in the sphere of pictorial, plastic and architectural formations,[26] all of the prevailing figurines and figures, all ornamental forms, as details and as wholes, are still through and through excerpts, departures, flights from themselves.[27] Easily movable interior spaces; anti-barracks in the city (an idea derived from ships); spanning bridges, which aptly are called bold; pictorial, and sculptural ciphers as drawn lines in things unfinished: all this touched the common point of orientation, inhabitability on the front where we now find ourselves. And only this would again constitute a true honesty of formation, a true justice done to function (but with horizons), both of which gave rise to training in the modern technical arts in the first place, and both of which, in spite of insistent warnings from the realms of painting and sculpture since the days of the 'Blauer Reiter', have been missing from this training thanks to the *sacrificio della fantasia*.

PART SEVEN

Bloch

At this point, it is especially advisable to overshoot the mark in order to hit it. Beauty and form which are more than noble simplicity and serene grandeur: without a doubt, this is the point at stake in the present discussion. But in trying to educate by means of pleasing (thus in the last analysis via classicistic, fixed forms) one must forget that it was precisely the Nazis who built and painted classicistically. One must also consider the young Goethe, standing in front of the Strasburg cathedral in the middle of classicism (to be sure the so-called genuine one), who certainly had no conception of the purity of a glass skyscraper in New York. Indeed, expressly, beauty à la Greque as one of a kind did not exist for him; certainly he did not consider beauty as the entrance way to or as the boundary or fixity of a single principle of art. Instead, the young Goethe discovered a startling principle which arched over the gap between an as yet hardly known primitive art and the Gothic. He daringly formulated this sweeping proposal: 'art is long in being formed[28] before it is beautiful, yet it is still true, great art, indeed often truer and more beautiful than the beautiful itself'. This statement, made by a man who was then still young, appeared in what was a revolutionary period, i.e. one of transcendent transition, when aesthetics provided for the *humanum*. Today the over-arching category of primitive Gothic has become self-evident; it has expanded and become great through its sympathetic reception in modern painting and sculpture, which have extended it to encompass suspended forms and elastically dynamic space. It has become a thoroughly ornamental style both pictorially and sculpturally: Exodus, as it turns out. Hence the conclusion: he, Goethe, alone exerting a rebellious influence radically different than in the first periods of modern technological art could, reconcile architecture not with the death of imagination *usque ad finem* but with the other fine arts,[29] those which were truly qualified. Then, finally, architecture would once again encompass the pictorial and the plastic, become the main figure in the still 'masked decorations of our innermost form' which had already been experimented with in painting and sculpture by Kandinsky and Archipenko. All this returns time and again to the problem of the new ornament, to sculptural excess – *in nuce* when it blossoms in the details of a building, *in entelechia* when it characterizes the all-encompassing principle of the entire building figure. The magnitude of architecture's sculptural loss can be measured precisely by the emptiness and lack of its ornamental force. There is and remains an abrupt breach of contract, which historically has never been fulfilled or terminated, a gap in the by no means consummated *entelechia* according to which architecture was conceived. Yet this breach can and may not stay unmediated; on the contrary, Vitruvius's postulated unity of *utilitas* and *venustas* (now of transparent fullness)[30] summons architecture more demandingly than ever to the fronts – to reassume its still recoverable position as the 'city crown' (to use a conceptually modified version of Bruno Taut's term) of all the optical fine and formative arts.[31]

NOTES

1   The flavour of the German is slightly lost here since Bloch uses a proverbial expression that we could not match in English. Unfortunately the characteristic mixture in Bloch's rhetoric of

Bloch   intricate dialectics and colloquialisms is not really conveyed by the Latinate English.

2   Literally 'founder time', the term used to refer to the German Empire at the end of the nineteenth century, according to Gordon A. Craigs' *Germany: 1866–1945* (Oxford University Press, 1978, p. 79), 'named after the great manipulators who 'founded' gigantic enterprises on the basis of paper and little else and who led millions of Germans in a frenzied dance around the statue of Mammon that ended in exhaustion and, for many, financial ruin'. The term is similar to the Victorian 'Wilhelmismus'.

3   'Education' here is *Erziehung*, the common word used for school education. 'Purposive-functional form' is *Zweckform* (literally 'purpose-form'), and is generally translated as 'functionalism' throughout.

4   'Functionalism' is here *Zweckform*.

5   The *Neue Sachlichkeit* movement, one of the main trends in German art in the early twentieth century, is commonly translated as 'New Objectivity'. The word *sachlich*, however, carries a series of connotations. Along with its emphasis on the 'thing' (*Sache*), it implies a frame of mind, of being 'matter of fact', 'down to earth'.

6   'Form' is here *Gestalt*, a slightly more neutral word than *Bildung*. 'Purposive' is *zweckmässig*, 'according to the purpose or end of the thing'.

7   'Formation of purpose' is *Zweckgestaltung*.

8   The pun is lost here. 'Birth forceps' are *Geburtszangen* and 'sugar tongs' are *Zuckerzangen*.

9   'Functional' here is *nützlich*, i.e. 'practical, useful'.

10   'Functionalism' again *Zweckform*.

11   The phrase is taken from Johann Joachim Winkelmann's 'Thoughts on the Imitation of Greek Painting and Sculpture' (1755). It characterizes the fundamental nature of Greek art and was the guiding spirit of German classicism of the late eighteenth and early nineteenth century.

12   'Railway-station character' is *Bahnhofhaftigkeit*, literally 'railway-stationness'.

13   The use of the word 'exorbiant' seems to rest on the Latin etymology of the word (especially since Bloch uses *Exorbitanten* and not the Germanized version whch would be more common). Namely, *exorbitare* (from *ex* + *orbitus*), 'to go out of the track'. This is supported by the extended spatial and wandering metaphors in this passage.

14   'High and low points' loses the pun and creativity of the German *Hoch- und Tiefstaplerisches*, thus a *Hochstapler* is a con-artist, while *Tiefstaplerisch* is an invention by Bloch (say, high and low con-artists).

15   'Fine, but still formative arts' are the *noch bildende Künste* which were above (page 47) called by their individual names, 'pictorial and plastic'.

16   'Dwelling cubicles' is even more drastic in German: *Wohnmaschinen*, literally 'dwelling machines'.

17   'Fine arts (those which form the essential)' loses the pun somewhat, namely *bildende Künste des Wesentlichen*, i.e., 'forming (= fine) arts of the essential.'

18   Again a proverbial expression or slogan, which translates literally: 'march separately, attack together'.

19   'Functionalist' again *Zweckform*.

20   'Fine arts' again *bildende Künste*.

21   This seems to be a reversal of the position in Part Five and below in the beginning of Part Six. In both those places he implies that technology (functionalist principles as applied to architecture) facilitated life, eased the burden of the inessential and hence made room for the essential (fine arts and their ornamentation). Here he associated the emancipation with the (Chagallian) fine arts and the concern for the essential with architecture.

22   'Formation' is *Bilden*, the substantive of the verb.

23   'Formative' is the adjective *bildend* from the verb (literally 'forming').

24   'Fine art' here and in the next line again *bildende Kunst*.

25   'This Exodus character' is in German *dieses Exodushafte*, literally 'this Exodusness'.

26   'Formations' again the substantive *Bilden*.

27   'Excerpts, departures, flights from themselves' is *Auszugsgestalten ihrer selbst*. *Auszug* means excerpt or abstract, but it is also the Germanization of the word Exodus (the flight from Egypt is the *Auszug*).

28   'Being formed' is again the progressive form of *bilden* (*bildend*). Of course for Goethe, one of the founders of the *Bildungsroman* tradition with his *Wilhelm Meister*, *bilden* was a key aesthetic concept.

29   The opposition here is between *Werkkunst* ('work art', 'technical art') and *bildende Kunst*.

30   This parenthetical statement stands in an unclear relationship to the 'postulated unity', though it is probably in aposition, a contemporary reformulation (*utilitas* – transparency, clarity; *venustas* – fullness, richness).

31   'Formative arts' again *bildende Künste*.

SIEGFRIED KRACAUER

German cultural theorist Siegfried Kracauer (1889–1966) is known principally for his later writings on film theory, such as *Theory of Film* and *From Caligari to Hitler*. Recent attention to his earlier work, however, has revealed him as wide-ranging cultural theorist, prominent within intellectual circles of Weimar Germany. Educated under Georg Simmel, Kracauer himself taught Theodor Adorno, and was a close acquaintance of various associates of the Frankfurt School, notably Walter Benjamin. Kracauer abandoned a career in architecture to become a journalist with the Frankfurter Zeitung. Forced out in 1933 under the growing anti-semitism, he subsequently fled to America where he made a name for himself as a film theorist.

Under the influence, no doubt, of Simmel, Kracauer focused his early articles on phenomena of everyday life, such as hotel lobbies, shopping arcades, cinemas and dance halls. Kracauer's observations of seemingly mundane subjects were under-pinned by a thoroughly considered philosophical position. As Kracauer himself commented, 'The surface-level expressions ... by virtue of their unconscious nature, provide unmediated access to the fundamental substance of the state of things. Conversely, knowledge of this state of things depends on the interpretation of these surface-level expressions.'[1] Above all, architectural space, for Kracauer, was a medium through which to understand society. 'Spatial images are the dreams of society. Wherever the hieroglyphics of any spatial image are deciphered, there the basis of social reality presents itself.'[2] Thus, for example, Kracauer reads the employment agency, the barren space which acts as a warehouse for the temporary rejects of society, as the embodiment of the empty despair of the unemployed, who are reduced to the level of objects of hygiene.

A central theme within Kracauer's work was the impoverishment of con-temporary existence, which had been emptied of all meaning. For Kracauer modernity was characterized by a form of transcendental homelessness, which was embodied in the hotel lobby, the space where silence reigns and where guests bury themselves in their newspapers to avoid exchanging glances. Kracauer blames this condition on the ascendency of capitalist *ratio*. This was not reason itself, but 'a murky form of reason'. *Ratio* 'is cut off from reason and bypasses man as it vanishes into the void of the abstract'.[3] In his famous analysis of the Tiller Girls, Kracauer expands on how capitalist *ratio* was expressed in the mass ornament of the synchronized cabaret dance routine, an abstracted form of rationality that had taken on various mythic traits. However, Kracauer was not critical of rationality *per se*. Rather he saw that rationality had been 'robbed of its progressive potential'. The problem of the contemporary condition for Kracauer was not an *excess* of rationality. In fact he believed that more rationality was required in order to

Kracauer   complete the disenchantment of the world. Kracauer therefore offered a qualified
endorsement of modernity.

NOTES

1   Siegfried Kracauer, 'The Mass Ornament' in *The Mass Ornament*, Thomas Y. Levin (trans.),
     Cambridge, Mass.: Harvard University Press, 1995, p. 75.
2   Kracauer, 'On Employment Agencies', p. 60.
3   Kracauer, *The Mass Ornament*, p. 84.

THE HOTEL LOBBY

Kracauer

. . . In the *house of God,* which presupposes an already extant community, the congregation accomplishes the task of making connections. Once the members of the congregation have abandoned the relation on which the place is founded, the house of God retains only a decorative significance. Even if it sinks into oblivion, civilized society at the height of its development still maintains privileged sites that testify to its own non-existence, just as the house of God testifies to the existence of the community united in reality. Admittedly society is unaware of this, for it cannot see beyond its own sphere; only the aesthetic construct, whose form renders the manifold as a projection, makes it possible to demonstrate this correspondence. The typical characteristics of the *hotel lobby,* which appears repeatedly in detective novels, indicate that it is conceived as the inverted image of the house of God. It is a negative church, and can be transformed into a church so long as one observes the conditions that govern the different spheres.

In both places people appear there *as guests.* But whereas the house of God is dedicated to the service of the one whom people have gone there to encounter, the hotel lobby accommodates all who go there to meet no one. It is the setting for those who neither seek nor find the one who is always sought, and who are therefore guests in space as such – a space that encompasses them and has no function other than to encompass them. The impersonal nothing represented by the hotel manager here occupies the position of the unknown one in whose name the church congregation gathers. And whereas the congregation invokes the name and dedicates itself to the service in order to fulfil the relation, the people dispersed in the lobby accept their host's incognito without question. Lacking any and all relation, they drip down into the vacuum with the same necessity that compels those striving in and for reality to lift themselves out of the nowhere toward their destination.

The congregation, which gathers in the house of God for prayer and worship, outgrows the imperfection of communal life in order not to overcome it but to bear it in mind and to reinsert it constantly into the tension. Its gathering is a *collectedness* and a unification of this directed life of the community, which belongs to two realms: the realm covered by law and the realm beyond law. At the site of the church – but of course not only here – these separate currents encounter each other; the law is broached here without being breached, and the paradoxical split is accorded legitimacy by the sporadic suspension of its languid continuity. Through the edification of the congregation, the community is always reconstructing itself, and this elevation above the everyday prevents the everyday itself from going under. The fact that such a returning of the community to its point of origin must submit to spatial and temporal limitations, that it steers away from worldly community, and that it is brought about through special celebrations – this is only a sign of man's dubious position between above and below, one that constantly forces him to establish on his own what is given or what has been conquered in the tension.

Since the determining characteristic of the lower region is its lack of tension, the togetherness in the hotel lobby has no meaning. While here, too, people certainly do become detached from everyday life, this detachment does not lead the community to assure itself of its existence as a congregation. Instead it merely displaces people from the unreality of the daily hustle and bustle to a place where they would encounter the void only if they were more than just reference points. The lobby, in which people find themselves *vis-à-vis de rien,* is a mere gap that does not even serve a purpose dictated by *Ratio* (like the conference room of a corporation), a purpose which at the very least could mask the directive that had been perceived in the relation. But if a sojourn in a hotel offers neither a perspective on nor an escape from the everyday, it does provide a groundless distance from it which can be exploited, if at all, aesthetically – the aesthetic being understood here as a category of the non-existent type of person, the residue of that positive aesthetic which makes it possible to put this non-existence into relief in the detective novel. The person sitting around idly is overcome by a disinterested satisfaction in the contemplation of a world creating itself, whose purposiveness is felt without being associated with any representation of a purpose. The Kantian definition of the beautiful is instantiated here in a way that takes seriously its isolation of the aesthetic and its lack of content. For in the emptied-out individuals of the detective novel – who, as rationally constructed complexes, are comparable to the transcendental subject – the aesthetic faculty is indeed detached from the existential stream of the total person. It is reduced to an unreal, purely formal relation that manifests the same indifference to the self as it does to matter. Kant himself was able to overlook this horrible last-minute sprint of the transcendental subject, since he still believed there was a seamless transition from the transcendental to the preformed subject-object world. The fact that he does not completely give up the total person even in the aesthetic realm is confirmed by his definition of the 'sublime', which takes the ethical into account and thereby attempts to reassemble the remaining pieces of the fractured whole. In the hotel lobby, admittedly, the aesthetic – lacking all qualities of sublimity – is presented without any regard for these upward-striving intentions, and the formula 'purposiveness without purpose'[1] also exhausts its content. Just as the lobby is the space that does not refer beyond itself, the aesthetic condition corresponding to it constitutes itself as its own limit. It is forbidden to go beyond this limit, so long as the tension that would propel the breakthrough is repressed and the marionettes of *Ratio* – who are not human beings – isolate themselves from their bustling activity. But the aesthetic that has become an end in itself pulls up its own roots; it obscures the higher level toward which it should refer and signifies only its own emptiness, which, according to the literal meaning of the Kantian definition, is a mere relation of faculties. It rises above a meaningless formal harmony only when it is in the service of something when instead of making claims to autonomy it inserts itself into the tension that does not concern it in particular. If human beings orient themselves beyond the form, then a kind of beauty may also mature that is a fulfilled beauty, because it is the consequence and not the aim – but where beauty is chosen as an aim without further consequences, all that remains is its empty shell. Both the hotel lobby and the house of God respond to the aesthetic sense that articulates its legitimate demands in them. But whereas in the latter the beautiful employs a language with which it also testifies against itself, in the former it is involuted in its muteness, incapable of finding the other. In tasteful lounge chairs a civilization intent on rationalization comes to an end, whereas the decorations

of the church pews are born from the tension that accords them a revelatory *Kracauer*
meaning. As a result, the chorales that are the expression of the divine service
turn into medleys whose strains encourage pure triviality, and devotion con-
geals into erotic desire that roams about without an object.

The *equality* of those who pray is likewise reflected in distorted form in the
hotel lobby. When a congregation forms, the differences between people disappear, because these beings all have one and the same destiny, and because, in
the encounter with the spirit that determines this destiny, anything that does
not determine that spirit simply ceases to exist – namely, the limit of necessity,
posited by man, and the separation, which is the work of nature. The
provisional status of communal life is experienced as such in the house of God,
and so the sinner enters into the 'we' in the same way as does the upright person
whose assurance is here disturbed. This – the fact that everything human is
oriented toward its own contingency – is what creates the equality of the
contingent. The great pales next to the small, and good and evil remain suspended when the congregation relates itself to that which no scale can measure.
Such a relativization of qualities does not lead to their confusion but instead
elevates them to the status of reality, since the relation to the last things
demands that the penultimate things be convulsed without being destroyed.
This equality is positive and essential, not a reduction and foreground; it is the
fulfilment of what has been differentiated, which must renounce its inde
pendent singular existence in order to save what is most singular. This
singularity is awaited and sought in the house of God. Relegated to the
shadows so long as merely human limits are imposed, it throws its own shadow
over those distinctions when man approaches the absolute limit.

In the hotel lobby, equality is based not on a relation to God but on a
relation to the nothing. Here, in the space of unrelatedness, the change of
environments does not leave purposive activity behind, but brackets it for the
sake of a freedom that can refer only to itself and therefore sinks into relaxation
and indifference. In the house of God, human differences diminish in the face of
their provisionality, exposed by a seriousness that dissipates the certainty of all
that is definitive. By contrast, an aimless lounging, to which no call is
addressed, leads to the mere play that elevates the unserious everyday to the
level of the serious. Simmel's definition of society as a 'play form of sociation' is
entirely legitimate, but does not get beyond mere description. What is presented
in the hotel lobby is the formal similarity of the figures, an equivalence that
signifies not fulfilment but evacuation. Removed from the hustle and bustle,
one does gain some distance from the distinctions of 'actual' life, but without
being subjected to a new determination that would circumscribe from above
the sphere of validity for these determinations. And it is in this way that a
person can vanish into an undetermined void, helplessly reduced to a 'member
of society as such' who stands superfluously off to the side and, when playing,
intoxicates himself. This invalidation of togetherness, itself already unreal, thus
does not lead up toward reality but is more of a sliding down into the doubly
unreal mixture of the undifferentiated atoms from which the world of appearance is constructed. Whereas in the house of God a creature emerges which sees
itself as a supporter of the community, in the hotel lobby what emerges is the
inessential foundation at the basis of rational socialization. It approaches the
nothing and takes shape by analogy with the abstract and formal *universal*

Kracauer   *concepts* through which thinking that has escaped from the tension believes it can grasp the world. These abstractions are inverted images of the universal concepts conceived within the relation; they rob the ungraspable given of its possible content, instead of raising it to the level of reality by relating it to the higher determinations. They are irrelevant to the oriented and total person who, the world in hand, meets them halfway; rather, they are posited by the transcendental subject, which allows them to become part of the powerlessness into which that transcendental subject degenerates as a result of its claim to be creator of the world. Even if free-floating *Ratio* – dimly aware of its limitation – does acknowledge the concepts of God, freedom and immortality, what it discovers are not the homonymic existential concepts, and the categorical imperative is surely no substitute for a commandment that arises out of an ethical resolution. Nevertheless, the weaving of these concepts into a system confirms that people do not want to abandon the reality that has been lost; yet, of course, they will not get hold of it precisely because they are seeking it by means of a kind of thinking which has repudiated all attachment to that reality. The desolation of *Ratio* is complete only when it removes its mask and hurls itself into the void of random abstractions that no longer mimic higher determinations, and when it renounces seductive consonances and desires itself even as a concept. The only immediacy it then retains is the now openly acknowledged nothing, in which, grasping upward from below, it tries to ground the reality to which it no longer has access. Just as God becomes, for the person situated in the tension, the beginning and end of all creation, so too does the intellect that has become totally self-absorbed create the appearance of a plenitude of figures from zero. It thinks it can wrench the world from this meaningless universal, which is situated closest to that zero and distinguishes itself from it only to the extent necessary in order to deduct a something. But the world is world only when it is interpreted by a universal that has been really experienced. The intellect reduces the relations that permeate the manifold to the common denominator of the concept of energy, which is separated merely by a thin layer from the zero. Or it robs historical events of their paradoxical nature and, having levelled them out, grasps them as progress in one-dimensional time. Or, seemingly betraying itself, it elevates irrational 'life' to the dignified status of an entity in order to recover itself, in its delimitation, from the now liberated residue of the totality of human being, and in order to traverse the realms across their entire expanse. If one takes as one's basis these extreme reductions of the real, then (as Simmel's philosophy of life confirms) one can obtain a distorted image of the discoveries made in the upper spheres – an image that is no less comprehensive than the one provided by the insistence of the words 'God' and 'spirit'. But even less ambiguously than the abusive employment of categories that have become incomprehensible, it is the deployment of empty abstractions that announces the actual position of a thinking that has slipped out of the tension. The visitors in the hotel lobby who allow the individual to disappear behind the peripheral equality of social masks, correspond to the exhausted terms that coerce differences out of the uniformity of the zero. Here, the visitors suspend the undetermined special being – which, in the house of God, gives way to that invisible equality of beings standing before God (out of which it both renews and determines itself) – by devolving into tuxedos. And the triviality of their conversation haphazardly aimed at utterly

insignificant objects so that one might encounter oneself in their exteriority, is   *Kracauer*
only the obverse of prayer, directing downward what they idly circumvent.

The observance of *silence,* no less obligatory in the hotel lobby than in the
house of God, indicates that in both places people consider themselves essentially as equals. In *Death in Venice* Thomas Mann formulates this as follows: 'A
solemn stillness reigned in the room, of the sort that is the pride of all large
hotels. The attentive waiters moved about on noiseless feet. A rattling of the tea
service, a half-whispered word was all that one could hear.' The contentless
solemnity of this conventionally imposed silence does not arise out of mutual
courtesy, of the sort one encounters everywhere, but rather serves to eliminate
differences. It is a silence that abstracts from the differentiating word and
compels one downward into the equality of the encounter with the nothing, an
equality that a voice resounding through space would disturb. In the house of
God, by contrast, silence signifies the individual collecting himself as firmly
directed self, and the word addressed to human beings is effaced solely in order
to release another word, which, whether uttered or not, sits in judgment over
human beings.

Since what counts here is not the dialogue of those who speak, the members
of the congregation are anonymous. They outgrow their names because the
very empirical being which these names designate disappears in prayer; thus,
they do not know one another as particular beings whose multiple determined
existences enmesh them in the world. If the proper name reveals its bearer, it
also separates him from those whose names have been called; it simultaneously
discloses and obscures, and it is with good reason that lovers want to destroy it,
as if it were the final wall separating them. It is only the relinquishing of the
name – which abolishes the semi-solidarity of the intermediate spheres – that
allows for the extensive solidarity of those who step out of the bright obscurity
of reciprocal contact and into the night and the light of the higher mystery.
Now that they do not know who the person closest to them is, their neighbour
becomes the closest, for out of his disintegrating appearance arises a creation
whose traits are also theirs. It is true that only those who stand before God are
sufficiently estranged from one another to discover they are brothers; only they
are exposed to such an extent that they can love one another without knowing
one another and without using names. At the limit of the human they rid themselves of their naming, so that the word might be bestowed upon them – a word
that strikes them more directly than any human law. And in the seclusion to
which such a relativization of form generally pushes them, they inquire about
their form. Having been initiated into the mystery that provides the name, and
having become transparent to one another in their relation to God, they enter
into the 'we' signifying a commonality of creatures that suspends and grounds
all those distinctions and associations adhering to the proper name.

This limit case 'we' of those who have dispossessed themselves of themselves
– a 'we' that is realized vicariously in the house of God due to human limitations – is transformed in the hotel lobby into the isolation of anonymous atoms.
Here profession is detached from the person and the name gets lost in the space,
since only the still unnamed crowd can serve *Ratio* as a point of attack. It
reduces to the level of the nothing – out of which it wants to produce the
world – even those pseudo-individuals it has deprived of individuality, since
their anonymity no longer serves any purpose other than meaningless

Kracauer   movement along the paths of convention. But if the meaning of this anonymity becomes nothing more than the representation of the insignificance of this beginning, the depiction of formal regularities, then it does not foster the solidarity of those liberated from the constraints of the name; instead, it deprives those encountering one another of the possibility of association that the name could have offered them. Remnants of individuals slip into the nirvana of relaxation, faces disappear behind newspapers, and the artificial continuous light illuminates nothing but mannequins. It is the coming and going of unfamiliar people who have become empty forms because they have lost their password, and who now file by as ungraspable flat ghosts. If they possessed an interior, it would have no windows at all, and they would perish aware of their endless abandonment, instead of knowing of their homeland as the congregation does. But as pure exterior, they escape themselves and express their non-being through the false aesthetic affirmation of the estrangement that has been installed between them. The presentation of the surface strikes them as an attraction; the tinge of exoticism gives them a pleasurable shudder. Indeed, in order to confirm the distance whose definitive character attracts them, they allow themselves to be bounced off a proximity that they themselves have conjured up: their monological fantasy attaches designations to the masks, designations that use the person facing them as a toy. And the fleeting exchange of glances which creates the possibility of exchange is acknowledged only because the illusion of that possibility confirms the reality of the distance. Just as in the house of God, here too namelessness unveils the meaning of naming; but whereas in the house of God it is an awaiting within the tension that reveals the preliminariness of names, in the hotel lobby it is a retreat into the unquestioned groundlessness that the intellect transforms into the names' site of origin. But where the call that unifies into the 'we' is not heard, those that have fled the form are irrevocably isolated.

In the congregation the entire community comes into being, for the immediate relation to the supralegal *mystery* inaugurates the paradox of the law that can be suspended in the actuality of the relation to God. That law is a penultimate term that withdraws when the connection occurs that humbles the self-assured and comforts those in danger. The tensionless people in the hotel lobby also represent the entire society, but not because transcendence here raises them up to its level; rather, this is because the hustle and bustle of immanence is still hidden. Instead of guiding people beyond themselves, the mystery slips between the masks; instead of penetrating the shells of the human, it is the veil that surrounds everything human; instead of confronting man with the question of the provisional, it paralyses the questioning that gives access to the realm of provisionality. In his all-too contemplative detective novel *Der Tod kehrt im Hotel ein* (Death Enters the Hotel), Sven Elvestad writes:

> Once again it is confirmed that a large hotel is a world unto itself and that this world is like the rest of the large world. The guests here roam about in their light-hearted, careless summer existence without suspecting anything of the strange mysteries circulating among them.

'Strange mysteries': the phrase is ironically ambiguous. On the one hand, it refers quite generally to the disguised quality of lived existence as such; on the *Kracauer* other, it refers to the higher mystery that finds distorted expression in the illegal activities that threaten safety. The clandestine character of all legal and illegal activities – to which the expression initially and immediately refers – indicates that in the hotel lobby the pseudo-life that is unfolding in pure immanence is being pushed back toward its undifferentiated origin. Were the mystery to come out of its shell, mere possibility would disappear in the fact: by detaching the illegal from the nothing, the Something would have appeared. The hotel management therefore thoughtfully conceals from its guests the real events which could put an end to the false aesthetic situation shrouding that nothing. Just as the formerly experienced higher mystery pushes those oriented toward it across the midpoint, whose limit is defined by the law, so does the mystery – which is the distortion of the higher ground and as such the utmost abstraction of the dangers that disrupt immanent life – relegate one to the lapsed neutrality of the meaningless beginning from which the pseudo-middle arises. It hinders the outbreak of differentiations in the service of emancipated *Ratio,* which strengthens its victory over the Something in the hotel lobby by helping the conventions take the upper hand. These are so worn out that the activity taking place in their name is at the same time an activity of dissimulation – an activity that serves as protection for legal life just as much as for illegal life, because as the empty form of all possible societies it is not oriented toward any particular thing but remains content with itself in its insignificance . . .

NOTE

1   This hallmark phrase from Kant's *Critique of Judgement* is put in quotation marks in the later republication of the essay.

ON EMPLOYMENT AGENCIES: THE CONSTRUCTION OF A SPACE

Each social stratum has a space that is associated with it. Thus, that *Neue Sachlichkeit* study, which one recognizes from films but which often fails to live up to the original, belongs to the managing director. One is deceived by sensational literature: most often it remains far behind reality in its inventiveness. As the characteristic location of the small dependent existences who still very much like to associate themselves with the sunken middle class, more and more suburbs are formed. The few inhabitable cubic metres, which cannot even be enlarged by the radio, correspond precisely to the narrow living space of this stratum. The typical space for the unemployed is more generously proportioned but as a result is the opposite of a home and certainly not a living space. It is the employment agency. An arcade, through which the unemployed should once more attain a gainfully employed existence. Today, unfortunately, the arcade is heavily congested.

I have visited several Berlin employment agencies. Not in order to indulge the enjoyment of the reporter who commonly with a sieve creates things out of life, but rather in order to ascertain what position the unemployed actually

Kracauer occupy in the system of our society. Neither the diverse commentaries on unemployment statistics nor the relevant parliamentary debates give any information on this. They are ideologically permeated and, in one sense or another, straighten out reality. In contrast, the space of the employment exchange is filled by reality itself. Each typical space is brought into being by typical social relationships that, without the distorting intervention of consciousness, express themselves in it. Everything that is disowned by consciousness, everything that would otherwise be intentionally overlooked, contributes to its construction. Spatial images are the dreams of society. Wherever the hieroglyphics of any spatial image are deciphered, there the basis of social reality presents itself.

The employment agency stands in the same relationship to the rule governed office as the financial support for the unemployed stands to the wage. It is usually more unfavourably located than the normal places of work; one notices that it is conceded to those who have been compulsorily liberated from society. Its accommodation in its own building, that might previously have been a school, already aspires to be little short of an exception. The director of a recently created agency for motor drivers, pilots, etc. informed me regretfully that his agency was so poorly located – in the interests of the employment agency. For the employers did not like to communicate in a district in which they would be afraid of leaving their often expensive vehicles unattended on the street. In actual fact, the surrounding area is peopled by Zille figures and is not the appropriate stopping place for fine car upholstery. Other employment agencies are located in the rear sections of large building complexes. One of them, in which positions for metal workers are dealt with, has just now been granted a place in the darkest regions. In order to make one's way to it, one must traverse two courtyards back from the street that are wedged in by morose brick walls. The pressure which the masses of stone exercise is raised by the fact that within them nonetheless work is still done. Finally, one detects no traces any more of the street. The employment agency itself is to be found three flights of stairs up at the furthest end of this world of nooks and crannies, and resembles an inverted fool's paradise in so far as on the way to it one has to first work one's way through the endless zone of smells of a public eating house. The fact that it makes the impression of a warehouse, contrary to the rear front, is totally justified. Likewise, the unemployed wait patiently in the rear front of the contemporary production process. They are secreted from it as waste products, they are the left-overs that remain. Under the prevailing circumstances, the space accorded to them can hardly have any other appearance than that of a junk room.

From the windows of the metal workers' employment agency one looks out at the industrial life that is played out in the front part of the buildings. The buildings, filled by the production and distribution process, mask the whole horizon of those who are unemployed. The unemployed person has no sun of his own, he has always only the employer in front of him who, at most, does not stand in his light if he offers work. 'We are primarily an organization for employers', a section manager explained to me. The fact that the rear part of the building of the employment agency exists in the shadow of the front building occupied by the employer is made pronounced in the arrangements. At specific hours, the particular relevant occupations are arranged: turner, pipe-layer, readymade clothing tailor, etc. An official mounts a small raised podium

in the middle of the hall and calls out the descriptions of the positions vacant. *Kracauer*
As a rule, dense crowds, who are waiting for work, surround him. Their
attention is riveted to the announcements that drip down upon them from the
heights of the realm of work, an ever-recurrent image that graphically confirms
the total dependency of the unemployed upon the powers in the front part of
the building. If these powers visit the employment agency then a special room
for employers is made available to them, in which they can negotiate with the
labour force. In the light of the present day state of the labour market, very few
can hope for an immediate transaction. As I learned in the agency for the textile
trade, 'out of 2,000 applications at the present time only around 10 are
successful'. Here and there in various places, I am given equally cheerless
figures that are pointless to repeat here since, without exception, they are to be
found in the statistics. More fundamental and more characteristic for the
locality is something else: namely, the aspect under which, viewed from here,
the production process appears. This production process weighs down like a
dark destiny upon the minds of men and women. Whereas in better off regions
one overlooks its natural course and strives to regulate it where not broken off,
in these storage spaces one speaks of it in a whispering tone and with a fatalism
as if it is misfortune. I was informed that, 'For three or four weeks, although
the level of redundancies has reduced, new orders have not arrived.' Or,
'Young, strong people are given greater attention than older ones.' Or, 'For
workers on gold, who are not at all in demand, unemployment often lasts for
three years and longer, whereas for better placed groups from six weeks to
three months.' Nothing but natural scientific statements, without a word of
criticism, which in this context would certainly not be appropriate. This is how
things are, and this is how they must be. The oppressive devotion to the
changing vicissitudes of market forces is plainly a typical characteristic of the
employment agencies. Here, behind the back of the all-powerful production
process, where one reprieves one's life, the categories that have stamped this
process as an unchangeable natural state of affairs still shed a faint glimmer of
their old bright glitter. Here it is still an idol and there exists nothing superior
to it.

In the employment agency, the concepts governing it ooze through all pores,
and if there is any place where they reign undisputed then it is in this space out
of its narrow sphere of power over the discharged workers. In the metal
workers' employment exchange there is mounted a warning with the following
content:

Unemployed! Protect and Preserve Common Property!

This warning is lacking for the textile workers who, on average, are of course
less powerfully built than, for instance, the locksmith. The furniture in the
waiting room consists of tables and benches, solid rectangular stuff that will
bear some hard knocks. Otherwise there falls under the rubric of common
property only the wall plastering which, by virtue of the permanent contact
with the masses of unemployed, appears not to be in good shape. It is to be
assumed that, with the narrowly developed feeling for language in Germany,
the public warning is harmlessly intended and is in fact also harmlessly paid
attention to. But the words easily disengage themselves from the user who does
not understand how to use them and reveal: not what he thought of but rather

Kracauer that which is so self-evident to him that he does not even have to consider it at all. And indeed the placard preaches the sacredness of property with an unceremoniousness such as only the sleepwalker possesses, he who does not concern himself with the provocative effect which such a sermon at such a place achieves if all participants were awake. Of course it states common property; yet for the unemployed, many of whom at present end up as objects of public welfare, the common property too is not common enough in order to forfeit its private character. To the point of superfluity they should still guard and defend this property from whose regular enjoyment, and without being themselves to blame, they are excluded. What is the whole expenditure of grandiose vocabulary for? For a couple of miserable tables and benches that neither deserve the pretentious name of common property, nor do they require preservation or even any special protection. Thus society preserves and protects property; it fences it in, even there where its defence is not at all necessary, with linguistic trenches and ramparts. It probably does it unintentionally, and perhaps one of those affected hardly notices that it does it. But that is precisely the genius of language; that it fulfils instructions that it has not been informed of, and erects bastions in the unconscious.

In the employment agency, the unemployed occupy themselves with waiting. Since in relation to their number that of positions vacant may at the moment be negligible, the activity of waiting becomes almost an end in itself. I have observed that, when the situations vacant are read out, many hardly still listen. They are already too indifferent to be capable of believing in being selected. Young lads and older people – in dense throngs they guard and defend common property without active employment. The fact that they mostly keep on their caps and hats may be a weak sign of freedom of the will. Only in the room does one remove the head-gear; but this space is actually not a room but, at most, a passageway, even though one wiles away one's time in it for months on end. I do not know of a spatial location in which the activity of waiting is so demoralizing. And this is quite aside from the fact that in these times of stagnation the goal is missing for them: above all what is lacking for them is the brightness. Here, the rebellious desire to make a noise is not permitted, nor does the enforced idleness retain any other kind of inspiration. On the contrary, idleness takes place completely in the shadows and must rely upon the social title of the autocracy who give birth to it. And yet much would be glossed over, for poverty is continuously exposed to its own glare. At one time, it spreads itself out with visible blotches and blemishes and, at another, it retreats in a bourgeois-prim manner into seclusion. In the case of a better dressed tailor, for instance, the cuff of the shirt was selected as the ultimate hidden recess. He contrived to hide it on some occasions whereas at others he outwardly exposed it all the more deliberately. The bodies are often neglected and a stuffy mist exhudes in the waiting rooms. Thus, abandoned to the unexplained association with one another, waiting becomes for the people a double burden. In every possible manner they seek to bide away the meaningless time but, in whichever direction they direct their efforts, the meaninglessness follows after them. They enter into conversations that should distract them from waiting and indeed at last should give up its unending background. They play dice, chess and cards, all of them games of chance that are jesting with lack of chance, because here the breakthrough of chance to happiness is prevented by the crisis that has risen

up to destiny. The older ones perhaps make friends with waiting as if with a *Kracauer*
comrade; in contrast, for the young unemployed it is a poison that slowly
permeates them.

I am witness to the following conversation. A man complains to the official:
'I have now been without work for a year and still have not obtained a job.' –
'But this person is already unemployed for a year and a half', is the reply given
to him. A reply of demonstrative clarity which succeeds on the basis of the
decision that in the case of the same qualifications the placement process
depends upon the length of unemployment. In some occupations, candidates
for employment can only be taken into consideration if they have been without
work beyond a certain time. The primitive justice that rules in the employment
agencies is intended for the masses, and the unemployed individual is a particle
of the mass. The fact that the masses go in and go out is imprinted by the rubber
stamp mark of the agency office. Time and time again these walls, these
theatrical stage props, witness the endless queues that form before the counters,
the shifting groups that coalesce and disperse, the patterns of people
crystallizing around the speaker. Where such a model of the massed is aroused,
justice can undertake nothing other than to muster the masses. It must balance
the quantities, the amounts of time and space that serve for its guidance. This is
all very well and no one would retain a bitter after-taste on their tongue if this
were not the case. In the employment agency for chauffeurs it was explained to
me: certainly, the longer a person is out of work the more likely it is that they
will be found employment. But the owners of valuable automobiles do not
willingly trust their vehicles to a chauffeur who has been out of employment for
months on end, but rather normally demand a man who has been out of work
for the shortest possible time. On this point, we must of course concede and act
against our principles . . . Justice in the low ground is thus intersected by an act
of arbitrary will that is, indeed, anything other than pure arbitrariness. It
travels into the lower strata like a flash of lightning from the serene heaven of
the upper strata. In the upper strata, the individual predominates instead of the
mass and a sense of justice could be adapted to it that decided in detail
according to the circumstances and which would be more precise than the
primitive justice. Each one of them knows that and the reason why it is not
factually in force there above, and in comparison with its caricature the
barbaric aspect of the utmost necessity certainly deserves the unconditional
precedence. Yet, due to its provisional nature, it is surrounded by affliction and
the fact that, now as always, questionable basic principles can be satisfied in a
sphere of individual claims removed from its grasp, and it acquires amongst
other things the appearance of inhumanity and increases still further the
affliction surrounding it. A bad individualism puts pressure on the good
crudeness, which must ignore the individual elements. Only with the mass itself
can a sense of justice rise to the higher sphere that is really just.

'In the interests of a smooth flow of persons, the orders of the hall porter
must be unquestioningly followed.' This regulation at the courtyard entrance of
a business block complex is sent on in advance of the employment agency, that
is to be found in the background, like the introduction of a book to its own
text. What is stated on the door plate and calculated to have an effect upon the
masses is thoroughly elaborated on the posters in the inside rooms. The posters
refer to the elementary needs of life that will legally come to the masses of

Kracauer unemployed. On the grounds of who knows what plausible building regulations or other such well considered reasons, smoking is always forbidden for them, and for still more valid reasons they nonetheless still smoke and for the most valid reasons the superintending staff close both their eyes to it. Alongside the need to smoke there is also hunger and love. The metal worker can himself silence each of these equally in the employment exchange itself. In one of the corners, a canteen has been installed which offers milk for sale as the main liquid refreshment. Milk is healthy, but how does one enjoy it? 'Never without something to eat', announces a prominently displayed notice . . . 'A glass of milk, drunk down at one go into an empty stomach, forms there a clump of cheese that is difficult to digest.' Sandwiches, that are therefore a basic precondition for healthy milk, are densely piled up on the adjacent buffet. The images of the clump of cheese and the empty stomach demonstrate in a drastic manner that the human beings in these spaces stand so nakedly and emptily like the walls, as an object of hygiene, that through its coarse directness throws away several possibilities. No aura graciously shrouds the bodily elements, rather the bodies step without any extenuation into the shrill light of the public sphere and the human beings who belong to these bodies are still merely systems that with the introduction of milk after the preceding meal will already function. In the back courts of society the human entrails are hung out like pieces of washing. It is to them that the posters are also addressed that pontificate upon sexually transmitted diseases and regulation of births. The fact that the elementary events of life are resolutely seized upon is as it should be and corresponds totally to the ordinances of primitive justice. But just as waiting in the labour exchange finds no fulfilment, except through the blind caprice of the production process, so too the elementary existence here is not built in and embraced. It stares into emptiness without being taken up by consciousness and its place being maintained. Ostensibly out of the need to brighten up the place a little, the walls have from time to time been adorned with coloured prints. Do landscapes interrupt the misery or artistic portraits? Not at all. Rather, pictures that are dedicated to the prevention of accidents. 'Think of your mother', stands under one of them that, like the rest, warns of the dangers to which the worker is subjected when working with machines. Astonishingly enough, the couple of illustrations of gloomy happenings shimmer in a friendly manner above the heads. Yet nothing typifies the character of this space more that the fact that in them even pictures of accidents become picture postcard greetings from the happy upper world. If the unemployed could be immediately transferred there from the employment agency, then the poster announcing 'Unnecessary waiting on the steps is not permitted', that adorns many staircase walls, would not be required. It sounds like an afterword to the collection of texts that is prefaced by the door plate at the entrance to the courtyard.

GEORG SIMMEL

Although marginalized for much of his academic career, the German sociologist and philosopher Georg Simmel (1858–1918) proved to be a highly original thinker who made a substantial contribution to establishing sociology as an autonomous field of study. Antipathy towards his individualized style of writing and unconventional subject matter, combined with anti-semitism and a resistance to sociology as an academic discipline, effectively prevented Simmel from obtaining a regular faculty appointment until late in life. Yet in his studies of seemingly mundane everyday phenomena, such as money, sexuality and contemporary urban life, Simmel is now recognized as having offered some penetrating insights into the consciousness of modernity.

In his essay 'The Metropolis and Mental Life' (1903) Simmel provides one of the most incisive snapshots of life in the modernist metropolis. The modern metropolitan individual is distinguished by a blasé attitude which is itself a product of the 'intensification of emotional life due to the swift and continuous shift of external and internal stimuli'. This engenders a certain autonomy, so that the modern individual becomes an intellectualized creature whose own disinterested circulation within the metropolis reflects the circulation of money and commodities themselves. Simmel's portrait of the metropolitan individual as overstimulated by sensory experience and distracted by the fragmentary existence of modern life matches that of Walter Benjamin. The blasé individual of Simmel's metropolis is comparable to the *flâneur* of Benjamin's arcade, although, unlike the *flâneur* he remains a creature of the crowd. The modern metropolitan type can thus be seen to be both a product of and a defence against the modern metropolitan existence.

In another famous essay, 'Bridge and Door', Simmel discusses the theme of connectedness and separation. The bridge and the door are concrete manifestations of fundamental human tendencies to connect and separate everything. 'The bridge indicates how humankind unifies the separatedness of merely natural being, and the door how it separates the uniform, continuous unity of natural being.' The door, however, is for Simmel superior to the bridge. It has 'richer and livelier significance'. Whereas the bridge tends to emphasize connectedness, the door emphasizes 'how separating and connecting are only two sides of precisely the same act'. The door, moreover, reminds us that 'the bounded and boundaryless adjoin one another . . . as the possibility of permanent interchange'. Simmel's evocation of the bridge makes a provocative comparison with that of Heidegger in the essay 'Building, Dwelling, Thinking' also contained in this volume.

Simmel

BRIDGE AND DOOR

The image of external things possesses for us the ambiguous dimension that in external nature everything can be considered to be connected, but also as separated. The uninterrupted transformations of materials as well as energies bring everything into relationship with everything else and make *one* cosmos out of all the individual elements. On the other hand, however, the objects remain banished in the merciless separation of space; no particle of matter can share its space with another and a real unity of the diverse does not exist in spatial terms. And, by virtue of this equal demand on self-excluding concepts, natural existence seems to resist any application of them at all.

Only to humanity, in contrast to nature, has the right to connect and separate been granted, and in the distinctive manner that one of these activities is always the presupposition of the other. By choosing two items from the undisturbed store of natural things in order to designate them as 'separate', we have already related them to one another in our consciousness, we have emphasized these two together against whatever lies between them. And conversely, we can only sense those things to be related which we have previously somehow isolated from one another; things must first be separated from one another in order to be together. Practically as well as logically, it would be meaningless to connect that which was not separated, and indeed that which also remains separated in some sense. The formula according to which both types of activity come together in human undertakings, whether the connectedness or the separation is felt to be what was naturally ordained and the respective alternative is felt to be our task, is something which can guide all our activity. In the immediate as well as the symbolic sense, in the physical as well as the intellectual sense, we are at any moment those who separate the connected or connect the separate.

The people who first built a path between two places performed one of the greatest human achievements. No matter how often they might have gone back and forth between the two and thus connected them subjectively, so to speak, it was only in visibly impressing the path into the surface of the earth that the places were objectively connected. The will to connection had become a shaping of things, a shaping that was available to the will at every repetition, without still being dependent on its frequency or rarity. Path building, one could say, is a specifically human achievement; the animal too continuously overcomes a separation and often in the cleverest and most ingenious ways, but its beginning and end remain unconnected, it does not accomplish the miracle of the road: freezing movement into a solid structure that commences from it and in which it terminates.

This achievement reaches its zenith in the construction of a bridge. Here the human will to connection seems to be confronted not only by the passive resistance of spatial separation but also by the active resistance of a special configuration. By overcoming this obstacle, the bridge symbolizes the extension of our volitional sphere over space. Only for us are the banks of a river not just apart but 'separated'; if we did not first connect them in our practical thoughts, in our needs and in our fantasy, then the concept of separation would have no meaning. But natural form here approaches this concept as if with a positive intention; here the separation seems imposed between the elements in and of themselves, over which the spirit now prevails, reconciling and uniting.

The bridge becomes an aesthetic value insofar as it accomplishes the connection between what is separated not only in reality and in order to fulfil practical goals, but in making it directly visible. The bridge gives to the eye the same support for connecting the sides of the landscape as it does to the body for practical reality. The mere dynamics of motion, in whose particular reality the 'purpose' of the bridge is exhausted, has become something visible and lasting, just as the portrait brings to a halt, as it were, the physical and mental life process in which the reality of humankind takes place and gathers the emotion of that reality, flowing and ebbing away in time, into a single timelessly stable visualization which reality never displays and never can display. The bridge confers an ultimate meaning elevated above all sensuousness, an individual meaning not mediated by any abstract reflection, an appearance that draws the practical purposive meaning of the bridge into itself, and brings it into a visible form in the same way as a work of art does with its 'object'. Yet the bridge reveals its difference from the work of art, in the fact that despite its synthesis transcending nature, in the end it fits into the image of nature. For the eye it stands in a much closer and much less fortuitous relationship to the banks that it connects than does, say, a house to its earth foundation, which disappears from sight beneath it. People quite generally regard a bridge in a landscape to be a 'picturesque' element, because through it the fortuitousness of that which is given by nature is elevated to a unity, which is indeed of a completely intellectual nature. Yet by means of its immediate spatial visibility it does indeed possess precisely that aesthetic value, whose purity art represents when it puts the spiritually gained unity of the merely natural into its island-like ideal enclosedness.

Whereas in the correlation of separateness and unity, the bridge always allows the accent to fall on the latter, and at the same time overcomes the separation of its anchor points that make them visible and measurable, the door represents in a more decisive manner how separating and connecting are only two sides of precisely the same act. The human being who first erected a hut, like the first road-builder, revealed the specifically human capacity over against nature, insofar as he or she cut a portion out of the continuity and infinity of space and arranged this into a particular unity in accordance with a *single* meaning. A piece of space was thereby brought together and separated from the whole remaining world. By virtue of the fact that the door forms, as it were, a linkage between the space of human beings and everything that remains outside it, it transcends the separation between the inner and the outer. Precisely because it can also be opened, its closure provides the feeling of a stronger isolation against everything outside this space than the mere unstructured wall. The latter is mute, but the door speaks. It is absolutely essential for humanity that it set itself a boundary, but with freedom, that is, in such a way that it can also remove this boundary again, that it can place itself outside it.

The finitude into which we have entered somehow always borders somewhere on the infinitude of physical or metaphysical being. Thus the door becomes the image of the boundary point at which human beings actually always stand or can stand. The finite unity, to which we have connected a part of infinite space designated for us, reconnects it to this latter; in the unity, the

Simmel   bounded and the boundaryless adjoint one another, not in the dead geometric
form of a mere separating wall, but rather as the possibility of a permanent
interchange – in contrast to the bridge which connects the finite with the finite.
Instead, the bridge removes us from this firmness in the act of walking on it
and, before we have become inured to it through daily habit, it must have
provided the wonderful feeling of floating for a moment between heaven and
earth. Whereas the bridge, as the line stretched between two points, prescribes
unconditional security and direction, life flows forth out of the door from the
limitation of isolated separate existence into the limitlessness of all possible
directions.

If the factors of separateness and connectedness meet in the bridge in such a
way that the former appears more as the concern of nature and the latter more
the concern of humankind, then in the case of the door, both are concentrated
more uniformly in human achievement *as* human achievement. This is the basis
for the richer and livelier significance of the door compared to the bridge,
which is also revealed in the fact that it makes no difference in meaning in
which direction one crosses a bridge, whereas the door displays a complete
difference of intention between entering and exiting. This completely distinguishes it from the significance of the window which, as a connection of inner
space with the external world, is otherwise related to the door. Yet the teleological emotion with respect to the window is directed almost exclusively
from inside to outside: it is there for looking out, not for looking in. It creates
the connection between the inner and the outer chronically and continually, as
it were, by virtue of its transparency; but the one-sided direction in which this
connection runs, just like the limitation upon it to be a path merely for the eye,
gives to the window only a part of the deeper and more fundamental significance of the door.

Of course, the particular situation can also emphasize one direction of the
latter's function more than the other. When the masonry openings in Gothic or
Romanesque cathedrals gradually taper down to the actual door and one
reaches it between rows of semi-columns and figures that approach each other
more and more closely, then the significance of these doors is obviously meant
to be that of a leading into but not a leading out of somewhere – the latter
existing rather as an unfortunately unavoidable accidental property. This
structure leads the person entering with certainty and with a gentle, natural
compulsion on the right way. (This meaning is extended, as I mention for the
sake of analogy here, by the rows of columns between the door and high altar.
By perspectivally moving closer together, they point the way, lead us onwards,
permit no wavering – which would not be the case if we actually observed the
real parallelism of the pillar; for then the end point would display no difference
from that of the beginning, there would be no marking to indicate that we must
start at the one point and end up at the other. Yet no matter how wonderfully
perspective is used here for the inner orientation of the church, it ultimately
also lends itself to the opposite effect and allows the row of pillars to direct us
to the door with the same narrowing from altar to door as the one that leads us
to its main point.) Only that external conical form of the door makes entering
in contrast to exiting its completely unambiguous meaning. But this is in fact a
totally unique situation which it symbolizes, namely, that the movement of life,
which goes equally from inside to outside and from outside to inside,

terminates at the church and is replaced by the only direction which is neces- *Simmel*
sary. Life on the earthly plane, however, as at every moment it throws a bridge
between the unconnectedness of things, likewise stands in every moment inside
or outside the door through which it will lead from its separate existence into
the world, or from the world into its separate existence.

The forms that dominate the dynamics of our lives are thus transferred by
bridge and door into the fixed permanence of visible creation. They do not
support the merely functional and teleological aspect of our movements as
tools; rather, in their form it solidifies, as it were, into immediately convincing
plasticity. Viewed in terms of the opposing emphases that prevail in their
impression, the bridge indicates how humankind unifies the separatedness of
merely natural being, and the door how it separates the uniform, continuous
unity of natural being. The basis for their distinctive value for the visual arts lies
in the general aesthetic significance which they gain through this visualization
of something metaphysical, this stabilization of something merely functional.
Even though one might also attribute the frequency with which painting
employs both to the artistic value of their mere form, there does indeed still
exist here that mysterious coincidence with which the purely artistic significance and perfection of an object at the same time always reveals the most
exhaustive expression of an actually non-visible spiritual or metaphysical
meaning. The purely artistic interest in, say, the human face, only concerned
with form and colour, is satisfied in the highest degree when its representation
includes the ultimate in inspiration and intellectual characterization.

Because the human being is the connecting creature who must always separate and cannot connect without separating – that is why we must first
conceive intellectually of the merely indifferent existence of two river banks as
something separated in order to connect them by means of a bridge. And the
human being is likewise the bordering creature who has no border. The
enclosure of his or her domestic being by the door means, to be sure, that they
have separated out a piece from the uninterrupted unity of natural being. But
just as the formless limitation takes on a shape, its limitedness finds its significance and dignity only in that which the mobility of the door illustrates: in the
possibility at any moment of stepping out of this limitation into freedom.

THE METROPOLIS AND MENTAL LIFE

The deepest problems of modern life flow from the attempt of the individual to
maintain the independence and individuality of his existence against the sovereign powers of society, against the weight of the historical heritage and the
external culture and technique of life. This antagonism represents the most
modern form of the conflict which primitive man must carry on with nature for
his own bodily existence. The eighteenth century may have called for liberation
from all the ties which grew up historically in politics, in religion, in morality
and in economics in order to permit the original natural virtue of man, which is
equal in everyone, to develop without inhibition; the nineteenth century may
have sought to promote, in addition to man's freedom, his individuality (which
is connected with the division of labour) and his achievements which make him

Simmel unique and indispensable but which at the same time make him so much the more dependent on the complementary activity of others; Nietzsche may have seen the relentless struggle of the individual as the prerequisite for his full development, while socialism found the same thing in the suppression of all competition – but in each of these the same fundamental motive was at work, namely the resistance of the individual to being levelled, swallowed up in the social-technological mechanism. When one inquires about the products of the specifically modern aspects of contemporary life with reference to their inner meaning – when, so to speak, one examines the body of culture with reference to the soul, as I am to do concerning the metropolis today – the answer will require the investigation of the relationship which such a social structure promotes between the individual aspects of life and those which transcend the existence of single individuals. It will require the investigation of the adaptations made by the personality in its adjustment to the forces that lie outside of it.

The psychological foundation, upon which the metropolitan individuality is erected, is the intensification of emotional life due to the swift and continuous shift of external and internal stimuli. Man is a creature whose existence is dependent on differences, i.e. his mind is stimulated by the difference between present impressions and those which have preceded. Lasting impressions, the slightness in their differences, the habituated regularity of their course and contrasts between them, consume, so to speak, less mental energy than the rapid telescoping of changing images, pronounced differences within what is grasped at a single glance, and the unexpectedness of violent stimuli. To the extent that the metropolis creates these psychological conditions – with every crossing of the street, with the tempo and multiplicity of economic, occupational and social life – it creates in the sensory foundations of mental life, and in the degree of awareness necessitated by our organization as creatures dependent on differences, a deep contrast with the slower, more habitual, more smoothly flowing rhythm of the sensory-mental phase of small town and rural existence. Thereby the essentially intellectualistic character of the mental life of the metropolis becomes intelligible as over against that of the small town which rests more on feelings and emotional relationships. These latter are rooted in the unconscious levels of the mind and develop most readily in the steady equilibrium of unbroken customs. The locus of reason, on the other hand, is in the lucid, conscious upper strata of the mind and it is the most adaptable of our inner forces. In order to adjust itself to the shifts and contradictions in events, it does not require the disturbances and inner upheavals which are the only means whereby more conservative personalities are able to adapt themselves to the same rhythm of events. Thus the metropolitan type – which naturally takes on a thousand individual modifications – creates a protective organ for itself against the profound disruption with which the fluctuations and discontinuities of the external milieu threaten it. Instead of reacting emotionally, the metropolitan type reacts primarily in a rational manner, thus creating a mental predominance through the intensification of consciousness, which in turn is caused by it. Thus the reaction of the metropolitan person to those events is moved to a sphere of mental activity which is least sensitive and which is furthest removed from the depths of the personality.

This intellectualistic quality which is thus recognized as a protection of the

inner life against the domination of the metropolis, becomes ramified into
numerous specific phenomena. The metropolis has always been the seat of
money economy because the many-sidedness and concentration of commercial
activity have given the medium of exchange an importance which it could not
have acquired in the commercial aspects of rural life. But money economy and
the domination of the intellect stand in the closest relationship to one another.
They have in common a purely matter-of-fact attitude in the treatment of
persons and things in which a formal justice is often combined with an
unrelenting hardness. The purely intellectualistic person is indifferent to all
things personal because, out of them, relationships and reactions develop
which are not to be completely understood by purely rational methods – just as
the unique element in events never enters into the principle of money. Money is
concerned only with what is common to all, i.e. with the exchange value which
reduces all quality and individuality to a purely quantitative level. All
emotional relationships between persons rest on their individuality, whereas
intellectual relationships deal with persons as with numbers, that is, as with
elements which, in themselves, are indifferent, but which are of interest only
insofar as they offer something objectively perceivable. It is in this very manner
that the inhabitant of the metropolis reckons with his merchant, his customer
and with his servant, and frequently with the persons with whom he is thrown
into obligatory association. These relationships stand in distinct contrast with
the nature of the smaller circle in which the inevitable knowledge of individual
characteristics produces, with an equal inevitability, an emotional tone in
conduct, a sphere which is beyond the mere objective weighting of tasks performed and payments made. What is essential here as regards the economic-
psychological aspect of the problem is that in less advanced cultures production
was for the customer who ordered the product so that the producer and the
purchaser knew one another. The modern city, however, is supplied almost
exclusively by production for the market, that is, for entirely unknown
purchasers who never appear in the actual field of vision of the producers
themselves. Thereby, the interests of each party acquire a relentless matter-of-
factness, and its rationally calculated economic egoism need not fear any
divergence from its set path because of the imponderability of personal
relationships. This is all the more the case in the money economy which dominates the metropolis in which the last remnants of domestic production and
direct barter of goods have been eradicated and in which the amount of
production on direct personal order is reduced daily. Furthermore, this psychological intellectualistic attitude and the money economy are in such close
integration that no one is able to say whether it was the former that effected the
latter or vice versa. What is certain is only that the form of life in the metropolis
is the soil which nourishes this interaction most fruitfully, a point which I shall
attempt to demonstrate only with the statement of the most outstanding
English constitutional historian to the effect that through the entire course of
English history London has never acted as the heart of England but often as its
intellect and always as its money bag.

In certain apparently insignificant characters or traits of the most external
aspects of life are to be found a number of characteristic mental tendencies. The
modern mind has become more and more a calculating one. The calculating
exactness of practical life which has resulted from a money economy

Simmel corresponds to the ideal of natural science, namely that of transforming the world into an arithmetical problem and of fixing every one of its parts in a mathematical formula. It has been money economy which has thus filled the daily life of so many people with weighing, calculating, enumerating and the reduction of qualitative values to quantitative terms. Because of the character of calculability which money has there has come into the relationships of the elements of life a precision and a degree of certainty in the definition of the equalities and inequalities and an unambiguousness in agreements and arrangements, just as externally this precision has been brought about through the general diffusion of pocket watches. It is, however, the conditions of the metropolis which are cause as well as effect for this essential characteristic. The relationships and concerns of the typical metropolitan resident are so manifold and complex that, especially as a result of the agglomeration of so many persons with such differentiated interests, their relationships and activities intertwine with one another into a many-membered organism. In view of this fact, the lack of the most exact punctuality in promises and performances would cause the whole to break down into an inextricable chaos. If all the watches in Berlin suddenly went wrong in different ways even only as much as an hour, its entire economic and commercial life would be derailed for some time. Even though this may seem more superficial in its significance, it transpires that the magnitude of distances results in making all waiting and the breaking of appointments an ill-afforded waste of time. For this reason the technique of metropolitan life in general is not conceivable without all of its activities and reciprocal relationships being organized and coordinated in the most punctual way into a firmly fixed framework of time which transcends all subjective elements. But here too there emerge those conclusions which are in general the whole task of this discussion, namely, that every event, however restricted to this superficial level it may appear, comes immediately into contact with the depths of the soul, and that the most banal externalities are, in the last analysis, bound up with the final decisions concerning the meaning and the style of life. Punctuality, calculability and exactness, which are required by the complications and extensiveness of metropolitan life, are not only most intimately connected with its capitalistic and intellectualistic character but also colour the content of life and are conducive to the exclusion of those irrational, instinctive, sovereign human traits and impulses which originally seek to determine the form of life from within instead of receiving it from the outside in a general, schematically precise form. Even though those lives which are autonomous and characterized by these vital impulses are not entirely impossible in the city, they are, none the less, opposed to it *in abstracto*. It is in the light of this that we can explain the passionate hatred of personalities like Ruskin and Nietzsche for the metropolis – personalities who found the value of life only in unschematized individual expressions which cannot be reduced to exact equivalents and in whom, on that account, there flowed from the same source as did that hatred, the hatred of the money economy and of the intellectualism of existence.

The same factors which, in the exactness and the minute precision of the form of life, have coalesced into a structure of the highest impersonality, have, on the other hand, an influence in a highly personal direction. There is perhaps no psychic phenomenon which is so unconditionally reserved to the city as the blasé outlook. It is at first the consequence of those rapidly shifting stimulations of the nerves which are thrown together in all their contrasts and from which it seems to us the intensification of metropolitan intellectuality seems to be derived. On that account it is not likely that stupid persons who have been hitherto intellectually dead will be blasé. Just as an immoderately sensuous life makes one blasé because it stimulates the nerves to their utmost reactivity until they finally can no longer produce any reaction at all, so, less harmful stimuli, through the rapidity and the contradictoriness of their shifts, force the nerves to make such violent responses, tear them about so brutally that they exhaust their last reserves of strength and, remaining in the same milieu, do not have time for new reserves to form. This incapacity to react to new stimulations with the required amount of energy constitutes in fact that blasé attitude which every child of a large city evinces when compared with the products of the more peaceful and more stable milieu.

Combined with this physiological source of the blasé metropolitan attitude there is another, which derives from a money economy. The essence of the blasé attitude is an indifference toward the distinctions between things. Not in the sense that they are not perceived, as is the case of mental dullness, but rather that the meaning and the value of the distinctions between things, and therewith of the things themselves, are experienced as meaningless. They appear to the blasé person in a homogeneous, flat and grey colour with no one of them worthy of being preferred to another. This psychic mood is the correct subjective reflection of a complete money economy to the extent that money takes the place of all the manifoldness of things and expresses all qualitative distinctions between them in the distinction of how much. To the extent that money, with its colourlessness and its indifferent quality, can become a common denominator of all values, it becomes the frightful leveller – it hollows out the core of things, their peculiarities, their specific values and their uniqueness and incomparability in a way which is beyond repair. They all float with the same specific gravity in the constantly moving stream of money. They all rest on the same level and are distinguished only by their amounts. In individual cases this colouring, or rather this de-colouring of things, through their equation with money, may be imperceptibly small. In the relationship, however, which the wealthy person has to objects which can be bought for money, perhaps indeed in the total character which, for this reason, public opinion now recognizes in these objects, it takes on very considerable proportions. This is why the metropolis is the seat of commerce and it is in it that the purchasability of things appears in quite a different aspect than in simpler economies. It is also the peculiar seat of the blasé attitude. In it is brought to a peak, in a certain way, that achievement in the concentration of purchasable things which stimulates the individual to the highest degree of nervous energy. Through the mere quantitative intensification of the same conditions this achievement is transformed into its opposite, into this peculiar adaptive phenomenon – the blasé attitude – in which the nerves reveal their final possibility of adjusting themselves to the content and the form of metropolitan life by renouncing the response to them. We see that the self-preservation of certain types of personalities is obtained at the cost of devaluing the entire objective world, ending inevitably in dragging the personality downward into a feeling of its own valuelessness.

Simmel   Whereas the subject of this form of existence must come to terms with it for himself, his self-preservation in the face of the great city requires of him a no less negative type of social conduct. The mental attitude of the people of the metropolis to one another may be designated formally as one of reserve. If the unceasing external contact of numbers of persons in the city should be met by the same number of inner reactions as in the small town, in which one knows almost every person he meets and to each of whom he has a positive relationship, one would be completely atomized internally and would fall into an unthinkable mental condition. Partly this psychological circumstance and partly the privilege of suspicion which we have in the face of the elements of metropolitan life (which are constantly touching one another in fleeting contact) necessitates in us that reserve, in consequence of which we do not know by sight neighbours of years standing and which permits us to appear to small-town folk so often as cold and uncongenial. Indeed, if I am not mistaken, the inner side of this external reserve is not only indifference but more frequently than we believe, it is a slight aversion, a mutual strangeness and repulsion which, in a close contact which has arisen any way whatever, can break out into hatred and conflict. The entire inner organization of such a type of extended commercial life rests on an extremely varied structure of sympathies, indifferences and aversions of the briefest as well as of the most enduring sort. This sphere of indifference is, for this reason, not as great as it seems superficially. Our minds respond, with some definite feeling, to almost every impression emanating from another person. The unconsciousness, the transitoriness and the shift of these feelings seem to raise them only into indifference. Actually this latter would be as unnatural to us as immersion into a chaos of unwished-for suggestions would be unbearable. From these two typical dangers of metropolitan life we are saved by antipathy which is the latent adumbration of actual antagonism since it brings about the sort of distantiation and deflection without which this type of life could not be carried on at all. Its extent and its mixture, the rhythm of its emergence and disappearance, the forms in which it is adequate – these constitute, with the simplified motives (in the narrower sense) an inseparable totality of the form of metropolitan life. What appears here directly as dissociation is in reality only one of the elementary forms of socialization.

This reserve with its overtone of concealed aversion appears once more, however, as the form or the wrappings of a much more general psychic trait of the metropolis. It assures the individual of a type and degree of personal freedom to which there is no analogy in other circumstances. It has its roots in one of the great developmental tendencies of social life as a whole; in one of the few for which an approximately exhaustive formula can be discovered. The most elementary stage of social organization which is to be found historically, as well as in the present, is this: a relatively small circle almost entirely closed against neighbouring foreign or otherwise antagonistic groups but which has however within itself such a narrow cohesion that the individual member has only a very slight area for the development of his own qualities and for free activity for which he himself is responsible. Political and familial groups began in this way as do political and religious communities; the self-preservation of very young associations requires a rigorous setting of boundaries and a centripetal unity and for that reason it cannot give room to freedom and the peculiarities of inner and external development of the individual. From this stage social evolution proceeds simultaneously in two divergent but none the less corresponding directions. In the measure that the group grows numerically, spatially, and in the meaningful content of life, its immediate inner unity and the definiteness of its original demarcation against others are weakened and rendered mild by reciprocal interactions and interconnections. And at the same time the individual gains a freedom of movement far beyond the first jealous delimitation, and gains also a peculiarity and individuality to which the division of labour in groups, which have become larger, gives both occasion and necessity. However much the particular conditions and forces of the individual situation might modify the general scheme, the state and Christianity, guilds and political parties and innumerable other groups have developed in accord with this formula. This tendency seems to me, however, to be quite clearly recognizable also in the development of individuality within the framework of city life. Small town life in antiquity as well as in the Middle Ages imposed such limits upon the movements of the individual in his relationships with the outside world and on his inner independence and differentiation that the modern person could not even breathe under such conditions. Even today the city dweller who is placed in a small town feels a type of narrowness which is very similar. The smaller the circle which forms our environment and the more limited the relationships which have the possibility of transcending the boundaries, the more anxiously the narrow community watches over the deeds, the conduct of life and the attitudes of the individual and the more will a quantitative and qualitative individuality tend to pass beyond the boundaries of such a community.

The ancient *polis* seems in this regard to have had a character of a small town. The incessant threat against its existence by enemies from near and far brought about that stern cohesion in political and military matters, that supervision of the citizen by other citizens, and that jealousy of the whole toward the individual whose own private life was repressed to such an extent that he could compensate himself only by acting as a despot in his own household. The tremendous agitation and excitement, and the unique colourfulness of Athenian life is perhaps explained by the fact that a people of incomparably individualized personalities were in constant struggle against the incessant inner and external oppression of a de-individualizing small town. This created an atmosphere of tension in which the weaker were held down and the stronger were impelled to the most passionate type of self-protection. And with this there blossomed in Athens, what, without being able to define it exactly, must be designated as 'the general human character' in the intellectual development of our species. For the correlation, the factual as well as the historical validity of which we are here maintaining, is that the broadest and the most general contents and forms of life are intimately bound up with the most individual ones. Both have a common prehistory and also common enemies in the narrow formations and groupings, whose striving for self-preservation set them in conflict with the broad and general on the outside, as well as the freely mobile and individual on the inside. Just as in feudal times the 'free' man was he who stood under the law of the land, that is, under the law of the largest social unit, but he was unfree who derived his legal rights only from the narrow circle of a feudal community – so today in an intellectualized and refined sense the citizen

Simmel   of the metropolis is 'free' in contrast with the trivialities and prejudices which bind the small town person. The mutual reserve and indifference, and the intellectual conditions of life in large social units are never more sharply appreciated in their significance for the independence of the individual than in the dense crowds of the metropolis, because the bodily closeness and lack of space make intellectual distance really perceivable for the first time. It is obviously only the obverse of this freedom that, under certain circumstances, one never feels as lonely and as deserted as in this metropolitan crush of persons. For here, as elsewhere, it is by no means necessary that the freedom of man reflect itself in his emotional life only as a pleasant experience.

It is not only the immediate size of the area and population which, on the basis of world-historical correlation between the increase in the size of the social unit and the degree of personal inner and outer freedom, makes the metropolis the locus of this condition. It is rather in transcending this purely tangible extensiveness that the metropolis also becomes the seat of cosmopolitanism. Comparable with the form of the development of wealth – (beyond a certain point property increases in ever more rapid progression as out of its own inner being) – the individual's horizon is enlarged. In the same way, economic, personal and intellectual relations in the city (which are its ideal reflection) grow in a geometrical progression as soon as, for the first time, a certain limit has been passed. Every dynamic extension becomes a preparation not only for a similar extension but rather for a larger one, and from every thread which is spun out of it there continue, growing as out of themselves, an endless number of others. This may be illustrated by the fact that within the city the 'unearned increment' of ground rent, through a mere increase in traffic, brings to the owner profits which are self-generating. At this point the quantitative aspects of life are transformed qualitatively. The sphere of life of the small town is, in the main, enclosed within itself. For the metropolis it is decisive that its inner life is extended in a wave-like motion over a broader national or international area. Weimar was no exception because its significance was dependent upon individual personalities and died with them, whereas the metropolis is characterized by its essential independence even of the most significant individual personalities; this is rather its antithesis and it is the price of independence which the individual living in it enjoys. The most significant aspect of the metropolis lies in this functional magnitude beyond its actual physical boundaries and this effectiveness reacts upon the latter and gives to it life, weight, importance and responsibility. A person does not end with the limits of his physical body or with the area to which his physical activity is immediately confined but embraces, rather, the totality of meaningful effects which emanates from him temporally and spatially. In the same way the city exists only in the totality of the effects which transcend their immediate sphere. These really are the actual extent in which their existence is expressed. This is already expressed in the fact that individual freedom, which is the logical historical complement of such extension, is not only to be understood in the negative sense as mere freedom of movement and emancipation from prejudices and philistinism. Its essential characteristic is rather to be found in the fact that the particularity and incomparability which ultimately every person possesses in some way is actually expressed, giving form to life. That we follow the laws of our inner nature – and this is what freedom is – becomes

perceptible and convincing to us and to others only when the expressions of   *Simmel*
this nature distinguish themselves from others; it is our irreplaceability by
others which shows that our mode of existence is not imposed upon us from
the outside.

Cities are above all the seat of the most advanced economic division of
labour. They produce such extreme phenomena as the lucrative vocation of the
quatorzieme in Paris. These are persons who may be recognized by shields on
their houses and who hold themselves ready at the dinner hour in appropriate
costumes so they can he called upon on short notice in case thirteen persons
find themselves at the table. Exactly in the measure of its extension, the city
offers to an increasing degree the determining conditions for the division of
labour. It is a unit which, because of its large size, is receptive to a highly
diversified plurality of achievements while at the same time the agglomeration
of individuals and their struggle for the customer forces the individual to a type
of specialized accomplishment in which he cannot be so easily exterminated by
the other. The decisive fact here is that in the life of a city, struggle with nature
for the means of life is transformed into a conflict with human beings, and the
gain which is fought for is granted, not by nature, but by man. For here we find
not only the previously mentioned source of specialization but rather the
deeper one in which the seller must seek to produce in the person to whom he
wishes to sell ever new and unique needs. The necessity to specialize one's
product in order to find a source of income which is not yet exhausted and also
to specialize a function which cannot be easily supplanted is conducive to
differentiation, refinement and enrichment of the needs of the public which
obviously must lead to increasing personal variation within this public.

All this leads to the narrower type of intellectual individuation of mental
qualities to which the city gives rise in proportion to its size. There is a whole
series of causes for this. First of all there is the difficulty of giving one's own
personality a certain status within the framework of metropolitan life. Where
quantitative increase of value and energy has reached its limits, one seizes on
qualitative distinctions, so that, through taking advantage of the existing
sensitivity to differences, the attention of the social world can, in some way, be
won for oneself. This leads ultimately to the strangest eccentricities, to
specifically metropolitan extravagances of self-distantiation, of caprice, of
fastidiousness, the meaning of which is no longer to be found in the content of
such activity itself but rather in its being a form of 'being different' – of making
oneself noticeable. For many types of persons these are still the only means of
saving for oneself, through the attention gained from others, some sort of self-
esteem and the sense of filling a position. In the same sense there operates an
apparently insignificant factor which in its effects however is perceptibly
cumulative, namely, the brevity and rarity of meetings which are allotted to
each individual as compared with social intercourse in a small city. For here we
find the attempt to appear to-the-point, clear-cut and individual with extra-
ordinarily greater frequency than where frequent and long association assures
to each person an unambiguous conception of the other's personality.

This appears to me to be the most profound cause of the fact that the
metropolis places emphasis on striving for the most individual forms of
personal existence – regardless of whether it is always correct or always
successful. The development of modern culture is characterized by the

Simmel predominance of what one can call the objective spirit over the subjective; that is, in language as well as in law, in the technique of production as well as in art, in science as well as in the objects of domestic environment, there is embodied a sort of spirit (*Geist*), the daily growth of which is followed only imperfectly and with an even greater lag by the intellectual development of the individual. If we survey, for instance, the vast culture which during the last century has been embodied in things and in knowledge, in institutions and in comforts, and if we compare them with the cultural progress of the individual during the same period – at least in the upper classes – we would see a frightful difference in rate of growth between the two which represents, in many points, rather a regression of the culture of the individual with reference to spirituality, delicacy and idealism. This discrepancy is in essence the result of the success of the growing division of labour. For it is this which requires from the individual an ever more one-sided type of achievement which, at its highest point, often permits his personality as a whole to fall into neglect. In any case this over-growlh of objective culture has been less and less satisfactory for the individual. Perhaps less conscious than in practical activity and in the obscure complex of feelings which flow from him, he is reduced to a negligible quantity. He becomes a single cog as over against the vast overwhelming organization of things and forces which gradually take out of his hands everything connected with progress, spirituality and value. The operation of these forces results in the transformation of the latter from a subjective form into one of purely objective existence. It need only be pointed out that the metropolis is the proper arena for this type of culture which has outgrown every personal element. Here in buildings and in educational institutions, in the wonders and comforts of space-conquering technique, in the formations of social life and in the concrete institutions of the State is to be found such a tremendous richness of crystal-lizing, de-personalized cultural accomplishments that the personality can, so to speak, scarcely maintain itself in the face of it. From one angle life is made infinitely more easy in the sense that stimulations, interests, and the taking up of time and attention, present themselves from all sides and carry it in a stream which scarcely requires any individual efforts for its ongoing. But from another angle, life is composed more and more of these impersonal cultural elements and existing goods and values which seek to suppress peculiar personal interests and incomparabilities. As a result, in order that this most personal element be saved, extremities and peculiarities and individualizations must be produced and they must be over-exaggerated merely to be brought into the awareness even of the individual himself. The atrophy of individual culture through the hypertrophy of objective culture lies at the root of the bitter hatred which the preachers of the most extreme individualism, in the footsteps of Nietzsche, directed against the metropolis. But it is also the explanation of why indeed they are so passionately loved in the metropolis and indeed appear to its residents as the saviours of their unsatisfied yearnings.

When both of these forms of individualism which are nourished by the quant-itative relationships of the metropolis, i.e. individual independence and the elaboration of personal peculiarities, are examined with reference to their historical position, the metropolis attains an entirely new value and meaning in the world history of the spirit. The eighteenth century found the individual in the grip of powerful bonds which had become meaningless – bonds of a political, agrarian, guild and religious nature – delimitations which imposed upon the human being at the same time an unnatural form and for a long time an unjust inequality. In this situation arose the cry for freedom and equality – the belief in the full freedom of movement of the individual in all his social and intellectual relationships which would then permit the same noble essence to emerge equally from all individuals as Nature had placed it in them and as it had been distorted by social life and historical development. Alongside of this liberalistic ideal there grew up in the nineteenth century from Goethe and the Romantics, on the one hand, and from the economic division of labour, on the other, the further tendency, namely, that individuals who had been liberated from their historical bonds sought now to distinguish themselves from one another. No longer was it the 'general human quality' in every individual but rather his qualitative uniqueness and irreplaceability that now became the criteria of his value. In the conflict and shifting interpretations of these two ways of defining the position of the individual within the totality is to be found the external as well as the internal history of our time. It is the function of the metropolis to make a place for the conflict and for the attempts at unification of both of these in the sense that its own peculiar conditions have been revealed to us as the occasion and the stimulus for the development of both. Thereby they attain a quite unique place, fruitful with an inexhaustible richness of meaning in the development of the mental life. They reveal themselves as one of those great historical structures in which conflicting life-embracing currents find themselves with equal legitimacy. Because of this, however, regardless of whether we are sympathetic or antipathetic with their individual expressions, they transcend the sphere in which a judge-like attitude on our part is appropriate. To the extent that such forces have been integrated, with the fleeting existence of a single cell, into the root as well as the crown of the totality of historical life to which we belong – it is our task not to complain or to condone but only to understand.

PART II

PHENOMENOLOGY

PHENOMENOLOGY

Phenomenology may be defined as the study of how phenomena appear. However, this is not limited to the visual domain. Phenomenology demands a receptivity to the full ontological potential of human experience. It therefore calls for a heightened receptivity of all the senses. Nor should this be perceived as some shallow, superficial level of reception. Phenomenology, as it was developed by Heidegger and Gadamer, necessarily entails a deeper, interpretative dimension in the form of hermeneutics. To engage with architecture involves an openness not only to the realm of the sensory, but also to the potential revelation of some truth. Hermeneutics allows for the reception and understanding of that truth. The nature of this revelation varies from thinker to thinker. For Heidegger and Gadamer the work of art 'represents' some form of symbolic truth, while for Lefebvre the process takes on an overtly political twist. Within the lived experience Lefebvre claims that there are 'moments' which reveal the emancipatory capacity of potential situations.

The writers within this section have been concerned broadly with exploring the ontological significance of architecture. Space for them is to be perceived not as abstract, neutral space, but as the space of lived experience. Their project has been to reclaim an ontological dimension to the built environment, a dimension that has been eroded progressively, according to Lefebvre, since the invention of linear perspective. There has been a tendency to perceive space as increasingly abstract and remote from the body and its sensations. In privileging the visual, perspective has impoverished our understanding of space. The other senses need to be addressed, and space needs to be perceived with all its phenomenological associations. Space should be experienced as much through the echoes of singing in the cathedral evoked by Lefebvre or the odour of drying raisins in Bachelard's oneiric house, as it is through any visual means of representation.

Phenomenology offers a depth model for understanding human existence, no less than structuralism or psychoanalysis. Yet the difference with structuralism is revealed throughout the texts included here. Structuralism, in the form of semiology, operates merely at the level of signs. Phenomenology, meanwhile, claims to have recourse to a deeper symbolic level; it seeks to go beyond the codifying capacity of semiology to reveal a richer understanding of the world. Yet it is in its very 'claims' that the weakness of the project is revealed.

As Derrida has convincingly exposed, there is an appropriation at work in the very moment of hermeneutics. Phenomenology is, in effect, a self-referential system. There can be nothing to legitimize its 'claims'. Phenomenology lacks, as Habermas observed, any normative foundations. There is a constant tendency to seek authority by slipping into the realm of the ontological, and to resort to a discourse of self-referential authenticity. It was precisely this 'jargon of authenticity' that Adorno attacked. Nevertheless, despite the epistemological fragility of its project, phenomenology continues to prove popular within architectural circles. Furthermore, the recent work of Vattimo is evidence that the questions raised by Heidegger, Bachelard and others are – if anything – more relevant today. Not least they offer a timely reminder that in an age of virtual reality the very corporeality of the body cannot be ignored when addressing the experience of space.

GASTON BACHELARD

French philosopher of science and phenomenologist Gaston Bachelard (1884–1962) trained originally as a scientist and as a philosopher, before developing a strong interest in phenomenology and the theory of the imagination. The seeds of his subsequent theorization of the imagination can be found in his early work on the philosophy of science. Bachelard stressed the dialectical relationship between rationalism (the world of thinking) and realism (the empirical world). Critical of the Cartesian drive towards simplicity, he emphasized instead complexity. In this Bachelard was heavily influenced by psychoanalysis and surrealism. He developed the concept of 'surrationalism', by which he sought to reinvigorate our understanding of the rational, by emphasizing the complexity of its material situation, rather as surrealism sought to invigorate realism by playing upon the dream world. In his later work the influence of psychoanalysis and the role of the imagination became increasingly dominant.

Gaston Bachelard

The introduction to Bachelard's influential work, *The Poetics of Space*, begins on a seemingly autobiographical note:

> A philosopher who has evolved his entire thinking from the fundamental themes of the philosophy of science, and followed the main line of the active, growing rationalism of contemporary science as closely as he could, must forget his learning and break with all his habits of philosophical research, if he wants to study the problems posed by the poetic imagination.

In the extract included here Bachelard pursues this question in the context of the house. In order to understand the house we must go beyond mere description and beyond the limited constraints of a realist (Cartesian) conception. We need to resort to the world of the daydream where 'memory and imagination remain associated'. Here in the realm of personal memories, in the realm of 'the odour of raisins drying on a wicker basket', the 'oneiric house', the house of dream-memory, can be retrieved. For daydreaming is more powerful than thought, and through its poetic dimension can recover the essence of the house that has been lost 'in a shadow of the beyond of the real past'. In emphasizing the daydream rather than the dream it is clear that Bachelard owes his psychoanalytic insights to Jung rather than to Freud.

Clear parallels may be drawn between Bachelard's French suburban house and Martin Heidegger's German peasant hut. Likewise Bachelard's subsequent account of the cellar begins to evoke Freud's distinction between the '*heimlich*' (homely) and '*unheimlich*' (uncanny), and comparisons can be made with references to the cellar in Lyotard's essay, '*Domus* and the Megalopolis'.

Bachelard   *POETICS OF SPACE* (EXTRACT)

PART ONE

A la porte de la maison qui viendra frapper?
Une porte ouverte on entre
Une porte fermée un antre
Le monde bat de l'autre côté de ma porte.

At the door of the house who will come knocking?
An open door, we enter
A closed door, a den
The world pulse beats beyond my door.
                    Pierre Albert Birot, *Les Amusements Naturels,* p. 217

The house, quite obviously, is a privileged entity for a phenomenological study of the intimate values of inside space, provided, of course, that we take it in both its unity and its complexity, and endeavour to integrate all the special values in one fundamental value. For the house furnishes us with dispersed images and a body of images at the same time. In both cases, I shall prove that imagination augments the values of reality. A sort of attraction for images concentrates them about the house. Transcending our memories of all the houses in which we have found shelter, above and beyond all the houses we have dreamed we lived in, can we isolate an intimate, concrete essence that would be a justification of the uncommon value of all of our images of protected intimacy? This, then, is the main problem.

In order to solve it, it is not enough to consider the house as an 'object' on which we can make our judgments and daydreams react. For a phenomenologist, a psychoanalyst or a psychologist (these three points of view being named in the order of decreasing efficacy), it is not a question of describing houses, or enumerating their picturesque features and analysing for which reasons they are comfortable. On the contrary, we must go beyond the problems of description – whether this description be objective or subjective, that is, whether it give facts or impressions – in order to attain to the primary virtues, those that reveal an attachment that is native in some way to the primary function of inhabiting. A geographer or an ethnographer can give us descriptions of very varied types of dwellings. In each variety, the phenomenologist makes the effort needed to seize upon the germ of the essential, sure, immediate well-being it encloses. In every dwelling, even the richest, the first task of the phenomenologist is to find the original shell.

But the related problems are many if we want to determine the profound reality of all the subtle shadings of our attachment for a chosen spot. For a phenomenologist, these shadings must be taken as the first rough outlines of a psychological phenomenon. The shading is not an additional, superficial colouring. We should therefore have to say how we inhabit our vital space, in accord with all the dialectics of life, how we take root, day after day, in a 'corner of the world'.

For our house is our corner of the world. As has often been said, it is our first universe, a real cosmos in every sense of the word. If we look at it intimately, the humblest dwelling has beauty. Authors of books on 'the humble home' often mention this feature of the poetics of space. But this mention is much too succinct. Finding little to describe in the humble home, they spend little time there; so they describe it as it actually is, without really experiencing its primitiveness, a primitiveness which belongs to all, rich and poor alike, if they are willing to dream.

But our adult life is so dispossessed of the essential benefits, its anthropocosmic ties have become so slack, that we do not feel their first attachment in the universe of the house. There is no dearth of abstract, 'world-conscious' philosophers who discover a universe by means of the dialectical game of the I and the non-I. In fact, they know the universe before they know the house, the far horizon before the resting-place; whereas the real beginnings of images, if we study them phenomenologically, will give concrete evidence of the values of inhabited space, of the non-I that protects the I.

Indeed, here we touch upon a converse whose images we shall have to explore: all really inhabited space bears the essence of the notion of home. In the course of this work, we shall see that the imagination functions in this direction whenever the human being has found the slightest shelter: we shall see the imagination build 'walls' of impalpable shadows, comfort itself with the illusion of protection – or, just the contrary, tremble behind thick walls, mistrust the staunchest ramparts. In short, in the most interminable of dialectics, the sheltered being gives perceptible limits to his shelter. He experiences the house in its reality and in its virtuality, by means of thought and dreams. It is no longer in its positive aspects that the house is really 'lived', nor is it only in the passing hour that we recognize its benefits. An entire past comes to dwell in a new house. The old saying: 'We bring our *lares* with us' has many variations. And the daydream deepens to the point where an immemorial domain opens up for the dreamer of a home beyond man's earliest memory. The house, like fire and water, will permit me, later in this work, to recall flashes of daydreams that illuminate the synthesis of immemorial and recollected. In this remote region, memory and imagination remain associated, each one working for their mutual deepening. In the order of values, they both constitute a community of memory and image. Thus the house is not experienced from day to day only, on the thread of a narrative, or in the telling of our own story. Through dreams, the various dwelling-places in our lives co-penetrate and retain the treasures of former days. And after we are in the new house, when memories of other places we have lived in come back to us, we travel to the land of Motionless Childhood, motionless the way all immemorial things are. We live fixations, fixations of happiness.[1] We comfort ourselves by reliving memories of protection. Something closed must retain our memories, while leaving them their original value as images. Memories of the outside world will never have the same tonality as those of home and, by recalling these memories, we add to our store of dreams; we are never real historians, but always near poets, and our emotion is perhaps nothing but an expression of a poetry that was lost.

Thus, by approaching the house images with care not to break up the solidarity of memory and imagination, we may hope to make others feel all the psychological elasticity of an image that moves us at an unimaginable depth. Through poems, perhaps more than through recollections, we touch the ultimate poetic depth of the space of the house.

Bachelard   This being the case, if I were asked to name the chief benefit of the house, I should say: the house shelters daydreaming, the house protects the dreamer, the house allows one to dream in peace. Thought and experience are not the only things that sanction human values. The values that belong to daydreaming mark humanity in its depths. Daydreaming even has a privilege of auto-valorization. It derives direct pleasure from its own being. Therefore, the places in which we have *experienced daydreaming* reconstitute themselves in a new daydream, and it is because our memories of former dwelling-places are relived as daydreams that these dwelling-places of the past remain in us for all time.

Now my aim is clear: I must show that the house is one of the greatest powers of integration for the thoughts, memories and dreams of mankind. The binding principle in this integration is the daydream. Past, present and future give the house different dynamisms, which often interfere, at times opposing, at others, stimulating one another. In the life of a man, the house thrusts aside contingencies, its councils of continuity are unceasing. Without it, man would be a dispersed being. It maintains him through the storms of the heavens and through those of life. It is body and soul. It is the human being's first world. Before he is 'cast into the world', as claimed by certain hasty metaphysics, man is laid in the cradle of the house. And always, in our daydreams, the house is a large cradle. A concrete metaphysics cannot neglect this fact, this simple fact, all the more, since this fact is a value, an important value, to which we return in our daydreaming. Being is already a value. Life begins well, it begins enclosed, protected, all warm in the bosom of the house.

From my viewpoint, from the phenomenologist's viewpoint, the conscious metaphysics that starts from the moment when the being is 'cast into the world' is a secondary metaphysics. It passes over the preliminaries, when being is being-well, when the human being is deposited in a being-well, in the well-being originally associated with being. To illustrate the metaphysics of consciousness we should have to wait for the experiences during which being is cast out, that is to say, thrown out, outside the being of the house, a circumstance in which the hostility of men and of the universe accumulates. But a complete metaphysics, englobing both the conscious and the unconscious, would leave the privilege of its values within. Within the being, in the being of within, an enveloping warmth welcomes being. Being reigns in a sort of earthly paradise of matter, dissolved in the comforts of an adequate matter. It is as though in this material paradise, the human being were bathed in nourishment, as though he were gratified with all the essential benefits.

When we dream of the house we were born in, in the utmost depths of revery, we participate in this original warmth, in this well-tempered matter of the material paradise. This is the environment in which the protective beings live. We shall come back to the maternal features of the house. For the moment, I should like to point out the original fullness of the house's being. Our daydreams carry us back to it. And the poet well knows that the house holds childhood motionless 'in its arms':[2]

> *Maison, pan de prairie, ô lumière du soir*
> *Soudain vous acquérez presque une face humaine*
> *Vous êtes près de nous, embrassants, embrassés.*

House, patch of meadow, oh evening light

Suddenly you acquire an almost human face   *Bachelard*
You are very near us, embracing and embraced.

PART TWO

Of course, thanks to the house, a great many of our memories are housed, and
if the house is a bit elaborate, if it has a cellar and a garret, nooks and corridors,
our memories have refuges that are all the more clearly delineated. All our lives
we come back to them in our daydreams. A psychoanalyst should, therefore,
turn his attention to this simple localization of our memories. I should like to
give the name of topoanalysis to this auxiliary of psychoanalysis. Topoanalysis,
then, would be the systematic psychological study of the sites of our intimate
lives. In the theatre of the past that is constituted by memory, the stage setting
maintains the characters in their dominant roles. At times we think we know
ourselves in time, when all we know is a sequence of fixations in the spaces of
the being's stability – a being who does not want to melt away, and who, even in
the past, when he sets out in search of things past, wants time to 'suspend' its
flight. In its countless alveoli, space contains compressed time. That is what
space is for.

And if we want to go beyond history, or even, while remaining in history,
detach from our own history the always too contingent history of the persons
who have encumbered it, we realize that the calendars of our lives can only be
established in its imagery. In order to analyse our being in the hierarchy of an
ontology, or to psychoanalyse our unconscious entrenched in primitive abodes,
it would be necessary, on the margin of normal psychoanalysis, to *desocialize*
our important memories, and attain to the plane of the daydreams that we used
to have in the places identified with our solitude. For investigations of this kind,
daydreams are more useful than dreams. They show moreover that daydreams
can be very different from dreams.[3]

And so, faced with these periods of solitude, the topoanalyst starts to ask
questions: Was the room a large one? Was the garret cluttered up? Was the
nook warm? How was it lighted? How, too, in these fragments of space, did the
human being achieve silence? How did he relish the very special silence of the
various retreats of solitary daydreaming?

Here space is everything, for time ceases to quicken memory. Memory –
what a strange thing it is! – does not record concrete duration, in the
Bergsonian sense of the word. We are unable to relive duration that has been
destroyed. We can only think of it, in the line of an abstract time that is
deprived of all thickness. The finest specimens of fossilized duration con-
cretized as a result of long sojourn, are to be found in and through space. The
unconscious abides. Memories are motionless, and the more securely they are
fixed in space, the sounder they are. To localize a memory in time is merely a
matter for the biographer and only corresponds to a sort of external history, for
external use, to be communicated to others. But hermeneutics, which is more
profound than biography, must determine the centres of fate by ridding history
of its conjunctive temporal tissue, which has no action on our fates. For a
knowledge of intimacy, localization in the spaces of our intimacy is more urgent
than determination of dates.

Psychoanalysis too often situates the passions 'in the century'. In reality,

Bachelard   however, the passions simmer and resimmer in solitude: the passionate being prepares his explosions and his exploits in this solitude.

And all the spaces of our past moments of solitude, the spaces in which we have suffered from solitude, enjoyed, desired and compromised solitude, remain indelible within us, and precisely because the human being wants them to remain so. He knows instinctively that this space identified with his solitude is creative; that even when it is forever expunged from the present, when, henceforth, it is alien to all the promises of the future, even when we no longer have a garret, when the attic room is lost and gone, there remains the fact that we once loved a garret, once lived in an attic. We return to them in our night dreams. These retreats have the value of a shell. And when we reach the very end of the labyrinths of sleep, when we attain to the regions of deep slumber, we may perhaps experience a type of repose that is pre-human; pre-human, in this case, approaching the immemorial. But in the daydream itself, the recollection of moments of confined, simple, shut-in space are experiences of heartwarming space, of a space that does not seek to become extended, but would like above all still to be possessed. In the past, the attic may have seemed too small, it may have seemed cold in winter and hot in summer. Now, however, in memory recaptured through daydreams, it is hard to say through what syncretism the attic is at once small and large, warm and cool, always comforting.

PART THREE

This being the case, we shall have to introduce a slight nuance at the very base of topoanalysis. I pointed out earlier that the unconscious is housed. It should be added that it is well and happily housed, in the space of its happiness. The normal unconscious knows how to make itself at home everywhere, and psychoanalysis comes to the assistance of the ousted unconscious, of the unconscious that has been roughly or insidiously dislodged. But psychoanalysis sets the human being in motion, rather than at rest. It calls on him to live outside the abodes of his unconscious, to enter into life's adventures, to come out of himself. And naturally, its action is a salutary one. Because we must also give an exterior destiny to the interior being. To accompany psychoanalysis in this salutary action, we should have to undertake a topoanalysis of all the space that has invited us to come out of ourselves.

> *Emmenez-moi, chemins! . . .*
> Carry me along, oh roads . . .

wrote Marceline Desbordes-Valmore, recalling her native Flanders (*Un Ruisseau de la Scarpe*).

And what a dynamic, handsome object is a path! How precise the familiar hill paths remain for our muscular consciousness! A poet has expressed all this dynamism in one single line:

> *O, mes chemins et leur cadence*
> Oh, my roads and their cadence.

>   Jean Caubère, *Déserts*

When I relive dynamically the road that 'climbed' the hill, I am quite sure that the road itself had muscles, or rather, counter-muscles. In my room in

Paris, it is a good exercise for me to think of the road in this way. As I write this   *Bachelard*
page, I feel freed of my duty to take a walk: I am sure of having gone out of my
house.

And indeed we should find countless intermediaries between reality and
symbols if we gave things all the movements they suggest. George Sand,
dreaming beside a path of yellow sand, saw life flowing by. 'What is more
beautiful than a road?' she wrote. 'It is the symbol and the image of an active,
varied life' (*Consuelo*, vol. II, p. 116).

Each one of us, then, should speak of his roads, his crossroads, his roadside
benches; each one of us should make a surveyor's map of his lost fields and
meadows. Thoreau said that he had the map of his fields engraved in his soul.
And Jean Wahl once wrote:

Le moutonnement des haies
C'est en moi que je l'ai.

The frothing of the hedges
I keep deep inside me.

Poème, p. 46

Thus we cover the universe with drawings we have lived. These drawings
need not be exact. They need only to be tonalized on the mode of our inner
space. But what a book would have to be written to decide all these problems!
Space calls for action, and before action, the imagination is at work. It mows
and ploughs. We should have to speak of the benefits of all these imaginary
actions. Psychoanalysis has made numerous observations on the subject of
projective behaviour, on the willingness of extroverted persons to exteriorize
their intimate impressions. An exteriorist topoanalysis would perhaps give
added precision to this projective behaviour by defining our daydreams of
objects. However, in this present work, I shall not be able to undertake, as
should be done, the two-fold imaginary geometrical and physical problem of
extroversion and introversion. Moreover, I do not believe that these two
branches of physics have the same psychic weight. My research is devoted to
the domain of intimacy, to the domain in which psychic weight is dominant.

I shall therefore put my trust in the power of attraction of all the domains of
intimacy. There does not exist a real intimacy that is repellent. All the spaces of
intimacy are designated by an attraction. Their being is well-being. In these
conditions, topoanalysis bears the stamp of a topophilia, and shelters and
rooms will be studied in the sense of this valorization.

PART FOUR

These virtues of shelter are so simple, so deeply rooted in our unconscious that
they may be recaptured through mere mention, rather than through minute
description. Here the nuance bespeaks the colour. A poet's word, because it
strikes true, moves the very depths of our being.

Over-picturesqueness in a house can conceal its intimacy. This is also true in
life. But it is truer still in daydreams. For the real houses of memory, the houses
to which we return in dreams, the houses that are rich in unalterable oneirism,
do not readily lend themselves to description. To describe them would be like

Bachelard showing them to visitors. We can perhaps tell everything about the present, but about the past! The first, the oneirically definitive house, must retain its shadows. For it belongs to the literature of depth, that is, to poetry, and not to the fluent type of literature that, in order to analyse intimacy, needs other people's stories. All I ought to say about my childhood home is just barely enough to place me, myself, in an oneiric situation, to set me on the threshold of a daydream in which I shall *find* repose in the past. Then I may hope that my page will possess a sonority that will ring true – a voice so remote within me, that it will be the voice we all hear when we listen as far back as memory reaches, on the very limits of memory, beyond memory perhaps, in the field of the immemorial. All we communicate to others is an *orientation* towards what is secret without ever being able to tell the secret objectively. What is secret never has total objectivity. In this respect, we orient oneirism but we do not accomplish it.[4]

What would be the use, for instance, in giving the plan of the room that was really *my* room, in describing the little room at the *end* of the garret, in saying that from the window, across the indentations of the roofs, one could see the hill. I alone, in my memories of another century, can open the deep cupboard that still retains for me alone that unique odour, the odour of raisins drying on a wicker tray. The odour of raisins! It is an odour that is beyond description, one that it takes a lot of imagination to smell. But I've already said too much. If I said more, the reader, back in his own room, would not open that unique wardrobe, with its unique smell, which is the signature of intimacy. Paradoxically, in order to suggest the values of intimacy, we have to induce in the reader a state of suspended reading. For it is not until his eyes have left the page that recollections of my room can become a threshold of oneirism for him. And when it is a poet speaking, the reader's soul reverberates; it experiences the kind of reverberation that, as Minkowski has shown, gives the energy of all origin to being.

It therefore makes sense from our standpoint of a philosophy of literature and poetry to say that we 'write a room', 'read a room' or 'read a house'. Thus, very quickly, at the very first word, at the first poetic overture, the reader who is 'reading a room' leaves off reading and starts to think of some place in his own past. You would like to tell everything about your room. You would like to interest the reader in yourself, whereas you have unlocked a door to daydreaming. The values of intimacy are so absorbing that the reader has ceased to read your room: he sees his own again. He is already far off, listening to the recollections of a father or a grandmother, of a mother or a servant, of 'the old faithful servant', in short, of the human being who dominates the corner of his most cherished memories.

And the house of memories becomes psychologically complex. Associated with the nooks and corners of solitude are the bedroom and the living room in which the leading characters held sway. The house we were born in is an inhabited house. In it the values of intimacy are scattered, they are not easily stabilized, they are subjected to dialectics. In how many tales of childhood – if tales of childhood were sincere – we should be told of a child that, lacking a room, went and sulked in his corner!

But over and beyond our memories, the house we were born in is physically inscribed in us. It is a group of organic habits. After twenty years, in spite of all

the other anonymous stairways; we would recapture the reflexes of the 'first   *Bachelard*
stairway', we would not stumble on that rather high step. The house's entire
being would open up, faithful to our own being. We would push the door that
creaks with the same gesture, we would find our way in the dark to the distant
attic. The feel of the tiniest latch has remained in our hands.

The successive houses in which we have lived have no doubt made our
gestures commonplace. But we are very surprised, when we return to the old
house, after an odyssey of many years, to find that the most delicate gestures,
the earliest gestures suddenly come alive, are still faultless. In short, the house
we were born in has engraved within us the hierarchy of the various functions
of inhabiting. We are the diagram of the functions of inhabiting that particular
house, and all the other houses are but variations on a fundamental theme. The
word habit is too worn a word to express this passionate liaison of our bodies,
which do not forget, with an unforgettable house.

But this area of detailed recollections that are easily retained because of the
names of things and people we knew in the first house, can be studied by means
of general psychology. Memories of dreams, however, which only poetic meditation can help us to recapture, are more confused, less clearly drawn. The
great function of poetry is to give us back the situations of our dreams. The
house we were born in is more than an embodiment of home, it is also an
embodiment of dreams. Each one of its nooks and corners was a resting-place
for daydreaming. And often the resting place particularized the daydream. Our
habits of a particular daydream were acquired there. The house, the bedroom,
the garret in which we were alone, furnished the framework for an interminable dream, one that poetry alone, through the creation of a poetic work, could
succeed in achieving completely. If we give their function of shelter for dreams
to all of these places of retreat, we may say, as I pointed out in an earlier work,[5]
that there exists for each one of us an oneiric house, a house of dream-memory,
that is lost in the shadow of a beyond of the real past. I called this oneiric house
the crypt of the house that we were born in. Here we find ourselves at a pivotal
point around which reciprocal interpretations of dreams through thought and
thought through dreams, keep turning. But the word *interpretation* hardens
this about-face unduly. In point of fact, we are in the unity of image and
memory, in the functional composite of imagination and memory. The
positivity of psychological history and geography cannot serve as a touchstone
for determining *the real being* of our childhood, for childhood is certainly
greater than reality. In order to sense, across the years, our attachment for the
house we were born in, dream is more powerful than thought. It is our
unconscious force that crystallizes our remotest memories. If a compact centre
of daydreams of repose had not existed in this first house, the very different
circumstances that surround actual life would have clouded our memories.
Except for a few medallions stamped with the likeness of our ancestors, our
child-memory contains only worn coins. It is on the plane of the daydream and
not on that of facts that childhood remains alive and poetically useful within
us. Through this permanent childhood, we maintain the poetry of the past. To
inhabit oneirically the house we were born in means more than to inhabit it in
memory; it means living in this house that is gone, the way we used to dream in
it.

What special depth there is in a child's daydream! And how happy the child

Bachelard who really possesses his moments of solitude! It is a good thing, it is even salutary, for a child to have periods of boredom, for him to learn to know the dialectics of exaggerated play and causeless, pure boredom. Alexander Dumas tells in his *Mémoires* that, as a child, he was bored, bored to tears. When his mother found him like that, weeping from sheer boredom, she said: 'And what is Dumas crying about?' 'Dumas is crying because Dumas has tears,' replied the six-year-old child. This is the kind of anecdote people tell in their memoirs. But how well it exemplifies absolute boredom, the boredom that is not the equivalent of the absence of playmates. There are children who will leave a game to go and be bored in a corner of the garret. How often have I wished for the attic of my boredom when the complications of life made me lose the very germ of all freedom!

And so, beyond all the positive values of protection, the house we were born in becomes imbued with dream values which remain after the house is gone. Centres of boredom, centres of solitude, centres of daydream group together to constitute the oneiric house which is more lasting than the scattered memories of our birthplace. Long phenomenological research would be needed to determine all these dream values, to plumb the depth of this dream ground in which our memories are rooted.

And we should not forget that these dream values communicate poetically from soul to soul. To read poetry is essentially to daydream.

PART FIVE

A house constitutes a body of images that give mankind proofs or illusions of stability. We are constantly re-imagining its reality: to distinguish all these images would be to describe the soul of the house; it would mean developing a veritable psychology of the house.

To bring order into these images, I believe that we should consider two principal connecting themes:

1   A house is imagined as a vertical being. It rises upward. It differentiates itself in terms of its verticality. It is one of the appeals to our consciousness of verticality.
2   A house is imagined as a concentrated being. It appeals to our consciousness of centrality.[6]

These themes are no doubt very abstractly stated. But with examples, it is not hard to recognize their psychologically concrete nature.

Verticality is ensured by the polarity of cellar and attic, the marks of which are so deep that, in a way, they open up two very different perspectives for a phenomenology of the imagination. Indeed, it is possible, almost without commentary, to oppose the rationality of the roof to the irrationality of the cellar. A roof tells its *raison d'être* right away: it gives mankind shelter from the rain and sun he fears. Geographers are constantly reminding us that, in every country, the slope of the roofs is one of the surest indications of the climate. We 'understand' the slant of a roof. Even a dreamer dreams rationally; for him, a pointed roof averts rain clouds. Up near the roof all our thoughts are clear. In the attic it is a pleasure to see the bare rafters of the strong framework. Here we participate in the carpenter's solid geometry.

As for the cellar, we shall no doubt find uses for it. It will be rationalized and   *Bachelard*
its conveniences enumerated. But it is first and foremost the *dark entity* of the
house, the one that partakes of subterranean forces. When we dream there, we
are in harmony with the irrationality of the depths.

We become aware of this dual vertical polarity of a house if we are
sufficiently aware of the function of inhabiting to consider it as an imaginary
response to the function of constructing. The dreamer constructs and recon-
structs the upper stories and the attic until they are well constructed. And, as I
said before, when we dream of the heights we are in the rational zone of
intellectualized projects. But for the cellar, the impassioned inhabitant digs and
redigs, making its very depth active. The fact is not enough, the dream is at
work. When it comes to excavated ground, dreams have no limit. I shall give
later some deep cellar reveries. But first let us remain in the space that is
polarized by the cellar and the attic, to see how this polarized space can serve to
illustrate very fine psychological nuances.

Here is how the psychoanalyst C. G. Jung has used the dual image of cellar
and attic to analyse the fears that inhabit a house. In Jung's *Modern Man in
Search of a Soul*[7] we find a comparison which is used to make us understand
the conscious being's hope of 'destroying the autonomy of complexes by debap-
tising them'. The image is the following:

> Here the conscious acts like a man who, hearing a suspicious noise in
> the cellar, hurries to the attic and, finding no burglars there decides,
> consequently, that the noise was pure imagination. In reality, this
> prudent man did not dare venture into the cellar.

To the extent that the explanatory image used by Jung convinces us, we
readers relive phenomenologically both fears: fear in the attic and fear in the
cellar. Instead of facing the cellar (the unconscious), Jung's 'prudent man' seeks
alibis for his courage in the attic. In the attic rats and mice can make considerable noise. But let the master of the house arrive unexpectedly and they return
to the silence of their holes. The creatures moving about in the cellar are slower,
less scampering, more mysterious.

In the attic, fears are easily 'rationalized'. Whereas in the cellar, even for a
more courageous man than the one Jung mentions, 'rationalization' is less
rapid and less clear; also it is never *definitive*. In the attic, the day's experiences
can always efface the fears of night. In the cellar, darkness prevails both day
and night, and even when we are carrying a lighted candle, we see shadows
dancing on the dark walls.

If we follow the inspiration of Jung's *explanatory* example to a complete
grasp of psychological reality, we encounter a cooperation between psychoanalysis and phenomenology which must be stressed if we are to dominate the
human phenomenon. As a matter of fact, the image has to be understood
phenomenologically in order to give it psychoanalytical efficacy. The phenomenologist, in this case, will accept the psychoanalyst's image in a spirit of shared
trepidation. He will revive the primitivity and the specificity of the fears. In our
civilization, which has the same light everywhere, and puts electricity in its
cellars, we no longer go to the cellar carrying a candle. But the unconscious
cannot be civilized. It takes a candle when it goes to the cellar. The psychoanalyst cannot cling to the superficiality of metaphors or comparisons, and the

Bachelard phenomenologist has to pursue every image to the very end. Here, so far from reducing and explaining, so far from comparing, the phenomenologist will exaggerate his exaggeration. Then, when they read Poe's *Tales* together, both the phenomenologist and the psychoanalyst will understand the value of this achievement. For these tales are the realization of childhood fears. The reader who is a 'devotee' of reading will hear the accursed cat, which is a symbol of unredeemed guilt, mewing behind the wall.[8] The cellar dreamer knows that the walls of the cellar are buried walls, that they are walls with a single casing, walls that have the entire earth behind them. And so the situation grows more dramatic, and fear becomes exaggerated. But where is the fear that does not become exaggerated? In this spirit of shared trepidation, the phenomenologist listens intently, as the poet Thoby Marcelin puts it, 'flush with madness'. The cellar then becomes buried madness, walled-in tragedy.

Stories of criminal cellars leave indelible marks on our memory, marks that we prefer not to deepen; who would like to re-read Poe's 'The Cask of Amontillado'? In this instance, the dramatic element is too facile, but it exploits natural fears, which are inherent to the dual nature of both man and house.

Although I have no intention of starting a file on the subject of human drama, I shall study a few ultra-cellars which prove that the cellar dream irrefutably increases reality.

If the dreamer's house is in a city it is not unusual that the dream is one of dominating in depth the surrounding cellars. His abode wants the undergrounds of legendary fortified castles, where mysterious passages that run under the enclosing walls, the ramparts and the moat put the heart of the castle into communication with the distant forest. The château planted on the hilltop had a cluster of cellars for roots. And what power it gave a simple house to be built on this underground clump!

In the novels of Henri Bosco, who is a great dreamer of houses, we come across ultra-cellars of this kind. Under the house in *L'Antiquaire* (*The Antique Dealer*, p. 60), there is a 'vaulted rotunda into which open four doors'. Four corridors lead from the four doors, dominating, as it were, the four cardinal points of an underground horizon. The door to the East opens and 'we advance subterraneously far under the houses in this neighbourhood ...'. There are traces of labyrinthine dreams in these pages. But associated with the labyrinths of the corridor, in which the air is 'heavy', are rotundas and chapels that are the sanctuaries of the secret. Thus, the cellar in *L'Antiquaire* is oneirically complex. The reader must explore it through dreams, certain of which refer to the suffering in the corridors, and others to the marvellous nature of underground palaces. He may become quite lost (actually as well as figuratively). At first he does not see very clearly the necessity for such a complicated geometry. Just here, a phenomenological analysis will prove to be effective. But what does the phenomenological attitude advise? It asks us to produce within ourselves a reading pride that will give us the illusion of participating in the work of the author of the book. Such an attitude could hardly be achieved on first reading, which remains too passive. For here the reader is still something of a child, a child who is entertained by reading. But every good book should be re-read as soon as it is finished. After the sketchiness of the first reading comes the creative work of reading. We must then know *the problem* that confronted the author. The second, then the third reading ... give us, little by little, the solution of this problem. Imperceptibly, we give ourselves the illusion that both *Bachelard* the problem and the solution are ours. The psychological nuance: 'I should have written that', establishes us as phenomenologists of reading. But so long as we have not acknowledged this nuance, we remain psychologists, or psychoanalysts.

NOTES

All footnotes for this article have been reproduced verbatim.

1   We should grant 'fixation' its virtues, independently of psychoanalytical literature which, because of its therapeutic function, is obliged to record, principally, processes of defixation.

2   Rainer Maria Rilke, translated into French by Claude Vigée, in *Les Lettres*, 4th year, Nos. 14–15–16, p. 11. *Editor's note:* In this work, all of the Rilke references will be to the French translations that inspired Bachelard's comments.

3   I plan to study these differences in a future work.

4   After giving a description of the Canaen estate (*Volupté*, p. 30), Sainte-Beuve adds:

> it is not so much for you, my friend, who never saw this place, and had you visited it, could not now feel the impressions and colours I feel, that I have gone over it in such detail, for which I must excuse myself. Nor should you try to see it as a result of what I have said; let the image float inside you; pass lightly; the slightest idea of it will suffice for you.

5   *La terre et les rêveries du repos*, Paris: Corti, p. 98.

6   For this second part, see Bachelard, *Poetics of Space*, Maria Jolas (trans.), Boston: Beacon Press, 1969, p. 29.

7   C.G. Jung, *Modern Man in Search of a Soul*, Harcourt, Brace & World, New York.

8   Edgar Allan Poe: 'The Black Cat'.

MARTIN HEIDEGGER

Martin
Heidegger

German philosopher Martin Heidegger (1889–1976) was educated in the phenomenological tradition under Edmund Husserl. While Heidegger has remained a controversial figure, largely because of his political affiliations with the National Socialists, he has proved to be a key figure within twentieth-century European thought and a significant influence on other thinkers such as Hans-Georg Gadamer and Jacques Derrida. Following the publication in 1927 of his seminal work, *Being and Time*, Heidegger pursued the whole problem of humankind's situatedness in the world, in a project centred on the key concepts of *dasein* and the question of 'Being'. Heidegger argued that the alienation of contemporary existence was based on the separation of thought from 'Being', a condition epitomized by the privileging of technology and calculative thinking in the modern world. His project was therefore an attempt to return humankind to some form of authentic existence.

A concern for the architectural underpins Heidegger's philosophy. For Heidegger the problem of man's situatedness in the world is inextricably bound up with the question of dwelling. Thus Heidegger stresses the link between dwelling and thinking, which he traces back etymologically to links between antique words. Not only does architecture allow for the possibility of dwelling, but it is also precisely part of that dwelling. To dwell authentically, for Heidegger, is to dwell *poetically*, since poetry is a manifestation of truth restored to its artistic dimension. Architecture becomes a setting into work of 'truth', and a means of making the 'world' visible. Fundamental to this process is the ancient Greek term *techne*, linked in Heidegger's mind to the term *tikto* – 'to bring forth or to produce' – a concept to be distinguished from the modern term 'technology' in which *techne* remains 'resolutely concealed'.

The extracts bring out the importance of context for Heidegger. The world is not 'in space', but 'space' is in the world. 'Space', for Heidegger, contains a sense of 'clearing-away', of releasing places from wilderness, and allowing the possibility of 'dwelling'. 'Space' is therefore linked to 'Being'. In his famous example of the Greek temple, Heidegger illustrates how the temple discloses the spatiality of Being through its 'standing there'. Fundamental to Heidegger's treatment of architecture is the situatedness of buildings – their *dasein*. Thus the temple grows out of the cleft rock, no less than the bridge 'gathers together' the banks of the river. Similarly the farmhouse in the Black Forest is born on and of the mountain slope where it sits, built by the 'dwelling' on peasants.

The centrality of Heidegger's thought to twentieth-century thinking is evident in the context of other essays in this volume. In particular, parallels may be drawn with the work of Gadamer, Vattimo and Bachelard, while contrasts may be made

with the work of Adorno, Benjamin, Derrida, Lefebvre and Lyotard. Heidegger's   *Heidegger*
discussion of the bridge in 'Building, Dwelling, Thinking' can be compared to that
of Simmel in 'Bridge and Door', while his treatment of *techne* can be compared to
that of Foucault in 'Space, Knowledge, Power'. Lyotard's article '*Domus* and the
Megalopolis' can be read as a riposte to Heidegger's celebration of dwelling.

———————

Heidegger   # BUILDING, DWELLING, THINKING

In what follows we shall try to think about dwelling and building. This thinking about building does not presume to discover architectural ideas, let alone to give rules for building. This venture in thought does not view building as an art or as a technique of construction; rather it traces building back into that domain to which everything that *is* belongs. We ask:

1   What is it to dwell?
2   How does building belong to dwelling?

PART ONE

We attain to dwelling, so it seems, only by means of building. The latter, building, has the former, dwelling, as its goal. Still, not every building is a dwelling. Bridges and hangars, stadiums and power stations are buildings but not dwellings; railway stations and highways, dams and market halls are built, but they are not dwelling places. Even so, these buildings are in the domain of our dwelling. That domain extends over these buildings and yet is not limited to the dwelling place. The truck driver is at home on the highway, but he does not have his shelter there; the working woman is at home in the spinning mill, but does not have her dwelling place there; the chief engineer is at home in the power station, but he does not dwell there. These buildings house man. He inhabits them and yet does not dwell in them, when to dwell means merely that we take shelter in them. In today's housing shortage even this much is reassuring and to the good; residential buildings do indeed provide shelter; today's houses may even be well planned, easy to keep, attractively cheap, open to air, light and sun, but – do the houses in themselves hold any guarantee that *dwelling* occurs in them? Yet those buildings that are not dwelling places remain in turn determined by dwelling insofar as they serve man's dwelling. Thus dwelling would in any case be the end that presides over all building. Dwelling and building are related as end and means. However, as long as this is all we have in mind, we take dwelling and building as two separate activities, an idea that has something correct in it. Yet at the same time by the means-end schema we block our view of the essential relations. For building is not merely a means and a way toward dwelling – to build is in itself already to dwell. Who tells us this? Who gives us a standard at all by which we can take the measure of the nature of dwelling and building?

It is language that tells us about the nature of a thing, provided that we respect language's own nature. In the meantime, to be sure, there rages round the earth an unbridled yet clever talking, writing and broadcasting of spoken words. Man acts as though *he* were the shaper and master of language, while in fact *language* remains the master of man. Perhaps it is before all else man's subversion of *this* relation of dominance that drives his nature into alienation. That we retain a concern for care in speaking is all to the good, but it is of no help to us as long as language still serves us even then only as a means of expression. Among all the appeals that we human beings, on our part, can help to be voiced, language is the highest and everywhere the first.

Heidegger

What, then, does *Bauen,* building, *mean?* The Old English and High German word for building, *buan,* means to dwell. This signifies: to remain, to stay in a place. The real meaning of the verb *bauen,* namely, to dwell, has been lost to us. But a covert trace of it has been preserved in the German word *Nachbar,* neighbour. The neighbour is in Old English the *neahgebur; neah,* near, and *gebur,* dweller. The Nachbar is the *Nachgebur,* the *Nachgebauer,* the near-dweller, he who dwells nearby. The verbs *buri, büren, beuren, beuron,* all signify dwelling, the abode, the place of dwelling. Now to be sure the old word *buan* not only tells us that *bauen,* to build, is really to dwell; it also gives us a clue as to how we have to think about the dwelling it signifies. When we speak of dwelling we usually think of an activity that man performs alongside many other activities. We work here and dwell there. We do not merely dwell – that would be virtual inactivity – we practise a profession, we do business, we travel and lodge on the way, now here, now there. *Bauen* originally means to dwell. Where the word *bauen* still speaks in its original sense it also says *how far* the nature of dwelling reaches. That is, *bauen, buan, bhu, beo* are our word *bin* in the versions: *ich bin,* I am, *du bist,* you are, the imperative form *bis,* be. What then does *ich bin* mean? The old word *bauen,* to which the *bin* belongs, answers: *ich bin, du bist* mean: I dwell, you dwell. The way in which you are and I am, the manner in which we humans *are* on the earth, is *Buan,* dwelling. To be a human being means to be on the earth as a mortal. It means to dwell. The old word *bauen* says that man *is* insofar as he *dwells,* this word *bauen* however *also* means at the same time to cherish and protect, to preserve and care for, specifically to till the soil, to cultivate the vine. Such building only takes care – it tends the growth that ripens into its fruit of its own accord. Building in the sense of preserving and nurturing is not making anything. Ship building and temple building, on the other hand, do in a certain way make their own works. Here building, in contrast with cultivating, is a constructing. Both modes of building – building as cultivating, Latin *colere, cultura,* and building as the raising up of edifices, *aedificare* – are comprised within genuine building, that is, dwelling. Building as dwelling, that is, as being on the earth, however, remains for man's everyday experience that which is from the outset 'habitual' – we inhabit it, as our language says so beautifully: it is the *Gewohnte.* For this reason it recedes behind the manifold ways in which dwelling is accomplished, the activities of cultivation and construction. These activities later claim the name of *bauen,* building, and with it the fact of building, exclusively for themselves. The real sense of *bauen,* namely dwelling, falls into oblivion.

At first sight this event looks as though it were no more than a change of meaning of mere terms. In truth, however, something decisive is concealed in it, namely, dwelling is not experienced as man's being; dwelling is never thought of as the basic character of human being.

That language in a way retracts the real meaning of the word *bauen,* which is dwelling, is evidence of the primal nature of these meanings; for with the essential words of language, their true meaning easily falls into oblivion in favour of foreground meanings. Man has hardly yet pondered the mystery of this process. Language withdraws from man its simple and high speech. But its primal call does not thereby become incapable of speech; it merely falls silent. Man, though, fails to heed this silence.

Heidegger   But if we listen to what language says in the word *bauen* we hear three things:

1   Building is really dwelling.
2   Dwelling is the manner in which mortals are on the earth.
3   Building as dwelling unfolds into the building that cultivates growing things and the building that erects buildings.

If we give thought to this threefold fact, we obtain a clue and note the following: as long as we do not bear in mind that all building is in itself a dwelling, we cannot even adequately *ask*, let alone properly decide, what the building of buildings might be in its nature. We do not dwell because we have built, but we build and have built because we dwell, that is, because we are *dwellers*. But in what does the nature of dwelling consist? Let us listen once more to what language says to us. The Old Saxon *wuon*, the Gothic *wunian*, like the old word *bauen*, mean to remain, to stay in a place. But the Gothic *wunian* says more distinctly how this remaining is experienced. *Wunian* means to be at peace, to be brought to peace, to remain in peace. The word for peace, *Friede*, means the free, *das Frye*, and *fry* means preserved from harm and danger, preserved from something, safeguarded. To free really means to spare. The sparing itself consists not only in the fact that we do not harm the one whom we spare. Real sparing is something *positive* and takes place when we leave something beforehand in its own nature, when we return it specifically to its being, when we 'free' it in the real sense of the word into a preserve of peace. To dwell, to be set at peace, means to remain at peace within the free, the preserve, the free sphere that safeguards each thing in its nature. *The fundamental character of dwelling is this sparing and preserving.* It pervades dwelling in its whole range. That range reveals itself to us as soon as we reflect that human being consists in dwelling and, indeed, dwelling in the sense of the stay of mortals on the earth.

But 'on the earth' already means 'under the sky'. Both of these *also* mean 'remaining before the divinities' and include a 'belonging to men's being with one another'. By *a primal* oneness the four – earth and sky, divinities and mortals – belong together in one.

Earth is the serving bearer, blossoming and fruiting, spreading out in rock and water, rising up into plant and animal. When we say earth, we are already thinking of the other three along with it, but we give no thought to the simple oneness of the four.

The sky is the vaulting path of the sun, the course of the changing moon, the wandering glitter of the stars, the year's seasons and their changes, the light and dusk of day, the gloom and glow of night, the clemency and inclemency of the weather, the drifting clouds and blue depth of the ether. When we say sky, we are already thinking of the other three along with it, but we give no thought to the simple oneness of the four.

The divinities are the beckoning messengers of the godhead. Out of the holy sway of the godhead, the god appears in his presence or withdraws into his concealment. When we speak of the divinities, we are already thinking of the other three along with them, but we give no thought to the simple oneness of the four.

The mortals are the human beings. They are called mortals because they can

die. To die means to be capable of death *as* death. Only man dies, and indeed   *Heidegger*
continually, as long as he remains on earth, under the sky, before the divinities.
When we speak of mortals, we are already thinking of the other three along
with them, but we give no thought to the simple oneness of the four.

This simple oneness of the four we call *the fourfold*. Mortals *are* in the fourfold by *dwelling*. But the basic character of dwelling is to spare, to preserve.
Mortals dwell in the way they preserve the fourfold in its essential being, its
presencing. Accordingly, the preserving that dwells is fourfold.

Mortals dwell in that they save the earth – taking the word in the old sense
still known to Lessing. Saving does not only snatch something from a danger.
To save really means to set something free into its own presencing. To save the
earth is more than to exploit it or even wear it out. Saving the earth does
not master the earth and does not subjugate it, which is merely one step from
spoliation.

Mortals dwell in that they receive the sky as sky. They leave to the sun and
the moon their journey, to the stars their courses, to the seasons their blessing
and their inclemency; they do not turn night into day nor day into a harassed
unrest.

Mortals dwell in that they await the divinities as divinities. In hope they hold
up to the divinities what is unhoped for. They wait for intimations of their
coming and do not mistake the signs of their absence. They do not make their
gods for themselves and do not worship idols. In the very depth of misfortune
they wait for the weal that has been withdrawn.

Mortals dwell in that they initiate their own nature – their being capable of
death as death – into the use and practice of this capacity, so that there may be
a good death. To initiate mortals into the nature of death in no way means to
make death, as empty Nothing, the goal. Nor does it mean to darken dwelling
by blindly staring toward the end.

In saving the earth, in receiving the sky, in awaiting the divinities, in initiat-
ing mortals, dwelling occurs as the fourfold preservation of the fourfold. To
spare and preserve means: to take under our care, to look after the fourfold in
its presencing. What we take under our care must be kept safe. But if dwelling
preserves the fourfold, where does it keep the fourfold's nature? How do
mortals make their dwelling such a preserving? Mortals would never be
capable of it if dwelling were merely a staying on earth under the sky, before the
divinities, among mortals. Rather, dwelling itself is always a staying with
things. Dwelling, as preserving, keeps the fourfold in that with which mortals
stay: in things.

Staying with things, however, is not merely something attached to this fourfold preserving as a fifth something. On the contrary: staying with things is the
only way in which the fourfold stay within the fourfold is accomplished at any
time in simple unity. Dwelling preserves the fourfold by bringing the presencing
of the fourfold into things. But things themselves secure the fourfold *only when*
they themselves *as* things are let be in their presencing. How is this done? In this
way, that mortals nurse and nurture the things that grow, and specially construct things that do not grow. Cultivating and construction are building in the
narrower sense. *Dwelling,* insofar as it keeps or secures the fourfold in things,
is, as this keeping, a *building*. With this, we are on our way to the second
question.

PART TWO

In what way does building belong to dwelling? The answer to this question will clarify for us what building, understood by way of the nature of dwelling, really is. We limit ourselves to building in the sense of constructing things and inquire: what is a built thing? A bridge may serve as an example for our reflections.

The bridge swings over the stream 'with ease and power'. It does not just connect banks that are already there. The banks emerge as banks only as the bridge crosses the stream. The bridge designedly causes them to lie across from each other. One side is set off against the other by the bridge. Nor do the banks stretch along the stream as indifferent border strips of the dry land. With the banks, the bridge brings to the stream the one and the other expanse of the landscape lying behind them. It brings stream and bank and land into each other's neighbourhood. The bridge *gathers* the earth as landscape around the stream. Thus it guides and attends the stream through the meadows. Resting upright in the stream's bed, the bridge-piers bear the swing of the arches that leave the stream's waters to run their course. The waters may wander on quiet and gay, the sky's floods from storm or thaw may shoot past the piers in torrential waves – the bridge is ready for the sky's weather and its fickle nature. Even where the bridge covers the stream, it holds its flow up to the sky by taking it for a moment under the vaulted gateway and then setting it free once more.

The bridge lets the stream run its course and at the same time grants their way to mortals so that they may come and go from shore to shore. Bridges lead in many ways. The city bridge leads from the precincts of the castle to the cathedral square, the river bridge near the country town brings wagons and horse teams to the surrounding villages. The old stone bridge's humble brook crossing gives to the harvest wagon its passage from the fields into the village and carries the lumber cart from the field path to the road. The highway bridge is tied into the network of long-distance traffic, paced as calculated for maximum yield. Always and ever differently the bridge escorts the lingering and hastening ways of men to and fro, so that they may get to other banks and in the end, as mortals, to the other side. Now in a high arch, now in a low, the bridge vaults over glen and stream – whether mortals keep in mind this vaulting of the bridge's course or forget that they, always themselves on their way to the last bridge, are actually striving to surmount all that is common and unsound in them in order to bring themselves before the haleness of the divinities. The bridge *gathers*, as a passage that crosses, before the divinities – whether we explicitly think of, and visibly *give thanks for,* their presence, as in the figure of the saint of the bridge, or whether that divine presence is obstructed or even pushed wholly aside.

The bridge *gathers* to itself in *its own* way earth and sky, divinities and mortals.

Gathering or assembly, by an ancient word of our language, is called 'thing'. The bridge is a thing – and, indeed, it is such *as* the gathering of the fourfold which we have described. To be sure, people think of the bridge as primarily and really *merely* a bridge; after that, and occasionally, it might possibly express much else besides; and as such an expression it would then become a symbol, for instance a symbol of those things we mentioned before. But the bridge, if it is a true bridge, is never first of all a mere bridge and then afterward a symbol. And just as little is the bridge in the first place exclusively a symbol, in the sense that it expresses something that strictly speaking does not belong to it. If we take the bridge strictly as such, it never appears as an expression. The bridge is a thing and *only that*. Only? As this thing it gathers the fourfold.

Our thinking has of course long been accustomed to *understate* the nature of the thing. The consequence, in the course of Western thought, has been that the thing is represented as an unknown X to which perceptible properties are attached. From this point of view, everything *that already belongs to the gathering nature of this thing* does, of course, appear as something that is afterward read into it. Yet the bridge would never be a mere bridge if it were not a thing.

To be sure, the bridge is a thing of its *own* kind; for it gathers the fourfold in *such* a way that it allows a *site* for it. But only something *that is itself a location* can make space for a site. The location is not already there before the bridge is. Before the bridge stands, there are of course many spots along the stream that can be occupied by something. One of them proves to be a location, and does so *because of the bridge*. Thus the bridge does not first come to a location to stand in it; rather, a location comes into existence only by virtue of the bridge. The bridge is a thing; it gathers the fourfold, but in such a way that it allows a site for the fourfold. By this site are determined the localities and ways by which a space is provided for.

Only things that are locations in this manner allow for spaces. What the word for space, *Raum, Rum*, designates is said by its ancient meaning. *Raum* means a place cleared or freed for settlement and lodging. A space is something that has been made room for, something that is cleared and free, namely within a boundary, Greek *peras*. A boundary is not that at which something stops but, as the Greeks recognized, the boundary is that from which something *begins its presencing*. That is why the concept is that of *horismos* that is, the horizon, the boundary. Space is in essence that for which room has been made, that which is let into its bounds. That for which room is made is always granted and hence is joined, that is, gathered, by virtue of a location, that is, by such a thing as the bridge. *Accordingly spaces receive their being from locations and not from 'space'*.

Things which, as locations, allow a site we now in anticipation call buildings. They are so called because they are made by a process of building construction. Of what sort this making – building – must be, however, we find out only after we have first given thought to the nature of those things which of themselves require building as the process by which they are made. These things are locations that allow a site for the fourfold, a site that in each case provides for a space. The relation between location and space lies in the nature of these things *qua* locations, but so does the relation of the location to the man who lives at that location. Therefore we shall now try to clarify the nature of these things that we call buildings by the following brief consideration.

For one thing, what is the relation between location and space? For another, what is the relation between man and space?

The bridge is a location. As such a thing, it allows a space into which earth and heaven, divinities and mortals are admitted. The space allowed by the bridge contains many places variously near or far from the bridge. These

Heidegger places, however, may be treated as mere positions between which there lies a measurable distance; a distance, in Greek *stadion*, always has room made for it, and indeed by bare positions. The space that is thus made by positions is space of a peculiar sort. As distance or 'stadion' it is what the same word, *stadion*, means in Latin, a *spatium*, an intervening space or interval. Thus nearness and remoteness between men and things can become mere distance, mere intervals of intervening space. In a space that is represented purely as *spatium*, the bridge now appears as a mere something at some position, which can be occupied at any time by something else or replaced by a mere marker. What is more, the mere dimensions of height, breadth and depth can be abstracted from space as intervals. What is so abstracted we represent as the pure manifold of the three dimensions. Yet the room made by this manifold is also no longer determined by distances; it is no longer a *spatium*, but now no more than *extensio* – extension. But from space as *extensio* a further abstraction can be made, to analytic-algebraic relations. What these relations make room for is the possibility of the purely mathematical construction of manifolds with an arbitrary number of dimensions. The space provided for in this mathematical manner may be called 'space', the 'one' space as such. But in this sense 'the' space, 'space', contains no spaces and no places. We never find in it any locations, that is, things of the kind the bridge is. As against that, however, in the spaces provided for by locations there is always space as interval, and in this interval in turn there is space as pure extension. *Spatium* and *extensio* afford at any time the possibility of measuring things and what they make room for, according to distances, spans and directions, and of computing these magnitudes. But the fact that they are *universally* applicable to everything that has extension can in no case make numerical magnitudes the *ground* of the nature of spaces and locations that are measurable with the aid of mathematics. How even modern physics was compelled by the facts themselves to represent the spatial medium of cosmic space as a field-unity determined by body as dynamic centre, cannot be discussed here.

The spaces through which we go daily are provided for by locations; their nature is grounded in things of the type of buildings. If we pay heed to these relations between locations and spaces, between spaces and space, we get a clue to help us in thinking of the relation of man and space.

When we speak of man and space, it sounds as though man stood on one side, space on the other. Yet space is not something that faces man. It is neither an external object nor an inner experience. It is not that there are men, and over and above them *space*; for when I say 'a man', and in saying this word think of a being who exists in a human manner – that is, who dwells – then by the name 'man' I already name the stay within the fourfold among things. Even when we relate ourselves to those things that are not in our immediate reach, we are staying with the things themselves. We do not represent distant things merely in our mind – as the textbooks have it – so that only mental representations of distant things run through our minds and heads as substitutes for the things. If all of us now think, from where we are right here, of the old bridge in Heidelberg, this thinking toward that location is not a mere experience inside the persons present here; rather, it belongs to the nature of our thinking *of* that bridge that *in itself* thinking gets through, persists through, the distance to that location. From this spot right here, we are there at the bridge – we are by no

means at some representational content in our consciousness. From right here
we may even be much nearer to that bridge and to what it makes room for than
someone who uses it daily as an indifferent river crossing. Spaces, and with
them space as such – 'space' – are always provided for already within the stay of
mortals. Spaces open up by the fact that they are let into the dwelling of man.
To say that mortals *are* is to say that *in dwelling* they persist through spaces by
virtue of their stay among things and locations. And only because mortals
pervade, persist through, spaces by their very nature are they able to go through
spaces. But in going through spaces we do not give up our standing in them.
Rather, we always go through spaces in such a way that we already experience
them by staying constantly with near and remote locations and things. When I
go toward the door of the lecture hall, I am already there, and I could not go to
it at all if I were not such that I am there. I am never here only, as this encap-
sulated body; rather, I am there, that is, I already pervade the room, and only
thus can I go through it.

Even when mortals turn 'inward,' taking stock of themselves, they do not
leave behind their belonging to the fourfold. When, as we say, we come to our
senses and reflect on ourselves, we come back to ourselves from things *without
ever abandoning* our stay among things. Indeed, the loss of rapport with things
that occurs in states of depression would be wholly impossible if even such a
state were not still what it is as a human state: that is, a staying *with* things.
Only if this stay already characterizes human being can the things among which
we are also *fail* to speak to us, *fail* to concern us any longer.

Man's relation to locations, and through locations to spaces, inheres in his
dwelling. The relationship between man and space is none other than dwelling,
strictly thought and spoken.

When we think, in the manner just attempted, about the relation between
location and space, but also about the relation of man and space, a light falls on
the nature of the things that are locations and that we call buildings.

The bridge is a thing of this sort. The location allows the simple onefold of
earth and sky, of divinities and mortals, to enter into a site by arranging the site
into spaces. The location makes room for the fourfold in a double sense. The
location *admits* the fourfold and it *installs* the fourfold. The two – making
room in the sense of admitting and in the sense of installing – belong together.
As a double space-making, the location is a shelter for the fourfold or, by the
same token, a house. Things like such locations shelter or house men's lives.
Things of this sort are housings, though not necessarily dwelling-houses in the
narrower sense.

The making of such things is building. Its nature consists in this, that it
corresponds to the character of these things. They are locations that allow
spaces. This is why building, by virtue of constructing locations, is a founding
and joining of spaces. Because building produces locations, the joining of the
spaces of these locations necessarily brings with it space, as *spatium* and as
extensio, into the thingly structure of buildings. But building never shapes pure
'space' as a single entity. Neither directly nor indirectly. Nevertheless, because it
produces things as locations, building is closer to the nature of spaces and to
the origin of the nature of 'space' than any geometry and mathematics. Building
puts up locations that make space and a site for the fourfold. From the simple
oneness in which earth and sky, divinities and mortals belong together, building

Heidegger   *receives the directive* for its erecting of locations. Building *takes over* from the fourfold the standard for all the traversing and measuring of the spaces that in each case are provided for by the locations that have been founded. The edifices guard the fourfold. They are things that in their own way preserve the fourfold. To preserve the fourfold, to save the earth, to receive the sky, to await the divinities, to escort mortals – this fourfold preserving is the simple nature, the presencing, of dwelling. In this way, then, do genuine buildings give form to dwelling in its presencing and house this presence.

Building thus characterized is a distinctive letting-dwell. Whenever it *is* such in fact, building already *has* responded to the summons of the fourfold. All planning remains grounded on this responding, and planning in turn opens up to the designer the precincts suitable for his designs.

As soon as we try to think of the nature of constructive building in terms of a letting-dwell, we come to know more clearly what that process of making consists in by which building is accomplished. Usually we take production to be an activity whose performance has a result, the finished structure, as its consequence. It is possible to conceive of making in that way; we thereby grasp something that is correct, and yet never touch its nature, which is a producing that brings something forth. For building brings the fourfold *hither* into a thing, the bridge, and brings *forth* the thing as a location, out into what is already there, room for which is only now made *by* this location.

The Greek for 'to bring forth or to produce' is *tikto*. The word *techne,* technique, belongs to the verb's root *tec.* To the Greeks *techne* means neither art nor handicraft but rather: to make something appear, within what is present, as this or that, in this way or that way. The Greeks conceive of *techne* producing, in terms of letting appear. *Techne* thus conceived has been concealed in the tectonics of architecture since ancient times. Of late it still remains concealed, and more resolutely, in the technology of power machinery. But the nature of the erecting of buildings cannot be understood adequately in terms either of architecture or of engineering construction, nor in terms of a mere combination of the two. The erecting of buildings would not be suitably defined *even if* we were to think of it in the sense of the original Greek *techne* as *solely* a letting-appear, which brings something made, as something present, among the things that are already present.

The nature of building is letting dwell. Building accomplishes its nature in the raising of locations by the joining of their spaces. *Only if we are capable of dwelling, only then can we build.* Let us think for a while of a farmhouse in the Black Forest, which was built some two hundred years ago by the dwelling of peasants. Here the self-sufficiency of the power to let earth and heaven, divinities and mortals enter *in simple oneness* into things, ordered the house. It placed the farm on the wind-sheltered mountain slope looking south, among the meadows close to the spring. It gave it the wide overhanging shingle roof whose proper slope bears up under the burden of snow, and which, reaching deep down, shields the chambers against the storms of the long winter nights. It did not forget the altar corner behind the community table; it made room in its chamber for the hallowed places of childbed and the 'tree of the dead' – for that is what they call a coffin there: the *Totenbaum* – and in this way it designed for the different generations under one roof the character of their journey through time. A craft which, itself sprung from dwelling, still uses its tools and frames as things, built the *Heidegger* farmhouse.

Only if we are capable of dwelling, only then can we build. Our reference to the Black Forest farm in no way means that we should or could go back to building such houses; rather, it illustrates by a dwelling that *has been* how *it* was able to build.

Dwelling, however, is *the basic character* of Being in keeping with which mortals exist. Perhaps this attempt to think about dwelling and building will bring out somewhat more clearly that building belongs to dwelling and how it receives its nature from dwelling. Enough will have been gained if dwelling and building have become *worthy of questioning* and thus have remained *worthy of thought*.

But that thinking itself belongs to dwelling in the same sense as building, although in a different way, may perhaps be attested to by the course of thought here attempted.

Building and thinking are, each in its own way, inescapable for dwelling. The two, however, are also insufficient for dwelling so long as each busies itself with its own affairs in separation instead of listening to one another. They are able to listen if both – building and thinking – belong to dwelling, if they remain within their limits and realize that the one as much as the other comes from the workshop of long experience and incessant practice.

We are attempting to trace in thought the nature of dwelling. The next step on this path would be the question: what is the state of dwelling in our precarious age? On all sides we hear talk about the housing shortage, and with good reason. Nor is there just talk; there is action too. We try to fill the need by providing houses, by promoting the building of houses, planning the whole architectural enterprise. However hard and bitter, however hampering and threatening the lack of houses remains, the *real plight of dwelling* does not lie merely in a lack of houses. The real plight of dwelling is indeed older than the world wars with their destruction, older also than the increase of the earth's population and the condition of the industrial workers. The real dwelling plight lies in this, that mortals ever search anew for the nature of dwelling, that they *must ever learn to dwell*. What if man's homelessness consisted in this, that man still does not even think of the *real* plight of dwelling as *the* plight? Yet as soon as man *gives thought* to his homelessness, it is a misery no longer. Rightly considered and kept well in mind, it is the sole summons that *calls* mortals into their dwelling.

But how else can mortals answer this summons than by trying on *their* part, on their own, to bring dwelling to the fullness of its nature? This they accomplish when they build out of dwelling, and think for the sake of dwelling.

. . . POETICALLY MAN DWELLS . . .

The phrase is taken from a late poem by Hölderlin, which comes to us by a curious route. It begins: 'In lovely blueness blooms the steeple with metal roof.' (Stuttgart edition 2, 1, pp. 372 ff.; Hellingrath VI, pp. 24 ff.) If we are to hear

Heidegger   the phrase 'poetically man dwells' rightly, we must restore it thoughtfully to the poem. For that reason let us give thought to the phrase. Let us clear up the doubts it immediately arouses. For otherwise we should lack the free readiness to respond to the phrase by following it.

'. . . poetically man dwells . . .'. If need be, we can imagine that poets do on occasion dwell poetically. But how is 'man' – and this means every man and all the time – supposed to dwell poetically? Does not all dwelling remain incompatible with the poetic? Our dwelling is harassed by the housing shortage. Even if that were not so, our dwelling today is harassed by work, made insecure by the hunt for gain and success, bewitched by the entertainment and recreation industry. But when there is still room left in today's dwelling for the poetic, and time is still set aside, what comes to pass is at best a preoccupation with aestheticizing, whether in writing or on the air. Poetry is either rejected as a frivolous mooning and vaporizing into the unknown, and a flight into dreamland, or is counted as a part of literature. And the validity of literature is assessed by the latest prevailing standard. The prevailing standard, in turn, is made and controlled by the organs for making public civilized opinions. One of its functionaries – at once driver and driven – is the literature industry. In such a setting poetry cannot appear otherwise than as literature. Where it is studied entirely in educational and scientific terms, it is the object of literary history. Western poetry goes under the general heading of 'European literature'.

But if the sole form in which poetry exists is literary to start with, then how can human dwelling be understood as based on the poetic? The phrase, 'man dwells poetically', comes indeed from a mere poet, and in fact from one who, we are told, could not cope with life. It is the way of poets to shut their eyes to actuality. Instead of acting, they dream. What they make is merely imagined. The things of imagination are merely made. Making is, in Greek, *poiesis*. And man's dwelling is supposed to be poetry and poetic? This can be assumed, surely, only by someone who stands aside from actuality and does not want to see the existent condition of man's historical-social life today – the sociologists call it the collective.

But before we so bluntly pronounce dwelling and poetry incompatible, it may be well to attend soberly to the poet's statement. It speaks of man's dwelling. It does not describe today's dwelling conditions. Above all, it does not assert that to dwell means to occupy a house, a dwelling place. Nor does it say that the poetic exhausts itself in an unreal play of poetic imagination. What thoughtful man, therefore, would presume to declare, unhesitatingly and from a somewhat dubious elevation, that dwelling and the poetic are incompatible? Perhaps the two can bear with each other. This is not all. Perhaps one even bears the other in such a way that dwelling rests on the poetic. If this is indeed what we suppose, then we are required to think of dwelling and poetry in terms of their essential nature. If we do not balk at this demand, we think of what is usually called the existence of man in terms of dwelling. In doing so, we do of course give up the customary notion of dwelling. According to that idea, dwelling remains merely one form of human behaviour alongside many others. We work in the city, but dwell outside it. We travel, and dwell now here, now there. Dwelling, so understood, is always merely the occupying of a lodging.

When Hölderlin speaks of dwelling, he has before his eyes the basic character of human existence. He sees the 'poetic', moreover, by way of its relation to this dwelling, thus understood essentially.   *Heidegger*

This does not mean, though, that the poetic is merely an ornament and bonus added to dwelling. Nor does the poetic character of dwelling mean merely that the poetic turns up in some way or other in all dwelling. Rather, the phrase 'poetically man dwells' says: poetry first causes dwelling to be dwelling. Poetry is what really lets us dwell. But through what do we attain to a dwelling place? Through building. Poetic creation, which lets us dwell, is a kind of building.

Thus we confront a double demand: for one thing, we are to think of what is called man's existence by way of the nature of dwelling; for another, we are to think of the nature of poetry as a letting-dwell, as a – perhaps even *the* – distinctive kind of building. If we search out the nature of poetry according to this viewpoint, then we arrive at the nature of dwelling.

But where do we humans get our information about the nature of dwelling and poetry? Where does man generally get the claim to arrive at the nature of something? Man can make such a claim only where he receives it. He receives it from the telling of language. Of course, only when and only as long as he respects language's own nature. Meanwhile, there rages round the earth an unbridled yet clever talking, writing and broadcasting of spoken words. Man acts as though he were the shaper and master of language, while in fact language remains the master of man. When this relation of dominance gets inverted, man hits upon strange manoeuvres. Language becomes the means of expression. As expression, language can decay into a mere medium for the printed word. That even in such employment of language we retain a concern for care in speaking is all to the good. But this alone will never help us to escape from the inversion of the true relation of dominance between language and man. For, strictly, it is language that speaks. Man first speaks when, and only when, he responds to language by listening to its appeal. Among all the appeals that we human beings, on our part, may help to be voiced, language is the highest and everywhere the first. Language beckons us, at first and then again at the end, toward a thing's nature. But that is not to say, ever, that in any word-meaning picked up at will language supplies us, straight away and definitively, with the transparent nature of the matter as if it were an object ready for use. But the responding in which man authentically listens to the appeal of language is that which speaks in the element of poetry. The more poetic a poet is – the freer (that is, the more open and ready for the unforeseen) his saying – the greater is the purity with which he submits what he says to an ever more painstaking listening, and the further what he says is from the mere propositional statement that is dealt with solely in regard to its correctness or incorrectness.

. . . poetically man dwells . . .

says the poet. We hear Hölderlin's words more clearly when we take them back into the poem in which they belong. First, let us listen only to the two lines from which we have detached and thus clipped the phrase. They run:

Full of merit, yet poetically, man
Dwells on this earth.

The keynote of the lines vibrates in the word 'poetically'. This word is set off in two directions: by what comes before it and by what follows.

Heidegger   Before it are the words: 'Full of merit, yet . . .'. They sound almost as if the next word, 'poetically', introduced a restriction on the profitable, meritorious dwelling of man. But it is just the reverse. The restriction is denoted by the expression 'Full of merit', to which we must add in thought a 'to be sure'. Man, to be sure, merits and earns much in his dwelling. For he cultivates the growing things of the earth and takes care of his increase. Cultivating and caring (*colere, cultura*) are a kind of building. But man not only cultivates what produces growth out of itself; he also builds in the sense of *aedificare,* by erecting things that cannot come into being and subsist by growing. Things that are built in this sense include not only buildings but all the works made by man's hands and through his arrangements. Merits due to this building, however, can never fill out the nature of dwelling. On the contrary, they even deny dwelling its own nature when they are pursued and acquired purely for their own sake. For in that case these merits, precisely by their abundance, would everywhere constrain dwelling within the bounds of this kind of building. Such building pursues the fulfilment of the needs of dwelling. Building in the sense of the farmer's cultivation of growing things, and of the erecting of edifices and works and the production of tools, is already a consequence of the nature of dwelling, but it is not its ground, let alone its grounding. This grounding must take place in a different building. Building of the usual kind, often practised exclusively and therefore the only one that is familiar, does of course bring an abundance of merits into dwelling. Yet man is capable of dwelling only if he has already built, is building, and remains disposed to build, in another way.

'Full of merit (to be sure), yet poetically, man dwells . . . .' This is followed in the text by the words: 'on this earth'. We might be inclined to think the addition superfluous; for dwelling, after all, already means man's stay on earth – on 'this' earth, to which every mortal knows himself to be entrusted and exposed. But when Hölderlin ventures to say that the dwelling of mortals is poetic, this statement, as soon as it is made, gives the impression that, on the contrary, 'poetic' dwelling snatches man away from the earth. For the 'poetic', when it is taken as poetry, is supposed to belong to the realm of fantasy. Poetic dwelling flies fantastically above reality. The poet counters this misgiving by saying expressly that poetic dwelling is a dwelling 'on this earth'. Hölderlin thus not only protects the 'poetic' from a likely misinterpretation, but by adding the words 'on this earth' expressly points to the nature of poetry. Poetry does not fly above and surmount the earth in order to escape it and hover over it. Poetry is what first brings man onto the earth, making him belong to it, and thus brings him into dwelling.

> Full of merit, yet poetically, man
> Dwells on this earth.

Do we know now why man dwells poetically? We still do not. We now even run the risk of intruding foreign thoughts into Hölderlin's poetic words. For Hölderlin indeed speaks of man's dwelling and his merit, but still he does not connect dwelling with building, as we have just done. He does not speak of building, either in the sense of cultivating and erecting, or in such a way as even to represent poetry as a special kind of building. Accordingly, Hölderlin does not speak of poetic dwelling as our own thinking does. Despite all this, we are thinking the same thing that Hölderlin is saying poetically.

It is, however, important to take note here of an essential point. A short Heidegger
parenthetical remark is needed. Poetry and thinking meet each other in one and
the same only when, and only as long as, they remain distinctly in the
distinctness of their nature. The same never coincides with the equal, not even
in the empty indifferent oneness of what is merely identical. The equal or
identical always moves toward the absence of difference, so that everything
may be reduced to a common denominator. The same, by contrast, is the
belonging together of what differs, through a gathering by way of the difference. We can only say 'the same' if we think difference. It is in the carrying
out and settling of differences that the gathering nature of sameness comes to
light. The same banishes all zeal always to level what is different into the equal
or identical. The same gathers what is distinct into an orginal being-at-one. The
equal, on the contrary, disperses them into the dull unity of mere uniformity.
Hölderlin, in his own way, knew of these relations. In an epigram which bears
the title 'Root of All Evil' (Stuttgart edition, 1, 1, p. 305) he says:

> Being at one is godlike and good; whence, then,
> this craze among men that there should exist only
> One, why should all be one?

When we follow in thought Hölderlin's poetic statement about the poetic
dwelling of man, we divine a path by which, through what is thought differently, we come nearer to thinking the same as that which the poet composes
in his poem.

But what does Hölderlin say of the poetic dwelling of man? We seek the
answer to the question by listening to lines 24 to 38 of our poem. For the two
lines on which we first commented are spoken from their region Hölderlin says:

> May, if life is sheer toil, a man
> Lift his eyes and say: so
> I too wish to be? Yes. As long as Kindness,
> The Pure, still stays with his heart, man
> Not unhappily measures himself
> Against the godhead. Is God unknown?
> Is he manifest like the sky? I'd sooner
> Believe the latter. It's the measure of man.
> Full of merit, yet poetically, man
> Dwells on this earth. But no purer
> Is the shade of the starry night,
> If I might put it so, than
> Man, who's called an image of the godhead.
> Is there a measure on earth? There is
> None.

We shall think over only a few points in these lines, and for the sole purpose of
hearing more clearly what Hölderlin means when he calls man's dwelling a
'poetic' one. The first lines (24 to 26) give us a clue. They are in the form of a
question that is answered confidently in the affirmative. The question is a
paraphrase of what the lines already expounded utter directly: 'Full of merit,
yet poetically, man dwells on this earth.' Hölderlin asks:

Heidegger   May, if life is sheer toil, a man
             Lift his eyes and say: so
             I too wish to be? Yes.

Only in the realm of sheer toil does man toil for 'merits'. There he obtains them
for himself in abundance. But at the same time, in this realm, man is allowed to
look up, out of it, through it, toward the divinities. The upward glance passes
aloft toward the sky, and yet it remains below on the earth. The upward glance
spans the between of sky and earth. This between is measured out for the
dwelling of man. We now call the span thus meted out the dimension. This
dimension does not arise from the fact that sky and earth are turned toward one
another. Rather, their facing each other itself depends on the dimension. Nor is
the dimension a stretch of space as ordinarily understood; for everything
spatial, as something for which space is made, is already in need of the dimension, that is, that into which it is admitted.

The nature of the dimension is the meting out – which is lightened and so can
be spanned – of the between: the upward to the sky as well as the downward to
earth. We leave the nature of the dimension without a name. According to
Hölderlin's words, man spans the dimension by measuring himself against the
heavenly. Man does not undertake this spanning just now and then; rather, man
is man at all only in such spanning. This is why he can indeed block this
spanning, trim it and disfigure it, but he can never evade it. Man, as man, has
always measured himself with and against something heavenly. Lucifer, too, is
descended from heaven. Therefore we read in the next lines (28 to 29): 'Man
measures himself against the godhead.' The godhead is the 'measure' with
which man measures out his dwelling, his stay on the earth beneath the sky.
Only insofar as man takes the measure of his dwelling in this way is he able to
be commensurately with his nature. Man's dwelling depends on an upward-
looking measure-taking of the dimension, in which the sky belongs just as
much as the earth. This measure-taking not only takes the measure of the earth,
ge, and accordingly it is no mere geo-metry. Just as little does it ever take the
measure of heaven, *ourauos,* for itself. Measure-taking is no science. Measure-
taking gauges the between, which brings the two, heaven and earth, to one
another. This measure-taking has its own *metron* and thus its own metric.

Man's taking measure in the dimension dealt out to him brings dwelling into
its ground plan. Taking the measure of the dimension is the element within
which human dwelling has its security, by which it securely endures. The taking
of measure is what is poetic in dwelling. Poetry is a measuring. But what is it to
measure? If poetry is to be understood as measuring, then obviously we may
not subsume it under just any idea of measuring and measure.

Poetry is presumably a high and special kind of measuring. But there is
more. Perhaps we have to pronounce the sentence, 'Poetry is a *measuring,*' with
a different stress. '*Poetry* is a measuring.' In poetry there takes place what all
measuring is in the ground of its being. Hence it is necessary to pay heed to the
basic act of measuring. That consists in man's first of all taking the measure
which then is applied in every measuring act. In poetry the taking of measure
occurs. To write poetry is measure-taking, understood in the strict sense of the
word, by which man first receives the measure for the breadth of his being.
Man exists as a mortal. He is called mortal because he can die. To be able to die

means: to be capable of death as death. Only man dies – and indeed continually,   *Heidegger*
so long as he stays on this earth, so long as he dwells. His dwelling, however,
rests in the poetic. Hölderlin sees the nature of the 'poetic' in the taking of the
measure by which the measure-taking of human being is accomplished.

Yet how shall we prove that Hölderlin thinks of the nature of poetry as
taking measure? We do not need to prove anything here. All proof is always
only a subsequent undertaking on the basis of presuppositions. Anything at all
can be proved, depending only on what presuppositions are made. But we can
here pay heed only to a few points. It is enough, then, if we attend to the poet's
own words. For in the next lines Hölderlin inquires, before anything else and in
fact exclusively, as to man's measure. That measure is the godhead against
which man measures himself. The question begins in line 29 with the words: 'Is
God unknown?' Manifestly not. For if he were unknown, how could he, being
unknown, ever be the measure? Yet – and this is what we must now listen to
and keep in mind – for Hölderlin God, as the one who he is, is unknown and it
is just as *this Unknown One* that he is the measure for the poet. This is also why
Hölderlin is perplexed by the exciting question: how can that which by its very
nature remains unknown ever become a measure? For something that man
measures himself by must after all impart itself, must appear. But if it appears,
it is known. The god, however, is unknown, and he is the measure nonetheless.
Not only this, but the god who remains unknown, must by showing *himself* as
the one he is, appear as the one who remains unknown. God's *manifestness* –
not only he himself – is mysterious. Therefore the poet immediately asks the
next question: 'Is he manifest like the sky?' Hölderlin answers: 'I'd sooner/
Believe the latter.'

Why – so *we* now ask – is the poet's surmise inclined in that way? The very
next words give the answer. They say tersely: 'It's the measure of man.' What is
the measure for human measuring? God? No. The sky? No. The manifestness
of the sky? No. The measure consists in the way in which the god who remains
unknown is revealed *as* such by the sky. God's appearance through the sky
consists in a disclosing that lets us see what conceals itself, but lets us see it not
by seeking to wrest what is concealed out of its concealedness, but only by
guarding the concealed in its self-concealment. Thus the unknown god appears
as the unknown by way of the sky's manifestness. This appearance is the
measure against which man measures himself.

A strange measure, perplexing it would seem to the common notions of
mortals, inconvenient to the cheap omniscience of everyday opinion, which
likes to claim that it is the standard for all thinking and reflection.

A strange measure for ordinary and in particular also for all merely scientific
ideas, certainly not a palpable stick or rod but in truth simpler to handle than
they, provided our hands do not abruptly grasp but are guided by gestures
befitting the measure here to be taken. This is done by a taking which at no time
clutches at the standard but rather takes it in a concentrated perception, a
gathered taking-in, that remains a listening.

But why should this measure, which is so strange to us men of today, be
addressed to man and imparted by the measure-taking of poetry? Because only
this measure gauges the very nature of man. For man dwells by spanning the 'on
the earth' and the 'beneath the sky'. This 'on' and 'beneath' belong together.
Their interplay is the span that man traverses at every moment insofar as he *is* as

an earthly being. In a fragment (Stuttgart edition, 2, 1, p. 334) Hölderlin says:

> Always, love! the earth
> moves and heaven holds.

Because man *is*, in his enduring the dimension, his being must now and again be measured out. That requires a measure which involves at once the whole dimension in one. To discern this measure, to gauge it as the measure, and to accept it as the measure, means for the poet to make poetry. Poetry is this measure-taking – its taking, indeed, for the dwelling of man. For immediately after the words 'It's the measure of man' there follow the lines: 'Full of merit, yet poetically, man dwells on this earth.'

Do we now know what the 'poetic' is for Hölderlin? Yes and no. Yes, because we receive an intimation about how poetry is to be thought of: namely, it is to be conceived as a distinctive kind of measuring. No, because poetry, as the gauging of that strange measure, becomes ever more mysterious. And so it must doubtless remain, if we are really prepared to make our stay in the domain of poetry's being.

Yet it strikes us as strange that Hölderlin thinks of poetry as a measuring. And rightly so, as long as we understand measuring only in the sense current *for us*. In this sense, by the use of something known – measuring rods and their number – something unknown is stepped off and thus made known, and so is confined within a quantity and order which can always be determined at a glance. Such measuring can vary with the type of apparatus employed. But who will guarantee that this customary kind of measuring, merely because it is common, touches the nature of measuring? When we hear of measure, we immediately think of number and imagine the two, measure and number, as quantitative. But the *nature* of measure is no more a quantum than is the *nature* of number. True, we can reckon with numbers – but not with the nature of number. When Hölderlin envisages poetry as a measuring, and above all himself achieves poetry as taking measure, then we, in order to think of poetry, must ever and again first give thought to the measure that is taken in poetry; we must pay heed to the kind of taking here, which does not consist in a clutching or any other kind of grasping, but rather in a letting come of what has been dealt out. What is the measure for poetry? The godhead; God, therefore? Who is the god? Perhaps this question is too hard for man, and asked too soon. Let us therefore first ask what may be said about God. Let us first ask merely: What is God?

Fortunately for us, and helpfully, some verses of Hölderlin's have been preserved which belong in substance and time to the ambience of the poem 'In lovely blueness . . . '. They begin (Stuttgart edition, 2, 1, p. 210):

> What is God? Unknown, yet
> Full of his qualities is the
> Face of the sky. For the lightnings
> Are the wrath of a god. The more something
> Is invisible, the more it yields to what's alien.

What remains alien to the god, the sight of the sky – this is what is familiar to man. And what is that? Everything that shimmers and blooms in the sky and thus under the sky and thus on earth, everything that sounds and is fragrant, rises and

comes – but also everything that goes and stumbles, moans and falls silent, pales
and darkens. Into this, which is intimate to man but alien to the god, the
unknown imparts himself, in order to remain guarded within it as the unknown.
But the poet calls all the brightness of the sights of the sky and every sound of its
courses and breezes into the singing word and there makes them shine and ring.
Yet the poet, if he is a poet, does not describe the mere appearance of sky and
earth. The poet calls, in the sights of the sky, that which in its very self-disclosure
causes the appearance of that which conceals itself, and indeed *as* that which
conceals itself. In the familiar appearances, the poet calls the alien as that to
which the invisible imparts itself in order to remain what it is – unknown.

The poet makes poetry only when he takes the measure, by saying the sights of
heaven in such a way that he submits to its appearances as to the alien element to
which the unknown god has 'yielded'. Our current name for the sight and
appearance of something is 'image'. The nature of the image is to let something
be seen. By contrast, copies and imitations are already mere variations on the
genuine image which, as a sight or spectacle, lets the invisible be seen and so
imagines the invisible in something alien to it. Because poetry takes that
mysterious measure, to wit, in the face of the sky, therefore it speaks in 'images'.
This is why poetic images are imaginings in a distinctive sense: not mere fancies
and illusions but imaginings that are visible inclusions of the alien in the sight of
the familiar. The poetic saying of images gathers the brightness and sound of the
heavenly appearances into one with the darkness and silence of what is alien. By
such sights the god surprises us. In this strangeness he proclaims his unfaltering
nearness. For that reason Hölderlin, after the lines 'Full of merit, yet poetically,
man Dwells on this earth,' can continue:

> . . . Yet no purer
> Is the shade of the starry night,
> If I might put it so, than
> Man, who's called an image of the godhead.

'The shade of the night' – the night itself is the shade, that darkness which can
never become a mere blackness because as shade it is wedded to light and
remains cast by it. The measure taken by poetry yields, imparts itself – as the
foreign element in which the invisible one preserves his presence – to what is
familiar in the sights of the sky. Hence, the measure is of the same nature as the
sky. But the sky is not sheer light. The radiance of its height is itself the darkness
of its all-sheltering breadth. The blue of the sky's lovely blueness is the colour of
depth. The radiance of the sky is the dawn and dusk of the twilight, which
shelters everything that can be proclaimed. This sky is the measure. This is why
the poet must ask:

> Is there a measure on earth?

And he must reply: 'There is none.' Why? Because what we signify when we say
'on the earth' exists only insofar as man dwells on the earth and in his dwelling
lets the earth be as earth.

But dwelling occurs only when poetry comes to pass and is present, and
indeed in the way whose nature we now have some idea of, as taking a
measure for all measuring. This measure-taking is itself an authentic measure-
taking, no mere gauging with ready-made measuring rods for the making of

Heidegger maps. Nor is poetry building in the sense of raising and fitting buildings. But poetry, as the authentic gauging of the dimension of dwelling, is the primal form of building. Poetry first of all admits man's dwelling into its very nature, its presencing being. Poetry is the original admission of dwelling.

The statement, *Man dwells in that he builds,* has now been given its proper sense. Man does not dwell in that he merely establishes his stay on the earth beneath the sky, by raising growing things and simultaneously raising buildings. Man is capable of such building only if he already builds in the sense of the poetic taking of measure. Authentic building occurs so far as there are poets, such poets as take the measure for architecture, the structure of dwelling.

On 12 March 1804 Hölderlin writes from Nürtingen to his friend Leo von Seckendorf: 'At present I am especially occupied with the fable, the poetic view of history, and the architectonics of the skies, especially of our nation's, so far as it differs from the Greek' (Hellingrath V2, p. 333).

'. . . poetically, man dwells . . .'

Poetry builds up the very nature of dwelling. Poetry and dwelling not only do not exclude each other; on the contrary, poetry and dwelling belong together, each calling for the other. 'Poetically man dwells.' Do *we* dwell poetically? Presumably we dwell altogether unpoetically. If that is so, does it give the lie to the poet's words; are they untrue? No. The truth of his utterance is confirmed in the most unearthly way. For dwelling can be unpoetic only because it is in essence poetic. For a man to be blind, he must remain a being by nature endowed with sight. A piece of wood can never go blind. But when man goes blind, there always remains the question whether his blindness derives from some defect and loss or lies in an abundance and excess. In the same poem that meditates on the measure for all measuring, Hölderlin says (lines 75–76): 'King Oedipus has perhaps one eye too many.' Thus it might be that our unpoetic dwelling, its incapacity to take the measure, derives from a curious excess of frantic measuring and calculating.

That we dwell unpoetically, and in what way, we can in any case learn only if we know the poetic. Whether, and when, we may come to a turning point in our unpoetic dwelling is something we may expect to happen only if we remain heedful of the poetic. How and to what extent our doings can share in this turn we alone can prove, if we take the poetic seriously.

The poetic is the basic capacity for human dwelling. But man is capable of poetry at any time only to the degree to which his being is appropriate to that which itself has a liking for man and therefore needs his presence. Poetry is authentic or inauthentic according to the degree of this appropriation.

That is why authentic poetry does not come to light appropriately in every period. When and for how long does authentic poetry exist? Hölderlin gives the answer in verses 26–69, already cited. Their explication has been purposely deferred until now. The verses run:

> . . . As long as Kindness,
> The Pure, still stays with his heart, man
> Not unhappily measures himself
> Against the Godhead. . . .

'Kindness' – what is it? A harmless word, but described by Hölderlin with the

capitalized epithet 'the Pure'. 'Kindness' – this word, if we take it literally, is   *Heidegger*
Hölderlin's magnificent translation for the Greek word *charis*. In his *Ajax*,
Sophocles says of *charis* (verse 522):

> *Charis charin gar estin he tiktous aei.*
> For kindness it is, that ever calls forth kindness.

'As long as Kindness, the Pure, still stays with his heart . . . .' Hölderlin says in
an idiom he liked to use: 'with his heart', not 'in his heart'. That is, it has come
to the dwelling being of man, come as the claim and appeal of the measure to
the heart in such a way that the heart turns to give heed to the measure.

As long as this arrival of kindness endures, so long does man succeed in
measuring himself not unhappily against the godhead. When this measuring
appropriately comes to light, man creates poetry from the very nature of the
poetic. When the poetic appropriately comes to light, then man dwells humanly
on this earth, and then – as Hölderlin says in his last poem – 'the life of man' is
a 'dwelling life' (Stuttgart edition, 2, 1, p. 312).

> *Vista*
> When far the dwelling life of man into the distance goes,
> Where, in that far distance, the grapevine's season glows,
> There too are summer's fields, emptied of their growing,
> And forest looms, its image darkly showing.
> That Nature paints the seasons so complete,
> That she abides, but they glide by so fleet,
> Comes of perfection; then heaven's radiant height
> Crowns man, as blossoms crown the trees, with light.

THE ORIGIN OF THE WORK OF ART (EXTRACTS)

THE TEMPLE

A building, a Greek temple, portrays nothing. It simply stands there in the
middle of the rock-cleft valley. The building encloses the figure of the god, and
in this concealment lets it stand out into the holy precinct through the open
portico. By means of the temple, the god is present in the temple. This presence
of the god is in itself the extension and delimitation of the precinct as a holy
precinct. The temple and its precinct, however, do not fade away into the
indefinite. It is the temple-work that first fits together and at the same time
gathers around itself the unity of those paths and relations in which birth and
death, disaster and blessing, victory and disgrace, endurance and decline
acquire the shape of destiny for human being. The all-governing expanse of this
open relational context is the world of this historical people. Only from and in
this expanse does the nation first return to itself for the fulfilment of its
vocation.

Standing there, the building rests on the rocky ground. This resting of the
work draws up out of the rock the mystery of that rock's clumsy yet spontaneous support. Standing there, the building holds its ground against the storm

Heidegger   raging above it and so first makes the storm itself manifest in its violence. The lustre and gleam of the stone, though itself apparently glowing only by the grace of the sun, yet first brings to light the light of the day, the breadth of the sky, the darkness of the night. The temple's firm towering makes visible the invisible space of air. The steadfastness of the work contrasts with the surge of the surf, and its own repose brings out the raging of the sea. Tree and grass, eagle and bull, snake and cricket first enter into their distinctive shapes and thus come to appear as what they are. The Greeks early called this emerging and rising in itself and in all things *phusis*. It clears and illuminates, also, that on which and in which man bases his dwelling. We call this ground the *earth*. What this word says is not to be associated with the idea of a mass of matter deposited somewhere, or with the merely astronomical idea of a planet. Earth is that whence the arising brings back and shelters everything that arises without violation. In the things that arise, earth is present as the sheltering agent.

The temple-work, standing there, opens up a world and at the same time sets this world back again on earth, which itself only thus emerges as native ground. But men and animals, plants and things, are never present and familiar as unchangeable objects, only to represent incidentally also a fitting environment for the temple, which one fine day is added to what is already there. We shall get closer to what *is*, rather, if we think of all this in reverse order, assuming of course that we have, to begin with, an eye for how differently everything then faces us. Mere reversing, done for its own sake, reveals nothing.

The temple, in its standing there, first gives to things their look and to men their outlook on themselves. This view remains open as long as the work is a work, as long as the god has not fled from it. It is the same with the sculpture of the god, votive offering of the victor in the athletic games. It is not a portrait whose purpose is to make it easier to realize how the god looks; rather, it is a work that lets the god himself be present and thus *is* the god himself. . . .

TECHNE

We think of creation as a bringing forth. But the making of equipment, too, is a bringing forth. Handicraft – a remarkable play of language – does not, to be sure, create works, not even when we contrast, as we must, the handmade with the factory product. But what is it that distinguishes bringing forth as creation from bringing forth in the mode of making? It is as difficult to track down the essential features of the creation of works and the making of equipment as it is easy to distinguish verbally between the two modes of bringing forth. Going along with first appearances we find the same procedure in the activity of potter and sculptor, of joiner and painter. The creation of a work requires craftsmanship. Great artists prize craftsmanship most highly. They are the first to call for its painstaking cultivation, based on complete mastery. They above all others constantly strive to educate themselves ever anew in thorough craftsmanship. It has often enough been pointed out that the Greeks, who knew quite a bit about works of art, use the same word *techne* for craft and art and call the craftsman and the artist by the same name: *technites*.

It thus seems advisable to define the nature of creative work in terms of its craft aspect. But reference to the linguistic usage of the Greeks, with their experience of the facts, must give us pause. However usual and convincing the

reference may be to the Greek practice of naming craft and art by the same   *Heidegger*
name, *techne,* it nevertheless remains oblique and superficial; for *techne*
signifies neither craft nor art, and not at all the technical in our present-day
sense; it never means a kind of practical performance.

The word *techne* denotes rather a mode of knowing. To know means to have
seen, in the widest sense of seeing, which means to apprehend what is present,
as such. For Greek thought the nature of knowing consists in *aletheia,* that is, in
the uncovering of beings. It supports and guides all comportment toward
beings. *Techne,* as knowledge experienced in the Greek manner, is a bringing
forth of beings in that it *brings forth* present beings as such beings *out of*
concealedness and specifically *into* the unconcealedness of their appearance;
techne never signifies the action of making.

ART AND SPACE

If one thinks much, one finds much wisdom inscribed in language.
Indeed, it is not probable that one brings everything into it by himself; rather, much wisdom lies therein, as in proverbs.

G. Chr. Lichtenberg

It appears, however, to be something overwhelming and hard to
grasp, the *topos.*

Aristotle, *Physics*, Book IV

The remarks on art, space and their interplay remain questions, even if they are
uttered in the form of assertions. These remarks are limited to the graphic arts,
and within these to sculpture. Sculptured structures are bodies. Their matter,
consisting of different materials, is variously formed. The forming of it happens
by demarcation as setting up an inclosing and excluding border. Herewith,
space comes into play. Becoming occupied by the sculptured structure, space
receives its special character as closed, breached and empty volume. A familiar
state of affairs, yet puzzling.

The sculptured body embodies something. Does it embody space? Is sculpture an occupying of space, a domination of space? Does sculpture match therewith the technical scientific conquest of space?

As art, of course, sculpture deals with artistic space. Art and scientific technology regard and work upon space toward diverse ends in diverse ways.

But space – does it remain the same? Is space itself not that space which
received its first determination from Galileo and Newton? Space – is it that
homogeneous expanse, not distinguished at any of its possible places,
equivalent toward each direction, but not perceptible with the senses?

Space – is it that which, since that time (Newton), challenges modern man
increasingly and ever more obstinately to its utter control? Does not modern
graphic art also follow this challenge in so far as it understands itself as dealing
with space? Does it not thereby find itself confirmed in its modern character?

Yet, can the physically-technologically projected space, however it may be
determined henceforth, be held as the sole genuine space? Compared with it,
are all other articulated spaces, artistic space, the space of everyday practice

Heidegger   and commerce, only subjectively conditioned prefigurations and modifications of one objective cosmic space?

But how can this be so, if the objectivity of the objective world-space remains, without question, the correlate of the subjectivity of a consciousness which was foreign to the epochs which preceded modern European times?

Even if we recognize the variety of space experiences of past epochs, would we win already an insight into the special character of space? The question, what space as space would be, is thereby not even asked, much less answered. In what manner space *is*, and whether Being in general can be attributed to it, remains undecided.

Space – does it belong to the primal phenomenon at the awareness of which men are overcome, as Goethe says, by an awe to the point of anxiety? For behind space, so it will appear, nothing more is given to which it could be traced back. Before space there is no retreat to something else. The special character of space must show forth from space itself. Can its special character still be uttered?

The urgency of such questions demands from us a confession: So long as we do not experience the special character of space, talk about artistic space also remains obscure. The way that space reigns throughout the work of art hangs, meantime, in indeterminateness.

The space, within which the sculptured structure can be met as an object present-at-hand; the space, which encloses the volume of the figure; the space, which subsists as the emptiness between volumes – are not these three spaces in the unity of their interplay always merely derivative of one physical-technological space, even if calculative measurement cannot be applied to artistic figures?

Once it is granted that art is the bringing-into-the-work of truth, and truth is the unconcealment of Being, then must not genuine space, namely what uncovers its authentic character, begin to hold sway in the work of graphic art?

Still, how can we find the special character of space? There is an emergency path which, to be sure, is a narrow and precarious one. Let us try to listen to language. Whereof does it speak in the word 'space'? Clearing-away (*Räumen*) is uttered therein. This means: to clear out (*roden*), to free from wilderness. Clearing-away brings forth the free, the openness for man's settling and dwelling. When thought in its own special character, clearing-away is the release of places toward which the fate of dwelling man turns in the preserve of the home or in the brokenness of homelessness or in complete indifference to the two. Clearing-away is release of the places at which a god appears, the places from which the gods have disappeared, the places at which the appearance of the godly tarries long. In each case, clearing-away brings forth locality preparing for dwelling. Secular spaces are always the privation of often very remote sacred spaces.

Clearing-away is release of places.

In clearing-away a happening at once speaks and conceals itself. This character of clearing-away is all too easily overlooked. And when it is seen, it always remains still difficult to determine; above all, so long as physical-technological space is held to be the space in which each spatial character should be oriented from the beginning.

How does clearing-away happen? Is it not making-room (*Einräumen*), and

this again in a twofold manner as granting and arranging? First, making-room   *Heidegger*
admits something. It lets openness hold sway which, among other things, grants
the appearance of things present to which human dwelling sees itself consigned.
On the other hand, making-room prepares for things the possibility to belong
to their relevant whither and, out of this, to each other.

In this twofold making-room, the yielding of places happens. The character
of this happening is such a yielding. Still, what is place, if its special character
must be determined from the guideline of releasing making-room?

Place always opens a region in which it gathers the things in their belonging
together.

Gathering (*Versammeln*) comes to play in the place in the sense of the
releasing sheltering of things in their region. And the region? The older form of
the word runs 'that-which-regions' (*die Gegnet*). It names the free expanse.
Through it the openness is urged to let each thing merge in its resting in itself.
This means at the same time: preserving, i.e. the gathering of things in their
belonging together.

The question comes up: Are places first and only the resultant issue of
making-room? Or does making-room take its special character from the reign
of gathering places? If this proves right, then we would have to search for the
special character of clearing-away in the grounding of locality, and we would
have to meditate on locality as the interplay of places. We would have then to
take heed that and how this play receives its reference to the belonging together
of things from the region's free expanse.

We would have to learn to recognize that things themselves are places and
do not merely belong to a place.

In this case, we would be obliged for a long time to come to accept an
estranging state of affairs:

Place is not located in a pre-given space, after the manner of physical-
technological space. The latter unfolds itself only through the reigning of places
of a region.

The interplay of art and space would have to be thought from out of the
experience of place and region. Art as sculpture: no occupying of space. Sculpture would not deal with space.

Sculpture would be the embodiment of places. Places, in preserving and
opening a region, hold something free gathered around them which grants the
tarrying of things under consideration and a dwelling for man in the midst of
things.

If it stands thus, what becomes of the volume of the sculptured, place
embodying structures? Presumably, volume will no longer demarcate spaces
from one another, in which surfaces surround an inner opposed to an outer.
What is named by the word 'volume', the meaning of which is only as old as
modern technological natural science, would have to lose its name.

The place seeking and place forming characteristics of sculptured embodiment would first remain nameless.

And what would become of the emptiness of space? Often enough it appears
to be a deficiency. Emptiness is held then to be a failure to fill up a cavity or gap.

Yet presumably the emptiness is closely allied to the special character of
place, and therefore no failure, but a bringing-forth. Again, language can give
us a hint. In the verb 'to empty' (*leeren*) the word 'collecting' (*Lesen*), taken in

Heidegger   the original sense of the gathering which reigns in place, is spoken. To empty a
glass means: To gather the glass, as that which can contain something, into its
having been freed.

To empty the collected fruit in a basket means: To prepare for them this
place.

Emptiness is not nothing. It is also no deficiency. In sculptural embodiment,
emptiness plays in the manner of a seeking-projecting instituting of places.

The preceding remarks certainly do not reach so far that they exhibit in
sufficient clarity the special character of sculpture as one of the graphic arts.
Sculpture: an embodying bringing-into-the-work of places, and with them a
disclosing of regions of possible dwellings for man, possible tarrying of things
surrounding and concerning man.

Sculpture: the embodiment of the truth of Being in its work of instituting
places.

Even a cautious insight into the special character of this art causes one to
suspect that truth, as unconcealment of Being, is not necessarily dependent on
embodiment.

Goethe said: 'It is not always necessary for the true to be embodied; it is
enough if it flutters nearby as spirit and generates a sort of concord, like when
the sound of bells floats as a friend in the air and as a bearer of peace.'[1]

NOTE

1   The translation of this quotation has been amended to accord with that given by Gianni
Vattimo in 'Ornament/Monument'.

HANS-GEORG GADAMER

German philosopher, Hans-Georg Gadamer (b. 1900) was a pupil of Martin Heidegger, and his work can be seen as an elaboration of Heidegger's thought. Central to Gadamer's contribution to the world of hermeneutics is the distinction which he draws between 'understanding' and 'explanation'. Against the shortcomings of earlier attempts to address such problems *methodologically*, Gadamer emphasizes how understanding is culturally conditioned and dependent upon an effective historical consciousness. We view texts according to our own cultural horizon. Thus the interpretation of the past becomes a 'fusion of horizons'.

The work of art is a primary concern for Gadamer, as it had been for Heidegger. Truth is to be found in the work of art no less than in scientific reason. The work of art plays a key ontological role in 'representing'. The viewer, meanwhile, needs to engage dynamically with the work of art, while recognizing that almost inevitably the work would have been intended to make a particular statement within a given cultural context. It is precisely this cultural situatedness that distinguishes authentic works of art from mere reproductions.

Gadamer elaborates upon these themes in the extract 'The Ontological Foundation of the Occasional and the Decorative'. Here 'occasionality' refers to the occasion, or situation, out of which works of art emerged. 'Occasionality,' Gadamer observes, 'means that their meaning is partly determined by the occasion for which they are intended.' He therefore draws the distinction between specific portraits and the anonymous use of models in paintings. The portrait is to be understood 'as a portrait', and even if displaced into a modern museum, the 'trace of its original purpose' would not be lost. The work of art goes beyond mere signification. Although not pure symbol, it also has an important symbolic dimension to it, which effectively enriches our understanding of its subject matter.

Architecture, for Gadamer, is of primary significance in that it points beyond itself to the totality of its context. A building has the dual purpose of fulfilling its functional requirements and contributing to its setting. A building would not be a work of art if it stood *anywhere*. Nor can it change its use without losing some of its 'reality'. Architecture, no less than the other arts that it embraced, has an ontological role of 'representing'. Here ornament is crucial, and Gadamer seeks to revise the received views on ornament. Ornament is not to be perceived as something additional or applied. 'Ornament,' Gadamer comments, 'is part of presentation. But presentation is an ontological event; it is representation.'

Obvious comparisons can be made between this extract and those by Heidegger and Vattimo included in this volume. Gadamer's treatment of the monument can also be contrasted with that of Lefebvre and Bataille.

Hans-Georg Gadamer

Gadamer

THE ONTOLOGICAL FOUNDATION OF THE OCCASIONAL AND THE DECORATIVE

If we proceed from the point of view that the work of art cannot be understood in terms of 'aesthetic consciousness', then many phenomena, which have a marginal importance for modern aesthetics, lose what is problematical about them and, indeed, even move into the centre of an 'aesthetic' questioning which is not artificially abbreviated.

I refer to things such as portraits, poems dedicated to someone, or even contemporary references in comedy. The aesthetic concepts of the portrait, the dedicated poem, the contemporary allusion are, of course, themselves cultivated by aesthetic consciousness. What is common to all of these is presented to aesthetic consciousness in the character of occasionality which such art forms possess. Occasionality means that their meaning is partly determined by the occasion for which they are intended, so that it contains more than it would without this occasion.[1] Hence the portrait contains a relation to the man represented, a relation that it does not need to be placed in, but which is expressly intended in the representation itself and is characteristic of it as portrait.

The important thing is that this occasionality is part of what the work is saying and is not something forced on it by its interpreter. This is why such art forms as the portrait, in which so much is obvious, have no real place in an aesthetics based on the concept of experience. A portrait contains, in its own pictorial content, its relation to the original. This does not mean simply that the picture is in fact painted after this original, but that it intends this.

This becomes clear from the way in which it differs from the model which the painter uses for a genre picture or for a figure composition. In the portrait the individuality of the man portrayed is represented. If, however, a picture shows the model as an individuality, as an interesting type whom the painter has got to sit for him, then this is an objection to the picture; for one then no longer sees in the picture what the painter presents, but something of the untransformed material. Hence it destroys the meaning of the picture of a figure if we recognize in it the well-known model of a painter. For a model is a disappearing schema. The relation to the original that served the painter must be extinguished in the picture.

We also call a 'model' that by means of which something else that cannot be seen becomes visible: e.g. the model of a planned house or the model of an atom. The painter's model is not meant as herself. She serves only to wear a costume or to make gestures clear – like a dressed-up doll. Contrariwise, someone represented in the portrait is so much himself that he does not appear to be dressed up, even if the splendid costume he is wearing attracts attention: for splendour of appearance is part of him. He is the person who he is for others.[2] To interpret a work of literature in terms of its biographical or historical sources is sometimes to do no more than the art historian who would look at the works of a painter in terms of his models.

The difference between the model and the portrait shows us what 'occasionality' means here. Occasionality in the sense intended clearly lies in a work's claim to significance, in contradistinction from whatever is observed in it or can be deduced from it that goes against this claim. A portrait desires to be understood as a portrait, even when the relation to the original is practically *Gadamer* crushed by the actual pictorial content of the picture. This is particularly clear in the case of pictures which are not portraits, but which contain, as one says, elements of portraiture. They too cause one to ask after the original that can be seen behind the picture, and therefore they are more than a mere model which is simply a schema that disappears. It is the same with works of literature in which literary protraits may be contained, without their therefore necessarily falling a victim to the pseudo-artistic indiscretion of being a roman à clef.[3]

However fluid and controversial the borderline between the allusion to something specific and the other documentary contents of a work, there is still the basic question whether one accepts the claim to meaning that the work makes, or simply regards it as a historical document that one merely consults. The historian will seek out all the elements that can communicate to him something of the past, even if it counters the work's claim to meaning. He will examine works of art in order to discover the models: that is, the connections with their own age that are woven into them, even if they were not recognized by the contemporary observer, and are not important for the meaning of the whole. This is not occasionality in the present sense, which is that it is part of a work's own claim to meaning to point to a particular original. It is not, then, left to the observer's whim to decide whether a work has such occasional elements or not. A portrait really is a portrait, and does not just become it through and for those who see in it the person portrayed. Although the relation to the original resides in the work itself, it is still right to call it 'occasional'. For the portrait does not say who the man portrayed is, but only that it is a particular individual (and not a type). We can only 'recognize' who it is if the man portrayed is known to us, and only be sure if there is a title or some other information to go on. At any rate there resides in the picture an unredeemed but fundamentally redeemable pledge of its meaning. This occasionality is part of the essential import of the 'picture', quite apart from whether or not it is known to the observer.

We can see this in the fact that a portrait also appears as a portrait (and the representation of a particular person in a picture appears portrait-like) even if one does not know the sitter. There is then something in the picture that is not fully realized by the viewer, namely that which is occasional about it. But what is not fully realized is not therefore not there; it is there in a quite unambiguous way. The same thing is true of many poetic phenomena. Pindar's poems of victory, a comedy that is critical of its age, but also such literary phenomena as the odes and satires of Horace are entirely occasional in nature. The occasional in such works has acquired so permanent a form that, even without being realized or understood, it is still part of the total meaning. Someone might explain to us the particular historical context, but this would be only secondary for the poem as a whole. He would be only filling out the meaning that exists in the poem itself.

It is important to recognize that what I call occasionality here is in no way a diminution of the artistic claim and meaning of such works. For that which presents itself to aesthetic subjectivity as 'the irruption of time into play',[4] and appeared in the age of experiential art as a lessening of the aesthetic meaning of a work, is in fact only the subjective aspect of that ontological relationship that has been developed above. A work of art belongs so closely to that to which it

Gadamer   is related that it enriches its being as if through a new event of being. To be
fixed in a picture, addressed in a poem, to be the object of an allusion from the
stage, are not incidental things remote from the essential nature, but they are
presentations of this nature itself. What was said in general about the ontological status of the picture includes these occasional elements. The element of
occasionality which we find in those things presents itself as the particular case
of a general relationship appropriate to the being of the work of art: namely, to
experience from the 'occasion' of its coming-to-presentation a continued determination of its significance.

This is seen most clearly in the interpretative arts, especially in drama and
music, which wait for the occasion in order to exist and find their form only
through that occasion. Hence the stage is a political institution because only the
performance brings out everything that is in the play, its allusions and its
echoes. No one knows beforehand what will come across and what will have
no resonance. Every performance is an event, but not one that would in any
way be separate from the work – the work itself is what 'takes place' in the
performative event. It is its nature to be occasional in such a way that the
occasion of the performance makes it speak and brings out what is in it. The
producer who stages the play shows his ability in being able to make use of the
occasion. But he acts according to the directions of the writer, whose whole
work is a stage direction. This is quite clearly the case with a musical work – the
score is really only a direction. Aesthetic differentiation may judge what the
music would be like in performance by the inner structure of sound read in the
score, but no one doubts that listening to music is not reading.

It is thus of the nature of dramatic or musical works that their performance
at different times and on different occasions is, and must be, different. Now it is
important to see that, *mutatis mutandis*, this is also true of the plastic arts. But
in the latter it is not the case either that the work exists *an sich* and only the
effect varies: it is the work of art itself that displays itself under different
conditions. The viewer of today not only sees in a different way, but he sees
different things. We only have to think of the way that the idea of the pale
marble of antiquity has ruled our taste, of our attitude to preservation, since the
Renaissance, or of the reflection of classicist feeling in the romantic north as
found in the purist spirituality of gothic cathedrals.

But specifically occasional art forms, such as the parabasis in classical
comedy or the caricature in politics, which are intended for a quite specific
occasion, and finally the portrait itself, are forms of the universal occasionality
characteristic of the work of art inasmuch as it determines itself anew from
occasion to occasion. Likewise, the unique determinateness through which an
element, occasional in this narrower sense, is fulfilled in the work of art, gains,
in the being of the work, a universality that renders it capable of yet further
fulfilment. The uniqueness of its relation to the occasion can never be fully
realized and it is this now unrealizable relation that remains present and
effective in the work itself. In this sense the portrait too is independent of the
uniqueness of its relation to the original, and contains the latter even in transcending it.

The portrait is only an intensified form of the general nature of a picture.
Every picture is an increase of being and is essentially determined as representation, as coming-to-presentation. In the special case of the portrait this

representation acquires a personal significance, in that here an individual is presented in a representative way. For this means that the man represented represents himself in his portrait and is represented by his portrait. The picture is not only a picture and certainly not only a copy, it belongs to the present or to the present memory of the man represented. This is its real nature. To this extent the portrait is a special case of the general ontological value assigned to the picture as such. What comes into being in it is not already contained in what his acquaintances see in the sitter. The best judges of a portrait are never the nearest relatives nor even the sitter himself. For a portrait never tries to reproduce the individual it represents as he appears in the eyes of the people near him. Of necessity, what it shows is an idealization, which can run through an infinite number of stages from the representative to the most intimate. This kind of idealization does not alter the fact that in a portrait an individual is represented, and not a type, however much the portrayed individual may be transformed in the portrait from the incidental and the private into the essential quality of his true appearance.

Religious or secular monuments display the universal ontological value of a picture more clearly than the intimate portrait does. For it is on this that their public function depends. A monument holds what is represented in it in a specific state of presentness which is obviously something quite different from that of the aesthetic consciousness.[5] It does not live only from the autonomous expressive power of a picture. This is clear from the fact that things other than works of art, e.g. symbols or inscriptions, can have the same function. The familiarity of that of which the monument should remind us, is always assumed: its potential presence, as it were. The figure of a god, the picture of a king, the memorial put up to someone, assume that the god, the king, the hero, the event, the victory, or the peace treaty already possess a presence affecting everyone. The statue that represents them thus adds nothing other than, say, an inscription: it holds it present in this general meaning. Nevertheless, if it is a work of art, this means not only that it adds something to this given meaning, but also that it can say something of its own, and thus becomes independent of the anterior knowledge of which it is the bearer.

What a picture is remains, despite all aesthetic differentiation, a manifestation of what it represents, even if it makes it manifest through its autonomous expressive power. This is obvious in the case of the religious picture; but the difference between the sacred and the secular is relative in a work of art. Even an individual portrait, if it is a work of art, shares in the mysterious radiation of being that flows from the level of being of that which is represented.

We may illustrate this by an example: Justi[6] once described Velasquez's *The Surrender of Breda* as a 'military sacrament'. He meant that the picture was not a group portrait, nor simply a historical picture. What is caught in this picture is not just a solemn event as such. The solemnity of this ceremony is present in the picture in this way because the ceremony itself has a pictorial quality and is performed like a sacrament. There are things that need to be, and are suitable for being, depicted; they are, as it were, perfected in their being only when represented in a picture. It is not accidental that religious terms seem appropriate when one is defending the particular level of being of works of fine art against an aesthetic levelling out.

It is consistent with the present viewpoint that the difference between profane (secular) and sacred should be only relative. We need only recall the meaning and the history of the word 'profane': the 'profane' is the place in the front of the sanctuary. The concept of the profane and of its derivative, profanation, always presuppose the sacred. Actually, the difference between profane and sacred could only be relative in classical antiquity from which it stems, since the whole sphere of life was sacrally ordered and determined. Only Christianity enables us to understand profaneness in a stricter sense. The New Testament de-demonized the world to such an extent that room was made for an absolute contrast between the profane and the religious. The Church's promise of salvation means that the world is still only 'this world'. The special nature of this claim of the Church also creates the tension between it and the State, which comes with the end of the classical world, and thus the concept of the profane acquires its own topicality. The entire history of the Middle Ages is dominated by the tension between Church and State. It is the spiritualistic deepening of the idea of the Christian Church that ultimately makes the secular State possible. The historical significance of the high Middle Ages is that it created the secular world, and gave its wide modern meaning to the notion of the 'profane'.[7] But that does not alter the fact that the profane has remained a concept related to the area of the sacred and determined by it alone. There is no such thing as profaneness by itself.[8]

The relativity of profane and sacred is not only part of the dialectic of concepts, but can be seen as a reality in the phenomenon of the picture. A work of art always has something sacred about it. True, a religious work of art or a monument on show in a museum can no longer be desecrated in the same sense as one that has remained in its original place. But this means only that it has in fact already suffered an injury, in that it has become an object in a museum. Obviously this is true not only of religious works of art. We sometimes have the same feeling in an antique shop when the old pieces on sale still have some trace of intimate life about them; it seems somehow scandalous to us, a kind of offence to piety, a profanation. Ultimately every work of art has something about it that protests against profanation.

This seems decisively proved by the fact that even pure aesthetic consciousness is familiar with the idea of profanation. It always experiences the destruction of works of art as a sacrilege.[9]

This is a characteristic feature of the modern aesthetic religion of culture, for which there is plenty of evidence. For example, the word 'vandalism', which goes back to mediaeval times, only became popular in the reaction against the destructiveness of the Jacobins in the French Revolution. To destroy works of art is to break into a world protected by its holiness. Even an 'autonomous' aesthetic consciousness cannot deny that art is more than it would admit to.

All these considerations justify a characterization of the mode of being of art in general in terms of presentation; this includes play and picture, communion and representation. The work of art is conceived as an ontological event and the abstraction to which aesthetic differentiation commits it is dissolved. A picture is an event of presentation. Its relation to the original is so far from being a reduction of the autonomy of its being that, on the contrary, I had to speak, in regard to the picture, of an 'increase of being'. The use of concepts from the sphere of the holy seemed appropriate.

Now it is important not to confuse the special sense of representation proper

to the work of art with the sacred representation performed by, say, the symbol. *Gadamer*
Not all forms of representation have the character of 'art'. Symbols and badges
are also forms of representation. They too indicate something, and this makes
them representations.

In the logical analysis of the nature of expression and meaning carried out in
this century, the structure of indicating, common to all these forms of representation, has been investigated in great detail.[10] I mention this work here for
another purpose. We are not concerned primarily with the problem of meaning,
but with the nature of a picture. We want to grasp its nature without being
confused by the abstraction performed by aesthetic consciousness. It behoves
us to examine the nature of indicating, in order to discover both similarities and
differences.

The essence of the picture stands, as it were, midway between two extremes:
these extremes of representation are pure indication (the essence of the sign),
and pure representation (the essence of the symbol). There is something of both
in a picture. Its representing includes the element of indicating what is represented in it. We saw that this emerges most clearly in specific forms such as the
portrait, for which the relation to the original is essential. At the same time a
picture is not a sign. For a sign is nothing but what its function demands; and
that is, to point away from itself. In order to be able to fulfil this function, of
course, it must first draw attention to itself. It must be striking: that is, it must
be clearly defined and present itself as an indicator, like a poster. But neither a
sign nor a poster is a picture. It should not attract attention to itself in a way
that would cause one to linger over it, for it is there only to make present something that is not present, and in such a way that the thing that is not present is
the only thing that is expressed.[11] It should not captivate by its own intrinsic
pictorial interest. The same is true of all signs: for instance, traffic signs, book-
markers, and the like. There is something schematic and abstract about them,
because they point not to themselves, but to what is not present, e.g. to the
curve ahead or to one's page. (Even natural signs, e.g. indications of the
weather, have their indicative function only through abstraction. If we look at
the sky and are filled with the beauty of what we see there and linger over it, we
experience a shift in the direction of our attention that causes its sign character
to retreat into the background.)

Of all signs, the memento seems to have most reality of its own. It refers to
the past and so is effectively a sign, but it is also precious in itself since, being an
element of the past that has not disappeared, it keeps the past present for us.
But it is clear that this characteristic is not grounded in the specific being of the
object. A memento only has value as a memento for someone who already – i.e.
still – recalls the past. Mementos lose their value when the past of which they
remind one no longer has any meaning. Furthermore, someone who not only
uses mementos to remind him, but makes a cult of them and lives in the past as
if it were the present, has a disturbed relation to reality.

Hence a picture is certainly not a sign. Even a memento does not cause us to
linger over it, but over the past that it represents for us. But a picture fulfils its
function of pointing to what it represents only through its own import. By
concentrating on it, we also put ourselves in contact with what is represented.
The picture points by causing us to linger over it. For its being is, as I pointed
out, that it is not absolutely different from what it represents, but shares in the

Gadamer   being of that. We say that what is represented comes to itself in the picture. It experiences an increase in being. But that means that it is there in the picture itself. It is merely an aesthetic reflection – I called it 'aesthetic differentiation' – that abstracts from this presence of the original in the picture.

The difference between a picture and a sign has an ontological basis. The picture does not disappear behind its pointing function but, in its own being, shares in what it represents.

This ontological sharing is part of the nature, not only of a picture, but of what we call a 'symbol'. Neither symbol nor picture indicate anything that is not at the same time present in themselves. Hence the problem arises of differentiating between the mode of being of a picture and the mode of being of a symbol.[12]

There is an obvious distinction between a symbol and a sign, in that the former is more like a picture. The representational function of a symbol is not merely to point to something that is not present. Instead, a symbol manifests as present something that really is present. This is seen in the original meaning of 'symbol'. When a symbol is used for a sign of recognition between separated friends or the scattered members of a religious community to show that they belong together, such a symbol undoubtedly functions as a sign. But it is more than a sign. It not only points to the fact that people belong together, but proves and visibly presents that fact. The *tessera hospitalis* is a relic of past living and proves through its existence what it indicates: it makes the past itself present again and causes it to be recognized as valid. It is especially true of religious symbols not only that they function as distinguishing marks, but that it is the meaning of these symbols that is understood by everyone, unites everyone and can therefore assume a sign function. Hence what is to be symbolized is undoubtedly in need of representation, inasmuch as it is itself non-sensible, infinite and unrepresentable, but it is also capable of it. It is only because it is present itself that it can be present in the symbol.

A symbol not only points to something, but it represents, in that it takes the place of something. But to take the place of something means to make something present that is not present. Thus the symbol takes the place of something in representing: that is, it makes something immediately present. Only because the symbol presents in this way the presence of what it represents, is it treated with the reverence due to that which it symbolizes. Such symbols as a crucifix, a flag, a uniform are so representative of what is revered that the latter is present in them.

That the concept of representation that was used above in describing the picture essentially belongs here is shown by the closeness between representation in the picture and the representative function of the symbol. In both cases, what they represent is itself present. At the same time a picture as such is not a symbol; symbols do not need to be pictorial. They perform their representative function through their mere existence and manifesting of themselves, but of themselves they say nothing about what they symbolize. They must be known, in the way that one must know a sign, if one is to understand what they indicate. Hence they do not mean an increase of being for what is represented. It is true that it is part of the being of what is represented to make itself present in symbols in this way. But its own being is not determined in its nature by the fact that the symbols are there and are shown. It is not there any more fully when they are there. They are merely representatives. Hence their own significance is of no importance, even if they have any. They are representatives and receive their representative function of being from what they are supposed to represent. The picture also represents, but through itself, through the extra significance that it brings. But that means that in it what is represented – the 'original' – is more fully there, more properly just as it truly is.

Hence a picture is equipoised halfway between a sign and a symbol. Its representative function is neither a pure pointing-to-something, nor a pure taking-the-place-of-something. It is this intermediate position which raises it to its own unique level of being. Artificial signs and symbols alike do not – like the picture – acquire their functional significance from their own content, but must be taken as signs or as symbols. We call this origin of their functional significance their 'institution'. It is decisive in determining the ontological quality of a picture (which is what we are concerned with), that in regard to a picture there is no such thing as an 'institution' in the same sense.

By 'institution' is meant the origin of the sign or of the symbolic function. The so-called 'natural' signs also, e.g. all the indications and presages of an event in nature are, in this fundamental sense, instituted. That means that they only have a sign function when they are taken as a sign. But they are only taken as a sign on the basis of a previous relationship between the sign and what is signified. This is true also of all artificial signs. Here the establishment of the sign is agreed by convention, and the originating act by which it is arrived at called 'institution'. On the institution of the sign depends primarily its indicative significance; for example, that of the traffic sign on the decision of the Ministry of Transport, that of the souvenir on the meaning given to its preservation, etc. Equally the symbol has to be instituted, for only this gives it its representative character. For it is not its own ontological content which gives it its significance, but an institution, a constitution, a consecration that gives significance to what is, in itself, without significance: for example, the sign of sovereignty, the flag, the crucifix.

It is important to see that a work of art, on the other hand, does not owe its real meaning to an institution of this kind, even if it is a religious picture or a secular memorial. The public act of consecration or unveiling which assigns to it its purpose does not give it its significance. Rather, it is already a structure with a signifying-function of its own, as a pictorial or non-pictorial representation, before it is assigned its function as a memorial. The setting-up and consecration of a memorial – and it is not by accident that we talk of religious and secular works of architecture as of architectural monuments, when historical distance has consecrated them – therefore only realizes a function that is already implied in the proper import of the work itself.

This is the reason why works of art can assume definite real functions and resist others: for instance, religious or secular public or private ones. They are instituted and set up as memorials of reverence, honour or piety, only because they themselves prescribe and help to fashion this kind of functional context. They themselves lay claim to their place, and even if they are displaced, e.g. are housed in a modern collection, the trace of their original purpose cannot be destroyed. It is part of their being because their being is representation.

If one considers the exemplary significance of these particular forms, one sees that forms of art which, from the point of view of the art of experience

(*Erlebniskunst*), are peripheral, become central: namely, all those whose proper import points beyond them into the totality of a context determined by them and for them. The greatest and most distinguished of these forms is architecture.

A work of architecture extends beyond itself in two ways. It is as much determined by the aim which it is to serve as by the place that it is to take up in a total spatial context. Every architect has to consider both these things. His plan is influenced by the fact that the building has to serve a particular living purpose and must be adapted to particular architectural circumstances. Hence we call a successful building a 'happy solution', and mean by this both that it perfectly fulfils its purpose and that its construction has added something new to the spatial dimensions of a town or a landscape. Through this dual ordering the building presents a true increase of being: it is a work of art.

It is not a work of art if it simply stands anywhere, as a building that is a blot on the landscape, but only if it represents the solution of a building problem. Aesthetics acknowledges only those works of art which are in some way memorable and calls these 'architectural monuments'. If a building is a work of art, then it is not only the artistic solution of a building problem posed by the contexts of purpose and of life to which it originally belongs, but somehow preserves these, so that it is visibly present even though the present manifestation of the original purposes is strange. Something in it points back to the original. Where the original intention has become completely unrecognizable or its unity destroyed by too many subsequent alterations, then the building itself will become incomprehensible. Thus architecture, this most 'statuary' of all art forms, shows how secondary 'aesthetic differentiation' is. A building is never primarily a work of art. Its purpose, through which it belongs in the context of life, cannot be separated from itself without its losing some of its reality. If it has become merely an object of the aesthetic consciousness, then it has merely a shadowy reality and lives a distorted life only in the degenerate form of an object of interest to tourists, or a subject for photography. The work of art in itself proves to be a pure abstraction.

In fact the presence of the great architectural monuments of the past in the modern world and its buildings poses the task of the integration of past and present. Works of architecture do not stand motionless on the shore of the stream of history, but are borne along by it. Even if historically minded ages seek to reconstruct the architecture of an earlier age, they cannot try to turn back the wheel of history, but must mediate in a new and better way between the past and the present. Even the restorer or the preserver of ancient monuments remains an artist of his time. The especial importance that architecture has for our enquiry is that in it too that element of mediation can be seen without which a work of art has no real 'presentness'. Thus even where representation does not take place through reproduction (which everyone knows belongs to its own present time), past and present are brought together in a work of art. That every work of art has its own world does not mean that when its original world is altered it has its reality in an alienated aesthetic consciousness. Architecture is an example of this, for its connections with the world are irredeemably part of it.

But this involves a further point. Architecture gives shape to space. Space is what surrounds everything that exists in space. That is why architecture embraces all the other forms of representation: all works of plastic art, all ornament. Moreover, to the representational arts of poetry, music, acting and dancing it gives their place. By embracing all the arts, it everywhere asserts its own perspective. That perspective is: decoration. Architecture preserves it even against those forms of art whose works are not decorative, but are gathered within themselves through the closedness of their circle of meaning. Modern research has begun to recall that this is true of all works of plastic art whose place was assigned them when they were commissioned. Even the free-standing statue on a pedestal is not really removed from the decorative context, but serves the representative heightening of a context of life in which it finds an ornamental place.[13] Even poetry and music, which have the freest mobility and can be read or performed anywhere, are not suited to any space whatever, but to one that is appropriate, a theatre, a concert-hall or a church. Here also it is not a question of subsequently finding an external setting for a work that is complete in itself, but the space-creating potentiality of the work itself has to be obeyed, which itself has to adapt as much to what is given as make its own conditions. (Think only of the problem of acoustics, which is not only technical, but architectural.)

Hence the comprehensive situation of architecture in relation to all the arts involves a twofold mediation. As the art which creates space it both shapes it and leaves it free. It not only embraces all the decorative aspects of the shaping of space, including ornament, but is itself decorative in nature. The nature of decoration consists in performing that two-sided mediation; namely to draw the attention of the viewer to itself, to satisfy his taste, and then to redirect it away from itself to the greater whole of the context of life which it accompanies.

This is true of the whole span of the decorative, from municipal architecture to the individual ornament. A building should certainly be the solution of an artistic problem and thus draw to itself the wonder and admiration of the viewer. At the same time it should fit into a living unity and not be an end in itself. It seeks to fit into this unity by providing ornament, a background of mood, or a framework. The same is true for each individual piece of work that the architect carries out, including ornament which should not draw attention to itself, but fulfil its accompanying decorative function. But even the extreme case of ornament still has something of the duality of decorative mediation about it. Certainly, it should not invite the attention to linger and be itself noticed as a decorative motif, but have merely an accompanying effect. Thus in general it will not have any objective content or will so iron it out through stylization or repetition that one's eye glides across it. It is not intended that the forms of nature used in an ornament should be recognized. If a repetitive pattern is seen as what it actually is, then its repetition becomes unbearably monotonous. But on the other hand, it should not have a dead or monotonous effect, for as an accompaniment it should have an enlivening effect and in this way must, to some extent, draw attention to itself.

On looking at the full extent of decorative tasks given to the architect, it is clear that it is the downfall of that prejudice of the aesthetic consciousness according to which the actual work of art is what is, outside all space and all time, the object of an aesthetic experience. One also sees that the usual distinction between a proper work of art and mere decoration demands revision.

Gadamer   The concept of the decorative is here obviously conceived as an antithesis to a 'real work of art' from its origin in 'the inspiration of genius'. The argument was more or less that what is only decorative is not the art of genius, but mere craftsmanship. It is only a means, subordinated to what it is supposed to decorate, and can therefore be replaced, like any other means subordinated to an end, by another appropriate means. It has no share in the uniqueness of the work of art.

In fact the concept of decoration must be freed from this antithetical relationship to the concept of the art of experience and be grounded in the ontological structure of representation, which we have seen as the mode of being of the work of art. We have only to remember that, in their original meaning, the ornamental and the decorative were the beautiful as such. It is necessary to recover this ancient insight. Ornament or decoration is determined by its relation to what it decorates, by what carries it. It does not possess an aesthetic import of its own which only afterwards acquires a limiting condition by its relation to what it is decorating. Even Kant, who endorsed this opinion, admits in his famous judgment on tattooing that ornament is ornament only when it suits the wearer.[14] It is part of taste not only to find something beautiful in itself, but also to know where it belongs and where not. Ornament is not primarily something by itself that is then applied to something else but belongs to the self-presentation of its wearer. Ornament is part of the presentation. But presentation is an ontological event; it is representation. An ornament, a decoration, a piece of sculpture set up in a chosen place are representative in the same sense that, say, the church in which they are to be found is itself representative.

Hence the concept of the decorative serves to complete our enquiry into the mode of being of the aesthetic . . . What we mean by representation is, at any rate, a universal ontological structural element of the aesthetic, an ontological event and not an experiential event which occurs at the moment of artistic creation and is only repeated each time in the mind of the viewer. Starting from the universal significance of play, we saw the ontological significance of representation in the fact that 'reproduction' is the original mode of being of the original art. Now we have confirmed that painting and the plastic arts in general are, ontologically speaking, of the same mode of being. The specific mode of the work of art's presence is the coming into representation of being.

NOTES

All notes for this article have been reproduced verbatim.

1   This is the sense of occasionality that has become customary in modern logic. A good example of the discrediting of occasionality by the aesthetics of experience is the mutilation of Hölderlin's *Rheinhymne* in the edition of 1826. The dedication to Sinclair seemed so alien that the last two stanzas were omitted and the whole described as a fragment.

2   Plato speaks of the proximity of the seemly (*prepon*) and the beautiful (*kalon*) Hipp. maj. 293e.

3   J. Burn's valuable book *Das literarische Porträt bei den Griechen* suffers from a lack of clarity on this point.

4   Cf Appendix II, p. 453, *Truth and Method*.

5   Cf p. 76, *Truth and Method*.

6   Karl Justi, *Diego Velasquez und sein Jahrhundert*, I, 1888, p. 366.

7   Cf Friedrich Heer, *Der Aufgang Europas*.

8   W. Kamlah in *Der Mensch in der Profanität* (1948) has tried to give the concept of the profane

this meaning to characterize the nature of modern science, but also sees this concept as *Gadamer* determined by its counter-concept, the 'acceptance of the beautiful'.

9 Translator's footnote: The German word *Frevel* is today rarely used except in the phrase *Kunst-Frevel*. *Frevel* = sacrilege, outrage; *Kunst* = art.

10 Above all in the first of E. Husserl's *Logische Untersuchungen*, in Dilthey's studies on the *Aufbau der geschichtlichen Welt* (Dilthey, VII) which are influenced by Husserl, and in M. Heidegger's analysis of the 'worldhood' of the world in *Being and Time*, sections 17 and 18.

11 I said above that the concept of a picture used here finds its historical fulfilment in the modern framed picture (p. 119, *Truth and Method*). Nevertheless, its 'transcendental' application seems legitimate. If, for historical purposes, mediaeval representations have been distinguished from the later 'picture' by being called *Bildzeichen* ('picture signs', D. Frey), much that is said in the text of the 'sign' is true of such representations, but still the difference between them and the sign is obvious. Picture signs are not a kind of sign, but a kind of picture.

12 Cf pp. 64–73, *Truth and Method*. The distinction, in terms of the history of the two ideas, between 'symbol' and 'allegory'.

13 Schleiermacher rightly stresses (as against Kant, *Ästhetik*, p. 201) that the art of gardening is not part of painting, but of architecture.

14 Kant, *Kritik der Urteilskraft*, 1799, p. 50, Meredith p. 73.

HENRI LEFEBVRE

*Henri
Lefebvre* French philosopher and social theorist Henri Lefebvre (1901–91) was a deeply political figure. A committed Marxist and leading intellectual within the French Communist Party, he perceived philosophy not as some isolated and specialized discipline, but as an activity that should be closely related to political practice. Although he became estranged from the French Communist Party in 1958, as it continued to support Stalinist beliefs, he remained committed to the revolutionary cause. Indeed he is regarded as one of the influential figures behind the events of May 1968, and the highly popular lectures which he gave as a professor of sociology at Nanterre are often viewed as one of the factors that helped to ignite the subsequent student uprisings.

Lefebvre set his philosophy in opposition to many of the dominant trends. Yet, although critical of structuralism, positivism, critical theory and certain strands of existentialist thought, he successfully appropriated elements of each along with aspects of psychoanalysis into his own philosophy, such that it is difficult to locate him within any particular category. Comparisons may be drawn with Situationist thought. Lefebvre developed, for example, the concept of the 'moment', a fleeting, intensely euphoric sensation which appeared as a point of rupture which revealed the totality of possibilities of daily existence. This was not dissimilar to the 'situation' in Situationist thought, although the Situationists criticized Lefebvre's 'moment' as being passive and temporal, in comparison with their active, spatio-temporal 'situation'.

Lefebvre's philosophy was one of lived experience, and his preoccupation with the urban environment as the location of this experience was a logical consequence of his concerns. In *The Production of Space* Lefebvre calls for a critique of space. He notes how the privileging of the image has led to a impoverished understanding of space, turning social space into a fetishised abstraction. The image 'kills' and cannot account for the richness of lived experience. Architects, in Lefebvre's eyes, are complicit within the whole alienating nature of contemporary existence. Not only are architects dominated by the dictates of bourgeois capitalism, but with their abstracted methods of representation they have reduced the world to a domain of blue-prints. Lefebvre calls instead for a restoration of concern for the body. Space should be experienced through all the senses. Nor can it be captured by the 'codifying approach of semiology'. 'What we are concerned with here,' Lefebvre observes, 'is not texts but texture.'

THE PRODUCTION OF SPACE (EXTRACTS) *Lefebvre*

THE MONUMENT

For millennia, *monumentality* took in all the following aspects of *spatiality* . . . : the perceived, the conceived and the lived; representations of space and representational spaces; the spaces proper to each faculty, from the sense of smell to speech; the gestural and the symbolic. Monumental space offered each member of a society an image of that membership, an image of his or her social visage. It thus constituted a collective mirror more faithful than any personal one. Such a 'recognition effect' has far greater import than the 'mirror effect' of the psychoanalysts. Of this social space, which embraced all the above-mentioned aspects while still according each its proper place, everyone partook, and partook fully – albeit, naturally, under the conditions of a generally accepted Power and a generally accepted Wisdom. The monument thus effected a 'consensus', and this in the strongest sense of the term, rendering it practical and concrete. The element of repression in it and the element of exaltation could scarcely be disentangled; or perhaps it would be more accurate to say that the repressive element was metamorphosed into exaltation. The codifying approach of semiology, which seeks to classify representations, impressions and evocations (as terms in the code of knowledge, the code of personal feelings, the symbolic code, or the hermeneutic code),[1] is quite unable to cover all facets of the monumental. Indeed, it does not even come close, for it is the residual, the irreducible – whatever cannot be classified or codified according to categories devised subsequent to production – which is, here as always, the most precious and the most essential, the diamond at the bottom of the melting-pot. The use of the cathedral's monumental space necessarily entails its supplying answers to all the questions that assail anyone who crosses the threshold. For visitors are bound to become aware of their own footsteps, and listen to the noises, the singing; they must breathe the incense-laden air, and plunge into a particular world, that of sin and redemption; they will partake of an ideology; they will contemplate and decipher the symbols around them; and they will thus, on the basis of their own bodies, experience a total being in a total space. Small wonder that from time immemorial conquerors and revolutionaries eager to destroy a society should so often have sought to do so by burning or razing that society's monuments. Sometimes, it is true, they contrive to redirect them to their own advantage. Here too, use goes further and deeper than the codes of exchange.

The most beautiful monuments are imposing in their durability. A cyclopean wall achieves monumental beauty because it seems eternal, because it seems to have escaped time. Monumentality transcends death, and hence also what is sometimes called the 'death instinct'. As both appearance and reality, this transcendence embeds itself in the monument as its irreducible foundation; the lineaments of atemporality overwhelm anxiety, even – and indeed above all – in funerary monuments. A *ne plus ultra* of art – form so thoroughly denying meaning that death itself is submerged. The Empress's Tomb in the Taj Mahal bathes in an atmosphere of gracefulness, whiteness and floral motifs. Every bit as much as a poem or a tragedy, a monument transmutes the fear of the passage of time, and anxiety about death, into splendour.

Monumental 'durability' is unable, however, to achieve a complete illusion. To put it in what pass for modern terms, its credibility is never total. It replaces a brutal reality with a materially realized appearance; reality is changed into appearance. What, after all, is the durable aside from the will to endure? Monumental imperishability bears the stamp of the will to power. Only Will, in its more elaborated forms – the wish for mastery, the will to will – can overcome, or believe it can overcome, death. Knowledge itself fails here, shrinking from the abyss. Only through the monument, through the intervention of the architect as demiurge, can the space of death be negated, transfigured into a living space which is an extension of the body; this is a transformation, however, which serves what religion, (political) power and knowledge have in common.

In order to define monumental space properly,[2] semiological categorization (codifying) and symbolic explanations must be restrained. But 'restrained' should not be taken to mean refused or rejected. I am not saying that the monument is not the outcome of a signifying practice, or of a particular way of proposing a meaning, but merely that it can be reduced neither to a language or discourse nor to the categories and concepts developed for the study of language. A spatial work (monument or architectural project) attains a complexity fundamentally different from the complexity of a text, whether prose or poetry. As I pointed out earlier, what we are concerned with here is not texts but texture. We already know that a texture is made up of a usually rather large space covered by networks or webs; monuments constitute the strong points, nexuses or anchors of such webs. The actions of social practice are expressible but not explicable through discourse: they are, precisely, *acted* – and not *read*. A monumental work, like a musical one, does not have a 'signified' (or 'signifieds'); rather, it has a *horizon of meaning*: a specific or indefinite multiplicity of meanings, a shifting hierarchy in which now one, now another meaning comes momentarily to the fore, by means of – and for the sake of – a particular action. The social and political operation of a monumental work traverses the various 'systems' and 'subsystems', or codes and subcodes, which constitute and found the society concerned. But it also surpasses such codes and subcodes, and implies a 'supercoding', in that it tends towards the all-embracing presence of the totality. To the degree that there are traces of violence and death, negativity and aggressiveness in social practice, the monumental work erases them and replaces them with a tranquil power and certitude which can encompass violence and terror. Thus the mortal 'moment' (or component) of the sign is temporarily abolished in monumental space. In and through the work in space, social practice transcends the limitations by which other 'signifying practices', and hence the other arts, including those texts known as 'literary', are bound; in this way a consensus, a profound agreement, is achieved. A Greek theatre presupposes tragedy and comedy, and by extension the presence of the city's people and their allegiance to their heroes and gods. In theatrical space, music, choruses, masks, tiering – all such elements converge with language and actors. A spatial action overcomes conflicts, at least momentarily, even though it does not resolve them; it opens a way from everyday concerns to collective joy.

Turmoil is inevitable once a monument loses its prestige, or can only retain it by means of admitted oppression and repression. When the subject – a city or a people – suffers dispersal, the *building* and its functions come into their own; by the same token, *housing* comes to prevail over *residence* within that city or amidst that people. The building has its roots in warehouses, barracks, depots and rental housing. Buildings have functions, forms and structures, but they do not integrate the formal, functional and structural 'moments' of social practice. And, inasmuch as sites, forms and functions are no longer focused and appropriated by monuments, the city's contexture or fabric – its streets, its underground levels, its frontiers – unravel, and generate not concord but violence. Indeed space as a whole becomes prone to sudden eruptions of violence.

The balance of forces between monuments and buildings has shifted. Buildings are to monuments as everyday life is to festival, products to works, lived experience to the merely perceived, concrete to stone, and so on. What we are seeing here is a new dialectical process, but one just as vast as its predecessors. How could the contradiction between building and monument be overcome and surpassed? How might that tendency be accelerated which has destroyed monumentality but which could well reinstitute it, within the sphere of buildings itself, by restoring the old unity at a higher level? So long as no such dialectical transcendence occurs, we can only expect the stagnation of crude interactions and intermixtures between 'moments' – in short, a continuing spatial chaos. Under this dispensation, buildings and dwelling-places have been dressed up in monumental *signs*: first their facades, and later their interiors. The homes of the moneyed classes have undergone a superficial 'socialization' with the introduction of reception areas, bars, nooks and furniture (divans, for instance) which bespeak some kind of erotic life. Pale echoes, in short, of the aristocratic palace or town house. The town, meanwhile, now effectively blown apart, has been 'privatized' no less superficially – thanks to urban 'decor' and 'design', and the development of fake environments. Instead, then, of a dialectical process with three stages which resolves a contradiction and 'creatively' transcends a conflictual situation, we have a stagnant opposition whose poles at first confront one another 'face to face', then relapse into muddle and confusion.

There is still a good deal to be said about the notion of the monument. It is especially worth emphasizing what a monument is *not,* because this will help avoid a number of misconceptions. Monuments should not be looked upon as collections of symbols (even though every monument embodies symbols – sometimes archaic and incomprehensible ones), nor as chains of signs (even though every monumental whole is made up of signs). A monument is neither an object nor an aggregation of diverse objects, even though its 'objectality', its position as a social object, is recalled at every moment, perhaps by the brutality of the materials or masses involved, perhaps, on the contrary, by their gentle qualities. It is neither a sculpture, nor a figure, nor simply the result of material procedures. The indispensable opposition between inside and outside, as indicated by thresholds, doors and frames, though often underestimated, simply does not suffice when it comes to defining monumental space. Such a space is determined by what may take place there, and consequently by what may not take place there (prescribed/proscribed, scene/obscene). What appears empty may turn out to be full – as is the case with sanctuaries, or with the 'ships' or

Lefebvre   naves of cathedrals. Alternatively, full space may be inverted over an almost heterotopic void at the same location (for instance, vaults, cupolas). The Taj Mahal, for instance, makes much play with the fullness of swelling curves suspended in a dramatic emptiness. Acoustic, gestural and ritual movements, elements grouped into vast ceremonial unities, breaches opening onto limitless perspectives, chains of meanings – all are organized into a monumental whole.

The affective level – which is to say, the level of the body, bound to symmetries and rhythms – is transformed into a 'property' of monumental space, into symbols which are generally intrinsic parts of a politico-religious whole, into co-ordinated symbols. The component elements of such wholes are disposed according to a strict order for the purposes of the use of space: some at a first level, the level of affective, bodily, lived experience, the level of the spoken word; some at a second level, that of the perceived, of socio-political signification; and some at a third level, the level of the conceived, where the dissemination of the written word and of knowledge welds the members of society into a 'consensus', and in doing so confers upon them the status of 'subjects'. Monumental space permits a continual back-and-forth between the private speech of ordinary conversations and the public speech of discourses, lectures, sermons, rallying-cries, and all theatrical forms of utterance.

Inasmuch as the poet through a poem gives voice to a way of living (loving, feeling, thinking, taking pleasure, or suffering), the experience of monumental space may be said to have some similarity to entering and sojourning in the poetic world. It is more easily understood, however, when compared with texts written for the theatre, which are composed of dialogues, rather than with poetry or other literary texts, which are monologues.

Monumental qualities are not solely plastic, not to be apprehended solely through looking. Monuments are also liable to possess acoustic properties, and when they do not this detracts from their monumentality. Silence itself, in a place of worship, has its music. In cloister or cathedral, space is measured by the ear: the sounds, voices and singing reverberate in an interplay analogous to that between the most basic sounds and tones; analogous also to the interplay set up when a reading voice breathes new life into a written text. Architectural volumes ensure a correlation between the rhythms that they entertain (gaits, ritual gestures, processions, parades, etc.) and their musical resonance. It is in this way, and at this level, in the *non-visible*, that bodies find one another. Should there be no echo to provide a reflection or acoustic mirror of presence, it falls to an object to supply this mediation between the inert and the living: bells tinkling at the slightest breeze, the play of fountains and running water, perhaps birds and caged animals.

Two 'primary processes', as described by certain psychoanalysts and linguists, might reasonably be expected to operate in monumental space: (1) displacement, implying metonymy, the shift from part to whole, and contiguity; and (2) condensation, involving substitution, metaphor and similarity. And, to a degree, this is so. Social space, the space of social practice, the space of the social relations of production and of work and non-work (relations which are to a greater or lesser extent codified) – this space is indeed condensed in monumental space. The notion of 'social condenser', as proposed by Russian architects in the 1920s, has a more general application. The 'properties' of a spatial texture are focused upon a single point: sanctuary, throne, seat, presidential chair, or the like. Thus each monumental space becomes the metaphorical and quasi-metaphysical underpinning of a society, this by virtue of a play of substitutions in which the religious and political realms symbolically (and ceremonially) exchange attributes – the attributes of power; in this way the authority of the sacred and the sacred aspect of authority are transferred back and forth, mutually reinforcing one another in the process. The horizontal chain of sites in space is thus replaced by vertical superimposition, by a hierarchy which follows its own route to the locus of power, whence it will determine the disposition of the sites in question. Any object – a vase, a chair, a garment – may be extracted from everyday practice and suffer a displacement which will transform it by transferring it into monumental space: the vase will become holy, the garment ceremonial, the chair the seat of authority. The famous bar which, according to the followers of Saussure, separates signifier from signified and desire from its object, is in fact transportable hither and thither at the whim of society, as a means of separating the sacred from the profane and of repressing those gestures which are not prescribed by monumental space – in short, as a means of banishing the obscene.

All of which has still not explained very much, for what we have said applies for all 'monumentality' and does not address the question of what particular power is in place. The obscene is a general category of social practice, and not of signifying processes as such: exclusion from the scene is pronounced silently by space itself.

THE SPACE OF ARCHITECTS

Cases are legion where the empirical approach to a given process refuses to carry its description to a conceptual level where a dialectical (conflictual) dynamic is likely to emerge. For example, countries in the throes of rapid development blithely destroy historic spaces – houses, palaces, military or civil structures. If advantage or profit is to be found in it, then the old is swept away. Later, however, perhaps towards the end of the period of accelerated growth, these same countries are liable to discover how such spaces may be pressed into the service of cultural consumption, of 'culture itself', and of the tourism and the leisure industries with their almost limitless prospects. When this happens, everything that they had so merrily demolished during the *belle époque* is reconstituted at great expense. Where destruction has not been complete, 'renovation' becomes the order of the day, or imitation, or replication, or neo-this or neo-that. In any case, what had been annihilated in the earlier frenzy of growth now becomes an object of adoration. And former objects of utility now pass for rare and precious works of art.

Let us for a moment consider the space of architecture and of architects, without attaching undue importance to what is said about this space. It is easy to imagine that the architect has before him a slice or piece of space cut from larger wholes, that he takes this portion of space as a 'given' and works on it according to his tastes, technical skills, ideas and preferences. In short, he receives his assignment and deals with it in complete freedom.

That is not what actually happens, however. The section of space assigned to the architect – perhaps by 'developers', perhaps by government agencies – is affected by calculations that he may have some intimation of but with which he is certainly not well acquainted. This space has nothing innocent about it: it answers to particular tactics and strategies; it is, quite simply, the space of the dominant mode of production, and hence the space of capitalism, governed by the bourgeoisie. It consists of 'lots' and is organized in a repressive manner as a function of the important features of the locality.

As for the eye of the architect, it is no more innocent than the lot he is given to build on or the blank sheet of paper on which he makes his first sketch. His 'subjective' space is freighted with all-too-objective meanings. It is a visual space, a space reduced to blueprints, to mere images – to that 'world of the image' which is the enemy of the imagination. These reductions are accentuated and justified by the rule of linear perspective. Such sterilizing tendencies were denounced long ago by Gromort, who demonstrated how they served to fetishize the facade – a volume made up of planes and lent spurious depth by means of decorative motifs.[3] The tendency to make reductions of this kind – reductions to parcels, to images, to façades that are made to be seen and to be seen from (thus reinforcing 'pure' visual space) – is a tendency that degrades space. The facade (to see and to be seen) was always a measure of social standing and prestige. A prison with a façade – which was also the prison of the family – became the epitome and modular form of bourgeoisified space.

It may thus be said of architectural discourse that it too often imitates or caricatures the discourse of power, and that it suffers from the delusion that 'objective' knowledge of 'reality' can be attained by means of graphic representations. This discourse no longer has any frame of reference or horizon. It only too easily becomes – as in the case of Le Corbusier – a moral discourse on straight lines, on right angles and straightness in general, combining a figurative appeal to nature (water, air, sunshine) with the worst kind of abstraction (plane geometry, modules, etc.).

Within the spatial practice of modern society, the architect ensconces himself in his own space. He has a *representation of this space*, one which is bound to graphic elements – to sheets of paper, plans, elevations, sections, perspective views of facades, modules, and so on. This *conceived* space is thought by those who make use of it to be *true*, despite the fact – or perhaps because of the fact – that it is geometrical: because it is a medium for objects, an object itself, and a locus of the objectification of plans. Its distant ancestor is the linear perspective developed as early as the Renaissance: a fixed observer, an immobile perceptual field, a stable visual world. The chief criterion of the architectural plan, which is 'unconsciously' determined by this perceptual field, is whether or not it is realizable: the plan is projected onto the field of architectural thought, there to be accepted or rejected. A vast number of representations (some would call them 'ideological' representations, but why bother with a term now so devalued by misuse?) take this route; any plan, to merit consideration, must be quantifiable, profitable, communicable and 'realistic'. Set aside or downplayed from the outset are all questions relating to what is too close or too distant, relating to the surroundings or 'environment', and relating to the relationship between private. and public. On the other hand, subdivisions (lots) and specializations (functional localizations) are quite admissible to this practically defined sphere. Much more than this, in fact: though the sphere in question seems passive with respect to operations of this kind, its very passive acceptance of them ensures their operational impact The division of labour, the division of needs and the division of objects (things), all localized, all pushed to the point of maximum separation of functions, people and things, are perfectly at home in this spatial field, no matter that it appears to be neutral and object-ive, no matter that it is apparently the repository of knowledge, *sans peur et sans reproche.*

Let us now turn our attention to the space of those who are referred to by means of such clumsy and pejorative labels as 'users' and 'inhabitants'. No well-defined terms with clear connotations have been found to designate these groups. Their marginalization by spatial practice thus extends even to language. The word 'user' (*usager*), for example, has something vague – and vaguely suspect – about it. 'User of what?' one tends to wonder. Clothes and cars are used (and wear out), just as houses are. But what is use value when set alongside exchange and its corollaries? As for 'inhabitants', the word desig-nates everyone – and no one. The fact is that the most basic demands of 'users' (suggesting 'underprivileged') and 'inhabitants' (suggesting 'marginal') find *expression* only with great difficulty, whereas the *signs* of their situation are constantly increasing and often stare us in the face.

The user's space is *lived* – not represented (or conceived). When compared with the abstract space of the experts (architects, urbanists, planners), the space of the everyday activities of users is a concrete one, which is to say, subjective. As a space of 'subjects' rather than of calculations, as a representational space, it has an origin, and that origin is childhood, with its hardships, its achieve-ments and its lacks. Lived space bears the stamp of the conflict between an inevitable, if long and difficult, maturation process and a failure to mature that leaves particular original resources and reserves untouched. It is in this space that the 'private' realm asserts itself, albeit more or less vigorously, and always in a conflictual way, against the public one.

It is possible, nevertheless, if only in a mediational or transitional way, to form a mental picture of a primacy of concrete spaces of semi-public, semi-private spaces, of meeting-places, pathways and passageways. This would mean the diversification of space, while the (relative) importance attached to functional distinctions would disappear. Appropriated places would be *fixed*, *semi-fixed*, *movable* or *vacant*. We should not forget that among the contra-dictions here a not unimportant part is played by the contradiction between the ephemeral and the stable (or, to use Heidegger's philosophical terminology, between Dwelling and Wandering). Although work – including a portion of household production (food preparation, etc.) – demands a fixed location, this is not true of sleep, nor of play, and in this respect the West might do well to take lessons from the East, with its great open spaces, and its low and easily movable furniture.

In the West the reign of the facade over space is certainly not over. The furniture, which is almost as heavy as the buildings themselves, continues to have facades; mirrored wardrobes, sideboards and chests still face out onto the sphere of private life, and so help dominate it. Any mobilization of 'private' life would be accompanied by a restoration of the body, and the contradictions of space would have to be brought out into the open. Inasmuch as the resulting space would be inhabited by *subjects,* it might legitimately be deemed 'situ-ational' or 'relational' – but these definitions or determinants would refer to sociological content rather than to any intrinsic properties of space as such.

Lefebvre   The restoration of the body means, first and foremost, the restoration of the sensory-sensual – of speech, of the voice, of smell, of hearing. In short, of the non-visual. And of the sexual – though not in the sense of sex considered in isolation, but rather in the sense of a sexual energy directed towards a specific discharge and flowing according to specific rhythms.

But these are no more than suggestions, or pointers.

NOTES

1   See Roland Barthes, *S/Z*, Paris: Seuil, 1970, pp. 25 ff. (English translation by Richard Miller: *S/Z*, New York: Hill & Wang, 1974, pp. 18 ff.)

2   Clearly we are not concerned here with architectural space understood as the preserve of a particular profession within the established social division of labour.

3   Cf. Georges Gromort, *Architecture et sculpture en France*, a volume in his *Histoire générale de l'art française de la Révolution à nos jours*, Paris: Librairie de France, 1923–5.

GIANNI VATTIMO

Italian philosopher Gianni Vattimo (b. 1936) has established himself as a prominent theorist of aesthetics and the leading phenomenological thinker in Italy. Vattimo, himself a former pupil of Hans-Georg Gadamer, has translated Gadamer's *Truth and Method* into Italian. He has also written extensively on Heidegger and Nietzsche. By focusing on the critique that these authors have made on modern thinking, Vattimo has explored the question of how these debates may then inform our understanding of postmodern thinking. He has thereby emerged also as a significant theorist of postmodernity.

Central to Vattimo's own contribution to the debate about postmodernity has been his introduction of the controversial notion of 'weak thought' (*il pensiero debole*). Here Vattimo argues that traditional metaphysics has privileged 'strong thought' in the form of 'reason'. In following nihilistic thinkers such as Nietzsche and Heidegger, Vattimo champions instead the ontological as a form of 'weak thought'. Thus Being itself becomes an 'unnoticed and marginal event'. This has important ramifications for works of art in general, and architecture in particular. In the essay 'Ornament/Monument' Vattimo observes how ornament and decor have been viewed traditionally as peripheral, and as expendable appendages to the work of art proper. Vattimo challenges this marginalization. There are clear parallels here with Derrida's thinking in *Truth in Painting*. Ornament for Vattimo, no less than the seemingly peripheral 'frame' (*parergon*) for Derrida, is precisely part of the work of art. Vattimo argues that the work of art is an example of 'weak ontology' and should itself be perceived in terms of ornament. Thus the ornamental is an intrinsic part of the work of art.

In his essay 'The End of Modernity, the End of the Project?' Vattimo challenges the 'strong' legitimation of humanist aesthetics with its emphasis on universals. The complexity of contemporary life should now be recognized as a multiplicity of 'language games' which should be reflected in its architecture. Likewise there is a need to attend to the relative shortage of the symbolic and the ornamental in contemporary architecture. Architects should see themselves as 'functionaries of society' and should respond more directly to the cultural conditions of place and community.

Vattimo's essay 'Ornament/Monument' provides a gloss to Gadamer's extract, 'The Ontological Foundation of the Occasional and the Decorative' contained in this volume. It also offers a provocative contrast to Bataille's and Lefebvre's discussions of the monument. Meanwhile Vattimo's essay 'The End of Modernity, the End of the Project?' evokes comparison with the extract from *The Seeds of Time* by Fredric Jameson, also contained within this volume.

Vattimo

THE END OF MODERNITY, THE END OF THE PROJECT?

The important thing to notice in the title of this essay is the question mark; one cannot insist on the equivalence of the 'end of modernity' and the 'end of the project'. I propose, therefore, to discuss the state of the project, and of the architectonic project in particular, in the light of a situation that in my view may be defined 'postmodern' – a term that is today still not in common usage, although this varies according to geographical area. By 1987, J.F. Lyotard had already declared the term 'postmodern' outworn, but listening to the topic of discussion in conferences and debates, there is reason enough not to consider the postmodern thematic obsolete, at least not in certain areas of *mitteleuropaisch* culture. I believe, then, that one can still say in all seriousness that we shall – or do – find ourselves in a postmodern condition. Moreover, its character may be such as to give the impression that the very notion of a project has become problematic.

To begin a general definition of the postmodern condition, which I have already spoken about on many occasions in my books and essays, I would like to refer to two lines from Hölderlin, often cited by Heidegger;

Voll Verdienst, doch dichterisch, wohnet
Der Mensch auf dieser Erde

Full of merit, yet poetically, man
Dwells on this earth.

These lines from Hölderlin define the condition of man in the moment of transition to the postmodern; the *doch*, the 'yet', is what signals the turn. One can think of modernity, then, as defined by the idea of a dwelling *voll verdienst*, of a life 'full of merit' – which is to say, full of activity. The most conventional image of modernity is certainly that according to which modern man has taken his destiny into his own hands. He has abandoned the transcendence, superstition and faith of the past and has taken his own fate upon himself. One could indeed take this *voll verdienst* to be the most conventional – but perhaps also the truest – representation of modernity. A vast historical and philosophical tradition concurs in this vision of modernity as immanentism, laicization, secularization. As is well known, this tradition began with Kant and his definition of *Aufklarung*. The *doch*, then, altogether beyond Hölderlin's intentions and perhaps those of Heidegger too, could mean the turn, the change in direction which brings us into the postmodern condition. Whereas, that is, modernity was characterized by an existence defined essentially in terms of projective activity and a drive towards the rationalization of reality by means of structures founded on thought and action, the postmodern would be the time when 'poetic' characteristics are rediscovered: '*doch dichterisch, wohnet/der Mensch auf dieser Erde*' – yet poetically man/Dwells on this earth.

I would like to underline just one feature of the 'poetic', namely, its indefiniteness. To dwell poetically does not mean to dwell in such a way that one needs poetry, but to dwell with a sensitivity to the poetic, characterized by the impossibility, in a sense, of defining clear-cut boundaries between reality and

imagination. If there is a passage from modernity to postmodernity, it seems
to lie in a wearing away of the boundaries between the real and the unreal, or,
at the very least, in a wearing away of the boundaries of the *real*. Without
entering into a sociological analysis, we can nonetheless say that contemporary reality seems to exhibit a tendency to posit itself entirely at the
level of simultaneity. Contemporary history is that phase of history in which
everything tends to be presented in the form of simultaneity. For example, one
could take the *terminus a quo* of the birth of contemporaneity to be the
diffusion of the daily press, or, better still, the invention of media such as
radio or television that are able to let us know what happens around the
world 'in real time', as one might say. The 'reality' of real time, then, is given
by the fact that there are technical means by which we can, so to speak,
'simultaneitize' events that take place all over the world. This 'simultaneitization' of history, of reality, is significant insofar as for apparently
different reasons – that may actually be the same – it occurs in a situation in
which historicity as diachrony tends to waste away to nothing.

The 'mediatization' and 'simultaneitization' of our historicity take place in a
world that is living through a crisis in the very notions of history and historicity. When we speak of History with a capital 'h', we assume that there is a
single course along which we can place events that occur in America, in Africa
or here in Italy. But this is no longer true. The historians were the first to lose
faith in this schema: above all in recent decades, but actually ever since the
expansion of schools like the French school of Annales, founded at the end of
the 1920s, the debates of historians have revolved around the problem of
knowing whether there is a dominant history, a history that would be the basis
for other different histories. For example, one speaks of the history of art, of
micro-histories such as the history of kitchen utensils, the history of economy,
as specialized histories that branch off from a principal history. Yet there
always emerges an awareness that this principal history is not objective and
external, but rather presupposes a subject with reasons for universalizing
certain schemata. One of the most common realizations in contemporary
historiography, then, is that history presupposes literary rhetorical schemata,
different ways of telling stories. History, therefore, is not history, but histories,
in the sense of stories that have been narrated and whose meaning depends
on the perspective, the coordinates or the point of view adopted for their
narration. We are witnessing a dissolution of historicity – in communal life,
conditioned by technology, no less than in methodology, historical consciousness and philosophical reflection. Now, in the tradition of Western metaphysics, history is real to the extent that it is a realization and an articulation of
a *Grund*, a foundation. This may be seen in the idea of 'revolution', a familiar
concept in the Western tradition. But could revolution not also be called 'innovation'? A revolution is an innovation that leads that which happens – history
back to its originary foundation: the Renaissance was a rebirth of Greece, in the
same way as the French Revolution, based on the thought of the *Aufklärung*, of
the Enlightenment, was itself set on returning to an original state, on regaining
an authentic human condition, etc. History, then, is affirmed as positively real
to the degree that it realizes a foundation already present in an implicit form.
But this conciliation between being and becoming presupposes the possibility
of speaking of history as if it were a single course, in order that a rational

Vattimo   schema may be identified within it. When it is no longer possible to speak of a single history, however, neither can there be any recourse to the rational schema. What is at stake in historicism is not merely establishing whether Hegel was right or wrong, but the fact that if one can no longer speak in terms of a single history, the only possibility of speaking of being as foundation is lost – as we see clearly in Nietzsche and Heidegger.

If these authors are read, that is, if Hegel, Nietzsche, Heidegger are read, one can no longer simply return to an earlier conception of the relation between the founded and the foundation. In our recent history, the development of the relation between founded and foundation has taken the form of historicism, which means that the rationality of reality is presented as the rational progress of events. Once it is no longer possible to speak of a rational progress of events because it is no longer possible to speak of progress (we are no longer imperial thinkers), then rationality as *Begrundung* (grounding) and as the substantial reality of that which is, is no longer given. What I mean to say, without insisting on further schematic philosophical detail, is that the 'simultaneitization' of reality in the contemporary world is, almost inevitably, also a 'simulacrization'. That which becomes simultaneous also becomes 'simulacral', in the sense that it concerns appearances that cannot be referred back to a basic rationality, to a true world – according to an expression Nietzsche uses in an aphorism from *Twighlight of the Idols* – since there is no longer the single thread of rationality that was found in historicism, and which served as the law of history.

In his *Zur Seinsfrage* (*The Question of Being*) Heidegger writes the word *Sein* with a cross through it. Clearly, it was not a way of writing the word *Sein* in order to mean something else. Instead, it seems to me that this way of writing 'being' should be interpreted as having more or less the same meaning as the *doch* of the 'yet poetically man/Dwells . . .'. Alternatively, perhaps it should be seen from the point of view of that which I have just described as 'simulacrization', or reality's turning into a simulacrum. In other words in our present historical condition, we are witnessing a manifestation of being marked by disappearance, by becoming lighter, less cogent, less definite. Will the processing of the world into information not also serve to open a way of being of things in which it is no longer a simple matter to tell reality from the fictions of the imagination? In the end, what do we know of reality? Ours is a world where the channels by which our experience of reality is mediated have become increasingly explicit. To be sure, one can say that in medieval times the experience of external reality was mediated. For example, it was by the preacher, the priest, that people who spent almost their entire lives in a tiny village were told of the history of the world, But then the mediation was not visible: there was a form of mediation sufficiently unitary to blend with reality almost without trace. Today, the 'simulacrization' of reality is a combined effect of invention, innovation in information technology and a loss of centrality in the vision of history. It is not a case of saying that only today is the information we have of the world mediated; perhaps it has always been so. But in the past, in the time when mediation did not occur in situations of conflict between images of the world, it was not visible. We live in a situation where the mediation has become visible by virtue of the proliferation of perspectives with, say, social and political origins that make it difficult to identify the image with reality about which, in turn, one no longer knows anything directly. We know only that if we want to produce an image of the world, we have to collect many different images. Yet even this does not absolutely guarantee that we shall be in a position to see the world as it 'truly' is, only that we shall no longer be conditioned by a single image, a single interpretation.

This is the framework within which, with particular attention to the theme of architecture, I shall try to redescribe the activity of the project.

Does planning a project in these conditions – those I have summarized with the notion of 'poetic dwelling' – open a way of being that is more free or less free? I don't know. But the task posed is to find legitimations for the project that no longer appeal to 'strong', natural, or even historical structures. For example, one can no longer say that there is a golden number, an ideal measure that can be used in the construction of buildings or the planning of cities, nor even that there are basic natural needs, since it is increasingly absurd to try to distinguish them from new needs induced by the market and therefore superfluous, not natural. It may be that as a philosopher I am particularly sensitive to this loss of 'foundation', but I believe that, at times, it may also be experienced by architects and planners as they reflect on their work. I know that often one receives a commission for a determinate project and then works from models. But even in this situation, it is increasingly difficult to find clear-cut and convincing criteria to which one can refer. Those concerned with planning cities accept that planning does not appeal to ideal guidelines and work instead in the knowledge that it is a contractual matter. It is in all cases a question of social rhetoric, of exchanges, deals, the planning of what one is setting out to do and its conciliation with that which is already there, that is, of taking into account so many variables that one can no longer speak of a plan.

In keeping with this idea of planning, architecture is sometimes defined by 'strong' aesthetic criteria: it is a matter of creating a good project and a beautiful building. The notion of 'beautiful' in this instance cannot be referred back to Kant's aesthetics, inasmuch as beauty is not defined by objective criteria and there are no models one has to measure up to – as, for example, there are in classicism. What, then, is the criterion? How, in the situation described here in a philosophical-sociological manner that has hardly anything to do directly with the projective activity of architects and planners, can one imagine the activity of projecting, the working conditions of the architect or the planner? It seems to me that here, in analogy with philosophy, the only way of finding criteria consists in appealing to memory or, as Heidegger says, to *Ueberlieferung*, to handing down. We possess no criteria that may be traced back to the rational structure of man, the world, nature or anything else; not even to the inevitable, providential or rational, course of history. In philosophy as in architecture, we have nothing by which to orient ourselves but indications that we have inherited from the past. This view is not far removed from Wittgenstein's notion of language games, which are precisely domains of rationality in which the rules in force are given by the game itself. From Wittgenstein's, and to some extent Heidegger's, point of view, our existence is defined as a multiplicity of language games, or games in a broad sense, having an internal normative character that we have always to confront, and which says something to us, regardless of whether we modify, accept or reject the

Vattimo games themselves. The rationality we have at our disposal today, in the epoch of the end of metaphysics, is no longer like this, at least not if one accepts the presuppositions I have just described. There are rules of games in force or, in more Heideggerian terms, there is an *Ueberlieferung,* a handing down, that issues from the past, but not only from the past. It may also issue from other cultures, other communities in this multiplicity of communities of values that come to light in the world of the simulacrum. It is the proliferation of the simulacra that shows the simulacra for what they are, and their proliferation amounts to minorities, disparate and ethnic groups, etc., having their say – which is precisely what occurs in the world of generalized information.

Does handing down, in this wide sense, offer up a meaning? Can it signify something more precise and detailed at the level of the project? In conclusion, I shall put forward, very briefly, three ideas that are really no more than consequences that may be drawn from these premises.

First and foremost, it should be underlined that the *Ueberlieferung,* the handing down, does not issue only from the past, but from all the communities that have found a voice in, to use Ricoeur's expression, the conflict of interpretations in which we live. In this sense, moreover, the legitimation of the project – and I use the term legitimation not only in a critical sense, but also to mean that which can guide and orient the one who plans and carries out the project – issues not from a strong metaphysical 'foundation', but from the voices of different communities, speaking not only from the past, but from the present too. At this point the difference emerges between the viewpoint that I am putting forward and the criterion of the 'beautiful' work. The idea of an aesthetic value to the architectonic work as such, which can coexist with the conception of planning as contractual and mediatory, leads back to a choice, to a historically enrooted taste. In other words, to construct a good building, one has to refer to a determinate community amongst the multiplicity of communities that speak in our society, and one has to represent it in a definite way, for example, by building a beautiful mosque in Rome, recalling the Arab culture, whether the Arabs from Rome (of whom there are only a few), or the Arabs of the Arab world (who are more numerous), etc. As a possible criterion, it derives from the metaphysical aesthetic tradition of the West, and in particular from Hegel, yet is applicable at the level of proliferation. In Hegel, the work of art represents absolute spirit in the form of the historical spirit of a people, which is to say, of a historical community. The work of art is classic – that is, valid when it is an accomplished expression of the world-view of a community which recognizes itself in it. But would Hegel have said this if he had lived in a world of proliferating communities? At bottom, Hegel identified the most evolved human community with the community of nineteenth-century Europe. The idea of a value, of a valid aesthetic linked to the complete representation of an historical community in a true or accomplished fashion, necessarily implies the idea that this historical community represents the highest point of evolutionary development. Hegel would never have maintained that a work of art could be perfect if it represented, for example, a bunch of criminals, in however accomplished a fashion it did so. He could not say this because a bunch of criminals does not have sufficient inner freedom to give themselves an accomplished representation. Hegel's judgment on the symbolic art of the

Asiatic peoples reached the same diagnosis. The symbolic art of which Hegel speaks precedes classic art and is imperfect insofar as spirit's inner freedom has not reached a degree such that it could achieve adequate expression in an image. This means that the criterion of recognizing aesthetic value in the ability to represent perfectly a living historical community necessarily implies a vision of history that comes back to historicism, or if one prefers, to an evolutionary view of history. In the context of the proliferation of communities, can we be satisfied with this criterion of representation typical of a world-view that lays out the other world-views and considers them from an external and privileged point of view? In my opinion, this has become problematic. I believe, rather, that the criterion of aesthetic value, in this world of multiple models of existence, cannot be legitimated except via the multiplicity, a multiplicity lived explicitly as such, without any realist reservations. Nowadays, it could be said that what is *kitsch* is precisely the work presented as classic, which naively readvances a 'natural' or objective criterion; it has the look of certain very formal rules of dress that are only observed now in marginal communities. *Kitsch* is nothing but that which has pretensions to classic status in the context of a proliferation of voices and tastes. The problem, therefore, is one of seeing how to bring a conscious multiplicity into effect within the construction of the work. I cannot propose a definite solution to this problem. But it is not true that the classic view of the work gives criteria that are any clearer: they only appear to be so, but in fact one has always to appeal to the Kantian genius, or in the terms we are using here, to the artist as one aware of the multiplicity of voices and *Weltanschauungen* and capable of thematizing them whilst standing outside them. This is all as regards the first point of my conclusion.

The second point regards the concept of monumentality: the ability to listen to the *Ueberlieferung*, the handing down, from the past no less than from the present, may also be expressed in the forms of a new monumentality, or in less solemn terms, in the forms of a new ensemble of recognizable characteristics, of a 'recognizableness'. It is neither a response to a nostalgia for relocalization, nor a new offer to enroot our experience in some stable reality. It responds to a perhaps affinitive need for a symbolic and ornamental dimension. It is as if to say that the need for monumentality makes itself felt when architecture and planning, in their reciprocal relation, no longer respond clearly to immediate needs – shelter, clothing . . . – but are left in that indefinite state that derives from the principle of reality having been worn away. In this situation a need arises for ornamentation, for that ornament which has been the object of polemic between, for example, many functionalist and rationalist architects and which, in the present situation, seems to be widely and strongly reaffirmed. We have needs that are not immediate and vital but symbolic, and which emerge all the more when every deducible, metaphysical reason founded on the nature of man, the needs of life, etc., is to some extent dissolved.

Viewed in this way, it is most instructive to consider what used to happen when the architects' clients were above all the monarch and the rich bourgeoisie, in contrast to the current proliferation of communities and value-systems. The comparison suggests – and I come here to the third point in my conclusion – that the position of architect is increasingly less that of 'genius' and more that of a

Vattimo   'symbolic operator' with a clear awareness of what he is doing. I don't know if, for example, the court architects that built the hunting villa of the Dukes of Savoy in Turin were conscious of expressing in their work the aesthetic expectations of a monarch. They probably believed they were conforming to the classical models they had taken as guides for their activity. Today, this conception of architectonic creation, more even than poetic or literary creation, is no longer possible. The architect is no longer the functionary of humanity, just as the philosopher no longer thinks of him or herself as a functionary of humanity or interpreter of a common vision of the world, despite having more reason for doing so. The philosopher is always the interpreter of a community. Yet this does not mean referring back to an ethnicity, to groups or places. The real problem of the post-modern condition is that one can no longer make any appeal to these 'realities', in however naive a manner. Even when one is said to refer back to a community, one no longer does; the innocence is lost and one has to be able to work in an inter-mediary zone between an enrootedness in a place – in a community – and an explicit consciousness of multiplicity. This is what I mean by a 'new monu-mentality': building cities where one recognizes oneself, not only in the sense that there is a perception of shared values, but also in the sense that one recognizes where one is, that there are distinguishing 'marks'. We need to be able to build in such a way that these marks are there from the beginning, and do not become marks only subsequently, like the monuments of present cities that are, so to speak, 'reduced' to being territorial markers, whereas originally they were or wished to be the incarnation of the idea in the sensible, as Hegel would say. We are in a situation of conscious historicity that could even block creativity – as Nietzsche said in one of his essays, the second *Untimely Meditations* – yet it is precisely this that we need. We need the ability to engage in building and in urban structure projects that satisfy these two 'conditions': an enrootedness in a place, and an explicit awareness of multiplicity.

I realize that these conclusions are not sufficient in themselves, but they may open up discussion. Once the architect is no longer the functionary of humanity, nor the deductive rationalist, nor the gifted interpreter of a world-view, but the functionary of a society made up of communities, then projection must become something both more complex and more indefinite. This means, for example, that there is a rhetorical aspect to urban planning (and perhaps also to architectural projection) that is not merely a response to the need to provide persuasive justifications to the listening public. Instead, it reveals the problem of links with non-technical cultural traditions – in the city, the regions or the state – that must be heard and which condition the creation and development of the plan. In this sense a plan is a contract, not something that the city can simply apply straight away. It has the form of a utopia, so to speak, that guides the real future project, but which will itself never actually be realized as a project 'put into action' and 'applied' on the landscape. Gathered together in this statutory form of the project are all the conditions of rhetoric, persuasion and argumentation regarding the cultural traditions of the place in question, those different cultural traditions within the community that significantly modify and redefine the activity of the contemporary architect and planner.

ORNAMENT/MONUMENT   *Vattimo*

A relatively little known and minor text by Heidegger dedicated to sculpture –
his lecture on 'Art and Space' (1969)[1] – ends with these words: 'it is not always
necessary for the true to be embodied; it is enough if it flutters nearby as spirit
and generates a sort of concord, like when the sound of bells floats as a friend in
the air and as a bearer of peace'. If on the one hand this lecture seems simp-
listically to return to the basic concepts of 'The Origin of the Work of Art',[2]
applying them this time to sculpture and the plastic arts, a careful reading
reveals that this 'application' gives rise to important modifications, or rather to
a new 'declension', as it were, of the definition of the work of art as a 'setting-
into-work of truth'. No doubt this can be understood as a part of the general
process of transformation of Heidegger's thought, and it is all the more interesting to us because it is not just a marginal aspect of the so-called *Kehre* said to
separate *Sein und Zeit* from the post-1930 works. Rather, it marks a movement
which takes place in the writings that are positioned after this 'turning-point' in
Heidegger's work. This is not, though, the place to examine this question in
such general terms.[3] In any event, it can be agreed that the 1969 lecture signals
the climactic moment of a process of rediscovery of 'spatiality' by Heidegger,
and thus a distancing not only from *Sein und Zeit* (in which temporality is the
key dimension for the reproposition of the problem of Being), but from a
number of subsequent ontological inquiries into the same problem. It is
difficult to decide exactly what this rediscovery of spatiality might mean for the
whole of Heidegger's thought, especially because there is a risk of seeing it as
opening onto possibilities which are too clearly mystical, or so it would seem.
Certainly, however, this emphasis on space in the so-called 'second period' of
Heidegger's work cannot be reductively interpreted as the mere stylistic
predominance of spatial metaphors, ranging from the *Lichtung* (or 'glade') to
the *Geviert* (or 'four fold' of earth and sky, mortals and divinities).[4]

In specific connection to Heidegger's concept of art and the aesthetic implications of his thought, the lecture on 'Art and Space' and the new attention that it
pays to spatiality appear to lead to an important clarification of the concept of
the work of art as a 'setting-into-work of truth' which also bears on the
Heideggerian concept of Being and the true. I propose to show that all this has
significant consequences for the aesthetic analysis of ornament.

Heidegger's theory of art would seem to be opposed to a recognition of the
legitimacy of ornament and decoration – at least, in its insistence on the truth-
fulness of the work of art, it has generally been interpreted in this way. The
work as a 'setting-into-work of truth' and as an inauguration of historical
worlds (as 'epochal' poetry) seems conceived above all on the model of the
great classical works – at least in the ordinary sense of this term, rather than in
the Hegelian one. This is the case because the 'setting-into-work of truth', as
Heidegger defines it, is realized not through a harmonization and perfect
matching of inside and outside, idea and appearance, but rather through the
persistence of the conflict between 'world' and 'earth' within the work. In spite
of this radical difference from the theory of Hegel, Heideggerian aesthetics
seems to consider the work to be 'classical' inasmuch as it conceives of the
work as founding history and as inaugurating and instituting models of

Vattimo historical/*geschicklich* existence: this constitutes precisely the work as the occurrence of truth, even if, as we shall see, it is not simply this alone.

The inaugural function of the work as a truth-event may occur, according to Heidegger, insofar as in the work the 'exhibition of a world',[5] along with the 'production of the earth', takes place. As long as these concepts are considered in regard to poetry, they tend to give rise to a predilection for a 'strong' notion of the inaugurality of art – and it seems likely that Heidegger thinks of the relation between the interpretative tradition and the great poetic works of the past in terms of the model provided by the relation between the Christian tradition and the Holy Scriptures. What happens if the exhibition of a world and the production of the earth are instead considered in relation to an art such as sculpture? Before the lecture on 'Art and Space', certain passages of Gadamer's *Truth and Method* take a first step towards providing us with some possible answers to this question. Gadamer reconsiders Heidegger's conclusions about the work of art as the occurrence of truth in an optic that assigns to architecture a sort of 'foundational' function in regard to all other arts, at least in the sense that it makes a 'place' for them and thus also 'embraces' them.[6] The words with which Heidegger's 1969 lecture ends, over and beyond their obvious spatial implications, appear difficult to fathom in reference to his concept of poetry. Precisely the fact that Heidegger here conceives of the 'opening' function of art with reference to a *spatial* art qualifies and clarifies at last what the conflict – in a positive sense – between world and earth means, together with the very significance of the term 'earth'. 'Art and Space', therefore, by no means restricts itself to applying the ideas of Heidegger's 1936 essay to the plastic arts, but provides a decisive explanation of the meaning of that essay – which is perhaps analogous to what occurs to the notion of being – towards death in the transition from *Sein und Zeit* to the ontological and hermeneutic works of Heidegger's final phase.[7] As is well known, in 'The Origin of the Work of Art' Heidegger theorizes a *dichterisch* essence of all the arts, both in the sense in which *dichten* means to 'create' and to 'invent', and in the more specific sense in which it indicates poetry as the art of the word. It is not entirely clear in this essay, however, how the conflict between world and earth is brought about in poetry as the art of the word; one of the clearest of the 'concrete' examples that Heidegger provides, after all, is taken from the plastic arts, namely the Greek temple (and, earlier in the essay, on Van Gogh's painting). If we agree with Heidegger that earth and world are not identifiable with the matter and form of the work, then their meaning in his 1936 essay appears to be that of the 'thematized' (or 'thematizable' – that is, the world) and the 'non-thematized' (or 'non-thematizable' – that is, the earth). In the work of art the earth is still a setting forth (*hergestellt*) as such, and this alone definitively distinguishes the work of art from the thing-instrument of everyday life. The obvious temptation – to which Heidegger's followers have certainly yielded – is that of understanding this as the distinction between an explicit meaning of the work (the world that it opens up and ex-poses) and a group of meanings which are always still in reserve (the earth). This may be legitimate to the degree that the earth is still wholly conceived of in terms of the dimension of temporality: if we think in purely temporal terms, the earth's keeping itself in reserve can only appear as the possibility of future worlds and further historical/*geschicklich* openings, that is, as an always available reserve of further ex-positions. It should be said that Heidegger never explicitly formulates his theory along these lines, probably because of a rightful unwillingness to reduce the earth to a not-yet-present (but still capable of being present) 'world'. The decisive step, though, is taken when Heidegger turns to the plastic arts, as he does in his 1969 text. Nor is this the only place where he does so; already in *Vorträge und Aufsätze* poetic dwelling is understood as an '*Einräumen*', as a making of space in the sense that is developed by Gadamer in the passages from *Truth and Method* mentioned above. In 'Art and Space', this *Einräumen* is visible in its two fundamental dimensions: it is both an 'arranging' of localities and a positioning of these places in relation to the 'free vastness of the region [*Gegend*]'.[8] In Gadamer's text, which serves as a sort of 'commentary' to Heidegger, the essence of the decorative and secondary arts is found in the fact that they operate in a double sense:

> the nature of decoration consists in performing that two-sided mediation; namely to draw the attention of the viewer to itself, to satisfy his taste, and then to redirect it away from itself to the greater whole of the context of life which it accompanies.[9]

May we legitimately consider this interplay between locality (*Ortschaft*) and region (*Gegend*) as a specification of the conflict between world and earth that is examined in 'The Origin of the Work of Art'? The answer is yes, if we keep in mind that Heidegger discovers this relation between *Ortschaft* and *Gegend* precisely at the point where, in 'Art and Space', he tries to explain how the 'setting-into-work of truth', which is the essence of art, could occur in sculpture. Sculpture is the 'setting-into-work of truth' insofar as it is the occurrence of authentic space (that is, in that which is proper to the latter); and this occurrence is precisely the interplay between locality and region in which the thing-work is foregrounded both as the agent of a (new) spatial ordering, and as a point of escape toward the free vastness of the region. The 'open' and the 'opening' (*das Offene, die Offenheit*) are the terms with which Heidegger – beginning in particular with his lecture on 'The Essence of Truth' (1930) – designates the truth in its originary meaning, that is, the one which also makes possible every occurrence of the 'true' as the conformity of the proposition to the thing. Perhaps, though, it never appears elsewhere so clearly as in this text on art and space that these terms do not only designate opening as an inaugurating and a founding, but also – and in an equally essential way – designate the act of opening as a dilation and a leaving free: it is, as it were, at once an ungrounding and a backgrounding, for what is placed in the background is also shown to possess a clearly limited and definite figure. In the play of *Ortschaft* and *Gegend* this double meaning of the opening as background is brought into focus for us. Heidegger's text on art and space thus leads us to see something that in his 1936 essay is left implicit or even not thought out: the definition of the work of art as the 'setting-into-work of truth' does not just concern the work of art, but also and above all the notion of truth. The truth that can occur and that can be 'set-into-work' is not simply the truth of metaphysics (as evidence and objective stability) with the additional characteristic of 'eventuality' rather than structure; that truth which occurs, in an event which for Heidegger is identified, almost without leaving any residue at all,[10] with art, is not the evidence of the *obiectum* giving itself to the *subiectum* but rather the

Vattimo play of appropriation and expropriation which elsewhere he calls the *Ereignis*.[11] If we look at sculpture and the other plastic arts in general, the play of transpropriation of the *Ereignis* – which is also that of the conflict between world and earth – arises as the interplay between the locality and the free vastness of the region.

It is here that significant indications for thinking about the notion of ornament may be found. In a long article on Gombrich's *The Sense of Order*,[12] Yves Michaud observes that Gombrich's interpretation of the urgency of the problem of ornament in art at the turn of the century, while it supplies crucial concepts for formulating the problem itself, does not place in question the distinction between 'an art that attracts attention to itself, on the one hand, and another art (that is, decorative art), which is supposedly the object of a strictly lateral interest, on the other'.[13] Michaud instead suggests that we radicalize Gombrich's argument, and puts forward the hypothesis that 'a large number of the most influential manifestations of contemporary art may consist precisely in the fact of shifting toward the centre and placing at the focal point of perception that which usually remains at its margins'.[14] This is not the place to enter into a broader and more direct discussion of Gombrich's work, in which other reasons for reflecting on the implications of Heidegger's theory in regard to a 'decorative' notion of art (in music, for instance) could easily be found; it may nonetheless be noted that, particularly from the point of view of 'Art and Space', the relation between centre and periphery does not have either the meaning of founding a typology alone (the distinction between an art that points openly and self-reflexively to itself and one which is the object of a strictly lateral interest on the part of the spectator), nor that of supplying an interpretive key to the development of contemporary art in relation to the art of the past. For Heidegger, it would appear, it is not merely a question of defining decorative art as a specific type of art, nor of determining the particular traits of contemporary art; rather, he seeks to acknowledge the decorative nature of all art. If we keep in mind Heidegger's insistence on the verbal sense of the term *Wesen*, or 'to essentialize', then it is possible to see that this question is connected to the reversal of centre and periphery that appears to characterize contemporary art in Michaud's eyes; for we accede to the essence of art in a situation in which it arises as an *event*, with precisely those same traits defined by Michaud; and this has to do with the essence of art in general, for it is the way in which art makes itself an essence in our own epoch of Being.

The occurrence of truth in art is a problem upon which Heidegger never ceases to reflect right up to his last works. In the light of 'Art and Space', his argument in the last analysis means that: (a) the truth which may occur does not possess the nature of truth as thematic evidence, but rather that of the 'opening' of the world, which signifies at the same time a thematization and a positioning of the work on the background, or an 'ungrounding'; and (b) if truth is understood in these terms, then art, as its setting-into-work, is definable in far less grandiose or emphatic terms than those which are customarily taken to belong to Heidegger's aesthetic thought. Gadamer, who is certainly well-informed about Heidegger's work, in *Truth and Method* assigns to architecture a more or less dominant and founding position among the arts. This gesture can legitimately be taken to imply that art in general has for Heidegger,

precisely inasmuch as it is the 'setting-into-work of truth', a decorative and   *Vattimo*
'marginal' essence.

The full implications of this cannot be understood unless placed within a
more general interpretation of Heideggerian ontology as 'weak ontology'. The
result of rethinking the meaning of Being is in fact, for Heidegger, the taking
leave of metaphysical Being and its strong traits, on the basis of which the
devaluation of the ornamental aspects of the work of art has always definitively
been legitimated, even if through more extensive chains of mediating concepts.
That which truly is (the *ontos on*) is not the centre which is opposed to the
periphery, nor is it the essence which is opposed to appearance, nor is it what
endures as opposed to the accidental and the mutable, nor is it the certainty of
the *obiectum* given to the subject as opposed to the vagueness and imprecision
of the horizon of the world. The occurrence of Being is rather, in Heideggerian
weak ontology, an unnoticed and marginal background event.

If we follow the archaeological work and continual remediation that
Heidegger dedicates to the poets, it is possible to see that this nevertheless does
not mean that we are confronted by the inapparent nature of the peripheral
occurrence of the beautiful, in a purely mystical sort of contemplation.
Heideggerian aesthetics does not induce interest in the small vibrations at the
edges of experience, but rather – and in spite of everything – maintains a monumental vision of the work of art. Even if the occurrence of truth in the work
happens in the form of marginality and decoration, it is still true that for it 'that
which remains is established by the poets'.[15] What 'remains', though, has the
nature of a residue rather than an *aere perennius*. The monument is made to
endure, but not as the full presence of the one whose memory it bears; this, on
the contrary, remains only as a memory (and the truth of Being itself, moreover,
can for Heidegger only arise in the form of a recollection). The techniques of
art, for example, and perhaps above all else poetic versification, can be seen as
stratagems – which themselves are, not coincidentally, minutely institutionalized and monumentalized – that transform the work of art into a residue and
into a monument capable of enduring because from the outset it is produced in
the form of that which is dead. It is capable of enduring not because of its force,
in other words, but because of its weakness.

From a Heideggerian point of view, the work of art as the occurrence of a
'weak' truth is understandable, in so many senses, as a monument. It may even
be thought of in the sense of an architectural monument that contributes to
form the background of our experience, but in itself generally remains the
object of a distracted perception. This is not the still grandiose metaphysical
sense that can be found in Ernst Bloch's concept of ornament in *The Spirit of
Utopia*;[16] for Bloch, ornament takes the form of a monument which is a
revelation of our truest nature, and this monumentality is still deeply classical
and Hegelian, even if Bloch tries to free it from these ties by displacing the
'perfect correspondence between inside and outside' to a future which is always
yet to come. In the monument that is art as the occurrence of truth in the
conflict between world and earth, there is no emergence and recognition of a
deep and essential truth. In this sense as well, essence is *Wesen* in its verbal
aspect; it is an occurrence in a form which neither reveals nor conceals a kernel
of truth, but in superimposing itself onto other ornaments constitutes the
ontological thickness of the truth-event.

Vattimo   We could uncover other meanings of Heideggerian weak ontology concerning an 'ornamental' and monumental notion of the work of art. In passing it could be pointed out, for instance, that Mikel Dufrenne,[17] starting from phenomenological premises, elaborates a notion of the 'poetic' which shares much of the same sense of *background* which can be found in Heidegger's work. What needs to be stressed is that ornamental art, both as a backdrop to which no attention is paid and as a surplus which has no possible legitimation in an authentic foundation (that is, in what is 'proper' to it), finds in Heideggerian ontology rather more than a marginal self-justification, for it becomes the central element of aesthetics and, in the last analysis, of ontological meditation itself – as the entire text of 'Art and Space' essentially shows. What is lost in the foundation and ungrounding which is ornament is the heuristic and critical function of the distinction between decoration as surplus and what is 'proper' to the thing and to the work. The critical validity of this distinction today appears completely exhausted, in particular at the level of the discourse of the arts and of militant criticism. Philosophy, in returning – although not exclusively – to the results of Heideggerian hermeneutic ontology, simply acknowledges the fact of this exhaustion, and tries to radicalize it with the aim of constructing different critical models.

NOTES

1   Martin Heidegger, 'Art and Space', pp. 120–3.
2   The Origin of the Work of Art' in *Poetry, Language, Thought*, Albert Hofstadter (trans), New York: Harper & Row, 1971; repr. 1975, pp. 163–86.
3   For an extremely careful and rich analysis and discussion of this, see E. Mazzarella, *Tecnica e metafisica. Saggio su Heidegger*, Naples: Guida, 1981, pt 1, ch. 3.
4   The most useful and complete of all the basic works on Heidegger's language, besides H. Feick's *Index zu Heideggers 'Sein und Zeit'*, 2nd edn (Tübingen: Niemeyer, 1968), is still E. Schofer's *Die Sprache Heideggers* (Pfullingen: Neske, 1962).
5   Here, as well as later on, I refer to the terminology and arguments provided by Heidegger in his essay on 'The Origin of the Work of Art', though I try not to bog down my discussion with notes for each term or concept that I consider. For a more detailed analysis of this essay, see my *Essere, storia e linguaggio in Heidegger* (Turin: Ed. di 'Filosofia', 1963), chapter 3.
6   Cf. H.-G. Gadamer, *Truth and Method*, Garrett Barden and John Cummings (trans.), 2nd edn, New York: Crossroads, 1975; repr. 1984, p. 139.
7   Here I refer the reader to the final chapters of my *Le aventure della differenza* (Milan: Feltrinelli, 1981).
8   Martin Heidegger, *Die Kunst und der Raum*; in *Gasamtausgabe*, vol. XIII, p. 207.
9   Cf. Gadamer, op. cit., p. 140. Repr. here, p. 134.
10 The essay on 'The Origin of the Work of Art' (in *Poetry, Language, Thought*, trans. Hofstadter), pp. 54–6, at one point discusses the different modes of occurrence of truth. None of these modes, though, not even that of philosophical thought, is taken up by Heidegger and developed in his subsequent works: the occurrence of truth remains tied to the 'setting-into-work of truth' that occurs in the work of art.
11 See especially the various texts published in *Vorträge und Aufsätze* (Pfullingen: Neske, 1954; repr. 1978).
12 E.H. Gombrich, *The Sense of Order: A Study in the Psychology of Decorative Art*, Ithaca: Cornell UP, 1979; Yves Michaud's article, 'L'Art auquel on ne fait pas attention', is found in *Critique*, 416, Jan. 1982, pp. 22–41.
13 Michaud, op. cit., p. 36.
14 Ibid., pp. 36–7.
15 For example, see Heidegger's lecture on 'Hölderlin and the Essence of Poetry' (1936) in *Erläuterungen zu Hölderlins Dichtung*, 3rd edn (Frankfurt: Klostermann, 1963).
16 Cf. Ernst Bloch, *Geist der Utopie* (1923), 2nd rev. edn, Frankfurt: Suhrkamp, 1977, p. 20 ff.
17 Cf. M. Dufrenne, *Le poétique*, Paris: PUF, 1963.

PART III

STRUCTURALISM

STRUCTURALISM

Structuralism is an inter-disciplinary movement that has sought to transcend the limitations of earlier *ad hoc* interpretation by grounding analysis in universal systems. It is, as Foucault observed, an 'attempt to establish between elements that may have been split over the course of time, a set of relationships that juxtapose them, set them in opposition or link them together, so as to create a sort of shape'.[1]

Structuralism was highly popular in the 1960s and early 1970s, but owes its origins to the work of the Swiss linguist Ferdinand de Saussure (1857–1913). Saussure drew the distinction between *langue* and *parole*, that is between language as a system and individual utterances. Saussure's concern was to understand the underlying system. Here it should be recognized that *langue* need not refer merely to literary systems. All cultural forms could be analysed by analogy with language, and could therefore be 'read'. Structuralism proved highly popular in a range of disciplines, not least anthropology, where Claude Lévi-Strauss, Mary Douglas and others based their research on patterns of kinship and so on.

Saussure was concerned with words as 'signs'. The sign is made up of the 'signifier' and the 'signified'. The 'signifier' refers to the form, whereas the 'signified' refers to the content or meaning. For Saussure, the relationship between the 'signified' and 'signifier' is arbitrary. There is no fixed relationship, for example, between the word 'cat' and the animal to which that word refers within the English language. In other languages different words would be used. Furthermore, the 'signified' is defined by what it is not. Thus a cat is a cat, because it is not a dog. The principle of opposition is fundamental to structuralism, and the world can be seen to be structured according to a system of paired opposites, of 'binary oppositions', such as theory/practice, inside/outside, male/female, etc.

Structuralism has obvious applications to the world of architecture through the discipline of semiology – the science of signs. Semiology offers a mechanism by which the built environment can be 'read' and 'decoded'. The work of Umberto Eco and Roland Barthes, no less than that of A. J. Greimas, has exposed the limitations of previous attempts by architects to 'read' the city, the best example of which has been provided by Kevin Lynch, who focused on the legibility of architectural features, rather than any semantic understanding of them. Later work by Diana Agrest, Mario Gandelsonas and Françoise Choay in particular has attempted to engage more directly with the field of semiology.

Structuralism as a system began to fall out of favour as its limitations became exposed. Poststructuralist theorists, for example, argued that, through its tendency to universalize, structuralism represented too rigid a system that could not account for the specificity of time or place. The exhaustion of the structuralist moment is evident in the article of Barthes, 'Semiology and the Urban', included here. Here Barthes stresses how readings are always only provisional and shift with time. Structuralism has also been attacked by ontological thinkers such as Henri Lefebvre, who argued that the world should be perceived not as 'text', but as 'texture', and that to understand the environment as a codified system of meaning is to privilege the eye over the other senses. The message of structuralism, however, has yet to be fully absorbed by the architectural community. Traditionally architects – often in contrast to the general public – have privileged technical considerations over the question of meaning. Semiology, however, offers architects a glimpse of the full semantic potential of architecture.

NOTE

1   Foucault, 'Of Other Spaces: Utopias and Heterotopias', p. 348.

ROLAND BARTHES

French writer and critic Roland Barthes (1915–80) remains a figure difficult to
categorize because of the range of his output and the shifts in his intellectual
position. His output stretched from works of a scientific orientation, such as *The
Fashion System*, to a more fluid style in his fictional and journalistic works. His
work was informed throughout by a clear intellectual project, although his
theoretical outlook shifted in the course of his career from a slightly unconventional structuralist position to a more overtly poststructuralist perspective in his
later works.

Barthes addresses the language of the city in 'Semiology and the Urban', an essay
which belongs to his later, poststructuralist period. 'The city is a discourse,' he
observes, 'and this discourse is truly a language.' Barthes warns that the relationship between signified and signifier should no longer be seen as a fixed one-to-one
relationship. While signifiers remain stable, signifieds are always transient,
'mythical creatures'. Equally there is the possibility of the empty signified, as in the
'empty centre' of Tokyo. Signifieds can never be enclosed within a full and final
signification, and can easily participate in an infinite chain of signification. Barthes
concludes that we should look to multiply not our surveys or 'functional studies' of
the city, but our readings of the city. For the city is like 'a poem which unfolds the
signifier and it is this unfolding that ultimately the semiology of the city should try
to grasp and make sing'.

Barthes further explores the question of signification in 'The Eiffel Tower'. The
tower attracts meaning in the way that 'a lightning rod attracts thunderbolts'. The
monument is a pure signifier on which men have attached meaning, without that
meaning ever being 'finite or fixed'. Barthes offers a fresh take on the question of
function, echoing the earlier sentiments of Adorno. Architecture for Barthes is both
dream and function. One should never overlook the symbolic dimension. Despite
Gustav Eiffel's initial attempts to justify his tower in terms of utility, the tower's
primary role has evolved as universal symbol of Paris. 'Use', Barthes observes,
'never does anything but shelter meaning.'

Barthes   # SEMIOLOGY AND THE URBAN

The subject of this discussion[1] involves a certain number of problems in urban semiology.

But I should add that whoever would outline a semiotics of the city needs to be at the same time semiologist (specialist in signs), geographer, historian, planner, architect and probably psychoanalyst. Since this is clearly not my case – in fact I am none of these things except perhaps a semiologist, and barely that – the reflections that I am going to present to you are the reflections of an amateur in the etymological sense of this word: amateur of signs, he who loves signs; amateur of cities, he who loves the city. For I love both the city and signs. And this double love (which probably is only one) leads me to believe, maybe with a certain presumption, in the possibility of a semiotics of the city. Under what conditions or rather with what precautions and what preliminaries would an urban semiotics be possible?

This is the theme of the reflections that I am going to present. I would like first of all to recall something very obvious which will serve as our starting point: human space in general (and not only urban space) has always been a satisfying space. Scientific geography and in particular modern cartography can be considered as a kind of obliteration, of censorship that objectivity has imposed on signification (objectivity which is a form like any other of the 'imaginary'). And before I speak of the city, I would like to recall certain facts about the cultural history of the West, more precisely of Greek antiquity. The human habitat, the *oecumenè*[2] such as we glimpse it through the first maps of the Greek geographers – Anaximander, Hecataeus – or through the mental cartography of someone like Herodotus, constitutes a veritable discourse with its symmetries, its oppositions of places, with its syntax and its paradigms. A map of the world of Herodotus in graphic form is constructed like a language, like a phrase, like a poem, on oppositions: hot lands and cold lands, known and unknown lands; then on the opposition between men on the one hand and monsters and chimaeras on the other, etc.

If from geographic space we pass now to urban space proper, I will recall that the notion of *Isonomia* forged for the Athens of the sixth century by a man like Clisthenes is a truly structural conception by which only the centre is privileged, since the relations of all citizens to it are at the same time both symmetrical and reversible.[3] At that time the conception of the city was exclusively a signifying one, since the utilitarian conception of an urban distribution based on functions and uses, which is incontestably predominant in our time, will appear later.

I wanted to remind you of this historical relativism in the conception of signifying spaces. Finally, it is in the recent past that a structuralist like Lévi-Strauss in his book *Tristes Tropiques* introduced urban semiology, although on a reduced scale, on the subject of a Bororo village whose space he studied using an essentially semantic approach.

It is odd that parallel to these strongly signifying conceptions of inhabited space, the theoretical elaborations of urban planners have up to now given, if I am not mistaken, only a very reduced place to the problems of signification.[4] To be sure, exceptions exist, many writers have spoken of the city in terms of signification. One of the authors who best expressed this essentially signifying *Barthes* nature of urban space is in my opinion Victor Hugo. In *Notre-Dame de Paris*, Hugo has written a very beautiful chapter, very subtle and perceptive, 'This will kill that'; 'this' meaning the book, 'that' meaning the monument. By expressing himself in such a way, Hugo gives proof of a rather modern way of conceiving the monument and the city, as a true text, as an inscription of man in space. This chapter by Victor Hugo is consecrated to the rivalry between two modes of writing, writing in stone and writing on paper. Indeed, this theme is very much current today in the remarks on writing of a philosopher like Jacques Derrida. Among the urban planners proper there is no talk of signification; only one name emerges, rightly so, that of the American Kevin Lynch, who seems to be closest to these problems of urban semantics in so far as he has been concerned with thinking about the city in the same terms as the consciousness perceiving it, which means discovering the image of the city among the readers of this city. But in reality the studies of Lynch, from the semantic point of view, remain rather ambiguous; on the one hand there is in his work a whole vocabulary of signification (for example, he lays great stress on the legibility of the city and this is a notion of great importance for us) and as a good semanticist he has the sense of *discrete units*; he has attempted to identify in urban space the discontinuous units which, *mutatis mutandis*, would bear some resemblance to phonemes and semantemes. These units he calls paths, edges, districts, nodes, landmarks. These are categories of units that would easily become semantic categories. But on the other hand, in spite of this vocabulary, Lynch has a conception of the city that remains more *Gestalt* than structural.

Beyond these authors who explicitly approach semantics of the city, we can observe a growing awareness of the functions of symbols in urban space. In many urban planning studies based on quantitative estimates and on opinion questionnaires, we nonetheless find mention, even if only as a note, of the purely qualitative issue of symbolization which even today is often used to explain facts of another nature. We find, for example, a technique fairly current in urban planning: simulation. Now, the technique of simulation, even if used in a fairly narrow and empirical manner, leads us to develop further the concept of model, which is a structural or at least pre-structural concept.

In another stage of these urban planning studies, the demand for meaning appears. We gradually discover that a kind of contradiction exists between signification and another order of phenomena and that consequently signification possesses irreducible specificity. For example, some planners or some of the scientists who study urban planning have had to notice that in certain cases a conflict exists between the functionalism of a part of a city, let us say of a neighbourhood, and what I will call its semantic contents (its semantic force). It is thus that they have remarked with a certain ingenuity (but maybe we must start from ingenuity) that Rome involves a permanent conflict between the functional necessities of modern life and the semantic charge given to the city by its history. And this conflict between signification and function is the despair of planners. There exists, furthermore, a conflict between signification and reason or, at least, between signification and the calculating reason which would have all the elements of a city uniformly assimilated by planning, while it is growing daily more evident that a city is a tissue formed not of equal elements whose functions we can enumerate, but of strong and neutral elements, or

Barthes rather, as the linguists say, of marked and unmarked elements (we know that the opposition between the sign and the absence of sign, between the full degree and the zero degree, constitutes one of the major processes of the elaboration of signification). Apparently every city possesses this kind of rhythm. Kevin Lynch has remarked that there exists in every city, from the moment that the city is truly inhabited by man and made by him, this fundamental rhythm of signification which is the opposition, the alternation and the juxtaposition of marked and of unmarked elements. Finally, there is a last conflict between signification and reality itself, at least between signification and that reality of objective geography, the reality of maps. Surveys directed by psycho-sociologists have shown, for example, that two neighbourhoods are adjoining, if we rely on the map, which means on the 'real', on objectivity, while, from the moment when they receive two different significations, they are radically separated in the image of the city. Signification, therefore, is experienced as in complete opposition to objective data.

The city is a discourse and this discourse is truly a language: the city speaks to its inhabitants, we speak our city, the city where we are, simply by living in it, by wandering through it, by looking at it. Still the problem is to bring an expression like 'the language of the city' out of the purely metaphorical stage. It is very easy metaphorically to speak of the language of the city as we speak of the language of the cinema or the language of flowers. The real scientific leap will be realized when we speak of a language of the city without metaphor. And we may say that this is exactly what happened to Freud when he for the first time spoke of the language of dreams, emptying this expression of its metaphorical meaning in order to give it real meaning. We also must face this problem: how to pass from metaphor to analysis when we speak of the language of the city. Once more I am referring to the specialists on the urban phenomenon, for even if they are quite far from these problems of urban semantics, they have nevertheless already noted (I quote the report of a survey) that: 'The data available in the social sciences presents a form poorly adapted to its integration in the models.' Well, if we have difficulty inserting in a model the data on the subject of the city provided us by psychology, sociology, geography, demography, it is precisely because we lack a last technique, that of symbols. Consequently, we need a new scientific energy in order to transform these data, to pass from metaphor to the description of signification, and it is in this that semiology (in the widest meaning of the term) could perhaps, by a development yet unforseeable, come to our aid. I do not intend to discuss here the discovery procedures of urban semiology. It is probable that these procedures would consist in decomposing the urban text into units, then distributing these units in formal classes and, thirdly, finding the rules of combination and transformation of these units and models. I will confine myself to three remarks which do not have a direct relation with the city but which could usefully point the way to an urban semiology in so far as they draw a summary balance sheet of current semiology and they take into consideration the fact that for the last few years the semiological 'landscape' is no longer the same.

My first remark is that 'symbolism' (which must be understood as a general discourse concerning signification) is no longer conceived today, at least as a general rule, as a regular correspondence between signifiers and signifieds. In other words, a notion of semantics which was fundamental some years ago has

become defunct; this is the notion of the lexicon as a set of lists of signifieds and   *Barthes*
their corresponding signifiers. This kind of crisis, of attrition of the notion of
lexicon, can be found in numerous sectors of research. First of all, there is the
distributive semantics of the disciples of Chomsky such as Katz and Fodor who
have launched a strong attack against the lexicon. If we leave the domain of
linguistics for that of literary criticism we find thematic criticism, which has
been dominant for fifteen or twenty years, at least in France, and which has
formed the essence of the studies in what we call the *Nouvelle Critique*, and
which is today being limited and remodelled to the detriment of the signifieds it
proposed to decipher.

In the domain of psychoanalysis, finally, we can no longer speak of a one-to-
one symbolism; this is clearly the dead part of Freud's work: a psychoanalytical
lexicon is no longer conceivable. All this has discredited the word 'symbol', for
this term has always allowed us to suppose till now that the relation of signification depended on the signified, on the presence of the signified. Personally, I
use the word 'symbol' to refer to an organization of meaning, syntagmatic and/
or paradigmatic but no longer semantic: we must make a very clear distinction
between the semantic dimension of the symbol and the syntagmatic or
paradigmatic nature of the same symbol.

In the same way, it would be an absurd enterprise to want to elaborate a
lexicon of the significations of the city, putting on one side places, neighbourhoods, functions, and on the other significations; or, rather, putting on one side
places uttered like signifiers and on the other functions uttered like signifieds.
The list of the functions that the neighbourhoods of a city can assume has been
known for a long time. We find approximately some thirty or so functions for a
neighbourhood of a city (at least for a neighbourhood of the city centre: a zone
that has been rather well studied from the sociological point of view). This list
can of course be completed, enriched, refined but it will constitute only an
extremely elementary level for semiological analysis, a level which will
probably have to be reviewed later: not only because of the weight and the
pressure exercised by history but because, precisely, the signifieds are like
mythical creatures, extremely imprecise, and at a certain point they always
become the signifiers of *something else*; the signifieds are transient, the
signifiers remain. The hunt for the signified can thus constitute only a provisional approach. The role of the signified when we succeed in discerning it is
only to be a kind of witness to a specific state of the distribution of signification. Besides we must note that we attribute an ever-growing importance to
the empty signified, to the empty space of the signified. In other words,
elements are understood as signifying rather by their own correlative position
than by their contents. Thus, Tokyo, which is one of the most tangled urban
complexes that we can imagine from the semantic point of view, nonetheless
has a kind of centre. But this centre, occupied by the imperial palace,
surrounded by a deep moat and hidden by greenery, is felt as an empty centre.
As a more general rule, the studies of the urban nucleus of different cities has
shown that the central point of the city centre (every city has a centre) which we
call 'solid nucleus', does not constitute the peak point of any particular activity
but a kind of empty 'focal point' for the image that the community develops of
the centre. We have here again a somehow empty place which is necessary for
the organization of the rest of the city.

Barthes   My second remark is that symbolism must be defined essentially as the world of signifiers, of correlations, and, especially, correlations that we can never enclose in a full signification, in a final signification. Henceforth, from the point of view of descriptive technique, the distribution of elements, meaning the signifiers, exhausts in a certain sense the semantic discovery. This is true for the Chomskian semantics of Katz and Fodor and even for the analyses of Lévi-Strauss, which are founded on the clarification of a relation which is no longer analogical but homological (a point demonstrated in his book on totemism which is rarely cited). Thus, we discover that when we wish to do the semiology of the city, we shall probably have to develop the division of signification further and in more detail. For this I appeal to my experience as amateur. We know that in certain cities, there exist spaces which offer a very elaborate specialization of functions: this is the case for example with the oriental souk, where a street is reserved for the tanners and another one for the goldsmiths; in Tokyo certain parts of the same neighbourhood are very homogeneous from the functional point of view: practically, we find there only bars or snackbars or places of entertainment. Well, we must go beyond this first aspect and not limit the semantic description of the city to this unit. We must try to decompose microstructures in the same way that we can isolate little fragments of phrases in a long period; we must then get in the habit of making a quite elaborate analysis which will lead us to these micro-structures and, inversely, we must get used to a broader analysis really arriving at the macro-structures. We all know that Tokyo is a polynuclear city; it has several cores around five or six centres. We must learn to differentiate semantically among these centres, which, in fact, are indicated by railroad stations. In other terms, even in this sector, the best model for the semantic study of the city will be provided, I believe, at least at the beginning, by the phrase of discourse. And here we rediscover Victor Hugo's old intuition: the city is a writing. He who moves about the city, e.g. the user of the city (what we all are), is a kind of reader who, following his obligations and his movements, appropriates fragments of the utterance in order to actualize them in secret. When we move about a city, we all are in the situation of the reader of the 100,000 million poems of Queneau, where one can find a different poem by changing a single line; unawares, we are somewhat like this avant-garde reader when we are in a city.

My third remark, finally, is that today semiology never supposes the existence of a definitive signified. This means that the signifieds are always signifiers for other signifieds and vice versa. In reality, in any cultural or even psychological complex, we are faced with infinite chains of metaphors whose signified is always retreating or becomes itself a signifier. This structure is currently being explored, as you know, in psychoanalysis by Jacques Lacan, and also in the study of writing, where it is postulated if not really explored. If we apply these ideas to the city we would doubtless be led to reveal a dimension which I must say I have never seen cited, at least explicitly, in the studies and surveys of urban planning. I will call it the *erotic* dimension. The eroticism of the city is the lesson we can draw from the infinitely metaphorical nature of urban discourse. I use the word eroticism in its widest meaning: it would be pointless to suppose that the eroticism of the city referred only to the area reserved for this kind of pleasure, for the concept of the place of pleasure is one

of the most tenacious mystifications of urban functionalism. It is a functional   *Barthes*
concept and not a semantic concept; I use eroticism or *sociality* inter-
changeably. The city, essentially and semantically, is the place of our meeting
with the *other*, and it is for this reason that the centre is the gathering place in
every city; the city centre is instituted above all by the young people, the
adolescents.

When they express their image of the city, they always have a tendency to
limit, to concentrate, to condense the centre; the city centre is felt as the place of
exchange of social activities and I would almost say erotic activities in the
broad sense of the word. Better still, the city centre is always felt as the space
where subversive forces, forces of rupture, ludic forces act and meet. Play is a
subject very often emphasized in the surveys on the centre; there is in France a
series of surveys concerning the appeal of Paris for the suburbs, and it has been
observed through these surveys that Paris as a centre was always experienced
semantically by the periphery as the privileged place where the other is and
where we ourselves are other, as the place where we play the other. In contrast,
all that is not the centre is precisely that which is not ludic space, everything
which is not otherness: family, residence, identity. Naturally, especially for the
city, we would have to discover the metaphorical chain, the chain substituted
for Eros. We must search more particularly in the direction of the large categories, of the major habits of man, for example nourishment, purchases,
which are really erotic activities in this consumer society. I am thinking once
again of the example of Tokyo: the huge railway stations which are the
landmarks of the principal neighbourhoods are also big shopping centres. And
it is certain that the Japanese railway station, the shop-station, has at bottom a
unique signification and that this signification is erotic: purchase or meeting.
We should then explore these deep images of the urban elements. For example,
numerous surveys have emphasized the imaginary function of the water course,
which in every city is experienced as a river, a channel, a body of water. There is
a relation between road and water and we are well aware that the cities which
are most resistant to signification and which incidentally often present difficulties of adaptation for the inhabitants are precisely the cities without water,
the cities without seashore, without a surface of water, without a lake, without
a river, without a stream: all these cities present difficulties of life, of legibility.

In conclusion, I would like to say only this: in the comments I have made
here I have not touched on the problem of methodology. Why? Because if we
want to undertake a semiology of the city, the best approach, in my opinion, as
indeed for every semantic venture, will be a certain ingenuity on the part of the
reader. Many of us should try to decipher the city we are in, starting if necessary
with a personal rapport. Dominating all these readings by different categories
of readers (for we have a complete scale of readers, from the native to the
stranger) we would thus work out the language of the city. This is why I would
say that it is not so important to multiply the surveys or the functional studies
of the city, but to multiply the readings of the city, of which unfortunately only
the writers have so far given us some examples.

Starting from these readings, from this reconstruction of a language or a
code of the city, we could then turn to means of a more scientific nature:
definition of units, syntax, etc., but always keeping in mind that we must never
seek to fix and rigidify the signified of the units discovered, because,

Barthes historically, these signifieds are always extremely vague, dubious and unmanageable.

We construct, we make every city a little in the image of the ship *Argo*, whose every piece was no longer the original piece but which still remained the ship *Argo*, that is, a set of significations easily readable and recognizable. In this attempt at a semantic approach to the city we should try to understand the play of signs, to understand that any city is a structure, but that we must never try and we must never want to fill in this structure.

For the city is a poem, as has often been said and as Hugo said better than anyone else, but it is not a classical poem, a poem tidily centred on a subject. It is a poem which unfolds the signifier and it is this unfolding that ultimately the semiology of the city should try to grasp and make sing.

NOTES

1   Lecture given on 16 May 1967, under the sponsorship of the *Institut Français*, the Institute of the History of Architecture at the University of Naples, published in *Op. Cit.*, 10 (1967).
2   *Oecumenè*: the word used by certain geographers to designate the inhabited world or an inhabited region. The Greek word means all the inhabited world.
3   Cf. P. Lévèque and P. Vidal-Naquet, *Clisthème l'Athénien*, Paris: Macula, 1983.
4   Cf. F. Choay, *L'Urbanisme: Utopie et Réalités*, Paris: Editions du Seuil, 1965.

THE EIFFEL TOWER

Maupassant often lunched at the restaurant in the tower, though he didn't care much for the food: 'It's the only place in Paris', he used to say, 'where I don't have to see it.' And it's true that you must take endless precautions, in Paris, not to see the Eiffel Tower; whatever the season, through mist and cloud, on overcast days or in sunshine, in rain – wherever you are, whatever the land-scape of roofs, domes, or branches separating you from it, *the Tower is there*; incorporated into daily life until you can no longer grant it any specific attribute, determined merely to persist, like a rock or the river, it is as literal as a phenomenon of nature whose meaning can be questioned to infinity but whose existence is incontestable. There is virtually no Parisian glance it fails to *touch* at some time of day; at the moment I begin writing these lines about it, the Tower is there, in front of me, framed by my window; and at the very moment the January night blurs it, apparently trying to make it invisible, to deny its presence, two little lights come on, winking gently as they revolve at its very tip: all this night, too, it will be there, connecting me above Paris to each of my friends that I know are seeing it: with it we all comprise a shifting figure of which it is the steady centre: the Tower is friendly.

The Tower is also present to the entire world. First of all as a universal symbol of Paris, it is everywhere on the globe where Paris is to be stated as an image; from the Midwest to Australia, there is no journey to France which isn't made, somehow, in the Tower's name, no schoolbook, poster, or film about France which fails to propose it as the major sign of a people and of a place: it belongs to the universal language of travel. Further: beyond its strictly Parisian statement, it touches the most general human image-repertoire: its simple,

primary shape confers upon it the vocation of an infinite cipher: in turn and   *Barthes*
according to the appeals of our imagination, the symbol of Paris, of modernity,
of communication, of science or of the nineteenth century, rocket, stem,
derrick, phallus, lightning rod or insect, confronting the great itineraries of our
dreams, it is the inevitable sign; just as there is no Parisian glance which is not
compelled to encounter it, there is no fantasy which fails, sooner or later, to
acknowledge its form and to be nourished by it; pick up a pencil and let your
hand, in other words your thoughts, wander, and it is often the Tower which
will appear, reduced to that simple line whose sole mythic function is to join, as
the poet says, *base and summit*, or again, *earth and heaven*.

This pure – virtually empty – sign – is ineluctible, *because it means every-*
thing. In order to negate the Eiffel Tower (though the temptation to do so is
rare, for this symbol offends nothing in us), you must, like Maupassant, get up
on it and, so to speak, identify yourself with it. Like man himself, who is the
only one not to know his own glance, the Tower is the only blind point of the
total optical system of which it is the centre and Paris the circumference. But in
this movement which seems to limit it, the Tower acquires a new power: an
object when we look at it, it becomes a lookout in its turn when we visit it, and
now constitutes as an object, simultaneously extended and collected beneath it,
that Paris which just now was looking at it. The Tower is an object which sees,
a glance which is seen; it is a complete verb, both active and passive, in which
no function, no *voice* (as we say in grammar, with a piquant ambiguity) is
defective. This dialectic is not in the least banal, it makes the Tower a singular
monument; for the world ordinarily produces either purely functional organisms (camera or eye) intended to see things but which then afford nothing to
sight, what *sees* being mythically linked to what remains *hidden* (this is the
theme of the voyeur), or else spectacles which themselves are blind and are left
in the pure passivity of the visible. The Tower (and this is one of its mythic
powers) transgresses this separation, this habitual divorce of *seeing* and *being*
seen, it achieves a sovereign circulation between the two functions; it is a
complete object which has, if one may say so, both sexes of sight. This radiant
position in the order of perception gives it a prodigious propensity to meaning:
the Tower attracts meaning the way a lightning rod attracts thunderbolts; for
all lovers of signification, it plays a glamorous part, that of a pure signifier, i.e.
of a form in which men unceasingly put *meaning* (which they extract at will
from their knowledge, their dreams, their history), without this meaning
thereby ever being finite and fixed: who can say what the Tower will be for
humanity tomorrow? But there can be no doubt it will always be something,
and something of humanity itself. Glance, object, symbol, such is the infinite
circuit of functions which permits it always to be something other and something much more than the Eiffel Tower.

In order to satisfy this great oneiric function, which makes it into a kind of
total monument, the Tower must escape reason. The first condition of this
victorious flight is that the Tower be an utterly *useless* monument. The Tower's
inutility has always been obscurely felt to be a scandal, i.e. a truth, one that is
precious and inadmissible. Even before it was built, it was blamed for being
useless, which, it was believed at the time, was suffcient to condemn it; it was
not in the spirit of a period commonly dedicated to rationality and to the
empiricism of great bourgeois enterprises to endure the notion of a useless

Barthes   object (unless it was declaratively an *objet d'art*, which was also unthinkable in relation to the Tower); hence Gustave Eiffel, in his own defence of his project in reply to the Artists' Petition, scrupulously lists all the future uses of the Tower: they are all, as we might expect of an engineer, scientific uses: aerodynamic measurements, studies of the resistance of substances, physiology of the climber, radio-electric research, problems of telecommunication, meteorological observations, etc. These uses are doubtless incontestable, but they seem quite ridiculous alongside the overwhelming myth of the Tower, of the human meaning which it has assumed throughout the world. This is because here the utilitarian excuses, however ennobled they may be by the myth of Science, are nothing in comparison to the great imaginary function which enables men to be strictly human. Yet, as always, the gratuitous meaning of the work is never avowed directly: it is rationalized under the rubric of *use*: Eiffel saw his Tower in the form of a serious object, rational, useful; men return it to him in the form of a great baroque dream which quite naturally touches on the borders of the irrational.

This double movement is a profound one: architecture is always dream and function, expression of a utopia and instrument of a convenience. Even before the Tower's birth, the nineteenth century (especially in America and in England) had often dreamed of structures whose height would be astonishing, for the century was given to technological feats, and the conquest of the sky once again preyed upon humanity. In 1881, shortly before the Tower, a French architect had elaborated the project of a sun tower; now this project, quite mad technologically, since it relied on masonry and not on steel, also put itself under the warrant of a thoroughly empirical utility; on the one hand, a bonfire placed on top of the structure was to illuminate the darkness of every nook and cranny in Paris by a system of mirrors (a system that was undoubtedly a complex one!), and on the other, the last storey of this sun tower (about 1,000 feet, like the Eiffel Tower) was to be reserved for a kind of sunroom, in which invalids would benefit from an air 'as pure as in the mountains'. And yet, here as in the case of the Tower, the naive utilitarianism of the enterprise is not separate from the oneiric, infinitely powerful function which, actually, inspires its creation: use never does anything but shelter meaning. Hence we might speak, among men, of a true Babel complex: Babel was supposed to *serve* to communicate with God, and yet Babel is a dream which touches much greater depths than that of the theological project; and just as this great ascensional dream, released from its utilitarian prop, is finally what remains in the countless Babels represented by the painters, as if the function of art were to reveal the profound uselessness of objects, just so the Tower, almost immediately disengaged from the scientific considerations which had authorized its birth (it matters very little here that the Tower should be in fact useful), has arisen from a great human dream in which movable and infinite meanings are mingled: it has reconquered the basic uselessness which makes it live in men's imagination. At first, it was sought – so paradoxical is the notion of an empty monument – to make it into a 'temple of Science'; but this is only a metaphor; as a matter of fact, the Tower is *nothing*, it achieves a kind of zero degree of the monument; it participates in no rite, in no cult, not even in Art; you cannot visit the Tower as a museum: there is nothing to see *inside* the Tower. This empty monument nevertheless receives each year twice as many visitors as the Louvre and considerably more than the largest movie house in Paris.

Then why do we visit the Eiffel Tower? No doubt in order to participate in a   *Barthes*
dream of which it is (and this is its originality) much more the crystallizer than
the true object. The Tower is not a usual spectacle; to enter the Tower, to scale
it, to run around its courses, is, in a manner both more elementary and more
profound, to accede to a *view* and to explore the interior of an object (though
an openwork one), to transform the touristic rite into an adventure of sight and
of the intelligence. It is this double function I should like to speak of briefly,
before passing in conclusion to the major symbolic function of the Tower,
which is its final meaning.

The Tower looks at Paris. To visit the Tower is to get oneself up onto the
balcony in order to perceive, comprehend and savour a certain essence of Paris.
And here again, the Tower is an original monument. Habitually, belvederes are
outlooks upon nature, whose elements – waters, valleys, forests – they assemble
beneath them, so that the tourism of the 'fine view' infallibly implies a naturist
mythology. Whereas the Tower overlooks not nature but the city; and yet, by its
very position of a visited outlook, the Tower makes the city into a kind of
nature; it constitutes the swarming of men into a landscape, it adds to the
frequently grim urban myth a romantic dimension, a harmony, a mitigation; by
it, starting from it, the city joins up with the great natural themes which are
offered to the curiosity of men: the ocean, the storm, the mountains, the snow,
the rivers. To visit the Tower, then, is to enter into contact not with a historical
Sacred, as is the case for the majority of monuments, but rather with a new
nature, that of human space: the Tower is not a trace, a souvenir, in short a
culture, but rather an immediate consumption of a humanity made natural by
that glance which transforms it into space.

One might say that for this reason the Tower materializes an imagination
which has had its first expression in literature (it is frequently the function of
the great books to achieve in advance what technology will merely put into
execution). The nineteenth century, fifty years before the Tower, produced
indeed two works in which the (perhaps very old) fantasy of a panoramic vision
received the guarantee of a major poetic writing (*écriture*). These are, on the one
hand, the chapter of *Notre-Dame de Paris* (*The Hunchback of Notre Dame*)
devoted to a bird's-eye view of Paris, and on the other, Michelet's *Tableau
chronologique*. Now, what is admirable in these two great inclusive visions,
one of Paris, the other of France, is that Hugo and Michelet clearly understood
that to the marvellous mitigation of altitude the panoramic vision added an
incomparable power of *intellection*. The bird's-eye view, which each visitor to
the Tower can assume in an instant for his own, gives us the world to *read* and
not only to perceive; this is why it corresponds to a new sensibility of vision; in
the past, to travel (we may recall certain – admirable, moreover – promenades
of Rousseau) was to be thrust into the midst of sensation, to perceive only a
kind of tidal wave of things; the bird's-eye view, on the contrary, represented by
our romantic writers as if they had anticipated both the construction of the
Tower and the birth of aviation, permits us to transcend sensation and to see
things *in their structure*. Hence it is the advent of a new perception, of an
intellectualist mode, which these literatures and these architectures of vision
mark out (born in the same century and probably from the same history): Paris
and France become under Hugo's pen and Michelet's (and under the glance of
the Tower) intelligible objects, yet without – and this is what is new – losing

Barthes   anything of their materiality; a new category appears, that of concrete abstraction; this, moreover, is the meaning which we can give today to the word *structure*: a corpus of intelligent forms.

Like Monsieur Jourdain confronted with prose, every visitor to the Tower makes structuralism without knowing it (which does not keep prose and structure from existing all the same); in Paris spread out beneath him, he spontaneously distinguishes separate – because known – points – and yet does not stop linking them, perceiving them within a great functional space; in short, he separates and groups; Paris offers itself to him as an object virtually *prepared*, exposed to the intelligence, but which he must himself construct by a final activity of the mind: nothing less passive than the *overall view* the Tower gives to Paris. This activity of the mind, conveyed by the tourist's modest glance, has a name: decipherment.

What, in fact, is a panorama? An image we attempt to decipher, in which we try to recognize known sites, to identify landmarks. Take some view of Paris taken from the Eiffel Tower; here you make out the hill sloping down from Chaillot, there the Bois de Boulogne; but where is the Arc de Triomphe? You don't see it, and this absence compels you to inspect the panorama once again, to look for this point which is missing in your structure; your knowledge (the knowledge you may have of Parisian topography) struggles with your perception, and in a sense, that is what intelligence is: to *reconstitute,* to make memory and sensation co-operate so as to produce in your mind a simulacrum of Paris, of which the elements are in front of you, real, ancestral, but nonetheless disoriented by the total space in which they are given to you, for this space was unknown to you. Hence we approach the complex, dialectical nature of all panoramic vision; on the one hand, it is a euphoric vision, for it can slide slowly, lightly the entire length of a continuous image of Paris, and initially no 'accident' manages to interrupt this great layer of mineral and vegetal strata, perceived in the distance in the bliss of altitude; but, on the other hand, this very continuity engages the mind in a certain struggle, it seeks to be deciphered, we must find *signs* within it, a familiarity proceeding from history and from myth. This is why a panorama can never be consumed as a work of art, the aesthetic interest of a painting ceasing once we try to *recognize* in it particular points derived from our knowledge; to say that there is a beauty to Paris stretched out at the feet of the Tower is doubtless to acknowledge this euphoria of aerial vision which recognizes nothing other than a nicely connected space; but it is also to mask the quite intellectual effort of the eye before an object which requires to be divided up, identified, reattached to memory; for the bliss of sensation (nothing happier than a lofty outlook) does not suffice to elude the questioning nature of the mind before any image.

This generally intellectual character of the panoramic vision is further attested by the following phenomenon, which Hugo and Michelet had moreover made into the mainspring of their bird's-eye views: to perceive Paris from above is infallibly to imagine a history; from the top of the Tower, the mind finds itself dreaming of the mutation of the landscape which it has before its eyes; through the astonishment of space, it plunges into the mystery of time, lets itself be affected by a kind of spontaneous anamnesis: it is duration itself which becomes panoramic. Let us put ourselves back (no difficult task) at the level of an average knowledge, an ordinary question put to the panorama of Paris; four

great moments immediately leap out to our vision, i.e. to our consciousness. *Barthes*
The first is that of prehistory; Paris was then covered by a layer of water, out of
which barely emerged a few solid points; set on the Tower's first floor, the
visitor would have had his nose level with the waves and would have seen only
some scattered islets, the Etoile, the Pantheon, a wooded island which was
Montmartre and two blue stakes in the distance, the towers of Notre-Dame,
then to his left, bordering this huge lake, the slopes of Mont Valérien; and
conversely, the traveller who chooses to put himself today on the heights of this
eminence, in foggy weather, would see emerging the two upper stories of the
Tower from a liquid base. This prehistoric relation of the Tower and the water
has been, so to speak, symbolically maintained down to our own days, for the
Tower is partly built on a thin arm of the Seine filled in (up to the Rue de
l'Université) and it still seems to rise from a gesture of the river whose bridges it
guards. The second history which lies before the Tower's gaze is the Middle
Ages; Cocteau once said that the Tower was the Notre-Dame of the Left Bank;
though the cathedral of Paris is not the highest of the city's monuments (the
Invalides, the Pantheon, Sacré-Coeur are higher), it forms with the tower a pair,
a symbolic couple, recognized, so to speak, by tourist folklore, which readily
reduces Paris to its Tower and its Cathedral: a symbol articulated on the
opposition of the past (the Middle Ages always represent a dense time) and the
present, of stone, old as the world, and metal, sign of modernity. The third
moment that can be read from the Tower is that of a broad history, undifferentiated since it proceeds from the Monarchy to the Empire, from the
Invalides to the Arc de Triomphe: this is strictly the History of France, as it is
experienced by French schoolchildren, and of which many episodes, present in
every schoolboy memory, touch Paris. Finally, the Tower surveys a fourth
history of Paris, the one which is being made now; certain modern monuments
(UNESCO, the Radio-Télévision building) are beginning to set signs of the
future within its space; the Tower permits harmonizing these unaccommodated
substances (glass, metal), these new forms, with the stones and domes of the
past; Paris, in its duration, under the Tower's gaze, composes itself like an
abstract canvas in which dark oblongs (derived from a very old past) are
contiguous with the white rectangles of modern architecture.

Once these points of history and of space are established by the eye, from the
top of the Tower, the imagination continues filling out the Parisian panorama,
giving it its structure; but what then intervenes are certain human functions.
Like the devil Asmodeus, by rising above Paris, the visitor to the Tower has the
illusion of raising the enormous lid which covers the private life of millions of
human beings; the city then becomes an intimacy whose functions, i.e. whose
connections, he deciphers. On the great polar axis, perpendicular to the
horizontal curve of the river, three zones are stacked one after the other, as
though along a prone body, three functions of human life: at the top, at the foot
of Montmartre, pleasure; at the centre, around the Opéra, materiality, business,
commerce; toward the bottom, at the foot of the Pantheon, knowledge, study;
then, to the right and left, enveloping this vital axis like two protective muffs,
two large zones of habitation, one residential, the other blue-collar; still farther,
two wooded strips, Boulogne and Vincennes. It has been observed that a kind
of very old law incites cities to develop toward the west, in the direction of the
setting sun; it is on this side that the wealth of the fine neighbourhoods

Barthes   proceeds, the east remaining the site of poverty; the Tower, by its very implantation, seems to follow this movement discreetly; one might say that it accompanies Paris in this westward shift, which our capital does not escape, and that it even invites the city toward its pole of development, to the south and to the west, where the sun is warmer, thereby participating in that great mythic function which makes every city into a living being: neither brain nor organ, situated a little apart from its vital zones, the Tower is merely the witness, the gaze which discreetly fixes, with its slender signal, the whole structure – geographical, historical, and social – of Paris space. This deciphering of Paris, performed by the Tower's gaze, is not only an act of the mind, it is also an initiation. To climb the Tower in order to contemplate Paris from it is the equivalent of that first journey, by which the young man from the provinces went up to Paris, in order to conquer the city. At the age of twelve, young Eiffel himself took the diligence from Dijon with his mother and discovered the 'magic' of Paris. The city, a kind of superlative capital, summons up that movement of accession to a superior order of pleasures, of values, of arts and luxuries; it is a kind of precious world of which knowledge makes the man, marks an entrance into a true life of passions and responsibilities; it is this myth – no doubt a very old one – which the trip to the Tower still allows us to suggest; for the tourist who climbs the Tower, however mild he may be, Paris laid out before his eyes by an individual and deliberate act of contemplation is still something of the Paris confronted, defied, possessed by Rastignac. Hence, of all the sites visited by the foreigner or the provincial, the Tower is the first obligatory monument; it is a Gateway, it marks the transition to a knowledge: one must sacrifice to the Tower by a rite of inclusion from which, precisely, the Parisian alone can excuse himself; the Tower is indeed the site which allows one to be incorporated into a race, and when it regards Paris, it is the very essence of the capital it gathers up and proffers to the foreigner who has paid to it his initiational tribute.

From Paris contemplated, we must now work our way back toward the Tower itself: the Tower which will live its life as an object (before being mobilized as a symbol). Ordinarily, for the tourist, every object is first of all an *inside*, for there is no visit without the exploration of an enclosed space. To visit a church, a museum, a palace is first of all to shut oneself up, to 'make the rounds' of an interior, a little in the manner of an owner: every exploration is an appropriation. This tour of the *inside* corresponds, moreover, to the question raised by the *outside*: the monument is a riddle, to enter it is to solve, to possess it. Here we recognize in the tourist visit that initiational function we have just invoked apropos of the trip to the Tower; the cohort of visitors which is enclosed by a monument and processionally follows its internal meanders before coming back outside is quite like the neophyte who, in order to accede to the initiate's status, is obliged to traverse a dark and unfamiliar route within the initiatory edifice. In the religious protocol as in the tourist enterprise, being enclosed is therefore a function of the rite. Here, too, the Tower is a paradoxical object: one cannot be shut up within it since what defines the Tower is its longilineal form and its open structure. How can you be enclosed within emptiness, how can you visit a line? Yet incontestably the Tower is visited: we linger within it, before using it as an observatory. What is happening? What becomes of the great exploratory function of the *inside* when it is applied to this

empty and depthless monument which might be said to consist entirely of an
exterior substance?

In order to understand how the modern visitor adapts himself to the paradoxical monument which is offered to his imagination, we need merely observe
what the Tower gives him, insofar as one sees in it an object and no longer a
lookout. On this point, the Tower's provisions are of two kinds. The first is of
a technical order; the Tower offers for consumption a certain number of
performances, or, if one prefers, of paradoxes, and the visitor then becomes an
engineer by proxy. These are, first of all, the four bases, and especially (for
enormity does not astonish) the exaggeratedly oblique insertion of the metal
pillars in the mineral mass; this obliquity is curious insofar as it gives birth to an
upright form, whose very verticality absorbs its departure in slanting forms,
and here there is a kind of agreeable challenge for the visitor. Then come the
elevators, quite surprising by their obliquity, for the ordinary imagination
requires that what rises mechanically slide along a vertical axis; and for anyone
who takes the stairs, there is the enlarged spectacle of all the details, plates,
beams, bolts, which *make* the Tower, the surprise of seeing how this rectilinear
form, which is consumed in every corner of Paris as a pure line, is composed of
countless segments, interlinked, crossed, divergent: an operation of reducing an
appearance (the straight line) to its contrary reality (a lacework of broken
substances), a kind of demystification provided by simple enlargement of the
level of perception, as in those photographs in which the curve of a face, by
enlargement, appears to be formed of a thousand tiny squares variously illuminated. Thus the Tower-as-object furnishes its observer, provided he insinuates
himself into it, a whole series of paradoxes, the delectable contraction of an
appearance and of its contrary reality.

The Tower's second provision, as an object, is that, despite its technical
singularity, it constitutes a familiar 'little world'; from the ground level, a whole
humble commerce accompanies its departure: vendors of postcards, souvenirs,
knick-knacks, balloons, toys, sunglasses, herald a commercial life which we
rediscover thoroughly installed on the first platform. Now any commerce has a
space-taming function; selling, buying, exchanging – it is by these simple
gestures that men truly dominate the wildest sites, the most sacred constructions. The myth of the moneylenders driven out of the Temple is actually an
ambiguous one, for such commerce testifies to a kind of affectionate familiarity
with regard to a monument whose singularity no longer intimidates, and it is by
a Christian sentiment (hence to a certain degree a special one) that the spiritual
excludes the familiar; in Antiquity, a great religious festival as well as a
theatrical representation, a veritable sacred ceremony, in no way prevented the
revelation of the most everyday gestures, such as eating or drinking: all
pleasures proceeded simultaneously, not by some heedless permissiveness but
because the ceremonial was never savage and certainly offered no contradiction
to the quotidian. The Tower is not a sacred monument, and no taboo can forbid
a commonplace life to develop there, but there can be no question, nonetheless,
of a trivial phenomenon here. The installation of a restaurant on the Tower, for
instance (food being the object of the most symbolic of trades), is a
phenomenon corresponding to a whole meaning of leisure; man always seems
disposed – if no constraints appear to stand in his way – to seek out a kind of
counterpoint in his pleasures: this is what is called comfort. The Eiffel Tower is

Barthes   a comfortable object, and moreover, it is in this that it is an object either very old (analogous, for instance, to the ancient Circus) or very modern (analogous to certain American institutions such as the drive-in movie, in which one can simultaneously enjoy the film, the car, the food and the freshness of the night air). Further, by affording its visitor a whole polyphony of pleasures, from technological wonder to haute cuisine, including the panorama, the Tower ultimately reunites with the essential function of all major human sites: autarchy. The Tower can live on itself: one can dream there, eat there, observe there, understand there, marvel there, shop there; as on an ocean liner (another mythic object that sets children dreaming), one can feel oneself cut off from the world and yet the owner of a world.

UMBERTO ECO

Italian semiotician Umberto Eco (b. 1932) is a thinker of great versatility, whose *Umberto* interests span from the mediaeval world of aesthetic theory to contemporary *Eco* debates about semiology, and whose publications address topics as diverse as the aesthetics of Thomas Aquinas and the sociology of jeans. He is also well known for his fictional writing which is informed by his academic work.

As a semiotician Eco adopts a middle ground with regard to language, and avoids an understanding of language as either univocal or deferring to infinite meaning. He therefore develops a model of an 'ideal' reader alert to the possibilities of language, if not to the infinite possibilities of language. Eco bases his semiotic theory on codes. He draws the distinction between specific and general codes, where specific codes refer to the language codes of particular languages, while general codes refer to the structure of language as a whole. At the same time he stresses that codes must be viewed within their cultural context. Thus he introduces a certain flexibility and a temporal dimension to an otherwise heavily structural understanding of language.

In his article 'Function and Sign: Semiotics of Architecture' Eco applies his general semiotic theory to the question of architecture and the built environment. Architecture, Eco notes, presents a special case as it is often intended to be primarily functional and not to to be communicative. Nonetheless, architecture does function as a form of mass communication. Eco draws the distinction between the denotative and the connotative. He therefore distinguishes between the primary function – architecture as functional object – and the secondary function – architecture as symbolic object. He notes that in both categories there is potential for 'losses, recoveries and substitutions'. Eco concludes that architects must design structures for 'variable primary functions and open secondary functions'.

In the extract 'How an Exposition Exposes Itself' Eco applies this theory to the context of the 1967 Expo World Fair. Such expositions, Eco observes, present extreme examples, in that the primary function of the pavilions is minimized while their secondary function is exaggerated. The pavilions serve less as functional buildings than as symbols of the values of their national culture.

Eco

FUNCTION AND SIGN: THE SEMIOTICS OF ARCHITECTURE

SEMIOTICS AND ARCHITECTURE

If semiotics, beyond being the science of recognized systems of signs, is really to be a science studying *all* cultural phenomena *as if* they were systems of signs – on the hypothesis that all cultural phenomena *are*, in reality, systems of signs, or that culture can be understood as *communication* – then one of the fields in which it will undoubtedly find itself most challenged is that of architecture.

It should be noted that the term *architecture* will be used in a broad sense here, indicating phenomena of industrial design and urban design as well as phenomena of architecture proper. (We will leave aside, however, the question of whether our notions on these phenomena would be applicable to *any type of design producing three-dimensional constructions destined to permit the fulfilment of some function connected with life in society*, a definition that would embrace the design of clothing, insofar as clothing is culturalized and a means of participating in society, and even the design of food, not as the production of something for the individual's nourishment, but insofar as it involves the construction of contexts that have social functions and symbolic connotations, such as particular menus, the accessories of a meal, etc. – a definition that would be understood to exclude, on the other hand, the production of three-dimensional objects destined primarily to be *contemplated* rather than utilized in society, such as works of art.)

Why is architecture a particular challenge to semiotics? First of all because apparently most architectural objects do not *communicate* (and are not designed to communicate), but *function*. No one can doubt that a roof fundamentally serves to cover, and a glass to hold liquids in such a way that one can then easily drink them. Indeed, this is so obviously and unquestionably the case as it might seem perverse to insist upon seeing as an act of communication something that is so well, and so easily, characterized as a *possibility of function*. One of the first questions for semiotics to face, then, if it aims to provide keys to the cultural phenomena in this field, is whether it is possible to interpret functions as having something to do with communication; and the point of it is that seeing functions from the semiotic point of view might permit one to understand and define them better, precisely as functions, and thereby to discover other types of functionality, which are just as essential but which a straight functionalist interpretation keeps one from perceiving.[1]

ARCHITECTURE AS COMMUNICATION

A phenomenological consideration of our relationship with architectural objects tells us that we commonly do experience architecture as communication, even while recognizing its functionality.

Let us imagine the point of view of the man who started the history of architecture. Still 'all wonder and ferocity' (to use Vico's phrase), driven by cold and rain and following the example of some animal or obeying an impulse in which instinct and reasoning are mixed in a confused way, this hypothetical

Stone Age man takes shelter in a recess, in some hole on the side of a mountain,   *Eco*
in a cave. Sheltered from the wind and rain, he examines the cave that shelters
him, by daylight or by the light of a fire (we will assume he has already
discovered fire). He notes the amplitude of the vault, and understands this as
the limit of an outside space, which is (with its wind and rain) *cut off*, and as the
beginning of an inside space, which is likely to evoke in him some unclear
nostalgia for the womb, imbue him with feelings of protection, and appear still
imprecise, and ambiguous to him, seen under a play of shadow and light. Once
the storm is over, he might leave the cave and reconsider it from the outside;
there he would note the entryway as 'hole that permits passage to the inside',
and the entrance would recall to his mind the image of the inside: entrance hole,
covering vault, walls (or continuous wall of rock) surrounding a space within.
Thus an 'idea of the cave' takes shape, which is useful at least as a mnemonic
device, enabling him to think of the cave later on as a possible objective in case
of rain; but it also enables him to recognize in another cave the same *possibility
of shelter* found in the first one. At the second cave he tries, the idea of that cave
is soon replaced by the idea of cave *tout court – a model, a type*, something that
does not exist concretely but on the basis of which he can recognize a certain
context of phenomena as 'cave'.

The model (or concept) functions so well that he can now recognize from a
distance someone else's cave or a cave he does not intend to make use of,
independently of whether he wants to take shelter in it or not. The man has
learned that the cave can assume various appearances. Now this would still be
a matter of an *individual's* realization of an abstract model, but in a sense the
model is *already codified*, not yet on a social level but on the level of this
individual who proposes and communicates it to himself, within his own mind.
And he would probably be able, at this point, to communicate the model of the
cave to other men, by means of graphic signs. The *architectural code* would
generate an *iconic code,* and the 'cave principle' would become an object of
communicative intercourse.

At this point the drawing of a cave or the image of a cave in the distance
becomes the communication of a possible function, and such it remains, even
when there is neither fulfilment of the function nor a wish to fulfil it.

What has happened, then, is what Roland Barthes is speaking about when
he says that 'as soon as there is a society, every usage is converted into a sign of
itself'.[2] To use a spoon to get food to one's mouth is still, of course, the fulfilment of a function, through the use of an artifact that allows and promotes that
function; yet to say that it 'promotes' the function indicates that the artifact
serves a communicative function as well: it *communicates the function to be
fulfilled*. Moreover, the fact that someone uses a spoon becomes, in the eyes of
the society that observes it, the communication of a conformity by him to
certain usages (as opposed to certain others, such as eating with one's hands or
sipping food directly from a dish).

The spoon promotes a *certain way of eating*, and *signifies that way of eating*,
just as the cave promotes the act of taking shelter and signifies the existence of
the possible functions; and both objects *signify even when they are not being
used* . . .

Eco   THE ARCHITECTURAL SIGN

With this semiotic framework, one is not obliged to characterize a sign on the basis of either behaviour that it stimulates or actual objects that would verify its meaning: it is characterized only on the basis of *codified meaning that in a given cultural context is attributed to the sign vehicle*. (It is true that even the processes of codification belong to the realm of social behaviour; but the codes do not admit of empirical verification either, for although based on constancies inferred from observation of *communicative usages*, they would always be constructed as *structural models*, postulated as a *theoretical hypothesis*.)

That a stair has obliged me to go up does not concern a theory of signification; but that occurring with certain formal characteristics that determine its nature as a *sign vehicle* (just as the verbal sign vehicle *stairs* occurs as an articulation of certain 'distinctive units'), the object communicates to me its possible function – this is a datum of culture, and can be established *independently of apparent behaviour, and even of a presumed mental reaction, on my part*. In other words, in the cultural context in which we live (and this is a model of culture that holds for several millennia of history as far as certain rather stable codes are concerned) there exists an architectural form that might be defined as 'an inclined progression of rigid horizontal surfaces upward in which the distance between successive surfaces in elevation, r, is set somewhere between 5 and 9 inches, in which the surfaces have a dimension in the direction of the progression in plan, t, set somewhere between 16 and 8 inches, and in which there is little or no distance between, or overlapping of, successive surfaces when projected orthographically on a horizontal plane, the sum total (or parts) falling somewhere between 17 and 48 degrees from horizontal'. (To this definition could of course be added the formula relating r to t.) And such a form *denotes* the *meaning* 'stair as a possibility of going up' on the basis of a code that I can work out and recognize as operative even if, in fact, no one is going up that stair at present and even though, in theory, no one might ever go up it again (even if stairs are never used again by anyone, just as no one is ever going to use a truncated pyramid again in making astronomical observations).

Thus what our semiotic framework would recognize in the architectural sign is *the presence of a sign vehicle whose denoted meaning is the function it makes possible* . . .

The semiotic perspective that we have preferred with its distinction between sign vehicles and meanings – the former observable and describable apart from the meanings we attribute to them, at least at some stage of the semiotic investigation, and the latter variable but determined by the codes in the light of which we read the sign vehicles – permits us to recognize in architectural signs *sign vehicles capable of being described and catalogued*, which can denote precise functions provided one interprets them in the light of certain codes, and *successive meanings* with which these sign vehicles are capable of being filled, whose attribution can occur, as we will see, not only by way of denotation, but also by way of connotation, on the basis of further codes.

Significative forms, codes worked out on the strength of inferences from usages and proposed as structural models of given communicative relations, denotative and connotative meanings attached to the sign vehicles on the basis of the codes – this is the semiotic universe in which a reading of architecture as

communication becomes viable, a universe in which verification through   *Eco*
observable physical behaviour and actual objects (whether denotata or
referents) would be simply irrelevant and in which the only concrete objects of
any relevance are *the architectural objects as significative forms*. Within these
bounds one can begin to see the various communicative possibilities of architecture.

ARCHITECTURAL DENOTATION

The object of use is, in its communicative capacity, the sign vehicle of a precisely and conventionally denoted meaning – its function. More loosely, it has
been said that the first meaning of a building is what one must do in order to
inhabit it – the architectural object denotes a 'form of inhabitation'. And it is
clear that this denotation occurs even when one is not availing oneself of the
denoted inhabitability (or, more generally, the denoted utility) of the architectural object. But we must remember from the outset that there is more to
architectural communication than this.

When I look at the windows on the façade of a building, for instance, their
denoted function may not be uppermost in my mind; my attention may be
turned to a window-meaning that is based on the function but in which the
function has receded to the extent that I may even forget it, for the moment,
concentrating on relationships through which the windows become elements of
an architectural rhythm – just as someone who is reading a poem may, without
entirely disregarding the meanings of the words there, let them recede into the
background and thereby enjoy a certain formal play in the sign vehicles'
contextual juxtaposition. And thus an architect might present one with some
false windows, whose denoted function would be illusory, and these windows
could still function as windows in the architectural context in which they occur
and be enjoyed (given the aesthetic function of the architectural message) as
windows.[3]

Moreover windows – in their form, their number, their disposition on a
façade (portholes, loopholes, curtain wall, etc.) – may, besides denoting a function, refer to a certain conception of inhabitation and use; they may *connote an
overall ideology* that has informed the architect's operation. Round arches,
pointed arches and ogee arches all function in the load-bearing sense and
denote this function, but they connote diverse ways of conceiving the function:
they begin to assume a symbolic function.

Let us return, however, to denotation and the primary, utilitarian function.
We said that the object of use denotes the function conventionally, according to
codes. Let us here consider some of the general conditions under which an
object denotes its function conventionally.

According to an immemorial architectural codification, a stair or a ramp
denotes the possibility of going up. But whether it is a simple set of steps in a
garden or a grand staircase by Vanvitelli, the winding stairs of the Eiffel Tower
or the spiralling ramp of Frank Lloyd Wright's Guggenheim Museum, one finds
oneself before a form whose interpretation involves not only a codified connection between the form and the function but also a conventional conception of
how one fulfils the function with the form. Recently, for example, one has been
able to go up also by means of an elevator, and the interpretation of the elevator

Eco   involves, besides the recognition of the possible function – and rather than being disposed to the motor activity of moving one's feet in a certain way – a conception of how to fulfil the function through the various accessory devices at one's disposal in the elevator. Now the 'legibility' of these features of the elevator might be taken for granted, and presumably their design is such that none of us would have any trouble interpreting them. But clearly a primitive man used to stairs or ramps would be at a loss in front of an elevator; the best intentions on the part of the designer would not result in making the thing clear to him. The designer may have had a conception of the push buttons, the graphic arrows indicating whether the elevator is about to go up or down, and the emphatic floor-level indicators, but the primitive, even if he can guess the function, does not know that these forms are the 'key' to the function. He simply has no real grasp of the code of the elevator. Likewise he might possess only fragments of the code of the revolving door and be determined to use one of these as if it were a matter of an ordinary door. We can see, then, that an architect's belief in form that 'follows function' would be rather naive unless it really rested on an understanding of the processes of codification involved.

In other words, the principle that form follows function might be restated: *the form of the object must, besides making the function possible, denote that function clearly enough to make it practicable as well as desirable*, clearly enough to dispose one to the actions through which it would be fulfilled.

Then all the ingenuity of an architect or designer cannot make a new form functional (and cannot give form to a new function) *without the support of existing processes of codification* . . .

A work of art can certainly be something new and highly informative; it can present articulations of elements that correspond to an idiolect of its own and not to pre-existing codes, for it is essentially an object intended to be contemplated, and it can communicate this new code, implicit in its makeup, precisely by fashioning it on the basis of the pre-existing codes, evoked and negated. Now an architectural object could likewise be something new and informative; and if intended to promote a new function, it could contain in its form (or in its relation to comparable familiar forms) indications for the 'decoding' of this function. It too would be playing upon elements of pre-existing codes, but rather than evoking and negating the codes, as the work of art might, and thus directing attention ultimately to itself, it would have to progressively transform them, progressively deforming already known forms and the functions conventionally referable to these forms. Otherwise the architectural object would become, not a functional object, but indeed a work of art: an ambiguous form, capable of being interpreted in the light of various different codes. Such is the case with 'kinetic' objects that simulate the outward appearance of objects of use; objects of use they are not, in effect, because of the underlying ambiguity that disposes them to any use imaginable and so to none in particular. (It should be noted that the situation of an object open to any use imaginable – and subject to none – is different from that of an object subject to a number of determinate uses, as we will see.)

One might well wish to go further into the nature of architectural denotation (here described only roughly, and with nothing in the way of detailed analysis). But we also mentioned possibilities of architectural connotation, which should be clarified.

ARCHITECTURAL CONNOTATION   *Eco*

We said that besides denoting its function the architectural object could connote a certain ideology of the function. But undoubtedly it can connote other things. The cave, in our hypothetical model of the beginning of architecture, came to denote a shelter function, but no doubt in time it would have begun to connote 'family' or 'group', 'security', 'familiar surroundings', etc. Then would its connotative nature, this symbolic 'function' of the object, be less *functional* than its first function? In other words, given that the cave denotes a certain basic *utilitas* (to borrow a term from Koenig), there is the question whether, with respect to life in society, the object would be any less *useful* in terms of its ability, as a symbol, to connote such things as closeness and familiarity. (From the semiotic point of view, the connotations would be founded on the denotation of the primary *utilitas*, but that would not diminish their importance.)

A seat tells me first of all that I can sit down on it. But if the seat is a throne, it must do more than seat one: it serves to seat one with a certain dignity, to corroborate its user's 'sitting in dignity' – perhaps through various accessory signs connoting 'regalness' (eagles on the arms, a high, crowned back, etc.). Indeed the connotation of dignity and regalness can become so functionally important that the basic function, to seat one, may even be slighted, or distorted: a throne, to connote regalness, often demands that the person sitting on it sit rigidly and uncomfortably (along with a sceptre in his right hand, a globe in the left, and a crown on his head), and therefore seats one 'poorly' with respect to the primary *utilitas*. Thus to seat one is only one of the functions of the throne – and only one of its meanings, the first but not the most important.

So the title *function* should be extended to all the uses of objects of use (in our perspective, to the various communicative, as well as to the denoted, functions), for with respect to life in society the 'symbolic' capacities of these objects are no less 'useful' than their 'functional' capacities. And it should be clear that we are not being metaphorical in calling the symbolic connotations functional, because although they may not be immediately identified with the 'functions' narrowly defined, they do represent (and indeed communicate) in each case a real social utility of the object. It is clear that the most important function of the throne is the 'symbolic' one, and clearly evening dress (which, instead of serving to cover one like most everyday clothing, often 'uncovers' for women, and for men covers poorly, lengthening to tails behind while leaving the chest practically bare) is functional because, thanks to the complex of conventions it connotes, it permits certain social relations, confirms them, shows their acceptance on the part of those who are communicating, with it, their social status, their decision to abide by certain rules, and so forth.[4]

ARCHITECTURAL COMMUNICATION AND HISTORY

PRIMARY FUNCTIONS AND SECONDARY FUNCTIONS

Since it would be awkward from here on to speak of 'functions' on the one hand, when referring to the denoted *utilitas* and of 'symbolic' connotations on the other, as if the latter did not likewise represent real functions, we will speak of a *'primary'* function (which is denoted) and of a complex of *secondary*

Eco   *functions* (which are connotative). It should be remembered, and is implied in
what has already been said, that the terms *primary* and *secondary* will be used
here to convey, not an axiological discrimination (as if the one function were
more important than the others), but rather a semiotic mechanism, in the sense
that the secondary functions rest on the denotation of the primary function
(just as when one has the connotation of 'bad tenor' from the word for 'dog' in
Italian, *cane*, it rests on the process of denotation).

Let us take a historical example where we can begin to see the intricacies of
these primary and secondary functions, comparing the records of interpretation history has left us. Architectural historians have long debated the
code of the Gothic, and particularly the structural value of the ogive. Three
major hypotheses have been advanced:

1   the ogive has a structural function, and the entire lofty and elegant
     structure of a cathedral stands upon it, by virtue of the miracle of
     equilibrium it allows;
2   the ogive has no structural value, even if it gives the opposite impres-
     sion; rather, it is the webs of the ogival vault that have the structural
     value;
3   the ogive had a structural value in the course of construction, func-
     tioning as a sort of provisional framework; later, the interplay of thrusts
     and counterthrusts was picked up by the webs and by the other elements
     of the structure, and in theory the ogives of the cross vaulting could
     have been eliminated.[5]

No matter which interpretation one might adhere to, no one has ever
doubted that the ogives of the cross vaulting *denoted* a structural function –
support reduced to the pure interplay of thrusts and counterthrusts along
slender, nervous elements; the controversy turns rather on the referent of that
denotation: is the denoted function an illusion? Even if it is illusory, then, the
communicative value of the ogival ribbing remains unquestionable; indeed if
the ribbing had been articulated only to *communicate* the function, and not to
permit it, that value would, while perhaps appearing more valid, simply be
more intentional. (Likewise, it cannot be denied that the word unicorn is a sign,
even though the unicorn does not exist, and even though its non-existence
might have been no surprise to those using the term.)

While they were debating the functional value of ogival ribbing, however,
historians and interpreters of all periods realized that the code of the Gothic
had also a 'symbolic' dimension (in other words, that the elements of the
Gothic cathedral had some complexes of secondary functions to them); one
knew that the ogival vault and the wall pierced with great windows had something connotative to communicate. Now what that something might be has
been defined time and again, on the basis of elaborate connotative subcodes
founded on the cultural conventions and intellectual patrimony of given groups
and given periods and determined by particular ideological perspectives, with
which they are congruent.

There is, for example, the standard romantic and proto-romantic interpretation, whereby the structure of the Gothic cathedral was intended to
reproduce the vault of Celtic forests, and thus the pre-Roman world, barbaric
and primitive, of druidical religiosity. And in the medieval period, legions of

commentators and allegorists put themselves to defining, according to codes of   *Eco*
formidable precision and subtlety, the individual meanings of every single
architectural element; it will suffice to refer the reader to the catalogue drawn
up, centuries later, by Joris Karl Juysmans in his *La cathédrale*.

But there is, after all, a singular document we could mention – a code's very
constitution – and that is the justification Suger gives of the cathedral in his *De
rebus in administratione sua gestis*, in the twelfth century.[6] There he lets it be
understood, in prose and in verse, that the light that penetrates in streams from
the windows into the dark naves (or the structure of the walls that permits the
light to be offered such ample access) must represent the very effusiveness of the
divine creative energy, a notion quite in keeping with certain Neoplatonic texts
and based on a codified equivalence between light and participation in the
divine essence.[7]

We could say with some assurance, then, that for men of the twelfth century
the Gothic windows and glazing (and in general the space of the naves traversed
by streams of light) connoted 'participation' (in the technical sense given the term
in medieval Neoplatonism); but the history of the interpretation of the Gothic
teaches us that over the centuries the same sign vehicle, in the light of different
subcodes, has been able to connote diverse things.

Indeed, in the nineteenth century one witnessed a phenomenon typical of the
history of art – when in a given period a code in its entirety (all artistic style, a
manner, a 'mode of forming', independently of the connotations of its individual manifestations in messages) comes to connote an ideology (with which it
was intimately united either at the moment of its birth or at the time of its most
characteristic affirmation). One had at that time the identification 'Gothic style
= religiosity', an identification that undoubtedly rested on the other, preceding
connotative identifications, such as 'vertical emphasis = elevation of the soul
Godward' or contrast of light streaming through great windows and naves in
'shadows = mysticism'. Now these are connotations so deeply rooted that even
today some effort is required to remember that the Greek temple too, balanced
and harmonious in its proportions, could connote, according to another
lexicon, the elevation of the spirit to the Gods, and that something like the altar
of Abraham on the top of a mountain could evoke mystical feelings; thus one
connotative lexicon may impose itself over others in the course of time and, for
example, the contrast of light and shadow becomes what one most deeply
associates with mystic states of mind.

A metropolis like New York is studded with neo-Gothic churches, whose
style (whose 'language') was chosen to express the presence of the divine. And
the curious fact is that, by convention, these churches still have (for the faithful)
the same value today, in spite of the fact that skyscrapers – by which they are
now hemmed in on every side, and made to appear very small, almost
miniaturized – have rendered the verticality emphasized in this architecture all
but indistinguishable. An example like this should be enough to remind us that
there are no mysterious 'expressive' values deriving simply from the nature of
the forms themselves, and that expressiveness arises instead from a dialectic
between significative forms and codes of interpretations; for otherwise the
Gothic churches of New York, which are no longer as distinctively attenuated
and vertical as they used to be, would no longer express what they used to,
while in fact they still do in some respects, and precisely because they are 'read'

Eco   on the basis of codes that permit one to recognize them as distinctively vertical in spite of the new formal context (and new code of reading), the advent of the skyscraper has now brought about.

ARCHITECTURAL MEANINGS AND HISTORY

It would be a mistake, however, to imagine that by their very nature architectural sign vehicles would denote stable primary functions, with only the secondary functions varying in the course of history. The example of ogival ribbing has already shown us a denoted function undergoing curious fluctuations – it was considered by some effective and essential, but by others provisional or illusory – and there is every reason to believe that in the course of time certain primary functions, no longer effective, would no longer even be denoted, the 'addresses' no longer possessing the requisite codes.

So, in the course of history, both primary and secondary functions might be found undergoing losses, recoveries and substitutions of various kinds. These losses, recoveries and substitutions are common to the life of forms in general, and constitute the norm in the course of the reading of works of art proper. If they seem more striking (and paradoxical) in the field of architectural forms, that is only because according to the common view one is dealing there with functional objects of an unequivocally indicated, and thus *univocally* communicative, nature; to give the lie to such a view, there is the story – its very currency puts its authenticity in doubt, but if untrue it is in any case credible – about the native wearing an alarm clock on his chest, an alarm clock interpreted as a pendant (as a kind of 'kinetic jewelry', one might say) rather than as a timepiece: the clock's measurement of time, and indeed the very notion of 'clock time', is the fruit of a codification and comprehensible only on the basis of it.

One type of fluctuation in the life of objects of use can therefore be seen in the variety of readings to which they are subject, regarding both primary and secondary functions . . .[8]

ARCHITECTURAL CODES

WHAT IS A CODE IN ARCHITECTURE?

Architectural signs as denotative and connotative according to codes, the codes and subcodes as making different readings possible in the course of history, the architect's operation as possibly a matter of 'facing' the likelihood of his work being subject to a variety of readings, to the vicissitudes of communication, by designing for variable primary functions and open secondary functions (open in the sense that they may be determined by unforseeable future codes) – everything that has been said so far might suggest that there is little question about what is meant by *code*.

As long as one confines oneself to verbal communication, the notion is fairly clear: there is a code-language, and there are certain connotative subcodes. But when, in another section of this study, we went on to consider visual codes, for example, we found we had to list a number of levels of codification (including, but not limited to, iconic and iconographic codes), and in the process to

introduce various 'clarifications' of the concept of code, and on the different *Eco*
types of articulation a code may provide for.[9] We also saw the importance of
the principle that the elements of articulation under a given code can be
syntagms of another, more 'analytic' code, or that the syntagms of one code can
turn out to be elements of articulation of another, more 'synthetic' code. This
should be kept in mind when considering codes in architecture, for one might
be tempted to attribute to an architectural code articulations that belong really
to some code, either more analytic or more synthetic, lying outside architecture.

We can expect some problems, then, in the definition of the codes of architecture. First of all, from the attempts there have been to date to spell out aspects
of architectural communication, we can see that there is the problem of
neglecting to consider whether what one is looking at is referable to a syntactic
code rather than a semantic code – that is, to rules concerning, rather than the
meanings conventionally attributed to, individual sign vehicles, the articulation
of certain significative structures separable from these sign vehicles and their
meanings – or for that matter to some underlying technical convention.

Catchwords like 'semantics of architecture' have led some to look for the
equivalent of the 'word' of verbal language in architectural signs, for units
endowed with definite meaning, indeed for symbols referring to referents. But
since we know there can be conventions concerning only the syntactic articulation of signs, it would be appropriate to look also for purely syntactic
codifications in architecture (finding such codifications and defining them with
precision, we might be in a better position to understand and classify, at least
from the point of view of semiotics, objects whose once denoted functions can
no longer be ascertained, such as the menhir, the dolmen, the Stonehenge
construction).

Then, too, in the case of architecture, codes of reading (and of construction)
of the object would have to be distinguished from codes of reading (and of
construction) of the *design* for the object (admittedly we are considering here
only a semiotics of architectural objects, and not a semiotics of architectural
designs). Of course the notational codes of the design, while conventionalized
independently, are to some extent derivatives of the codes of the object: they
provide ways in which to 'transcribe' the object, just as to transcribe spoken
language there are conventions for representing such elements as sounds,
syllables or words. But that does not mean a semiotic investigation of the architectural design would be without some interesting problems of its own – there
are in a design, for example, various systems of notation (the codes operative in
a plan are not quite the same as those operative in a section or in a wiring
diagram for a building),[10] and in these systems of notation there can be found
iconic signs, diagrams, indices, symbols, qualisigns, sinsigns, etc., perhaps
enough to fill the entire gamut of signs proposed by Peirce.

Much of the discussion of architecture as communication has centred on
typological codes, especially semantic typological codes, those concerning
functional and sociological types; it has been pointed out that there are in architecture configurations clearly indicating 'church', 'railroad station', 'palace',
etc. We will return to typological codes later, but it is clear that they constitute
only one, if perhaps the most conspicuous, of the level of codification in
architecture.

Eco   In attempting to move progressively back from a level at which the codes are so complex and temporal – for it is clear that 'church' has found different articulations at different moments in history – one might be tempted to hypothesize for architecture something like the 'double articulation' found in verbal languages, and assume that the most basic level of articulation (that is, the units constituting the 'second' articulation) would be a matter of geometry.

If architecture is the art of the articulation of spaces,[11] then perhaps we already have, in Euclid's geometry, a good definition of the rudimentary code of architecture. Let us say that the second articulation is based on the Euclidean *stoicheia* (the 'elements' of classical geometry); then the 'first' articulation would involve certain higher-level spatial units, which could be called *choremes*, with these combining into spatial syntagms of one kind or another.[12] In other words, the angle, the straight line, the various curves, the point, etc., might be elements of a second articulation, a level at which the units are not yet *significant* (endowed with meaning) but are *distinctive* (having differential value); the square, the triangle, the parallelogram, the ellipse – even rather complicated irregular figures, as long as they could be defined with geometric equations of some kind – might be elements of a first articulation, a level at which the units begin to be significant; and one rectangle within another might be an elementary syntagmatic combination (as in some window–wall relationship), with more complex syntagms to be found in such things as space-enclosing combinations of rectangles or articulations based on the Greek-cross plan. Of course solid geometry suggests the possibility of a third level of articulation, and it could be assumed that further articulative possibilities would come to light with the recognition of non-Euclidean geometries.

The trouble is that this geometric code *would not pertain specifically to architecture*. Besides lying behind some artistic phenomena – and not just those of abstract, geometric art (Mondrian), because it has long been held that the configurations in representational art can be reduced to an articulation, if perhaps a quite complex one, of primordial geometric elements – the code clearly underlies the formulations of geometry in the etymological sense of the word (surveying) and other types of 'transcription' of terrain (topographic, geodetic, etc.). It might even be identified with a 'gestaltic' code presiding over our perception of all such forms. What we have here, then, is an example of one sort of code one can arrive at when attempting to analyse the elements of articulation of a certain 'language': a code capable of serving as a *metalanguage* for it, and for a number of other more synthetic codes as well.

So it would be better to pass over a code of this kind, just as in linguistics one passes over the possibility of going beyond 'distinctive features' in analysing phonemes. Admittedly such analytic possibilities might have to be explored if one had to compare architectural phenomena with phenomena belonging to some other 'language', and thus had to find a metalanguage capable of describing them in the same terms – for instance, one might wish to 'code' a certain landscape in such a way as to be able to compare it with certain proposed architectural solutions, to determine what architectural artifacts to insert in the context of that landscape, and if one resorted to elements of the code of solid geometry (pyramid, cone, etc.) in defining the structure of the landscape, then it would make sense to describe the architecture in the light of that geometric code, taken as a metalanguage.[13] *But the fact that architecture*

can be described in terms of geometry does not indicate that architecture as   Eco
such is founded on a geometric code.

After all, that both Chinese and words articulated in the phonemes of the
Italian language can be seen as a matter of amplitudes, frequencies, wave
forms, etc., in radio-acoustics or when converted into grooves on a disk does
not indicate that Chinese and Italian rest on one and the same code; it simply
shows that the languages admit of that type of analysis, that for certain
purposes they can be *reduced* to a common system of transcription. In fact
there are few physical phenomena that would not permit analysis in terms of
chemistry or physics at the molecular level, and in turn an atomic code, but that
does not lead us to believe that the *Mona Lisa* should be analysed with the same
instruments used in analysing a mineral specimen.

Then what more properly architectural codes have emerged in various
analyses or, recently, 'semiotic' readings of architecture?

VARIETIES OF ARCHITECTURAL CODE

It would appear, from those that have come to light, that architectural codes
could be broken down roughly as follows:

1 Technical codes

To this category would belong, to take a ready example, articulations of the
kind dealt with in the science of architectural engineering. The architectural
form resolves into beams, flooring systems, columns, plates, reinforced-
concrete elements, insulation, wiring, etc. There is at this level of codification
no communicative 'content', except of course in cases where a structural (or
technical) function or technique itself becomes such; there is only a structural
logic, or structural conditions behind architecture and architectural signification conditions that might therefore be seen as somewhat analogous to a
second articulation in verbal languages, where though one is still short of
meanings there are certain formal conditions of signification.[14]

2 Syntactic codes

These are exemplified by typological codes concerning articulation into spatial
types (circular plan, Greek-cross plan, 'open' plan, labyrinth, high-rise, etc.),
but there are certainly other syntactic conventions to be considered (a stairway
does not as a rule go through a window, a bedroom is generally adjacent to a
bathroom, etc.).

3 Semantic codes

These concern the significant units of architecture, or the relations established
between individual architectural sign vehicles (even some architectural
syntagms) and their denotative and connotative meanings. They might be
subdivided as to whether, through them, the units

   (a)   denote *primary functions* (roof, stairway, window);

Eco (b) have connotative *secondary functions* (tympanum, triumphal arch, neo-Gothic arch);

(c) connote *ideologies of inhabitation* (common room, dining room, parlour); or

(d) at a larger scale have typological meaning under certain *functional and sociological types* (hospital, villa, school, palace, railroad station).[15]

The inventory could of course become quite elaborate – there should, for instance, be a special place for types like 'garden city' and 'new town', and for the codifications emerging from certain recent *modi operandi* (derived from avant-garde aesthetics) that have already created something of a tradition, a manner, of their own.

But what stands out about these codes is that on the whole they would appear to be, as communicative systems go, rather limited in operational possibilities. They are, that is, codifications of *already worked-out solutions*, codifications yielding *standardized messages* – this instead of constituting, as would codes truly on the model of those of verbal languages, a system of possible relationships from which countless significantly different messages could be generated.

A verbal language serves the formulation of messages of all kinds, messages connoting the most diverse ideologies (and is inherently neither a class instrument nor the superstructure of a particular economic base).[16] Indeed the diversity of the messages produced under the codes of a verbal language makes it all but impossible to identify any overall ideological connotations in considering broad samplings of them. Of course this characterization might be challenged, for there is some evidence to support the theory that the very way in which a language is articulated obliges one speaking it to see the world in a particular way (there might be, then, ideological bias and connotation of some kind inherent in the language).[17] But even given that, on the most profound, ultimate level, one could take a verbal language as a *field of (nearly absolute) freedom*, in which the speaker is free to improvise novel messages to suit unexpected situations. And in architecture, if the codes are really those indicated above, that does not seem to be the case.

The point is not that in articulating a church, for example, the architect is in the first place obeying a socio-architectural prescription that churches be made and used (about this sort of determinant we will have more to say later). And in the end he would be free to try to find and exploit some way in which to make a church that while conforming to its type would be somewhat different from any that had yet appeared, a church that would thereby provide a somewhat unaccustomed, 'refreshing' context in which to worship and imagine the relationship with God. But if at the same time, in order for it to be a church, he must unfailingly articulate the building in manifold conformity to a type ('down to the hardware', one might say), if the codes operative in architecture allow only slight differences from a standardized message, however appealing, then architecture is not the field of creative freedom some have imagined it to be, but a system of rules for giving society what it expects in the way of architecture.

In that case architecture might be considered not the service some have imagined it to be – a mission for men of unusual culture and vision, continually readying new propositions to put before the social body – but a service in the sense in which waste disposal, water supply and mass transit are services: an *Eco* operation that is, even with changes and technical refinements from time to time, the routine satisfaction of some preconstituted demand.

It would appear to be rather impoverished as an art, then, also, if it is characteristic of art, as we have suggested elsewhere, to put before the public things they have not yet come to expect (Eco, 1968, op. cit., ch. A.3).

So the codes that have been mentioned would amount to little more than lexicons on the model of those of iconographic, stylistic and other specialized systems, or limited repertories of set constructions. They establish not generative possibilities but ready-made solutions, not open forms for extemporary 'speech' but fossilized forms – at best, 'figures of speech', or schemes providing for formulaic presentation of the unexpected (as a complement to the system of established, identified and never really disturbed expectations), rather than relationships from which communication varying in information content as determined by the 'speaker' could be improvised. The codes of architecture would then constitute a rhetoric in the narrow sense of the word: a store of *tried and true discursive formulas*. (That is, they would constitute a rhetoric in the sense of the term discussed in Eco, 1968, op. cit., par. A.4.2.2.)

And this could be said not only of the semantic codes, but also of the syntactic codifications, which clearly confine us to a certain quite specialized 'grammar' of building, and the technical codes, for it is obvious that even this body of 'empty' forms underlying architecture (column, beam, etc.) is too specialized to permit every conceivable architectural message: it permits a kind of architecture to which civilization in its evolving technologies has accustomed us, a kind relating to certain principles of statics and dynamics, certain geometric concepts, many of them from Euclid's geometry, certain elements and systems of construction – the principles, concepts, elements and systems that, proving relatively stable and resistant to wear and tear, are found codified under the science of architectural engineering.

ARCHITECTURE AS MASS COMMUNICATION?

MASS APPEAL IN ARCHITECTURE

If architecture is a system of rhetorical formulas producing just those messages the community of users has come to expect (seasoned with a judicious measure of the unexpected), what then distinguishes it from various forms of mass culture? The notion that architecture is a form of mass culture has become rather popular,[18] and as a communicative operation directed toward large groups of people and confirming certain widely subscribed to attitudes and ways of life while meeting their expectations, it could certainly be called mass communication loosely, without bothering about any detailed criteria.

But even under more careful consideration,[19] architectural objects seem to have characteristics in common with the messages of mass communication. To mention a few:

- Architectural 'discourse' generally *aims at mass appeal*: it starts with accepted premises, builds upon them well-known or readily acceptable 'arguments', and thereby elicits a certain type of consent. ('This

Eco   proposition is to our liking; it is in most respects something we are already familiar with, and the differences involved only represent a welcome improvement or variation of some kind.')

- Architectural discourse is *psychologically persuasive*: with a gentle hand (even if one is not aware of this as a form of manipulation) one is prompted to follow the 'instructions' implicit in the architectural message; functions are not only signified but also promoted and induced, just as certain products and attitudes are promoted through 'hidden persuasion', sexual associations, etc.

- Architectural discourse is *experienced inattentively*, in the same way in which we experience the discourse of movies and television, the comics or advertising – not, that is, in the way in which one is meant to experience works of art and other more demanding messages, which call for concentration, absorption, wholehearted interest in interpreting the message, interest in the intentions of the 'addresser.'[20]

- Architectural messages *can never be interpreted in an aberrant way*, and without the 'addressee' being aware of thereby perverting them. Most of us would have some sense of being engaged in a perversion of the object if we were to use the Venus de Milo for erotic purposes or religious vestments as dustcloths, but we use the cover of an elevated roadway for getting out of the rain or hang laundry out to dry over a railing and see no perversion in this.

- Thus architecture *fluctuates between being rather coercive*, implying that you will live in such and such a way with it, *and rather indifferent*, letting you use it as you see fit.

- Architecture *belongs to the realm of everyday life*, just like pop music and most ready-to-wear clothing, instead of being set apart like 'serious' music and high fashion.

- Architecture is *a business*.[21] It is produced under economic conditions very similar to the ones governing much of mass culture, and in this too differs from other forms of culture. Painters may deal with galleries, and writers with publishers, but for the most part that has to do with their livelihood and need not have anything to do with what they find themselves painting and writing; the painter can always pursue painting independently, perhaps while making a living in some other way, and the writer can produce works for which there is no market, perhaps with no thought of having them published, but the architect cannot be engaged in the practice of architecture without inserting himself into a given economy and technology and trying to embrace the logic he finds there, even when he would like to contest it . . .

EXTERNAL CODES

ARCHITECTURE AS BASED ON CODES EXTERNAL TO IT

To recapitulate:

1   we began with the premise that architecture would, to be able to communicate the functions it permits and promotes, have to be based on codes;

2   we have seen that the codes that could properly be called architectural   *Eco*
     establish rather limited operational possibilities, that they function not
     on the model of a language but as a system of rhetorical formulas and
     already produced message-solutions;
3   resting on these codes, the architectural message becomes something of
     mass appeal, something that may be taken for granted, something that
     one would expect;
4   yet it seems that architecture may also move in the direction of innov-
     ation and higher information-content, going against existing rhetorical
     and ideological expectations;
5   it cannot be the case, however, that when architecture moves in this
     direction it departs from given codes entirely, for without the basis of a
     code of some kind, there would be no effective communication . . .

It goes without saying, for instance, that an urban designer could lay out a
street on the basis of the lexicon that embraces and defines the type 'street'; he
could even, with a minor dialectic between redundancy and information, make
it somewhat different from previous ones while still operating within the
traditional urbanistic system.

When, however, Le Corbusier proposes his elevated streets (closer to the type
'bridge' than to the type 'street'), he moves outside the accepted typology, which
has streets at ground level or, if elevated, elevated in a different fashion and for
different reasons – and yet he does so with a certain assurance, believing that this
new sign, along with the rest of his proposed city, would be accepted and
comprehended by the users. Now whether such a belief is justified or not, it
would have to be based on something like this: the architect has preceded
architectural design with an examination of certain new social exigencies, certain
'existential' desiderata, certain tendencies in the development of the modern city
and life within it, and has traced out, so to speak, a semantic system of certain
future exigencies (developing from the current situation) on the basis of which
new functions and new architectural forms might come into being.

In other words, the architect would have identified:

1   a series of social exigencies, presumably as a system of some kind;
2   a system of functions that would satisfy the exigencies, and that would
     become sign vehicles of those exigencies; and
3   a system of forms that would correspond to the functions, and that
     would become sign vehicles of those functions.

From the point of view of common sense, this means that to produce the new
architecture Le Corbusier was obliged, before thinking like an architect, to
think like a sociologist, an anthropologist, a psychologist, an ideologist, etc.,
and we will return to that shortly. But first we might consider the peculiarity of
the phenomenon from the semiotic point of view.

Only at the last level, the level of point 3 above, do we find forms that could
be understood as 'architecture'. So while the elements of architecture constitute
themselves a system, they become a code only when coupled with systems that
lie outside architecture . . .

What about architecture, then, if we accept the hypotheses above? Let us use
X for the system of architectural forms, *Y* for the system of functions, and *K* for

Eco   the system of social exigencies, or the anthropological system – an x might be a table of a certain width, which permits and signifies a certain function y (to eat at a considerable distance from one another, let us say), which in turn allows the realization of an anthropological value k ('formal' relationship), whose sign vehicle that function has become.

Then the units in X, as spatial forms, admit of several kinds of description – two dimensional (through a set of drawings or a photograph), verbal (through an oral or written description), mathematical (through a series of equations), etc.; the units in Y, as functions, admit of either verbal description or representation in terms of some iconic (cinematographic, for example), kinesic, or other kind of system for 'transcribing' functions; and the units in K, as anthropological values, can be described verbally.

Now it is clear that while a form x is being used it might seem (to the user) quite closely tied to a function y and an anthropological value k – just as closely as a meaning seems (to the speaker) tied to a verbal sign vehicle. But from the point of view of semiotics, it is possible to *describe the units of each of these three systems independently*, without, that is, having recourse to the units of either of the other two.

This is something that was never envisaged by those who have considered the notion of meaning suspect, because up to now studies in semantics have been conducted inside the circle of verbal 'interpretants'. So above and beyond what else it offers, semiotics shows us the possibility of investigating systems of signs where the planes of expression and content are not inseparable – or at least where they can be more successfully separated.

THE ANTHROPOLOGICAL SYSTEM

But in introducing this K, this anthropological system, have we jeopardized the semiotic framework behind everything we said before?

Having said that architecture has to elaborate its sign vehicles and messages with reference to something that lies *outside* it, are we forced to admit its signs cannot, after all, be adequately characterized without bringing something like *referents* back into the picture?

We have argued that semiotics must confine itself to the *left side* of the Ogden-Richards triangle – because in semiotics one studies codes as phenomena of culture – and, leaving aside verifiable realities to which the signs may refer, examine only the communicative rules established within a social body: rules of the equivalence between sign vehicles and meanings (the definition of the latter being possible only through interpretants or other sign vehicles by means of which the meanings may be signified), and rules regarding the syntagmatic combination of the elements of the paradigmatic repertories. This means not that the referent is non-existent, but that it is the object of *other* sciences (physics, biology, etc.): semiotics can, and must, confine itself to the universe of the cultural conventions governing communicative intercourse.

If for architecture, then, or for any other system of signs, we had to admit that the plane of content involved something that did not belong to the semiotic universe, we would be faced with a phenomenon confounding semiotics, or at any rate confounding all the notions we have elaborated, here and elsewhere, on semiosis.[22]

So it is not casually that we have been referring to an anthropological *Eco* 'system'; we have been referring, that is, to facts that while belonging to the universe of the social sciences may nevertheless be seen as *already codified*, and thus reduced to a cultural system . . .

To put it differently, let us say that the architect has decided to restructure the urban fabric of a city (or the 'shape of landscape' in a certain area) from the point of view of the perceptibility of its 'image.'[23] He might then base his operation upon rules of a code concerned precisely with phenomena of image-recognition and orientation (a code that could be elaborated on the basis of data from interviews and basic research on perception, and perhaps even take into account exigencies of commerce or circulation, medical findings on factors contributing to stress, etc.). But then the validity and significance of the operation, based on that code, would depend upon confining oneself to that particular point of view. As soon as it became necessary for the architect to relate his architecture to some other system of social phenomena as well – the one dealt with in proxemics, let us say – the code concerned with image-recognition and orientation would have to be broken down and integrated with a code concerning proxemic phenomena; and since there would no doubt be more than just these two external systems to relate to, it would become necessary to find the relations between a number of different systems tracing them all back to an underlying *Ur-code* common to all of them, on which elaboration of the new architectural solutions would ultimately have to be based.[24]

So the architect, in practice, is continually obliged to be something other than an architect. Time and again he is forced to become something of a sociologist, a psychologist, an anthropologist, a semiotician . . . And that he can rely in this to some extent on teamwork – that is, on having experts in the various fields working with him – does not change the situation very much, even if teamwork makes it seem less a matter of guesswork. Forced to find forms that will give form to systems over which *he has no power*, forced to articulate a language that has always to express something external to it – we said there were possibilities of the poetic function and self-reflexiveness in architecture, but the fact remains that because of its very nature (and even though it has traditionally been understood as a matter of pure 'arrangement', regarding only its own forms) these can never 'take over' in it, as they can in other types of discourse, such as in poetry, painting or music – the architect finds himself obliged in his work to *think in terms of the totality*, and this he must do no matter how much he may seem to have become a technician, a specialist, someone intent on specific operations rather than general questions.

CONCLUSION

One might at this point be left with the idea that having the role of supplying 'words' to signify 'things' lying outside its province, architecture is powerless to proceed without a prior determination of exactly what those 'things' are (or are going to be).

Or one might have come to a somewhat different conclusion: that even though the systems of functions and values it is to convey are external to it, architecture has the power, through the operation of its system of stimulative

Eco sign-vehicles, to determine what those functions and values are going to be – restricting men to a particular way of life dictating laws to events.

These both go too far, and they go along with two unfortunate ideas of the role of the architect. According to the first, he has only to find the proper forms to answer to what he can take as 'programmatic' givens; here he may accept on faith certain sociological and ideological determinations made by others, which may not be well founded. According to the second, the architect (and we know what currency this delusion has enjoyed) becomes a demiurge, an artificer of history.

This alternative to these varieties of overconfidence has already been suggested: *the architect should be designing for variable primary functions and open secondary functions.*

NOTES

1 Christian Norberg-Schutz, *Intentions in Architecture*, Cambridge, Mass.: MIT Press, 1965.

2 Roland Barthes, *Elements of Sociology*, Annette Lavers and Colin Smith (trans.), New York: Hill & Wang, 1968.

3 In this case it is the aesthetic function that is predominant in the architectural message, what Roman Jakobson, speaking of acts of verbal communication, has termed the poetic function (Jakobson, 'Linguistics and Poetics', in Thomas A. Sebeok, ed., *Style in Language*, Cambridge, Mass.: MIT Press, 1966, pp. 350–77.). But architectural messages display also the five other communicative functions listed by Jakobson: architecture involves communication that is connative (or imperative, making one inhabit it in a certain way), emotive (think of the calm of a Greek temple, the turbulence of a baroque church), phatic (obviously in the many attention-getting devices of architecture – the phatic function might be found to be predominant, then, in such messages as obelisks, arches, and tympana – but also at the level of urban fabric, where 'channels' are opened and established for architectural messages, as in a piazza's ensuring continued attention to the facades of the buildings that surround it), metalingual (where, for one example, to relieve any confusion about the code for interpreting the message architecture assumes a self-explaining, or 'glossing', function – think of the benches built into certain otherwise inhospitable American plazas), and of course referential (what we will be concerned with here for the most part – that is, the denotations and connotations of architectural objects).

4 We should note that the symbolic value of forms was not entirely ignored by the theorists of functionalism: see Louis Sullivan, 'The Tall Office Building Artistically Reconsidered', in *Kindergarten Chats and Other Writings*, New York: Wittenborn, Shultz 1947, pp. 202–13; and Renato de Fusco (*L'idea di architettura*, Milan, Communità, 1964) shows that their symbolic value was important not only to Sullivan but also to Le Corbusier. On the connotative value of forms at the level of urban design – turning to the relational forms in the fabric of large urban areas – see Kevin Lynch, *The Image of the City*, Cambridge, Mass.: MIT Press, 1960: esp. p. 91: cities are to be given forms that can stand as symbols for urban life.

5 For a bibliography on this question see Paul Frankl, *The Gothic Literary Sources and Interpretation Through Eight Centuries*, Princeton: Princeton University Press, 1960.

6 Abbot Suger, *Oeuvres complètes de Suger*, Richard Albert Lecoy de la Marche, ed., Paris 1967. Abbot Suger, *Abbot Suger on the Abbey Church of St Denis and its Art Treasures*, Erwin Panofsky ed. and trans., Princeton: Princeton University Press, 1946.

7 Umberto Eco, *Il problema estetico in San Tommaso*, Turin: Edizioni di 'Filosofia', 1956. Umberto Eco, 'Sviluppo dell' estetica medievale', in *Momenti e problemi di storia dell' estetica*, Milan: Marzorati, 1968.

8 See Giulio Carlo Argan, *Progetto e destino*, Milan: Il Saggiatore, 1965. Giulio Carlo Argan *et al.*, 'Designe mass media', in *Op. Cit.* (Selezione della critica d'arte contemporanea), 2, particularly the title essay, where the notion of works that remain 'open' (the 'opera aperta') is applied to architectural design. One way of understanding the 'openness' of architectural and urbanistic objects is suggested in Roland Barthes' 'Semiology and the Urban' [see pp. 166–72, this volume]. Agreeing with certain views held by Jacques Lacan – discussed in Eco, 1968 op. cit., ch. D. 5, 'La struttura e l'assenza' – Barthes believes that with regard to the city the question of meaning becomes less important than a detailed analysis of abstracted 'signifiers'. Thus, 'in this attempt at a semantic approach to the city we should try to understand the play of signs, to understand that any city is a structure, but that we must never try and we must never want

to fill in this structure', for 'semiology at present never posits the existence of a final signified', *Eco*
and 'any cultural (or, for that matter, psychological) complex confronts us with infinite
metaphorical chains, in which the signified is always deferred or becomes itself a signifier'. Now
it is true that any city confronts us with phenomena of enrichment (and substitution) of
meaning, but the semantic value of the city emerges not only when one sees it as a structure that
generates meaning: it emerges also when, in experiencing it, one is filling it with concrete
significations. Indeed, to oppose to the concrete process of signification – in the light of which
the city is designed – the notion of a free play of pure sign-vehicles might be to empty the activity
of architecture of much of its creative thrust. For if this notion were carried to an extreme, and
the significative power of a city considered really infinite – as infinite as the significative power
of verbal languages, which in spite of the fact that man has little say with regard to their
constitution and laws still permit him to be adequately 'spoken' – then there would no longer
seem to be any point in designing a 'new' city: in any existing city there would already be the
elements of an infinite number of possible combinations, permitting every type of life within
that form. In reality, the problem of architecture is that of defining the limit beyond which an
existing form no longer allows the type of life one has in mind, the limit beyond which the
architectural sign-vehicles that pass before one appear no longer as a matrix of freedom but as
the very image of a domination, of an ideology that imposes, through the rhetorical forms it has
generated, various modes of enslavement.

9   Eco, 1968, op. cit., ch. B.1–3, 'I codici visivi', 'Il mito della doppia articolazione' and
    'Articolazioni dei codici visivi'.

10 Through the use of the wrong code, then, a plan might be read as a section of vice versa; see
    the amusing situation described in Giovanni Klaus Koenig *Analisi del linguaggio
    architettonico*, Florence: Fiorentina, 1964, ch. 8, and *L'invecchiamento dell' architettura
    moderna ed altre dodici note*, 2nd edn, Florence: Fiorentina, 1967.

11 Bruno Zevi, *Architecture as Space: How to Look at Architecture*, Joseph Barty, ed., Milton
    Gendel (trans.), New York: Horizon Press, 1957, and *Architettura in nuce*, Venice and Rome:
    Instituto per la Collaborazione Cutturale, 1960.

12 The term choreme is derived from *chora* ('space, place'). For a theoretical consideration of the
    stoicheia as primary elements of the spatial arts, including architecture, see the remarks by
    Mondrian discussed in Fusco 1964, op. cit., pp. 143–5, and *L'architettura come mass-
    medium: Note per una semiologia architettonica*, Bari: Dedalo Libri, 1967.

13 See Christian Norberg-Schulz, *Intentions in Architecture*, Cambridge, Mass.: MIT Press, 1965.

14 On these, and on the codes that follow, see Klaus Koenig, 1964, op. cit., pp. 38–52,
    'L'articolazione del linguaggio architettonico'; and Gillo Dorfles, *Simbolo, comunicazione,
    consumo*, Turin: Einaudi, 1962.

15 On the concept of 'type', see, besides Dorfles and Koenig, the text entitled 'Sul concetto di
    tipologia architettonica' in Argan's work (1965, op. cit.), where the proper parallel is drawn
    between architectural typology and iconography; type is defined as *progetto di forma*, which
    comes close to the definition of figures of speech (as *relazioni generali di inaspettatezza*, or
    general schemes providing for formulaic presentation of the unexpected) given in Eco 1968,
    op. cit., par. A.4.2.2; see also Sergio Bettini 'Semantic criticism and the historical continuity of
    European architecture', *Zodiac 2*, 1958 and Vittorio Gregotti *Il territorio dell' architettura*,
    Milan: Fetrinelli, 1966.

16 For Joseph Stalin's well-known views on linguistics see Josef Stalin, *Marxism and Linguistics*,
    New York: International, 1951.

17 That language determines the way in which one sees reality, see Benjamin Lee Whorf,
    Language, Thought and Reality, John Carrol, ed., Cambridge, Mass.: MIT Press, 1956, 1964.

18 See Argan *et al.*, 1965, op. cit. and Filiberto Menna, 'Design, communicazione estetica e mass
    media', *Edilizia Moderna*, 85, 1965; see for that matter the whole of issue 85 of *Edilizia
    Moderna*, and note the slant of the graphics.

19 For perhaps the most comprehensive study to date, see Fusco, 1967, op. cit.

20 To quote Walter Benjamin:

> Distraction and concentration form polar opposites which may be stated as follows: A
> man who concentrates before a work of art is absorbed by it. He enters into this work of
> art the way legend tells of the Chinese painter when he viewed his finished painting. In
> contrast, the distracted mass absorbs the work of art. This is most obvious with regard to
> buildings. Architecture has always represented the prototype of a work of art the reception
> of which is consummated by a collectivity in a state of distraction. ('The Work of Art in the
> Age of Mechanical Reproduction', in Hannah Arendt, ed., *Illuminations*, Harry Zohn
> (trans.), New York: Harcourt, Brace & World, 1968, p. 241.)

21 See the issue of *Edilizia Moderna* dedicated to 'design', cited above, and in particular the
    introduction, 'Problemi del design'.

Eco 22   Reviewing the first version of this text, Maria Corti, Review, *Strumenti Critici*, 1967, 1 (4): pp. 447–50, commented that the introduction of the anthropological system into the discussion was 'a trap', one that reopened the problem of the autonomy of semiotics as a science. While I acknowledge there might have been some malicious intent to it, I would like to point out that I was really trying to resolve the problem, which would have come up in any case, and that her comments, together with a series of doubts advanced by Vittorio Gregotti in conversation, have driven me to making this point a little clearer, even to me.

23   See Lynch, 1960, op. cit.; Luciana de Rosa 'La poetica urbanistica di Lynch', op. cit. 2 and also Donald Appleyard, Kevin Lynch and John Myer, *The View from the Road*, Cambridge, Mass.: MIT Press, 1964.

24   For an example of research on procedures of codification at the level of 'ultimate' structures, see Christopher Alexander, *Notes on the Synthesis of Form*, Cambridge: Harvard University Press, 1964. For a parallel drawn between Alexander's work and that of structuralists, see Maria Bottero 'Lo strutturalismo funzionale di Christopher Alexander', *Communità*, 1958, pp. 148–9.

HOW AN EXPOSITION EXPOSES ITSELF

In contemporary expositions a country no longer says, 'Look what I produce' but 'Look how smart I am in presenting what I produce.' The 'planetary society' has already standardized industrial production to such a degree that the fact of showing a tractor or a space capsule no longer differentiates one image of civilization from another. The only solution left is symbolic. Each country shows itself by the way in which it is able to present the same thing other countries could also present. The prestige game is won by the country that best tells what it does, independently of what it actually does. The architectural solutions confirm this view of expositions.

In order to understand the problem better, let us assume that architecture (and design, in its overall sense) is an act of communication, a message, of which the parts or the whole can perform the double action of every communication, connotation and denotation. A word or a phrase can denote something. The word 'moonlight', for example, means, unequivocally, the light that the earth's satellite gives off. At the same time it has a broader connotation depending on the historical period and education of the person who communicates or receives a message using the word. Thus it could connote 'a romantic situation', 'love', 'feeling', and so on. In architecture, it seems at first that the inherent function of every item prevents us from regarding it as a message, as a medium of communication (a staircase is used for going up, a chair for sitting); if architecture communicates something, it is in the form of a symbol. The colonnade by Bernini in St Peter's Square in Rome can be interpreted as an immense pair of arms, open to embrace all the faithful. Aside from this, a product of architecture or design is simply like a mechanism that suggests a function and acts on the user only as a stimulus that requires a behavioural response: a staircase, because it is one step after another, does not allow one to walk on a plane, but stimulates the walker to ascend. A stimulus is not a symbol; a stimulus acts directly at the physiological level and has nothing to do with culture.

But as Roland Barthes wrote in his *Elements of Semiology*, as soon as society can be said to exist, every use also becomes the sign of that same use. The staircase becomes for everybody the conventional sign to denote ascending, whether or not anyone ascends a given staircase in fact. The known connection between form and function mainly means this: the form of the object must *Eco* fundamentally and unequivocally communicate the function for which the object was designed, and only if it denotes this function unambiguously is one stimulated to use it the way it was intended. The architectural product acts as a stimulus only if it first acts as a sign. So the object, according to the linguistic theory of de Saussure, is the signifier, denoting exactly and conventionally that signified which is its function. Nevertheless, even if a chair communicates immediately the fact of sitting, the chair does not fulfil only this function and does not have only this meaning. If the chair is a throne, its use is not only to have somebody sitting on it; it has to make somebody sit with dignity, and should stress the act of sitting with dignity, through various details appropriate to royalty. For example, it might have eagles on the arms of the chair and a crown surmounting the back. These connotations of royalty are functions of a throne and are so important that as long as they are there, one can minimize or even forget the primary function of sitting comfortably. Frequently, for that matter, a throne, in order to indicate royalty, demands that the occupant sit stiffly (that is, uncomfortably) because providing a seat is only one of the meanings of a throne and not the most important one. More important are the symbolic connotations that the throne must communicate and whose communication reinforces its social function.

This continuous oscillation between primary function (the conventional use of the object, or its most direct or elementary meaning) and secondary functions (its related meanings, based on cultural conventions, and mental and semantic associations) forms the object as a system of signs, a message. The history of architecture and design is the history of the dialectic between these two functions. The history of civilization influences the history of architecture in such a way that objects in which the two functions were harmoniously integrated are in time deprived of one of these functions, so that the other becomes dominant; or else the original functions change, creating quite a different object. The ruins of the Greek and Roman temples and amphitheatres provide an example of the first case, where the primary function, which was to gather people for prayer or entertainment, is largely absent from the mind of the contemporary viewer, who sees them in terms of their secondary functions, in the light of notions like 'paganism' and 'classicism' and the expression of a particular sense of harmony, rhythm and monumentality. The Egyptian pyramids offer an example of the second case. Not only is their primary function, that of a tomb, lost to us today; even their original connotation, based on astrological and mathematical symbolism, in which the pyramidal shape had exact communicative functions, has lost its meaning. What is left is a series of connotations established by history and 'carried' by the monument. We recognize these connotations in the monument because we are educated to the same symbolism.

With its voracious vitality, history robs architecture of its meaning and endows it with new meaning. Some massive forms that have lost all original capacity to communicate, such as the statues on Easter Island or the stones of Stonehenge, now appear to be enormous messages, overcomplex in relation to the actual information they can communicate to us. But they may spur us to find new meanings instead, just as Chateaubriand, who could not understand the original social function of the Gothic cathedrals, interpreted them in new ways.

Eco   The architecture of the contemporary exposition is used to connote symbolic meanings, minimizing its primary functions. Naturally, an exposition building must allow people to come in and circulate and see something. But its utilitarian function is too small in comparison with its semantic apparatus, which aims at other types of communication. In an exposition, architecture and design explode their dual communicative nature, sacrificing denotation to very widespread connotation. If we look at the buildings in an exposition as structures to live in or pass through, they are out of scale, but they make sense if we look at them as media of communication and suggestion. The paradox in an exposition is that the buildings, which are supposed to last just a few months, look as if they have survived, or will survive, for centuries. In an exposition, architecture proves to be message first, then utility; meaning first, then stimulus. To conclude: in an exposition we show not the objects but the exposition itself. The basic ideology of an exposition is that the packaging is more important than the product, meaning that the building and the objects in it should communicate the value of a culture, the image of a civilization.

PART IV

POSTMODERNISM

POSTMODERNISM

Postmodernism is often understood in opposition to modernism, as a corrective movement that comes after – 'post' – modernism. As Derrida notes, 'If modernism distinguishes itself by striving for absolute domination, then postmodernism might be the realisation or the experience of its end, the end of the plan of domination.'[1] Not all, however, would accept this temporal distinction between modernism and postmodernism. Jürgen Habermas, for example, criticizes the prefix 'post' as being not only misguided in its 'rejection' of the past, but also weak in its failure to give the present a name. Meanwhile, for Jean-François Lyotard, whose *Postmodern Condition: A Report on Knowledge* remains a seminal work of postmodernist theory, the postmodern is precisely part of the modern. It amounts to a moment of recuperation within a cyclical process which leads to ever new modernisms.

Postmodernism takes a variety of manifestations in its varying cultural contexts. Critics such as Hal Foster have detected two seemingly contradictory strains in postmodernism, a postmodernism of reaction which repudiates modernism and celebrates the status quo, and a postmodernism of resistance that attempts to continue the project of modernism while subjecting it to critical re-evaluation. Clearly postmodernism, no less than modernism, is a term that defies any easy definition. We may start, however, by challenging Charles Jencks's limited appropriation of the term to refer to an architectural style popular in commercial developments in the 1980s, which relies heavily on historicist motifs. Rather we may wish to focus on the very processes of commodification which underpinned such commercial architecture, and subscribe instead to Fredric Jameson's more sophisticated understanding of the term as necessarily linked to the cultural conditions of late capitalist society.

Jameson is indebted here, as is Jean Baudrillard, to the insights of thinkers such as Guy Debord. Although Jameson and Baudrillard diverge in their theoretical positions, as is evident in their respective critiques of the Bonaventure Hotel in Los Angeles, they share a common inheritance in Debord's analysis of the 'Society of the Spectacle'. It is hardly surprising that the privileging of the commodified image observed by Debord should find its logical conclusion in the commercial office block championed by Jencks, and in the advertising hoardings of a gambling town such as Las Vegas celebrated equally uncritically by Robert Venturi and Denise Scott-Brown.

With the exception of the article by Lyotard, '*Domus* and the Megalopolis', which is largely a critique of phenomenology and the politics implicit in the work of Martin Heidegger, many of the essays in this section are directed against postmodernism. Yet even this opposition is by no means straightforward. Much of the writing, not least that of Jameson and Baudrillard, comes across as somewhat ambivalent. Their critiques appear to falter under the obvious fascination that postmodernism holds over them. Therein perhaps lies the strength of postmodernism.

NOTE

1   Jacques Derrida, 'Architecture Where The Desire May Live', pp. 320–1.

JEAN BAUDRILLARD

French sociologist Jean Baudrillard (b. 1929) has established himself as an influential and highly original theorist of postmodernity. His writing is characterized by a 'fatal strategy' of pushing his analyses to an extreme, so that his work becomes less a representation of reality than a transcendence of it. Emerging out of a Marxist tradition, yet also registering a psychoanalytic impulse, Baudrillard relies on a semiological model to understand the world of the commodity. Against more traditional measures such as use-value, Baudrillard emphasizes the sign value. Our present society, according to Baudrillard, is a media society, a world saturated by images and communication, a world where Marshall McLuhan's 'the medium is the message' comes true. Culture is now dominated by simulation. Objects and discourses no longer have any firm referent or grounding. Instead the real has been bypassed. The image has supplanted reality, inducing what Baudrillard has termed a condition of hyperreality, a world of self-referential signs.

Jean Baudrillard

In 'Beaubourg-Effect: Implosion and Deterrence' Baudrillard offers a complex reworking of thoughts which have their origin in his *Symbolic Exchange and Death*, published just one year earlier. Beaubourg – the Centre Pompidou – is presented as a confused cultural object, the embodiment of a paradox deeply embedded within the contemporary cultural condition. The exterior represents the recyclable and transient – the ethos of the oil refinery – of flux and flow. It speaks of simulation, a hyperreal version of culture. The interior, by contrast, houses 'culture' in the form of temporary art exhibitions. Yet it has the paradoxical air of the hypermarket – a hypermarket of art – and has abandoned any sense of memory in favour of art as 'stock'. Thus, for Baudrillard, the true culture of Beaubourg is an anti-culture.

Just like the Bastille – the very site of popular uprising – which had been given over to a new opera house, Beaubourg is an attempt by the elite to introduce culture to the masses. Yet the masses have always been antithetical to such culture. A further paradox emerges. Seduced by the attraction of the crowd, the masses may potentially destroy this house of culture through their very weight – they threaten to 'make Beaubourg buckle'. This violent implosion, this panic in slow motion, is a model of saturation which underwrites culture at large. Culture risks imploding in on itself in a metaphor which evokes the Big Bang theory of science.

Baudrillard reveals himself as one of the most incisive commentators of the urban realm in his various 'city portraits' which seem to owe their origin to Walter Benjamin and the tradition of the theoretically informed European essay. A clear parallel develops between Benjamin and Baudrillard, between a theorist of the modern 'arcades' and a theorist of the postmodern shopping mall. Meanwhile, Baudrillard's description of the Bonaventure Hotel makes an interesting comparison with that of Fredric Jameson.

Baudrillard   # THE BEAUBOURG-EFFECT: IMPLOSION AND DETERRENCE

Beaubourg-Effect . . . Beaubourg-Machine . . . Beaubourg-*Thing* – how can we name it? The puzzle of this carcass of signs and flux, of networks and circuits . . . the ultimate gesture toward translation of an unnameable structure: that of social relations consigned to a system of surface ventilation (animation, self-regulation, information, media) and an in-depth, irreversible implosion. A monument to mass simulation effects, the Centre functions like an incinerator, absorbing and devouring all cultural energy, rather like the black monolith of *2001* – a mad convection current for the materialization, absorption and destruction of all the contents within it.

The neighbourhood all around is merely a buffer zone, recoated, disinfected by snobbish and hygienic design, psychologically. It's a vacuum-making machine, somewhat like nuclear power centres. Their real danger lies not in lack of safety, pollution, explosion, but in the maximum-security system that radiates from them, the zone of surveillance and deterrence that spreads by degrees over the entire terrain – a technical, ecological, economic, geopolitical buffer zone. What does the nucleus matter? The centre is a matrix for developing a model of *absolute* security, subject to generalization on all social levels, one that is most profoundly a model of deterrence. (It is the very same one that serves to regulate us globally under the sign of peaceful coexistence and the simulation of atomic peril.)

With allowances made for scale, the same model is developed through the Centre: cultural fission, political deterrence. This being said, the circulation of fluids is uneven. All the traditional fluids – exhaust, coolant, electricity – flow smoothly. But already the circulation of human masses is less assured (the archaic solution of escalators moving through plastic tubes . . . they should have used suction, propulsion, or what have you, some kind of motion in the image of that baroque theatricality of flux which makes for the originality of the carcass). And as for the stock – works of art, objects, books – as well as the so-called polyvalent interior workspace: there the flow has stopped entirely. The deeper you penetrate into the interior, the less circulation you find. It's the exact opposite of Roissy, where after moving through a space-age, futuristic design radiating outward from a centre, you end up prosaically at . . . ordinary airplanes. But the incoherence is the same. (And what of money, that other fluid, what of its mode of circulation, emulsion and fall-out in Beaubourg?)

The contradiction prevails even in the behaviour of the personnel assigned to the 'polyvalent' space and thus with no private place to work. Standing and on the move, the staff effects a laid-back, flexible style: very high-tech, very adapted to the 'structure' of a 'modern' space. But seated in their cubicles which aren't really even cubicles, they strain to secrete an artificial solitude, to spin themselves a bubble. Here is another fine strategy of deterrence: they are condemned to expend all their energy on this individual defensive. Here again we find the real contradiction at the centre of the Beaubourg-Thing: a fluid commutative exterior – cool and modern – and an interior uptight with old values.

This space of deterrence, linked to the ideology of visibility, transparency polyvalence, consensus, contact, and sanctioned by the threat to security, is

virtually that of all social relations today. The whole of social discourse is there
and on both this level and that of cultural manipulation, Beaubourg is – in total
contradiction to its stated objectives – a brilliant monument of modernity.
There is pleasure in the realization that the idea for this was generated not by a
revolutionary mind, but by logicians of the establishment wholly lacking in
critical spirit, and thus closer to the truth, capable, in their very obstinacy, of
setting up a basically uncontrollable mechanism, which even by its success
escapes them and offers, through its very contradictions, the most exact reflection possible of the present state of affairs.

Granted, the entire cultural contents of Beaubourg are anachronistic, since
only an interior void could have corresponded to this architectural envelope.
Given the general impression that everything here has long been comatose, that
the attempt at animation is nothing but reanimation, and that this is so because
the culture itself is dead, Beaubourg figures this forth admirably well, though
shamefacedly, when this death called for a triumphant acceptance and the
erection of a monument – or antimonument – equal to the phallic inanity, in its
time, of the Eiffel Tower. A monument to total disconnectlon, to hyperreality,
and to the cultural implosion actually created by transistor networks continually threatened by a huge short-circuit.

Beaubourg is really a compression sculpture by César: the image of a culture
flattened by its own weight, the mobile automobile suddenly frozen into a
geometric block. Like César's cars, survivors of an ideal accident, Beaubourg is
no longer external but internal to the metallic and mechanical structure, which
has made of it a pile of cubes of metal scrap, whose chaos of tubes, levers,
chassis, of metal and human flesh within, is cut to the geometric measure of the
smallest possible space. So culture at Beaubourg is crushed, twisted, cut out and
stamped into its tiniest basic elements – a bunch of transmissions and defunct
metabolism, frozen like a science-fiction mechanoid.

Yet, within this carcass, which looks, in any event, like a compression sculpture, instead of crushing and breaking all culture, they *exhibit* César. Dubuffet
is shown, as is the counterculture – whose imagery of opposition merely
functions to refer to the defunct culture. Within this carcass that might have
served as a mausoleum for the hapless operation of signs, Tinguely's ephemeral,
self-destructing machines are re-exhibited under the rubric of the eternal life of
culture. Thus everything is neutralized at the same time: Tinguely is embalmed
in the museological institution and Beaubourg is trapped within its so-called
artistic contents.

Happily, this whole simulacrum of cultural values is undermined from the
very outset by the architectural shell.[1] For, with its armatures of tubing and its
look of a world's fair pavilion, with its (calculated?) fragility that argues against
traditional mentality or monumentality, this *thing* openly declares that our age
will no longer be one of duration, that our only temporal mode is that of the
accelerated cycle and of recycling: the time of transistors and fluid flow. Our
only culture is basically that of hydrocarbons – that of the refining, the
cracking, the breaking up of cultural molecules, and of their recombination
into synthetic products. This, Beaubourg-Museum wants to hide; but
Beaubourg-Carcass proclaims it. And here, truly, is the source of the shell's
beauty and the disaster of the interior spaces. The very ideology of 'cultural
production' is, in any case, antithetical to culture, just as visibility and multi-

Baudrillard   purpose spaces are; for culture is a precinct of secrecy, seduction, initiation and symbolic exchange, highly ritualized and restrained. It can't be helped. Too bad for populism. Tough on Beaubourg.

What, then, should have been put inside Beaubourg?

Nothing. Emptiness would signify the complete disappearance of a culture of meaning and of aesthetic sensibility. But even this is too romantic and agonizing; this empty space might have suited a masterpiece of anti-culture.

Perhaps a spinning of strobe lights and gyroscopes, streaking the space whose moving pedestal is created by the crowd?

Beaubourg, however, actually illustrates the fact that an order of simulacra is maintained only by the alibi of a preceding order. A body entirely composed of flux and surface connections chooses for its content the traditional culture of depth. Thus, an anterior order of simulacra (the one of meaning) now supplies the empty substance of a later order: one which no longer even recognizes the distinction between signifier and signified, between container and contents. Therefore the question 'What should be in Beaubourg?' is absurd. It can't be answered because the local distinction between inside and outside can no longer be posited. There is our truth, the truth of Moebius – a utopia that surely is unrealizable, but one which Beaubourg confirms in the sense that any one of its contents is an (internal) contradiction, destroyed from the outset by the container.

And yet ... and yet ... if Beaubourg really had to contain something it should be a labyrinth, a library of infinite permutations, a game or a lottery for the chance reparcelling of destinies – in short, a Borgesian world, or better still, a Circular Ruin: a linkage of individuals each dreamed by the other (not a Disneyland of Dream, but a laboratory of practical fiction). An experiment in all the different processes of representation: diffraction, implosion, multiplication, chance connections and disconnections – a little like the Exploratorium in San Francisco or the novels of Philip Dick: simply, then, a culture of simulation and fascination, and no longer a culture of production and meaning. Here a proposal of something other than a miserable anticulture.

Is it possible? Clearly not here. But this culture is happening elsewhere, everywhere, nowhere. Henceforth, the only true cultural practice, that of the masses as of ourselves (there is no longer any difference), involves the chance labyrinthine, manipulatory play of signs without meaning.

It is, in another sense, not true that Beaubourg displays an incoherence between container and contents. If we give credence to the official cultural project this is true. But what really takes place is the exact reverse. Beaubourg is nothing but a huge mutational operation at work on this splendid traditional culture of meaning, transmuting it into a random order of signs and of simulacra that are now (on this third level) completely homogeneous with the flux and tubing of the facade. And it is really to prepare the masses for this new semiurgic system that they are summoned – under the pretext of indoctrination into meaning and depth.

We must, therefore, start with the axiom: Beaubourg is a *monument of cultural deterrence*. By means of a museological script which is there only to rescue the fiction of humanist culture, the actual labour of the death of culture is enacted. It is to this – *a real cultural work of mourning* – that the masses are joyfully summoned.

Baudrillard

And they stampede to it. That's the supreme irony of Beaubourg: the masses rush there not because they slaver for this culture which has been denied them for centuries, but because, for the first time, they have a chance to participate, *en masse*, in this immense work of mourning for a culture they have always detested.

If, therefore, we denounce Beaubourg as a cultural mystification of the masses, the misunderstanding is total. The masses fall on Beaubourg to enjoy this execution, this dismembering, this operational prostitution of a culture that is at last truly liquidated, including all counterculture, which is nothing but its apotheosis. The masses charge at Beaubourg as they do to the scenes of catastrophes, and with the same irresistible impulse. Even better: they *are* the catastrophe of Beaubourg. Their number, their trampling, their fascination, their itch to see and touch everything comprise a behaviour that is in point of fact deadly, catastrophic, for the whole business. Not only does their weight threaten the building, but their adhesion and their curiosity destroy the very contents of this cultural spectacle.

This stampede is totally out of scale with the cultural objectives proposed; this rush is, in its very excess and 'success', their radical negation. The masses, then, serve as the agent of catastrophe for this structure of catastrophe: *the masses themselves will finish off mass culture.*

Flowing through the transparent space they are, to be sure, converted into pure movement; but at the same time, by their very opaqueness and inertia, they put an end to the 'polyvalence' of this space. They are summoned to participate, to interact, to simulate, to play with the models . . . and they do it well. They interact and manipulate so well that they eradicate all the meaning imputed to this operation and threaten even the infrastructure of the building. Thus, a type of parody, of oversimulation in response to the simulation of culture: the masses, meant only to be cultural livestock, are always transformed into the slaughterers of a culture of which Beaubourg is just the shameful incarnation.

We should applaud this success in cultural deterrence. All those anti-artists, leftists and culture haters have never so much as approached the deterrent efficacy of this huge black hole, this Beaubourg. This operation is truly revolutionary, exactly because it is involuntary, *mad and meaningless*, uncontrolled, when every reasonable operation to liquidate culture has – as we know – only revived it.

Frankly, the only contents of Beaubourg are the masses themselves, which the building treats like a converter, a black box, or in terms of input/output, just like a refinery handling petroleum products or a flow of raw material.

Never has it been so clear that the contents – here culture, elsewhere information or merchandise – are merely the ghostly support for the opposition of the medium whose function is still that of beguiling the masses, of producing a homogeneous flow of men and minds. The huge surges of coming and going are like the crowds of suburban commuters: absorbed and disgorged by their places of work at fixed hours. And of course it is work that is at issue here: the work of testing, probing, directed questioning. People come here to choose the objectified response to all the questions they can ask, or rather *they themselves come as an answer to* the functional, directed questions posed by the objects. No more forced labour. The restraints of programmatic discipline are hidden

Baudrillard   beneath a varnish of tolerance. Well beyond the traditional institutions of
capital, the hypermarket, or Beaubourg the 'hypermarket of culture' is already
the model of all future forms of controlled 'socialization': the retotalization of
all the dispersed functions of the body and of social life (work, leisure, media,
culture) within a single, homogeneous space-time; it is the retranscription of all
contradictory movements in terms of integrated circuits. It is the space-time of
the whole operational simulation of social life.

This requires that the mass of consumers become equivalent or homologous
to the mass of products. And it is this very confrontation and fusion of the two
masses that occurs in the hypermarket as at Beaubourg, producing something
quite different from traditional cultural settings: museums, monuments,
galleries, libraries, cultural centres. It is here that a condition of *critical mass*
develops, surpassing that of merchandise become hypermerchandise, or culture
become hyperculture – a *critical mass* that is no longer tied to specific
exchanges or to determinate needs but to a kind of total universe of signals;
through this integrated circuit impulses travel everywhere in a ceaseless transit
of selections, readings, references, marks, decodings. Like consumer objects
elsewhere, the cultural objects here have no other purpose than that of maintaining one in a state of integrated mass, of transistorized flux, of magnetized
molecularity. That's what we've learned from the hypermarket, the hyperreality
of the merchandise; and that's what one comes to learn at Beaubourg, the
hyperreality of culture.

The traditional museum had already begun this process of excising
regrouping, and interfering with all cultures – this unconditional aestheticiza-
tion that produces the hyperreality of culture – but the museum still had a
memory. Never as here has culture so lost its memory to the profit of inventory
and functional redistribution. And this records a more general fact: everywhere
in the 'civilized' world the build-up of stockpiles of objects entails the complementary process of human stockpiling: lines, waiting, bottlenecks, concen-
trations, camps. That's what 'mass production' is – not massive production or a
utilization of the masses for production, but rather a production *of the
mass(es)*. The mass(es) is now a final product of all societal relations, delivering
the final blow to those relations, because this crowd that they want us to
believe is the social fabric, is instead only the place of social implosion. *The
mass(es) is that space of ever greater density into which everything societal is
imploded and ground up in an uninterrupted process of simulation.*

Thus this concave mirror: it's because they see the mass(es) inside it that the
masses will be tempted to crowd in. It's a typical marketing device from which
the whole ideology of transparency draws meaning. Or put another way, in
presenting an idealized miniature model they hope to produce an accelerated
gravitational pull, an automatic agglutination of culture as an automatic
agglomeration of the masses. The process is the same: the nuclear chain
reaction, or, the specular operation of white magic.

Thus for the first time, at Beaubourg, there is a supermarketing of culture
which operates at the same level as the supermarketing of merchandise: *the
perfectly circular* function by which anything, no matter what (merchandise,
culture, crowds, compressed air), is demonstrated by means of its *own
accelerated circulation.*

But if the stockpiling of objects entails the pile up of people, the violence latent within the object-inventory entails an inverse human violence.   *Baudrillard*

There is violence in stockpiling due to the fact of implosion; and in the massing of people there is also a violence proper to its own specific gravity, to the increase in its specific density around its own centre of inertia. The mass(es) is a centre of inertia and thus a centre of a wholly new violence – inexplicable and different from explosive violence.

Critical mass. Implosive mass. Above 30,000 it threatens to 'buckle' Beaubourg's structure. That this mass, magnetized by the structure, should become a factor of potential destruction for that very structure . . . what if this were intended by those who conceived the project (but it is beyond one's hopes) . . . if it were part of something they had programmed, the chance to finish off both architecture and culture in one blow . . . well, Beaubourg would then be the most audacious object and successful happening of the century.

MAKE BEAUBOURG BUCKLE! A new revolutionary slogan. No need to torch it or to fight it; just go there! That's the best way to destroy it. Beaubourg's success is no mystery; people go there *just for that*. The fragility of this edifice already exudes catastrophe, and they stampede it just to make it buckle.

Sure, they obey the commands of deterrence, for they have been given an object to consume, a culture to devour, a physical structure to manipulate. But at the same time they aim expressly and unknowingly for this annihilation. The only act, as such, that the mass(es) can produce is the stampede – a projectile mass, defying the edifice of mass culture, defiantly responds to the culturalism promoted by Beaubourg by means of its own weight, its most meaningless, stupid, least cultural aspect. In defiance of a mass indoctrination into a sterile culture, the crowd replies with a burst of destruction extended as brute physical manipulation. Thus to mental deterrence the crowd responds with direct physical deterrence. This is the mass's own form of defiance. Its tactic is to reply in the same terms in which it is solicited, but beyond that, to respond to the simulation within which it is confined by a social enthusiasm which outstrips its objects and functions as a destructive hypersimulation.[2]

The people want to accept everything, swipe everything, eat everything, touch everything. Looking, deciphering, studying doesn't move them. The one mass affect is that of touching, or manipulating. The organizers (and the artists, and the intellectuals) are alarmed by this uncontrollable impulse, for they reckoned only with the apprenticeship of the masses to the *spectacle* of culture. They never anticipated this active, destructive fascination – this original and brutal response to the gift of an incomprehensible culture, this attraction which has all the semblance of housebreaking or the sacking of a shrine.

The day after the opening Beaubourg could or should have disappeared, dismantled and kidnapped by the crowd as the only possible response to the absurd challenge of the transparency and the democracy of culture: each person would have carried away a bolt as a fetish of this fetishized culture.

People come to touch, and they view as if they were touching, their glance being only an aspect of tactile manipulation. It's really a world of touch, no longer one of visuality or discourse. People are now directly implicated in process: manipulate/be manipulated, ventilate/be ventilated, circulate/be circulated. And this process is no longer part of the order of representation or of distance or reflection. It is something connected with panic, and with a world in panic.

Baudrillard Panic in slow motion, without external movement. It is the internal violence of a saturated whole: *implosion*.

Beaubourg can hardly burn; all precautions have been taken. Fire, explosion, destruction are no longer the imaginary alternatives for this type of edifice. The abolition of this 'quaternary' world – cybernetic and permutational – takes the form of implosion.

Subversion and violent destruction are the forms of response to a world of production. To a universe of networks, permutations and flux, the response is reversion and implosion.

This holds true as well for institutions, the state, power, and so forth. The dream of seeing all that explode through the force of its own contradictions is, precisely, only a dream. In fact what will happen is that the institutions will implode themselves by the power of ramification, feedback, overdeveloped control circuitry. *Power implodes*; that is its real form of disappearance.

And so it is with cities. Fire, wars, plague, revolutions, criminal marginality, catastrophes: the whole problematic of the anti-city, of hostility to the city from without or within, all this has something archaic about it in relation to the real modality of the city's annihilation.

The scenario of the underground city – the Chinese version of burying structure – is also naive. Cities no longer repeat themselves according to a schema of reproduction still dependent on a general schema of production, or according to a schema of resemblance still dependent on the schematic of representation. (That was the type of restoration that followed the Second World War.) Cities no longer renew themselves, even in their depths. They get remade according to a sort of genetic code that allows for an indefinite number of repetitions according to a cumulative cybernetic memory. Even the utopia of Borges – the map that is coextensive with its terrain, reduplicating it completely – is finished. Today the simulacrum no longer works through doubling and reduplication but rather through genetic miniaturization. No more representation, as implosion – there also – of all space occurs within an infinitesimal memory that forgets nothing and belongs to no one. Simulation of an irreversible, immanent order, increasingly dense and saturated to capacity, that will never again know the liberation of explosion.

We *used to be* a culture of liberating violence (reason). Whether this is seen as a function of capital, of the free play of productive forces, of the irreversible extension of the field of reason and the field of value, of the conquest and colonization of space all the way to the cosmos – or whether we view it as a function of revolution which anticipates the future forces of society and of social energy – the same schema applies: that of a sphere expanding in either slow or violent phases, that of released energy, the image-repertory of radiation.

The violence that goes with this is the kind that engenders a larger world, the violence of production. This kind of violence is dialectical, energetic, cathartic. It is the kind we've learned to analyse and which is familiar to us, the kind that lays out the paths of socialization and leads to a saturation of the whole social field. This violence is analytic, liberating, *determinate*.

The violence appearing today is of an altogether different kind, one we no longer know how to analyse because it eludes the traditional model of explosive violence. It is an *implosive* violence no longer resulting from the extension of a system but from its saturation and contraction – as in the physical systems of stars. Violence as a consequence of unlimited increase in social density, resulting from an overregulated system, from overloaded networks (of knowledge, information, power?), and from hypertrophied controls that invade all the interstitial paths of facilitation.

This violence is unintelligible to us because our entire image-repertory is oriented to the logic of expanding systems. Indeterminate, this violence is nonetheless indecipherable because it is no longer consistent with models of indeterminacy. Because these models of the operations of randomness have replaced the models of determinacy and classical causality from which they are not fundamentally different. They all express the passage from definite systems of expansion to multi-directional systems of production and expansion – no matter whether star- or rhizome-like in structure. All philosophies of the release of energy, of the radiation of intensity, and of the molecularization of desire tend in the same direction: that networks are capable of infinite and interstitial saturation. The difference between the molar and the molecular is only one of modulation – perhaps the last – within the fundamental processes of energy within systems of expansion.

But it's quite another thing if we pass from the millennium of liberation and energy release, after a sort of maximal radiation, into a phase of implosion, a phase of *social inversion* – the enormous inversion of a field once the point of saturation has been reached. (Reconsider in this sense Bataille's concepts of loss and expenditure, and the solar myth of an unlimited radiation as the basis for his sumptuary anthropology: this is the last myth of explosion and radiation within our philosophical tradition, the terminal fireworks of a general economy, although the myth is no longer meaningful for us.) After all, stars don't cease to exist once their radiational energy has been expended. They implode according to a process that is slow at first but then accelerates exponentially; they contract at a fabulous pace to become involuted systems that absorb all the surrounding energy until they become black holes where the world as we understand it – that is, as radiation and unlimited potential of energy – is destroyed.

Perhaps the great metropolises – these surely, if this hypothesis makes sense – have become implosive centres in the sense of centres of absorption and reabsorption of a society whose golden age (contemporary with the double concept of capital and revolution) is undoubtedly past. Society closes in on itself slowly – or brutally – within a field of inertia that already envelops all politics (is this inverse energy?) We must be careful not to understand implosion as a negative, inert, regressive process, as language tends to force us to do by glorifying the inverse terms of evolution or revolution. Implosion is a specific process with incalculable consequences. Undoubtedly May 1968 was the first implosive episode – which is to say (contrary to its rewriting as the very personification of revolution) a first violent reaction of social saturation, a retraction, a defiance of social hegemony, even though this was in contradiction to the ideology of the participants themselves who thought they were pushing social structures forward – such is the imaginary that continues to dominate us. Even though a large part of the events of 1968 could still be a function of revolutionary dynamism and explosive violence, other things began to happen at the same time: the violent involution of society around this focal point; the

Baudrillard   consequent, sudden implosion of power, beginning after a brief lag in time but never stopping once it began. That is what continues underground: the implosion of social structure, institutions, power; and not some matchless revolutionary dynamic. On the contrary, revolution, or rather the very idea of revolution, has imploded with far heavier consequences than revolution itself.

In Italy something of the same type is in play. In the actions of students, Metropolitan Indians, radio-pirates, something goes on which no longer partakes of the category of universality, having nothing to do either with classical solidarity (politics) or with the information diffusion of the media (curiously neither the media nor the international 'revolutionary' movement reverberated with the slightest echo of what went on in February–March of 1977). In order that mechanisms of such universality cease functioning, something must have changed, something must have taken place for the effect of subversion to move in some sense *in the inverse direction, toward the interior, in defiance of the universal.* Universality is subverted by an action within a limited, circumscribed sphere, one that is very concentrated, very dense, *one that is exhausted by its own revolution.* Here we have an absolutely new process.

Such indeed are the radio-pirates, no longer broadcasting centres, but multiple points of implosion, points in an ungraspable swarm. They are a shifting landmass, but a landmass nonetheless, resistant to the homogeneity of political space. That is why the system must reduce them. Not for their political or militant content, but because, non-extensible, non-explosive, non-generalizable, they are dangerous localizations, drawing their uniqueness and their peculiar violence from their refusal to be a system of expansion.

NOTES

1   One more thing undermines Beaubourg's cultural project: the very mass of people that swarms in to enjoy it (to which we shall return further on).
2   In relation to the critical mass and the radicality of its comprehension of Beaubourg, how silly was the demonstration of the Vincennes students on the evening of the opening!

AMERICA

NEW YORK

In New York there is this double miracle: each of the great buildings and each of the ethnic groups dominates or has dominated the city – after its own fashion. Here crowdedness lends sparkle to each of the ingredients in the mix whereas elsewhere it tends to cancel out differences. In Montreal, all the same elements are present – ethnic groups, buildings and space on the grand American scale – but the sparkle and violence of American cities are missing.

Clouds spoil our European skies. Compared with the immense skies of America and their thick clouds, our little fleecy skies and little fleecy clouds resemble our fleecy thoughts, which are never thoughts of wide open spaces . . . In Paris, the sky never takes off. It doesn't soar above us. It remains caught up in the backdrop of sickly buildings, all living in each other's shade, as though it

were a little piece of private property. It is not, as here in the great capital New *Baudrillard*
York, the vertiginous glass facade reflecting each building to the others. Europe
has never been a continent. You can see that by its skies. As soon as you set foot
in America, you feel the presence of an entire continent – space there is the very
form of thought.

By contrast with the American 'downtown areas' and their blocks of sky-
scrapers, la Défense has forfeited the architectural benefits of verticality and
excess by squeezing its high-rise blocks into an Italian-style setting, into a
closed theatre bounded by a ring-road. It is very much a garden *à la française*: a
bunch of buildings with a ribbon around it. All this has closed off the
possibility that these monsters might engender others to infinity, that they
might battle it out within a space rendered dramatic by their very competition
(New York, Chicago, Houston, Seattle, Toronto). It is in such a space that the
pure architectural object is born, an object beyond the control of architects,
which roundly repudiates the city and its uses, repudiates the interests of the
collectivity and individuals and persists in its own madness. That object has no
equivalent, except perhaps the arrogance of the cities of the Renaissance.

No, architecture should not be humanized. Anti-architecture, the true sort
(not the kind you find in Arcosanti, Arizona, which gathers together all the
'soft' technologies in the heart of the desert), the wild, inhuman type that is
beyond the measure of man was made here – made itself here – in New York,
without considerations of setting, well-being or ideal ecology. It opted for hard
technologies, exaggerated all dimensions, gambled on heaven and hell . . . Eco-
architecture, eco-society . . . this is the gentle hell of the Roman Empire in its
decline.

Modern demolition is truly wonderful. As a spectacle it is the opposite of a
rocket launch. The twenty-storey block remains perfectly vertical as it slides
towards the centre of the earth. It falls straight, with no loss of its upright
bearing, like a tailor's dummy falling through a trap-door, and its own surface
area absorbs the rubble. What a marvellous modern art form this is, a match
for the firework displays of our childhood.

They say the streets are alive in Europe, but dead in America. They are wrong.
Nothing could be more intense, electrifying, turbulent and vital than the streets of
New York. They are filled with crowds, bustle and advertisements, each by turns
aggressive or casual. There are millions of people in the streets, wandering, care-
free, violent, as if they had nothing better to do – and doubtless they have nothing
else to do – than produce the permanent scenario of the city. There is music
everywhere; the activity is intense, relatively violent, and silent (it is not the
agitated, theatrical activity you find in Italy). The streets and avenues never
empty, but the neat, spacious geometry of the city is far removed from the
thronging intimacy of the narrow streets of Europe.

In Europe, the street only lives in sudden surges, in historic moments of
revolution and barricades. At other times people move along briskly, no one
really hangs around (no one wanders any more). It is the same with European
cars. No one actually lives in them; there isn't enough space. The cities, too, do
not have enough space, or rather that space is deemed public and bears all the
marks of the public arena, which forbids you to cross it or wander around it as
though it were a desert or some indifferent area.

The American street has not, perhaps, known these historic moments, but it

Baudrillard is always turbulent, lively, kinetic and cinematic, like the country itself, where the specifically historical and political stage counts for little, but where change, whether spurred by technology, racial differences or the media, assumes virulent forms: its violence is the very violence of the way of life.

SANTA BARBARA

On the aromatic hillsides of Santa Barbara, the villas are all like funeral homes. Between the gardenias and the eucalyptus trees, among the profusion of plant genuses and the monotony of the human species, lies the tragedy of a utopian dream made reality. In the very heartland of wealth and liberation, you always hear the same question: 'What are you doing after the orgy?' What do you do when everything is available – sex, flowers, the stereotypes of life and death? This is America's problem and, through America, it has become the whole world's problem.

All dwellings have something of the grave about them, but here the fake serenity is complete. The unspeakable house plants, lurking everywhere like the obsessive fear of death, the picture windows looking like Snow White's glass coffin, the clumps of pale, dwarf flowers stretched out in patches like sclerosis, the proliferation of technical gadgetry inside the house, beneath it, around it, like drips in an intensive care ward, the TV, stereo and video which provide communication with the beyond, the car (or cars) that connect one up to that great shoppers' funeral parlour, the supermarket, and, lastly, the wife and children, as glowing symptoms of success . . . everything here testifies to death having found its ideal home.

THE BONAVENTURE HOTEL, LOS ANGELES

The top of the Bonaventure Hotel. Its metal structure and its plate-glass windows rotate slowly around the cocktail bar. The movement of the sky-scrapers outside is almost imperceptible. Then you realize that it is the platform of the bar that is moving, while the rest of the building remains still. In the end I get to see the whole city revolve around the top of the hotel. A dizzy feeling, which continues inside the hotel as a result of its labyrinthine convolution. Is this still architecture, this pure illusionism, this mere box of spatio-temporal tricks? Ludic and hallucinogenic, is this postmodern architecture?

No interior/exterior interface. The glass facades merely reflect the environment, sending back its own image. This makes them much more formidable than any wall of stone. It's just like people who wear dark glasses. Their eyes are hidden and others see only their own reflection. Everywhere the transparency of interfaces ends in internal refraction. Everything pretentiously termed 'communication' and 'interaction' – walkman, dark glasses, automatic household appliances, hi-tech cars, even the perpetual dialogue with the computer – ends up with each monad retreating into the shade of its own formula, into its self-regulating little corner and its artificial immunity. Blocks like the Bonaventure building claim to be perfect, self-sufficient miniature cities. But they cut themselves off from the city more than they interact with it. They stop seeing it. They refract it like a dark surface. And you cannot get out of the building itself. You cannot fathom out its internal space, but it has no mystery;

it is just like those games where you have to join all the dots together without   *Baudrillard*
any line crossing another. Here too everything connects, without any two pairs
of eyes ever meeting.

It is the same outside.

A camouflaged individual, with a long beak, feathers and a yellow cagoule,
a madman in fancy dress, wanders along the sidewalks downtown, and
nobody, but nobody, looks at him. They do not look at other people here. They
are much too afraid they will throw themselves upon them with unbearable,
sexual demands, requests for money or affection. Everything is charged with a
somnambulic violence and you must avoid contact to escape its potential discharge. Now that the mad have been let out of the asylums everyone is seen as
a potential madman. Everything is so informal, there is so little in the way of
reserve or manners (except for that eternal film of a smile, which offers only a
very flimsy protection), that you feel anything could blow up at any moment.
By some chain reaction, all this latent hysteria could be released at a stroke. The
same feeling in New York, where panic is almost the characteristic smell of the
city streets. Sometimes it takes the form of a gigantic breakdown, as in 1976.

All around, the tinted glass facades of the buildings are like faces: frosted
surfaces. It is as though there were no one inside the buildings, as if there were no
one behind the faces. And there *really* is no one. This is what the ideal city is like.

SALT LAKE CITY

Pompous Mormon symmetry. Everywhere marble: flawless, funereal (the
Capitol, the organ in the Visitor Centre). Yet a Los-Angelic modernity, too – all
the requisite gadgetry for a minimalist, extraterrestrial comfort. The Christ-
topped dome (all the Christs here are copied from Thorwaldsen's and look like
Bjorn Borg) straight out of *Close Encounters*: religion as special effects. In fact
the whole city has the transparency and supernatural, otherworldly cleanness
of a thing from outer space. A symmetrical, luminous, overpowering abstraction. At every intersection in the Tabernacle area – all marble and roses, and
evangelical marketing – an electronic cuckoo-clock sings out: such Puritan
obsessiveness is astonishing in this heat, in the heart of the desert, alongside this
leaden lake, its waters also hyperreal from sheer density of salt. And, beyond
the lake, the Great Salt Lake Desert, where they had to invent the speed of
prototype cars to cope with the absolute horizontality . . . But the city itself is
like a jewel, with its purity of air and its plunging urban vistas more breath-
taking even than those of Los Angeles. What stunning brilliance, what modern
veracity these Mormons show, these rich bankers, musicians, international
genealogists, polygamists (the Empire State in New York has something of this
same funereal Puritanism raised to the *n*th power). It is the capitalist, trans-
sexual pride of a people of mutants that gives the city its magic, equal and
opposite to that of Las Vegas, that great whore on the other side of the desert.

DISNEYLAND

Disneyland is a perfect model of all the entangled orders of simulacra. It is first
of all a play of illusions and phantasms: the Pirates, the Frontier, the Future
World, etc. This imaginary world is supposed to ensure the success of the

operation. But what attracts the crowds the most is without a doubt the social microcosm, the religious, miniaturized pleasure of real America, of its constraints and joys. One parks outside and stands in line inside, one is altogether abandoned at the exit. The only phantasmagoria in this imaginary world lies in the tenderness and warmth of the crowd, and in the sufficient and excessive number of gadgets necessary to create the multitudinous effect. The contrast with the absolute solitude of the parking lot – a veritable concentration camp – is total. Or, rather: inside, a whole panoply of gadgets magnetizes the crowd in directed flows – outside, solitude is directed at a single gadget: the automobile. By an extraordinary coincidence (but this derives without a doubt from the enchantment inherent to this universe), this frozen, child-like world is found to have been conceived and realized by a man who is himself now cryogenized: Walt Disney, who awaits his resurrection through an increase of 180 degrees centigrade.

Thus, everywhere in Disneyland the objective profile of America, down to the morphology of individuals and of the crowd, is drawn. All its values are exalted by the miniature and the comic strip. Embalmed and pacified. Whence the possibility of an ideological analysis of Disneyland (L. Marin did it very well in *Utopiques, jeux d'espace* [Utopias, play of space]): digest of the American way of life, panegyric of American values, idealized transposition of a contradictory reality. Certainly. But this masks something else and this 'ideological' blanket functions as a cover for a *simulation of the third order*: Disneyland exists in order to hide that it is the 'real' country, all of 'real' America that is Disneyland (a bit like prisons are there to hide that it is the social in its entirety, in its banal omnipresence, that is carceral). Disneyland is presented as imaginary in order to make us believe that the rest is real, whereas all of Los Angeles and the America that surrounds it are no longer real, but belong to the hyperreal order and to the order of simulation. It is no longer a question of a false representation of reality (ideology) but of concealing the fact that the real is no longer real, and thus saving the reality principle.

The imaginary of Disneyland is neither true nor false. It is a deterrence machine set up in order to rejuvenate the fiction of the real in the opposite camp. Whence the debility of this imaginary, its infantile degeneration. This world wants to be childish in order to make us believe that the adults are elsewhere, in the 'real' world, and to conceal the fact that true childishness is everywhere – that it is that of the adults themselves who come here to act the child in order to foster illusions as to their real childishness.

Disneyland is not the only one, however. Enchanted Village, Magic Mountain, Marine World: Los Angeles is surrounded by these imaginary stations that feed reality, the energy of the real to a city whose mystery is precisely that of no longer being anything but a network of incessant, unreal circulation – a city of incredible proportions but without space, without dimension. As much as electrical and atomic power stations, as much as cinema studios, this city, which is no longer anything but an immense scenario and a perpetual pan shot, needs this old imaginary like a sympathetic nervous system made up of childhood signals and faked phantasms . . .

LAS VEGAS   *Baudrillard*

When one sees Las Vegas at dusk rise whole from the desert in the radiance of advertising, and return to the desert when dawn breaks, one sees that advertising is not what brightens or decorates the walls; it is what effaces the walls, effaces the streets, the façades and all the architecture, effaces any support and any depth, and that it is this liquidation, this reabsorption of everything into the surface ... that plunges us into this stupefied, hyperreal euphoria that we would not exchange for anything else, and that is the empty and inescapable form of seduction.

AMERICA

I speak of the American deserts and of the cities which are not cities. No oases, no monuments; infinite panning shots over mineral landscapes and freeways. Everywhere: Los Angeles or Twenty-Nine Palms, Las Vegas or Borrego Springs ...

No desire: the desert. Desire is still something deeply natural, we live off its vestiges in Europe, and off the vestiges of a moribund critical culture. Here the cities are mobile deserts. No monuments and no history: the exaltation of mobile deserts and simulation. There is the same wildness in the endless, indifferent cities as in the intact silence of the Badlands. Why is LA, why are the deserts so fascinating? It is because you are delivered from all depth there – a brilliant, mobile, superficial neutrality, a challenge to meaning and profundity, a challenge to nature and culture, an outer hyperspace, with no origin, no reference-points.

No charm, no seduction in all this. Seduction is elsewhere, in Italy, in certain landscapes that have become paintings, as culturalized and refined in their design as the cities and museums that house them. Circumscribed, traced-out, highly seductive spaces where meaning, at these heights of luxury, has finally become adornment. It is exactly the reverse here: there is no seduction, but there is an absolute fascination – the fascination of the very disappearance of all aesthetic and critical forms of life in the irradiation of an objectless neutrality. Immanent and solar. The fascination of the desert: immobility without desire. Of Los Angeles: insane circulation without desire. The end of aesthetics.

It is not just the aesthetics of decor (of nature or architecture) that vanishes into thin air, but the aesthetics of bodies and language, of everything that forms the European's – especially the Latin European's – mental and social *habitus*, that continual *commedia dell'arte*, the pathos and rhetoric of social relations, the dramatization of speech, the subtle play of language, the aura of make-up and artificial gesture. The whole aesthetic and rhetorical system of seduction, of taste, of charm, of theatre, but also of contradictions, of violence always reappropriated by speech, by play, by distance, by artifice. Our universe is never desert-like, always theatrical. Always ambiguous. Always cultural, and faintly ridiculous in its hereditary culturality.

What is arresting here is the absence of all these things – both the absence of architecture in the cities, which are nothing but long tracking shots of signals, and the dizzying absence of emotion and character in the faces and bodies. Handsome, fluid, supple or cool, or grotesquely obese, probably less as the

Baudrillard   result of compulsive bulimia than a general incoherence, which results in a
casualness about the body or language, food or the city: a loose network of
individual, successive functions, a hypertrophied cell tissue proliferating in all
directions.

Thus the only tissue of the city is that of the freeways, a vehicular, or rather
an incessant transurbanistic, tissue, the extraordinary spectacle of cars moving
at the same speed, in both directions, headlights full on in broad daylight, on
the Ventura Freeway, coming from nowhere, going nowhere: an immense
collective act, rolling along, ceaselessly unrolling, without aggression, without
objectives – transferential sociality, doubtless the only kind in a hyperreal,
technological, soft-mobile era, exhausting itself in surfaces, networks and soft
technologies. No elevator or subway in Los Angeles. No verticality or underground, no intimacy or collectivity, no streets or façades, no centre or monuments: a fantastic space, a spectral and discontinuous succession of all the
various functions, of all signs with no hierarchical ordering – an extravaganza
of indifference, extravaganza of undifferentiated surfaces – the power of pure
open space, the kind you find in the deserts. The power of the desert form: it is
the erasure of traces in the desert, of the signified of signs in the cities, of any
psychology in bodies. An animal and metaphysical fascination – the direct
fascination of space, the immanent fascination of dryness and sterility.

JÜRGEN HABERMAS

As a prominent member of the Frankfurt Institute for Social Research, German philosopher and social theorist Jürgen Habermas (b. 1929) inherited the mantle of Adorno and Horkheimer. His theoretical outlook can be seen as both a development and critique of the earlier Frankfurt School project. He rejects the pessimism of its earlier outlook, especially in its critique of enlightenment rationality. Habermas is careful to distinguish between normative and instrumental rationality. The latter is positivistic in its outlook and serves to impoverish cultural life. A normative rationality, on the other hand, may serve as a force of social change. Habermas therefore endorses modernism as a continuation of the enlightenment project, and supports rationality as a potential source of emancipation.

Habermas places great emphasis on the public sphere as the realm of communicative action. Here he subscribes to a form of inter-subjective communication as a means of overcoming the potential relativism of the 'language games' celebrated by various theorists of postmodernity. This emphasis on the public sphere has led others to employ Habermas's theories in various areas of public participation. John Forrester, for example, has applied the principles of Habermas's thinking to the field of planning.

Habermas has proved to be one of the most outspoken critics of postmodernism. His position on this question is outlined articulately in the article 'Modernity, an Incomplete Project', which he opens with a criticism of the conservatism of the architectural exhibits at the Venice Biennale of 1980. He develops this criticism further in his article 'Modernism versus Postmodernism in Architecture'. Modernism, according to Habermas, suffers from being overburdened and instrumentalized. Habermas himself would favour a self-critical continuation of the Modern Movement. By way of contrast, he outlines three oppositional trends which repudiate rather than attempt to rework the Modern Movement: neo-historicism, postmodernism (as defined by Charles Jencks) and 'alternative architecture'.

Habermas criticizes neo-historicism as a conservative escapist reaction which 'transfroms department stores into Medieval rows of houses, and underground ventilation shafts into pocket-book size Palladian villas'. Likewise he attacks postmodern architects like Hollein and Venturi as 'surrealist stage designers' who 'utilise modern design methods in order to coax picturesque effects from aggressively mixed styles'. Finally – and perhaps most surprisingly – he condemns the 'alternative architecture' of interest groups who are concerned with questions of ecology and preservation of historic centres. While 'initiatives which aim at a

Habermas communal participatory architecture' might subscribe to his celebration of communicative action, they all too often lead to 'the cult of the vernacular and reverence for the banal'. In its time this 'architecture without architects' led to the monumentalism of Führer-architecture.

MODERN AND POSTMODERN ARCHITECTURE   *Habermas*

The exhibition 'The Other Tradition – Architecture in Munich from 1800 up to today' offers an opportunity to consider the meaning of a preposition. This preposition has inconspicuously become part of the dispute on Post- or late-Modern Architecture. With the prefix *post*, the protagonists wish to dismiss the past, unable as yet to give the present a *new* name. To the recognizable problems of the future, they, that is to say, we, do not yet have the answer.

At first the expression 'postmodern' had only been used to denote novel variations within the broad spectrum of the 'late-modern', when it was used during the 1950s and 1960s in the United States for literary trends that intended to set themselves apart from earlier modern writings. Postmodernism only became an emotionally loaded, outright political war cry in the 1970s, when two contrasting camps seized the expression. On the one hand the 'neo-conservatives', who wanted to rid themselves of the supposedly subversive contents of a 'hostile culture', in favour of reawakened traditions; on the other hand, certain *critics of economic growth*, for whom the New Building (*Neues Bauen*) had become the symbol of the destruction brought on by modern-ization. Thus for the first time architectural movements which had still shared the theoretical position of the Modern Architecture – and which have rightfully been described by Charles Jencks as Late-Modern – happened to have been dragged into the 'conservative' wake of the 1970s, paving the way for an intellectually playful yet provocative repudiation of the moral principles of Modern Architecture.

It is not easy to disentangle the frontiers for all parties agree in the critique of the soulless 'container' architecture, of the absence of a relationship with the environment and the solitary arrogance of the unarticulated office block, of the monstrous department stores, monumental universities and congress centres, of the lack of urbanity and the misanthropy of the satellite towns, of the heaps of speculative buildings, the brutal successor to the 'bunker architecture' – the mass production of pitch-roofed dog houses, the destruction of cities in the name of the automobile, and so forth . . . So many slogans with no disagree-ment whatsoever!

Indeed what one side calls *immanent criticism*, the other side considers to be *opposition to the 'modern'*. The same reasons that encourage the one side to a critical continuation of an irreplaceable tradition are sufficient for the other side to proclaim a postmodern era. Furthermore these opponents draw con-trasting conclusions according to whether they confront the evil in terms of cosmetics or in terms of criticism of the system.

Those of a *conservative disposition* satisfy themselves with a stylistic cover-up of that which nonetheless exists, either like the traditionalist von Branca or like the pop-artist Venturi today, who transforms the spirit of the Modern Movement into a quotation and mixes it ironically with other quotations, like dazzling radiant neon light texts. The radical *anti-modernists*, on the other hand, tackle the problem at a more fundamental level, seeking to undermine the economic and administrative constraints of industrial constructions. Their aim is a de-differentiation of the architectural culture. What the one side considers as problems of style, the other perceives as problems of the

Habermas decolonization of lost human habitats. Thus those who wish to continue the incomplete project of the shaken Modern Movement see themselves confronted by various opponents who agree only in as much as they are determined to break away from modern architecture. Modern architecture which has even left its mark on everyday life, after all, is still the first and only unifying style since the days of classicism. It has developed out of both the organic as well as rationalistic origins of a Frank Lloyd Wright and an Adolf Loos, and flourished in the most successful work of a Gropius and a Mies van der Rohe, a Le Corbusier and an Alvar Aalto. It is the only architectural movement to originate from the avant-garde spirit: it is equivalent to avant-garde painting, music and literature of our century. It continued along the traditional line of occidental rationalism and was powerful enough to create its own models; in other words, it became classic itself and set the foundations of a tradition that from the very beginning crossed national boundaries. How are such hardly disputable facts reconcilable with the fact that in the very name of this International Style those unanimously condemned deformations which followed the Second World War, could have come about? Might it be that the real face of Modern Architecture is revealed in these atrocities, or are they misrepresentations of its true spirit?

THE CHALLENGE OF THE NINETEENTH CENTURY TO ARCHITECTURE

I should like to attempt a provisional answer by:

1   Listing the problems which faced architecture in the nineteenth century.
2   Giving an account of the programmatic answers which the Modern Movement offered in response to the problems.
3   Pointing out the kind of problems which could not be solved by this programme. Finally,
4   These considerations should help to make a judgement on the suggestion, which this exhibition attempts to make (presuming its intentions have been correctly understood).

How good is the recommendation to adopt the modern tradition unerringly and to continue it critically instead of following 'the escapist movements' which are currently dominant: be it tradition-conscious 'neo-historicism', the ultra-modern 'stage-set' architecture that was presented at the Venice Biennale in 1980, or the 'vitalism' of simplified life in anonymous, de-professionalized, vernacular architecture? The Industrial Revolution and the accelerated social modernization that followed introduced a new situation to nineteenth-century architecture and town planning. I would like to mention the three best-known challenges:

•   the qualitatively new requirements in architectural design;
•   the new materials and construction techniques; and finally
•   the subjugation of architecture to new functional, above all economic, imperatives.

Industrial capitalism created *new interest spheres* that evaded both courtly-ecclesiastical architecture, as well as the old European urban and rural

architectural culture. The diffusion of culture and the formation of a wider, *Habermas*
educated public, interested in the arts, called for new libraries and schools,
opera houses and theatres. However, these were conventional tasks. Entirely
different is the challenge presented by the transport network which was
revolutionized by the railway; not only did it give to the already familiar
transport structures, the bridges and tunnels, a different meaning, but it introduced a new task: the construction of railway stations. Railway stations are
characteristic places for dense and varied as well as anonymous and fleeting
encounters, in other words, for the type of interactions which were to mark the
atmosphere of life in the big cities, described by Benjamin as overflowing with
excitement but lacking in contact. As the motorways, airports and television
towers have shown, the development of transport and communication networks have initiated innovations time and again.

This also applied to the development for commercial communication. It not
only created the demand for a new scale of warehouses and market-halls, but
introduced unconventional construction projects as well: the department store
and the exhibition hall. Above all, however, industrial production with its
factories, workers' housing estates and goods produced for mass consumption,
created new spheres of life into which formal design and architectural articulation was not able to penetrate at first.

In the second half of the nineteenth century those mass products for daily
use, which had escaped the stylistic force of the traditional arts and crafts, were
the first to be perceived as an aesthetic problem. John Ruskin and William
Morris sought to bridge the gap that had opened between utility and beauty in
the everyday life of the industrial world by reforming the applied arts. The
reform movement was led by a wider forward-looking architectural notion
which accompanied the claim to form, from an architectural point of view, the
entire physical environment of bourgeois society. Morris in particular recognized the contradiction between the democratic demands for universal participation in culture and the fact that, within industrial capitalism, increasing
domains of human activity were being alienated from the creative cultural
forces.

The second challenge to architecture arose from the development of *new
materials* (such as glass and iron, steel and cement) and *new methods of
production* (above all the use of prefabricated elements). In the course of the
nineteenth century the engineers advanced the techniques of construction,
thereby developing new design possibilities which shattered the classical limits
of the constructional handling of planes and volumes. Originating from greenhouse construction, the glass palaces of the first industrial exhibitions in
London, Munich and Paris, built from standardized parts, conveyed to their
fascinated contemporaries the first impressions of new orders of magnitude and
of constructional principles. They revolutionized visual experience and
altered the spectators' concept of space, as dramatically as the railway changed
the passengers' concept of time. The interior of the centreless repetitive London
Crystal Palace must have had the effect of transcendence of all known dimensions of designed space.

Finally, the third challenge was the capitalist *mobilization* of labour, real
estate and buildings, in general of all *urban living conditions*. This led to the
concentration of large masses and to the incursion of speculation in the field of

private housing. The reason for today's protests in Kreuzberg and elsewhere originates in that period. As housing construction became an amortizeable investment, so decisions about the purchase and the sale of estate, and construction, demolition and reconstruction, about renting and vacating property were freed from the ties of family and local traditions; in other words they made themselves independent of use-value considerations. The laws of the building and housing market altered the attitude towards building and dwelling. Economic imperatives also determined the uncontrolled growth of cities. Out of these arose the requirements of a kind of town planning which cannot be compared to baroque city developments. The way these two sorts of functional imperatives, those of the market with those of communal and state planning, intersect, and the way they entangle architecture in a new system of subordinations, is demonstrated in a grand style by the redevelopment of Paris by Haussmann, under Napoleon III. The architects played no noteworthy part in these plans.

FAILURE OF HISTORICISM, MODERNISM'S ANSWER

In order to understand the impulse from which modern architecture developed, one has to bear in mind that the architecture of the second part of the nineteenth century was not only overwhelmed by this third requirement of industrial capitalism, but, although the other two challenges were recognized, it has still not mastered them. The arbitrary disposition of scientifically objectified styles, having been torn from their formative context, enabled historicism to side-step into an idealism which had become impotent, and to separate the field of architecture from the banalities of everyday bourgeois life. By setting utilitarian architecture free from artistic demands, a virtue was made of the necessity of the new domains of human concerns which had been alienated from architectural design. The opportunities offered by the new possibilities of technical design were only grasped in order to divide the world between architects and engineers, style and function, impressive facades on the exterior and autonomous spatial disposition in the interior. Thus historical architecture did not have much more to set against the immanent dynamic of economic growth, to the mobilization of urban living conditions, to the social plight of the masses, than the escape into the triumph of spirit and culture over the (disguised) material bases.

In the reformist tendencies of the *Jugendstil*, from which modern architecture emerged, the protest was already raised against this falsity, against an architecture of repression and symptom formation. It was no coincidence that, in the same period, Sigmund Freud developed the foundations of his theory of neurosis.

The Modern Movement took on the challenges for which the nineteenth-century architecture was no match. It overcame the stylistic pluralism and such differentiations and subdivisions with which architecture had come to terms. It gave an answer to the alienation from culture and industrial capitalism domains with the claim for a style that would not only make a mark on prestige buildings, but would also penetrate everyday practice. The spirit of modernism was to participate in the totality of social manifestations. Industrial design was able to take up the reform of the applied arts: the functional design of utility

buildings was able to take up the engineering skills demonstrated in transport   *Habermas*
and commercial buildings; the concept of commercial quarters was able to take
up the models of the Chicago School. Over and above that, the new architectural language seized on the exclusive fields of monumental architecture, of
churches, theatres, law courts, ministries, townhalls, universities, spas, etc. On
the other hand it expanded into key areas of industrial production, into settlements, social housing and factories.

WHAT DOES FUNCTIONALISM REALLY MEAN?

The New Style could certainly not have penetrated into all spheres of life had
modern architecture not assimilated the second challenge, that is, the
immensely widened range of technical design possibilities with a determined
aesthetic approach. The term 'functionalism' incorporates certain key notions –
principles for the construction of rooms, for the use of materials and methods
of production and organization. 'Functionalism' is based on the conviction that
forms should express the use-functions for which a building is produced. But
the expression 'functionalism' also suggests false concepts. If nothing else it
conceals the fact that the qualities of modern buildings result from a consistently applied autonomous system of aesthetic rules. That which is wrongly
attributed to functionalism it owes in fact to an aesthetically motivated
constructivism, following independently from new problem definitions posed
in art. Through constructivism, modern architecture followed the experimental
trail of avant-garde painting.

Modern architecture found itself at a paradoxical point of departure. On the
one hand architecture has always been a use-orientated art. As opposed to
music, painting and poetry, architecture cannot escape from its practical
contextual relations any more than prose of a high literary standard can evade
the use of colloquial speech. These arts remain tied to the network of common
practice and everyday communication. It is for that reason that Adolf Loos
considered architecture, together with anything else that serves a purpose, to be
excluded from the sphere of art.

On the other hand architecture is dominated by the laws of modern culture
– it is subject, as is art in general, to the compulsion of attaining radical
autonomy. The avant-garde art, that freed itself from perspective perception of
the object and from tonality, from immitation and harmony, and that turned to
its own means of representation, has been characterized by Adorno with key-
words like construction, experiment and montage.

According to Adorno, the paradigmatic works indulge in an esoteric
absolutism,

> at the expense of real appropriateness, within which functional
> objects, as for example bridges and industrial facilities, seek their
> own formal laws. . . . On the contrary, the autonomous work of art,
> functional only within its immanent teleology, seeks to attain that
> which was once called beauty.

Thus Adorno contrasts the work of art, functioning 'within itself', with the
use-object, functioning for 'exterior purposes'. However, modern architecture
in its most convincing examples does not comply with the dichotomy outlined

Habermas by Adorno. Its functionalism rather coincides with the inner logic of a development of art. Above all, three groups worked on the problem which had arisen out of cubist painting: the group of purists around Le Corbusier, the constructivists around Malevich, and in particular the De-Stijl movement (with van Doesburg, Mondrian and Oud). Just as de Saussure had analysed language structures at that time, the Dutch Neoplasticists, as they called themselves, investigated the grammar of the means of expression and design of the most general techniques used in the applied arts in order to incorporate them in a total work of art involving the comprehensive architectural articulation of the environment. In Malevich's and Oud's very early house plans one can see how those objects of the functionalist Bauhaus architecture emerge from the experimental approach using pure means of design. It is precisely in Bruno Taut's catch-phrase: 'what functions well, looks good', that the *aesthetic significance of functionalism*, expressed so clearly in Taut's own buildings, is lost.

While the Modern Movement recognized the challenges of the qualitatively new requirements and the new technical design possibilities, and while it essentially responded correctly, it reacted rather helplessly to the pressures of the market and the planning bureaucracies.

The broadened architectural concept, which had encouraged the Modern Movement to overcome a stylistic pluralism that stood out against everyday reality, was a mixed blessing. Not only did it focus attention on the important relations between industrial design, interior design and the architecture of housing and town planning, but it also acted as a sponsor when the theoreticians of the New Architecture (*Neues Bauen*) wanted to see total forms of the life completely subjugated to the dictates of their design tasks. However, such totalities extend beyond the powers of design. When Le Corbusier finally managed to realize his design for a '*unité jardin verticale*', it was the communal facilities that remained unused or were eradicated. The utopia of preconceived forms of life which had already inspired the designs of Owen and Fourier could not be filled with life. Not only because of a hopeless underestimation of the diversity, complexity and variability of modern aspects of life, but also because modernized societies with their functional interdependencies go beyond the dimensions of living conditions, which could be gauged by the planner with his imagination. The crisis which has become apparent today within modern architecture cannot be traced back to a crisis in architecture itself, but to the fact that it had readily allowed itself to be overburdened.

THE COMPULSION OF THE SYSTEM. ARCHITECTURE AND THE WILL TO LIFE

Moreover, modern architecture, with the indistinctions of functionalist ideology was poorly armed against the dangers brought about by the post-Second World War reconstruction, the period during which the International Style broadly asserted itself for the first time. Gropius certainly emphasized the close relations that architecture and town planning had with industry, commerce, politics and administration. In those early days he already perceived the character of the process of planning. However, within the Bauhaus, these problems only appeared in a 'format', which was tailored only to didactic purposes. Furthermore, the success of the Modern Movement led the pioneers

to the unjustified expectation that 'unity of culture and production' could be   *Habermas*
achieved in another sense as well. The economic and politico-administrative
limitations to which the design of the environment was subjected appeared in
this transfigured viewpoint to be a mere question of organization. When in
1949 the American Architects Association sought to insert in its statute the
condition that architects should not operate as building contractors, Gropius
protested – not against the insufficiency of the means, but against the purpose
and reason for the proposal. He persisted in his belief:

> Art, that has become a cultural factor in general, will be in a
> position to give the social environment the unity, which will be the
> true basis for a culture embracing every object, from a simple chair
> to a house of prayer.

Within this grand synthesis, all the contradictions characterizing capitalistic
modernization, especially in the field of town planning, disappear – the contradictions between the requirements of a structured environment on the one
hand, and the imperatives shared by money and power on the other.

RESTORATION OF URBANITY?

No doubt development met with a linguistic misunderstanding. Those means,
that are suitable for a certain purpose, are called 'functional'. In this sense one
can understand 'functionalism' as seeking to construct buildings according to
the measure of the users' purposes. The term 'functional', however, also
characterizes decisions which stabilize an anonymous relation of activities,
without the system's existence having necessarily been called for or even
noticed by any of the participants. In this sense, what is considered as 'system
functional' for the economy and administration, for example an increase in the
density of inner city areas with rising prices in real estate and increasing tax
revenues, by no means has to prove to be functional in the background of the
lives of both inhabitants and neighbouring residents. The problems of town
planning are not primarily problems of design but problems of controlling and
dealing with the anonymous system imperatives that influence the spheres of
city life and threaten to devastate the urban fabric.

Today, everyone is talking about recalling the traditional European city.
However, as early as 1889, Camillo Sitte, who was one of the first to compare
the medieval town with the modern city, had warned against such forced lack
of constraints. After a century's criticism of the large city, after innumerable,
repeated and disillusioned attempts to keep a balance in the cities, to save the
inner cities, to divide urban space into residential areas and commercial
quarters, industrial facilities and garden suburbs; private and public zones; to
build habitable satellite towns; to rehabilitate slum areas; to regulate traffic
most sensibly, etc., the question that is brought to mind is whether the actual
notion of the city has not itself been superseded As a comprehensible habitat,
the city could at one time be architecturally designed and mentally represented.
The social functions of urban life, political and economic, private and public,
the assignments of cultural and religious representation, of work habitation,
recreation and celebration could be *translated* into use-purposes, into functions
of temporally regulated use of designed spaces. However, by the nineteenth

Habermas century at the latest the city became the intersection point of a different kind of functional relationship. It was embedded in abstract systems which could no longer be captured aesthetically in an intelligible presence. The fact that from the middle of the nineteenth century until the late 1880s the great industrial exhibitions were planned as big architectural events reveals an impulse which seems touching today. Whilst for the purpose of international competition arranging a festive and vivid display of their industrial products in magnificent halls for the general public, the governments literally wanted to set the stage for the world market and bring it back within the limits of the human habitat. However, not even the railway stations, which had brought their passengers into contact with the transport network, could represent the network's functions in the same way as the city gates had once represented the actual connections to the nearby villages and neighbouring towns. Besides, airports today are situated way outside cities, for good reasons. In the characterless office buildings which dominate the town centres, in the banks and ministeries, the law courts and corporate administrations, the publishing and printing houses, the private and public bureaucracies, one cannot recognize the functional relations whose point of intersection they form. The graphics of company trademarks and of neon-light advertisements demonstrate that differentiation must take place by means of that other than the formal language of architecture. Another indication that the urban habitat is increasingly being mediated by systemic relations, which cannot be given concrete form, is the failure of perhaps the most ambitious project of the new architecture (*Neues Bauen*). To this day it has not been possible to integrate social housing and factories within the city. The urban agglomerations have outgrown the old concept of the city which people so cherish. However, that is the failure of neither modern architecture, nor of any other architecture.

PERPLEXITY AND REACTIONS

Assuming this diagnosis is not absolutely wrong, then it first of all merely confirms the dominating perplexity and the need to search for new solutions. Of course, it also raises doubts as to the reactions which have been set off by the disaster of the simultaneously overburdened and instrumentalized architecture of the Modern Movement (*Neues Bauen*). In order to at least provisionally orientate myself within the complex terrain of counter-movements, I have distinguished three tendencies which have one thing in common: contrary to the self-critical continuation of the Modern Movement, they break away from the Modern Style. They want to dissolve the ties of the avant-garde formal language and the inflexible functionalistic principles; programmatically, form and function are to be separated once again.

On a trivial level, this holds true for neo-historicism, which transforms department stores into mediaeval rows of houses, and underground ventilation shafts into pocket-book size Palladian villas. As in the past century, the return to eclecticism is due to compensatory needs. This traditionalism falls under the heading of political neo-conservatism, not unknown to Bavaria, insofar as it redefines problems which lie on a *different level*, in terms of questions of style, thus removing it from the consciousness of the public. The escapist reaction is related to a tendency for the affirmative: all that remains should stay as it is.

The separation of form and function also applies to the postmodern movement, *Habermas* which corresponds to Charles Jencks's definitions and which is free of nostalgia – whether it is Eisenmann or Graves who automize the formal repertoire of the 1920s artistically, or whether it is Hollein or Venturi, who, like surrealist stage designers, utilize modern design methods in order to coax picturesque effects from aggressively mixed styles. The language of this stage-set architecture indulges in a rhetoric that still seeks to express in ciphers systemic relationships which can no longer be architecturally formulated. Finally, the unity of form and function is broken in a different way by the *'Alternative Architecture'* which is based on the problems of ecology and of the preservation of historically developed urban districts. These trends, often characterized as 'vitalistic', are primarily aimed at relating architectural design to spatial, cultural and historical contexts. Therein survive some of the impulses of the Modern Movement, now obviously on the defensive. Above all, it is worth noting some of the initiatives which aim at a communal 'participatory architecture', which designs urban areas in a dialogue with the clients. When the guiding mechanisms of the market and the town planning administration function in such a way as to have disfunctional consequences on the lives of those concerned, failing the 'functionalism' as it was understood, then it only follows that the formative communication of the participants be allowed to compete with the media of money and power.

However, the nostalgia for the de-differentiated forms of existence often bestows upon these tendencies an air of anti-modernism. They are then linked to the cult of the vernacular and to reverence for the banal. This ideology of the uncomplicated denies the sensible potential and the specificity of cultural modernism. The praise of the anonymous architecture, of architecture without architects, has a price which this vitalism, having become critical of the whole system, is willing to pay – even if it has another 'Volksgeist' in mind, as for example, the one whose transfiguration in its time brought the monumentalism of the Führer-architecture to its ultimate completion.

A good deal of truth also lies in this form of opposition. It takes on the unanswered problems which modern architecture had left in the background – that is to say – the colonization of the human habitat by the imperatives of autonomized systems of economic and administrative processes. However, it will only be possible to learn something from all these oppositions if we keep one thing in mind. At a certain fortunate moment in modern architecture, the aesthetic identity of constructivism met with the practical spirit of strict functionalism and cohered informally. Traditions can only live through such historic moments.

FREDRIC JAMESON

Fredric
*Jameson*American literary and cultural theorist Fredric Jameson (b. 1934) is one of the key
theorists of postmodernism. Jameson addresses the question of cultural theory
from the perspective of Marxism and the New Left, and under the strong influences
of Adorno and Lukacs. He is concerned with the possibility for effective social
action in transforming Western societies, against the backdrop of a seemingly all-
consuming capitalism.

Jameson looks to culture both as a means of understanding the postmodern
condition, and as a potential mechanism to mediate against that condition. For
Jameson the contemporary age is dominated by capitalism. There is no space outside exchange society. Within postmodern culture everything is immediately co-
opted into commodities and images. Jameson focuses on aesthetics as a response to
this condition. What is required is a cognitively viable aesthetics that reinserts the
individual in the community. Architecture assumes a pivotal role in Jameson's
thought. For it is here that 'modifications in the aesthetic production are most
dramatically visible'. Within the postmodern urban environment, Jameson is
concerned to develop a viable form of cognitive mapping to resist the otherwise
totally homogenizing space of global multi-nationalism. For Jameson the problem
of today is how to live in postmodern space productively, and how to develop a new
art to deal with new forms of being.

In the very opening chapter of his highly influential work, *Postmodernism, or
the Cultural Logic of Late Capitalism*, Jameson undertakes an analysis of the
Bonaventure Hotel in Los Angeles – a commercial development overlooked by
mainstream architectural discourse. Several major themes of Jameson's project
come together here in what proved to be a seminal account, which spawned many
responses, including one by Baudrillard also included in this volume. The mirror
glass exterior embodies the glazed superficiality of the commodity in late
capitalism, while the disorientating interior exemplifies problems of cognitive
mapping in such an environment.

Jameson further pursues the theme of the all-consuming nature of multinational capitalism in 'The Constraints of Postmodernism', a critique of Kenneth
Frampton's 'Towards a Critical Regionalism', itself a canonical work of architectural theory. In a study of sustained rigour and penetrating insight, Jameson
challenges Frampton on a number of issues, and ends with the provocative
suggestion that the call for 'difference' which underpins Frampton's position might
itself be a product of the very multi-national capitalism that it attempts to oppose.

Jameson pursues similar themes in 'Is Space Political?', where he argues that

calls for the 'chaotic' and 'organic' can be seen as the products of neo-Fordist,   *Jameson*
postmodern marketing. He challenges many accepted tenets within architecture,
highlighting the reactionary utopianism of phenomenology and questioning the
capacity for architecture to be 'critical'. Jameson argues that political 'content' in
architecture, no less than in art, is merely allegorical. Architecture in itself is inert.
The political may be read as apolitical, while that which is decorative may be
rewritten as political 'with energetic interpretation'.

Jameson   # THE CULTURAL LOGIC OF LATE CAPITALISM

The last few years have been marked by an inverted millenarianism in which premonitions of the future, catastrophic or redemptive, have been replaced by senses of the end of this or that (the end of ideology, art or social class; the 'crisis' of Leninism, social democracy or the welfare state etc., etc.); taken together, all of these perhaps constitute what is increasingly called post-modernism. The case for its existence depends on the hypothesis of some radical break or *coupure*, generally traced back to the end of the 1950s or the early 1960s.

As the word itself suggests, this break is most often related to notions of the waning or extinction of the hundred-year-old Modern Movement (or to its ideological or aesthetic repudiation). Thus abstract expressionism in painting, existentialism in philosophy, the final forms of representation in the novel, the films of the great auteurs, or the modernist school of poetry (as institutionalized and canonized in the works of Wallace Stevens) all are now seen as the final, extraordinary flowering of a high-modernist impulse which is spent and exhausted with them. The enumeration of what follows, then, at once becomes empirical, chaotic and heterogeneous: Andy Warhol and pop art, but also photo-realism, and beyond it, the 'new expressionism'; the moment, in music, of John Cage, but also the synthesis of classical and 'popular' styles found in composers like Phil Glass and Terry Riley, and also punk and new wave rock (the Beatles and the Stones now standing as the high-modernist moment of that more recent and rapidly evolving tradition); in film, Godard, post-Godard, and experimental cinema and video, but also a whole new type of commercial film (about which more below); Burroughs, Pynchon or Ishmael Reed, on the one hand, and the French *nouveau roman* and its succession, on the other, along with alarming new kinds of literary criticism based on some new aesthetic of textuality or *écriture*. . . . The list might be extended indefinitely: but does it imply any more fundamental change or break than the periodic style and fashion changes determined by an older high-modernist imperative of stylistic innovation?

It is in the realm of architecture, however, that modifications in aesthetic production are most dramatically visible, and that their theoretical problems have been most centrally raised and articulated: it was indeed from architectural debates that my own conception of postmodernism – as it will be outlined in the following pages – initially began to emerge. More decisively than in the other arts or media, postmodernist positions in architecture have been inseparable from an implacable critique of architectural high modernism and of Frank Lloyd Wright or the so-called international style (Le Corbusier, Mies, etc), where formal criticism and analysis (of the high-modernist trans-formation of the building into a virtual sculpture, or monumental 'duck': as Robert Venturi puts it)[1] are at one with reconsiderations on the level of urbanism and of the aesthetic institution. High modernism is thus credited with the destruction of the fabric of the traditional city and its older neighbourhood culture (by way of the radical disjunction of the new Utopian high-modernist building from its surrounding context), while the prophetic elitism and authoritarianism of the Modern Movement are remorselessly identified in the imperious gesture of the charismatic Master.

Postmodernism in architecture will then logically enough stage itself as a kind of aesthetic populism, as the very title of Venturi's influential manifesto, *Learning from Las Vegas*, suggests. However we may ultimately wish to evaluate this populist rhetoric,[2] it has at least the merit of drawing our attention to one fundamental feature of all the postmodernisms enumerated above: namely, the effacement in them of the older (essentially high-modernist) frontier between high culture and so-called mass or commercial culture, and the emergence of new kinds of texts infused with the forms, categories and contents of that very culture industry so passionately denounced by all the ideologues of the modern, from Leavis and the American New Criticism all the way to Adorno and the Frankfurt School. The postmodernisms have, in fact, been fascinated precisely by this whole 'degraded' landscape of schlock and kitsch, of TV series and *Reader's Digest* culture, of advertising and motels, of the late show and the grade-B Hollywood film, of so-called paraliterature, with its airport paperback categories of the gothic and the romance, the popular biography, the murder mystery, and the science fiction or fantasy novel: materials they no longer simply 'quote', as a Joyce or a Mahler might have done, but incorporate into their very substance.

Nor should the break in question be thought of as a purely cultural affair: indeed, theories of the postmodern – whether celebratory or couched in the language of moral revulsion and denunciation – bear a strong family resemblance to all those more ambitious sociological generalizations which, at much the same time, bring us the news of the arrival and inauguration of a whole new type of society, most famously baptized 'postindustrial society' (Daniel Bell) but often also designated consumer society, media society, information society, electronic society or high tech, and the like. Such theories have the obvious ideological mission of demonstrating, to their own relief, that the new social formation in question no longer obeys the laws of classical capitalism, namely, the primacy of industrial production and the omnipresence of class struggle. The Marxist tradition has therefore resisted them with vehemence, with the signal exception of the economist Ernest Mandel, whose book *Late Capitalism* sets out not merely to anatomize the historic originality of this new society (which he sees as a third stage or moment in the evolution of capital) but also to demonstrate that it is, if anything, a purer stage of capitalism than any of the moments that preceded it. I will return to this argument later: suffice it for the moment to anticipate a point that will be argued . . . , namely, that every position on postmodernism in culture – whether apologia or stigmatization – is also at one and the same time, and necessarily, an implicitly or explicitly political stance on the nature of multinational capitalism today.

A last preliminary word on method: what follows is not to be read as stylistic description, as the account of one cultural style or movement among others. I have rather meant to offer a periodizing hypothesis, and that at a moment in which the very conception of historical periodization has come to seem most problematical indeed. I have argued elsewhere that all isolated or discrete cultural analysis always involves a buried or repressed theory of historical periodization: in any case, the conception of the 'genealogy' largely lays to rest traditional theoretical worries about so-called linear history, theories of 'stages,' and teleological historiography. In the present context,

Jameson however, lengthier theoretical discussion of such (very real) issues can perhaps be replaced by a few substantive remarks.

One of the concerns frequently aroused by periodizing hypotheses is that these tend to obliterate difference and to project an idea of the historical period as massive homogeneity (bounded on either side by inexplicable chronological metamorphoses and punctuation marks). This is, however, precisely why it seems to me essential to grasp postmodernism not as a style but rather as a cultural dominant: a conception which allows for the presence and coexistence of a range of very different, yet subordinate, features.

Consider, for example, the powerful alternative position that postmodernism is itself little more than one more stage of modernism proper (if not, indeed, of the even older romanticism): it may indeed be conceded that all the features of postmodernism I am about to enumerate can be detected, full-blown, in this or that preceding modernism (including such astonishing genealogical precursors as Gertrude Stein, Raymond Roussel or Marcel Duchamp, who may be considered outright postmodernists, *avant la lettre*). What has not been taken into account by this view, however, is the social position of the older modernism, or better still, its passionate repudiation by an older Victorian and post-Victorian bourgeoisie for whom its forms and ethos are received as being variously ugly, dissonant, obscure, scandalous, immoral, subversive, and generally 'antisocial'. It will be argued here, however, that a mutation in the sphere of culture has rendered such attitudes archaic. Not only are Picasso and Joyce no longer ugly; they now strike us, on the whole, as rather 'realistic', and this is the result of a canonization and academic institutionalization of the Modern Movement generally that can be traced to the late 1950s. This is surely one of the most plausible explanations for the emergence of postmodernism itself, since the younger generation of the 1960s will now confront the formerly oppositional modern movement as a set of dead classics, which 'weigh like a nightmare on the brains of the living', as Marx once said in a different context.

As for the postmodern revolt against all that, however, it must equally be stressed that its own offensive features – from obscurity and sexually explicit material to psychological squalour and overt expressions of social and political defiance, which transcend anything that might have been imagined at the most extreme moments of high modernism – no longer scandalize anyone and are not only received with the greatest complacency but have themselves become institutionalized and are at one with the official or public culture of Western society.

What has happened is that aesthetic production today has become integrated into commodity production generally: the frantic economic urgency of producing fresh waves of ever more novel-seeming goods (from clothing to airplanes), at ever greater rates of turnover, now assigns an increasingly essential structural function and position to aesthetic innovation and experimentation. Such economic necessities then find recognition in the varied kinds of institutional support available for the newer art, from foundations and grants to museums and other forms of patronage. Of all the arts, architecture is the closest constitutively to the economic, with which, in the form of commissions and land values, it has a virtually unmediated relationship. It will therefore not be surprising to find the extraordinary flowering of the new postmodern architecture grounded in the patronage of multinational business, whose expansion

Jameson

and development is strictly contemporaneous with it. Later I will suggest that these two new phenomena have an even deeper dialectical interrelationship than the simple one-to-one financing of this or that individual project. Yet this is the point at which I must remind the reader of the obvious; namely, that this whole global, yet American, postmodern culture is the internal and superstructural expression of a whole new wave of American military and economic domination throughout the world: in this sense. as throughout class history, the underside of culture is blood, torture, death and terror.

The first point to be made about the conception of periodization in dominance, therefore, is that even if all the constitutive features of postmodernism were identical with and continuous to those of an older modernism – a position I feel to be demonstrably erroneous but which only an even lengthier analysis of modernism proper could dispel – the two phenomena would still remain utterly distinct in their meaning and social function, owing to the very different positioning of postmodernism in the economic system of late capital and, beyond that, to the transformation of the very sphere of culture in contemporary society . . .

I must now briefly address a different kind of objection to periodization, a concern about its possible obliteration of heterogeneity, one most often expressed by the Left. And it is certain that there is a strange quasi-Sartrean irony – a 'winner loses' logic – which tends to surround any effort to describe a 'system', a totalizing dynamic, as these are detected in the movement of contemporary society. What happens is that the more powerful the vision of some increasingly total system or logic – the Foucault of the prisons book is the obvious example – the more powerless the reader comes to feel. Insofar as the theorist wins, therefore, by constructing an increasingly closed and terrifying machine, to that very degree he loses, since the critical capacity of his work is thereby paralysed, and the impulses of negation and revolt, not to speak of those of social transformation, are increasingly perceived as vain and trivial in the face of the model itself.

I have felt, however, that it was only in the light of some conception of a dominant cultural logic or hegemonic norm that genuine difference could be measured and assessed. I am very far from feeling that all cultural production today is 'postmodern' in the broad sense I will be conferring on this term. The postmodern is, however, the force field in which very different kinds of cultural impulses – what Raymond Williams has usefully termed 'residual' and 'emergent' forms of cultural production – must make their way. If we do not achieve some general sense of a cultural dominant, then we fall back into a view of present history as sheer heterogeneity, random difference, a coexistence of a host of distinct forces whose effectivity is undecidable. At any rate, this has been the political spirit in which the following analysis was devised: to project some conception of a new systematic cultural norm and its reproduction in order to reflect more adequately on the most effective forms of any radical cultural politics today.

The exposition will take up in turn the following constitutive features of the postmodern: a new depthlessness, which finds its prolongation both in contemporary 'theory' and in a whole new culture of the image or the simulacrum; a consequent weakening of historicity, both in our relationship to public history and in the new forms of our private temporality, whose 'schizophrenic'

Jameson structure (following Lacan) will determine new types of syntax or syntagmatic relationships in the more temporal arts; a whole new type of emotional ground tone – what I will call 'intensities' – which can best be grasped by a return to older theories of the sublime; the deep constitutive relationships of all this to a whole new technology, which is itself a figure for a whole new economic world system; and, after a brief account of postmodernist mutations in the lived experience of built space itself, some reflections on the mission of political art in the bewildering new world space of late or multinational capital. . . .

Now, before concluding, I want to sketch an analysis of a full-blown postmodern building – a work which is in many ways uncharacteristic of that postmodern architecture whose principal proponents are Robert Venturi, Charles Moore, Michael Graves and, more recently, Frank Gehry, but which to my mind offers some very striking lessons about the originality of postmodernist space. Let me amplify the figure which has run through the preceding remarks and make it even more explicit: I am proposing the notion that we are here in the presence of something like a mutation in built space itself. My implication is that we ourselves, the human subjects who happen into this new space, have not kept pace with that evolution; there has been a mutation in the object unaccompanied as yet by any equivalent mutation in the subject. We do not yet possess the perceptual equipment to match this new hyperspace, as I will call it, in part because our perceptual habits were formed in that older kind of space I have called the space of high modernism. The newer architecture therefore – like many of the other cultural products I have evoked in the preceding remarks – stands as something like an imperative to grow new organs, to expand our sensorium and our body to some new, yet unimaginable, perhaps ultimately impossible, dimensions.

The building whose features I will very rapidly enumerate is the Westin Bonaventure Hotel, built in the new Los Angeles downtown by the architect and developer John Portman, whose other works include the various Hyatt Regencies, the Peachtree Center in Atlanta, and the Renaissance Center in Detroit. I have mentioned the populist aspect of the rhetorical defence of postmodernism against the elite (and Utopian) austerities of the great architectural modernisms. It is generally affirmed, in other words, that these newer buildings are popular works, on the one hand, and that they respect the vernacular of the American city fabric, on the other; that is to say, they no longer attempt, as did the masterworks and monuments of high modernism, to insert a different, a distinct, an elevated, a new Utopian language into the tawdry and commercial sign system of the surrounding city, but rather they seek to speak that very language, using its lexicon and syntax as that has been emblematically 'learned from Las Vegas'.

On the first of these counts Portman's Bonaventure fully confirms the claim: it is a popular building, visited with enthusiasm by locals and tourists alike (although Portman's other buildings are even more successful in this respect). The populist insertion into the city fabric is, however, another matter, and it is with this that we will begin. There are three entrances to the Bonaventure, one from Figueroa and the other two by way of elevated gardens on the other side of the hotel, which is built into the remaining slope of the former Bunker Hill. None of these is anything like the old hotel marquee, or the monumental *porte-cochère* with which the sumptuous buildings of yesteryear were wont to stage your passage from city street to the interior. The entryways of the Bonaventure are, as it were, lateral and rather backdoor affairs: the gardens in the back admit you to the sixth floor of the towers, and even there you must walk down one flight to find the elevator by which you gain access to the lobby. Meanwhile, what one is still tempted to think of as the front entry, on Figueroa, admits you, baggage and all, onto the second-storey shopping balcony, from which you must take an escalator down to the main registration desk. What I first want to suggest about these curiously unmarked ways in is that they seem to have been imposed by some new category of closure governing the inner space of the hotel itself (and this over and above the material constraints under which Portman had to work). I believe that, with a certain number of other characteristic postmodern buildings, such as the Beaubourg in Paris or the Eaton Centre in Toronto, the Bonaventure aspires to being a total space, a complete world, a kind of miniature city; to this new total space, meanwhile, corresponds a new collective practice, a new mode in which individuals move and congregate, something like the practice of a new and historically original kind of hypercrowd. In this sense, then, ideally the minicity of Portman's Bonaventure ought not to have entrances at all, since the entryway is always the seam that links the building to the rest of the city that surrounds it: for it does not wish to be a part of the city but rather its equivalent and replacement or substitute. That is obviously not possible, whence the downplaying of the entrance to its bare minimum.[3] But this disjunction from the surrounding city is different from that of the monuments of the International Style, in which the act of disjunction was violent, visible and had a very real symbolic significance – as in Le Corbusier's great *pilotis*, whose gesture radically separates the new Utopian space of the modern from the degraded and fallen city fabric which it thereby explicitly repudiates (although the gamble of the modern was that this new Utopian space, in the virulence of its novum, would fan out and eventually transform its surroundings by the very power of its new spatial language). The Bonaventure, however, is content to 'let the fallen city fabric continue to be in its being' (to parody Heidegger); no further effects, no larger protopolitical Utopian transformation, is either expected or desired.

This diagnosis is confirmed by the great reflective glass skin of the Bonaventure, whose function I will now interpret rather differently than I did a moment ago when I saw the phenomenon of reflection generally as developing a thematics of reproductive technology (the two readings are, however, not incompatible). Now one would want rather to stress the way in which the glass skin repels the city outside, a repulsion for which we have analogies in those reflector sunglasses which make it impossible for your interlocutor to see your own eyes and thereby achieve a certain aggressivity toward and power over the Other. In a similar way, the glass skin achieves a peculiar and placeless dissociation of the Bonaventure from its neighbourhood: it is not even an exterior, inasmuch as when you seek to look at the hotel's outer walls you cannot see the hotel itself but only the distorted images of everything that surrounds it.

Now consider the escalators and elevators. Given their very real pleasures in Portman, particularly the latter, which the artist has termed 'gigantic kinetic sculptures' and which certainly account for much of the spectacle and excitement of the hotel interior – particularly in the Hyatts, where like great Japanese

Jameson lanterns or gondolas they ceaselessly rise and fall – given such a deliberate marking and foregrounding in their own right, I believe one has to see such 'people movers' (Portman's own term, adapted from Disney) as somewhat more significant than mere functions and engineering components. We know in any case that recent architectural theory has begun to borrow from narrative analysis in other fields and to attempt to see our physical trajectories through such buildings as virtual narratives or stories, as dynamic paths and narrative paradigms which we as visitors are asked to fulfil and to complete with our own bodies and movements. In the Bonaventure, however, we find a dialectical heightening of this process: it seems to me that the escalators and elevators here henceforth replace movement but also, and above all, designate themselves as new reflexive signs and emblems of movement proper (something which will become evident when we come to the question of what remains of older forms of movement in this building, most notably walking itself). Here the narrative stroll has been underscored, symbolized, reified and replaced by a transportation machine which becomes the allegorical signifier of that older promenade we are no longer allowed to conduct on our own: and this is a dialectical intensification of the autoreferentiality of all modern culture, which tends to turn upon itself and designate its own cultural production as its content.

I am more at a loss when it comes to conveying the thing itself, the experience of space you undergo when you step off such allegorical devices into the lobby or atrium, with its great central column surrounded by a miniature lake, the whole positioned between the four symmetrical residential towers with their elevators, and surrounded by rising balconies capped by a kind of greenhouse roof at the sixth level. I am tempted to say that such space makes it impossible for us to use the language of volume or volumes any longer, since these are impossible to seize. Hanging streamers indeed suffuse this empty space in such a way as to distract systematically and deliberately from whatever form it might be supposed to have, while a constant busyness gives the feeling that emptiness is here absolutely packed, that it is an element within which you yourself are immersed, without any of that distance that formerly enabled the perception of perspective or volume. You are in this hyperspace up to your eyes and your body: and if it seemed before that that suppression of depth I spoke of in postmodern painting or literature would necessarily be difficult to achieve in architecture itself, perhaps this bewildering immersion may now serve as the formal equivalent in the new medium.

Yet escalator and elevator are also in this context dialectical opposites: and we may suggest that the glorious movement of the elevator gondola is also a dialectical compensation for this filled space of the atrium – it gives us the chance at a radically different, but complementary, spatial experience: that of rapidly shooting up through the ceiling and outside, along one of the four symmetrical towers, with the referent, Los Angeles itself, spread out breathtakingly and even alarmingly before us. But even this vertical movement is contained: the elevator lifts you to one of those revolving cocktail lounges, in which, seated, you are again passively rotated about and offered a contemplative spectacle of the city itself, now transformed into its own images by the glass windows through which you view it.

We may conclude all this by returning to the central space of the lobby itself (with the passing observation that the hotel rooms are visibly marginalized: the corridors in the residential sections are low-ceilinged and dark, most depressingly functional, while one understands that the rooms are in the worst of taste). The descent is dramatic enough, plummeting back down through the roof to splash down in the lake. What happens when you get there is something else, which can only be characterized as milling confusion, something like the vengeance this space takes on those who still seek to walk through it. Given the absolute symmetry of the four towers, it is quite impossible to get your bearings in this lobby; recently, colour coding and directional signals have been added in a pitiful and revealing, rather desperate, attempt to restore the co-ordinates of an older space. I will take as the most dramatic practical result of this spatial mutation the notorious dilemma of the shopkeepers on the various balconies. It has been obvious since the opening of the hotel in 1977 that nobody could ever find any of these stores, and even if you once located the appropriate boutique, you would be most unlikely to be as fortunate a second time. As a consequence, the commercial tenants are in despair and all the merchandise is marked down to bargain prices. When you recall that Portman is a businessman as well as an architect and a millionaire developer, an artist who is at one and the same time a capitalist in his own right, one cannot but feel that here too something of a 'return of the repressed' is involved.

So I come finally to my principal point here, that this latest mutation in space – postmodern hyperspace – has finally succeeded in transcending the capacities of the individual human body to locate itself, to organize its immediate surroundings perceptually, and cognitively to map its position in a mappable external world. It may now be suggested that this alarming disjunction point between the body and its built environment – which is to the initial bewilderment of the older modernism as the velocities of spacecraft to those of the automobile – can itself stand as the symbol and analogon of that even sharper dilemma which is the incapacity of our minds, at least at present, to map the great global multinational and decentred communicational network in which we find ourselves caught as individual subjects.

But as I am anxious that Portman's space not be perceived as something either exceptional or seemingly marginalized and leisure-specialized on the order of Disneyland, I will conclude by juxtaposing this complacent and entertaining (although bewildering) leisure-time space with its analogue in a very different area, namely, the space of postmodern warfare, in particular as Michael Herr evokes it in *Dispatches*, his great book on the experience of Vietnam. The extraordinary linguistic innovations of this work may still be considered postmodern, in the eclectic way in which its language impersonally fuses a whole range of contemporary collective idiolects, most notably rock language and black language: but the fusion is dictated by problems of content. This first terrible postmodernist war cannot be told in any of the traditional paradigms of the war novel or movie – indeed, that breakdown of all previous narrative paradigms is, along with the breakdown of any shared language through which a veteran might convey such experience, among the principal subjects of the book and may be said to open up the place of a whole new reflexivity. Benjamin's account of Baudelaire, and of the emergence of modernism from a new experience of city technology which transcends all the older habits of bodily perception, is both singularly relevant and singularly

Jameson antiquated in the light of this new and virtually unimaginable quantum leap in technological alienation:

> He was a moving-target-survivor subscriber, a true child of the war, because except for the rare times when you were pinned or stranded the system was geared to keep you mobile, if that was what you thought you wanted. As a technique for staying alive it seemed to make as much sense as anything, given naturally that you were there to begin with and wanted to see it close: it started out sound and straight but it formed a cone as it progressed, because the more you moved the more you saw, the more you saw the more besides death and mutilation you risked, and the more you risked of that the more you would have to let go of one day as a 'survivor.' Some of us moved around the war like crazy people until we couldn't see which way the run was taking us anymore, only the war all over its surface with occasional, unexpected penetration. As long as we could have choppers like taxis it took real exhaustion or depression near shock or a dozen pipes of opium to keep us even apparently quiet, we'd still be running around inside our skins like something was after us, ha ha, La Vida Loca. In the months after I got back the hundreds of helicopters I'd flown in began to draw together until they formed a collective meta-chopper, and in my mind it was the sexiest thing going; saver-destroyer, provider-waster, right hand-left hand, nimble, fluent, canny and human: hot steel, grease, jungle-saturated canvas webbing, sweat cooling and warming up again, cassette rock and roll in one ear and door-gun fire in the other, fuel, heat, vitality and death, death itself, hardly an intruder.[4]

In this new machine, which does not, like the older modernist machinery of the locomotive or the airplane, represent motion, but which can only be represented in motion, something of the mystery of the new postmodernist space is concentrated.

NOTES

1   Robert Venturi and Denise Scott Brown, *Learning from Las Vegas*, Cambridge, Mass.: 1972.
2   The originality of Charles Jencks's pathbreaking *Language of Postmodern Architecture* (London: Academy, 1978) lay in its well-nigh dialectical combination of postmodern architecture and a certain kind of semiotics, each being appealed to justify the existence of the other. Semiotics becomes appropriate as a mode of analysis of the newer architecture by virtue of the latter's populism, which does emit signs and messages to a spatial 'reading public', unlike the monumentality of the high modern. Meanwhile, the newer architecture is itself thereby validated, in so far as it is accessible to semiotic analysis and thus proves to be an essentially aesthetic object (rather than the tranaesthetic constructions of the high modern). Here, then, aesthetics reinforces an ideology of communication and vice versa. Beside Jencks' many valuable contributions, see also Heinrich Klotz, *History of Postmodern Architecture* (Cambridge, Mass., 1988); Pier Paolo Portoghesi, *After Modern Architecture* (New York, 1982).
3   'To say that a structure of this type 'turns its back away' is surely an understatement, while to speak of its 'popular' character is to miss the point of its systematic segregation from the great Hispanic-Asian city outside (whose crowds prefer the open space of the old Plaza). Indeed, it is virtually to endorse the master illusion that Portman seeks to convey: that he has re-created within the precious spaces of his super-lobbies the genuine popular texture of city life.

    (In fact, Portman has only built large vivariums for the upper middle classes, protected by astonishingly complex security systems. Most of the new downtown centres might as well have been built on the third moon of Jupiter. Their fundamental logic is that of a claustrophobic space colony attempting to miniaturize nature within itself. Thus the Bonaventure reconstructs a nostalgic Southern California in aspic: orange trees, fountains, flowering vines and clean air. Outside in a smog-poisoned reality, vast mirrored surfaces reflect away not only the misery of the larger city, but also its irrepressible vibrancy and quest for authenticity, including the most exciting neighbourhood mural movement in North Africa). Mike Davis, 'Urban Renaissance and the Spirit of Postmodernism,' *New Left Review*, 151, May–June 1985: p. 112).

Davis imagines I am being complacent or corrupt about this bit of second-order urban renewal; his article is as full of useful urban information as it is of bad faith. Lessons in economics from someone who thinks that sweatshops are 'precapitalist' are not helpful; meanwhile it is unclear what mileage is to be gained by crediting our side ('the ghetto rebel-lions of the late 1960s') with the formative influence in bringing postmodernism into being (a hegemonic or 'ruling class' style if ever there was one), let alone gentrification. The sequence is obviously the other way round: capital (and its multitudinous 'penetrations') comes first, and only then can 'resistance' to it develop, even though it might be pretty to think otherwise. ('The association of the workers as it appears in the factory is not posited by them but by capital. Their combination is not *their* being, but the being of capital. To the individual worker it appears fortuitous. He relates to his own association with other workers and to his cooperation with them as *alien*, as to modes of operation of capital,' [Karl Marx, *The Grundrisse* in *Collected Works*, volume 28, Moscow, 1986, p. 505].)

Davis's reply is characteristic of some of the more 'militant' sounds from the Left; right-wing reactions to my article generally take the form of aesthetic handwringing, and (for example) deplore my apparent identification of postmodern architecture generally with a figure like Portman, who is, as it were, the Coppola (if not the Harold Robbins) of the new downtowns.

4   Michael Herr, *Dispatches*, New York: Knopf, 1978, pp. 8–9.

THE CONSTRAINTS OF POSTMODERNISM (EXTRACT)

What Kenneth Frampton (following Tzonis and Lefaivre) calls Critical Regionalism, is for one thing virtually by definition not a movement: he himself calls it a 'critical category oriented towards certain common features',[1] but there seems no good reason for us not to go on to characterize it as an exemplar of that virtually extinct conceptual species, an *aesthetic*, for it is certain that Critical Regionalism knows, perhaps in untraditional proportions, the same fundamental tension between the descriptive and the prescriptive that marks all philosophical (but also all vanguard) aesthetics. Such systems – and it would be appropriate to limit its history as a project to the bourgeois era as such, from the mid-eighteenth to the mid-twentieth centuries – in effect seek, by describing the constitutive features of authentic works of art as they already exist, to suggest invariants and norms for the production of future works. To put it this way is to realize how unseasonable this project is today, and how unfashionable the very conception of aesthetics must be in an age of artistic nominalism and antinomianism. It can be argued that the 'second modernism' of the avant-gardes represented any number of efforts to free art from aesthetics (I take this to be Peter Bürger's position in *Theory of the Avant-Garde*); it can also be argued that aesthetics emerges as a problematic with secular modernism, whose contradictions finally render it impossible (this would at least be one way of reading Adorno's *Aesthetic Theory*). Meanwhile, on any philosophical view, the totalizing normativity of this kind of traditional philosophical discourse is

Jameson clearly very unpostmodern indeed: it sins against the poststructural and post-modern repudiation of the conception of a philosophical system, and is some-how un- and antitheoretical in its values and procedures (if one takes the position that what is called theory today, or 'theoretical discourse', constitutes a displacement of traditional philosophy and a replacement of or substitute for it).

Yet it is equally clear, not merely that Frampton is aware of all this but also that a certain deliberate retrogression is built into the project itself where it is underscored by the slogan of an *arrière-garde* or rearguard action, whose untimely status is further emphasized by Frampton's insistence that whatever Critical Regionalism turns out to be, in its various regions of possibility, it must necessarily remain a 'marginal practice'.[2]

But these features suggest a second paradox in any typology that associates the aesthetic of Critical Regionalism with the stylistic postmodernisms of the relevant (mainly North American) contemporary architects: for while it can be said that Critical Regionalism shares with them a systematic repudiation of certain essential traits of high modernism, it distinguishes itself by attempting at one and the same time to negate a whole series of postmodern negations of modernism as well, and can in some respects be seen as antimodern and antipostmodern simultaneously, in a 'negation of the negation' that is far from returning us to our starting point or from making Critical Regionalism over into a belated form of modernism.

Such is, for example, very precisely the stand outlined here on the matter of the avant-garde, which remained, in high modernism, both Enlightenment and Utopian, sought to out-trump the vulgar bourgeois conception of progress, and retained the belief in the possibilities of a liberatory dimension to technology and scientific development. But the postcontemporary forms of such 'progress', in global modernization, corporate hegemony and the universal standard-ization of commodities and 'life styles', are precisely what Critical Regionalism seeks to resist. It thus shares the doxa of the postmodern generally with respect to the end of the avant-garde, the perniciousness of Utopianism, and the fear of a universalizing homogeneity or identity. Yet its slogan of an *arrière-garde* would also seem incompatible with a postmodern 'end of history' and repud-iation of historical teleology, since Critical Regionalism continues to seek a certain deeper historical logic in the past of this system, if not its future: a rearguard retains overtones of a collective resistance, and not the anarchy of trans-avant-garde pluralism that characterizes many of the postmodern ideologies of Difference as such. Meanwhile, if the current slogans of marginality and resistance are also evoked by Frampton, they would appear to carry rather different connotations than those employed in, say, current evocations of multiculturalism, which are urban and internal First World, rather than geographically remote, as in his systematically semiperipheral examples, located in Denmark, Catalunia, Portugal, Mexico, California in the 1920s and 1930s, Ticino, Japan and Greece.[3] The enumeration warns us, to begin with, that 'region' in this aesthetic programme is very different from the sentimental localism we have discussed on the occasion of Buford's view of the new American short-story writers: here it designates, not a rural place that resists the nation and its power structures but rather a whole culturally coherent zone (which may also correspond to political autonomy) in tension

Jameson

with the standardizing world system as a whole.

Such areas are not so much characterized by the emergence of strong collective identities as they are by their relative distance from the full force of global modernization, a distance that provided a shelter or an eco-niche in which regional traditions could still develop. The model shows some similarities to Eric Wolf's remarkable *Peasant Wars of the Twentieth Century*, which posits a relationship between remoteness from colonization and the ultimate possibility of organizing popular resistance to it. Obviously, social and collective organization has to provide a mediation in both cases: in Wolf, it is the fact that a collective or village culture was left relatively intact that enables the formation of conscious popular insurgencies (I take it that the multiculturalisms see such forms of resistance in terms of reconquest and reconstruction rather than in terms of the survival of residual traditions). Frampton quotes the California architect Harwell Hamilton Harris to something of the same effect:

> In California in the late Twenties and Thirties modern European ideas met a still developing regionalism. In New England, on the other hand, European Modernism met a rigid and restrictive regionalism that at first resisted and then surrendered. New England accepted European Modernism whole because its own regionalism had been reduced to a collection of restrictions.[4]

It should be added, in view of Frampton's explicit dissociation of Critical Regionalism from populism,[5] that this is not to be understood as a political movement as such (another feature that distinguishes it from the essentially political conception of the modernist avant-gardes). Indeed, the untheorized nature of its relationship to the social and political movements that might be expected to accompany its development, to serve as a cultural context or to lend morale and support, is something of a problem here. What seems clear is that a mediation of intellectuals and professionals is foreseen in which these strata retain a kind of semi-autonomy: we may then conjecture a political situation in which the status of national professionals, of the local architects and engineers, is threatened by the increasing control of global technocracies and long-distance corporate decision-makers and their staffs. In such a situation, then, the matter of the survival of national autonomy as such, and the suggestion of idealism that may accompany a defence of the survival of national artistic styles is regrounded in social existence and practice.

There is thus a sense in which Critical Regionalism can be opposed both to modernism and to postmodernism alike. On the other hand, if one wished rather to stress its more fundamental vocation to resist a range of postmodern trends and temptations, Frampton offers a revised account of architectural history that would document a continuity between a certain High Modernism and the critical-regional practice of the present day:

> A tectonic impulse may be traced across the century uniting diverse works irrespective of their different origins ... Thus for all their stylistic idiosyncrasies a very similar level of tectonic articulation patently links Henrik Petrus Berlage's Stock Exchange of 1895 to Frank Lloyd Wright's Larkin Building of 1904 and Herman Hertzberger's Central Beheer office complex of 1974. In each

instance there is a similar concatenation of span and support that amounts to a tectonic syntax in which gravitational force passes from purlin to truss, to pad stone, to corbel, to arch, to pediment and abutment. The technical transfer of this load passes through a series of appropriately articulated transitions and joints . . . We find a comparable concern for the revealed joint in the architecture of both Auguste Perret and Louis Kahn.[6]

We will return in a moment to the formal implications of this historical revision in which it is modernism (and in particular the work of Frank Lloyd Wright) whose essential telos is now located in a tectonic vocation.

On the other hand, with a little ingenuity, Critical Regionalism could be readjusted to its postmodern position in our scheme, on the basis of its post-Utopian disillusionment and its retreat from the overweening high modernist conception of the monument and the megastructure, and of the spatial innovation powerful enough to change the world in a genuinely revolutionary way. From this perspective, Critical Regionalism could be seen to share postmodernism's more general contextualism; as for the valorization of the part or fragment, it is a kind of thinking that here returns in an unexpected way, namely, via the synecdochic function whereby the individual building comes to stand for the local spatial culture generally. In this sense, Critical Regionalism could be characterized as a kind of postmodernism of the global system as a whole (or at least of the semiperiphery if not the Third World), as opposed to the First World's own internal and external postmodernisms that I have described earlier.

But it will be more useful, in conclusion, to sketch out the oppositions and tensions between the critical-regionalist aesthetic and the features of an actually existing postmodernism. . . . The new schema suggests some interesting formal aspects, in addition to the logical possibilities of new lateral syntheses or combinations that are intriguing enough to be left for another time. The crucial issues to be touched on now are, however, the theme of 'joints and supports' as well as that of the tectonic generally; the matter of the scenographic and also of the 'grid'; and finally the role of technology in all this, or in other words of the truest bearer of modernity (if not of modernism) in the architectural process.

It is at any rate by way of form itself that the new aesthetic is best approached, for in this area Frampton provides a series of features that are systematically defined in opposition to current doxa, and in particular to Venturi's influential description of the essentials of any building in terms of the 'decorated shed' or in other words the façade with its ornament and the space that is constructed and projected behind it. Both these features are categories of the representational for Frampton, and it is indeed the very primacy of representation in contemporary architecture that the notion of a Critical Regionalism is designed fundamentally to challenge. He does not engage in any elaborate polemic with the idea of the spatial, save to observe everything that is abstract about it (when contrasted to place):[7] an abstraction in the concept that itself replicates abstraction in the instrumental relationship to the world itself. Indeed, his selection of a remark by Vittorio Gregotti – 'The worst enemy of modern architecture is the idea of space considered solely in terms of its economic and technical exigencies indifferent to the idea of the site' – would seem to authorize a dialectical continuation, for which a certain aesthetic abstraction of space could be grasped as the correlative to the economic and technical one evoked here. Space can indeed not be seen as such, and in that sense a 'space' is difficult to theorize as an aesthetic object in its own right; yet it is perhaps because the critique of visual representation (that will come into its own in the related discussion of the facade) does not take directly on this abstract aesthetization of space, that the diagnosis of the 'scenographic' is here so brilliantly proposed and deployed. Flamboyant spaces become visible as the scene of imaginary gestures and dramas, and it is by way of this supplement of the melodramatic and the theatrical that a critique of commodity form can enter the more properly architectural diagnosis (it would for example be of no little interest to prolong this analysis in the direction of Michael Fried's historical theory of modernism as a tendential resistance of 'absorption' to 'theatricality'). Frampton's own working philosophical categories here are 'ontological' (as opposed to 'representational') categories; besides invoking Heidegger's conception of the relationship of dwelling to building, he would seem to rely heavily on the more problematical (or 'humanist') notion of 'experience' as an alternative to the spectacle and commodity conceptions of the visual and the scenographic.

In fact, however, Frampton has a more formal alternative to these particular aesthetic modes: an alternative framed by the tripartite values of the tactile, the tectonic and the telluric which frame the notion of space in such a way that it turns back slowly into a conception of place once again. This alternative tends now to displace those parts of the building that are visible (and thus lend themselves to categories of the visual arts) in favour of a 'privileging of the joint as the primordial tectonic element': a non-visual and non-representational category which Frampton attributes to Gottfried Semper and which for him constitutes 'the fundamental nexus around which building comes into being, that is to say, comes to be articulated as a presence in itself'.[8] The category of the joint as a primal articulation of the two forces that meet in it (along with its correlative of the 'break or "dis-joint" . . . that point at which things break against each other rather than connect: that significant fulcrum at which one system, surface or material abruptly ends to give way to another')[9] would seem to be the fundamental innovation of the aesthetic of Critical Regionalism, whose non- or antirepresentational equivalent for the other arts (or literature) remains to be worked out.

In my view, Frampton's more conventional emphasis on the tactile features of such buildings is best grasped by way of this more fundamentally structural one of forces in opposition, rather than as the privileging of one type of bodily sense ('touch') as opposed to another ('sight'). Indeed, his illustrations – the relationship between a solid parquet and 'the momentum of an induced gait and the relative inertia of the body' in Visconti's *The Damned,* for example[10] – would seem to authorize an interpretation whereby it is the isolation of the individual sense that becomes the fundamental symptom of postmodern alienation, an isolation most often visual, but which one could just as easily imagine in terms of tactility (as for example in the gleaming – but obviously highly tactile – surfaces of Venturi's Gordon Wu Hall, or the remarkable film of running water of Norman Foster's Century Tower in Tokyo, where paper-thin water itself becomes virtually a new and undiscovered Science-Fictional element akin to polished concrete or steel). The aesthetic of Critical Regionalism would presumably have to insist on the synaesthetic or structural-relational sensoriality of even the tactile as a vehicle for that more fundamental category and value that is the tectonic itself.

The related value of the 'telluric' can also be grasped in this way, as a seemingly Heideggerian and archaic, 'rear-guard' emphasis on the earth itself and on traditional sacred structures, which can also be read far more contemporaneously as a systematic negation of that emphasis on the grid (that is to say, on abstract and homogeneous corporate space) that we have found both Koolhaas and Eisenman obliged to engage in one way or another in their only partially 'postmodern' forms of production. Here it is the way in which the tectonic and its fundamental category, the joint, necessarily enforces a downward distribution of pressures and forces that can be said, not merely to reveal and acknowledge the site as such but even in some creative sense to unveil and to produce it as though for the first time (Gregotti is again quoted to the effect that such 'siting' constitutes 'an act of knowledge of the context that comes out of its architectural modification').[11] But at that point, the negation of the value of the grid ceases to be a merely ideological option (a kind of humanist preference for place over against the alienated poststructural and postmodern dehumanization of space) and expresses a positive and formal architectural value in its own right: a value that goes a long way toward 'regrounding' (in all the senses of this word) Frampton's defence of the various forms of local or regional 'critical' architecture in the global differentiation of the 'ground' thus 'marked' and 'broken' by a truly telluric-tactile construction.

We must now finally come to the role of technology and modernity in this aesthetic for it is in the unique relationship of Critical Regionalism to such 'Western' realities that this proposal most fundamentally distinguishes itself from the populist or cultural-nationalist, Third World, and anti-Western or antimodern responses with which we are familiar. However deliberately regressive and tradition-oriented this aesthetic may seem, insisting as it does on what Raymond Williams would have called a cultural politics of the 'residual' rather than the 'emergent' in the contemporary situation, it equally explicitly acknowledges the existence and the necessity of modern technology in ways whose originality must now be shown. We have already seen, for example, how Koolhaas acknowledged the constraint and 'necessity' of technological modernity (that 'one third of the section of a building . . . [is] inaccessible to architectural thought') by concentrating it into the single fixed point of a kind of architectural 'condensor' (the 1811 Manhattan grid plan for urbanism, the elevator for the individual building) whose acceptance released the surrounding space to a new kind of freedom or innovation.

Frampton's conception of the acknowledgment of this necessity seems both less programmatic in that it does not foresee a single kind of solution to the matter the way Koolhaas seems to do, and more 'philosophical' or even ideological insofar as the dualistic nature of the opposition between technology and its other is somehow through his various examples always maintained (this is the sense, for example, in which he can even evoke Norman Foster's work – here the Sainsbury centre of 1978 – with its 'discrimination between servant and served spaces' as an articulation still distantly redolent of properly tectonic

values[12] rather than as the outright 'late-modern' technological and corporate   *Jameson*
celebration seen by other analysts such as Jencks).

Still, two of his crucial illustrations for the exemplification of an already
existing Critical Regionalism would seem to open up this dualism in a suggest-
ively new way and to stage this aesthetic as a strategy for somehow including
and defusing technological modernity, for outsmarting it in the very constructional process itself. Thus he shows how Jorn Utzon's Bagsvaerd Church
projects a kind of double life, its exterior 'combination of modular assembly
and *in-situ* casting' constituting 'an appropriate integration of the full range of
concrete techniques which are now at our disposal' and 'not only accord[ing]
with the values of universal civilisation but also represent[ing] its capacity for
normative application';[13] while the interior of the church suddenly projects a
vault that goes well beyond its customary signification of 'the sacred in Western
culture' and indeed incorporates 'the subtle and contrary allusions' deployed
by the Chinese pagoda roof (along with the 'Nordic vernacular of the stave
church'), whose ideological consequences as an architectural 'symbolic act'
Frampton here analyses with exemplary perspicuity.[14]

A rather different, if not inverted, way of dealing with the modern Frampton
then deduces from the practice of Tadao Ando, whose very theory (itself no
doubt a development out of the uniquely Japanese philosophical attention to
what was in the 1930s and 1940s called the problem of 'overcoming modernity')
characterizes it as the strategy of an 'enclosed modernity': here the technological
is as it were wrapped within the renewal of more authentic Japanese attention to
light and detail and thus ultimately to what Frampton calls the tectonic.[15] The
procedure here would seem to be something like the reversal or inversion of
Utzon's move, described above; yet both hold out the possibility of inventing
some new relationship to the technological beyond nostalgic repudiation or
mindless corporate celebration. If Critical Regionalism is to have any genuine
content, it will do so only on the strength of such invention and its capacity to
'enclose' or to reopen and transfigure the burden of the modern.

It is, however, worth emphasizing the degree to which the very concept and
programme of Critical Regionalism reflects its moment in history, and in particular expresses the pathos of a situation in which the possibility of a radical
alternative to late capitalist technologies (in both architecture and urbanism
alike) has decisively receded. Here not the emergent but the residual is
emphasized (out of historical necessity), and the theoretical problem is at one
with a political one, namely, how to fashion a progressive strategy out of what
are necessarily the materials of tradition and nostalgia? How to use the attempt
to conserve in an actively liberatory and transformational way? The problem
has its historical roots in the specificity of postmodern technology and
urbanism, where 'progress' – if the concept exists at all any longer – involves a
very different ratio of the introduction of new machinery to the transformation
of the built environment than it did in the nineteenth century (in which a
different kind of technology obtained, with a very different, more visible and
stylistic impact on nature than is the case with the information technologies).
So it is that today very often some of the most militant urban or neighbourhood
movements draw their vitality from the attempt to prevent an older city fabric
from being disaggregated or destroyed altogether: something that foretells
significant and ominous dilemmas in co-ordinating such 'chains of equivalence'

Jameson   (to speak like Laclau and Mouffe again) with those of 'new social movements' that necessarily refuse such conservative family-and-neighbourhood ideological motivations.

Frampton's conceptual proposal, however, is not an internal but rather a geopolitical one: it seeks to mobilize a pluralism of 'regional' styles (a term selected, no doubt, in order to forestall the unwanted connotations of the terms national and international alike), with a view toward resisting the standard-izations of a henceforth global late capitalism and corporatism, whose 'vernacular' is as omnipresent as its power over local decisions (and indeed, after the end of the Cold War, over local governments and individual nation states as well).

It is thus politically important, returning to the problem of parts or com-ponents, to emphasize the degree to which the concept of Critical Regionalism is necessarily allegorical. What the individual buildings are henceforth here a unit of is no longer a unique vision of city planning (such as the Baroque) nor a specific city fabric (like Las Vegas) but rather a distinctive regional culture as a whole, for which the distinctive individual building becomes a metonym. The construction of such a building resembles the two previously discussed move-ments of a stylistic postmodernism and Italian neo-rationalism to the degree to which it must also deploy a storehouse of pre-existing forms and traditional motifs, as signs and markers by which to 'decorate' what generally remains a relatively conventional Western 'shed'.

In order for this kind of building to make a different kind of statement, its decorations must also be grasped as recognizable elements in a cultural-national discourse, and the building of the building must be grasped at one and the same time as a physical structure and as a symbolic act that reaffirms the regional-national culture as a collective possibility in its moment of besiegement and crisis. But perhaps it is with allegory as with the mythical that its effects remain wanting unless the object has been labelled in advance and we have been told beforehand that it is an allegorical effect that has been sought after? This interesting theoretical problem, however, becomes visible only when a 'text' is isolated from the social ground in which its effects are generated. In the present instance, for example, it should be clear enough that an architectural form of Critical Regionalism would lack all political and allegorical efficacy unless it were co-ordinated with a variety of other local, social and cultural movements that aimed at securing national autonomy. It was one of the signal errors of the artistic activism of the 1960s to suppose that there existed, in advance, forms that were in and of themselves endowed with a political, and even revolutionary, potential by virtue of their own intrinsic properties. On the other hand, there remains a danger of idealism implicit in all forms of cultural nationalism as such, which tends to overestimate the effectivity of culture and consciousness and to neglect the concomitant requirement of economic autonomy. But it is precisely economic autonomy that has been everywhere called back into question in the post-modernity of a genuinely global late capitalism.

An even graver objection to the strategies of Critical Regionalism, as to the various postmodernisms generally when they claim a political vocation for themselves, is awakened by the value of pluralism and the slogan of difference they all in one way or another endorse. The objection does not consist in some conviction that pluralism is always a liberal, rather than a truly radical, value –

a dogmatic and doctrinaire position that the examination of any number of   *Jameson*
active moments of history would be enough to dispel. No, the uneasiness stems
from the very nature of late capitalism itself, about which it can be wondered
whether pluralism and difference are not somehow related to its own deeper
internal dynamics.

It is a feeling raised, for example, by the new strategies of what is now called
post-Fordism: the term can be seen as one of the optional variants for such terms
as *postmodernity* or *late capitalism*, with which it is roughly synonymous.
However, it underscores one of the originalities of multinational capitalism today
in a way that tends to problematize the assumptions of the strategy of Critical
Regionalism itself. Where Fordism and classical imperialism, in other words,
designed their products centrally and then imposed them by fiat on an emergent
public (you do have a choice of colour with the Model-T: black!), post-Fordism
puts the new computerized technology to work by custom-designing its products
for individual markets. This has indeed been called postmodern marketing, and it
can be thought to 'respect' the values and cultures of the local population by
adapting its various goods to suit those vernacular languages and practices.
Unfortunately this inserts the corporations into the very heart of local and
regional culture, about which it becomes difficult to decide whether it is authentic
any longer (and indeed whether that term still means anything). It is the EPCOT
syndrome raised to a global scale and returns us to the question of the 'critical'
with a vengeance, since now the 'regional' as such becomes the business of global
American Disneyland-related corporations, who will redo your own native
architecture for you more exactly than you can do it yourself. Is global Difference
the same today as global Identity?

NOTES

1 Kenneth Frampton, 'Critical Regionalism: Modern Architecture and Cultural Identity' in
   Modern Architecture: A Cultural History, London: Thames & Hudson, 1985, p. 326.
2 Ibid., p. 327.
3 Ibid., pp. 314–26.
4 Ibid., p. 320.
5 Kenneth Frampton, 'Towards a Critical Regionalism: Six Points for an Architecture of
   Resistance', in Hal Foster (ed.) *The Anti-Aesthetic*, Seattle: Bay Press, 1983, pp. 20–1.
6 Kenneth Frampton, 'Rappel à l'ordre: The Case for the Tectonic', *Architectural Design* 50, 3/
   4, 1991, p. 24.
7 Frampton, 'Towards a Critical Regionalism', pp. 24–5.
8 Frampton, 'Rappel à l'ordre', p. 22.
9 Ibid., p. 24.
10 Frampton, 'Towards a Critical Regionalism', p. 28.
11 Frampton, 'Rappel à l'ordre', p. 24.
12 Ibid., p. 25.
13 Frampton, 'Critical Regionalism', p. 314.
14 Ibid., p. 315.
15 Ibid., p. 324.

IS SPACE POLITICAL?

The clever title 'The Residence of Architecture in Politics' usefully suggests that
architecture can somehow never get out of politics, but must learn to dwell in it

Jameson on a permanent if uneasy basis; and also that we have to do here, not with inventing or forging a relationship between architecture and politics where presumably none existed before, but rather simply with revealing what was there all along, what we may choose not to see but what can, in the last analysis, scarcely be avoided. Building codes, zoning, city ordinances, local politics, wards and parishes, bosses, payoffs, unions, the Mafia – I suppose all this comes to mind first when we think of attempting to refocus our object so that an architecture space can slowly be seen as persisting in the middle of politics. But this is complicated by the remembrance that at least two different meanings are deployed when we use the word *politics*. One is politics as the specialized, local thing, the empirical activity; as, for example, when speaking of a political novel, we mean a novel about government and general elections, about Quebec City or Washington, about people in power and their techniques and specific tasks. The other is politics in the global sense, of the founding and transformation, the conservation and revolutionizing, of society as a whole, of the collective, of what organizes human relationships generally and enables or sponsors, or limits and maims, human possibilities. This larger acceptation of the word *politics* often seems non-empirical, on the grounds that one cannot see vast entities like society itself; perhaps we should characterize this distinction as that between the particular and the general or universal. Regardless, two very different dimensions come into play here, neither of which can be sacrificed without serious damage to thought and experience, but which cannot be simply synthesized or unified either. I want to propose that these two dimensions acquire an essentially allegorical relationship to each other, which runs in both directions. Thus the empirical institutions and situations of the city stand as allegories of the invisible substance of society as a whole; while the very concept that citizens are able to form of society as a whole becomes allegorical of their empirical possibilities, their constraints and restrictions or, on the other hand, their new potentialities and future openings.

But this is only the beginning of the oppositions or antinomies a political architecture has to face. There is also, for example, the fundamental tension between architecture as the art of the individual building and urbanism as the attempt to organize the life and circulation of the larger city space: this may not exactly correspond to the role division between architect and engineer to which it is obviously somehow related. Nor does it correspond exactly to the allegorical relationship I suggested above: for although a larger entity, never fully totalizable, the city is not exactly non-empirical; while the individual house or building, tangible enough and presumably accessible to the senses, can probably not be thought of as fully empirical either (maybe nothing really is), since our concept of the building as a whole must always accompany every segment we intuit.

Nothing in the other arts quite corresponds to this tension or contradiction, although it is sometimes suggestive for them when we try out this building/city opposition as an analogy. Architecture is business as well as culture, and outright value fully as much as ideal representation: the seam architecture shares with economics also has no parallel in the other arts, although commercial art – rock music, for example – comes close in certain ways; but even that analogy serves to underscore the differences. However the other arts react to the market, they somehow work outside of it and then offer their wares

for sale. Architecture seems to be first for sale and only later on, after it is built, *Jameson*
to leave the market and somehow become art or culture as such.

Then there is the public/private opposition, which equally does not seem to register in quite the same fashion in the other arts: theatre versus literature does not quite capture the difference between the symbolic meaning of public buildings – the symbolism they acquire (connotation of fascist public art, for example) fully as much as the symbolism they were intended to have (the glory of the sovereign, the power of the collectivity or of law as such, or of the republic) – and the more quotidian meaning of private space, which comments on the way people live after hours and how they try to reproduce the labour force after the official activities of labour are over. Perhaps that is also part of the building/city opposition, but only part of it; or perhaps it is subsumed under that in some uneven way, since the city also includes the street and consumption, and not merely working and dwelling: the late capitalist city above all has to make a very large place for these spaces which are neither public nor private.

Now politics would also seem to include some notion of change, even when that involves running to stay in the same place (as in ordinary city or even national or state government). But in its most dramatic embodiments, politics surely always has the vocation of realizing a collective ideal, fulfilling or at least staging the great collective project. And this is precisely an allegorical matter. None of the individual projects that makes up politics has the supreme value of the whole collective activity, but each must participate in its value in some way other than as a mere part of the whole: they are allegorical of it, each in its own local and modest way; the revolution (of whatever kind) is realized fully in each small effort that makes it up.

How can artistic works be read in these political senses? How they can be expected to participate in a collective project is perhaps the most difficult question, unless we want to remain with the easy answer that, as monumental public construction, they ratify its success and remind the passing collectivity of its own achievements, symbolically offering the occasion to restage and recelebrate the inaugural act, the foundation of collectivity, the sealing of the social contract itself (Rousseau spoke of festivals, but architecture is a more durable festival). I doubt if many of us today, however significant and indispensable we may feel public monuments to be, find enormous aesthetic excitement in the contemplation of projects like this; the general deterioration of public values has clearly drawn such architecture with it in its wake; people often loosely attribute this to the suspicion of politics, the corruption of public officials, voter apathy, post-Watergate, and the like, but it probably has more to do with the privatization of the public sphere, the displacement of governmental initiative by the great corporations, the increasing centrality of multinational business in late capitalism. Thus our public buildings are now the great insurance centres and the great banks, the great office buildings, the ring of towers whose construction around the outskirts of Paris was authorized by Georges Pompidou as a tangible symbol of the financial centrality of Paris in the new Europe. These buildings show an obvious kind of symbolic political meaning; but there can be more subtle connotative meanings that affirm this or that aspect of contemporary business society. I wonder, for example, whether the general low-rise modernist glass-box style of yesterday did not fulfil a

Jameson symbolic function with respect to the social (and not merely represent a quick and undistinguished financial and spatial solution), just as the deplorable omnipresent pastel postmodern buildings do today: they remain messages, even though their content may be little more than mere repetition.

Symbolic meaning is as volatile as the arbitrariness of the sign: in other words, as in dreams, the spatial unconscious can associate anything with anything else – a dead body meaning jubilatory euphoria, a loved one's photograph triggering violent xenophobia. It is not enough to say that opposites mean each other: they especially mean each other. As St Augustine says in his treatise on scriptural allegory and interpretation: a thing can mean itself or its own opposite – Noah's drunken nakedness means disrespect or respect, 'depending on the context'. What is arbitrary then is that old and time-honoured mechanism called the 'association of ideas': in Proust, for example, the 'modern style' in buildings is incorporated into the Verdurins' cultural offensive and documents the cutting-edge superiority of the former 'little clan', now become the most advanced salon in all of Paris: 'In the first years of the XXth century, the "modern style" knows great success in Munich, where it is considered, in architecture, to be a reaction against the greco-roman pastiches of the period of Ludwig II, and, in interior decoration as a "protest against apartments crammed with over-heavy furniture".'[1]

It is altogether logical then that, in the high tide of the war effort and of Germanophobia, this particular trait (a 'Munich' style) should be the operator of a complete reversal of meaning. In any case, according to the fatal evolution of an aestheticism that ends up biting its own tail, the Verdurins claimed no longer to be able to stand the modern style (in any case it was associated with Munich) nor white bare apartments, and now exclusively favoured antique French furniture in a darkened setting.

In the same way, a sugar-candy postmodern decoration can for a moment stand as a heroic repudiation of the dominant, old, repressive modern glass-box international style, only in another blink of an eye to become 'indissolubly' (at least for this moment and this particular, equally ephemeral, present) associated with the high- and low-life ultraconsumerist speculation of a Reagan 1980s destined to join the 1920s in the history books for sheer upper-class indulgence. I'm not sure whether this really means that anything can carry a symbolic charge of 'anything else', as St Augustine thinks (remember, he only has in mind two alternate and available messages: it either does or doesn't figure the inscription of God's providence; is either positive or negative as far as eternity is concerned); but it certainly foretells caution in the a priori deduction of social meaning from the internal content of any particular work of art. It is the extraordinary capacity of content itself to undergo ceaseless and convulsive metamorphoses in its own right that ought to give the interpreter pause; and that inspires the kneejerk appeal to that not very meaningful thing called 'context' (let alone 'contextual', 'contextualism', etc., which are often intended to mean something like social or sociological analysis, but which may prove to be poisoned gifts in the arsenal of the various Lefts who brandish them).

If an architecture wished to dissent from the status quo, how would it go about doing this? I have come to think that no work of art or culture can set out to be political once and for all, no matter how ostentatiously it labels itself as such, for there can never be any guarantee it will be used the way it demands. A great political art (Brecht) can be taken as a pure and apolitical art; art that seems to want to be merely aesthetic and decorative can be rewritten as political with energetic interpretation. The political rewriting or appropriation then, the political use, must also be allegorical; you have to know that this is what it is supposed to be or mean – in itself it is inert. Nor is this only a matter of use or reception by the public; it must be an active, interpretative reception or use (in other words, a reading, what Heidegger calls the *qua* or the *als*). In this particular area, and by comparison with the other arts, architecture is the most repressible: all other arts demand some minimal effort of reading (which may not seem to go so far as interpretation but which perhaps none the less still minimally includes it or implies it). Even a painting demands a glance; whereas architecture can be lived in, be moved around in, and simultaneously ignored. Much of US culture could be discussed in terms of just this repression of space and of architecture. Perhaps this explains the paradoxes of Manfredo Tafuri's work, for example, for whom you can intervene in thinking about architecture but not in the building of it. Many of us, however, feel that Tafuri's is a peculiarly frustrating position that we would at least like to try to transcend, and my suggestions now will be little more than that clumsy attempt, fraught with traces of that same frustration.

I want to suggest that the political relationship of works of art to the societies they reside in can be determined according to the difference between replication (reproduction of the logic of that society) and opposition (the attempt to establish the elements of a Utopian space radically different from the one in which we reside). At their extremes, both these stances raise some questions: for example, can even the most undistinguished work still altogether replicate or reproduce the hegemonic spatial logic? If we see it allegorically as an example of that very spatial logic, are we not in the process of lifting it from its context and making it somehow exemplary, even of the status quo? But does this not amount to endowing it already with a certain aesthetic value? This is perhaps the place to raise the Venturi question, as it were, namely, whether intellectuals can ever really speak the vernacular. Or, to put it another way, is irony in architecture possible? Is it possible, as Venturi suggests, to replicate the city fabric, to reproduce its logic, and yet maintain that minimal distance that is called irony and that allows you to dissociate yourself ever so slightly, but ever so absolutely, from that status quo? If so, it is clearly that minimal distance that would allow your building to qualify as art, rather than as construction. At the point of that minimal distance you could wage an argument against absolute conformity, and could claim a certain implicit critical function for your work; that it was not the same as the buildings around it but was just slightly different, and that it put those undistinguished structures in perspective and judged them as shoddy and worthless in comparison. But at this minimal, almost imperceptible point, replication turns around into negation; only the ironic stance makes it possible for the reversal to go unseen, since notoriously (and ironically) irony is by definition what can never be definitively identified as being ironic. You have to be able to take it the other way as well; the condition of irony is to be able to remain invisible as irony.

How then could a building establish itself as critical and put its context in negative or critical perspective? The perplexity of our political reflections on architecture finds itself concentrated in this question: since architecture

Jameson becomes being itself, how can the *negative find any place in it*? In the other arts, again, the negative is lodged in the very medium and the material: words are not, and can never become, things; distance in literature is thereby secured. Indeed, nowhere is Venturi's argument more powerful than in his critique and reversal of the project of a Utopian modern architecture, which sought to create a radically different and other space within this one, and ended up producing not buildings and dwellings but sculptures, falling inertly back into the space of being with a vengeance.

Other more dialectical critiques of the Utopian (such as Herbert Marcuse's essay *On the Affirmative Function of Culture*) have argued that excessive Utopianism in a cultural artifact ends up itself reproducing the system, and ratifying, reconfirming the uses of culture as mere window dressing, a sandbox, an inoffensive area of sheer aesthetic play that changes nothing.

On the other hand, the idea of Utopian space, the Utopian building, or even the Utopian city plan, dies hard; for it alone can embody the political aspiration for radical change and transfiguration. Even in aesthetic terms, it is hard to see how any ambitious artist could elude the inveterate impulse to create something different, minimally distinct from the space of what already is all around it (we have just seen how Venturi's irony opens the door onto precisely that slightly different space). Hard to see, then, how the modern could really be terminated, the habit of thinking in terms of the new, of making something even slightly different. The mechanism which enforces this irrepressible modernist teleology is, of course, the market itself, which has to demand new products and fashions in spite of itself. Yet how Utopian projections fare in post-modernity, and what forms they can take in a period in which everybody talks as though they had done with Innovation and with Utopia, is the interesting question for us today. It is also an interesting political issue.

But the logical contradiction lies elsewhere, in the difficulty of producing difference out of the same. It is a difficulty compounded by our conviction as to the increasing systematicity of this system, of its closure as a totality from which, as Foucault taught us again and again, we can scarcely hope to escape. In that case, what we think of as a radically different space from our own is little more than a fantasy projection of difference, it is the same masquerading itself as difference: the real future, if it comes and if it is radically different from this present, will by definition scarcely resemble the fantasies of the present about difference and about the future. From within the system you cannot hope to generate anything that negates the system as a whole or portends the experience of something other than the system, or outside of the system. This was Tafuri's position, whose perplexities are as salutary for us as Zeno's paradoxes, and as unresolvable.

But perhaps his particular paradox can be turned inside out. 'A mode of speech', Wittgenstein said, 'is a mode of life.' Perhaps we can see whether any of the new forms we have imagined might secretly correspond to new modes of life emerging even partially. Perhaps indeed we might start to do this at the existential level, at the level of daily life, asking ourselves whether we can think of spaces that demand new kinds or types of living that demand new kinds of space.

How strong is the wall? And can we imagine anything to replace the room? Does this particular question, for example, have the speculative value that its analogies might have in the other arts: as when the Modern Movement asked whether we could do without story-telling or narrative, or modern music asked whether we could do without tonality (and all the forms and developments – closure and event – inherent to that system)? I once imagined framing this problem in terms of the sentence itself, speculating that it may be misleading to frame the social consequences of spatial innovation in terms of space itself – the indirection of some third term or interpretant drawn from another realm or medium seems to impose itself. Such was the case in film studies a few years ago when Christian Metz elaborated his film semiotics in a vast rewriting programme in which the essentials of filmic structure were reformulated in terms of language and sign systems. The tangible result of such a rewriting programme was to produce a dual problem that might never have been articulated or brought into focus had it remained couched in purely cinematographic terms – the problem of the minimal unities and macroforms of what, in the image, might correspond to the sign and its components, not to speak of the word itself; and of what in filmic diegesis might be considered to be a complete utterance, if not a sentence, let alone a larger 'textual' paragraph of some sort. But such problems are 'produced' within the framework of a larger pseudo-problem that looks ontological (or metaphysical, which amounts to the same thing), and which can take the form of the unanswerable question of whether film is a kind of language (even to assert that it is like a language – or like Language – sets off metaphysical resonance). This particular period of film studies seems to have ended, not when the ontological question was identified as a false one, but when the local work of transcoding had reached the limit of its objects, at which point the judgment of the pseudo-problem could be allowed to take its course.

Such a rewriting programme may be useful in our present architectural context, provided it is not confused with a semiotics of architecture (which already exists), and provided a second historical and Utopian step is added onto this key one, whose function is not to raise analogous ontological questions (as to whether built space is a kind of language), but rather to awaken the question of the conditions of possibility of this or that spatial form.

As in film, the first questions are those of minimal units: the words of built space, or at least its substantives, would seem to be rooms, categories which are syntactically or syncategorematically related and articulated by the various spatial verbs and adverbs – corridors, doorways and staircases, for example, modified in turn by adjectives in the form of paint and furnishings, decoration and ornament (whose puritanical denunciation by Adolf Loos offers some interesting linguistic and literary parallels). Meanwhile, these 'sentences' – if that indeed is what a building can be said to 'be' – are read by readers whose bodies fill the various shifter-slots and subject-positions; while the larger text into which such units are inserted can be assigned to the text-grammar of the urban as such (or perhaps, in a world system, to even vaster geographies and their syntactic laws).

Once these equivalents have been laid in place, the more interesting questions of historical identity begin to pose themselves – questions not implicit in the linguistic or semiotic apparatus, which begin to obtain when this is itself dialectically challenged. How, for example. are we to think of the fundamental category of the room (as minimal unity)? Are private rooms public rooms, and

Jameson   rooms for work (white-collar office space, for instance) to be thought of as the same kind of substantive? Can they all be deployed indifferently within the same kind of sentence structure? On one historical reading, however, the modern room comes into being only as a consequence of the invention of the corridor in the seventeenth century; its privacies have little enough to do with those indifferent sleeping spaces that a person used to negotiate by passing through a rat's nest of other rooms and stepping over sleeping bodies. This innovation, thus renarrativized, now generates cognate questions about the origins of the nuclear family and the construction or formation of bourgeois subjectivity fully – as much as do queries about related architectural techniques. But it also raises serious doubts about the philosophies of language that in effect produced the formulation in the first place: what is, indeed, the transhistorical status of the word and the sentence? Following Heidegger and Emile Benveniste in their different ways, modern philosophy significantly modified its vision of its own history as well as its conception of its function when it began to appreciate the relationship of its most fundamental (Western) categories to the grammatical structure of ancient Greek (let alone the latter's approximations in Latin). The repudiation of the category of substance in modern philosophy can be said to be one response to the impact of this experience of historicity, which seemed to discredit the substantive as such. It is not clear that anything similar took place on the macrolevel of the sentence proper, even though the constitutive relationship of linguistics as a discipline to the sentence as its largest conceivable object of study has come to be understood (and is reinforced, rather than dispelled, by the attempt to invent compensatory disciplines like semantics or text-grammar, which dramatically designate the frontiers they would desperately like to transgress or abolish).

Historical speculation is here only exacerbated by the drawing of political and social consequences. The question of the origins of language itself (the urformation of the sentence and the word in some galactic magma at the dawn of human time) has been declared illicit by everyone from Kant to Lévi-Strauss, even though it is accompanied by a question about the origins of the social itself (and used to be accompanied by another related one about the origins of the family). But that of the possible evolution and modification of language is still conceivable and entertains a vital relationship to the Utopian question about the possible modification of society (where that is itself still conceivable). Indeed, the forms taken by just such debates will seem philosophically receivable or, on the contrary, antiquated and superstitious in strict proportions to your deeper convictions as to whether postmodern society can be changed any longer or not. Debate in the Soviet Union over the theories of N.J. Marr, for example, has been categorized with Lysenko as a scientific aberration, largely owing to Marr's hypothesis that the very form and structure of language itself altered according to the mode of production of which it was a superstructure. As Russian had not sensibly evolved since the tsarist period, Stalin put an abrupt end to this speculation with a famous pamphlet ('Marxism and Linguistics'). In our own time, feminism has been virtually alone in attempting to envision the Utopian languages spoken in societies in which gender domination and inequality would have ceased to exist: the result was more than just a glorious moment in recent science fiction, and should continue to set the example for the political value of the Utopian imagination as a form of praxis.

It is precisely from the perspective of such Utopian praxis that we can return   *Jameson*
to the problem of the judgment to be made on the innovations of the Modern
Movement in architecture. For just as the expansion of the sentence plays a
fundamental role in literary modernism from Mallarmé to Faulkner, so too the
metamorphosis of the minimal unit is fundamental to architectural modernism,
which may be said to have attempted to transcend the sentence (as such) in its
abolition of the street. Le Corbusier's 'free plan' may be said in much the same
sense to challenge the existence of the traditional room as a syntactic category
and to produce an imperative to dwell in some new way, to invent new forms of
living and habitation as an ethical and political (and perhaps psychoanalytic)
consequence of formal mutation. Everything turns, then, on whether you think
the free plan is just another room, albeit of a novel type, or whether it
transcends that category altogether (just as a language beyond the sentence
would transcend our Western conceptuality and sociality alike). Nor is it only a
question of demolishing the older forms, as in the iconoclastic and purifying
therapy of Dada: this kind of modernism promised the articulation of new
spatial categories that might properly merit characterization as Utopian. It is
well known that postmodernism is at one with a negative judgment on these
aspirations of the high modern, which it claims to have abandoned. But the
new name, the sense of a radical break, the enthusiasm that greeted the new
kinds of buildings, all testify to the persistence of some notion of novelty or
innovation that seems to have survived the modern itself.[2]

But there are also more obvious and immediate ways in which space can be
considered to be ideological: indeed, one of the most important and influential
modern Utopian novels, Edward Bellamy's *Looking Backward* (1887),
abolishes kitchens in individual apartments as a feminist gesture in order to
dramatize the move toward more genuinely collective living, which is unavoidably enforced by the collective dining halls and their great collective kitchens.
Here a feature of building space carries a deeply inscribed symbolic meaning or
connotation which is not cancelled by the tensions and vibrations introduced
by two other contradictory features, namely, the actual place of women in the
citizenship system of this Utopia, and the still individualistic nature of the living
and sleeping arrangements (as distinguished from the dining ones). This spatial
symbolism is evidently a macrostructural effect, despite its apparent intervention in a single component (the kitchen) of the larger plan: for the removal
of the latter is possible only on the condition of the reorganization of the
housing complex as a whole, and the presence in it of collective dining and
cooking spaces. I once served on a jury for a student project designed to fulfil a
Cuban programme for a new city outside Havana. It was explained to me that
American architecture students almost never have the opportunity to design
collective spaces of this kind any more. This is, therefore, the example of a
specific kind of ideology – the ideology of individualism – being reinforced by
omission, rather than by positive features: a strategy of containment that
prevents the issue from coming into view in the first place (and it was very
much in this way that Lukacs described the operations of ideology in *History
and Class Consciousness*). One did note, in passing, the absence of Bellamy's
collective kitchens, and the persistence of single-family apartment spaces
(including individual cooking and eating areas), as signs that the Cuban
Revolution was perhaps not yet as Utopian as the bourgeois revolutionary

Jameson   Bellamy. On the other hand, this particular example brings starkly home the
relationship between the possibility of certain symbolic meanings and the
possibility of radical social and systemic change: it is only if wholesale social
changes, such as those betokened by collective kitchens, were even discursive
possibilities in American politics – it is only if some minor but actually existing
party flew these changes on their bannerhead as future possibilities – that a
certain kind of building could hold onto an intentional political symbolism, by
including a non-operative collective dining space somewhere in the apartment
structure, for example (let alone a space for collective tenants' meetings or
neighbourhood theatre, or even the most realistic and virulent of all these
symbolic signals, perhaps, room for child care for the apartment dwellers).

Still, one can think speculatively of other ways in which certain kinds of
spatial ideologies are expressed, and I enumerate them in no special order. I
believe one can posit a certain ideology of privacy as the other face and positive
form of the repression of the collective in Western life, along with the
expression of that form we call private property, as it generates equivalents for
itself at every level of social life (thus, for example, William James famously
linked up the feeling of personal identity, the unity and centredness of the
subject or psyche, to my private property, my ownership of my own memories:
as soon as I lose title to them, I lapse into schizophrenic dissolution).

Privacy – no doubt ritually acted out as far back as the violation of the body
and the ban on touching – dramatically enacts its relations with private
property in the form of the great estates, enormous wooded tracts into which
outsiders cannot penetrate uninvited. There is here a dual dialectic of the
senses, of seeing and hearing: no one is to be allowed to see me (as James Hall
pointed out, the distances felt to constitute a violation of my person or, on the
other hand, a worshipful inspection, are variable from culture to culture), and
my money buys me the freedom from hearing anyone else: sound also violates,
and submission to other people's sounds is a symbolic index of powerlessness
and vulnerability. All of this suggests some deeper drive to repress the social
and sociability as such: my reward for acquiring a fortune is my possibility of
withdrawing from everything that might remind me of the existence of other
people in the first place. Or rather, the other way around, my submission to
those reminders, day-in and day-out, my immersion in the social (and the at
least formerly collective), is itself a mark of weakness. Just as commodity
reification in capitalism is determined by the attempt to flee class guilt and, in
particular, to efface the traces of production and of other people's labour from
the product, so here too, in the great estates (imaginatively reinvented in E.L.
Doctorow's *Loon Lake*), my deepest social longing lies in the will to escape the
social altogether, as though it were a curse, matter or animality from which
privacy allows an escape into some angelic realm. It is a contradictory longing,
to be sure, whose 'comeuppance' Orson Welles displays for us in Citizen Kane's
old age, or in the remorse of the last heir of the Ambersons.

Still, the right to repression runs deep, and the privilege of escaping from the
polis and from politics in general is supremely acted out in this separation of
private life from work or public space. That it may be symbolic only of the
privileges of the head of the household might be deduced from the rather
different dynamic of privacy within the apartment or dwelling space itself.
There, sexuality and power, or control, seem to be the not so symbolic stakes:

who has a right to close his door, and upon what, is a question that goes hand   *Jameson*
in hand with the other one about the right to determine the use of the television
set (or the living room).

Space otherwise notoriously underscores and reinforces whatever division of
labour is active in the social order in question: what would be at stake
aesthetically and practically in the planning of a building that deliberately
transgressed those divisions? On the other hand, what would that building
have been in the first place? The factory might at best afford a space for
expressing Japanese team styles, rather than the Fordist assembly line (it is true
that this distinction has often been ideologically deployed as a genuine marker
of distinct cultural systems, of the truly pre- or post-individualistic as
contrasted with the Western exploitative). The office building, meanwhile,
could at best offer the occasion for dramatizing different management
methods, as opposed to radically different labour processes and relationships
to property itself.

I raise these political questions about built space not because they are the
only ones, but in order to show their instability and, on the one hand, the ways
in which they tend to slip into culturalism (how differently did the Victorians,
or do the Japanese for that matter, think their spaces and their existential
practices?) and, on the other, the revolutionary or systemic, the Utopian (the
Tafuri option again: it is useless to speculate on changing something until we
are in a position to change everything). The question can be asked in reverse, of
course: and then (still paranoid) it reads – to what degree are we necessarily
locked into our own system, so that even our fantasies of change reflect its
internal logic, rather than our genuine discovery of something else, something
radically different or other? This is a question various intellectual movements
have sometimes tried to respond to by teaching that imprisonment, rather than
offering a glimpse of something else: yet architecture drawn to those strategic
specifics would presumably not be a very cheerful place to live in at any length.

Still, it seems possible to posit, alongside the political and social ideology
that architecture might under certain circumstances be thought to express,
those rather different ideologies or specific ideologemes that are at work all
around us in social life and that architecture might only incidentally reinforce.
I want to conclude with two of those, which I will identify as humanism and
chaos respectively, and then mention the burning political problem which the
concept of politics exercised here seems to prevent us from raising.

PART ONE

By way of historical reconstruction and also in order to gauge the profound
conservatism of the present moment, I have lately been trying to reflect on
exactly what it was we used to stigmatize as humanism in the bad sense: old-
fashioned philosophy and literary criticism, metaphysics, the centred subject,
narrativity as such (with or without a happy end)? Liberal politics and social
rhetoric? The Western great books and the great Western Judeo-Christian
tradition? The valorization of 'Man' (very much in the ironic feminist mode)?
In architecture, however, the strong form of humanism is not particularly
traditional (in the sense, for example, of some antimodern tastes and values
that would confront the various architectural modernities with indignation and

Jameson call for the restoration of Victorian cityscapes and historicist forms). Rather it is phenomenology itself, as that has made itself felt in the area of space: and it must be said that however self-enclosed Husserl's phenomenology was in the problem of the structure and nature of mental operations and intellectual acts – however much Heidegger then found urgency in the relationship of human beings to time and anxiety (and following him, Sartre, to decisions and freedom) – the work of Merleau-Ponty was always significantly committed to a life in space. The analysis of perception and the Utopian vocation to restore bodily experience to a kind of prelapsarian plenitude – which make up everything glorious about Merleau-Ponty's philosophical writings – necessarily had as their complement the experience of space itself in all its imaginable varieties. It is easy to see how this conception of the vocation of philosophy would find its ally in an aesthetics of perception, that is, in a defence of art as what dispels a numbness and a habituation of perception and restores a more vibrant and articulated life in the world (clearly not all aesthetics offer this justification and defence of art by any means; but it has been influential in modern times, and not only in the idiosyncratic version of the Russian Formalists). Here too a vocation of the art critic is inscribed, as someone who will open up our perception of the works (and thereby presumably of the world itself): Ruskin and then Proust.

But in architecture, the building really is the world, or almost: so that opening up our capacities to perceive architectural space is already, and not even virtually, to extend our capacities for perception itself in general. But it is a two-way street: the architects who are seduced by this view of their vocation must then accept the human body as the ultimate criterion and build buildings to its scale. Or rather, since it is already supposed that this was done by the tradition, whence the valorization of antiquity and then of its development in the Renaissance, architects are thereby bound to return to some of those physical and tactile values, and to eschew the dissonances of what exceeds or maims or diminishes the human frame: what administers shocks to it for whatever purpose.

The same set of values can of course also be detected in urbanism: 'good city form', the ideal of the city somehow memorizable and mappable (Kevin Lynch) and organized around the human body to a human scale – this is phenomenological humanism on the level of the urban itself. It may well involve a certain tension with purely architectural phenomenology, asking certain buildings to accept a reduced position within the perception of the whole, rather than to strive to become themselves microcosms and models of the totality (and thereby the totality of perception). But the same implicit belief in the scale of the human is at work here.

Now these visions are glorious moments in our history, and reflect certain extreme conquests: one can deconstruct them, as Derrida did with Husserl; one can also make an ideological analysis of their function at a given time in which they are re-elaborated with a whole inner situation logic. Thus it seems clear that they represent a response to spatial alienation and an attempt to restore non-alienated experience to the modern industrial city. But the modern was also a response to that alienation, of a radically different type; and we can grasp something about what makes the phenomenological-humanist position reactionary by comparing its harmonious serenity to the desperate violence of the modern itself.

The phenomenological view of architecture is Utopian, in so far as it   *Jameson*
promises to restore or to resurrect from within the fallen body of the modern
city-dweller – with clogged and diminished senses, therapeutically lowered and
adjusted feelers and organs of perception, maimed language and shoddy,
standardized mass-produced feelings – the glorious Utopian body of an
unfallen being who can once again take the measure of an unfallen nature.
Architecture serves as the intermediary of this resurrection by exercising those
new or heightened faculties in a therapeutic way and organizing the external
world for perception itself. Heidegger does not altogether fall into this
category, yet his notion of the way in which the building stands at the centre of
the universe and articulates, indeed, reinvents, what he calls the *Geviert*: the
relationship between heaven and earth, between man and the gods, is somehow
analogous to the aims of phenomenology and a good illustration of one
dramatic version of that programme.

This is the case when you read Christian Norberg Schulz (or as I have said in
a different way for the city: Kevin Lynch). It is difficult to argue against these
visions, since such an argument would seem to stand out for ugliness and
squalour, for lack of perception, and so forth. But two things need to be pointed
out: first, that this is bad Utopianism in Marx and Engels' early sense: it asks
for resurrection without paying the price; change without politics; transformation by simple persuasion and common sense – people will react directly
to this beauty and demand it (whereas the argument started from the premise
that people could no longer perceive fully in the first place).

The second point is a class one: when one then reads something like Roger
Scruton's *Aesthetics of Architecture*, it becomes clearer that we have to do not
merely with a class vision, a description of the way in which the upper classes
(like Hölderlin's gods) inhabit their spacious dwellings and live their bodies,
but with even more, all the complex mirror-dialectics of envy involved in class
perceptions. What is being excited here is not the will to restore my perceptions, but rather the envy of those full perceptions as they are exercised by
another class (and not by the bourgeoisie, but by the aristocracy: thus these
are middle-class envies that survive in the general form of culture after the
bourgeois revolution itself). It becomes then a little more complicated to
distinguish between an attempt to restore older kinds of space and the incite-
ment of collective fantasies whose very different function is that of
legitimating a nobler way of life (and thereby excusing whatever has to be
done, economically and politically, to perpetuate that way of life which
virtually by definition is not for everyone, but whose minority experience
somewhere is nonetheless supposed to redeem the fallen lives the rest of us
have to lead).

PART TWO

As far as spatial ideologemes in the urban area are concerned, I think I can do
nothing better than refer to the recent novel by William Gibson, *Virtual Light*
(1993), a book inspired by a collaboration with the architects Ming Fung and
Craig Hodgetts on reimagining San Francisco. I want to point out the
persistence, through this exciting narrative, of a now standard opposition
between the planned – the boring, totalitarian or corporate (as in the malls of

Jameson this novel) – and the chaotic, somehow natural, 'grown in the wild' structure called The Bridge:

> But none of it done to any plan that he could see. Not like a mall, where they plug a business into a slot and wait to see whether it works or not. This place had just *grown*, it looked like, one thing patched onto the next, until the whole span was wrapped in this formless mass of *stuff*, and no two pieces of it matched. There was a different material anywhere you looked . . . (p. 178).

It is worth exploring the genesis of this particular binary opposition – deeply entrenched in postmodern doxa, where it stands for pluralism, neo-Fordist flexibility, postmodern marketing, and so forth, as opposed to bureaucracy. This is a hangover of cold war propaganda, in which socialist planning is grasped as imposing an unwanted order on human life, in contrast to which capitalism becomes celebrated as a place of freedom, a kind of jungle play-ground of consumption, with plenty of interstices for those who want to drop out of the system. Clearly, it is an opposition ill calculated to measure the degree to which late capitalism is a form of standardization, and a lifeless application of grids and prefabricated forms. To be sure, in the new moment, chaos is derived as it were fractally from prefabricated modules (whence the term flexibility): freedom is thus apparently achieved on the far side of human production by means of computers and cybernetic techniques.

But how can an architect plan such productive chaos? Can it be built into the city or into the individual building, particularly when that building is a megastructure that wants to rival the city? Is not the mall, which prophetically passes before us as the antithesis in Gibson's account, the final sorry result of the attempt to generate a rich simulacrum of wild life in the project not to plan? I don't particularly care about the answers to these questions, but they serve to highlight the omnipresence of this stereotypical opposition between intention, plan and praxis, on the one hand, and, on the other, chaos, the informational, the late capitalist and consumption.

PART THREE

The business of identifying ideologemes is a crucial one; it is a necessary part of politics (although not all of it), and architecture is a useful experimental laboratory in detecting and observing the operations of ideologemes one would not normally expect to find there. But I confess that in none of what I have said do I find any reference to the most significant political development (and issue) of our own period, namely, globalization itself, and by the same token I find no reference to the important question of what architecture might have to do with globalization and how it can offer possible political interventions into the new world system. As this conference itself, in its mobility, presupposes globalization, and as contemporary architecture, with its multiple projects all over the world, is unthinkable without it (more unthinkable than a modernism which could well be imagined fulfilling itself within a single national regime), I wonder how I have managed to evade the question of the multiple levels in which all thought has to move today, namely, the local, the regional, the national and the global: buildings are as locked into these as are concepts; politics must engage them (I'm thinking of _Jameson_ the meshes on a flywheel) as substantively as aesthetics or theory. But I suspect that in order to reach globalization as a reality, or a kind of thing-in-itself, we will first have to spend considerable time in identifying its various ideologies, not least the spatial ones.

NOTES

1   _Le temps retrouvé_, Éditions de la Pléiade, vol. 3. Gallimard, 1989, p. 1204.
2   F. Jameson, _Postmodernism_, Duke University Press, 1992, pp. 104–7.

JEAN-FRANÇOIS LYOTARD

Jean-François Lyotard French philosopher Jean-François Lyotard (b. 1924) is the author of one of the key texts on postmodernism. His work, *The Postmodern Condition: A Report on Knowledge*, commissioned by the Quebec government, challenges many of the assumptions of modernism. Here Lyotard is concerned with the legitimation of knowledge, especially scientific knowledge, and observes famously the crisis of legitimation within the postmodern condition. For Lyotard the principle of the 'Grand Narrative' (liberalism, Christianity, Communism, etc.) has been called into question, and the world should now be understood in terms of small or local narratives. Knowledge is now legitimated no longer according to any notion of human emancipation or speculative spirit, but solely through performative discourses of economics and technology.

Lyotard's position should not be taken as a criticism of science *per se*, but rather of 'techno-science'. Indeed his overall outlook would seem to support more recent theoretical developments in science such as theories of complexity which break down traditional epistemologies of science. Likewise his critique of 'Grand Narratives' and his affirmation of the specificity of genres of discourse should not be taken as an espousal of relativism. Indeed, while earlier on Lyotard had been extremely active politically, much of his later work was taken up with the problems of political agency and ethical imperatives. Moreover, he questions the ethical consequences of Heidegger's position in his book *Heidegger and 'the jews'*, published shortly after revelations were made public of Heidegger's political affiliation with the National Socialists. It was not only Heidegger's silence which was to be faulted, but the 'forgetting' which is inherent in *all* thought.

This theme of the totalitarianism potentially sanctioned by Heidegger's philosophy of the soil takes on a specifically architectural dimension in the essay '*Domus* and the Megalopolis'. Here Lyotard exposes the potential violence that underwrites the domesticated household. In a critique of received attitudes towards the domestic idyll, he reveals the dark side of the *domus*. The influence of Freud noticeable elsewhere in much of Lyotard's earlier work is again evident here, and Freud's discussion of the 'uncanny' seemingly underpins the essay, where '*heimlich*' is the figure of both the familiar and the open, the secret and the repressed. Comparisons might also be made with the work of Gaston Bachelard, where the cellar is read as the site of the sinister in line with Jung's use of it as an architectural metaphor.

DOMUS AND THE MEGALOPOLIS   *Lyotard*

The representation of a facade. Fairly wide, not necessarily high. Lots of windows and doors, yet blind. As it does not look at the visitor, so it does not expect the visitor's look. What is it turned towards? Not much activity. Let's suppose that it's pretty hot outside. The courtyard is surrounded by walls and farm buildings. A large tree of some kind, willow, horse chestnut, lime, a clump of pines. Dovecots, swallows. The child raises its eyes. Say it's seven o'clock in the evening. Onto the kitchen table arrive in their place the milk, the basket of eggs, the skinned rabbit. Then each of the *fruges* goes to its destination, the dairy, the cool scullery, the cooking pot, the shelf. The men come home. Glasses of fresh wine. A cross is made in the middle of the large loaf. Supper. Who will get up to serve out? Common time, common sense, common place. That of the *domus,* that of its representation, mine, here.

There are varieties of the common place, cottage, manor. The ostentation of the facades. The commoners move around at a distance from the masters' residences. In place of pastures and ploughed fields, parks and pleasant gardens offer themselves to the facade. Pleasure and work divide space-time and are shared out among the bodies. It's a serious question, a historian's or sociologist's question, this division. But basically, extended or not, divided or not in its exploitation, the basis remains domestic. It is the sphere of reference of the estate, a monad. A mode of space, time and body under the regime (of) nature. A state of mind, of perception, of memory confined to its limits, but where the universe is represented. It is the secret of the façades. Similarly with action. The *fruges* are obtained by nature and from nature. They produce, destroy and reproduce themselves stubbornly and according to the order of things. According to nature's care for itself, which is called frugality. *Alla domenica, domus* gives thanks for what has taken place and had its moment and prays for what will take place and have its moment. The temporal regime of the *domus* is rhythm or rhyme.

Domestic language is rhythmic. There are stories: the generations, the locality, the seasons, wisdom and madness. The story makes beginning and end rhyme, scars over the interruptions. Everyone in the house finds their place and their name here, and the episodes annexed. Their births and deaths are also inscribed, will be inscribed in the circle of things and souls with them. You are dependent on God, on nature. All you do is serve the will, unknown and well known, of *physis*, place yourself in the service of its urge, of the *phyein* which urges living matter to grow, decrease and grow again. This service is called labour. (With the dubious wish sometimes, to profit also, that the estate should profit, from growth? One wonders. Rhythmed wisdom protects itself against *pleonexia*, the delirium of a growth with no return, a story with no pause for breath.)

Ancilla, the female servant. From *ambi* and *colere, ambicilla*, she who turns all the way round, the old sense of *colere*, to cultivate, to surround with care. Culture has two meanings: cult of the gods, but the gods also *colunt domum*, cultivate the dwelling, they surround it with their care, cultivate it with their circumspection. The female servant protects the mistress, for to serve is to keep. When she gets up to serve at table, it is the nature-god who cultivates the house,

Lyotard   is content there, is at home. The domestic space is entwined and intertwined
with circumvolutions, with the comings and goings of conversations. Service is
given and returned without any contract. Natural duties and rights. I find it
hard to believe that this organic life was the 'primitive form of exchange', as
Mauss put it.

It is a community of work. It does not cease to work. It works its works
itself. These operate and are distributed spontaneously, out of custom. The
child is one of these works, the first, the first-fruit, the *offspring*. The child will
bear fruit. Within the domestic rhythm, it is the moment, the suspension of
beginning again, the seed. It is what will have been. It is the surprise, the story
starting over again. Speechless, *infans*, it will babble, speak, tell stories, will
have told stories, will have stories told about it, will have had stories told about
it. The common work is the *domus* itself, in other words the community. It is
the work of a repeated domestication. Custom domesticates time, including the
time of incidents and accidents, and also space, even the border regions.
Memory is inscribed not only in narratives, but in gestures, in the body's
mannerisms. And the narratives are like gestures, related to gestures, places,
proper names. The stories speak themselves on their own. They are language
honouring the house, and the house serving language. The bodies make a
pause, and speech takes over from them indoors, in the fields, in the middle of
the woods. Such rich hours, even those of the poor. The past repeats itself in
work. It is fixed, which is to say it is held back and forgotten, in legends. The
domus is the space-time of this reiteration.

Exclusion is not essential to the domestic monad. The poor man, the solitary
traveller, has a place at the table. Let him give his opinions, show his talent, tell
his story. People get up for him, too. Brief silence, an angel is passing. Be
careful. What if he were a messenger? Then they will make sure he is remembered, domesticated.

Bucolic tableau. *Boukolein* does not only mean keeping the flock. Keeping
humans, too, serving them. Yet the *domus* has a bucolic air only from outside,
from afar, from the city. The city spends centuries, millennia slowly gnawing
away at the *domus* and its community. The political city, imperial or
republican, then the city of economic affairs, today the megalopolis spread out
over what used to be the countryside. It stifles and reduces *res domesticae*,
turns them over to tourism and vacation. It knows only the residence
(*domicile*). It provides residences for the presidents of families, the *domini*, it
bends them to egalitarian citizenship, to the workforce and to another memory,
the public archive, which is written, mechanographically operated, electronic.
It does surveys of the estates and disperses their order. It breaks up god-nature,
its returns, its times of offering and reward. With another regulation of space-
time set in place, it is in relation to this that the bucolic regime is perceived as a
melancholic survival. Sad tropics seen from the north.

A savouring of the sounds. Come from the near distance, the depths of the
stables, cacklings, a silence hollowed out round the call of the owls when Venus
shines out at dusk, crackling of the alder branches thrown onto the hearth,
clogs on the thresholds, conversation on the hill opposite, wasps round the
melon, shouts of encouragement to the autumn oxen, swifts madly chasing
each other around the darkening roofs. The sounds are toned to the measure of
the bittersweet, the smoky, the tastelessness of the boiled beans, the pungent

dung, the ferment of the hot straw. The tones eat each other up. The minor   *Lyotard*
senses were honoured in the physical *domus*.

What I say about it, the domestic community, can be understood only from
where I speak, the human world become megalopolis. From after the death of
Virgil. From after the end of the houses. (At the end of the *Buddenbrooks*.)
Now that we have to gain time and space, gain with and against them, gain or
earn our livings. When the regulation of things, humans and capacities happens
exclusively between humans, with no nature to serve, according to the principle
of a generalized exchange aiming for more. . . . In the 'pragmatic' busyness,
which disperses the ancient domestic monads and hands over the care for
memory to the anonymity of archives. No one's memory, without custom, or
story or rhythm. A memory controlled by the principle of reason, which
despises tradition, where everyone seeks and will find as best s/he can the
information needed to make a living, which makes no sense (*ne rime à rien*).
The birth of individualities amid dispersion, as Marx said, of singularities in
liberty, according to Nancy. The estate façades still standing, because we
conserve them, attest to the old absent *ethos*. Cracked as they are by radiation
and telecommunications. Businesses that they are by means of interfacing.

We know all that by heart, sick of it, today. This slow retreat of domestic,
neolithic life, we know what does indeed have to be named, from here, the
revolution of the spatio-temporal regime of being-together. Not too difficult,
doubtless, to show that Heidegger's *Gestell* is thought only, in return, through
the conservation of an idea of service, which is domestic. Which does not only,
to a large extent, lead to the motif of his *Dichtung* filtered through Hölderlin,
but to the *Dienst* divided into three (the service of thinking, war and work, as in
Dumézil) deployed by the *Rectorship Address*. So we know how much our
melancholy for the *domus* is relative to its loss. Even Greek tragedy, that
enigma, must, we know, be decoded by means of the grid of de-domination, de-
domestication. The new law, that of the *polis* and its right. *Themis* goes beyond
the ancestral domestic regulation of the *genos*. But this historico-sociological
account does not acquit us of tragedy. Our distance, our anti-domestic
violence, makes discernible another scene in the tableau of the houses.

In this scene, the female servant with the heart of gold is impure. The service
is suspect, ironic. The common work is haunted by disaster. The respect is
feigned, the hospitality despotic, common sense obsessed by the banishing of
the mad, its burial within. Something remains untamed in the domination, and
capable of interrupting the cycles. The domestic monad is torn, full of stories
and scenes, haunted by secrets. Acts of violence stretch it to breaking point,
inexplicable injustices, refused offers of affection, lies, seductions accepted and
unbearable, petty thefts, lusts. Freud makes us reread, via Sophocles and
Shakespeare, the tragedy of the Greek families in this penumbra of madness.
The generous purposiveness of the god-nature, dressed up by the philosophers
with the name of love, reconciliation, being-together as a whole, everyone in
their place, of which the *domus* is the wise figure, the awaited birth and the
beautiful death, all this is cracked by evil. An evil not even committed. An evil
before evil, a pain both more ancient and younger than the sufferings
experienced. A pain always new. In the lowest depths of the *domus*, rumour of
anti-nature, threat of *stasis*, of sedition. Father, mother, child, female servant

with the heart of gold, niece, old man-servant, shepherd and ploughman, gardener, cook, all the figures of wisdom, the corner of the park under the fig tree, the little passage for whispering, the attic and its chests - everything is matter for obscene crimes. Something in the *domus* did not want the bucolic.

Something does not want this recurrent inscription, and it isn't *me*. But as to its place in the domestic hegemony, there the ego does want its share in memory, to make and remake its place in space-time and in the narrative. The son to become the *dominus*, in his turn. The daughter, the *domina*. And the man-servant, of course, the master, here or elsewhere. As long as it's that, in other words the business and busyness of the ego, the ambivalences, hesitations and contradictions, the little ruses and strategies, then domestic nature remains untouched. It pursues its ends through intrigue, it can repair, it will repair. It will inscribe that in its memory, an episode in caution, in conservation. But the rest? What is not resolved in sacrifice, in offering, in being received? The prodigal, the dissipated, the fury? That is not a member of the domestic organism, that is banished into its entrails.

Even more than the city, the republic or even the flabby and permissive association of interests and opinions called contemporary society - it is strange that, even more than with any of these states of assembling the diverse, the *domus* gives the untameable a chance to appear. As though the god-nature which cultivates it were doubling himself with an anti-god, an anti-nature, desperate to make the bucolic lie. The violence I am speaking of exceeds ordinary war and economic and social crisis. Conversely, and in spite of their generality, or because of it, crisis and war do not become desperate unless they are infiltrated with the breath and the asphyxia of the domestic. Even if the houses have long been ruined, it is enough to activate the memory of a lost domain and legend (a living common space, the myth of a pure common origin) for the political and economic community to parade and parody itself as a *gens*, as a *domus* mocked. So then conflict, crisis change into *stasis* and *seditio*, as though they were affecting some domestic *habitus* that had been thought abandoned. The undominated, the untamed, in earlier times concealed in the *domus*, is unleashed in the *homo politicus* and *economicus* but under the ancient aegis of service, *Dienst*. It's necessary, one might say, that shareable matter be densified to the narrow scale of domesticity for anti-matter to deliver its hatred from each body. *Homo re-domesticus* in power kills in the street shouting 'You are not one of ours.' He takes the visitor hostage. He persecutes anything that migrates. He hides it away in his cellars, reduces it to ashes in the furthest ends of his lowlands. It is not war - he devastates. *Hybris* break apart the domestic *modus*. And the domestic remodelling will have served to unleash *hybris*.

The ruin of the *domus* makes possible this fury, which it contained, and which is exercised in its name. But apart from this case, the case of evil, I find it hard to think that in general the emancipation of singularities from out of domestic space-time favours, on its own, freedom of thought. Perhaps thinking's lot is just to bear witness to the rest, to the untameable, to what is incommensurable with it. But to say witness is to say trace, and to say trace is to say inscription. *Retention*, dwelling. Now all memory makes a work. So that at the very moment when thought bears witness that the *domus* has become impossible, and that the façade is indeed blind, it starts appealing to the house and to the work, in which it inscribes this witnessing. And the fact that there *Lyotard* are many houses in the megalopolis nowadays does not mean that there are no longer any works, nor any works to be produced. It means that works are destined to be left idle, deprived of façades, effaced by their heaping up. Libraries, museums: their richness is in fact the misery of the great conglomerates of council flats. The *domus* remains, remains as impossible. My common place. But *impossible* is not only the opposite of *possible*, it is a case of it, the *zero* case.

We wake up and we are not happy. No question of remaking a real new house. But no question either of stifling the old childhood which murmurs at our waking. Thinking awakens in the middle of it, from the middle of very old words, loaded with a thousand domesticities. Our servants, our masters. To think, which is to write, means to awaken in them a childhood which these old folk have not yet had. That does not happen without a certain lack of respect, assuredly, but not without respect either. You go on, untameable, but with care. Forced to it. You go on, but the past in words awaits there in front of you. It mocks us. And that does not mean that you advance backwards, like Benjamin's angel. At any rate, it is only for the last of men, the nihilist, that the disaster of the *domus* and the rise of the megalopolis to the stars can procure an (evil) delight. Not only for the ingenious one who rushes ahead of what is coming in order to control it, but for his cousin, the well-meaning philosopher, who makes a virtue out of redundancy. It is impossible to think or write without some façade of a house at least rising up, a phantom, to receive and to make a work of our peregrinations. Lost behind our thoughts, the *domus* is also a mirage in front, the impossible dwelling. Prodigal sons, we engender its patriarchal frugality.

Thus things past are remembered ahead. The beginning the awakening, offers itself only at the end as its inscription by the writing of the remembrance, in its working-out. Always to be reread, redone. And the dwelling of the work is built only from this passage from awakening to the inscription of the awakening. And this passage itself does not cease to pass. And there is no roof where, at the end, the awakening will be over, where we will be awake, and the inscription will have ceased to inscribe. There is no *domus* as the rhyme of time that is so. But nostalgia for the lost *domus* is what awakens, and our domain nowadays is the inscription of this awakening. So only transit, transfer, translation and difference. It is not the house passing away, like a mobile home or the shepherd's hut, it is in passing that we dwell.

The only kind of thought - but an abject, objective, rejective thought - which is capable of thinking the end of the *domus*, is perhaps the thought suggested by techno-science. The domestic monad was still almost 'naked', to use Leibniz's terms, not a large enough means of memorizing, practising, inscribing. It is decomposed as the big monad forms in its greater complexity, the one that Heidegger, coming from a quite other kind of thinking, from thinking which determined itself quite otherwise, names the *Gestell*. Much more complete, much more capable of programming, of neutralizing the event and storing it, of mediating what happens, of conserving what has happened. Including, of course, and first of all, the untameable, the uncontrolled domestic remainder. End of tragedy, flexibility, permissiveness. The control is no longer territorialized or historicized. It is computerized. There is a process of complexification, they say, which is initiated and desired by no one, no self, not even that of humanity. A cosmic zone, once called the earth, now a miniscule planet of a small stellar system in a galaxy of pretty moderate size – but a zone where neg-entropy is rife. The *domus* was too simple, it left too much remainder that it did not succeed in taming. The big techno-scientific monad has no need of our terrestrial bodies, of passions and writings that used to be kept in the *domus*. What it needs is 'our' wonderful brains. When it evacuates the dying solar system, the big monad, which is cosmically competitive, will not take the untameable along with it. Before imploding, like the other celestial bodies, with its sun, little Earth will have bequeathed to the great spatial megalopolitan monad the memory that was momentarily confided to the most intelligent of earthly species. But the only one of any use for the navigation of the monad in the cosmos. So they say.

Metaphysics is realized in the physics, broad sense, operating in the techno-science of today. It certainly requires of us another mourning than the kind required by the philosophy of disaster and redundancy. The line taken is not that of the untameable, but of its neglect. To do the (quasi-Leibnizian) physics of the unconscious, we might say. No need for writing, childhood, pain. To think consists in contributing to the amelioration of the big monad. It is that which is obsessively demanded of us. You must think in a communicable way. Make culture. Not think according to the welcome of what comes about, singularly. To pre-vent it, rather. To success is to process.[1] Improve performances. It's a domestication, if you will, but with no *domus*. A physics with no god-nature. An economy in which everything is taken, nothing received. And so necessarily, an illiteracy. The respect and lack of respect of severe and serene reading of the text, of writing with regard to language, this vast and still unexplored house, the indispensable comings and goings in the maze of its inhabited, always deserted rooms – the big monad doesn't give a damn about all this. It just goes and builds. Promotion. That's what it demands of humans. In the name of 'communicative action', 'conversation' and the relegation of philosophy, in the name of performativity, we are begged to think useful. Useful for the composition of the megalopolis. I'm amazed that this consensualist demand can still nowadays be picked up as though it emanated from the idea of the Enlightenment. Whereas it results from the complexification of material ensembles, say the ingenious.

There was still some *domus* in the metropolis, *polis-mètèr*, city mother, *mater* and patrimony. The metropolis refers only to a size which exceeds the domestic scale. Filiation and concern for the past are not its forte. It is not a city but an *urbs*. An *urbs* become its own *orbs*. We were hoping for a *cosmopolitès*, there is no need for a *megapolitès*. We need ingenious people. As many monads as the enormous megalopolitan memory will allow must be combined. Its electrical circuits contain a power of which humans have no need and no idea stored energy, and potential capacity. With the ancient idea of *dynamis*, the world was schematized like a nature, and nature like a *domus*. Domestic events in a unique, sensitive finality. As for the megalopolis, it conceives scenarios of cosmic exile by assembling particles.

Baudelaire, Benjamin, Adorno. How to inhabit the megalopolis? By bearing witness to the impossible work, by citing the lost *domus*. Only the quality of suffering counts as bearing witness. Including, of course, the suffering due to language. We inhabit the megalopolis only to the extent that we declare it uninhabitable. Otherwise, we are just lodged there. In the closure of time paid off (security), await the catastrophe of the instant, wrote Benjamin. In the inevitable transformation of works into cultural commodities, keep up a searing witness to the impossibility of the work, wrote Adorno. To inhabit the uninhabitable is the condition of the ghetto. The ghetto is the impossibility of the *domus*. Thought is not *in* the ghetto. Every work to which prodigal thought resolves itself *secretes* the wall of its ghetto, serves to neutralize thought. It can only leave its trace upon the brick. Making media graffiti, ultimate prodigality, last homage to the lost frugality.

What domesticity regulated – savagery – it demanded. It had to have its off-stage within itself. The stories it tells speak only of that, of the *seditio* smouldering up at its heart. Solitude is *seditio*. Love is *seditio*. All love is criminal. It has no concern for the regulation of services, places, moments. And the solitude of the adolescent in the *domus* is seditious because in the suspense of its melancholy it bears the whole order of nature and culture. In the secrecy of his bedroom, he inscribes upon nothing, on the intimate surface of his diary, the idea of another house, of the vanity of any house. Like Orwell's Winston, he inscribes the drama of his incapacity before the law. Like Kafka. And lovers do not even have anything to tell. They are committed to *deixis*: this, now, yesterday, you. Committed to presence, deprived of representation. But the *domus* made legends and representations out of these silences and these inscriptions. In place of which the megalopolis displays, commentates on them, and explains them, makes them communicable. It calls melancholy being autistic and love sex. Like the way that it calls *fruges* agro-alimentry products. Secrets must be put into circuits, writings programmed, tragedies transcribed into bits of information. Protocols of transparency, scenarios of operationality. After all, I'll take it, your *domus,* it's saleable, your nostalgia, your love, let me get on with it. It might come in useful. The secret is capitalized swiftly and efficiently. But that the secret should be a secret of nothing, be uncultivated, senseless, already in the *domus*, the megalopolis has no idea. Or rather, it has only the idea. Whereas the secret, because it consists only in the timbre of a sensitive, sentimental matter, is inaccessible except to stupor.

I wanted to say only this, it seems. Not that the *domus* is the figure of community that can provide an alternative to the megalopolis. Domesticity is over, and probably it never existed, except as a dream of the old child awakening and destroying it on awakening. Of the child whose awakening displaces it to the future horizon of his thoughts and writing, to a coming which will always have to be deferred. It is thus, not even like some surface of inscription which is there, well and truly there, but like an unknown astral body exercising its attraction on writing and thought from afar; rather, then, like a mirage which sets requirements than like a required condition - it is thus that the domestic world does not cease to operate on our passibility to writing, right up to the disaster of the houses. Thought today makes no appeal cannot appeal, to the memory which is tradition, to bucolic *physis* to rhyming time, to perfect beauty. In going back to these phantoms, it is sure to get it wrong - what I mean is, it will make a fortune out of the retro distributed by the megalopolis just as well (it might come in useful). Thought cannot want its house. But the house haunts it.

Lyotard   The house does not haunt contemporary thought in the way that it once pierced the untameable, forcing it into the tragic mode. The untameable was tragic because it was lodged in the heart of the *domus*. The domestic schema resisted the violence of a timbre that was none the less irresistible. The tragic *cursus* stages this incommensurability, between the beautiful ordinance of a rhymed space-time and the amazement procured by the sublime encounter with an unprepared material, the tone of a voice, the nuance of an iris or a petal the fragrance of a smell. A no-saying amid the always already said: stupor. A stupid passion rises in the domestic dough. As though the god were dropping the share he took in the common bake. Were letting the matter of time and space be touched in the raw. All the same, this abandon, this bankruptcy can still be taken up by the *domus*, it represents them as tragedy. Untameable dominated, sublime held to the rules of the beautiful, outside-the-law redestined. Here is the reason why the megalopolis does not permit writing, inscribing 'living' not only pastoral poems, but even tragedies. Having dispersed the domestic schemas. So the untameable is not representable there. Timbre is consigned by the megalopolis to the ghetto. And it's not the 'good old' ghetto tolerated by the *domus*, itself a somewhat domestic and domesticated ghetto. It is the Warsaw ghetto, administratively committed to *Vernichtung*, the 'rear' of the megalopolitan front. It must be exterminated because it constitutes an empty opacity for the programme of total mobilization in view of transparency.

Where the untameable finds a way of gripping on, is domestic flesh. Either it devastates it, or else the flesh reduces it, tames and eliminates it. They go together, in their insoluble *différend*. With Nazism the big monad in the process of forming mimicked the *domus*. Whence the exceptional tenacity, which arose from the (artificial) reconstitution of flesh. Does that remain a constant temptation, after Nazism? At any rate the untameable has to be controlled, if the big monad is to be competent and competitive. Everything must be possible, without remainder, with a bit of ingenuity. But that's just it, the *domus* isn't ingenious enough, the extermination betrays too much *hybris*, there has to be a more rational and open way of operating. More operational, less reactively earthly. Secrecy must not surround the destruction of the secret. Communication and culture accomplish this destruction, and much better. Timbre will get analysed, its elements will be put into a memory, it will be reproduced at will, it may come in useful. The important thing is not that the result is a simulacrum: so was tragedy. The important thing is to dominate - not even that, to treat – everything that was rebellious to the *domus*, as much as possible. As to what's left, it is condemned to extinction, denied, *vernichtet*.

And I wanted to say this too. Well, we say to ourselves (who, 'we'?), well, at least in the ghetto we shall go on. As far as it is possible. Thinking, writing, is, in our sense, to bear witness for the secret timbre. That this witnessing should make up an oeuvre and that this oeuvre might be able, in a few cases, at the price of the worst misunderstanding (*méprise*), of the worst contempt (*mépris*), to be placed on the circuits of the mediated megalopolis, is inevitable, but what is also inevitable is that the oeuvre promoted in this way be undone again, deconstructed, made redundant (*désoeuvrée*), deterritorialized, by the work of thinking some more, and by the bewildering encounter with a material (with the help not of god or of the devil, but of chance). Let us at least bear witness, and again, and for no one, to thinking as disaster, nomadism, difference and

redundancy. Let's write our graffiti since we can't engrave. That seems to be a *Lyotard*
matter of real gravity. But still I say to myself: even the one who goes on bearing
witness, and witness to what is condemned, it's that she isn't condemned, and
that she survives the extermination of suffering. That she hasn't suffered
enough, as when the suffering of having to inscribe what cannot be inscribed
without a remainder is of itself the only grave witnessing. The witness of the
wrongs and the suffering engendered by thinking's *différend* with what it does
not manage to think, this witness, the writer, the megalopolis is quite happy to
have him or her, his or her witnessing may come in useful. Attested, suffering
and the untameable are as if already destroyed. I mean that in witnessing, one
also exterminates. The witness is a traitor.

NOTE

1   In English in original. (Translators' note.)

PART V

POSTSTRUCTURALISM

POSTSTRUCTURALISM

Poststructuralism refers to an inter-disciplinary movement popular from the late 1970s, which could be seen as a supplement to structuralism, and as an attempt to problematize and challenge many of its assumptions. As with the relationship between postmodernism and modernism, so too that between poststructuralism and structuralism is more complex than might at first appear. Poststructuralism does not lend itself to any clear-cut definition. Broadly speaking, however, poststructuralism sought to redress the universalizing tendencies of structuralism by introducing a certain specificity into discourse. Thus against the static and universal models of structuralism, poststructuralism introduced notions of time and difference. The bar that separates signified from signifier was seen by poststructuralists as less stable. Meaning, in other words, was never fixed, and always subject to differals and play. Likewise poststructuralism challenged the treatment of binary oppositions in structuralism, and sought to expose the fact that within such oppositions one term is invariably privileged over the other. Nonetheless poststructuralism should be understood not as a negation of structuralism, but as a problematization, intent on augmenting and improving the structuralist project.

The problematization of structuralism was evident already in the work of Barthes, where he stressed the transiency of the signified. Barthes called for an increase not in functional studies of the city, but in readings of the city. Hélène Cixous seemingly responds to Barthes's call in her evocative readings of Prague. One may detect a similar tendency in Jacques Derrida's description of Bernard Tschumi's follies at the Parc de la Villette. For Derrida the follies in their folly become the site of play of meaning, of the meaning of meaning. In effect Derrida reads his own philosophical project into the forms of Tschumi's architecture. Throughout the primacy of the text is stressed. The world becomes treated as 'text' to be read inter-textually.

This shift from the static universalization of structuralism is evident in Foucault's later work, where he emphasizes not the simple, structured classification of space, but the power/knowledge axis which controls social behaviour. Deleuze takes this argument further. Human beings can be seen to be controlled no longer by physical walls, but by more 'gaseous' concepts such as credit. Virilio also addresses the erosion of the authority of the architectonic. The physicality of the traditional door and window must give way to the metaphorical window of the VDU console. Andrew Benjamin fits less happily into this category. Yet within his engagement with Peter Eisenman there is evidence of a strategic challenging of received concepts, which is the hallmark of poststructuralism.

Poststructuralism has been accused by its critics of leading to a possible relativism, and always threatening negation. The potential for a constant deferral of meaning, they would claim, seems to infer that we can never fully access the object of our reading. Yet supporters of poststructuralism would claim that this criticism is misguided. Indeed, as Derrida has convincing argued, it is rather hermeneutics which risks a potential relativism. By contrast, deconstruction, for example, serves as an epistemological check against the appropriations of hermeneutics. Thus, far from promoting relativism, in some respects poststructuralism could be seen as a defence against relativism. Likewise, far from advocating negation, poststructuralism could be seen to be premised on affirmation, although the possibility for negation must always be left open.

ANDREW BENJAMIN

═══════════

Australian Andrew Benjamin (b. 1952) is one of relatively few philosophers from the English speaking world who have engaged with the continental tradition. He has published extensively on the work of Martin Heidegger, Theodor Adorno, Walter Benjamin, Julia Kristeva and Jean-François Lyotard. Andrew Benjamin belongs to an emerging group of contemporary thinkers who have pursued what might be termed an 'aesthetic turn' in philosophy, echoing the earlier 'literary turn'. Here he recognizes the interdependency of philosophy and the visual arts, and architecture especially. 'Philosophy can never be free of architecture.' To this end he has engaged in a vigorous exploration of the interaction between these two traditionally quite distinct fields with a view not to denying the specificity of the individual disciplines, but rather to exploring how each may inform the other. *Andrew Benjamin*

The essay, 'Eisenman and the Housing of Tradition', is part of this project. By bringing together Descartes, a philosopher who thinks 'architecturally', and Peter Eisenman, an avant-garde architect who is at once theorist and practitioner, Benjamin seeks to explore the question of tradition and the way in which it is 'housed'. He exposes some of the tensions in the thought of Descartes who had pursued the question of the 'break' with tradition via an architectural metaphor – as a 'refounding' of philosophy. As Benjamin argues, in Descartes' terms an absolute 'break' with tradition is impossible. Rather it is a question of recognizing 'the reinscription of a repetition within an attempt to break down the repetition of tradition'. Thus Benjamin formulates an understanding of the project of the avant-garde in terms of a 'reworking' of the past, not dissimilar to Freud's concept of 'Nachträglichkeit' ('working through'). Eisenman's work, Benjamin argues, must be seen as an overcoming of the complacency of tradition, an ongoing struggle open to a plurality of possibilities where 'becoming triumphs over being'. Above all, it 'opens up the need to think philosophically beyond the recuperative and nihilistic unfolding of tradition'. The interdependancy of architecture and philosophy is thereby affirmed. Benjamin concludes by observing that from now on what is required of both philosophy and architecture are 'works with open doors'.

───────────

Benjamin   ## EISENMAN AND THE HOUSING OF TRADITION

J'ai sans doute mal lu l'oeuvre de Derrida, mais mal lire c'est
finalement une façon de créer, et c'est en lisant mal que j'arrive à
vivre dans la réalité et que je pourrais travailler avec lui.

Peter Eisenman

Locating architecture would seem to be unproblematic. Architecture houses. It
is at home in – and provides a home for – philosophy, aesthetics and those
discourses which are thought to describe it. And yet it is precisely the generality
as well as the singularity of these claims that makes such a description or
location problematic. In each instance something remains unquestioned. The
assertion – even the argument – that architecture houses, fails in a concrete,
philosophical and political sense to address housing. Equally the interplay
between architecture and the home in which philosophy, aesthetics and discourse may be located, works with the assumption that the nature of what is
housed is such that the act of housing it will not call into question the specificity
of the act itself. In other words the unified nature of philosophy is assumed and
thus is thought to have been provided either by the unity of tradition or the
singularity of its object. What needs to be examined therefore are some of the
elements at work within these assumptions; their premises and therefore that
on which they are built. Philosophy can never be free of architecture. The
impossibility of pure freedom, of pure positivity and thus of a radical and
absolute break entails that what is at stake here is, as a consequence, precisely
philosophy and architecture themselves. Of the many locations that can be
given to Eisenman's work one is to situate it within the act of rethinking both
architecture and philosophy. A way towards an understanding of the
impossibility of an absolute break and therefore of this location of Eisenman's
work may stem from a consideration of Descartes' use of an architectural
metaphor in the *Discours de la méthode*. Descartes' attempt to refound philosophy in the wake of a complete break with the past is presented within
architectural terms. What must be traced is the founding of this attempt.[1]

DESCARTES' ARCHITECTURE

For philosophy what is at stake in the question of the relationship between
architecture and tradition is the possibility of a rethinking of architectural
thought. Tradition emerges as the site that occasions both an understanding of
dominance – the categories and concepts which are handed down and which
thus determine thinking within and as tradition – and the possibility of a
thinking which, while it maintains (houses) the dominant, is neither reducible
to nor explicable in terms of it. In sum, tradition allows for history to be
thought within philosophy. In addition the tension that marks the corresponding non-correspondence of a thinking (be it architectural or philosophical)
that is situated within tradition, and a thinking that cannot be thus situated,
provides a way to renew the concept of the avant-garde as well as providing
access to an understanding of the accompanying mode of experience (that is
sensibility) proper to the avant-garde.

Descartes' architectural 'metaphor' is a familiar point of entry. It goes with-   *Benjamin*
out saying that within Descartes' architecture there is an explicit confrontation
with tradition. The location of this 'metaphor' is the Second Part of the
Discours de la méthode. The context concerns the possibility of philosophy, of
a new philosophical thinking, and thus whether tradition can be refurbished –
what has been handed down by and as tradition – or, on the contrary, whether
philosophy is constrained to start again. It is not difficult to see in the very
formulation of the problem that Descartes thinks that tradition may be, in fact,
left behind. In other words that an absolute break with the past can be
established. Consequently, in discussing Descartes it will be essential to analyse
the unfolding of the metaphor as well as to examine or assess the possibility of
this purported complete departure. Descartes' metaphor is an 'example' of the
general problem of how change occurs and, of course, who should bring it
about. (It is thus not *just* a metaphor.) He notes that

> there is not usually so much perfection in works composed of
> several parts and produced by various different craftsmen as in the
> works of one man. Thus we see that buildings undertaken and
> completed by a single architect are usually more attractive and
> better planned than those which several have tried to patch up by
> adapting old walls built for different purposes. Again, ancient
> towns which have gradually grown from mere villages into large
> towns are usually ill-proportioned, compared with those ordinary
> towns that planners lay out as the fancy (*fantaisie*) on level ground.
> Looking at the buildings of the former individually, you will often
> find as much art in them, if not more, than in those of the latter; but
> in view of their arrangement – a tall one here, a small one there –
> and the way they make the streets crooked and irregular, you would
> say it is chance (*fortune*) rather than the will of men using reason
> (*raison*) that placed them so. And when you consider that there
> have always been certain officials whose job is to see that private
> buildings embellish public places, you will understand how difficult
> it is to make something perfect by working only on what others
> have produced (*les ouvrages d'autrui*).[2]

This passage warrants careful analysis. It is not an isolated instance within
Descartes' writings. It should be remembered, for example, that the actuality of
starting again is articulated within architectural terms in the First Meditation,
where he describes his task in the following way:

> to start once again from the foundations
> *commencer tout de nouveau dès les fondements.*[3]

It is the possibility of this 'new' beginning that defines the relation to as well as
the conception of tradition at work in both the *Méditations* and the *Discours
de la méthode*. Now, returning to the passage from the *Discours de la méthode*,
it is essential to note both the presentation of tradition, its interarticulation
within the language of architecture, and thus its putting into play as well as
demanding a specific conception of experience and thereby of the aesthetic.
Rather than working on, '*les ouvrages d'autrui*', the implicit suggestion is
that the philosopher like the architect (the philosopher as architect) should

Benjamin 'begin again'. The '*autrui*' of this passage can be interpreted as standing for tradition. Inscribed therefore within the more general architectural metaphor is an additional trope. The relationship between self and other has become mapped onto the possibility of a departure from tradition. Tradition here, within this framework, is presented as the other. The other is the already present. The other here is history. The self becomes that possibility that emerges within the break from that conception of the self/other relation that views both parts as inextricably linked. The self must emerge as new – in a perpetual state of renewal – from this linkage. It is precisely in this sense that Descartes' juxtaposition of the solitary individual working alone and a team – the '*divers maîtres*' – needs to be understood.

Descartes' refusal of tradition is connected therefore to the emergence of the individual subject. It is thus that Cartesian thought establishes the centrality, both within architecture and philosophy, of the subject, and thus of subjectivism. Cartesianism is the emergence of the centrality of the subject; the subject of epistemology as well as the subject of sentiment. Rather than pursuing this particular path, however, it is essential to move to a more detailed analysis of what is at play in the rejection of tradition. Fundamental to the possibility of this rejection will be a specific construal of repetition. This has to be the case since Descartes believes that the break with the work of others (a break or rupture within repetition and therefore occasioning the cessation of repetition) establishes, and defines, the new. There can be no sense, within the terms of his own argument, that repetition can operate if repetition is understood as the repetition of a tradition. It will be seen, however, that there is another sense in which Descartes cannot escape another repetition. It is this sense that, it will be suggested, checks his claim concerning that which has already been described in terms of the possibility of an absolutely new beginning. The detour into repetition will take us to the centre of the problem of tradition, explanation, interpretation and therefore of a more generalized aesthetic – general in the sense that its stakes are not reducible simply to architecture.

Descartes understands tradition's repetition not necessarily in terms of the repetition of an unchanging and identical content, but rather as a continuity of content; one determined and structured by the precepts of medieval Aristotelianism, that is, Scholasticism. The break would be the refusal both to occasion and to sanction the repetition of these precepts; to take them over and hand them on. The resistance is to their continuity. Two questions arise here. First, if there is a radical break – one in which it is possible to *begin again* – how is the break to be maintained, housed, within Descartes' own philosophical adventure? Second, how does the break figure within the implicit conception of tradition at work in the departure itself? Before it is possible to answer these questions it is vital to try and understand repetition beyond the confines of Cartesianism. What is at stake now, therefore, is to move from the relationship between repetition and tradition within Descartes to a more generalized conception – remembering, of course, that for Descartes it is possible to call a halt to continuity. Indeed it is possible to interpret the doubt of the First Meditation as the break, and the subsequent overcoming of doubt as the recommencement.

There is a sense in which Descartes is correct. Tradition in general terms can be understood as the *determination in advance*. The way tradition operates is invariably in terms of teleology. There is a *telos* established within and as tradition. In the case of architecture, the *telos* refers to function and thus to housing. Architecture must house. Its being as architecture is, within the terms set by the dominant tradition, to be determined if not evaluated by the success of any architectural instance – any building – to fulfil such a criterion. It is, of course, a criterion determined in advance. The incorporation of teleology into tradition and into architecture does not preclude the possibility of excess. Indeed excess has to be understood not as a subversive element within a more general economy but as a designation that flows from the centrality of function. It is therefore essential to distinguish between excess and transgression. Excess is always going to be the addition that sustains the law or rule. Transgression is that which robs them of their power, while maintaining that power as a remnant. It endures but no longer as itself. Within the purview of teleology, however, the history of architecture, in fact the philosophy of architecture, have become as a result the history and philosophy of a specific process: one marked by an origin, a goal and a creator. This is not, however, the only way in which teleology figures within architecture.

The important additional dimension concerns the effect that specific elements within a building or house are supposed to have. The effect is continually thought to have been predictable. Whether or not the prediction is valid, what is at work within such an architectural practice is a thinking that involves the inclusion within itself and within the 'house' of either a repetitive monotony or a decorative excess that enacts no more than the attempt to mask the specific effect; the effect as the effect of function. The necessity, both within architecture and philosophy, of rethinking repetition – of moving on from the domination of the Same – cannot be over-emphasized. Now it could be argued that the attempt to subvert the dominance of the Same is precisely what Descartes is doing. The problem here is to identify on exactly what level the Same is to be located.

In regards to architecture the Same is explicable, for the most part, in terms of teleology and thus in terms of function. The instance becomes, as was mentioned, either a particular instantiation of the general designation in the sense that the particular is coextensive with the general, or the particular is viewed in terms of its excess; that is that state of affairs where the general functional designation defines the excess. The repetition of the Same therefore is the repetition of function. Now the question here is, what would an architectural thinking be that was no longer dominated by the *telos* given by tradition to architecture? It is by returning to Descartes that an answer to this question can be given.

Within Descartes' attempt to establish the completely new – absolute originality – a certain philosophical strategy was deployed. Of the many philosophical oppositions within which Descartes' architectural 'metaphor' is positioned (thereby positioning itself and the oppositions) the two which were the most central were reason and chance and the one and the many. It is clear that they are related. Within the Cartesian texts the oppositions are advanced in terms, for example, of the distinction between the understanding and the imagination. In addition it is a retention and repetition of these terms, amongst others, that defines – defines in the sense of reorientates – the philosophical task. Furthermore it is the presentation of the opposition between reason and

Benjamin chance and the one and the many that sustains, supports, perhaps even provides the architectural metaphor's foundation. In other words it is the repetition of these oppositions that provides the conditions of possibility for Descartes' arguments within the 'metaphor'. The city of reason as opposed to the city of chance is one that has been constructed without any retention of that which preceded it. It needs to be the work of one mind – the subject of epistemological certainty – as opposed to the joint operation of diverse minds. The consequence of this is that the possibility of breaking with tradition, in the Cartesian sense, that is of ending repetition, can itself take place only if the oppositions that sustain this possibility are themselves repeated. The Cartesian break with tradition ends up reinscribing tradition as that which allows for the possibility of the break. It is only if the oppositions that characterize the history of philosophy are allowed to be repeated that Descartes' desire to 'begin again' is in fact possible. Now there are two important conclusions that can be drawn from this reinscription of tradition.

The first is that it makes clear in what sense the Cartesian conception of tradition is to be understood. The second is that it allows for a critical understanding of what is at stake in the claim that an absolute break with tradition is impossible. It now emerges that a refusal of dominance still has to house what had hitherto dominated. The architectural question, even within philosophy, can never be ignored. In addition it can now be understood that the question of tradition involves a repetition in which concepts and categories are handed down. Moreover repetition is not neutral but involves dominance and therefore power. The resistance to, or refusal of, tradition must take place in relation to the conceptual and categorial. (The way in which dominance and power figure here gives rise to another philosophical task.) They need to be housed while their domination is resisted. This interplay of resistance and inclusion marks the tension within the domain of contemporary interpretation. It goes without saying that there are many works of philosophy or architecture that involve a simple repetition of tradition. Descartes conceived of his philosophical task as avoiding nihilistic repetition. The task failed as it was premised on the reinscription of another repetition.

Understood ontologically, therefore, the repetition within Cartesianism becomes the repetition of the same within the Same. This repetition is linked to the particular conception of the object within Cartesianism. In the *Discours de la méthode* Descartes describes the connection between truth and the object: 'there being only one truth about each thing whosoever finds it knows as much about that thing as can be known.'[4] The object of knowledge like the subject of knowledge must be a unity. Subject and object must be homological in themselves as well as constructing a homological relation within the act of knowing. Ontologically therefore they must be the same. The origin must be unified if knowledge is to be possible. Repetition is the repetition of Sameness. What Cartesian repetition cannot include is a conception of repetition that is not articulated within and therefore as the Same. This takes place in the positive sense in terms of a repetition of and within the Same and in the negative in terms of the postulated complete rejection of repetition. If repetition is to be rethought then what has to emerge as central is the ontology that sanctions a repetition in which what comes to be repeated is at the same time same and different. (The time of this simultaneity is complex.)

These tentative deliberations concerning ontology can be taken a step *Benjamin* further. One way of interpreting Descartes' reinscription of a repetition within the attempt to break down the repetition of tradition is that the work – Descartes' own text – as an object of interpretation thereby becomes a site that is no longer reconciled with itself. Its desire for original unity was rendered impossible by that which intended to establish it as a unity; as unified. The aspiration (understood as intentional logic) for an initial and original unity gives way, within the recognition of its impossibility (an impossible possibility), to an original heterogeneity; that is to anoriginal heterogeneity. The origin has become redescribed. The foundations are renewed within repetition such that they are then repeated for the first time. The consequence of this means that if there is to be a refusal to take over and carry on that which tradition hands down then there has to be another way in which this task can be understood. It is precisely in these terms that it will be necessary to rethink the force of the claim that 'architecture houses'.

THE HOUSING OF ARCHITECTURES

The limit already emerging within the architectural constraints determined by teleology are also at work within philosophy. There are two aspects that are of strategic importance here. The first is the envisaged relationship between philosophy and its object, and the second emerges from the consideration of what is to be understood by philosophy both within the terms set by tradition and, in addition, in the resistance to the dominance and domination of tradition. Clearly the second of these provides the place to start. In a sense, however, it opens up much larger problems concerning history, naming, inter-pretation, the political, etc., all of which are central to any understanding of Eisenman's work.

What is at stake in asking the question 'what is philosophy?' arises not from the specificity of a particular response but from the recognition that an answer has already been determined in advance of the question; this determination in advance is tradition.[5] The tradition within which philosophy is enacted – and hence which it enacts – has decreed what is going to count as philosophical and therefore what will fall beyond the borders it constructs. The repetition of philosophy within, by and as tradition reduces it to the repetition of an ideal essence. It must not be assumed, of course, that that essence need be at hand. Indeed it is possible to present a conception of philosophy where its object and its nature are in some sense hidden, and thus what becomes fundamental to, if not descriptive of, the philosophical task is the revelation of that which is not at hand. Here repetition is the repetition of that which is essential though concealed.

Countering a conception of philosophy that defines its identity in terms of an ideal essence means allowing the question 'what is philosophy?' to be re-posed. The re-posing of this question unfolds within a repetition that changes the stakes of the question (recalling the ontology of the object with Cartesianism). The repetition of this question breaks with the control exercised by the Same. It sanctions a repetition in which the same is different. The reason for this being the case is explicable in terms of the different ontologico-temporal dimensions at work within, on the one hand, a repetition that resists

Benjamin   the dominance of the Same, and, on the other, one that repeats it.

The repetition of an ideal essence, whether it be of philosophy or architecture, necessitates the repetition of that which cannot change. The essence of philosophy or architecture – an essence which shows itself within their *arché* and *telos* – has to endure. Its endurance must enact and take place within an ontology and temporality of stasis. The question of the essence therefore comes to be re-posed within that specific ontologico-temporal concatenation proper to stasis. The unstated premise at work here is that the name 'philosophy' – though this will be equally true of the name 'architecture' – names that essence. (This premise also operates in those cases where the essence is assumed even though it is yet to be revealed.) It is clear therefore that re-posing the question of philosophy or architecture – sanctioning a repetition beyond the Same – involves a reconsideration of naming as well as of time and existence. If the assumption, that the nature of philosophy and architecture is not determined by tradition (tradition as the determination in advance), is accepted then this gives rise to three important and difficult questions: How are the names philosophy and architecture to be understood? What do they name? and finally, How do they house tradition?

In a sense all these question are related in so far as they pivot around the problem of identity and hence of the ontology of identity. On the basis that the identity of philosophy, and equally of architecture, need not be reduced to the identity handed down by tradition and which is thus determined in advance, then this will mean that the repetition of an ideal essence is no longer under consideration as providing the means whereby the questions of identity and naming can be answered.[6] Furthermore it means that the borders established by tradition to fend off 'outside' claims to be philosophical or architectural, that were, by definition, not sanctioned by tradition, are no longer in place. Their displacement means that the question of identity is such that it can never be finally settled. It will remain open. The question 'what is philosophy?' will henceforth include within its range all those answers (answers which will be potentially or actually conflictual) that claim to be answers to the question. Philosophy, and by extension all such names, will name the continual attempt to provide an answer to the question of the identity, both named and demanded, within the question. The resistance to tradition here becomes the refusal to take over the answer to the question of identity. The taking over of what is handed down is the repetition of tradition; a repetition articulated within and by the Same. This will occasion the possibility of a rereading or rather a reworking of texts (that is objects of interpretation, books, paintings, sculptures, buildings, etc.) that comprise the history – the past – of the specific name in question. The temporality of this reworking is extremely complex since it involves a doubling of the object of interpretation within the act of interpretation. A way of understanding this particular interplay between time and interpretation is provided by the Freudian conception of *Nachträglichkeit*.

Rethinking naming, both the name and what is named, cannot be adequately undertaken without reference to the ontologico-temporal dimension within which it is situated. It has already been argued that what marked the repetition of the Same was an ideal essence articulated within an ontology and temporality of stasis; in other words within the premises of a philosophy of Being. The conception of naming alluded to above demands a different understanding of the relationship between time and existence. It follows from the claim that the question of identity remains an open question, that it is, by definition, impossible to understand within those categories which demand either an ideal essence or a unique and singular referent. (This point can, of course, be extended to include teleology within it.) Furthermore if the answer to the question 'what is . . . ?' necessitates an initial acceptance of that plurality of answers that are answers to the question in so far as they intend to be answers, then their clash will provide precisely what the name within the 'what is . . . ?' question actually names. In sum, therefore, identity will henceforth be understood as the continual struggle to establish identity. It is at the very least because of the emphasis on the continuity of struggle (Heraclitean 'strife') and the plurality of possible answers (a plurality that is of necessity differential) that this particular understanding of identity and naming cannot be incorporated into a philosophy of Being; here, therefore, becoming triumphs over being. It is not surprising that Eisenman situates his own work within this triumph:

> architecture cannot be except as it continuously distances itself
> from its own boundaries; it is always in the process of becoming, of
> changing, while it is also establishing, institutionalising.[7]

It must be added that, in addition, the absence and impossibility of an ideal essence needs to be understood as resisting tradition. It also means that the ways in which tradition can be resisted are themselves plural and do not have an ideal essence. Were they to be single in nature then this would construct – if only because it necessitated – an ontological homology between each answer and the tradition. However there is more at play here than mere refusal.

The plurality and affirmation of heterogeneity that marks the refusal of tradition cannot be reduced to a simple negativity. Negativity is incorporated, located – houses still have to shelter – in what is at play here, but the experimentations and developments within art, architecture and philosophy that signal the affirmative within the present are themselves not explicable in terms of that negativity.[8] They are not the simple negation of dominance. This is because there is a necessary discontinuity between the interpretive apparatus handed down by tradition and experimentation. The avant-garde demands experimentation within philosophy, interpretation, etc., as well as in works of art, architecture and literature. Works situated within this discontinuity – the site of tension – are affirmative. They mark what could be described as the co-presence of negation and creativity. It goes without saying that this is the site of Eisenman's work. Its relation to tradition, to teleology, to there being an ideal essence of architecture, all enact this interpretive, conceptual and philosophical tension. Indeed it is precisely in these terms that it is possible to understand the developments within Eisenman's work. 'Scaling', 'decomposition' and 'dislocation' are all means whereby resistance and affirmation take place.

Eisenman's development as an architect is to be understood as the continual search for the means – both material and philosophical – to overcome the 'complacency' of tradition. He writes of House VI in the following terms:

> The design process of this house, as with all the architectural work
> in this book, intended to move the act of architecture from its

Benjamin complacent relationship with the metaphysic of architecture by reactivating its capacity to dislocate; thereby extending the search into the possibilities of occupiable form.[9]

In a recent interview he links the practice of dislocation to that of location, thereby indicating how the question of the housing of tradition is to be understood. It is an answer that highlights the specificity of architecture though at the same time allowing it to be extended beyond the range of material habitation.

> architecture faces a difficult task: to dislocate that which it locates. This is the paradox of architecture. Because of the imperative of presence, the importance of the architectural object to the experience of the here and now, architecture faces this paradox as does no other discipline.[10]

While the importance of this particular paradox within architecture cannot be denied, it is also present within other areas of study research and artistic practice. Location within architecture is repeated elsewhere in terms of the imperative of sense. No matter how disruptive or subversive a text or work of art may be the possibility of meaning must none the less inhere. The recognition of the necessary interplay between location and dislocation and the grounds for arguing for its extension are outlined by Eisenman in terms of function; that is in teleological terms.

> while a house today must still shelter, it does not need to symbolise or romanticise its sheltering function, to the contrary such symbols are today meaningless and merely nostalgic.[11]

It is precisely in these terms that it is possible to speak of the housing of tradition; that is a form of housing that contains within it the tradition of housing and yet is neither reducible to nor explicable in the terms set by that tradition. This is the paradox referred to earlier and which is marked by the interplay between dislocation and location.

Before trying to trace the consequences of this relationship beyond the borders of architecture it is essential to describe this paradox in greater detail. In fact it is only a paradox in the most conventional sense. What is at play here – and this is also true of all Eisenman's architectural strategies – is, to use his own formulation, an attempt 'to question the accumulated tradition of the institution of dwelling'. It is a questioning, however, that is neither theoretical nor abstract but which is enacted in the buildings themselves. It does not take place outside, as though there were an outside. Not only does this check the assumed and often unquestioned viability of the distinction between theory and practice, it brings to the fore the twofold need for a new aesthetics and, perhaps more importantly, a new conception of sensibility; understood, of course as part of a re-expression of experience.

Eisenman's plans for the Bio-Centrum at the University of Frankfurt provide a more concrete way of extending these preliminary comments. The Centre is being constructed for advance work in biological research. It is this 'use' that in the first instance determines the elements that are involved. They enact – architecturally – the codes used by the biologists in their own scientific work. Mark Wigley has, with great accuracy and care, described the consequences of the interplay between the code and the basic forms of the 'modernist blocks': *Benjamin*

> these intersections of modernist abstraction and an arbitrary
> figurative code, which act as the basic form, are then progressively
> distorted to provide the functionally specific social and technical
> spaces. This distortion is effected by systematically adding further
> shapes in a way that clashes – new shapes that come out of the same
> system of four basic shapes that they distort.[12]

This description both highlights the difficulty of Eisenman's recent work and
indicates how the site – the project – is itself enacted in terms of an initial
heterogeneity which is, by definition, incapable of synthesis. 'Distortion' is
creative. The addition of new elements brought about a change in the aesthetic
reception or response to the earlier ones. The complexity of the interrelationship between the elements of the project means, as Wigley has argued,
that the elements combine in a complex and unending 'dialogue'. There is
therefore an original and multiple babble whose end is the absence of ends. The
function rather than functionality has determined the initial structure. At the
same time it not only sanctions but also determines its own distortion. This
unpredictable and creative inter-connection means that it is impossible to
privilege any particular part of the 'project'. Indeed the criteria in terms of
which evaluation, response, etc., would take place are themselves no longer
straightforward. This decentring function is at the same time the subversion of
the centrality and dominance of aesthetic and evaluative universality. While the
project as an object of interpretation appears to be self-referential, located
within that self-referentiality is the tradition, though now displaced and dis-
seminated it can no longer be thematized. It is no longer itself. It is repeated
though it is no longer the same as itself. Homology has become heterology: not
after the event but in its being reworked. This is precisely what is at stake in
dislocation. Eisenman's own description of the strategy of allowing the interplay of a rethinking of biology and architecture attests to the creative potential
of this location of dislocation; perhaps even a relocation that dislocates.

> As biology today dislocates the traditions of science, so the
> architecture of our Bio-Centrum project dislocates the traditions of
> architecture. While architecture's role is traditionally seen to be that
> of accommodating and representing function, this project does not
> simply accommodate the methods by which research into biological
> process is carried out, rather it articulates those processes them-
> selves. Indeed it could be said its architecture is produced by those
> very processes.[13]

The inapplicability of function opens up a space that can no longer be filled by
prediction. Prediction is the determination inscribed within the building that is
generated by, and hence which also sustains, the dominance of use. The space,
in opening the building, of robbing prediction of its predictive power, once
again constructs the building as an object – an object of interpretation – which
can never be self-referential. There is always the space that cannot be filled. The
temporality of past, present and future understood within sequential continuity
is no longer, even in this instance, viable. This state of affairs has already been
noted when Eisenman writes of a design that extends 'the search into the

Benjamin possibilities of occupiable form'. The search opens out. The end cannot be predicted; though it can always, in the end, be located. Opening limits self-referentiality.

The question of self-referentiality is in addition linked to the paradox mentioned above. In Eisenman's House VI the presence of columns in the dining room that neither aid (in terms of function or decoration) nor hinder the intended activity, 'have according to the occupants of the house changed the dining experience in a real and more importantly unpredictable sense'.[14] The experience of dislocating, expressed in a light, almost glancing way in the above, opens up two related paths of investigation, if not of experimentation. The first concerns the question of experience, while the second concerns how the connection (if indeed connection is the right term) between homogeneity and heterogeneity is to be understood, since they neither involve nor take place within either an either/or, or a binary opposition. Understanding this 'connection', beyond the purview of these oppositions, involves rethinking the relationship between time and interpretation. (Because of the complexity of this problem all that will be presented here is a brief sketch of some of the issues involved.)

The ascription of heterogeneity and homogeneity within the object of interpretation take place within tradition. In other words the assumed homogeneity of the object of interpretation – and indeed of the philosophical enterprise itself – is both an assumption and a consequence of tradition understood as the determination in advance. This means that within the frame designated by tradition the homogeneous is original. Now, it is not the case that Eisenman's work enacts, or is to be understood in terms of its enacting, a countering move, that is one where the purported initial homogeneity is contrasted with or opposed by an initial heterogeneity. In either sense that would be to repeat the either/or. There is, in fact, an additional premise at work here.

The tradition, in its attempt to make the heterogeneous (for example the figurative) a secondary event that presupposed a homogeneous original event (for example the literal), always privileged the Same over diversity. The temporality here is straightforward; one precedes the other. Unity, identity, the Same, in other words any conception of the homogeneous or the self-identical, is positioned as being prior and thereby as having priority. However this priority, that which was prior, is, in Nietzsche's sense of the term, a 'fiction'. It is an attempt both to still becoming and to naturalize that which was always a secondary event. Naturalization here means that an event becomes redescribed (for the 'first' time). It appears to be original because the act and effect of this first 'redescription' has been forgotten. The forgetting therefore is fundamental both to the positioning of unity, the homogeneous, the Same, etc., as original, as well as accounting for how this particular designation is repeated in and as tradition. Overcoming forgetting is, here, the recognition of forgetting. It is thus that the object/event is reworked, giving rise to a mode of interpretation.

The result of accepting this description is that not only does the 'original' event become the site of heterogeneity, thereby calling into question any straightforward opposition between heterogeneity and homogeneity; the 'literal' becomes a trope, thereby undermining the distinction between the literal and the figural. Works, objects of interpretation have to be reworked and thereby reread and reinterpreted. The initial object/event/site of interpretation

will no longer be the same as itself. Self-identity will have become fractured.   *Benjamin*
The work will have been repeated. But now the repetition will no longer take
place under the reign of the Same. Here, in the reworking the work will become
repeated and therefore re-presented for the first time.

The obvious consequence of locating the heterogeneous as prior is that it
provides a way of interpreting works in terms of the attempt to suppress (to
forget) that original heterogeneity. (The philosophical enterprise associated
with Derrida can, in part, be situated here.)[15] The suppression is demanded by
tradition and yet it is precisely the activity of suppression that marks the
unfolding, if not the very possibility, of the strategy enacted by the text/work/
object of interpretation. There are, of course, those works which, rather than
assuming an initial homogeneity and therefore necessitating that form of interpretation whereby that initial assumption is shown to be impossible, attempt to
present, within the plurality of ways it is possible, the reality of an initial
heterogeneity. Such works are affirmative. The works, writings, buildings of
Peter Eisenman are in this sense affirmative.[16] This does, in a sense, mark their
importance. They count as developments within architecture. They mark either
a break or refusal of nihilistic repetition. It also opens up the problem of
sensibility; of the experience of that which can no longer be assimilated nor
understood in terms of the categories and concepts handed down as the
unfolding of tradition. In sum this could be described as the problem of avant-
garde experience.

BUILDING EXPERIENCE

The problem of experience must continually traverse any attempt to dwell on
or to present either modernism or the present. In order to take these deliberations a step forward it is essential to take up – perhaps even to redeem –
elements of Burke's aesthetics. The value of Burke lies in the importance that is
attributed to experience. It is an emphasis that springs from the almost
physiological foundation he gives to the aesthetic. None the less within Burke's
body – the body as place – lies the possibility of drawing, withdrawing, specific
elements that will be fundamental to a conception of avant-garde experience.

These elements emerge with greatest clarity when Burke is attempting to
distinguish between terror and delight as part of a general clarification of the
sublime.

> When danger or pain press too nearly, they are incapable of giving
> any delight, and are simply terrible, but at *a certain distance*, and
> with *slight modification*, they may be and are delightful, as we every
> day experience.[17] (My emphasis)

This particular passage is of central importance. It introduces time into
experience. There is a more or less straightforward sense in which 'distance'
can be seen to involve time. It would seem, on the surface at least, to be the
temporality at work in Turner's painting *The Morning after the Storm*. Here
the storm is over and its absence marked by the choppy water, the heavy
condensation. Distance, however, does not mean simply 'after' or 'over'. Were
it to be the case then the temporality signalled in the passage from Burke, as
well as in Turner's painting, would involve a backward and forward movement

Benjamin structured by the temporality of sequential continuity (with its related ontological considerations). That Burke can be read otherwise, and thus that Turner's painting demands more sophisticated and complex temporal and ontological considerations, provides a way forward. It is only in the wake of this adventure, perhaps only in its calmer waters, that it will be possible to take up the problem of avant-garde experience.

There is another problem that is at stake within the interpretation of architecture. It concerns the relationship between an architect's writings and the buildings themselves. Clearly both are objects of interpretation. The problem concerns their identity *qua* objects of interpretation and their difference within that designation. Experience will provide, in the case of Eisenman, a way of approaching this problem. It is perhaps not surprising that Eisenman's own writings nearly always refer to the experience of buildings. In so doing the event of experience and the experience of the event come to be rethought in their being reworked. Prior to taking up the interpretive possibilities implicit in Burke's conception of the sublime – possibilities stemming for the most part from the conception of temporality proper to the sublime – it is essential to note, once again, the centrality attributed by Eisenman to experience.

Writing about the work undertaken on a loft in New York he notes that:

> The structure of the loft space is understood piece by piece as one glimpses fragments of the integrating text. The entire space has the effect of being a rare, isolated glimpse of some larger usually invisible context of vectors, currents and coded messages.[18]

This description needs to be read in relation to the already cited passage detailing the consequences of dining in House VI. There is, however, an additional important element that is introduced here and while it cannot be pursued it must, at least, be noted. It concerns the relationship between the visible and the invisible. The question that must be asked is what type of totality is the 'context' invoked by Eisenman. (A way towards understanding the complexity of this question may be provided by Burke's description of succession as conveying the artificial sublime.) The problem of the precise nature of the totality is also linked to the openness marking the overcoming of prediction.

The centrality of experience within Eisenman's writings does not mean that experience needs to be taken at face value. There are no experiences as such. Experience, as will be suggested, involves a complex doubling. The question within which a start can be made, is why it is that, when in Burke's terms, 'danger and pain press too nearly, they are incapable of giving any delight, and are more simply terrible'. The experience of 'danger and pain' is such that they are not within the actuality of their presence also objects of experience. There is therefore no sense in which there is a split such that it would then be possible to posit the reality of a recognition of experience that is coterminous with the experience itself. The body, fear and terror are present as one. The possibility of delight and hence of the sublime occurs only after 'a certain distance' and with 'certain modifications'. The terms 'distance' and 'modification' refer to a complex state of affairs.

The first element that must be noted is the causal relationship between the

source of terror and the state of terror. Neither, however, can be said to exist as
an object of experience in which there is any sense of reflexivity. The unity of
body, fear and terror predominates. The instant, as a consequence, must be
understood as excluding objectivity. Now the distance that emerges is the
breakdown of this unity in which the causal relation itself becomes an object of
experience. Its becoming an object is founded on the emergence within it of
alterity.

Benjamin

The same movement also occurs in the passage quoted (in fact misquoted)
from Pope earlier in the *Enquiry*. The passage as cited by Burke reads:

> As when a wretch, who conscious of his crime
> Pursued for murder from his native clime,
> Just gains sure frontier, breathless pale amaz'd
> All gaze, all wonder.[19]

After which Burke adds:

> when we have suffered from some violent emotion, the mind
> naturally continues in something like the same conditions after the
> cause which first produced it ceases to function.[20]

While the argument Burke advances concerns the relationship between
pleasure and pain in terms of which it will be possible to distinguish between
delight and pleasure, it is the internal operation of these passages that is
important here. They rehearse the movement that has already been noted. In
the lines from Pope the sublime effect emerges only when the terror no longer
dominates and is itself therefore taken as an object. The amazement marks the
emergence of the object and therefore of the causal relation also as an object.

In both passages distance creates the conditions in which objectivity
becomes possible. This distance, however, is not simple distance. It involves
doubling. With terror, within the all-encompassing power of a 'violent
emotion', there is no split between cause and effect such that the cause and the
effect are themselves possible objects of experience This possibility becomes
real with – and within – the split itself. The split creates the distance within
which the object becomes reworked and repeated such that it presents itself –
qua object of experience – for the first time. For Burke, therefore, the sublime
experience involves objects that are both the same and different. Amazement is
the re-recognition that is original. Distance involves a repetition in which the
object is reworked; hence the use of the term 'modification'. The distance is not
one of simple chronology in that the object is not re-presented; it is never just
given again within an atemporal sequence governed by similitude.[21] Hence the
analogy with the Freudian conception of *Nachträglichkeit*.[22] The action
engendering the sublime is deferred.

The doubling of the object within repetition in which it is presented again
for the first time is not sublime. It is rather that the Burkean conception of the
sublime allows for such a conception of the object to be understood. The use of
Burke is not intended to establish an analogy between avant-garde experience
and the sublime, but rather to provide the temporality proper to this particular
form of experience. The analogy, if there is one, is between the experience of an
object that resists understanding and explanation in the terms provided by
tradition (understood as the determination in advance), and 'terror' or 'violent

Benjamin emotion'. It is only with distance in which the experience itself becomes an object of experience that it is possible to break through shock and overcome silence. (The work of art remains a step ahead.)

The way therefore that tradition comes to be known emerges out of the work – both the work as object and the work as the process of objectification within interpretation. The truth of the object of avant-garde experience will be to mark the distance it constructs between sensibility and understanding. The understanding here is not the one equipped with regulative ideas. Understanding is the process that emerges out of sensibility. It is the understanding that is involved in the recognition of 'terror' and 'violent emotions' as objects of experience. Understanding will contain sensibility since it occasions delight. The postulated existence of regulative ideas is, when removed from the realm of the cognitive, the analogue of tradition. It is the resistance to them, transgression, felt within avant-garde experience, that comes to be grasped by the understanding, in its having found objectivity. The grasp is never complete.

It is within the domain of the avant-garde that the heterological will be affirmative. The re-reading of the tradition in which anoriginal heterogeneity is rediscovered for the first time will involve a particular conception of philosophical activity; the task of affirmation. It is clear that such a conception of interpretation bears the same relation to tradition as Eisenman's 'buildings' do to the tradition of architecture.

WORKS WITH OPEN DOORS

Eisenman's work, the experience of that work, the philosophy demanded by it, opens up the need to think philosophically beyond the recuperative and nihilistic unfolding of tradition. Tradition is housed – since there is no pure beyond – but the housing of tradition takes place within a plurality of possibilities that can no longer be foreclosed by function, by teleology or by the aesthetics of form. Works with open doors must be what are henceforth demanded by philosophy and architecture.

NOTES

1   I have discussed Descartes' architectural 'metaphor' in relation to Derrida's writings on architecture in 'Derrida, architecture and philosophy', *Architectural Design*, vol. 58, no. 3/4, 1988.
2   R. Descartes, *Discours de la méthode*, Paris: Edition Vrin, 1979, pp. 59–60.
3   R. Descartes, 'Meditations', in *Oeuvres Philosophiques*, F. Alquié (ed.), Paris: Garnier, 1963.
4   R. Descartes, *Discours de la méthode*, p. 74.
5   The question 'what is philosophy?' takes the place of all questions of the 'what is . . . ?' form. It is a question that seeks the identity of that which is named within the question. Consequently architecture, painting, sculpture, and even interpretation and aesthetics, could all come to be posed within this form of questioning. This point is outlined in slightly greater detail further on.
6   It is, of course, not just the essence that is in question here. The point could equally be made in relation to a singular and unique referent that was not expressed in terms of having an essence. This possibility means that what is, in fact, at stake is the necessity that what the name names is at the same time homogeneous and excludes the possibility of an initial heterogeneity. It is precisely this twofold necessity that contemporary philosophical writing, especially that associated with Derrida, has shown to be impossible.
7   P. Eisenman, *Houses of Cards*, New York: Oxford University Press, 1987, pp. 182–3.
8   The affirmative – a term 'borrowed' from Nietzsche and Derrida – has been redeployed here in

order to describe/locate those experimentations within the present that demand forms of *Benjamin* philosophical, aesthetic, political, physical responses that have not been handed down by tradition. In this sense the affirmative becomes a way of redeeming the avant-garde.

9   P. Eisenman, op. cit., p. 169.

10   P. Eisenman, 'The Blue Line Text,' in *Architectural Design*, vol. 58, no. 7/8, August 1988.

11   Ibid., p. 172.

12   P. Johnson and M. Wigley, *Deconstructive Architecture*, New York: Museum of Modern Art, 1988, p. 56.

13   P. Eisenman, 'Bio-Centrum Frankfurt', in *Architectural Design,* vol. 59, no. 1/2, 1989.

14   Eisenman, *Houses of Cards*, p. 181.

15   I have attempted to sketch this interconnection in 'Deconstruction and art/the art of deconstruction', in C. Norris and A. Benjamin, *What is Deconstruction?* (London: Academy Editions, 1988).

16   While he does not use the term 'affirmative', Alain Pélissier provides an excellent analysis of Eisenman's work, and especially of *House El Even Odd*, that attempts to identify what has been designated by it. See 'Microcosmos' in *Cahiers du CCI*, no. 1, *Architecture: récits, figures, fictions*, Paris: AA, 1986.

17   E. Burke, *A Philosophical Enquiry into the Origin of our Ideas of the Sublime and the Beautiful*, J. T. Boulton (ed.), Notre Dame: University of Notre Dame Press, 1968, p. 40.

18   P. Eisenman and F. Yorgancioglu, 'Tom's loft, New York,' in *Architectural Design*, vol. 58, no. 7/8, 1988, p. 35.

19   Burke, op. cit., p. 34.

20   Ibid., p. 35.

21   The problem of the relationship between writings and buildings can be, at least in part, resolved by the recognition that Eisenman in his writings is writing after and before the experience. The writings cannot set the conditions of possibility for experience. The writings do not come to be experienced as buildings. The writings mark the object. One can never be the other. And yet, of course, they are mutually informing. They both demand a different understanding of experience and of the act of interpretation. Their relationship will always be marked by the heterological.

22   I have dealt with the relationship between *Nachträglichkeit* and interpretation in considerable detail in 'Translating Origins: Philosophy and Psychoanalysis' in L. Venuti ed., *Rethinking Translation: Discourse, Subjectivity and Ideology* (London: Routledge, 1992).

HÉLÈNE CIXOUS

_____

Hélène Cixous

Hélène Cixous (b. 1937) is a versatile French writer and critic who has worked in a variety of areas – fiction, theatre and theoretical writing – in a style frequently transgressive of genre. Associated with the *'Psychanalyse et Politique'* group of feminists, her work has been informed by a strong psychoanalytic impulse which seeks to challenge unconscious structures of exclusion. Cixous has argued instead for a sexual difference based on openness to the other, and has promoted a 'feminine writing' – *écriture féminine* – as a strategy of exploring difference in a non-exclusionary mode. Such writing is not limited to women, however, and some of the best examples have been the works of male authors such as James Joyce.

Like much of her other writing, 'Attacks of the Castle' contains traces of autobiographical material and a significant psychoanalytic dimension. It draws in particular on her earlier work on Kafka's short story 'Before the Law', which had been used by Cixous as an allegory for female exclusion under patriarchy. In Kafka's story a man arrives before the door to the Law, but remains convinced of his own exclusion, even though the door remains open. The theme of access and denial runs throughout 'Attacks of the Castle'. Prague is a city that can never be fully captured by the onto-hermeneutical process. It is not Prague, but Pragues, promised Pragues to which the author, like the character in Kafka's tale, would never gain entry. 'Promised Pragues. You dream of going. You cannot go. What would happen if you went?' The theme of Prague as a city of multiple interpretations echoes Cixous' earlier observations on Monet's twenty-six paintings, each an attempt to 'capture' Rouen Cathedral. The 'truth' of Rouen Cathedral is in fact twenty-six cathedrals. It is in her own very painterly and self-reflexive writing on Prague – a Prague of traces, memories and meanings erased by repetition – that Cixous opens up the possibility of a new way of writing about the city.

_____

ATTACKS OF THE CASTLE

Cixous

I was in Prague two weeks ago, it was the first time and the only thing I absolutely wanted to see was Kafka's tomb. But to-see-Kafka's-tomb does not simply mean to see Kafka's tomb. I was at last in Prague and I wanted at last to see the hand, the trace, the footprint, that is to say the natural and naked fleshy face of the author of the Letter, that is to say the eyelids of god. It is now thirty-five years that I have fought for this day, a long combat and obscure like all combats. One never knows in the heat of the struggle who one is everything being mixed up, desire, fear, hostility of love, one fights, desire is a battle between oneself against oneself, an imagination of obstacles to stop oneself from going off to lose the war.

But finally I was there, too bad. The long-awaited day was inevitable. I wanted to see Kafka's tomb. Knowing perfectly well (having verified it so many times) that you cannot see what you want to see, I went to the cemetery to see what I could not see. It's the law. All is law. It's because of desire. The law makes its nest in the peel of desire. Go on: you will not enter. If you did not desire to go, there would be a chance that the door would open. I went to Israelica Street. And then the cemetery was closed. So we went around the cemetery which is immense. I had no hope. Every now and again there were portals of forged iron, the car drove by the portals, heavily chained. All were closed. At one particular moment, the car stopped near a large rusted portal with chained iron bars. I pressed myself against the portal, because it was written you will press yourself against the rusted portal of the promised land, I had forgotten. And there before me was Kafka's tomb, and I was before him.

It is a clean tomb, modern, the stone is a raised stone, those who have seen it before me say it is black, but this one is white, my one, the one I saw standing facing me standing facing it was thin white upright, *my size*. It was turned toward me and on its brow the words Dr Franz Kafka looked at me.

I have already seen this tomb look at me with eyes metamorphosed into letters of a name. It was in the cemetery of Algiers, I looked at my father look at me with his eyes that said his name gravely to me, as do children and dead people: Dr Georges Cixous.

So standing face to face my hands on the rusted bars I knew that I always looked for the same face solemnly simplified to childhood.

The tomb and I were separated by the high locked portal, and it was good. Desire and fear answered together was unhoped-for. I clutched the bars.

There are three cities I would like to go to and I will never make it. Though I can do everything to try to get there, in reality I do not make it, I mean it's impossible for me to find myself there in the flesh in the streets in the squares in the roads in the walls bridges towers cathedrals façades courtyards quays rivers and oceans, they are still well guarded. These are the cities I have the most meditated on, lay siege to frequented and run through in dreams in stories in guides I have studied them in dictionaries I have lived in them if not in this life then in another life.

Promised Pragues. You dream of going. You cannot go. What would happen if you went?

Cixous   How can one not go to Athens even while going there? Freud asked himself
for decades until the September day when he decided to go to Corfu from
Trieste where he was staying with his brother. 'Corfu?!' a friend said to him. 'In
the middle of summer? Insanity! You would be better off going to Athens for 3
days.' And indeed the Lloyd's steamer left that afternoon, but the two brothers
were not at all sure. Therefore they were quite surprised when in spite of everything that was opposed to Athens they found themselves there, they were
standing on the Acropolis in reality, but Freud only half believed it: it all existed
as the two brothers had learned in school. From the schoolbook to the landscape the consequence was quite good. It was too beautiful to be true. But
Freud never would have been able to find himself in Athens either totally or
half-way if he had not decided to go to Corfu.

And where should I go, to what city other than Prague so as to arrive in
Prague only by guile or by chance without having wanted it?

I went to Vienna. Walking down the Berggasse at a sharp slope to ring at Dr
Freud's door, I felt Prague breathing a short distance away. There we were on
the road that separates-unites Vienna and Prague. The car went neither to the
right nor to the left. We passed a few kilometers from Trnava where Michael
Klein my grandfather was born. I have never been there. But Trnava exists in
the Atlas. At the time the border floated in the wind and you were one day
Czech one day Austrian and every day Bohemian. An inhabitant of Turnau of
Trnava. One day Dr Franz Kafka of Prague came to stay at Turnau, at the hotel
where my grandfather Michael Klein had come to deliver fresh produce from
the farm yesterday. I lived all of this. It is like the day Dr Freud had just left the
Berggasse to go to Gmund when Dr Kafka passed in front of Dr Freud's house
his head lowered, because it was a dream of a missed encounter.

I did not go to Turnau where I will never go, but my life passed close by.
Fields of poppies and of blue flax spread between us the blue and red sheet of
separation.

For centuries my desire has been haunted by a being called sometimes die
Altneusynagoge sometimes Staronova Synagoga and that I call the Oldyoung
Synagogue. And always I roam outside the Old Jewish Cemetery, Alt Jüdischen
Friedhof, absolute desire without commentary blind confident. What do I
want? I will see. I am expected. I am expecting it. I am waiting for myself there.

In dreams I have often gone there. The cemetery there is immense and sweet
like an ocean. Squirrels dance around pine trees, merry reincarnations of the
dead. I search. I want to see the tomb that is my cradle. I want to see my cradle,
the cradle of my tombs, the tomb of my childhood, the source of my dreams
and of my worries.

Everyone has gone to the Old Jewish Cemetery except me. My children my
friends my loves everyone has gone without me before me for me beyond me to
lean over my cradles. My mother too, except me.

Nevertheless I was waiting for the possibility. I cannot go lightly to see the
tomb of my cradles. I was waiting for the person who would accompany me,
the being who would be necessary enough delicate enough to break with me the
bread of awaiting. The messiah of the Oldyoung synagogue. But if he did not
come, ever?

But on the other hand, we cannot never have gone to our tomb-cradle; it is
an obligation. We must go to the sources before the hour of death. It's that all

human destinies are launched from a tomb. We do not always know it, but in   *Cixous*
the end we return to port.

One day I thought everything started from there, enough backing away since
in the end I will go let's go there now so I went there as a lone woman as a silent
woman as a widow, as a person and on the exterior of all dream.

No sooner inside – there I was pushed back like an attack. How to take it? I
look everywhere for the door, the entrance, the defect. Passing by the Charles
Bridge and its squads of statues planted like impassive saints coming off on the
side of Mala Strana, by the alley of the Saxons, then by Velkoprevorske Square
by Prokopka Alley up to Malostravske Namesti at a brisk pace passing in front
of the Schönborn Palace then going up by Bretislavova until the Nerudova and
there you go back down the slope until Mala Strana without ever managing to
penetrate.

The next day, second try: on the quays up to the National Theatre, then
coming back up to Starometske, passing by Miners' Road, it was fleeing just in
front of me. Ten times I asked directions in German, they stared at me as a false
ghost, no one spoke the tongue of my parents any more. Effacement effacement
thy name is City.

Thirdly by Celetna Road passing in front of the house at the Golden Angel
up to Ovocny Square, the fruit market, from there up to the Tyl Theatre the
flowered balconies of which had thrown themselves out of the interior stage of
the Opera by the window on that day – because the play takes place at this very
moment on the Old City Square. It was Sunday. Then, on the square, instead of
the black and plump monument to Jan Hus, there is no monument, no square
everything is conjured away, neither can you see the Starometsky Orlo, the
clock on which yesterday the sun and the moon still turned, nor the palaces,
nor the houses, the centre of the universe is covered this Sunday with a flood of
feet in sneakers. It was the marathon that had attacked the city introducing the
virus of the Sneaker. The City had fallen? Sneaker, Praguean horse, so with your
Synecdoche you have vanquished the impregnable city!? Around the tank to
Jan Hus topped with hundreds of sneakers the air was fluorescent blue. Venus
of the whole country, the victorious sneakers rolled thousands of cans with the
effigy of Coca-cola under the chaos of their hooves. Suddenly exhausted, the
macabre carnival collapsed, loosing its masks. A universal tee-shirt enveloped
the remains of the disembowelled City. From the shroud emerged only the two
untamable horns of the Tyn church.

But the next day the Castle began again.

There has never been a more pricked-up city.

A City? An army. There is none more combative more erect, more
provocative. A City? A heroine, called Prague. At dawn barely is one rising, she is
already up, her lances standing, her helmets pricked. From the heights of her hills
she apostrophes you: Try to take me! She stamps her foot, she envelops herself in
her stone coat. Wherever one is, raising one's head, she is there – brandished
phallic modest, omnipresent and inaccessible. There is none more impregnable.
Certain cities remain intact, the crowds believe they trample them – the regiments
of tourists banderilla it with foreign flags, course through the roads, occupy the
arcades, no attack will ever force the City to surrender.

Over the centuries suitors had presented themselves, had conquered it,

Cixous tamed it they thought; they hurried to build their palaces, during the construction anxiety aged them, knowing that the walls would outlive them made their flesh sweat. But one after another, they constructed, it was the City that wanted it. It was fate to build until you're done in; then there was a gust of wind, the lords fell successively: into ashes and into bloods and the palaces were there, calm under the snow.

No, this is not a City.

A reserve of centuries of alleys of tombs.

Centuries: alleys: tombs: it is all interchangeable.

I do not know why, why Prague, Prague, why so many centuries flow in your alleys? Full of powder of generations, flasks of constructions.

Stratigraphy of the layers of the Praguean bark. Columns of dates, piles of styles.

10th century – 1050, ca. 1050 – ca. 1260, ca. 1260 – 1310, 1310 – 1419, ca. 1450 – 1526, 1538 – 1580, ca. 1580 – 1620, 1611 – 1690, 1690 – 1745, 1745 – 1780, 1780 – 1830, 1895 – 1914, 1918 – 1939: spreading Gothic high Baroque neo-Renaissance, neo-Baroque Functionalism and Constructivism Late Renaissance (Mannerism) pre-Romanesque architecture (Prague Castle, Vysehrad, Brevnov) primitive Gothic Rococo (late Baroque) Art Nouveau (Secession) high Renaissance Romanesque architecture Romantic Historicism: neo-Romanesque style, neo-Gothic primitive Baroque late Gothic (flamboyant, of Vladislav).

Everything started with the Castle, Vysehrad in 1050 Otto architecture, and the Castle gave to the site the tables of the law: and you shall build on the Red Sea, and you shall build hotels and churches on the dark lake of blood. All will end with the Castle. But this is a fable: and that is the Castle of Babble with sleeping inhabitants. A single dead person keeps watch still, like a candle lit in a match box at 22 Alchemists Road.

Everywhere cranes rise in an assault of the sky. No this is not yet a city, it's an idea, it's a fury of interminable inconstruction. Nothing but Pelions and Ossases. The idea is at the end to build the city one day on the summit of the heap.

I was in Prague for the first time and Prague was not there. She had just left, or else it was he, the spirit of the City, the doctor K, the inhabitant of our 'Right this minute' house. We have heard about it this Odradek, this bobbin that is not a bobbin, that is not only a bobbin, and that stands on two small sticks as on two legs. One could think that it was useful once and that it is broken, but that is a mistake. It is something that was described by Dr Franz Kafka standing on two small stick legs, it has all the appearance of the thing that has lost its meaning, but one cannot speak without being mistaken, because Odradek is extremely mobile, while I speak, he runs off and he is no longer here. One can only look for him.

So where is he? Is he in the dictionary, in a museum? No, 'he is now in the attic, now in the stairwell, now in the halls and now in the entranceway'. He gets around a lot. He has no lodgings, he is in all the parts of the house that do not lodge, that are not counted, places where one only passes through or else disappears.

Or else was it I who was not there? When we are alive we do not know we are ghosts.

Cixous

What are we in the promised cities? The contemporary dead of our descendants, the future returning ghosts. It is Sunday today I pass in front of the 'Right this moment' house that K. left just now sixty years ago to go to his office. He went out the door and he took off. A person who is not yet born will pass by here in forty years, and will wind the cut string onto our bobbin.

Time is a square wheel. Running fast enough in the alleys I could perhaps catch him who passed through here even before I was born before I was born.

For this it suffices that the centuries be well guarded inside the Castle.

Imaginary memories, imaginary life: I have already lived here we lived on the fourth floor, by the window of the living room you could see the corner of the City Hall. No more imaginary a life than my other ancient lives. The country of the past belongs to the same continent as the imagined country. They meet and mingle their fields, their squares, their sweet salt waters. At the back of the picture the streets of Oran intersect the streets of Prague.

We dream of going to Prague. We do not know how to go. We fear. We go. Once inside we do not find it. We wander for a long time in the Castle. If there had not been the minuscule door 22 Zlata Ulicke, the minuscule door in Gold Street, to cast the anchor for a minute, we would never even have landed at all.

Where is the Synagogue? Where is the door?

Happily, we never get there. It was too late. It had just closed. We would not have succeeded in entering.

Blessed be the closed doors and the rusted portals. You wanted to enter?

Happily we failed.

Where is the Oldyoung Jewish cemetery enchanted with squirrels? – Here, here, between the dark severe walls, just in front of your nose. Above our humiliated heads powerful volleys of crows scream their brusque abrupt menaces. It is a harsh miracle, these crows: they caw like lions inside a minuscule square of sky just vertical to the minuscule hanky-full of dead people. The old Jewish cemetery raises its invisible well filled with tombs up to the feet of the sky, you do not see the end of it, the crows scream up there: it's here, it's here. I had never seen a cemetery so high and so small, like a roll of dead people that climbs and descends from the bottom of the earth up to the bottom of the sky. Make room, thunder the crows, let the dead climb past!

I had not been told that the cemetery was so small. I had not been told that the thousand year city leaves only the end of its nose of tombs and a few worn teeth visible at the surface of the century. The tombs bury the tombs. Twelve layers of tombs.

I had not been told of the doll houses, the doll Synagogue, the doll people. Everything dwarfed. Everything sacred.

Your Prague is not in Prague, as you can well see. Promised Prague is in the sky under the earth.

I clutched the bars in my rusted hands. In front of me svelte distracted white the tomb looked at me with its bright eyes of words. How alive and young you are, I thought. While all the other ghosts in the palaces, behind the sgraffitoed walls, all the ghosts are dead. 'You have not changed,' I said.

GILLES DELEUZE

French philosopher Gilles Deleuze (1925–95) has enjoyed a reputation as one of the most innovatory thinkers in an age increasingly preoccupied with the question of complexity. Indeed Michel Foucault once predicted that the twentieth century would be known as Deleuzian. Deleuze's thought is a combination of commentary on other thinkers – notably Nietzsche and Foucault – and his own highly original investigations, suffused in his later work by the influence of his collaborator, the radical psychoanalyst Félix Guattari.

Deleuze was above all a theorist of flux, plurality and movement. He rejected the more traditional concepts of sameness and representation in favour of repetition, proliferation and difference. He elaborated a series of concepts such as the 'monad', the 'striated' and the 'fold', and in particular championed the 'rhizome'. It would be doing an injustice to the sophistication of Deleuze's thought to attempt any short-hand definition of such terms. It is precisely the fluidity of his thought that denies such totalizing strategies.

The extract 'City/State' reflects Deleuze's increasing preoccupation with the theme of connection. Here he examines, in collaboration with Guattari, the opposition between town and state, 'two forms, two speeds of deterritorialization'. The town should be perceived as a 'correlate of the road', as a 'function of circulation and of circuits'. The town is a circuit-point within a network of flow, 'a phenomenon of transconsistency'. The state, by comparison, offers a more restrictive model. It is a 'phenomenon of intraconsistency', an internal and isolated circuit, whose power is dependent on stratification and subordination. Space can be seen as a complex interaction between these two models, each warding off and anticipating the other in a process of 'reciprocal presupposition', such that the state could even be read as a component within a 'worldwide axiomatic that is like a single city'.

Deleuze's essay, 'Postscript on the Societies of Control', elaborates themes raised initially by Foucault. The disciplinary societies have now given way to societies of control. Emblematic of this is the shift from factories to corporations and from machines to computers. Physical discipline has been replaced by more gaseous systems of control, where the credit card has supplanted the gaze of the foreman. Humankind is no longer enclosed by physical space, but forever trapped by debt, ensnared in a system of limitless postponement. 'The burrows of the molehill' have been replaced by the complex 'coils of the serpent'.

Deleuze's project can be seen to be highly relevant to the world of architecture. Not least, his insights on societies of control have offered a crucial retake on the influence of architectural form on human behaviour. Yet his work is directed primarily towards processes of thought and not practices of building. Too often his sophisticated theory has been appropriated in a simplistic fashion and translated crudely into a manifesto for complex architectural forms.

POSTSCRIPT ON THE SOCIETIES OF CONTROL *Deleuze*

HISTORICAL

Foucault located the *disciplinary societies* in the eighteenth and nineteenth centuries; they reach their height at the outset of the twentieth. They initiate the organization of vast spaces of enclosure. The individual never ceases passing from one closed environment to another, each having its own laws: first, the family; then the school ('you are no longer in your family'); then the barracks ('you are no longer at school'); then the factory; from time to time the hospital; possibly the prison, the pre-eminent instance of the enclosed environment. It's the prison that serves as the analogical model: at the sight of some labourers, the heroine of Rossellini's *Europa '51* could exclaim, 'I thought I was seeing convicts.'

Foucault has brilliantly analysed the ideal project of these environments of enclosure, particularly visible within the factory: to concentrate; to distribute in space; to order in time; to compose a productive force within the dimension of space-time whose effect will be greater than the sum of its component forces. But what Foucault recognized as well was the transience of this model: it succeeded that of the *societies of sovereignty*, the goal and functions of which were something quite different (to tax rather than to organize production, to rule on death rather than to administer life); the transition took place over time, and Napoleon seemed to effect the large-scale conversion from one society to the other. But in their turn the disciplines underwent a crisis to the benefit of new forces that were gradually instituted and which accelerated after the Second World War: a disciplinary society was what we already no longer were, what we had ceased to be.

We are in a generalized crisis in relation to all the environments of enclosure – prison, hospital, factory, school, family. The family is an 'interior', in crisis like all other interiors – scholarly, professional, etc. The administrations in charge never cease announcing supposedly necessary reforms: to reform schools, to reform industries, hospitals, the armed forces, prisons. But everyone knows that these institutions are finished, whatever the length of their expiration periods. It's only a matter of administering their last rites and of keeping people employed until the installation of the new forces knocking at the door. These are the *societies of control*, which are in the process of replacing the disciplinary societies. 'Control' is the name Burroughs proposes as a term for the new monster, one that Foucault recognizes as our immediate future. Paul Virilio also is continually analysing the ultrarapid forms of free-floating control that replaced the old disciplines operating in the time frame of a closed system. There is no need here to invoke the extraordinary pharmaceutical productions, the molecular engineering, the genetic manipulations, although these are slated to enter into the new process. There is no need to ask which is the toughest or most tolerable regime, for it's within each of them that liberating and enslaving forces confront one another. For example, in the crisis of the hospital as environment of enclosure, neighbourhood clinics, hospices and day care could at first express new freedom, but they could participate as well in mechanisms of control that are equal to the harshest of confinements. There is no need to fear or hope, but only to look for new weapons.

Deleuze   LOGIC

The different internments or spaces of enclosure through which the individual passes are independent variables: each time one is supposed to start from zero, and although a common language for all these places exists, it is *analogical*. On the other hand, the different control mechanisms are inseparable variations, forming a system of variable geometry the language of which is *numerical* (which doesn't necessarily mean binary). Enclosures are *moulds*, distinct castings, but controls are a *modulation*, like a self-deforming cast that will continuously change from one moment to the other, or like a sieve whose mesh will transmute from point to point.

This is obvious in the matter of salaries: the factory was a body that contained its internal forces at a level of equilibrium, the highest possible in terms of production, the lowest possible in terms of wages; but in a society of control, the corporation has replaced the factory, and the corporation is a spirit, a gas. Of course the factory was already familiar with the system of bonuses, but the corporation works more deeply to impose a modulation of each salary, in states of perpetual metastability that operate through challenges, contests and highly comic group sessions. If the most idiotic television game shows are so successful, it's because they express the corporate situation with great precision. The factory constituted individuals as a single body to the double advantage of the boss who surveyed each element within the mass and the unions who mobilized a mass resistance; but the corporation constantly presents the brashest rivalry as a healthy form of emulation, an excellent motivational force that opposes individuals against one another and runs through each, dividing each within. The modulating principle of 'salary according to merit' has not failed to tempt national education itself. Indeed, just as the corporation replaces the factory, *perpetual training* tends to replace the *school*, and continuous control to replace the examination. Which is the surest way of delivering the school over to the corporation.

In the disciplinary societies one was always starting again (from school to the barracks, from the barracks to the factory), while in the societies of control one is never finished with anything – the corporation, the educational system, the armed services being metastable states coexisting in one and the same modulation, like a universal system of deformation. In *The Trial*, Kafka, who had already placed himself at the pivotal point between two types of social formation, described the most fearsome of juridical forms. The *apparent acquittal* of the disciplinary societies (between two incarcerations); and the *limitless postponements* of the societies of control (in continuous variation) are two very different modes of juridical life, and if our law is hesitant, itself in crisis, it's because we are leaving one in order to enter into the other. The disciplinary societies have two poles: the signature that designates the *individual*, and the number or administrative numeration that indicates his or her position within a *mass*. This is because the disciplines never saw any incompatibility between these two, and because at the same time power individualizes and masses together, that is, constitutes those over whom it exercises power into a body and moulds the individuality of each member of that body. (Foucault saw the origin of this double charge in the pastoral power of the priest – the flock and each of its animals – but civil power moves in turn and by other means to

make itself lay 'priest'.) In the societies of control, on the other hand, what is   *Deleuze*
important is no longer either a signature or a number, but a code: the code is a
password, while on the other hand the disciplinary societies are regulated by
watchwords (as much from the point of view of integration as from that of
resistance). The numerical language of control is made of codes that mark
access to information, or reject it. We no longer find ourselves dealing with the
mass/individual pair. Individuals have become '*dividuals*', and masses, samples,
data, markets or '*banks*'. Perhaps it is money that expresses the distinction
between the two societies best, since discipline always referred back to minted
money that locks gold in as numerical standard, while control relates to
floating rates of exchange, modulated according to a rate established by a set of
standard currencies. The old monetary mole is the animal of the spaces of
enclosure, but the serpent is that of the societies of control. We have passed
from one animal to the other, from the mole to the serpent, in the system under
which we live, but also in our manner of living and in our relations with others.
The disciplinary man was a discontinuous producer of energy, but the man of
control is undulatory, in orbit, in a continuous network. Everywhere *surfing*
has already replaced the older *sports*.

Types of machines are easily matched with each type of society – not that
machines are determining, but because they express those social forms capable
of generating them and using them. The old societies of sovereignty made use of
simple machines – levers, pulleys, clocks; but the recent disciplinary societies
equipped themselves with machines involving energy, with the passive danger
of entropy and the active danger of sabotage; the societies of control operate
with machines of a third type, computers, whose passive danger is jamming and
whose active one is piracy and the introduction of viruses. This technological
evolution must be, even more profoundly, a mutation of capitalism, an
already well-known or familiar mutation that can be summed up as follows:
nineteenth-century capitalism is a capitalism of concentration, for production
and for property. It therefore erects the factory as a space of enclosure, the
capitalist being the owner of the means of production but also, progressively,
the owner of other spaces conceived through analogy (the worker's familial
house, the school). As for markets, they are conquered sometimes by
specialization, sometimes by colonization, sometimes by lowering the costs of
production. But, in the present situation, capitalism is no longer involved in
production, which it often relegates to the Third World, even for the complex
forms of textiles, metallurgy, or oil production. It's a capitalism of higher-order
production. It no longer buys raw materials and no longer sells the finished
products: it buys the finished products or assembles parts. What it wants to sell
is services and what it wants to buy is stocks. This is no longer a capitalism for
production but for the product, which is to say, for being sold or marketed.
Thus it is essentially dispersive, and the factory has given way to the corporation. The family, the school, the army, the factory are no longer the distinct
analogical spaces that converge towards an owner – state or private power –
but coded figures – deformable and transformable – of a single corporation that
now has only stockholders. Even art has left the spaces of enclosure in order to
enter into the open circuits of the bank. The conquests of the market are made
by grabbing control and no longer by disciplinary training, by fixing the
exchange rate much more than by lowering costs, by transformation of the

Deleuze product more than by specialization of production. Corruption thereby gains a new power. Marketing has become the centre or the 'soul' of the corporation. We are taught that corporations have a soul, which is the most terrifying news in the world. The operation of markets is now the instrument of social control and forms the impudent breed of our masters. Control is short-term and of rapid rates of turnover, but also continuous and without limit, while discipline was of long duration, infinite and discontinuous. Man is no longer man enclosed, but man in debt. It is true that capitalism has retained as a constant the extreme poverty of three-quarters of humanity, too poor for debt, too numerous for confinement: control will not only have to deal with erosions of frontiers but with the explosions within shanty towns or ghettos.

PROGRAMME

The conception of a control mechanism, giving the position of any element within an open environment at any given instant (whether animal in a reserve or human in a corporation, as with an electronic collar), is not necessarily one of science fiction. Félix Guattari has imagined a city where one would be able to leave one's apartment, one's street, one's neighbourhood, thanks to one's (dividual) electronic card that raises a given barrier; but the card could just as easily be rejected on a given day or between certain hours; what counts is not the barrier but the computer that tracks each person's position – licit or illicit – and effects a universal modulation.

The socio-technological study of the mechanisms of control, grasped at their inception, would have to be categorical and to describe what is already in the process of substitution for the disciplinary sites of enclosure, whose crisis is everywhere proclaimed. It may be that older methods, borrowed from the former societies of sovereignty, will return to the fore, but with the necessary modifications. What counts is that we are at the beginning of something. In the *prison system*: the attempt to find penalties of 'substitution', at least for petty crimes, and the use of electronic collars that force the convicted person to stay at home during certain hours. For the *school system*: continuous forms of control, and the effect on the school of perpetual training, the corresponding abandonment of all university research, the introduction of the 'corporation' at all levels of schooling. For the *hospital system*: the new medicine 'without doctor or patient' that singles out potential sick people and subjects at risk, which in no way attests to individuation – as they say – but substitutes for the individual or numerical body the code of a 'dividual' material to be controlled. In the *corporate system*: new ways of handling money, profits and humans that no longer pass through the old factory form. These are very small examples, but ones that will allow for better understanding of what is meant by the crisis of the institutions, which is to say, the progressive and dispersed installation of a new system of domination. One of the most important questions will concern the ineptitude of the unions: tied to the whole of their history of struggle against the disciplines or within the spaces of enclosure, will they be able to adapt themselves or will they give way to new forms of resistance against the societies of control? Can we already grasp the rough outlines of these coming forms, capable of threatening the joys of marketing? Many young people strangely boast of being 'motivated'; they re-request apprenticeships and

permanent training. It's up to them to discover what they're being made to   *Deleuze*
serve, just as their elders discovered, not without difficulty, the *telos* of the
disciplines. The coils of a serpent are even more complex than the burrows of a
molehill.

CITY/STATE (with Félix Guattari)

In so-called primitive societies there exist collective mechanisms which
simultaneously ward off and anticipate the formation of a central power. The
appearance of a central power is thus a function of a threshold or degree
beyond which what is conjured away ceases to be so and arrives. This threshold
of consistency or of constraint is not evolutionary, but coexists with what has
not crossed it. What is more, a distinction must be made between different
thresholds of consistency: the town and the State, however complementary, are
not the same thing. The 'urban revolution' and the 'state revolution' may
coincide, but are not one. In both cases there is a central power, but it does not
assume the same figure. Certain authors have made a distinction between the
palatial or imperial system (palace temple) and the urban town system. In both
cases there is a town, but in one case the town is an outgrowth of the palace or
temple and in the other the palace or the temple is a concretion of the town. In
one case the town par excellence is the capital, and in the other the metropolis.
Sumer already attests to a town-solution, as opposed to the imperial solution of
Egypt. But to an even greater extent, it was the Mediterranean world, with the
Pelasgians, Phoenicians, Greeks and Carthaginians, that created an urban
tissue distinct from the imperial organisms of the Orient.[1] Once again, the
question is not one of evolution, but of two thresholds of consistency that are
themselves coexistent. They differ in several respects.

The town is the correlate of the road. The town exists only as a function of
circulation and of circuits; it is a singular point on the circuits which create it
and which it creates. It is defined by entries and exits: something must enter it
and exit from it. It imposes a frequency. It effects a polarization of matter, inert,
living or human; it causes the *phylum*, the flow, to pass through specific places,
along horizontal lines. It is a phenomenon of transconsistency, a network,
because it is fundamentally in contact with other towns. It represents a threshold of deterritorialization because whatever the material involved, it must be
deterritorialized enough to enter the network, to submit to the polarization, to
follow the circuit of urban and road recoding. The maximum deterritorialization appears in the tendency of maritime and commercial towns to separate
from the backcountry, from the countryside (Athens, Carthage, Venice). The
commercial character of the town has often been emphasized, but the commerce in question is also spiritual, as in a network of monasteries or temple-
cities. Towns are points-circuits of every kind, which enter into counterpoint
along horizontal lines; they operate a complete but local town-by-town
integration. Each one constitutes a central power, but is a power of polarization
or of the middle (*milieu*), of forced co-ordination. That is why this kind of
power has egalitarian pretensions, regardless of the form it takes: tyrannical,
democratic, oligarchic, aristocratic. . . . Town power invents the idea of the

Deleuze magistrature, which is very different from the State civil-service sector (*fonctionnariat*).[2] Who can say where the greatest civil violence resides?

The State proceeds otherwise: it is a phenomenon of intraconsistency. It makes points resonate together, points that are not necessarily already town-poles, but even diverse points of order – geographic, ethnic, linguistic, moral, economic, technological particularities. The State makes the town resonate with the countryside. It operates by stratification: in other words, it forms a vertical, hierarchized aggregate that spans the horizontal lines in a dimension of depth. In retaining given elements, it necessarily cuts off their relations with other elements, which become exterior; it inhibits, slows down or controls those relations. If the State has a circuit of its own, it is an internal circuit dependent primarily upon resonance; it is a zone of recurrence that isolates itself from the remainder of the network, even if in order to do so it must exert even stricter controls over its relations with that remainder. The question is not to find out whether what is retained is natural or artificial (borders) because in any event there is deterritorialization. But in this case deterritorialization is a result of the territory itself being taken as an object, as a material to stratify, to make resonate. Thus the central power of the State is hierarchical and constitutes a civil-service sector; the centre is not in the middle (*au milieu*) but on top because the only way it can recombine what it isolates is through subordination. Of course, there is a multiplicity of States no less than of towns, but it is not the same type of multiplicity: there are as many States as there are vertical cross-sections in dimension of depth, each separated off from the others, whereas the town is inseparable from the horizontal network of towns. Each State is a global (not local) integration, a redundancy of resonance (not of frequency), an operation of the stratification of the territory (not of the polarization of the milieu).

It is possible to reconstruct how primitive societies warded off both thresholds, while at the same time anticipating them. Lévi-Strauss has shown that the same villages are susceptible to two presentations, one segmentary and egalitarian, the other encompassing and hierarchized. These are like two potentials, one anticipating a central point common to two horizontal segments, the other anticipating a central point external to a straight line.[3] Primitive societies do not lack formations of power; they even have many of them. But what prevents the potential central points from crystallizing, from taking on consistency, are precisely those mechanisms that keep the formations of power both from resonating together in a higher point and from becoming polarized at a common point: the circles are not concentric, and the two segments have need of a third segment through which to communicate.[4] This is the sense in which primitive societies have not crossed either the town-threshold or the State-threshold.

If we now turn our attention to the two thresholds of consistency, it is clear that they imply a deterritorialization in relation to the primitive territorial code. It is futile to ask which came first, the city or the State, the urban or state revolution, because the two are in reciprocal presupposition. Both the melodic line of the towns and the harmonic cross-sections of the States are necessary to effect the striation of space. The only question that arises is the possibility that there may be an inverse relation at the heart of this reciprocity. For although the archaic imperial State necessarily included towns of considerable size, they

remained all the more strictly subordinated to the State the more it extended its   *Deleuze*
monopoly over foreign trade. On the other hand, the town tended to break free
when the State's overcoding itself provoked decoded flows. A decoding was
coupled with the deterritorialization and amplified it: the necessary recoding
was then achieved through a certain autonomy of the towns or else directly
through corporative and commercial towns freed from the State-form. Thus
towns arose that no longer had a connection to their own land because they
assured the trade between empires or, better, because they themselves
constituted a free commercial network with other towns. There is therefore an
adventure proper to towns in the zones where the most intense decoding
occurs: for example, the ancient Aegean world or the Western world of the
Middle Ages and the Renaissance. Could it not be said that capitalism is the
fruit of the towns and arises when an urban recoding tends to replace State
overcoding? This, however, was not the case. The towns did not create
capitalism. The banking and commercial towns, being unproductive and indifferent to the backcountry, did not perform a recoding without also inhibiting
the general conjunction of decoded flows. If it is true that they anticipated
capitalism, they in turn did not anticipate it without also warding it off. They
do not cross this new threshold. Thus it is necessary to expand the hypothesis
of mechanisms both anticipatory and inhibiting: these mechanisms are at play
not only in primitive societies, but also in the conflict of towns 'against' the
State and 'against' capitalism. Finally, it was through the State-form and not
the town-form that capitalism triumphed: this occurred when the Western
States became models of realization for an axiomatic of decoded flows, and in
that way resubjugated the towns. As Braudel says, there were '*always two
runners*, the state and the town' – two forms and two speeds of deterritorialization – and 'the state usually won . . . everywhere in Europe, it disciplined the towns with instinctive relentlessness, whether or not it used
violence . . . the states caught up with the forward gallop of the towns.'[5] But the
relation is a reciprocal one: if it is the modern State that gives capitalism its
models of realization, what is thus realized is an independent, worldwide
axiomatic that is like a single City, megalopolis or 'megamachine' of which the
States are parts or neighbourhoods.

NOTES

1   On Chinese towns and their subordination to the imperial principle see Etienne Balazs,
     Chinese Civilisation and Bureaucracy, H.M. Wright (trans.), New Haven: Yale University
     Press, 1964, p. 410: 'The social structures in both India and China automatically rejected the
     town and offered, as it were, refractory, substandard material to it. It was because society was
     well and truly frozen in a sort of irreducible system, a previous crystallization.'
2   From all of these standpoints, François Châtelet questions the classical notion of the city-state
     and doubts that the Athenian city can be equated with any variety of State ('La Grèce
     classique, la Raison, L'Etat' in Alberto Asor Rosa *et al.*, *En marge, l'Occident et ses autres*,
     Paris: Aubier Montaigne, 1978. Islam was to confront analogous problems, as would Italy,
     Germany and Flanders beginning in the eleventh century: in these cases, political power does
     not imply the State-form. An example is the community of Hanseatic towns, which lacked
     functionaries, an army and even legal status. The town is always inside a network of towns,
     but the 'network of towns' does not coincide with the 'mosaic of States': on all of these points,
     see the analyses of François Fourquet and Lion Murard, *Généalogie des équipments collectifs*,
     Paris, 10/18, pp. 79–106.
3   Claude Lévi-Strauss, *Structural Anthropology*, Claire Jacobson and Brooke Grundfest Schrept
     (trans.), New York: Basic Books, 1963, pp. 150–1.

Deleuze   4   Louis Berthe analyses a specific example of the need for a 'third village' to prevent the directional circuit from closing: 'Aines et cadets, l'alliance et la hierarchie chez les Baduj', *L'Homme*, vol. 5, no. 3/4, July–December 1965, pp. 214–15.

         5   Femand Braudel, *Capitalism and Material Life*, New York: Harper & Row, 1973, pp. 398, 405, 411; italics added. (On town–State relations in the West, see pp. 396–406.) As Braudel notes, one of the reasons for the victory of the States over the towns starting in the beginning of the fifteenth century was that the State alone had the ability fully to appropriate the war machine: by means of the territorial recruitment of men, material investment, the industrialization of war (it was more in the arms factories than in the pin factories that mass production and mechanical division appeared). The commercial towns, on the other hand, required wars of short duration, resorted to mercenaries and were only able to encast the war machine.

JACQUES DERRIDA

French philosopher Jacques Derrida (b. 1930) has had a considerable impact on the world of architecture. On the one hand, he has been directly involved in the actual design process through his collaboration with Peter Eisenman on a section of the Parc de la Villette at the instigation of Bernard Tschumi, who won the competition for the overall project. On the other, it was he has who coined the term 'deconstruction', which has been associated – very problematically – with an architectural style.

Broadly speaking, deconstruction in philosophy is a project which seeks to expose the paradoxes and value-laden hierarchies which exist within the discourse of Western metaphysics. In opposition to structuralism, it stresses the 'differal' – the play and slippage of meaning – that is always at work in the process of signification. Although deconstruction 'dismantles' concepts, its links with architecture are clearly only metaphorical. In the sense in which it is used by Derrida, deconstruction is not a style, and has little – if anything – in common with what passes for 'deconstruction' in architecture. Nonetheless it has obvious applications within the world of architecture, and offers a powerful conceptual tool.

Within architectural circles much confusion surrounds the term 'deconstruction'. Derrida attempts to dispel this in the interview, 'Architecture Where the Desire May Live'. Here Derrida explores the possibility of a way of thinking linked to the architectural moment. He raises the question of deconstruction, which, he observes, 'resembles an architectural metaphor'. However, Derrida stresses that deconstruction is not simply a technique of reversed construction. Rather it is a 'probing' which 'touches the technique itself upon the authority of the architectural metaphor, and thereby constitutes its own architectural rhetoric'. Derrida sees architecture as a form of writing, and hence as a way of living. He calls for a new inventive faculty of 'architectural difference'. Architecture must produce 'places where desire can recognise itself, where it can live'.

In 'Point de Folie – maintenant l'architecture', a dense but poetic piece of writing, Derrida offers an incisive analysis of Bernard Tschumi's follies at the Parc de la Villette. In effect he reads his own philosophical project into the architectural forms. The follies represent the instability – the play – of meaning. The red fragmented cubes of Tschumi's 'follies' are seen as 'dice' which breathe new life into architecture. They give architecture 'a chance'. 'They revive, perhaps, an energy which was infinitely anaesthetised, walled-in, buried in a common grave or sepulchral nostalgia.' Derrida challenges the accepted authority of external imperatives, such as economic, aesthetic or techno-utilitarian norms in architecture. 'These norms will be taken into account, but they will find themselves

Derrida   subordinated and reinscribed .. in a space where they no longer command in the final instance.'

Finally, in 'Why Peter Eisenman Writes Such Good Books' Derrida documents his own collaboration with Eisenman in the Parc de la Villette. As he illustrates, the work was not based on a division of labour whereby Eisenman supplied the architectural forms, and Derrida the discourse. Rather it was a process of collaboration, with Derrida suggesting the initial idea for the architectural form, and Eisenman inventing the title, 'Choral Works'. In characteristic fashion Derrida plays on this term and draws out its various 'differals' of meaning.

———

ARCHITECTURE WHERE THE DESIRE MAY LIVE   *Derrida*

JD   Let us consider architectural thinking. By that I don't mean to conceive architecture as a technique separate from thought and therefore possibly suitable to represent it in space, to constitute almost an embodiment of thinking, but rather to raise the question of architecture as a possibility of thought, which cannot be reduced to the status of a representation of thought.

    Since you refer to the separation of theory and practice, one might start by asking oneself how this working separation came about. It seems to me that from the moment one separates *Theorem* and *Pratem*, one considers architecture as a simple technique and detaches it from thought, whereas there may be an undiscovered way of thinking belonging to the architectural moment, to desire, to creation.

EM   If one is going to envisage architecture as a metaphor and thereby constantly point to the necessity of the embodiment of thinking, how can it be reintroduced into thinking in a non-metaphorical way? Possibly not necessarily leading to an embodiment, but which remain along the way, in a labyrinth for example?

JD   We will talk about the labyrinth later. First of all, I would like to outline how the philosophical tradition has used the architectural model as a metaphor for a kind of thinking which in itself cannot be architectural. In Descartes, for instance, you find the metaphor of the founding of a town, and this foundation is in fact what is supposed to support the building, the architectonic construction, the town at the base. There is consequently a kind of urbanistic metaphor in philosophy. The 'Meditations', the 'Discourse on Method' are full of these architectonic representations which, in addition, always have political relevance. When Aristotle wants to give an example of theory and practice, he quotes the '*architekton*': he knows the origin of things, he is a theorist who can also teach and has at his command the labourers who are incapable of independent thought. And with that a political hierarchy is established: architectonics is defined as an art of systems, as an art therefore suitable for the rational organization of complete branches of knowledge. It is evident that architectural reference is useful in rhetoric in a language which in itself has retained no architecturality whatsoever. I consequently ask myself how, before the separation between theory and practice, between thinking and architecture, a way of thinking linked to the architectural event could have existed. If each language proposes a spatialization, an arrangement in space which doesn't dominate it but which approaches it by approximation, then it is to be compared with a kind of pioneering, with the clearing of a path. A path which does not have to be discovered but to be created. And this creation of a path is not at all alien to architecture. Each architectural place, each habitation has one precondition: that the building should be located on a path, at a crossroads at which arrival and departure are both possible. There is no building without streets leading towards it or away from it; nor is there

Derrida   one without paths inside, without corridors, staircases, passages, doors. And if language cannot control these paths towards and within a building, then that only signifies that language is enmeshed in these structures, that it is 'on the way'. 'On the move towards language' (Heidegger), on the way to reaching itself. The way is not a method, that must be clear. The method is a technique, a procedure in order to gain control of the way, in order to make it viable.

EM   And what is the way, then?

JD   I refer once more to Heidegger who says that '*odos*', the way, is not '*methodos*', that there is a way which cannot be reduced to the definition of method. The definition of the way as a method is interpreted by Heidegger as an epoch in the history of philosophy starting with Descartes, Leibniz and Hegel and concealing its nature of being a way, making it slip into oblivion whereas in fact it indicates an infinity of thinking: thinking is always a way. If thinking doesn't rise above the way, if the language of thinking or the thinking system of the language is not understood as meta-language on the way, that means that language is a way and so has always had a certain connection with habitability and with architecture. This constant 'being on the move', the habitability of the way offering no way out entangles you in a labyrinth without any escape. More precisely it is a trap, a calculated device such as Joyce's labyrinth of Daedalus.

The question of architecture is in fact that of the place, of the taking place in space. The establishing of a place which didn't exist until then and is in keeping with what will take place there one day, that is a place. As Mallarmé puts it, '*ce qui a lieu, c'est le lieu*'. It is not at all natural. The setting up of a habitable place is an event and obviously the setting up is always something technical. It invents something which didn't exist beforehand and yet at the same time there is the inhabitant, man or God, who requires the place prior to its invention or causing it. Therefore one doesn't quite know where to pin down the origin of the place. Maybe there is a labyrinth which is neither natural nor artificial and which we inhabit within the history of graeco-occidental philosophy where the opposition between nature and technology originated. From this opposition arises the distinction between the two labyrinths. Let us return to the place, to spatiality and writing. For some time something like a deconstructive procedure has been establishing itself an attempt to free oneself from the oppositions imposed by the history of philosophy such as *physis/teckne*, God/man, philosophy/architecture. Deconstruction therefore analyses and questions conceptual pairs which are currently accepted as self-evident and natural as if they hadn't been institutionalized at some precise point, as if they had no history. Because of being taken for granted they restrict thinking.

Now the concept of deconstruction itself resembles an architectural metaphor. It is often said to have a negative attitude. Something has been constructed, a philosophical system, a tradition, a culture, and along comes a deconstructor and destroys it stone by stone, analyses the structure and dissolves it. Often enough this is the case. One looks, at a

system – Platonic/Hegelian – and examines how it was built, which key- *Derrida*
stone, which angle of vision supports the building; one shifts them and
thereby frees oneself from the authority of the system. It seems to me, however, that this is not the essence of deconstruction. It is not simply the
technique of an architect who knows how to deconstruct what has been
constructed, but a probing which touches upon the technique itself, upon
the authority of the architectural metaphor and thereby constitutes its own
architectural rhetoric. Deconstruction is not simply – as its name seems to
indicate – the technique of a reversed construction when it is able to conceive for itself the idea of construction. One could say that there is nothing
more architectural than deconstruction but also nothing less architectural.
Architectural thinking can only be deconstructive in the following sense: as
an attempt to visualize that which establishes the authority of the architectural concatenation in philosophy. From this point we can go back to
what connects deconstruction with writing: its spatiality, thinking in terms
of a path, of the opening up of a way which – without knowing where it
will lead to – inscribes its traces. Looking at it like that, one can say that the
opening up of a path is a writing which cannot be attributed to either man
or God or animal since it designates in its widest sense the place from
which this classification – man/God/animal – can take shape. This writing
is truly like a labyrinth since it has neither beginning nor end. One is
always on the move. The opposition between time and space, between the
time of speech and the space of the temple or the house has no longer any
sense. One lives in writing. Writing is a way of living.

EM At this point I would like to bring into play the forms of writing of the
architect himself. Since the introduction of the orthogonal projection,
ground plan and sectional drawings have become the primary means of
notation in architecture. They also provide the principles according to
which architecture is defined. Looking at floor plans by Palladio,
Bramante, Scamozzi, one can read the transition from a theocentric to an
anthropocentric world view in that the shape of the cross opens up
increasingly in platonic squares and rectangles to be finally totally resolved
in them. Modernism, on the other hand, distinguishes itself by a criticism
of this humanistic position. Le Corbusier's Maison Domino is an example
of this: a new type of construction made of cubic elements with a flat roof
and large windows rationally articulated without any constructional ornaments. In short, an architecture which no longer represents man but which
– as Peter Eisenman puts it – becomes a self-referential sign. A self-
explanatory architecture gives information on what is inherent in itself. It
reflects a fundamentally new relationship between man and object, house
and inhabitants. One possibility of representing such an architecture is
axonometry: a guide to the reading of a building which doesn't presuppose
its habitability. It seems to me that this self-reflection of architecture within
architecture shows a development which can be connected with your work
on deconstruction because of its starting point which is deeply critical of
methodology and therefore also of philosophic nature. If the house in
which one feels 'at home' becomes open to imitation and intrudes upon
reality then a changed concept of building has been introduced, not as an

Derrida   application but as a condition of thinking. Would it be conceivable that the theocentric and the anthropocentric world view, together with its 'being a place', could be transformed into a new and more diversified network of references?

JD   What emerges here can be grasped as the opening of architecture, as the beginning of a non-representative architecture. In this context it might be interesting to recall the fact that at the outset architecture was not an art of representation, whereas painting, drawing and sculpture can always imitate something which is supposed to already exist. I would like to remind you once more of Heidegger and above all of the 'Origin of the Work of Art' in which he refers to the '*Riß*' (rip-break-up drawings). It is a '*Riß*' which should be thought of in its original sense independently of modifications such as '*Grundriß*' (ground plan), '*Aufriß*' (vertical section), '*Skizze*' (draft). In architecture there is an imitation of the '*Riß*', of the engraving, the action of ripping. This has to be associated with writing. From here originates the attempt of modern and postmodern architecture to create a different kind of living which no longer fits the old circumstances, where the plan is not oriented towards domination, controlling communication, the economy and transport, etc. A completely new rapport between surface – the drawing – and space – architecture – is emerging. This relationship has long been important. In order to talk about the impossibility of absolute objectification, let us move from the labyrinth to the building of the tower of Babel. There too the sky is to be conquered in an act of name-giving, which yet remains inseparably linked with the natural language. A tribe, the Semites, whose name means 'name', a tribe therefore called 'name' want to erect a tower supposed to reach the sky, according to the Scriptures, with the aim of making a name for itself. This conquest of the sky, this taking up of a position in the sky means giving oneself a name and from this power, from the power of the name, from the height of the meta-language, to dominate the other tribes, the other languages, to colonize them. But God descends and spoils the enterprise by uttering one word: 'Babel', and this word is a name which resembles a noun meaning confusion. With this word he condemns mankind to the diversity of languages. Therefore they have to renounce their plan of domination by means of a language which would be universal.

The fact that this intervention in architecture, with a construction – and that also means: de-construction – represents the failure or the limitation imposed on a universal language in order to foil the plan for political and linguistic domination of the world says something about the impossibility of mastering the diversity of languages, about the impossibility of there being a universal translation. This also means that the construction of architecture will always remain labyrinthine. The issue is not to give up one point of view for the sake of another, which would be the only one and absolute, but to see a diversity of possible points of view.

If the tower had been completed there would be no architecture. Only the incompletion of the tower makes it possible for architecture as well as the multitude of languages to have a history. This history always has to be understood in relation to a divine being who is finite. Perhaps it is characteristic of postmodernism to take this failure into account. If modernism distinguishes itself by the striving for absolute domination, then postmodernism might be the realization of the experience of its end, the end of the plan of domination. Postmodernism could develop a new relationship with the divine which would no longer be manifest in the traditional shapes of the Greek, Christian or other deities, but would still set the conditions for architectural thinking. Perhaps there is no architectural thinking. But should there be such thinking, then it could only be conveyed by the dimension of the High, the Supreme, the Sublime. Viewed as such, architecture is not a matter of space but an experience of the Supreme which is not higher but in a sense more ancient than space and therefore is a spatialization of time.

EM   Could this 'spatialization' be thought of as a postmodern conception of a process involving the subject in its machination to such an extent that it cannot recognize itself in it? How can we understand this as a technique if it does not imply any reacquisition, any dominion?

JD   All the questions we have raised so far point to the question of doctrine and that can only be placed in a political context. How is it possible, for instance, to develop a new inventive faculty that would allow the architect to use the possibilities of the new technology without aspiring to uniformity, without developing models for the whole world? An inventive faculty of the architectural difference which would bring out a new type of diversity with different limitations, other heterogeneities than the existing ones and which would not be reduced to the technique of planning? At the 'Collège International de Philosophie', a seminar is held where philosophers and architects work together because it became evident that the planning of the 'Collège' also has to be an architectural venture. The 'Collège' cannot take place if one cannot find a place, an architectural form for it which bears resemblance to what might be thought in it. The 'Collège' has to be habitable in a totally different way from a university. Until now, there has been no building for the 'Collège'. You take a room here, a hall there. As architecture, the 'Collège' does not exist yet and perhaps never will. There is a formless desire for another form. The desire for a new location, new arcades, new corridors, new ways of living and of thinking.

That is a promise. And when I said that the 'Collège' does not exist as architecture yet, it might also mean that the community it requires does not exist yet and therefore the place is not being constituted. A community must accept the commitment and work so that architectural thinking takes place. A new relationship between the individual and the community, between the original and the reproduction is emerging. Think of China and Japan, for example, where they build temples out of wood and renew them regularly and entirely without them losing their originality, which obviously is not contained in the sensitive body but in something else. That too is Babel: the diversity of relationships with the architectural event from one culture to another. To know that a promise is being given even if it is not kept in its visible form. Places where desire can recognize itself, where it can live.

Derrida **POINT DE FOLIE – MAINTENANT L'ARCHITECTURE**

PART ONE

Maintenant,[1] this French word will not be translated. Why? For reasons, a whole series of reasons, which may appear along the way, or even at the end of the road. For here I am undertaking one road or, rather, one course among other possible and concurrent ones: a series of cursive notations through the *Folies* of Bernard Tschumi, from point to point, and hazardous, discontinuous, aleatory.

Why *maintenant*? I put away or place in reserve, I set *aside* the reason to maintain the seal or stamp of this idiom: it would recall the Parc de la Villette in France, and that a pretext gave rise to these *Folies*. Only a pretext, no doubt, along the way – a station, phase, or pause in a trajectory. Nevertheless, the pretext was offered in France. In French we say that a chance is offered but also, do not forget, to offer a resistance.

PART TWO

Maintenant, the word will not flutter like the banner of the moment, it will not introduce burning questions: What about architecture today? What are we to think about the current state of architecture? What is new in this domain? For architecture no longer defines a domain. *Maintenant:* neither a modernist signal nor even a salute to postmodernity. The *post-s* and *posters* which proliferate today (poststructuralism, postmodernism, etc.) still surrender to the historicist urge. Everything marks an era, even the decentring of the subject: posthumanism. It is as if one again wished to put a linear succession in order, to periodize, to distinguish between before and after, to limit the risks of reversibility or repetition, transformation or permutation: an ideology of progress.

PART THREE

Maintenant: if the word still designates what happens, has just happened, promises to happen *to* architecture as well as *through* architecture, this imminence of the *just* (*just* happens, *just* happened, is *just* about to happen) no longer lets itself be inscribed in the ordered sequence of a history: it is neither a fashion, a period or an era. The *just maintenant* [just now] does not remain a stranger to history, of course, but the relation would be different. And if this happens to *us*, we must be prepared to receive these two words. On the one hand, it does not happen to a constituted *us*, to a human subjectivity whose essence would be arrested and which would *then* find itself affected by the history of this thing called architecture. We appear to ourselves only through an experience of spacing which is already marked by architecture. What happens through architecture both constructs and instructs this *us*. The latter *finds itself* engaged by architecture before it becomes the subject of it: master and possessor. On the other hand, the imminence of what happens to us *maintenant* announces not only an architectural event but, more particularly, a writing of space, a mode of spacing which makes a place for the event. If Tschumi's work

indeed describes an architecture of the event, it is not only in that it constructs *Derrida*
places in which something should happen or to make the construction itself be,
as we say, an event. This is not what is essential. The dimension of the event is
subsumed in the very structure of the architectural apparatus: sequence, open
series, narrativity, the cinematic, dramaturgy, choreography.

PART FOUR

Is an architecture of events possible? If what happens to us thus does not come
from outside, or rather, if this outside engages us in the very thing we are, is
there a *maintenant* of architecture and in what sense *[sens]*? Everything indeed
[justement] comes down to the question of meaning *[sens]*. We shall not reply
by indicating a means of access, for example, through a given form of architecture: preamble, *pronaos,* threshold, methodical route, circle or circulation,
labyrinth, flight of stairs, ascent, archaeological regression towards a foundation, etc. Even less through the form of a system, that is, through architectonics:
the art of systems, as Kant says. We will not reply by giving access to some final
meaning, whose assumption would be finally promised us. No, it is justly
[justement] a question of what happens to meaning: not in the sense of what
would finally allow us to arrive at meaning, but of what happens to it, to meaning, to the meaning of meaning. And so – and this is the event – what happens
to it through an event which, no longer precisely or simply falling into the
domain of meaning, would be intimately linked to something like madness *[la
folie]* .

PART FIVE

Not madness *[la Folie],* the allegorical hypostasis of Unreason, non-sense, but
the *madnesses [les folies]*. We will have to account with this plural. The *folies,*
then, Bernard Tschumi's *folies.* Henceforth we will speak of them through
metonymy and in a metonymically metonymic manner since, as we will see, this
figure carries itself away; it has no means within itself to stop itself, any more
than the number of *Folies* in the Parc de la Villette. *Folies:* it is first of all the
name, a proper name in a way, and a signature. Tschumi names in this manner
the point-grid which distributes a non-finite number of elements in a space
which it in fact spaces but does not fill. Metonymy, then, since *folies,* at first,
designates only a part, a series of parts, precisely the pinpoint weave of an
ensemble which also includes lines and surfaces, a 'sound-track' and an 'image-
track'. We will return to the function assigned to this multiplicity of red points.
Here, let us note only that it maintains a metonymic relation to the whole of the
Parc. Through this proper name, in fact, the *folies* are a common denominator,
the 'largest common denominator' of this 'programmatic deconstruction'. But,
in addition, the red point of each *folie* remains divisible in turn, a point without
a point, offered up in its articulated structure to substitutions or combinatory
permutations which relate it to other *folies* as much as to its own parts. Open
point and closed point. This double metonymy becomes abyssal when it
determines or overdetermines what opens this proper name (the *'Folies'* of
Bernard Tschumi) to the vast semantics of the concept of madness, the great
name or common denominator of all that happens to meaning when it leaves

Derrida   itself, alienates and dissociates itself without ever having been subject, exposes itself to the outside and spaces itself out in what is not itself: not the semantics but, first of all, the asemantics of *Folies*.

PART SIX

The *folies*, then, these *folies* in every sense – *for once* we can say that they are not on the road to ruin, the ruin of defeat or nostalgia. They do not amount to the 'absence of the work' – that fate of *madness in the classical period* of which Foucault speaks. Instead, they make up a work; they put into operation. How? How can we think that the work can possibly *maintain itself* in this madness? How can we think the *maintenant* of the architectural work? Through a certain adventure of the point, we're coming to it, *maintenant* the work *maintenant* is the point – this very instant, the point of its implosion. The *folies* put into operation a general dislocation; they draw into it everything that, until *maintenant*, seems to have given architecture meaning. More precisely, everything that seems to have given architecture over to meaning. They deconstruct first of all, but not only, the semantics of architecture.

PART SEVEN

Let us never forget that there is an architecture of architecture. Down even to its archaic foundation, the most fundamental concept of architecture has been *constructed*. This naturalized architecture is bequeathed to us: we inhabit it, it inhabits us, we think it is destined for habitation, and it is no longer an object for us at all. But we must recognize in it an *artefact,* a *construction,* a monument. It did not fall from the sky; it is not natural, even if it informs a specific scheme of relations to *physis,* the sky, the earth, the human and the divine. This architecture of architecture has a history; it is historical through and through. Its heritage inaugurates the intimacy of our economy, the law of our hearth *(oikos),* our familial, religious and political oikonomy, all the places of birth and death, temple, school, stadium, agora, square, sepulchre. It goes right through us *[nous transit]* to the point that we forget its very historicity: we take it for nature. It is common sense itself.

PART EIGHT

The concept of architecture is itself an inhabited *constructum*, a heritage which comprehends us even before we could submit it to thought. Certain invariables remain, constant, through all the mutations of architecture. Impassible, imperturbable, an axiomatic traverses the whole history of architecture. An axiomatic, that is to say, an organized ensemble of fundamental and always presupposed evaluations. This hierarchy has fixed itself in stone; henceforth, it informs the entirety of social space. What are these invariables? I will distinguish four, the slightly artificial charter of four traits, let us say, rather, of four points. They translate one and the same postulation: *architecture must have a meaning*, it must *present* it and, through it, *signify*. The signifying or symbolical value of this meaning must direct the structure and syntax, the form and function of architecture. It must direct it *from outside,* according to a

principle *(arché),* a fundamental or foundation, a transcendence or finality   *Derrida*
(telos) whose locations are not themselves architectural. The anarchitectural
topic of this semanticism from which, inevitably, *four points* of invariance
derive:

- The experience of meaning must be *dwelling,* the law of *oikos,* the
  economy of men or gods. In its non-representational presence which (as
  distinct from the other arts) seems to refer only to itself, the
  architectural work seems to have been destined for the presence of men
  and gods. The arrangement, occupation and investment of locations
  must be measured against this economy. Heidegger still alludes to it
  when he interprets homelessness *(Heimatlösigkeit)* as the symptom of
  onto-theology and, more precisely, of modern technology. Behind the
  housing crisis he encourages us to reflect properly on the real distress,
  poverty and destitution of dwelling itself *(die eigentliche Not des
  Wohnens).* Mortals must first learn to dwell *(sie das Wohnen erst lernen
  müssen),* listen to what *calls* them to dwell. This is not a deconstruction,
  but rather a call to repeat the very fundamentals of the architecture that
  we inhabit, that we should learn again how to inhabit, the origin of its
  meaning. Of course, if the *folies* think through and dislocate this origin,
  they should not give in either to the jubilation of modern technology or
  to the maniacal mastery of its powers. That would be a new turn in the
  same metaphysics. Hence the difficulty of what justly – *maintenant* –
  arises.
- Centred and hierarchized, the architectural organization had to fall in
  line with the anamnesis of the origin and the seating of the foundation.
  Not only from the time of its foundation on the ground of the earth but
  also since its juridico-political foundation, the institution which com-
  memorates the myths of the city, heroes or founding gods. Despite
  appearances, this religious or political memory, this historicism, has not
  deserted architecture. Modern architecture retains nostalgia for it: it is
  its destiny to be a guardian. An always-hierarchizing nostalgia:
  architecture will materialize the hierarchy in stone or wood *(hylè);* it is a
  hyletics of the sacred *(hieros)* and the principle *(arché),* an *archi-
  hieratics.*
- This economy remains, of necessity, a *teleology* of dwelling. It
  subscribes to all the rules of finality. Ethico-political finality, religious
  duty, utilitarian or functional ends: it is always a question of putting
  architecture *in service,* and *at service.* This end is the principle of the
  archi-hieratical order.
- Regardless of mode, period or dominant style, this order ultimately
  depends on the fine arts. The value of beauty, harmony and totality still
  reigns.

These four points of invariability do not adjoin. They delineate the chart of a
system from the angles of a frame. We will not say only that they come together
and remain inseparable, which is true. They give rise to a specific experience of
assembling, that of the coherent totality and continuity of the system. Thus,
they determine a network of evaluations; they induce and inform, even if
indirectly, all the theory and criticism of architecture, from the most specialized

Derrida to the most trivial. Such evaluation inscribes the hierarchy in a hyletics, as well as in the space of a formal distribution of values. But this architectonics of invariable points also regulates all of what is called Western culture, far beyond its architecture. Hence the contradiction, the *double bind* or antinomy which at once animates and disturbs this history. On the one hand, this general architectonics *effaces* or *exceeds* the sharp specificity of architecture; it is valid for other arts and regions of experience as well. On the other hand, architecture forms its most powerful metonymy; it gives it its most solid *consistency*, objective substance. By consistency, I do not mean only logical coherence, which implicates all dimensions of human experience in the same network: there is no work of architecture without interpretation, or even economic, religious, political, aesthetic or philosophical decree. But by consistency I also mean duration, hardness, the monumental, mineral or ligneous subsistence, the hyletics of tradition. Hence the *resistance:* the resistance of materials as much as of consciousnesses and unconsciouses which instate this architecture as the last fortress of metaphysics. Resistance and transference. Any consequent deconstruction would be negligible if it did not take account of this resistance and this transference; it would do little if it did not go after architecture as much as architectonics. To go after it: not in order to attack, destroy or deroute it, to criticize or disqualify it. Rather, in order to *think* it in fact, to detach itself sufficiently to apprehend it in a thought which goes beyond the theorem – and becomes a work in its turn.

PART NINE

Maintenant we will take the measure of the *folies*, of what others would call the immeasurable *hybris* of Bernard Tschumi and of what it offers to our thought. These *folies* destabilize meaning, the meaning of meaning, the signifying ensemble of this powerful architectonics. They put in question, dislocate, destabilize or deconstruct the edifice of this configuration. It will be said that they are 'madness' in this. For in a *polemos* which is without aggression, without the destructive drive that would still betray a reactive affect within the hierarchy, they do battle with the very meaning of architectural meaning, as it has been bequeathed to us and as we still inhabit it. We should not avoid the issue: if this configuration presides over what in the West is called architecture, do these *folies* not raze it to the ground? Do they not lead back to the desert of anarchitecture, a zero degree of architectural writing where this writing would lose itself, henceforth without finality, aesthetic aura, fundamentals, hierarchical principles or symbolic signification, in short, in a prose made of abstract, neutral, inhuman, useless, uninhabitable and meaningless volumes?

Precisely not. The *folies* affirm, and engage their affirmation beyond this ultimately annihilating, secretly nihilistic repetition of metaphysical architecture. They enter into the *maintenant* of which I speak; they maintain, renew and reinscribe architecture. They revive, perhaps, an energy which was infinitely anaesthetized, walled-in, buried in a common grave or sepulchral nostalgia. For we must begin by emphasizing this: the charter or metaphysical frame whose configuration has just been sketched was already, one could say, the end of architecture, its 'reign of ends' in the figure of death.

This charter had come to arraign the work, it imposes on it norms or

meanings which were extrinsic, if not accidental. It made its attributes into an   *Derrida*
essence: formal beauty, finality, utility, functionalism, inhabitable value, its
religious or political economy – all the *services,* so many non-architectural or
meta-architectural predicates. By withdrawing architecture *maintenant* – what
I keep referring to in this way, using a paleonym, so as to maintain a muffled
appeal – by ceasing to impose these alien norms on the work, the *folies* return
architecture, faithfully, to what architecture, since the very eve of its origin,
should have signed. The *maintenant* that I speak of will be this, most
irreducible, signature. It does not contravene the charter, but rather draws it
into another text; it even subscribes to, and directs others to subscribe to, what
we will again call, later, a *contract,* another play of the trait, of attraction and
contraction.

A proposition that I do not make without caution and warnings. Still, the
signal of two red points:

- These *folies* do not destroy. Tschumi always talks about 'decon-
  struction/reconstruction', particularly concerning the *folie* and the
  generation of its cube (formal combinations and transformational
  relations). What is in question in *The Manhattan Transcripts* is the
  invention of 'new relations, in which the traditional components of
  architecture are broken down and reconstructed along other axes'.
  Without nostalgia, the most living act of memory. Nothing, here, of that
  nihilistic gesture which would fulfil a certain theme of metaphysics; no
  reversal of values aimed at an unaesthetic, uninhabitable, unusable, a-
  symbolical and meaningless architecture, an architecture simply left
  vacant after the retreat of gods and men. And the *folies* – like *la folie* in
  general – are anything but anarchic chaos. Yet without proposing a
  'new order' they locate the architectural work in another place where, at
  least in its principle, its essential impetus, it will no longer obey these
  external imperatives. Tschumi's 'first' concern will no longer be to
  organize space as a function or in view of economic, aesthetic, epiphanic
  or techno-utilitarian norms. These norms will be taken into consideration, but they will find themselves subordinated and reinscribed in one
  place in the text and in a space which they no longer command in the
  final instance. By pushing 'architecture towards its limits', a place will
  be made for 'pleasure'; each *folie* will be destined for a given 'use', with
  its own cultural, ludic, pedagogical, scientific and philosophical
  finalities. We will say more later about its powers of 'attraction'. All of
  this answers to a programme of transfers, transformations or
  permutations over which these external norms no longer hold the final
  word. They will not have presided over the work, since Tschumi has
  folded them into the general operation.
- Yes, folded. What is the fold? The aim of re-establishing architecture in
  what should have been specifically its own is not to reconstitute a *simple*
  of architecture, a simply architectural architecture, through a purist or
  integratist obsession. It is no longer a question of saving its own in the
  virginal immanence of its economy and of returning it to its inalienable
  presence, a presence which, ultimately, is non-representational, non-
  mimetic and refers only to itself. This autonomy of architecture, which

would thus pretend to reconcile a formalism and a semanticism in their extremes, would only fulfil the metaphysics it pretended to deconstruct. The invention, in this case, consists in crossing the architectural motif with what is most singular and most parallel in other writings which are themselves drawn into the said madness, in its plural, meaning photographic, cinematographic, choreographic, and even mythographic writings. As *The Manhattan Transcripts* demonstrated (the same is true, though in a different way, of La Villette), a narrative montage of great complexity explodes, outside, the narrative which mythologies contracted or effaced in the hieratic presence of the 'memorable' monument. An architectural writing interprets (in the Nietzschean sense of active, productive, violent, transforming interpretation) events which are *marked* by photography or cinematography. Marked: provoked, determined *or* transcribed, captured, in any case always mobilized in a scenography of passage (transference, translation, transgression from one place to another, from a place of writing to another, graft, hybridization). Neither architecture nor anarchitecture: transarchitecture. It has it out with the event; it no longer offers its work to users, believers or dwellers, to contemplators, aesthetes or consumers. Instead, it appeals to the other to invent, in turn, the event, sign, consign or *countersign:* advanced by an advance made at the other – and *maintenant* architecture.

(I am aware of a murmur: but doesn't this event you speak of, which reinvents architecture in a series of 'only onces' which are always unique in their repetition, isn't it what takes place each time not *in* a church or a temple, or even *in* a political place – not *in* them, but rather, *as* them, reviving them, for example, during each Mass when the body of Christ, etc., when the body of the King or of the nation presents or announces itself? Why not, if at least it could happen again, happen through (across) architecture, or even up to it? Without venturing further in this direction, although still acknowledging its necessity, I will say only that Tschumi's architectural *folies make us think* about what *takes place* when, *for example,* the eucharistic event goes through *[transir]* a church, *ici, maintenant* [here, now], or when a date, a seal, the trace of the other are finally laid on the body of stone, this time in the movement of its disappearance.)

PART TEN

Therefore, we can no longer speak of a *properly* architectural moment, the hieratic impassibility of the monument, this hyle-morphic complex that is given once and for all, permitting no trace to appear on its body because it afforded no chance of transformation, permutation or substitutions. In the *folies* of which we speak, on the contrary, the event undoubtedly undergoes this trial of the monumental moment; however, it inscribes it, as well, in a series of *experiences*. As its name indicates, an experience traverses: voyage, trajectory, translation, transference. Not with the object of a final presentation, a face-to-face with the thing itself, nor in order to complete an odyssey of consciousness, the phenomenology of mind as an architectural step. The route through the

folies is undoubtedly prescribed, from point to point, to the extent that the   *Derrida*
point-grid counts on a *programme* of possible experiences and new
experiments (cinema, botanical garden, video workshop, library, skating rink,
gymnasium). But the structure of the grid[2] and of each cube – for these points
are cubes – leaves opportunity for chance, formal invention, combinatory
transformation, wandering. Such opportunity is not given to the inhabitant or
the believer, the user or the architectural theorist, but to whoever engages, in
turn, in architectural writing: without reservation, which implies an inventive
reading, the restlessness of a whole culture and the body's signature. This body
would no longer simply be content to *walk,* circulate, stroll around *in* a place or
on paths, but would transform its elementary motions by giving rise to them; it
would receive from this other spacing the invention of its gestures.

PART ELEVEN

The *folie* does not stop: neither in the hieratic monument, nor in the circular
path. Neither impassibility nor pace. Seriality inscribes itself in stone, iron or
wood, but this seriality does not stop there. And it had begun earlier. The series
of *trials* (experiments or artist's proofs) that are naively called sketches, essays,
photographs, models, films or writings (for example, what is gathered together
for a while in this volume) fully belongs to the *experience* of the *folies: folies at
work.* We can no longer give them the value of documents, supplementary
illustrations, preparatory or pedagogical notes – *hors d'oeuvre,* in short, or the
equivalent of theatrical rehearsals. No – and this is what appears as the greatest
danger to the architectural desire which still inhabits us. The immovable mass
of stone, the vertical glass or metal plane that we had taken to be the very object
of architecture *(die Sache selbst* or *the real thing),* its indisplaceable effectivity,
is apprehended *maintenant* in the voluminous text of multiple writings: superimposition of a *Wunderblock* (to signal a text by Freud – and Tschumi exposes
architecture to psychoanalysis, introducing the theme of the transference, for
example, as well as the schiz), palimpsest grid, supersedimented textuality,
bottomless stratigraphy that is mobile, light and abyssal, foliated, foliiform.
Foliated folly, foliage and *folle* [mad] not to seek reassurance in any solidity:
not in ground or tree, horizontality or verticality, nature or culture, form or
foundation or finality. The architect who once wrote with stones now places
lithographs in a volume, and Tschumi speaks of them as *folios.* Something
weaves through this foliation whose stratagem, as well as coincidence, reminds
me of Littré's suspicion. Regarding the second meaning of the word *folie,* that
of the houses bearing their signers' name, the name of 'the one who has had
them built or of the place in which they are located', Littré hazards the
following, in the name of etymology: 'Usually one sees in this the word
madness [folie]. But this becomes uncertain when one finds in the texts from
the Middle Ages: *foleia quae erat ante domum,* and *domum foleyae,* and *folia
Johannis Morelli;* one suspects that this involves an alteration of the word
feuillie or feuillée' [foliage] . The word *folie* has no common sense anymore: it
has lost even the reassuring unity of its meaning. Tschumi's *folies* no doubt play
on this 'alteration' and superimpose, against common sense, common meaning,
this other meaning, the meaning of the other, of the other language, the
madness of this asemantics.

PART TWELVE

When I discovered Bernard Tschumi's work, I had to dismiss one easy
hypothesis: recourse to the language of deconstruction, to what in it has
become coded, to its most insistent words and motifs, to some of its strategies
would only be an analogical transposition or even an architectural application.
In any case, impossibility itself. For according to the logic of this hypothesis
(which quickly became untenable), we could have inquired: what could a
deconstructive architecture be? Isn't what deconstructive strategies begin or
end by destabilizing exactly the structural principle of architecture (system,
architectonics, structure, foundation, construction, etc.)? Instead, the last
question led me towards another turn of interpretation: what *The Manhattan
Transcripts* and the *Folies* of La Villette urge us towards is the obligatory route
of deconstruction in one of its most intense, affirmative and necessary imple-
mentations. Not deconstruction *itself,* since there never was such a thing;
rather, what carries its jolt beyond semantic analysis, critique of discourses and
ideologies, concepts or texts, in the traditional sense of the term. Decon-
structions would be feeble if they were negative, if they did not construct, and
above all, if they did not first measure themselves against institutions in their
solidity, *at the place of their greatest resistance:* political structures, levers of
economic decision, the material and phantasmatic apparatuses which connect
state, civil society, capital, bureaucracy, cultural power and architectural
education – a remarkably sensitive relay; but in addition, those which join the
arts, from the fine arts to martial arts, science and technology, the old and the
new. All these are so many forces which quickly harden or cement into a large-
scale architectural operation, particularly when it approaches the body of a
metropolis and involves transactions with the state. This is the case here.

PART THIRTEEN

One does not declare war. Another strategy weaves itself between hostilities
and negotiations. Taken in its strictest, if not most literal, sense, the grid of
folies introduces a specific device into the space of the transaction. The
meaning of 'grid' does not achieve assembled totality. It crosses through. To
establish a grid is to cross through, to go through a channel. It is the experience
of a permeability. Furthermore, such crossing does not move through an
already-existing texture; it weaves this texture, it invents the histological
structure of a text, of what one would call in English a 'fabric'. Fabric in
English recalls *fabrique,* a French noun with an entirely different meaning
which some decision-makers proposed substituting for the disquieting title of
folies.

    Architect-weaver. He plots grids, twining the threads of a chain, his writing
holds out a net. A weave always weaves in several directions, several meanings,
and beyond meaning. A network-stratagem, and thus a singular device. Which?
A dissociated series of 'points', red points, constitutes the grid, spacing a
multiplicity of matrices or generative cells whose transformations will never let
themselves be calmed, stabilized, installed, identified in a continuum. Divisible
themselves, these cells also point towards instants of rupture, discontinuity,
disjunction. But simultaneously, or rather, through a series of mishaps,

rhythmed anachromies or aphoristical gaps, the point of *folie* [Fr. *point de folie*   *Derrida*
= no *folie*] gathers together what it has just dispersed; it reassembles it as
dispersion. It gathers into a multiplicity of *red* points. Resemblance and
reassembly are not confined to colour, but the *chromographic* reminder plays a
necessary part in it.

What then, is a point, *this* point of *folie*? How does it stop *folie*? For it
suspends it and, in this movement, brings it to a halt, but *as folie*. Arrest of
folie: point de folie, no or node-*folie*, more *folie, no* more *folie*, no *folie* at all.
At the same time it settles the question, but by which decree, which arrest – and
which aphoristic justness? What does the law accomplish? Who accomplishes
the law? The law divides *and* arrests division; it *maintains* this point of *folie*,
this chromosomal cell, as the generative principle. How can we analyse the
architectural *chromosome*, its colour, this labour of division and individuation
which no longer pertains to the domain of biogenetics?

We are getting there, but only after a detour. We must pass through one more
point.

PART FOURTEEN

There are strong words in Tschumi's lexicon. They locate the points of greatest
intensity. These are the words beginning with *trans-* (transcript, transference,
etc.) and, above all, *de-* or *dis-*. These words speak of destabilization, deconstruction, dehiscence and, first of all, dissociation, disjunction, disruption,
difference. An architecture of heterogeneity, interruption, non-coincidence. But
who would ever have built in this manner? Who would have counted on only
the energies in *dis-* or *de-?* No work results from a simple displacement or
dislocation. Therefore, invention is needed. A path must be traced for another
writing. Without renouncing the deconstructive affirmation whose necessity we
have tested – indeed, on the contrary, so as to give it new impetus – this writing
maintains the *dis-jointed* as such; it joins up the *dis-* by maintaining
[maintenant] the distance; it gathers together the difference. This assembling
will be singular. What holds together does not necessarily take the form of a
system; it does not always depend on architectonics and can disobey the logic
of synthesis or the order of syntax. The *maintenant* of architecture would be
this manoeuvre to inscribe the *dis-* and make it into a work in itself. Abiding
and maintaining *[maintenant]*, this work does not pour the difference into
concrete; it does not erase the differential trait, nor does it reduce or embed this
track, the distract or abs-tract, in a homogeneous mass *(concrete)*. Architectonics (or the art of the system) represents only one epoch, says Heidegger, in
the history of the *Mitsein*. It is only a specific possibility of the assembling.
This, then, would be both the task and the wager, a preoccupation with the
impossible: to give dissociation its due, but to implement it *as such* in the space
of reassembly. A transaction aimed at a spacing and at a *socius* of dissociation
which, furthermore, would allow the negotiation of *even this*, difference, with
received norms, the politico-economic powers of architectonics, the mastery of
the *maîtres d'oeuvre*. This 'difficulty' is Tschumi's experience. He does not hide
it, 'this is not without difficulty':

At La Villette, it is a matter of forming, of acting out dissociation

Derrida   (. . .) This is not without difficulty. Putting dissociation into form
necessitates that the support structure (the Parc, the institution) be
structured as a reassembling system. The red point of *folies* is the
focus of this dissociated space.[3]

PART FIFTEEN

A force joins up and holds together the dis-jointed as such. Its effect upon the
dis- is not external. The *dis-joint* itself, *maintenant* architecture, architecture
that arrests the *madness* in its dislocation. It is not only *a* point: an open multiplicity of red points resists its totalization, even by metonymy. These points
might fragment, but I would not define them as fragments. A fragment still
signals to a lost or promised totality.

Multiplicity does not open each point *from outside*. In order to understand
how it also develops from inside we must analyse the double bind whose knot
the point of *folie* tightens, without forgetting what can bind a double bind to
schiz and madness.

On the one hand, the point concentrates, folds back towards itself the
greatest force of attraction, *contracting* lines towards the centre. Wholly self-
referential, within a grid which is also autonomous, it fascinates and
magnetizes, seduces through what could be called its self-sufficiency and
'narcissism'. At the same time, through its force of magnetic attraction
(Tschumi speaks here of a magnet which would 'reassemble' the 'fragments of
an exploded system'), the point seems to bind, as Freud would say, the energy
freely available within a given field. It exerts its attraction through its very
punctuality, the *stigmè* of instantaneous *maintenant towards* which everything converges and where it seems to individuate itself; but also from the fact
that in stopping madness, it constitutes the point of transaction with the
architecture which it, in turn, deconstructs or divides. A discontinuous series
of instants and *attractions:* in each point of *folie* the attractions of the Parc,
useful or playful activities, finalities, meanings, economic or ecological
investments, services will again find their place on the programme. Bound
energy and semantic recharge. Hence, also, the distinction and the transaction between what Tschumi terms the normality and deviation of the *folies.*
Each point is a breaking point: it interrupts, absolutely, the continuity of the
text or of the grid. But the inter-ruptor maintains together *both* the rupture
and the relation to the other, which is itself structured as both attraction and
interruption, interference and difference: a relation without relation. What is
contracted here passes a 'mad' contract between the *socius* and dissociation.
And this without dialectic, without that *Aufhebung* whose process Hegel
explains to us and which can always reappropriate such a *maintenant:* the
point negates space and, in this spatial negation of itself, generates the line in
which it maintains itself by cancelling itself *(als sich aufhebend).* Thus, the
line would be the truth of the point, the surface the truth of the line, time the
truth of space and, finally, the *maintenant* the truth of the point
(Encyclopédie, §256-7). Here I permit myself to refer to my text, *Ousia et
grammè*[4] Under the same name, the *maintenant* I speak of would mark the
interruption of this dialectic.

But on the other hand, if dissociation does not happen to the point from

outside, it is because the point is *both* divisible and indivisible. It appears   *Derrida*
atomic, and thus has the function and individualizing form of the point only
according to a *point of view,* according to the perspective of the serial
ensemble which it punctuates, organizes and subtends without ever being its
simple support. As it is seen, and seen from outside, it simultaneously scans
and interrupts, maintains and divides, puts colour and rhythm into the
spacing of the grid. But this point of view does not see; it is blind to what
happens *in* the *folie.* For if we consider it *absolutely,* abstracted from the
ensemble and in itself (it is also destined to abstract, distract or subtract
itself), the point is not a point anymore; it no longer has the atomic
indivisibility that is bestowed on the geometrical point. Opened inside to a
void that gives play to the pieces, it constructs/deconstructs itself like a cube
given over to formal combination. The articulated pieces separate, compose
and recompose. By articulating pieces that are more than pieces – pieces of a
game, theatre pieces, pieces of an a-partment [Fr. *pièce,* room] at once places
and spaces of *movement* – the *dis*-joint forms that are *destined* for events: in
order for them to take place.

PART SIXTEEN

For it was necessary to speak of promise and pledge, of promise as affirmation,
the promise that provides the privileged example of a performative writing.
More than an example: the very condition of such writing. Without accepting
what would be retained as presuppositions by theories of performative
language and *speech acts* – relayed here by an architectural pragmatics (for
example, the value of presence, of the *maintenant* as present) – and without
being able to discuss it here, let us focus on this single trait: the provocation of
the event I speak of ('I promise', for example), that I describe or trace; the event
that I *make* happen or *let* happen by marking it. The mark or trait must be
emphasized so as to remove this performativity from the hegemony of speech
and of what is called human speech. The performative mark *spaces*: is the event
of spacing. The red points space, maintaining architecture in the dissociation of
spacing. But this *maintenant* does not only maintain a past and a tradition; it
does not ensure a synthesis. It maintains the interruption, in other words, the
relation to the other as such. To the other in the magnetic field of attraction, of
the 'common denominator' or 'hearth' to other points of rupture as well, but
first of all to the Other: the one through whom the promised event will happen
or will not. For he is called, only called to countersign the pledge *[gage],* the
engagement or the wager. This Other never presents itself; he is not present,
maintenant. He can be represented by what is too quickly referred to as Power,
the politico-economic decision-makers, users, representatives of domains, of
cultural domination, and here, in particular, of a philosophy of architecture.
This other will be anyone, not yet *[point encore]* a subject, ego or conscience
and not a man *[point l'homme];* anyone who comes and answers to the
promise, who first answers *for* the promise, the to-come of an event which
would maintain spacing, the *maintenant* in dissociation, the relation to the
other as such. Not the hand being held *[main tenue]* but the hand outstretched
[main tendue] above the abyss.

PART SEVENTEEN

Overlaid by the entire history of architecture and laid open to the hazards of a future that cannot be anticipated, this other architecture, this architecture of the other is nothing that exists. It is not a present, the memory of a past present, the purchase or pre-comprehension of a future present. It presents neither a constative theory nor a politics nor an ethics of architecture. Not even a narrative, although it opens this space to all narrative matrices, to sound-tracks and image-tracks (as I write this, I think of *La Folie du Jour* by Blanchot, and of the demand for, and impossibility of, narration that is made evident there. Everything I have been able to write about it, most notably in *Parages,* is directly and sometimes, literally concerned – I am aware of this after the fact, thanks to Tschumi – with the madness of architecture: step, threshold, stair-case, labyrinth, hotel, hospital, wall, enclosure, edges, room, the inhabitation of the uninhabitable. And since all of this, dealing with the madness of the trait, the spacing of dis-traction, will be published in English, I also think of that idiomatic manner of referring to the fool, the absent-minded, the wanderer: *the one who is spacy, or spaced out.*)

But if it presents neither theory, nor ethics, nor politics, nor narration ('No, no narrative, never again', *La Folie du Jour)* it gives a place to them all. It writes and signs in advance – *maintenant* a divided line on the edge of meaning, before any presentation, beyond it – the very other, who engages architecture, its discourse, political scenography, economy and ethics. Pledge but also wager, symbolic order and gamble: these red cubes are thrown like the dice of architecture. The throw not only programmes a strategy of events, as I suggested earlier; it anticipates the architecture to come. It runs the risk and gives us the chance.

NOTES

1   *Maintenant*, Fr. adv., now; from *maintenir*, keeping in position, supporting, upholding; from *se maintenir*, v. remaining, lasting; from *main tenant*, the hand that holds.

   Folie, Fr., n. madness, delusion, mania; folly; country pleasure-house. In general the French spelling of the word *folie* has been kept in this translation, according to Bernard Tschumi's own usage, so as to retain the connotation of madness. [Note added by translator.]

2   *Trane*, Fr., woof, weft, web, thread; also plot, conspiracy; (Phot. Engr.) screen. [Note added by translator.]

3   Bernard Tschumi, 'Madness and the Combinative', *Précis V*, New York: Columbia University, 1984.

4   Jacques Derrida, *La paraphrase: point, ligne, surface*, in *Marges*, Minuit *1972, Margins*, University of Chicago Press.

WHY PETER EISENMAN WRITES SUCH GOOD BOOKS

This title barely conceals a quotation from another, well-known title. It lifts a fragment, or rather a person. By translating the title 'Why I write such good books' *(Warum ich so gute Bücher schreibe)* into the third person, by

summoning Nietzsche's *Ecce Homo* to bear witness, I take it upon myself to   *Derrida*
clear Eisenman of all suspicion. It is not he who speaks, it is I. I who write. I
who, using displacements, withdrawals, fragmentations, play with identities,
with persons and their titles, with the integrity of their proper names. Has one
the right to do this? But who will declare the right? And in whose name?

By abusing metonymy as well as pseudonymy, following Nietzsche's
example, I propose to undertake many things – all at once, or one by one. But I
will not reveal them all, and certainly not to begin with. Without giving away
all the leads, the threads, I will reveal neither the route, nor the connections. Is
this not the best condition for writing good texts? Whoever assumes from a
simple reading of my title that I am going to diagnose the paranoia of some
Nietzsche of modern architecture has mistaken the address.

First I propose to draw attention to the art with which Eisenman himself
knows how to play with titles. We will take a few examples, among which, first
of all, there are the titles of his books. They are made up of words. But what are
words for an architect? Or books?

I also want to propose, with the allusion to *Ecce Homo*, that Eisenman is, in
the realm of architecture, if you will, the most anti-Wagnerian creator of our
time. What might be a Wagnerian architecture? Where would one find its
remains or its disguised presence today? These questions will remain
unanswered here. But isn't it true that questions of art or politics are worthy of
being pondered, if not posed?

I propose to speak of music, of musical instruments in one of Eisenman's
works in progress. It is unnecessary to recall the fact that *Ecce Homo* is above
all a book on music, and not only in its last chapter, *Der Fall Wagner, Ein
Musikanten-Problem*.

Finally, I propose to note that the architectural value, the very axiom of
architecture that Eisenman begins by overturning, is the measure of man, that
which proportions everything to a human, all too human, scale: *Menschliches,
Allzumenschliches, Mit zwei Fortsetzungen,* to cite another chapter of *Ecce
Homo*. Already at the entry to the labyrinth of *Moving Arrows, Eros, and
Other Errors,* one can read: 'Architecture traditionally has been related to
human scale.' For the 'metaphysics of scale' which Eisenman's 'scaling'
attempts to destabilize is, first of all, a humanism or an anthropocentrism. It is
a human, all too human, desire for 'presence' and 'origin'. Even in its
theological dimensions, this architecture of originary presence returns to man
under the law of representation and aesthetics: 'In destabilizing presence and
origin, the value that architecture gives to representation and the aesthetic
object is also called into question' (ibid.).

We should not, however, simply conclude that such an architecture will be
Nietzschean. We shall not borrow *themes* or rather the *philosophemes* from
Ecce Homo, but rather some figures (or tropes), some staging and apostrophes,
and then a lexicon, similar to those computerized palettes where colours may
be summoned up by a keystroke before beginning to type. So, I take this phrase
which in a moment you will read on the screen (I write on my computer and
you well know that Nietzsche was one of the first writers to use a typewriter); it
is from the beginning of *Ecce Homo*. It concerns a 'labyrinth', the labyrinth of
knowledge, his very own, the most dangerous of all, to which some would wish
to forbid entry: *'man wird niemals in dies Labyrinth verwegener Erkenntnisse*

Derrida *eintreten;'* a little further on, there is a citation from *Zarathustra,* and then an allusion to those who hold 'an Ariadne's thread in a cowardly hand'. Between these two phrases, one may also lift the allusion to those bold searchers who 'embark on terrible seas' *('auf furchtbare Meere')* and to those whose soul is lured by flutes toward all the dangerous whirlpools *('deren Seele mit Floeten zu jedem Irrschlunde gelockt wird').* In brief, let us agree that what we retain from the chapter 'Why I Write Such Good Books' in *Ecce Homo* is only this: the seduction of music, the musical instrument, the sea or the abyss, and the labyrinth.

A strange introduction to architecture, you will say, and especially to that of Peter Eisenman. In which hand must the thread be held? And firmly or loosely?

It is true that this is doubtless not my subject. I would rather speak of meetings, and of what a particular *meeting* means, what takes *place* at the inter-section of chance and program, of the aleatory and the necessary.

When I met Peter Eisenman, I thought in my naïveté that *discourse* would be my realm and that architecture 'properly speaking' – places, spaces, drawing, the silent calculation, stones, the resistance of materials – would be his. Of course I was not so naïve; I knew that discourse and language did not count for nothing in the activity of architects and above all in Eisenman's. I even had reason to think that they were more important than the architects themselves realized. But I did not understand to what extent, and above all in what way, his architecture confronted the very conditions of discourse, grammar and semantics. Nor did I then understand why Eisenman is a writer – which, far from distancing him from architecture and making him one of those 'theoreticians' (who, as those who do neither say, write more than they build), on the contrary opens a space in which two writings, the verbal and the archi-tectural, are inscribed, the one within the other, outside the traditional hierarchies. That is to say, what Eisenman writes 'with words' is not limited to a so-called theoretical reflection on the architectural object, which attempts to define what this object has been or what it ought to be. Certainly this aspect is to be found in Eisenman, but there is still something else, something that does not simply develop as a metalanguage on (or about) a certain traditional authority of discourse in architecture. This may be characterized as another treatment of the word, of another 'poetics', if you like, which participates with full legitimacy in the invention of architecture without submitting it to the order of discourse.

Our meeting was indeed a chance for me. But the *aléa* — as with all encounters – must have been programmed within an unfathomable agenda which I will not take the risk of analysing here. Let us begin at the point when Bernard Tschumi proposed to both of us that we collaborate in the conception of what was called, by convention, a 'garden' in the Parc de La Villette, a rather strange garden in that it does not admit any vegetation, only liquids and solids, water and minerals. I will not elaborate here on my first contribution, which was a text on the Chora in Plato's *Timaeus.* The unfathomable enigma of what Plato says about the architect-demiurge, of the place, of the inscription which imprints in it (in the place) the images of paradigms, etc., all this seemed to me to merit a kind of architectural test, a rigorous challenge: a challenge at once rigorous and necessary, inevitably rigorous, to all the text's poetic, rhetorical and political stakes, with all the difficulties of reading which have resisted

centuries of interpretation. But once again, I do not wish to speak here of what   *Derrida*
happened on my side of the proposition that I put forward, even as I put myself
forward with the greatest misgivings. What is important here is what came
from the other side, from Peter Eisenman.

As things seemed to have begun with words and a book, I quickly had to
accept the obvious. Eisenman does not only take great pleasure, jubilation, in
playing with language, with languages, at the meeting, the crossing of many
idioms, welcoming chances, attentive to risk, to transplants, to the slippings
and derivations of the letter. He also takes this play seriously, if one can say this,
and without giving himself the principal, inductive, role in a work that one
hesitates to call properly or purely architectural, without setting up this play of
the letter as a *determining origin* (such a thing never exists for Eisenman), he
does not leave it *outside the work*. For him, words are not *exergues*.

I will cite only two examples.

After he had translated, or rather transferred and transformed, certain
motifs appropriated by himself and for himself from my Chora text in a first
architectural project, a limitless palimpsest, with 'scaling', 'quarry' and 'labyrinth', I insisted, and Eisenman fully agreed, on the need to give our common
work a title, and an inventive title at that, one which did not have as its sole
function the gathering of collective meaning, the production of those effects of
legitimizing identification which one expects from titles in general. On the
other hand, precisely because what we were making was not a garden (the
category under which the administration of La Villette naïvely classified the
space entrusted to us), but something else, a place yet without name, if not
unnameable, it was necessary to give it a name, and with this naming make a
new gesture, a supplementary element of the project itself, something other
than a simple reference to a thing that would exist in any case without its name,
outside the name.

Three conditions seemed to be required.

1   That this title would be as strong, as subsuming, and as economical of
    the work as possible. Such was the 'classic' and normally referential
    function of the title and the name.
2   That this title, while designating the work from outside, should also be
    part of the work, imprinting it from within with an indispensable
    motion, so that the letters of the name would participate in this way in
    the very body of the architecture.
3   That the verbal structure should maintain such a relationship to the *aléa*
    of meeting of such a kind that no semantic order could stop the play, or
    totalize it from a centre, an origin or a principle.

Choral Work, this was the title invented by Eisenman.

Even though it surfaced at a moment when long discussions had already
given rise to the first 'drawings' and the principle schema of the work, this title
seemed to have imposed itself all of a sudden: by chance, but also as the result
of calculation. No arguing, no reservations were possible. The title was perfect.

1   It names in the most apt fashion, by means of the most efficient and
    economic reference, a work that in its own way interprets, in a
    dimension that is both discursive and architectural, a reading of the

platonic *chora*. The name *chora* is carried over into song (choral) and even into choreography. With the final *l*, chora*l*: *chora* becomes more liquid or more aerial, I do not dare to say, more feminine.

2   It becomes indissociable from a construction on which it imposes from within a new dimension: choreographic, musical and vocal at the same time. Speech, even song, are thus inscribed in the work, taking their place within a rhythmic composition. To give way to, or to take place is, in either sense, to make an architectural event out of music, or rather out of a choir.

3   In addition to being a musical allusion – and even a choreographic one in Plato's *chora* – this title is more than a title. It also designs a signature, a plural signature, written by both of us in concert. Eisenman had just done what he said he was doing. The performance, the felicitous efficacy of the performative, consisted in inventing by himself the form of a signature that not only signed for both of us, but enunciated in itself the plurality of the choral signature, the cosignature or the counter-signature. He gives me his signature in the sense one says of someone giving to a collaborator the 'power' to sign in his place. The work becomes musical, an architecture for many voices, at once different and harmonized in their very alterity. This comprises a gift as precious as it is petrified, a coral *(corail)*. As if water had naturally allied itself with minerals for this simulacrum of spontaneous creation in the unconscious depths of some shared or divided ocean. *Ecce Homo:* the abyss of depths without bottom, music, a hyperbolic labyrinth.

The law is at the same time respected and mocked because the commission that we had been given also prescribed this: only water and stone should be used for this pseudo-garden and above all, no vegetation. And this was what had been created with a single blow, with a wave of the magic wand, in two words, so close to silence: the magic wand is also the baton of an orchestra conductor. I still hear it now, like the masterpiece of a maker of fireworks, the explosion of a firecracker. And how could I not be reminded of the *Music for the Royal Fireworks,* of the chorale, of Corelli's influence, of that 'architectural sense' we always admire in Handel.

The elements are thus brought to light, exposed to the air: earth, water and fire – as in the *Timaeus,* at the moment of the formation of the *cosmos*. But it is impossible to assign an order, a hierarchy or principle of deduction or derivation to all the meanings that intersect as if from a chance meeting, in hardly more than ten letters, sealed, forged *(coined)* in the idiomatic forge *(forgery)* of a single language. The 'title' is condensed in the stamp, the seal or the initials of this countersignature (because this was also a way not to sign while signing), but at the same time, it opens up the whole to which it seems to belong. Thus there is no capital role to be played by this title, itself open to other interpretations or, one might say, other performances, other musicians, other choreographers, or even other voices. Totalization is impossible.

We might draw out some other threads, other chords in this labyrinthine skein. Eisenman often refers to the labyrinth to describe the routes called for by certain of his works:

These superpositions appear in a labyrinth, which is located at the

site of the castle of Juliet. Like the story of Romeo and Juliet, it is an   *Derrida*
analogic expression of the unresolved tension between fate and free
will. Here the labyrinth, like the castle sites, becomes a palimpsest.

Like the work it names, the title *Choral Work* is at the same time palimpsest
and labyrinth, a maze of superimposed structures (Plato's text, the reading of it
that I have proposed in my text, the slaughterhouses of La Villette, Eisenman's
project for Venice (Cannaregio) and Tschumi's Follies). In French, in a phrase
that remains untranslatable, one would say: the title *se donne carrière*.
'Carrière' means quarry. But '*se donner carrière*' is also to give free rein, to
appropriate a space with a certain joyful insolence. Literally, I understand it in
the sense of '*carrière*' which at once gives itself graciously, offering up its own
resources, but belongs first and foremost to the very space it enriches. How can
one *give* in this way? How can one, while drawing from it, enrich the totality of
which it forms a part? What is this strange economy of the gift? In *Choral Work*
and elsewhere, Eisenman plays the game of constituting a part of the whole '*en
carrière*' (as quarry), as a mine of materials to be displaced for the rest at the
interior of the same ensemble. The quarry is at the same time inside and
outside, the resources are included. And the structure of our title obeys the
same law, it has the same form of potentiality, the same power: the dynamics of
an immanent invention. Everything is found inside but it is almost
unforeseeable.

For my second example, I must pluck another chord/string. This musical and
choreographic architecture was going to point toward, as if it incorporated or
cited them in itself, both a poetic genre, that is, the *lyric*, and the stringed
instrument which corresponds to this genre – the lyre.

The title was already given and we had progressed in the preparation of
Choral Work, when Eisenman suggested that I finally take an initiative that
was not solely discursive, theoretical or 'philosophical' (I place this word
between quotations marks because the reading of the *chora* that I propose
perhaps no longer belongs to the realm of philosophical thought, but we will
leave this aside). He wanted, with justification, our choir to be more than the
simple aggregation of two soloists, a writer and an architect. If the architect
signed and 'designated', de-signed with words, I should for my part project or
design visible forms. On returning from New York, in the airplane, I wrote
Eisenman a letter containing a design and its interpretation. Thinking of one of
the most enigmatic (to my mind) passages in Plato's *Timaeus*, I wanted the
figure of a sieve to be inscribed on, in and within the *Choral Work* itself, as the
memory of a synecdoche or an errant metonomy. It would be errant in the sense
that no reprise would be possible in any totality of which it would figure only a
detached piece: neither fragment nor ruin. For the *Timaeus*, in effect, utilizes
what one no doubt calls abusively a metaphor, that of the sieve, in order to
describe the way in which the place (the *chora*) filters the 'types,' the forces or
seeds that have been impressed on it:

> The nurse of becoming was characterized by the qualities of water
> and fire, of earth and air, and by others that go with them, and its
> visual appearance was therefore varied; but as there was no
> homogeneity or balance in the forces that filled it, no part of it was
> in equilibrium, but it swayed unevenly under the impact of their

motion, and in turn communicated its motion to them. And its contents were in constant process of movement and separation, rather like the contents of a winnowing basket or similar implement for cleaning corn, in which the solid and heavy stuff is sifted out and settles on one side, the light and insubstantial on another so the four basic constituents were shaken by the receptacle, which acted as a kind of shaking implement.[1]

This is not the place to explain why I have always found this passage to be provocative and fascinating by reason of the very resistance it offers to reading. This is of little importance here. As if to give a body to this fascination, I thus wrote this letter to Eisenman on the airplane, a fragment of which you will permit me to cite:

> You will recall what we envisaged when we were together at Yale: that in order to finish, I would 'write', so to speak, without a single word, a heterogeneous piece, without origin or apparent destination, as if it were a fragment arriving, without indicating any totality (lost or promised), in order to break the circle of reappropriation, the triad of the three sites (Eisenman-Derrida, Tschumi, La Villette); to break, in short, the totalization, the still too-historical configuration, so that it would be open to a general decipherment. And nevertheless I thought that, without giving any assurance on this subject, that some detached and enigmatic metonymy, rebelling against the history of the three sites and even against the palimpsest, should 'recall' by chance if one encountered it, something, the most incomprehensible of all, of the *chora*. For myself, today, that which I find the most enigmatic, which resists and provokes the most, in the reading which I am undertaking of the *Timaeus* is (we can talk about this again later), the allusion to the figure of the sieve *(plokanon,* a work or braided cord, 52e), and to the *chora* as *sieve* (sieve, sift, I also love these English words). There is in the *Timaeus* a figural allusion which I do not know how to interpret and which nevertheless seems to me decisive. It speaks of something like movement, the shaking *(seiesthai, seien, seiomena),* the tremor in the course of which a selection of the forces or seeds *takes place;* a sorting, a filtering in the very place where, nevertheless, the place remains impassive, indeterminate, amorphous, etc. It seems to me that this passage in the *Timaeus* is as erratic, as difficult to integrate, as deprived of origin and of manifest *telos* as that piece we have imagined for our *Choral Work.*
>
> Thus I propose the following approximate 'representation', 'materialization', 'formation': in one or three examples (if there are three, then each with different scalings), a *guilded* metal object (there is gold in the passage from the *Timaeus,* on the *chora,* and in your Cannaregio project) to be planted obliquely in the earth. Neither vertical, nor horizontal, an extremely solid frame that would resemble at once a web, a sieve, or a grill (grid) and a stringed musical instrument (piano, harp, lyre?: strings, stringed instrument, vocal chord, etc.). As a grill, grid, etc., it would have a certain

Derrida

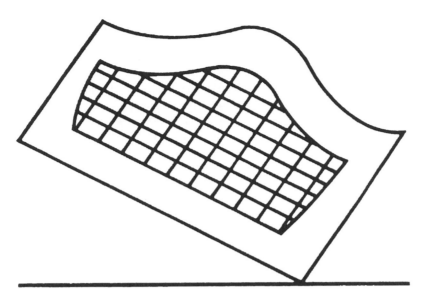

Figure 1 Sketch by Jacques Derrida for *Choral Work* project
Source: G. Bennington and J. Derrida, *Jacques Derrida*, London, The University of Chicago Press, 1993

relationship with the *filter* (a telescope or a photographic acid bath, or a machine which has fallen from the sky having photographed or X-rayed – filtered – an aerial view). This would be both an interpretive and *selective* filter which would allow the reading and the sieving of the three sites and the three layers (Eisenman-Derrida, Tschumi, La Villette). As a stringed instrument, it would announce the concert and the multiple chorale, the *chora* of *Choral Work*.

I do not think that anything should be inscribed on this sculpture (for this is a sculpture), save perhaps the title, and a signature might figure somewhere (i.e. *Choral Work*, by . . . 1986), as well as one or two Greek words *(plokanon, seiomena,* etc.). We should discuss this, among other things . . . (30 May 1986)

One will note in this passage, the allusion to the filtering of a selective interpretation that evokes, in my letter, Nietzsche and a certain scene played out between Nietzsche and the pre-Socratics – those same figures that seem to haunt a given passage in the *Timaeus* (Democritus, for example).

So what does Eisenman do? He interprets in his turn, actively and selectively. He translates, transposes, transforms and appropriates my letter, rewriting it in *his* language, in his *languages,* both architectural structure (a structure that is already quite fixed): that of a lyre, lying down at an oblique angle. Then, in a change of scale, he re-inscribes it in its very interior, as a small lyre within a large one. He is not content to create a metonomy *en abyme*[2] at the bottom of the ocean where the coral is deposited in sediments, in order to outsmart the ruses of totalizing reason. Among all the stringed instruments evoked in my letter (piano, harp, lyre) he chooses one, whose play he reinvents in his own language, English. And in inventing another architectural device, he transcribes this linguistic reinvention, one which is his, his own.

Derrida   What then in fact happens? First he adds another justification and another
dimension to the open title *Choral Work,* which then finds itself enriched and
overdetermined. Then, on all the semantic and even formal strings/chords of the
word which happens to be homographic in both French and English – we hear
the resonance of different texts. These are added, superposed, superimposed one
within the other, *on* or *under* the other according to an apparently impossible and
unrepresentable topology seen through a surface; an invisible surface, certainly,
but one which is audible from the internal reflection of many resonant layers.
These resonant layers are also layers of meaning, but you immediately recognize
what is implied in a quasi-homophonic way, in the English word *layer* which
both takes its place in the series of layers I have noted and designates the totality.

The strata of this palimpsest, its 'layers' are thus bottomless, since, for the
reasons I have given, they do not allow of totalization.

Now, this structure of the non-totalizable palimpsest which draws from one
of its elements the resources for the others (their *carrière* or quarry), and which
makes an unrepresentable and unobjectifiable labyrinth out of this play of
internal differences (scale without end, *scaling* without hierarchy): this is
precisely the structure of *Choral Work.* Its structure of stone and metal, the
superposition of layers (La Villette, the Eisenman-Derrida project, Tschumi's
Follies, etc.) plunges into the abyss of the 'platonic' *chora.* 'Lyre', 'layers',
would thus be a good title, over-title, or sub-title for *Choral Work.* And this
title is inscribed *in* the work, like a piece of the very thing which it names. It
says the truth of the work in the body of the work; it says the truth in a word
which is many words, a kind of many leaved book, but that is also the visible
figure of a lyre, the visibility of an instrument which foments the invisible:
music. And everything that 'lyric', in a word, may suggest.

But, for these same reasons, the truth of *Choral Work,* the truth which *lyre*
or *layer* says and does and gives is not a truth: it is not presentable, representable, totalizable; it never shows itself. It gives rise to no revelation of
presence, still less to an adequation. It is an irreducible inadequation which we
have just evoked; and also a challenge to the *subjectile.* For all these layers of
meaning and forms, of visibility and invisibility extend (lie, as in layers) *into*
each other, *on* or *under* each other, *in front of* or *behind* each other, but the
truth of the relationship is never established, never stabilized in any judgment.
It always causes something else to be said – allegorically – than that which is
said. *In a word,* it causes one to lie. The truth of the work lies in this lying
strength, this liar who accompanies all our representations (as Kant notes of the
'I think') but who also accompanies them as a lyre can accompany a choir.

Without equivalent and therefore without opposition. In this abyssal
palimpsest, no truth can establish itself on any primitive or final presence of the
meaning. In the labyrinth of this coral, the truth is the non-truth, the errance of
one of those 'errors' which belong to the title of another labyrinth, another
palimpsest, another 'quarry'. I have been speaking about this other for some
time now without naming it directly. I speak of Romeo and Juliet, an entire
story of names and contretemps about which I have also written elsewhere;[3]
here, I speak of Eisenman's Romeo and Juliet, *Moving Arrows, Eros and Other
Errors.* Have I not then lied? Have I not allegorically been speaking all this
while about something other than that which you believed? Yes and no. The lie
is without contrary, both absolute and null. It does not mislead in error, but in

those 'moving errors' whose erring is at once finite and infinite, random and programmed. For this lie without contrary, there is no liar to be found. What remains 'is' the unfindable, something entirely different from a signatory, conscious and assured of its mastery, entirely different from a subject; rather an infinite series of subjectiles and countersignatories, you among them, ready to take, to pay or miss the pleasure given by the passing of Eros. Liar or lyre, this is the royal name, for the moment, one of the best names, by which to signify, that is, the homonym and the pseudonym, the multiple voice of this secret signatory, the encrypted title of *Choral Work*. But if I say that we owe this to language more than to Peter Eisenman, you will ask me, 'which language?' There are so many. Do you mean the *meeting* of languages? An architecture which is at least tri- or quadrilingual, of polyglot stones or metals?

But if I tell you that we owe this chance to Peter Eisenman, whose own name, as you know, embodies both stone and metal, will you believe me? Nevertheless, I tell you the truth. It is the truth of this man of iron, determined to break with the anthropomorphic scale, with 'man the measure of all things': he writes such good books! I swear it to you!

This is of course what all the liars say; they would not be lying if they did not say that they were telling the truth.

I see that you do not believe me; let us explain things in another way. What is it that I hoped to have shown, about the subject of the *Choral Work*, all the while proposing with the other hand an autobiographical description of my meeting with Peter Eisenman, in all of the languages which are at work within him? All of this in truth refers to two other works, the *Fin d'Ou T Hou S* and *Moving Arrows, Eros, and Other Errors*. That which Jeffrey Kipnis correctly analysed as 'the endless play of readings'[4] is equally valuable for these three works. Each of the three is at the same time bigger and smaller than the series, which no doubt also includes the project for Venice (Cannaregio) and several others. And I had to find an economic way of speaking about all three at once and in a few pages, those which were allowed me. Similarly, at La Villette, we had little space, a single space with which we had to work. We had already multiplied it or divided it by three within itself and we hoped to multiply it by three again in the future. For the moment we have to find a structure which multiplies within a given economy, *faisant flèche de tout bois* (literally, 'making an arrow out of any piece of wood', i.e. making the best of one's resources), as we say in French, when meaning is displaced like an arrow, without ever being allowed to stop or collect itself, we will no longer oppose the errors which it provokes and which indeed are no longer lies, to the truth. Among *errors, eros* and *arrows,* the transformation is endless, and the contamination at once inevitable and aleatory. None of Eisenman's three projects presides at the meeting. They intersect like arrows, making a generative force out of mis-readings, mis-spellings, mispronunciations, a force which speaks of pleasure at the same time as procuring it. If I had enough time and enough space, I would analyse the stratagems with which Peter Eisenman plays, and what he has to do in his books, that is to say, in his constructions also, in order to fly like an arrow all the while avoiding being trapped by oppositions with which he nevertheless has to negotiate. The absence which he speaks of in *Moving Arrows . . .* is not opposed, and above all, is not dialectically opposed to presence. Linked as it is to the discontinuous structure of 'scaling', it is not a mere void. Determined by

Derrida   recursivity and by the internal–external difference of 'self-similarity', this absence 'produces', it 'is' (without being, nor being an origin or a productive cause) a *text,* better and something other than a 'good book'; more that *a* book, more than one; a text like 'an unending *transformation* of properties': 'Rather than an aesthetic object, the object becomes a text . . .' That which overturns the opposition presence/absence, and thus an entire ontology, must nevertheless be advanced within the language that it transforms in this way, within which is inscribed that which this language literally contains *without* containing, is found imprinted. Eisenman's architecture marks this 'without' (which I prefer to write in English), with/without, within and out, etc. We are related to this 'without' of the language, by dominating it in order to play with it, and at the same time in order to be subjected to the law, its law which is the law of the language, of languages, in truth of all marks. We are in this sense at the same time both passive and active. And we could say something *analogous* on the subject of this active/passive opposition in the texts of Eisenman, something analogous as well on the subject of analogies. But one must also know how to stop an arrow. He too knows how to do it.

We might be tempted to speak here of an architectural *Witz,* of a new textual economy (and *oikos,* after all, *is* the house; Eisenman also builds houses), an economy in which we no longer have to exclude the invisible from the visible, to oppose the temporal and the spatial, discourse and architecture. Not that we confuse them, but we distribute them according to another hierarchy, a hierarchy without an 'arché', a memory without origin, a hierarchy without hierarchy.

What there is there (there is, *es gibt*) is something beyond *Witz,* as in beyond the pleasure principle, if at least we understand these two words, *Witz* and *plaisir* as implying the intractable law of saving and economy.

Finally, to raise the question of the book once more: there are those who would like sometimes to imply somewhat facilely, that the most innovative 'theoretician' architects write books instead of building. It should not be forgotten that those who hold to this dogma generally do neither one nor the other. Eisenman writes, in effect. But in order to break with the norms and the authority of the existing economy, he needed, by means of something which still resembled a book *effectively* to clear a new space in which this an-economy would be at the same time possible and, to a certain point, legitimized, negotiated. This negotiation takes place within time, and it needs time with the powers and the cultures of the moment. For beyond the economy, beyond the book, whose form still displays this encompassing mania of speech, he writes something else.

It is a *topos:* monuments have often been compared to books.[5] Eisenman's 'libretti' are, no doubt, no longer books. Nor are they at all 'good and beautiful'. They pass the test of calligraphy or of the *callistique,* that ancient name for the aesthetic. I would not say that they are, notwithstanding, sublime. In its very disproportionateness, the sublime is still a human measure. *Ecce Homo:* end, the end of all, *la fin de tout.*

NOTES

1   Desmond Lee (trans.), Plato, *Timaeus and Critias.* Middlesex, England and New York: Penguin Classics, 1971, p. 72, 52e–53a.

2   *en abyme:* French expression meaning telescoping image, that is, an image which gets smaller   *Derrida*
    in constant multiplication of itself (trans. note).
3   *L'aphorism à Contretemps,* in *Romeo et Juliette, le Livre,* Paris: Papiers, 1986 (to be
    published in English).
4   So an endless play of readings: 'find out house', 'fine doubt house', 'find either or', 'end of
    where', 'end of covering' (in the wealth of reading possibilities, two of an 'inside' nature that
    have recently arisen might be interesting to indicate. 'Fin d'Ou T' can also suggest the French
    fin d'août, the end of August, the period, in fact, when the work on the project was
    completed. In addition, an English reader affecting French might well mispronounce the same
    fragment as 'fondu', a Swiss cooking technique (from the French *fondu* for melted, also a
    ballet term for bending at the knee) alluding to the presence of a Swiss-trained architect,
    Pieter Versteegh, as a principal design assistant!) etc., is provoked by regulated manipulations
    of the spaces – between letters, between languages, between image and writing – a
    manipulation that is in every way formal, in every way writing, yet blatantly independent of
    the manipulations that the foundations (of French or English) would permit.
    Jeffrey Kipnis, *Architecture Unbound, Consequences of the recent work of Peter Eisenman,*
                                                                    in *Fin d'Ou T Hou S,* p. 19.
5   Or the book to a monument. Hugo, for example, in *Notre Dame de Paris:* 'The book will kill
    the edifice,' but also 'The bible of stone and the bible of paper' ... 'the cathedral of
    Shakespeare ...' 'the mosque of Byron ...'.

MICHEL FOUCAULT

Michel
Foucault French philosopher Michel Foucault (1926–84) was concerned with examining the past as a means of diagnosing the present. For Foucault there was no essential order or meaning behind things, and everything was therefore to be judged according to a framework of knowledge which was forever changing. Foucault referred to the broad changes in intellectual outlook as *epistemes*, periodizations of knowledge not dissimilar to Thomas Kuhn's 'paradigms'. History, for Foucault, had to be understood according to the *epistemes* and discourses of the past. It was through a 'genealogical' analysis of the past that we would inevitably gain some insight into the way in which the present had been 'produced'. Foucault's own intellectual project in some sense mirrored the shifting preoccupations of his time. Thus, for example, Foucault's early work, *The Order of Things*, reflected the predominance of structuralism in the 1960s, while his later historical works, *Discipline and Punish* and, to a greater degree, *The History of Sexuality*, reflected the subsequent so-called 'poststructuralist' move away from the rigidities of structuralism.

The question of space is central to Foucault's thinking, and his work therefore has a special relevance to architecture. His treatment of this matter reflects shifts in his broader intellectual developments. The essay 'Of Other Spaces: Utopias and Heterotopias', for example, belongs to Foucault's early structuralist phase. Here Foucault is concerned with space as an institutionalized demarcation of structures of power. The discussion of Bentham's panopticon, by contrast, belongs to a transitional phase when Foucault was becoming increasingly preoccupied with the exercise of power in its more diffuse forms. The panopticon provides a model which encapsulates the characteristics of a society founded on discipline. It embodies a system in which surveillance plays a crucial role, and in which knowledge is inseparably bound to power. The very architectural layout of the panopticon affords various techniques of control, which, Foucault thought, would in themselves assure almost automatically the subjection and the subjectification of the inmates.

Foucault revisits the example of the panopticon in a subsequent interview, 'Space, Knowledge and Power', where he appears to qualify his earlier comments. On the subject of liberty, Foucault stresses that architecture in itself cannot act as a force of either liberation or oppression. 'I think that it can never be inherent in the structure of things to guarantee the exercise of freedom. The guarantee of freedom is freedom.' Architectural form, according to Foucault, cannot in itself address such questions, although it could produce 'positive effects' when the 'liberating intentions of the architect' coincide with 'the real practice of people in the exercise of their freedom'. Foucault is therefore not contradicting but merely qualifying his earlier comments on the panopticon. It is not the form of the panopticon which *Foucault* controls behaviour, but the power differential between warden and inmates. The efficient layout of the architecture is merely supporting the exercise of this power. Foucault thereby provides a crucial insight into the capacity for architecture to influence human behaviour.

Gilles Deleuze has offered a provocative gloss on the subject of the panopticon in his article, 'Postscripts on the Societies of Control'.

————

Foucault   # OF OTHER SPACES: UTOPIAS AND HETEROTOPIAS

As is well known, the great and obsessive dread of the nineteenth century was history, with its themes of development and stagnation, crisis and cycle, the accumulation of the past, the surplus of the dead and the world threatened by cooling. The nineteenth century found the quintessence of its mythological resources in the second law of thermodynamics. Our own era, on the other hand, seems to be that of space. We are in the age of the simultaneous, of juxtaposition, the near and the far, the side by side and the scattered. A period in which, in my view, the world is putting itself to the test, not so much as a great way of life destined to grow in time but as a net that links points together and creates its own muddle. It might be said that certain ideological conflicts which underlie the controversies of our day take place between pious descendants of time and tenacious inhabitants of space. Structuralism – or at least what is lumped together under this rather too vague label – is the attempt to establish between elements that may have been split over the course of time, a set of relationships that juxtapose them, set them in opposition or link them together, so as to create a sort of shape. Actually it is not so much a question of denying time as of a certain way of dealing with what we call time and which goes by the name of history.

For one thing the space which now looms on the horizon of our preoccupations, our theories and our systems, is not an innovation in Western history, having a history of its own. Nor is it possible to deny its fatal entanglement with time. To provide a very rough outline of its history, it could be said that there was a hierarchical system of places in the Middle Ages: places that were sacred and profane, protected and, on the contrary, open and undefended, urban places and rural places (for the real life of men anyhow). In cosmological theory, supercelestial places existed, in contrast to the celestial place, opposed in its turn to the terrestrial place; there were places where things could be found because they had been shifted there by violence and there were other places where, on the contrary, things found their natural position and rest. This hierarchy, contrast and mingling of places made up that which might, very approximately, be called medieval space. That is to say, the space of localization.

This space of localization was opened up by Galileo, for the real scandal caused by Galileo's work was not the discovery, or rediscovery, of the earth's movement around the sun, but the assertion of an infinite and infinitely open space, in which the space of the Middle Ages was to some extent dissolved. The location of a thing, in fact, was no longer anything more than a point in its movement, its rest nothing but its movement slowed down infinitely. In other words, from Galileo onward, ever since the seventeenth century, localization was replaced by extension.

Nowadays arrangement has taken over from extension, which had once replaced localization. It is defined by relationships of neighbourhood between points and elements, which can be described formally as series, trees and networks.

On the other hand, we know very well the importance of the problems of arrangements in contemporary technology: storage of information or of the partial results of a calculation in the memory of a machine; circulation of discrete elements to random outlets (automobiles, for instance, or even sounds transmitted over telephone lines); location of labelled or coded elements within a randomly divided set, or one that is classified according to univocal or multiple systems, etc.

In a still more concrete manner, the problem of position is posed for men in demographic terms. The question of the arrangement of the earth's inhabitants is not just one of knowing whether there will be enough room for all of them – a problem that is in any case of the greatest importance – but also one of knowing what are the relations of vicinity, what kind of storage, circulation, reference and classification of human elements should take preference in this or that situation, according to the objective that is being sought. In our era, space presents itself to us in the form of patterns of ordering.

In any case, I feel that current anxiety is fundamentally concerned with space, much more than with time: the latter, probably, merely appears to us as one of the many possible patterns of distribution between elements that are scattered over space.

Now, it may be that contemporary space has not yet lost those sacred characteristics (which time certainly lost in the nineteenth century), in spite of all the techniques that assail it and the web of knowledge that allows it to be defined and formalized. Of course, a theoretical desanctification of space, for which Galileo's work gave the signal, has already occurred: it remains to be seen whether we have achieved its desanctification in practice. It may be, in fact, that our lives are still ruled by a certain number of unrelenting opposites, which institution and practice have not dared to erode. I refer here to opposites that we take for granted, such as the contrast between public and private space, family and social space, cultural and utilitarian space, the space of pleasure and the space of work – all opposites that are still actuated by a veiled sacredness.

The (immense) work of Bachelard and the descriptions of the phenomenologists have taught us that we do not live in a homogeneous and empty space, but in a space that is saturated with qualities, and that may even be pervaded by a spectral aura. The space of our primary perception, of our dreams and of our passions, holds within itself almost intrinsic qualities: it is light, ethereal, transparent, or dark, uneven, cluttered. Again, it is a space of height, of peaks, or on the contrary, of the depths of mud; space that flows, like spring water, or fixed space, like stone or crystal.

In any case, these analyses, however fundamental for contemporary thought, are primarily concerned with inner space. But it is about external space that I would like to speak now. The space in which we live, from which we are drawn out of ourselves, just where the erosion of our lives, our time, our history takes place, this space that wears us down and consumes us, is in itself heterogeneous. In other words, we do not live in a sort of a vacuum, within which individuals and things can be located, or that may take on so many different fleeting colours, but in a set of relationships that define positions which cannot be equated or in any way superimposed.

Certainly, one could undertake the description of these different arrangements, looking for the set of relationships that defines them. For instance, by describing the set of relationships that defines arrangements of transition, roads, trains (and, with regard to the latter, think of the extraordinary bundle

Foucault   of relations represented by something through which one passes, by means of which we pass from one point to another, and which, in its turn, has the power of passing). Through the sets of relationships that define them, one could describe arrangements where one makes a temporary halt: cafes, cinemas, beaches. It would be equally possible to define, through its network of relations, the arrangements of rest, closed or partly open, that make up the house, the bedroom, the bed, etc. . . . However I am only interested in a few of these arrangements: to be precise, those which are endowed with the curious property of being in relation with all the others, but in such a way as to suspend, neutralize or invert the set of relationships designed, reflected or mirrored by themselves. These spaces, which are in rapport in some way with all the others, and yet contradict them, are of two general types.

First of all, the utopias. These are arrangements which have no real space. Arrangements which have a general relationship of direct or inverse analogy with the real space of society. They represent society itself brought to perfection, or its reverse, and in any case utopias are spaces that are by their very essence fundamentally unreal.

There also exist, and this is probably true for all cultures and all civilizations, real and effective spaces which are outlined in the very institution of society, but which constitute a sort of counter-arrangement, of effectively realized utopia, in which all the real arrangements, all the other real arrangements that can be found within society, are at one and the same time represented, challenged and overturned: a sort of place that lies outside all places and yet is actually localizable. In contrast to the utopias, these places which are absolutely *other* with respect to all the arrangements that they reflect and of which they speak might be described as heterotopias. Between these two, I would then set that sort of mixed experience which partakes of the qualities of both types of location, the mirror. It is, after all, a utopia, in that it is a place without a place. In it, I see myself where I am not, in an unreal space that opens up potentially beyond its surface; there I am down there where I am not, a sort of shadow that makes my appearance visible to myself, allowing me to look at myself where I do not exist: utopia of the mirror. At the same time, we are dealing with a heterotopia. The mirror really exists and has a kind of come-back effect on the place that I occupy: starting from it, in fact. I find myself absent from the place where I am, in that I see myself in there.

Starting from that gaze which to some extent is brought to bear on me, from the depths of that virtual space which is on the other side of the mirror, I turn back on myself, beginning to turn my eyes on myself and reconstitute myself where I am in reality. Hence the mirror functions as a heterotopia, since it makes the place that I occupy, whenever I look at myself in the glass, both absolutely real – it is in fact linked to all the surrounding space and absolutely unreal, for in order to be perceived it has of necessity to pass that virtual point that is situated down there.

As for the heterotopias in the proper sense of the word, how can we describe them? What meaning do they have? We might postulate, not a science, a now overworked word, but a sort of systematic description. Given a particular society, this would have as its object the study, analysis, description and 'reading', as it is the fashion to call it nowadays, of those different spaces, those other places, in a kind of both mythical and real contestation of the space in which we live. Such a description might be called heterotopology. Its first principle is that there is probably not a single culture in the world that is not made up of heterotopias. It is a constant feature of all human groups. It is evident, though, that heterotopias assume a wide variety of forms, to the extent that a single, absolutely universal form may not exist. In any case, it is possible to classify them into two main types. In so-called primitive societies, there is a certain kind of heterotopia which I would describe as that of crisis; it comprises privileged or sacred or forbidden places that are reserved for the individual who finds himself in a state of crisis with respect to the society or the environment in which he lives: adolescents, women during the menstrual period or in labour, the old, etc.

In our own society, these heterotopias of crisis are steadily disappearing, even though some vestiges of them are bound to survive. For instance, the boarding school in its nineteenth-century form or military service for young men has played a role of this kind, so that the first manifestations of male sexuality could occur 'elsewhere', away from the family. For girls there was, up until the middle of this century, the tradition of the honeymoon, or *'voyage de noces'* as it is called in French, an ancestral theme. The girl's defloration could not take place 'anywhere' and at that time, the train or the honeymoon hotel represented that place which was not located anywhere, a heterotopia without geographical co-ordinates.

Yet these heterotopias of crisis are vanishing today, only to be replaced, I believe, by others which could be described as heterotopias of deviance, occupied by individuals whose behaviour deviates from the current average or standard. They are the rest homes, psychiatric clinics and, let us be clear, prisons, in a list which must undoubtedly be extended to cover old-people's homes, in a way on the border between the heterotopia of crisis and that of deviance. This is because in a society like our own, where pleasure is the rule, the inactivity of old age constitutes not only a crisis but a deviation.

The second element of my description: over the course of its history, a society may take an existing heterotopia, which has never vanished, and make it function in a very different way. Actually, each heterotopia has a precise and well-defined function within society and the same heterotopia can, in accordance with the synchroneity of the culture in which it is located, have a different function.

Let us take, for example, the curious heterotopia of the cemetery. This is certainly an 'other' place with respect to ordinary cultural spaces, and yet it is connected with all the locations of the city, the society, the village, and so on, since every family has some relative there. In Western culture, one might say that it has always existed. And yet it has undergone important changes.

Up until the end of the eighteenth century, the cemetery was located in the very heart of the city, near the church.

Within it, there existed a hierarchy of every possible type of tomb. There was an ossuary where the corpses lost their last traces of individuality, there were some individual tombs, and there were the graves inside the church, which conformed to two models: either a simple slab of marble, or a mausoleum with statues, etc. The cemetery, situated in the sacred space of the church, has taken on quite another character in modern civilization. It is curious to note that in an age which has been very roughly defined as 'atheist', Western culture has inaugurated the so-called cult of the dead.

After all, it was very natural that, as long as people actually believed in the resurrection of the body and the immortality of the soul, not a great deal of importance was given to the mortal remains. On the contrary, from the moment when people were no longer so certain of survival after death, it became logical to take much more care with the remains of the dead, the only trace, in the end, of our existence in the world and in words.

In any case, it is from the nineteenth century onward that each of us has had the right to his own little box for his little personal decomposition, but it is only from the nineteenth century on that the cemetery began to be shifted to the outskirts of the city. In parallel to this individualization of death and the bourgeois appropriation of the cemetery, an obsession with death as 'sickness' has emerged. It is supposed that the dead transmit sickness to the living and that their presence and proximity to the houses and church, almost in the middle of the street, spreads death. This great concern with the spread of sickness by contagion from cemeteries began to appear with insistence toward the end of the eighteenth century, but the cemeteries only moved out to the suburbs during the course of the nineteenth. From then on, they no longer constituted the sacred and immortal wind of the city, but the 'other city', where each family possessed its gloomy dwelling.

Third principle. The heterotopia has the power of juxtaposing in a single real place different spaces and locations that are incompatible with each other. Thus on the rectangle of its stage, the theatre alternates as a series of places that are alien to each other; thus the cinema appears as a very curious rectangular hall, at the back of which a three-dimensional space is projected onto a two-dimensional screen. Perhaps the oldest example of these heterotopias in the form of contradictory locations is the garden. Let us not forget that this astounding and age-old creation had very profound meanings in the East, and that these seemed to be superimposed. The traditional garden of the Persians was a sacred space that was supposed to unite four separate parts within its rectangle, representing the four parts of the world, as well as one space still more sacred than the others, a space that was like the navel, the centre of the world brought into the garden (it was here that the basin and jet of water were located). All the vegetation was concentrated in this zone, as if in a sort of microcosm. As for carpets. they originally set out to reproduce gardens, since the garden was a carpet where the world in its entirety achieved symbolic perfection, and the carpet a sort of movable garden in space. The garden is the smallest fragment of the world and, at the same time, represents its totality, forming right from the remotest times a sort of felicitous and universal heterotopia (from which are derived our own zoological gardens).

Fourth principle. Heterotopias are linked for the most part to bits and pieces of time, i.e. they open up through what we might define as a pure symmetry of heterochronisms. The heterotopia enters fully into function when men find themselves in a sort of total breach of their traditional time. Then it is easy to see how the cemetery is a highly heterotopian place, in that it begins with that strange heterochronism that is, for a human being, the loss of life and of that quasi-eternity in which, however, he does not cease to dissolve and be erased.

Generally speaking, in a society like ours, heterotopia and heterochronism   *Foucault*
are organized and arranged in a relatively complex fashion. In the first place
there are the heterotopias of time which accumulate *ad infinitum*, such as
museums and libraries. These are heterotopias in which time does not cease to
accumulate, perching, so to speak, on its own summit. Yet up until the end of
the seventeenth century, these had still been the expression of an individual
choice. The idea of accumulating everything, on the contrary, of creating a sort
of universal archive, the desire to enclose all times, all eras, forms and styles
within a single place, the concept of making all times into one place, and yet a
place that is outside time, inaccessible to the wear and tear of the years,
according to a plan of almost perpetual and unlimited accumulation within an
irremovable place, all this belongs entirely to our modern outlook. Museums
and libraries are heterotopias typical of nineteenth-century Western culture.

Along with this type, bound up with the accumulation of time, there are
other heterotopias linked to time in its more futile, transitory and precarious
aspects, a time viewed as celebration. These then are heterotopias without a
bias toward the eternal. They are absolutely time-bound. To this class belong
the fairs, those marvelous empty zones outside the city limits, that fill up twice
a year with booths, showcases, miscellaneous objects, wrestlers, snake-women,
optimistic fortune-tellers, etc. Very recently, a new form of chronic heterotopia
has been invented, that of the holiday village: a sort of Polynesian village which
offers three short weeks of primitive and eternal nudity to city dwellers. It is
easy to see, on the other hand, how the two types of heterotopia, that of the
festival and that of the eternity of accumulating time, come together: the huts
on the island of Jerba are relatives in a way of the libraries and museums. And
in fact, by rediscovering Polynesian life, is not time abolished at the very
moment in which it is found again? It is the whole story of humanity that dates
right back to the origins, like a kind of great and immediate knowledge.

Fifth principle. Heterotopias always presuppose a system of opening and
closing that isolates them and makes them penetrable at one and the same time.
Usually, one does not get into a heterotopian location by one's own will. Either
one is forced, as in the case of the barracks or the prison, or one must submit to
rites of purification. One can only enter by special permission and after one has
completed a certain number of gestures. Heterotopias also exist that are
entirely devoted to practices of purification that are half religious, half hygienic
(the Muslim 'hammams'), or apparently solely hygienic (Scandinavian saunas).

Other heterotopias, on the contrary, have the appearance of pure and simple
openings, although they usually conceal curious exclusions. Anyone can enter
one of these heterotopian locations, but, in reality, they are nothing more than
an illusion: one thinks one has entered and, by the sole fact of entering, one is
excluded. I am reminded, for instance, of those famous rooms to be found on
big farms in Brazil and throughout South America in general. The front door
did not give onto the main part of the house, where the family lived, so that any
person who happened to pass by, any traveller, had the right to push open that
door, enter the room, and spend the night there. Now, the rooms were arranged
in such a way that anyone who went in there could never reach to the heart of
the family: more than ever a passing visitor, never a true guest. This type of
heterotopia, which has now almost entirely vanished from our civilization,
might perhaps be recognized in the American 'motel' room, which one enters

with one's own vehicle and lover and where illicit sex is totally protected and totally concealed at one and the same time, set apart and yet not under an open sky.

Finally, the last characteristic of heterotopias is that they have, in relation to the rest of space, a function that takes place between two opposite poles. On the one hand they perform the task of creating a space of illusion that reveals how all of real space is more illusory, all the locations within which life is fragmented. On the other, they have the function of forming another space, another real space, as perfect, meticulous and well-arranged as ours is disordered, ill-conceived and in a sketchy state. This heterotopia is not one of illusion but of compensation, and I wonder if it is not somewhat in this manner that certain colonies have functioned.

In a number of cases they have played, at the level of the general organization of terrestrial space, the genuine role of a heterotopia. An example of this, from the first wave of colonization in the seventeenth century, might be some of the Puritan colonies founded by the English in America, which were absolutely perfect places.

Or those extraordinary Jesuit colonies, set up in South America: wonderful, totally regulated colonies, in which human perfection was actually reached. The Jesuits of Paraguay had established settlements in which existence was regulated point by point. The village was laid out according to a strict pattern around a rectangular square at one end of which stood the church; on one side, the college, on the other the cemetery, while, facing the church, there was a street which met another at a right angle. Each family's hut lay on one of these two axes, reproducing exactly the symbol of Christ. Thus Christianity made its fundamental mark on the space and geography of the American world.

The daily life of individuals was regulated not by the whistle, but by the bell: the same hour of awakening laid down for all, with meals at midday and five o'clock. Afterward people went to bed and, at midnight, came what was known as the conjugal awakening: at this sound of the monastery's bell, each of them did his and her duty.

Brothels and colonies, here are two extreme types of heterotopia. Think of the ship: it is a floating part of space, a placeless place, that lives by itself, closed in on itself and at the same time poised in the infinite ocean, and yet, from port to port, tack by tack, from brothel to brothel, it goes as far as the colonies, looking for the most precious things hidden in their gardens. Then you will understand why it has been not only and obviously the main means of economic growth (which I do not intend to go into here), but at the same time the greatest reserve of imagination for our civilization from the sixteenth century down to the present day. The ship is the heterotopia *par excellence*. In civilizations where it is lacking, dreams dry up, adventure is replaced by espionage, and privateers by the police.

PANOPTICISM (EXTRACT)

The following, according to an order published at the end of the seventeenth century, were the measures to be taken when the plague appeared in a town.[1]

First, a strict spatial partitioning: the closing of the town and its outlying   *Foucault*
districts, a prohibition to leave the town on pain of death, the killing of all stray
animals; the division of the town into distinct quarters, each governed by an
intendant. Each street is placed under the authority of a syndic, who keeps it
under surveillance; if he leaves the street, he will be condemned to death. On
the appointed day, everyone is ordered to stay indoors: it is forbidden to leave
on pain of death. The syndic himself comes to lock the door of each house from
the outside; he takes the key with him and hands it over to the intendant of the
quarter; the intendant keeps it until the end of the quarantine. Each family will
have made its own provisions; but, for bread and wine, small wooden canals
are set up between the street and the interior of the houses, thus allowing each
person to receive his ration without communicating with the suppliers and
other residents; meat, fish and herbs will be hoisted up into the houses with
pulleys and baskets. If it is absolutely necessary to leave the house, it will be
done in turn, avoiding any meeting. Only the intendants, syndics and guards
will move about the streets and also, between the infected houses, from one
corpse to another, the 'crows', who can be left to die: these are 'people of little
substance who carry the sick, bury the dead, clean and do many vile and abject
offices'. It is a segmented, immobile, frozen space. Each individual is fixed in
his place. And, if he moves, he does so at the risk of his life, contagion or
punishment.

Inspection functions ceaselessly. The gaze is alert everywhere: 'A considerable body of militia, commanded by good officers and men of substance',
guards at the gates, at the town hall and in every quarter to ensure the prompt
obedience of the people and the most absolute authority of the magistrates, 'as
also to observe all disorder theft and extortion'. At each of the town gates there
will be an observation post; at the end of each street sentinels. Every day, the
intendant visits the quarter in his charge, inquires whether the syndics have
carried out their tasks, whether the inhabitants have anything to complain of;
they 'observe their actions'. Every day, too, the syndic goes into the street for
which he is responsible; stops before each house: gets all the inhabitants to
appear at the windows (those who live overlooking the courtyard will be
allocated a window looking onto the street at which no one but they may show
themselves); he calls each of them by name; informs himself as to the state of
each and every one of them – 'in which respect the inhabitants will be compelled to speak the truth under pain of death', if someone does not appear at the
window, the syndic must ask why: 'In this way he will find out easily enough
whether dead or sick are being concealed.' Everyone locked up in his cage,
everyone at his window, answering to his name and showing himself when
asked – it is the great review of the living and the dead.

This surveillance is based on a system of permanent registration: reports
from the syndics to the intendants, from the intendants to the magistrates or
mayor. At the beginning of the 'lock up', the role of each of the inhabitants
present in the town is laid down, one by one; this document bears 'the name,
age, sex of everyone, notwithstanding his condition': a copy is sent to the
intendant of the quarter, another to the office of the town hall, another to
enable the syndic to make his daily roll call. Everything that may be observed
during the course of the visits – deaths, illnesses, complaints, irregularities – is
noted down and transmitted to the intendants and magistrates. The magistrates

Foucault   have complete control over medical treatment; they have appointed a physician in charge; no other practitioner may treat, no apothecary prepare medicine, no confessor visit a sick person without having received from him a written note 'to prevent anyone from concealing and dealing with those sick of the contagion unknown to the magistrates'. The registration of the pathological must be constantly centralized. The relation of each individual to his disease and to his death passes through the representatives of power, the registration they make of it, the decisions they take on it.

Five or six days after the beginning of the quarantine, the process of purifying the houses one by one is begun. All the inhabitants are made to leave; in each room 'the furniture and goods' are raised from the ground or suspended from the air; perfume is poured around the room; after carefully sealing the windows, doors and even the keyholes with wax, the perfume is set alight. Finally, the entire house is closed while the perfume is consumed; those who have carried out the work are searched, as they were on entry, 'in the presence of the residents of the house, to see that they did not have something on their persons as they left that they did not have on entering'. Four hours later, the residents are allowed to re-enter their homes.

This enclosed, segmented space, observed at every point, in which the individuals are inserted in a fixed place, in which the slightest movements are supervised, in which all events are recorded, in which an uninterrupted work of writing links the centre and periphery, in which power is exercised without division, according to a continuous hierarchical figure, in which each individual is constantly located, examined and distributed among the living beings, the sick and the dead – all this constitutes a compact model of the disciplinary mechanism. The plague is met by order; its function is to sort out every possible confusion: that of the disease, which is transmitted when bodies are mixed together; that of the evil, which is increased when fear and death overcome prohibitions. It lays down for each individual his place, his body, his disease and his death, his well-being, by means of an omnipresent and omniscient power that subdivides itself in a regular, uninterrupted way even to the ultimate determination of the individual, of what characterizes him, of what belongs to him, of what happens to him. Against the plague, which is a mixture, discipline brings into play its power, which is one of analysis. A whole literary fiction of the festival grew up around the plague: suspended laws, lifted prohibitions, the frenzy of passing time, bodies mingling together without respect, individuals unmasked, abandoning their statutory identity and the figure under which they had been recognized, allowing a quite different truth to appear. But there was also a political dream of the plague, which was exactly its reverse: not the collective festival but strict divisions; not laws transgressed, but the penetration of regulation into even the smallest details of everyday life through the mediation of the complete hierarchy that assured the capillary functioning of power; not masks that were put on and taken off, but the assignment to each individual of his 'true' name, his 'true' place, his true body, his 'true' disease. The plague as a form, at once real and imaginary, of disorder had as its medical and political correlative discipline. Behind the disciplinary mechanisms can be read the haunting memory of 'contagions', of the plague, of rebellions, crimes, vagabondage, desertions, people who appear and disappear, live and die in disorder.

If it is true that the leper gave rise to rituals of exclusion, which to a certain _Foucault_ extent provided the model for and general form of the great Confinement, then the plague gave rise to disciplinary projects. Rather than the massive, binary division between one set of people and another, it called for multiple separations, individualizing distributions, an organization in depth of surveillance and control, an intensification and a ramification of power. The leper was caught up in a practice of rejection, of exile-enclosure; he was left to his doom in a mass among which it was useless to differentiate – those sick of the plague were caught up in a meticulous tactical partitioning in which individual differentiations were the constricting effects of a power that multiplied, articulated and subdivided itself; the great confinement on the one hand; the correct training on the other The leper and his separation; the plague and its segmentations. The first is marked; the second analysed and distributed. The exile of the leper and the arrest of the plague do not bring with them the same political dream. The first is that of a pure community, the second that of a disciplined society. Two ways of exercising power over men, of controlling their relations, of separating out their dangerous mixtures. The plague-stricken town, traversed throughout with hierarchy, surveillance, observation, writing; the town immobilized by the functioning of an extensive power that bears in a distinct way over all individual bodies – this is the utopia of the perfectly governed city. The plague (envisaged as a possibility at least) is the trial in the course of which one may define ideally the exercise of disciplinary power. In order to make rights and laws function according to pure theory, the jurists place themselves in imagination in the state of nature; in order to see perfect disciplines functioning, rulers dreamt of the state of plague. Underlying disciplinary projects the image of the plague stands for all forms of confusion and disorder; just as the image of the leper, cut off from all human contact, underlies projects of exclusion.

They are different projects, then, but not incompatible ones. We see them coming slowly together, and it is the peculiarity of the nineteenth century that it applied to the space of exclusion of which the leper was the symbolic inhabitant (beggars, vagabonds, madmen and the disorderly formed the real population) the technique of power proper to disciplinary partitioning. Treat 'lepers' as 'plague victims', project the subtle segmentations of discipline onto the confused space of internment, combine it with the methods of analytical distribution proper to power, individualize the excluded, but use procedures of individualization to mark exclusion – this is what was operated regularly by disciplinary power from the beginning of the nineteenth century in the psychiatric asylum, the penitentiary, the reformatory, the approved school and, to some extent, the hospital. Generally speaking, all the authorities exercising individual control function according to a double mode; that of binary division and branding (mad/sane; dangerous/harmless; normal/abnormal); and that of coercive assignment, of differential distribution (who he is; where he must be; how he is to be characterized; how he is to be recognized; how a constant surveillance is to be exercised over him in an individual way, etc.). On the one hand, the lepers are treated as plague victims; the tactics of individualizing disciplines are imposed on the excluded; and, on the other hand, the universality of disciplinary controls makes it possible to brand the 'leper' and to bring into play against him the dualistic mechanisms of exclusion. The constant

Foucault   division between the normal and the abnormal, to which every individual is subjected, brings us back to our own time, by applying the binary branding and exile of the leper to quite different objects; the existence of a whole set of techniques and institutions for measuring, supervising and correcting the abnormal brings into play the disciplinary mechanisms to which the fear of the plague gave rise. All the mechanisms of power which, even today, are disposed around the abnormal individual, to brand him and to alter him, are composed of those two forms from which they distantly derive.

Bentham's *Panopticon* is the architectural figure of this composition. We know the principle on which it was based: at the periphery an annular building; at the centre, a tower; this tower is pierced with wide windows that open onto the inner side of the ring; the peripheric building is divided into cells, each of which extends the whole width of the building; they have two windows, one on the inside, corresponding to the windows of the tower; the other, on the outside, allows the light to cross the cell from one end to the other. All that is needed, then, is to place a supervisor in the central tower and to shut up in each cell a madman, a patient, a condemned man, a worker or a schoolboy. By the

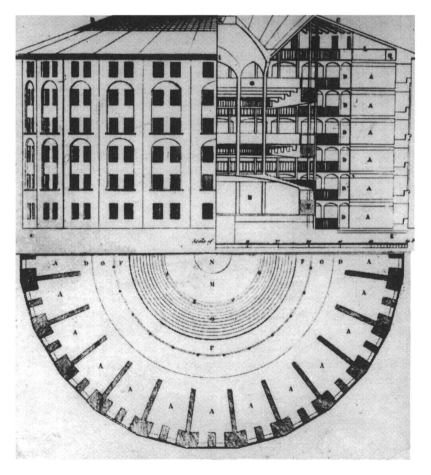

Figure 2 Bentham's Panopticon (1791)
Source: J. Bentham, *Panopticon; Postscript*, London, 1791

effect of backlighting, one can observe from the tower, standing out precisely *Foucault* against the light, the small captive shadows in the cells of the periphery. They are like so many cages, so many small theatres, in which each actor is alone, perfectly individualized and constantly visible. The panoptic mechanism arranges spatial unities that make it possible to see constantly and to recognize immediately. In short, it reverses the principle of the dungeon; or rather of its three functions – to enclose, to deprive of light and to hide – it preserves only the first and eliminates the other two. Full lighting and the eye of a supervisor capture better than darkness, which ultimately protected. Visibility is a trap.

To begin with, this made it possible – as a negative effect – to avoid those compact, swarming, howling masses that were to be found in places of confinement, those painted by Goya or described by Howard. Each individual, in his place, is securely confined to a cell from which he is seen from the front by the supervisor; but the side walls prevent him from coming into contact with his companions. He is seen, but he does not see; he is the object of information, never a subject in communication. The arrangement of his room, opposite the central tower, imposes on him an axial visibility; but the divisions of the ring, those separated cells, imply a lateral invisibility. And this invisibility is a guarantee of order. If the inmates are convicts, there is no danger of a plot, an attempt at collective escape, the planning of new crimes for the future, bad reciprocal influences; if they are patients, there is no danger of contagion; if they are madmen, there is no risk of their committing violence upon one another; if they are schoolchildren, there is no copying, no noise, no chatter, no waste of time; if they are workers, there are no disorders, no theft, no coalitions, none of those distractions that slow down the rate of work, make it less perfect or cause accidents. The crowd, a compact mass, a locus of multiple exchanges, individualities merging together, a collective effect, is abolished and replaced by a collection of separated individualities. From the point of view of the guardian, it is replaced by a multiplicity that can be numbered and supervised; from the point of view of the inmates, by a sequestered and observed solitude.[2]

Hence the major effect of the Panopticon: to induce in the inmate a state of conscious and permanent visibility that assures the automatic functioning of power. So to arrange things that the surveillance is permanent in its effects, even if it is discontinuous in its action; that the perfection of power should tend to render its actual exercise unnecessary; that this architectural apparatus should be a machine for creating and sustaining a power relation independent of the person who exercises it; in short, that the inmates should be caught up in a power situation of which they are themselves the bearers. To achieve this, it is at once too much and too little that the prisoner should be constantly observed by an inspector: too little, for what matters is that he knows himself to be observed; too much, because he has no need in fact of being so. In view of this, Bentham laid down the principle that power should be visible and unverifiable. Visible: the inmate will constantly have before his eyes the tall outline of the central tower from which he is spied upon. Unverifiable: the inmate must never know whether he is being looked at at any one moment; but he must be sure that he may always be so. In order to make the presence or absence of the inspector unverifiable, so that the prisoners, in their cells, cannot even see a shadow, Bentham envisaged not only venetian blinds on the windows of the central observation hall, but, on the inside, partitions that intersected the hall at right angles and, in order to pass from one quarter to the other, not doors but zig-zag openings; for the slightest noise, a gleam of light, a brightness in a half-opened door would betray the presence of the guardian.[3] The Panopticon is a machine for dissociating the see/being seen dyad: in the peripheric ring, one is totally seen, without ever seeing; in the central tower, one sees everything without ever being seen.[4]

It is an important mechanism, for it automatizes and disindividualizes power. Power has its principle not so much in a person as in a certain concerted distribution of bodies, surfaces, lights, gazes; in an arrangement whose internal mechanisms produce the relation in which individuals are caught up. The ceremonies, the rituals, the marks by which the sovereign's surplus power was manifested are useless. There is a machinery that assures dissymmetry, disequilibrium, difference. Consequently, it does not matter who exercises power. Any individual, taken almost at random, can operate the machine: in the absence of the director, his family, his friends, his visitors, even his servants.[5] Similarly, it does not matter what motive animates him: the curiosity of the indiscreet, the malice of a child, the thirst for knowledge of a philosopher who wishes to visit this museum of human nature, or the perversity of those who take pleasure in spying and punishing. The more numerous those anonymous and temporary observers are, the greater the risk for the inmate of being surprised and the greater his anxious awareness of being observed. The Panopticon is a marvellous machine which, whatever use one may wish to put it to, produces homogeneous effects of power.

A real subjection is born mechanically from a fictitious relation. So it is not necessary to use force to constrain the convict to good behaviour, the madman to calm, the worker to work, the schoolboy to application, the patient to the observation of the regulations. Bentham was surprised that panoptic institutions could be so light: there were no more bars, no more chains, no more heavy locks; all that was needed was that the separations should be clear and the openings well arranged. The heaviness of the old 'houses of security' with their fortress-like architecture, could be replaced by the simple, economic geometry of a 'house of certainty'. The efficiency of power, its constraining force have, in a sense, passed over to the other side – to the side of its surface of application. He who is subjected to a field of visibility, and who knows it, assumes responsibility for the constraints of power; he makes them play spontaneously upon himself; he inscribes in himself the power relation in which he simultaneously plays both roles; he becomes the principle of his own subjection. By this very fact, the external power may throw off its physical weight; it tends to the non-corporal; and, the more it approaches this limit, the more constant, profound and permanent are its effects: it is a perpetual victory that avoids any physical confrontation and which is always decided in advance.

Bentham does not say whether he was inspired, in his project, by Le Vaux's menagerie at Versailles: the first menagerie in which the different elements are not, as they traditionally were, distributed in a park.[6] At the centre was an octagonal pavilion which, on the first floor, consisted of only a single room, the king's *salon*; on every side large windows looked out onto seven cages (the eighth side was reserved for the entrance), containing different species of animals. By Bentham's time, this menagerie had disappeared. But one finds in

Foucault

the programme of the Panopticon a similar concern with individualizing observation, with characterization and classification, with the analytical arrangement of space. The Panopticon is a royal menagerie; the animal is replaced by man, individual distribution by specific grouping and the king by the machinery of a furtive power. With this exception, the Panopticon also does the work of a naturalist. It makes it possible to draw up differences: among patients, to observe the symptoms of each individual, without the proximity of beds, the circulation of miasmas, the effects of contagion confusing the clinical tables; among schoolchildren, it makes it possible to observe performances (without there being any imitation or copying), to map aptitudes, to assess characters, to draw up rigorous classifications and, in relation to normal development, to distinguish 'laziness and stubbornness' from 'incurable imbecility'; among workers, it makes it possible to note the aptitudes of each worker, compare the time he takes to perform a task and, if they are paid by the day, to calculate their wages.[7]

So much for the question of observation. But the Panopticon was also a laboratory; it could be used as a machine to carry out experiments, to alter behaviour, to train or correct individuals. To experiment with medicines and monitor their effects. To try out different punishments on prisoners, according to their crimes and character, and to seek the most effective ones. To teach different techniques simultaneously to the workers, to decide which is the best. To try out pedagogical experiments – and in particular to take up once again the well-debated problem of secluded education, by using orphans. One would see what would happen when, in their sixteenth or eighteenth year, they were presented with other boys or girls; one could verify whether, as Helvetius thought, anyone could learn anything; one would follow 'the genealogy of every observable idea'; one could bring up different children according to different systems of thought, making certain children believe that two and two do not make four or that the moon is a cheese, then put them together when they are twenty or twenty-five years old; one would then have discussions that would be worth a great deal more than the sermons or lectures on which so much money is spent; one would have at least an opportunity of making discoveries in the domain of metaphysics. The Panopticon is a privileged place for experiments on men, and for analysing with complete certainty the transformations that may be obtained from them. The Panopticon may even provide an apparatus for supervising its own mechanisms. In this central tower, the director may spy on all the employees that he has under his orders: nurses, doctors, foremen, teachers, warders; he will be able to judge them continuously, alter their behaviour, impose upon them the methods he thinks best; and it will even be possible to observe the director himself. An inspector arriving unexpectedly at the centre of the Panopticon will be able to judge at a glance, without anything being concealed from him, how the entire establishment is functioning. And, in any case, enclosed as he is in the middle of this architectural mechanism, is not the director's own fate entirely bound up with it? The incompetent physician who has allowed contagion to spread, the incompetent prison governor or workshop manager will be the first victims of an epidemic or a revolt. "By every tie I could devise', said the master of the Panopticon, 'my own fate had been bound up by me with theirs" '.[8] The Panopticon functions as a kind of laboratory of power. Thanks to its

Foucault mechanisms of observation, it gains in efficiency and in the ability to penetrate into men's behaviour; knowledge follows the advances of power, discovering new objects of knowledge over all the surfaces on which power is exercised.

The plague-stricken town, the panoptic establishment – the differences are important. They mark, at a distance of a century and a half, the transformations of the disciplinary programme. In the first case, there is an exceptional situation: against an extraordinary evil, power is mobilized; it makes itself everywhere present and visible; it invents new mechanisms; it separates, it immobilizes, it partitions; it constructs for a time what is both a counter-city and the perfect society; it imposes an ideal functioning, but one that is reduced, in the final analysis, like the evil that it combats, to a simple dualism of life and death: that which moves brings death, and one kills that which moves. The Panopticon, on the other hand, must be understood as a generalizable model of functioning; a way of defining power relations in terms of the everyday life of men. No doubt Bentham presents it as a particular institution, closed in upon itself. Utopias, perfectly closed in upon themselves, are common enough. As opposed to the ruined prisons, littered with mechanisms of torture, to be seen in Piranesi's engravings, the Panopticon presents a cruel, ingenious cage. The fact that it should have given rise, even in our own time, to so many variations, projected or realized, is evidence of the imaginary intensity that it has possessed for almost two hundred years. But the Panopticon must not be understood as a dream building: it is the diagram of a mechanism of power reduced to its ideal form; its functioning, abstracted from any obstacle, resistance or friction, must be represented as a pure architectural and optical system: it is in fact a figure of political technology that may and must be detached from any specific use.

It is polyvalent in its applications; it serves to reform prisoners, but also to treat patients, to instruct schoolchildren, to confine the insane, to supervise workers, to put beggars and idlers to work. It is a type of location of bodies in space, of distribution of individuals in relation to one another, of hierarchical organization, of disposition of centres and channels of power, of definition of the instruments and modes of intervention of power, which can be implemented in hospitals, workshops, schools, prisons. Whenever one is dealing with a multiplicity of individuals on whom a task or a particular form of behaviour must be imposed, the panoptic schema may be used. It is – necessary modifications apart – applicable 'to all establishments whatsoever, in which, within a space not too large to be covered or commanded by buildings, a number of persons are meant to be kept under inspection';[9] (although Bentham takes the penitentiary house as his prime example, it is because it has many different functions to fulfil – safe custody, confinement, solitude, forced labour and instruction).

In each of its applications, it makes it possible to perfect the exercise of power. It does this in several ways: because it can reduce the number of those who exercise it, while increasing the number of those on whom it is exercised. Because it is possible to intervene at any moment and because the constant pressure acts even before the offences, mistakes or crimes have been committed. Because, in these conditions, its strength is that it never intervenes, it is exercised spontaneously and without noise, it constitutes a mechanism whose effects follow from one another. Because, without any physical instrument

other than architecture and geometry, it acts directly on individuals; it gives   *Foucault*
'power of mind over mind'. The panoptic schema makes any apparatus of
power more intense: it assures its economy (in material, in personnel, in time);
it assures its efficacity by its preventative character, its continuous functioning
and its automatic mechanisms. It is a way of obtaining from power 'in hitherto
unexampled quantity', 'a great and new instrument of government ...; its
great excellence consists in the great strength it is capable of giving to *any*
institution it may be thought proper to apply it to'.[10]

It's a case of 'it's easy once you've thought of it' in the political sphere. It can
in fact be integrated into any function (education, medical treatment, production, punishment); it can increase the effect of this function, by being linked
closely with it; it can constitute a mixed mechanism in which relations of power
(and of knowledge) may be precisely adjusted, in the smallest detail, to the
processes that are to be supervised; it can establish a direct proportion between
'surplus power' and 'surplus production'. In short, it arranges things in such a
way that the exercise of power is not added on from the outside, like a rigid,
heavy constraint, to the functions it invests, but is so subtly present in them as
to increase their efficiency by itself increasing its own points of contact. The
panoptic mechanism is not simply a hinge, a point of exchange between a
mechanism of power and a function; it is a way of making power relations
function in a function, and of making a function function through these power
relations. Bentham's Preface to *Panopticon* opens with a list of the benefits to
be obtained from his 'inspection-house': '*Morals reformed – health preserved –
industry invigorated – instruction diffused – public burthens lightened –*
Economy seated, as it were, upon a rock – the gordian knot of the Poor-Laws
not cut, but untied – all by a simple idea in architecture!'.[11]

Furthermore, the arrangement of this machine is such that its enclosed
nature does not preclude a permanent presence from the outside: we have seen
that anyone may come and exercise in the central tower the functions of
surveillance, and that, this being the case, he can gain a clear idea of the way in
which the surveillance is practised. In fact, any panoptic institution, even if it is
as rigorously closed as a penitentiary, may without difficulty be subjected to
such irregular and constant inspections: and not only by the appointed
inspectors, but also by the public; any member of society will have the right to
come and see with his own eyes how the schools, hospitals, factories, prisons
function. There is no risk, therefore, that the increase of power created by the
panoptic machine may degenerate into tyranny; the disciplinary mechanism
will be democratically controlled, since it will be constantly accessible 'to the
great tribunal committee of the world'.[12] This Panopticon, subtly arranged so
that an observer may observe, at a glance, so many different individuals, also
enables everyone to come and observe any of the observers. The seeing machine
was once a sort of dark room into which individuals spied; it has become a
transparent building in which the exercise of power may be supervised by
society as a whole.

The panoptic schema, without disappearing as such or losing any of its
properties, was destined to spread throughout the social body; its vocation was
to become a generalized function. The plague-stricken town provided an
exceptional disciplinary model: perfect, but absolutely violent; to the disease
that brought death, power opposed its perpetual threat of death; life inside It

Foucault was reduced to its simplest expression; it was, against the power of death, the meticulous exercise of the right of the sword. The Panopticon, on the other hand, has a role of amplification; although it arranges power, although it is intended to make it more economic and more effective, it does so not for power itself, nor for the immediate salvation of a threatened society: its aim is to strengthen the social forces – to increase production, to develop the economy, spread education, raise the level of public morality; to increase and multiply.

How is power to be strengthened in such a way that, far from impeding progress, far from weighing upon it with its rules and regulations, it actually facilitates such progress? What intensificator of power will be able at the same time to be a multiplicator of production? How will power, by increasing its forces, be able to increase those of society instead of confiscating them or impeding them? The Panopticon's solution to this problem is that the productive increase of power can be assured only if, on the one hand, it can be exercised continuously in the very foundations of society, in the subtlest possible way, and if, on the other hand, it functions outside these sudden, violent, discontinuous forms that are bound up with the exercise of sovereignty. The body of the king, with its strange material and physical presence, with the force that he himself deploys or transmits to some few others, is at the opposite extreme of this new physics of power represented by panopticism; the domain of panopticism is, on the contrary, that whole lower region, that region of irregular bodies, with their details, their multiple movements, their heterogeneous forces, their spatial relations; what are required are mechanisms that analyse distributions, gaps, series, combinations, and which use instruments that render visible, record, differentiate and compare: a physics of a relational and multiple power, which has its maximum intensity not in the person of the king, but in the bodies that can be individualized by these relations. At the theoretical level, Bentham defines another way of analysing the social body and the power relations that traverse it; in terms of practice, he defines a procedure of subordination of bodies and forces that must increase the utility of power while dispensing with the need for the prince. Panopticism is the general principle of a new 'political anatomy' whose object and end are not the relations of sovereignty but the relations of discipline.

The celebrated, transparent, circular cage, with its high tower, powerful and knowing, may have been for Bentham a project of a perfect disciplinary institution; but he also set out to show how one may 'unlock' the disciplines and get them to function in a diffused, multiple, polyvalent way throughout the whole social body. These disciplines, which the classical age had elaborated in specific, relatively enclosed places – barracks, schools, workshops – and whose total implementation had been imagined only at the limited and temporary scale of a plague-stricken town, Bentham dreamt of transforming into a network of mechanisms that would be everywhere and always alert, running through society without interruption in space or in time. The panoptic arrangement provides the formula for this generalization. It programmes, at the level of an elementary and easily transferable mechanism, the basic functioning of a society penetrated through and through with disciplinary mechanisms.

There are two images, then, of discipline. At one extreme, the discipline-blockade, the enclosed institution, established on the edges of society, turned inwards towards negative functions: arresting evil, breaking communications,

suspending time. At the other extreme, with panopticism, is the discipline-   *Foucault*
mechanism: a functional mechanism that must improve the exercise of power
by making it lighter, more rapid, more effective, a design of subtle coercion for
a society to come. The movement from one project to the other, from a schema
of exceptional discipline to one of a generalized surveillance, rests on a
historical transformation: the gradual extension of the mechanisms of discipline throughout the seventeenth and eighteenth centuries, their spread
throughout the whole social body, the formation of what might be called in
general the disciplinary society.

NOTES

1 Archives militaires de Vincennes, A 1,516 91 sc. Pièce. This regulation is broadly similar to a
  whole series of others that date from the same period and earlier.
2 J. Bentham, *Works*, ed. Bowring, IV, 1843, pp. 60–4.
3 In the *Panopticon; Postscript*, 1791, Bentham adds dark inspection galleries painted in black
  around the inspector's lodge, each making it possible to observe two stories of cells.
4 In his first version of the *Panopticon*, Bentham had also imagined an acoustic surveillance,
  operated by means of pipes leading from the cells to the central tower. In the *Postscript* he
  abandoned the idea, perhaps because he could not introduce into it the principle of dissymétry
  and prevent the prisoners from hearing the inspector as well as the inspector hearing them.
  Julius tried to develop a system of dissymetrical listening. (N. H. Julius, *Leçons sur les
  prisons*, I, 1831).
5 Bentham, *Works*, p. 45.
6 G. Loisel, *Histoire des Ménageries*, II, 1912, pp. 104–7.
7 Bentham, *Works*, pp. 60–4.
8 Ibid., p. 177.
9 Ibid., p. 40.
10 Ibid., p. 66.
11 Ibid., p. 39.
12 Imagining this continuous flow of visitors entering the central tower by an underground
   passage and then observing the circular landscape of the Panopticon, was Bentham aware of
   the panoramas that Barker was producing at exactly the same period (the first seems to date
   from 1787) and in which the visitors, occupying the central place, saw unfolding around them
   a landscape, a city or a battle? The visitors occupied exactly the place of the sovereign gaze.

SPACE, KNOWLEDGE AND POWER (INTERVIEW CONDUCTED WITH PAUL RABINOW)

PR   In your interview with geographers at *Herodote*, you said that architecture
     becomes[1] political at the end of the eighteenth century. Obviously, it was
     political in earlier periods, too, such as during the Roman Empire. What is
     particular about the eighteenth century?

MF   My statement was awkward in that form. Of course I did not mean to say
     that architecture was not political before, becoming so only at that time. I
     only meant to say that in the eighteenth century one sees the development
     of reflection upon architecture as a function of the aims and techniques of
     the government of societies. One begins to see a form of political literature
     that addresses what the order of a society should be, what a city should be,
     given the requirements of the maintenance of order; given that one should
     avoid epidemics, avoid revolts, permit a decent and moral family life, and

so on. In terms of these objectives, how is one to conceive of both the organization of a city and the construction of a collective infrastructure? And how should houses be built? I am not saying that this sort of reflection appears only in the eighteenth century, but only that in the eighteenth century a very broad and general reflection on these questions takes place. If one opens a police report of the times – the treatises that are devoted to the techniques of government – one finds that architecture and urbanism occupy a place of considerable importance. That is what I meant to say.

PR   Among the ancients, in Rome or Greece, what was the difference?

MF   In discussing Rome, one sees that the problem revolves around Vitruvius. Vitruvius was reinterpreted from the sixteenth century on, but one can find in the sixteenth century – and no doubt in the Middle Ages as well – many considerations of the same order as Vitruvius; if you consider them as *reflections upon*. The treatises on politics, on the art of government, on the manner of good government, did not generally include chapters or analyses devoted to the organization of cities or to architecture. The *Republic* of Jean Bodin does not contain extended discussions of the role of architecture, whereas the police treatises of the eighteenth century are full of them.[2]

PR   Do you mean there were techniques and practices, but the discourse did not exist?

MF   I did not say that discourses upon architecture did not exist before the eighteenth century. Nor do I mean to say that the discussions of architecture before the eighteenth century lacked any political dimension or significance. What I wish to point out is that from the eighteenth century on, every discussion of politics as the art of the government of men necessarily includes a chapter or a series of chapters on urbanism, on collective facilities, on hygiene, and on private architecture. Such chapters are not found in the discussions of the art of government of the sixteenth century. This change is perhaps not in the reflections of architects upon architecture, but it is quite clearly seen in the reflections of political men.

PR   So it was not necessarily a change within the theory of architecture itself?

MF   That's right. It was not necessarily a change in the minds of architects, or in their techniques although that remains to be seen – but in the minds of political men in the choice and the form of attention that they bring to bear upon the objects that are of concern to them. Architecture became one of these during the seventeenth and eighteenth centuries.

PR   Could you tell us why?

MF   Well, I think that it was linked to a number of phenomena, such as the question of the city and the idea that was clearly formulated at the beginning of the seventeenth century that the government of a large state like France should ultimately think of its territory on the model of the city. The city was no longer perceived as a place of privilege, as an exception in a territory of fields, forests and roads. The cities were no longer islands beyond the common law. Instead, the cities, with the problems that they

raised, and the particular forms that they took, served as the models for the *Foucault*
governmental rationality that was to apply to the whole of the territory.

There is an entire series of utopias or projects for governing territory
that developed on the premise that a state is like a large city; the capital is
like its main square; the roads are like its streets. A state will be well
organized when a system of policing as tight and efficient as that of the
cities extends over the entire territory. At the outset, the notion of police
applied only to the set of regulations that were to assure the tranquillity of
a city, but at that moment the police become the very *type* of rationality for
the government of the whole territory. The model of the city became the
matrix for the regulations that apply to a whole state.

The notion of police, even in France today, is frequently misunderstood.
When one speaks to a Frenchman about police, he can only think of people
in uniform or in the secret service. In the seventeenth and eighteenth
centuries, 'police' signified a programme of government rationality. This
can be characterized as a project to create a system of regulation of the
general conduct of individuals whereby everything would be controlled to
the point of self-sustenance, without the need for intervention. This is the
rather typically French effort of policing. The English, for a number of
reasons, did not develop a comparable system, mainly because of the
parliamentary tradition on one hand, and the tradition of local, communal
autonomy on the other, not to mention the religious system.

One can place Napoleon almost exactly at the break between the old
organization of the eighteenth-century police state (understood, of course,
in the sense we have been discussing, not in the sense of the 'police state' as
we have come to know it) and the forms of the modern state, which he
invented. At any rate, it seems that, during the eighteenth and nineteenth
centuries, there appeared – rather quickly in the case of commerce and
more slowly in all the other domains – this idea of a police that would
manage to penetrate, to stimulate, to regulate, and to render almost automatic all the mechanisms of society.

This idea has since been abandoned. The question has been turned
around. No longer do we ask: What is the form of governmental rationality that will be able to penetrate the body politic to its most fundamental
elements? but rather: How is government possible? That is, what is the
principle of limitation that applies to governmental actions such that
things will occur for the best, in conformity with the rationality of government, and without intervention?

It is here that the question of liberalism comes up. It seems to me that at
that very moment it became apparent that if one governed too much, one
did not govern at all – that one provoked results contrary to those one
desired. What was discovered at that time and this was one of the great
discoveries of political thought at the end of the eighteenth century – was
the idea of *society*. That is to say, that government not only has to deal with
a territory, with a domain, and with its subjects, but that it also has to deal
with a complex and independent reality that has its own laws and mechanisms of reaction, its regulations as well as its possibilities of disturbance.
This new reality is society. From the moment that one is to manipulate a
society, one cannot consider it completely penetrable by police. One must

Foucault   take into account what it is. It becomes necessary to reflect upon it, upon
its specific characteristics, its constants and its variables . . .

PR   So there is a change in the importance of space. In the eighteenth century
there was a territory and the problem of governing people in this territory:
one can choose as an example *La Métropolite* (1682) of Alexandre
LeMaitre – a utopian treatise on how to build a capital city – or one can
understand a city as a metaphor or symbol for the territory and how to
govern it. All of this is quite spatial, whereas after Napoleon, society is not
necessarily so *spatialized* . . .

MF   That's right. On one hand, it is not so spatialized, yet at the same time a
certain number of problems that are properly seen as spatial emerged.
Urban space has its own dangers: disease, such as the epidemics of cholera
in Europe from 1830 to about 1880; and revolution, such as the series of
urban revolts that shook all of Europe during the same period. These
spatial problems, which were perhaps not new, took on a new importance.
   Second, a new aspect of the relations of space and power was the railroads. These were to establish a network of communication no longer
corresponding necessarily to the traditional network of roads, but they
nonetheless had to take into account the nature of society and its history.
In addition, there are all the social phenomena that railroads gave rise to,
be they the resistances they provoked, the transformations of population,
or changes in the behaviour of people. Europe was immediately sensitive to
the changes in behaviour that the railroads entailed. What was going to
happen, for example, if it was possible to get married between Bordeaux
and Nantes? Something that was not possible before. What was going to
happen when people in Germany and France might get to know one
another? Would war still be possible once there were railroads? In France a
theory developed that the railroads would increase familiarity among
people and that the new forms of human universality made possible would
render war impossible. But what the people did not foresee – although the
German military command was fully aware of it, since they were much
cleverer than their French counterpart – was that, on the contrary, the railroads rendered war far easier to wage. The third development, which came
later, was electricity.
   So there were problems in the links between the exercise of political
power and the space of a territory, or the space of cities – links that were
completely new.

PR   So it was less a matter of architecture than before. These are sorts of
technics of space . . .

MF   The major problems of space, from the nineteenth century on, were indeed
of a different type. Which is not to say that problems of an architectural
nature were forgotten. In terms of the first ones I referred to – disease and
the political problems – architecture has a very important role to play. The
reflections on urbanism and on the design of workers' housing – all of
these questions – are an area of reflection upon architecture.

PR   But architecture itself, the École des Beaux-Arts, belongs to a completely
different set of spatial issues.

MF   That's right. With the birth of these new technologies and these new economic processes, one sees the birth of a sort of thinking about space that is no longer modelled on the police state of the urbanization of the territory, but that extends far beyond the limits of urbanism and architecture.

PR   Consequently, the École des Ponts et Chaussées . . .

MF   That's right. The École des Ponts et Chaussées and its capital importance in political rationality in France are part of this. It was not architects, but engineers and builders of bridges, roads, viaducts, railways, as well as the polytechnicians (who practically controlled the French railroads) – those are the people who thought out space.

PR   Has this situation continued up to the present, or are we witnessing a change in relations between the technicians of space?

MF   We may well witness some changes, but I think that we have until now remained with the developers of the territory, the people of the Ponts et Chaussées, etc.

PR   So architects are not necessarily the masters of space that they once were, or believe themselves to be.

MF   That's right. They are not the technicians or engineers of the three great variables – territory, communication and speed. These escape the domain of architects.

PR   Do you see any particular architectural projects, either in the past or the present, as forces of liberation or resistance?

MF   I do not think that it is possible to say that one thing is of the order of 'liberation' and another is of the order of 'oppression'. There are a certain number of things that one can say with some certainty about a concentration camp to the effect that it is not an instrument of liberation, but one should still take into account – and this is not generally acknowledged – that, aside from torture and execution, which preclude any resistance, no matter how terrifying a given system may be, there always remain the possibilities of resistance, disobedience and oppositional groupings.

     On the other hand, I do not think that there is anything that is functionally – by its very nature – absolutely liberating. Liberty is a *practice*. So there may, in fact, always be a certain number of projects whose aim is to modify some constraints, to loosen, or even to break them, but none of these projects can, simply by its nature, assure that people will have liberty automatically, that it will be established by the project itself. The liberty of men is never assured by the institutions and laws that are intended to guarantee them. This is why almost all of these laws and institutions are quite capable of being turned around. Not because they are ambiguous, but simply because 'liberty' is what must be exercised.

PR   Are there urban examples of this? Or examples where architects succeeded?

Foucault   MF   Well, up to a point there is Le Corbusier, who is described today – with a sort of cruelty that I find perfectly useless – as a sort of crypto-Stalinist. He was, I am sure, someone full of good intentions and what he did was in fact dedicated to liberating effects. Perhaps the means that he proposed were in the end less liberating than he thought, but, once again, I think that it can never be inherent in the structure of things to guarantee the exercise of freedom. The guarantee of freedom is freedom.

PR   So you do not think of Le Corbusier as an example of success. You are simply saying that his intention was liberating. Can you give us a successful example?

MF   No. It *cannot* succeed. If one were to find a place, and perhaps there are some, where liberty is effectively exercised, one would find that this is not owing to the order of objects, but, once again, owing to the practice of liberty. Which is not to say that, after all, one may as well leave people in slums, thinking that they can simply exercise their rights there.

PR   Meaning that architecture in itself cannot resolve social problems?

MF   I think that it can and does produce positive effects when the liberating intentions of the architect coincide with the real practice of people in the exercise of their freedom.

PR   But the same architecture can serve other ends?

MF   Absolutely. Let me bring up another example: the *Familistère* of Jean-Baptiste Godin at Guise (1859). The architecture of Godin was clearly intended for the freedom of people. Here was something that manifested the power of ordinary workers to participate in the exercise of their trade. It was a rather important sign and instrument of autonomy for a group of workers. Yet no one could enter or leave the place without being seen by everyone – an aspect of the architecture that could be totally oppressive. But it could only be oppressive if people were prepared to use their own presence in order to watch over others. Let's imagine a community of unlimited sexual practices that might be established there. It would once again become a place of freedom. I think it is somewhat arbitrary to try to dissociate the effective practice of freedom by people, the practice of social relations, and the spatial distributions in which they find themselves. If they are separated, they become impossible to understand. Each can only be understood through the other.

PR   Yet people have often attempted to find utopian schemes to liberate people, or to oppress them.

MF   Men have dreamed of liberating machines. But there are no machines of freedom, by definition. This is not to say that the exercise of freedom is completely indifferent to spatial distribution, but it can only function when there is a certain convergence; in the case of divergence or distortion, it immediately becomes the opposite of that which had been intended. The panoptic qualities of Guise could perfectly well have allowed it to be used as a prison. Nothing could be simpler. It is clear that, in fact, the *Familistère* may well have served as an instrument for discipline and a rather unbearable group pressure.

PR So, once again, the intention of the architect is not the fundamental   *Foucault*
    determining factor.

MF Nothing is fundamental. That is what is interesting in the analysis of
    society. That is why nothing irritates me as much as these inquiries – which
    are by definition metaphysical – on the foundations of power in a society
    or the self-institution of a society, etc. These are not fundamental
    phenomena. There are only reciprocal relations, and the perpetual gaps
    between intentions in relation to one another.

PR You have singled out doctors, prison wardens, priests, judges and
    psychiatrists as key figures in the political configurations that involve
    domination. Would you put architects on this list?

MF You know, I was not really attempting to describe figures of domination
    when I referred to doctors and people like that, but rather to describe
    people through whom power passed or who are important in the fields of
    power relations. A patient in a mental institution is placed within a field of
    fairly complicated power relations, which Erving Goffman analysed very
    well. The pastor in a Christian or Catholic church (in Protestant churches
    it is somewhat different) is an important link in a set of power relations.
    The architect is not an individual of that sort. After all, the architect has no
    power over me. If I want to tear down or change a house he built for me,
    put up new partitions, add a chimney, the architect has no control. So the
    architect should be placed in another category – which is not to say that he
    is not totally foreign to the organization, the implementation, and all the
    techniques of power that are exercised in a society. I would say that one
    must take *him* – his mentality, his attitude – into account as well as his
    projects, in order to understand a certain number of the techniques of
    power that are invested in architecture, but he is not comparable to a
    doctor, a priest, a psychiatrist or a prison warden.

PR 'Postmodernism' has received a great deal of attention recently in
    architectural circles. It is also being talked about in philosophy, notably by
    Jean-François Lyotard and Jürgen Habermas. Clearly, historical reference
    and language play an important role in the modern episteme. How do you
    see postmodernism, both as architecture and in terms of the historical and
    philosophical questions that are posed by it?

MF I think that there is a widespread and facile tendency, which one should
    combat, to designate that which has just occurred as the primary enemy, as
    if this were always the principal form of oppression from which one had to
    liberate oneself. Now this simple attitude entails a number of dangerous
    consequences: first, an inclination to seek out some cheap form of
    archaism or some imaginary past forms of happiness that people did not, in
    fact, have at all. For instance, in the areas that interest me, it is very
    amusing to see how contemporary sexuality is described as something
    absolutely terrible. To think that it is only possible now to make love after
    turning off the television! and in mass-produced beds! 'Not like that
    wonderful time when . . .' Well, what about those wonderful times when
    people worked eighteen hours a day and there were six people in a bed, if

Foucault   one was lucky enough to have a bed! There is in this hatred of the present or the immediate past a dangerous tendency to invoke a completely mythical past. Second, there is the problem raised by Habermas: if one abandons the work of Kant or Weber, for example, one runs the risk of lapsing into irrationality.

I am completely in agreement with this, but at the same time, our question is quite different: I think that the central issue of philosophy and critical thought since the eighteenth century has always been, still is, and will, I hope, remain the question: *What* is this Reason that we use? What are its historical effects? What are its limits, and what are its dangers? How can we exist as rational beings, fortunately committed to practising a rationality that is unfortunately criss-crossed by intrinsic dangers? One should remain as close to this question as possible, keeping in mind that it is both central and extremely difficult to resolve. In addition, if it is extremely dangerous to say that Reason is the enemy that should be eliminated, it is just as dangerous to say that any critical questioning of this rationality risks sending us into irrationality. One should not forget – and I'm not saying this in order to criticize rationality, but in order to show how ambiguous things are – it was on the basis of the flamboyant rationality of social Darwinism that racism was formulated, becoming one of the most enduring and powerful ingredients of Nazism. This was, of course, an irrationality, but an irrationality that was at the same time, after all, a certain form of rationality . . .

This is the situation that we are in and that we must combat. If intellectuals in general are to have a function, if critical thought itself has a function, and, even more specifically, if philosophy has a function within critical thought, it is precisely to accept this sort of spiral, this sort of revolving door of rationality that refers us to its necessity, to its indispensability, and at the same time, to its intrinsic dangers.

PR   All that being said, it would be fair to say that you are much less afraid of historicism and the play of historical references than someone like Habermas is; also, that this issue has been posed in architecture as almost a crisis of civilization by the defenders of modernism, who contend that if we abandon modern architecture for a frivolous return to decoration and motifs, we are somehow abandoning civilization. On the other hand, some postmodernists have claimed that historical references *per se* are somehow meaningful and are going to protect us from the dangers of an overly rationalized world.

MF   Although it may not answer your question, I would say this: one should totally and absolutely suspect anything that claims to be a return. One reason is a logical one; there is in fact no such thing as a return. History, and the meticulous interest applied to history, is certainly one of the best defences against this theme of the return. For me, the history of madness or the studies of the prison . . . were done in that precise manner because I knew full well – this is in fact what aggravated many people – that I was carrying out a historical analysis in such a manner that people *could* criticize the present, but it was impossible for them to say, 'Let's go back to the good old days when madmen in the eighteenth century . . .' or, 'Let's go back to the days when the prison was not one of the principal instruments. . . .' No; I think that history preserves us from that sort of ideology of the return.

PR   Hence, the simple opposition between reason and history is rather silly . . . choosing sides between the two . . .

MF   Yes. Well, the problem for Habermas is, after all, to make a transcendental mode of thought spring forth against any historicism. I am, indeed, far more historicist and Nietzschean. I do not think that there is a proper usage of history or a proper usage of intrahistorical analysis – which is fairly lucid, by the way – that works precisely against this ideology of the return. A good study of peasant architecture in Europe, for example, would show the utter vanity of wanting to return to the little individual house with its thatched roof. History protects us from historicism – from a historicism that calls on the past to resolve the questions of the present.

PR   It also reminds us that there is always a history; that those modernists who wanted to suppress any reference to the past were making a mistake.

MF   Of course.

PR   Your next two books deal with sexuality among the Greeks and the early Christians. Are there any particular architectural dimensions to the issues you discuss?

MF   I didn't find any; absolutely none. But what is interesting is that in imperial Rome there were, in fact, brothels, pleasure quarters, criminal areas, etc., and there was also one sort of quasi-public place of pleasure: the baths, the *thermes*. The baths were a very important place of pleasure and encounter, which slowly disappeared in Europe. In the Middle Ages, the baths were still a place of encounter between men and women as well as of men with men and women with women, although that is rarely talked about. What were referred to and condemned, as well as practised, were the encounters between men and women, which disappeared over the course of the sixteenth and seventeenth centuries.

PR   In the Arab world it continues.

MF   Yes; but in France it has largely ceased. It still existed in the nineteenth century. One sees it in *Les Enfants du Paradis*, and it is historically exact. One of the characters, Lacenaire, was – no one mentions it – a swine and a pimp who used young boys to attract older men and then blackmailed them; there is a scene that refers to this. It required all the naiveté and anti-homosexuality of the Surrealists to overlook that fact. So the baths continued to exist, as a place of sexual encounters. The bath was a sort of cathedral of pleasure at the heart of the city, where people could go as often as they want, where they walked about, picked each other up, met each other, took their pleasure, ate, drank, discussed . . .

PR   So sex was not separated from the other pleasures. It was inscribed in the centre of the cities. It was public; it served a purpose . . .

MF   That's right. Sexuality was obviously considered a social pleasure for the

Greeks and the Romans. What is interesting about male homosexuality today – this has apparently been the case of female homosexuals for some time – is that their sexual relations are immediately translated into social relations and the social relations are understood as sexual relations. For the Greeks and the Romans, in a different fashion, sexual relations were located within social relations in the widest sense of the term. The baths were a place of sociality that included sexual relations.

One can directly compare the bath and the brothel. The brothel is in fact a place, and an architecture, of pleasure. There is, in fact, a very interesting form of sociality that was studied by Alain Corbin in *Les Filles de noces*.[3] The men of the city met at the brothel; they were tied to one another by the fact that the same women passed through their hands, that the same diseases and infections were communicated to them. There was a sociality of the brothel, but the sociality of the baths as it existed among the ancients – a new version of which could perhaps exist again – was completely different from the sociality of the brothel.

PR   We now know a great deal about disciplinary architecture. What about confessional architecture – the kind of architecture that would be associated with a confessional technology?

MF   You mean religious architecture? I think that it has been studied. There is the whole problem of a monastery as xenophobic. There one finds precise regulations concerning life in common; affecting sleeping, eating, prayer, the place of each individual in all of that, the cells. All of this was programmed from very early on.

PR   In a technology of power, of confession as opposed to discipline, space seems to play a central role as well.

MF   Yes. Space is fundamental in any form of communal life; space is fundamental in any exercise of power. To make a parenthetical remark, I recall having been invited, in 1966, by a group of architects to do a study of space, of something that I called at that time 'heterotopias', those singular spaces to be found in some given social spaces whose functions are different or even the opposite of others. The architects worked on this, and at the end of the study someone spoke up – a Sartrean psychologist – who firebombed me, saying that *space* is reactionary and capitalist, but *history* and *becoming* are revolutionary. This absurd discourse was not at all unusual at the time. Today everyone would be convulsed with laughter at such a pronouncement, but not then.

PR   Architects in particular, if they do choose to analyse an institutional building such as a hospital or a school in terms of its disciplinary function, would tend to focus primarily on the walls. After all, that is what they design. Your approach is perhaps more concerned with space, rather than architecture, in that the physical walls are only one aspect of the institution. How would you characterize the difference between these two approaches, between the building itself and space?

MF   I think there is a difference in method and approach. It is true that for me, architecture, in the very vague analyses of it that I have been able to

conduct, is only taken as an element of support, to ensure a certain   *Foucault*
allocation of people in space, a *canalization* of their circulation, as well as
the coding of their reciprocal relations. So it is not only considered as an
element in space, but is especially thought of as a plunge into a field of
social relations in which it brings about some specific effects.

For example, I know that there is a historian who is carrying out some
interesting studies of the archaeology of the Middle Ages, in which he takes
up the problem of architecture, of houses in the Middle Ages, in terms of
the problem of the chimney. I think that he is in the process of showing that
beginning at a certain moment it was possible to build a chimney inside the
house – a chimney with a hearth, not simply an open room or a chimney
outside the house; that at that moment all sorts of things changed and
relations between individuals became possible. All of this seems very
interesting to me, but the conclusion that he presented in an article was
that the history of ideas and thoughts is useless.

What is, in fact, interesting is that the two are rigorously indivisible.
Why did people struggle to find the way to put a chimney inside a house?
Or why did they put their techniques to this use? So often in the history of
techniques it takes years or even centuries to implement them. It is certain,
and of capital importance, that this technique was a formative influence on
new human relations, but it is impossible to think that it would have been
developed and adapted had there not been in the play and strategy of
human relations something which tended in that direction. What is
interesting is always interconnection, not the primacy of this over that,
which never has any meaning.

PR In your book *The Order of Things* you constructed certain vivid spatial
metaphors to describe structures of thought. Why do you think spatial
images are so evocative for these references? What is the relationship
between these spatial metaphors describing disciplines and more concrete
descriptions of institutional spaces?

MF It is quite possible that since I was interested in the problems of space, I
used quite a number of spatial metaphors in *The Order of Things,* but
usually these metaphors were not ones that I advanced, but ones that I was
studying as objects. What is striking in the epistemological mutations and
transformations of the seventeenth century is to see how the spatialization
of knowledge was one of the factors in the constitution of this knowledge
as a science. If the natural history and the classifications of Linneaus were
possible, it is for a certain number of reasons: on the one hand, there was
literally a spatialization of the very object of their analyses, since they gave
themselves the rule of studying and classifying a plant only on the basis of
that which was visible. They didn't even want to use a microscope. All the
traditional elements of knowledge, such as the medical functions of the
plant, fell away. The object was spatialized. Subsequently, it was
spatialized insofar as the principles of classification had to be found in the
very structure of the plant: the number of elements, how they were
arranged, their size, etc., and certain other elements, like the height of the
plant. Then there was the spatialization into illustrations within books,
which was only possible with certain printing techniques. Then the

Foucault   spatialization of the reproduction of the plants themselves, which was represented in books. All of these are spatial techniques, not metaphors.

PR   Is the actual plan for a building – the precise drawing that becomes walls and windows – the same form of discourse as, say, a hierarchical pyramid that describes rather precisely relations between people, not only in space, but also in social life?

MF   Well, I think there are a few simple and exceptional examples in which the architectural means reproduce, with more or less emphasis, the social hierarchies. There is the model of the military camp, where the military hierarchy is to be read in the ground itself, by the place occupied by the tents and the buildings reserved for each rank. It reproduces precisely through architecture a pyramid of power; but this is an exceptional example, as is everything military – privileged in society and of an extreme simplicity.

PR   But the plan itself is not always an account of relations or power.

MF   No. Fortunately for human imagination, things are a little more complicated than that.

PR   Architecture is not, of course, a constant: it has a long tradition of changing preoccupations, changing systems, different rules. The *savoir* of architecture is partly the history of the profession, partly the evolution of a science of construction, and partly a rewriting of aesthetic theories. What do you think is particular about this form of *savoir*? Is it more like a natural science, or what you have called a 'dubious science'?

MF   I can't exactly say that this distinction between sciences that are certain and those that are uncertain is of no interest – that would be avoiding the question – but I must say that what interests me more is to focus on what the Greeks called the *techne,* that is to say, a practical rationality governed by a conscious goal. I am not even sure if it is worth constantly asking the question of whether government can be the object of an exact science. On the other hand, if architecture, like the practice of government and the practice of other forms of social organization, is considered as a *techne,* possibly using elements of sciences like physics, for example, or statistics, etc. . . . , that is what is interesting. But if one wanted to do a history of architecture, I think that it should be much more along the lines of that general history of the *techne,* rather than the histories of either the exact sciences or the inexact ones. The disadvantage of this word *techne,* I realize, is its relation to the word 'technology', which has a very specific meaning. A very narrow meaning is given to 'technology': one thinks of hard technology, the technology of wood, of fire, of electricity. Whereas government is also a function of technology: the government of individuals, the government of souls, the government of the self by the self, the government of families, the government of children, and so on. I believe that if one placed the history of architecture back in this general history of *techne,* in this wide sense of the word, one would have a more interesting guiding concept than by considering opposition between the exact sciences and the inexact ones.

NOTES

1   See the article on Foucault in *Skyline*, March 1982, p. 14.
2   Jean Bodin, *Republic*, Paris, 1577.
3   Alain Corbin, *Les Filles de noces*, Aubier, 1978.

PAUL VIRILIO

Paul
Virilio French theorist and self-styled urbanist Paul Virilio (b. 1932) has pursued a long involvement with architecture. A partner of Claude Parent, he explored for some time the theory of the 'oblique', which has been considered influential in the origins of deconstruction. Amongst his other early work was a study of the architecture of wartime bunkers. Virilio was appointed director of the École Spéciale d'Architecture in Paris in the reforms following the events of May 1968, in which he took an active part.

Virilio is now known above all as a theorist of speed and time. Technical developments in the field of telecommunications and transportation have led to an erosion of the physical, to the point where 'the loss of material space leads to the government of nothing but time'. This has an obvious consequence for a discipline such as architecture which has exerted its influence through materiality. In 'The Overexposed City' Virilio explores a number of themes that arise from this condition. Symbolically – but also practically – the city is no longer governed by physical boundaries but by systems of electronic surveillance. Thus the city gate gives way to the security gateway at the airport. Within the home too the traditional physical window gives way to the interface of the screen. Everywhere architecture is going through a crisis as the hegemony of physical presence is being eroded, and notions such as 'near' and 'far' have lost their traditional authority – '*speed distance* obliterates the notion of physical dimension'.

Virilio could be criticized for the utopianism of his futuristic vision, and for failing to take sufficient account of the corporeality of the body in his thinking. Likewise it could be argued that the homogenization of global communications, far from promoting a simple placelessness, may have a counter-effect of a renewed celebration of the specificity of material place. Yet there is an undeniable prescience in Virilio's vision. With the advent of the Internet, Virilio's observation that the screen has become the city square, 'the cross roads of all mass media', reveals the far-sightedness of much of Virilio's thought. In the age of cyberspace, Virilio has emerged as a leading theorist.

THE OVEREXPOSED CITY   *Virilio*

At the beginning of the 1960s, with black ghettoes rioting, the mayor of Philadelphia announced: 'From here on in, the frontiers of the State pass to the interior of the cities.' While this sentence translated the political reality for all Americans who were being discriminated against, it also pointed to an even larger dimension, given the construction of the Berlin Wall, on 13 August 1961, in the heart of the ancient capital of the Reich.

Since then, this assertion has been confirmed time and again: Belfast, Londonderry where not so long ago certain streets bore a yellow band separating the Catholic side from the Protestant, so that neither would move too far, leaving a chain-link no man's land to divide their communities even more clearly. And then there's Beirut with its East and West sections, its tortured internal boundaries, its tunnels and its mined boulevards.

Basically, the American mayor's statement revealed a general phenomenon that was just beginning to hit the capital cities as well as the provincial towns and hamlets, the phenomenon of obligatory introversion in which the City sustained the first effects of a multinational economy modelled along the lines of industrial enterprises, a real urban redeployment which soon contributed to the gutting of certain worker cities such as Liverpool and Sheffield in England, Detroit and Saint Louis in the United States, Dortmund in West Germany, and all of this at the very moment in which other areas were being built up, around tremendous international airports, a METROPLEX, a metropolitan complex such as Dallas/Fort Worth. Since the 1970s and the beginnings of the world economic crisis, the construction of these airports was further subjected to the imperatives of the defence against air pirates.

Construction no longer derived simply from traditional technical constraint. The plan had become a function of the risks of 'terrorist contamination' and the disposition of sites conceived of as sterile zones for departures and non-sterile zones for arrivals. Suddenly, all forms of loading and unloading – regardless of passenger, baggage or freight status – and all manner of airport transit had to be submitted to a system of interior/exterior traffic control. The architecture that resulted from this had little to do with the architect's personality. It emerged instead from perceived public security requirements.

As the last gateway to the State, the airport came to resemble the fort, port or railway station of earlier days. As airports were turned into theatres of necessary regulation of exchange and communication, they also became breeding and testing grounds for high-pressured experiments in control and aerial surveillance performed for and by a new 'air and border patrol', whose anti-terrorist exploits began to make headlines with the intervention of the German GS.G9 border guards in the Mogadishu hijacking, several thousand miles away from Germany.

At that instant, the strategy of confining the sick or the suspect gave way to a tactic of mid-voyage interception. Practically, this meant examining clothing and baggage, which explains the sudden proliferation of cameras, radars and detectors in all restricted passageways. When the French built 'maximum security cell-blocks', they used the magnetized doorways that airports had had for years. Paradoxically, the equipment that ensured maximal freedom in travel

Virilio formed part of the core of penitentiary incarceration. At the same time, in a number of residential areas in the United States, security was maintained exclusively through closed-circuit television hook-ups with a central police station. In banks, in supermarkets, and on major highways, where toll-booths resembled the ancient city gates, the rite of passage was no longer intermittent. It had become immanent.

In this new perspective devoid of horizon, the city was entered not through a gate nor through an *arc de triomphe,* but rather through an electronic audience system. Users of the road were no longer understood to be inhabitants or privileged residents. They were now interlocutors in permanent transit. From this moment on, continuity no longer breaks down in space, not in the physical space of urban lots nor in the juridical space of their property tax records. From here, continuity is ruptured in time, in a time that advanced technologies and industrial redeployment incessantly arrange through a series of interruptions, such as plant closings, unemployment, casual labour and successive or simultaneous disappearing acts. These serve to organize and then disorganize the urban environment to the point of provoking the irreversible decay and degradation of neighbourhoods, as in the housing development near Lyon where the occupants' 'rate of rotation' became so great – people staying for a year and then moving on – that it contributed to the ruin of a place that each inhabitant found adequate . . .

In fact, since the originary enclosures, the concept of boundary has undergone numerous changes as regards both the façade and the neighbourhood it fronts. From the palisade to the screen, by way of stone ramparts, the boundary-surface has recorded innumerable perceptible and imperceptible transformations, of which the latest is probably that of the interface. Once again, we have to approach the question of access to the City in a new manner. For example, does the metropolis possess its own façade? At which moment does the city show us its face?

The phrase 'to go into town', which replaced the nineteenth-century's 'to go to town', indicates the uncertainty of the encounter, as if we could no longer stand before the city but rather abide forever within. If the metropolis is still a place, a geographic site, it no longer has anything to do with the classical oppositions of city/country nor centre/periphery. The city is no longer organized into a localized and axial estate. While the suburbs contributed to this dissolution, in fact the intramural–extramural opposition collapsed with the transport revolutions and the development of communication and telecommunications technologies. These promoted the merger of disconnected metropolitan fringes into a single urban mass.

In effect, we are witnessing a paradoxical moment in which the opacity of building materials is reduced to zero. With the invention of the steel skeleton construction, curtain walls made of light and transparent materials, such as glass or plastics, replace stone façades, just as tracing paper, acetate and plexiglass replace the opacity of paper in the designing phase.

On the other hand, with the screen interface of computers, television and teleconferences, the surface of inscription, hitherto devoid of depth, becomes a kind of 'distance', a depth of field of a new kind of representation, a visibility without any face-to-face encounter in which the *vis-à-vis* of the ancient streets disappears and is erased. In this situation, a difference of position blurs into

Virilio

fusion and confusion. Deprived of objective boundaries, the architectonic element begins to drift and float in an electronic ether, devoid of spatial dimensions, but inscribed in the singular temporality of an instantaneous diffusion. From here on, people can't be separated by physical obstacles or by temporal distances. With the interfacing of computer terminals and video monitors, distinctions of *here* and *there* no longer mean anything.

This sudden reversion of boundaries and oppositions introduces into everyday, common space an element which until now was reserved for the world of microscopes. There is no *plenum*; space is not filled with matter. Instead, an unbounded expanse appears in the false perspective of the machines' luminous emissions. From here on, constructed space occurs within an electronic topology where the framing of perspective and the gridwork weft of numerical images renovate the division of urban property. The ancient private/public occultation and the distinction between housing and traffic are replaced by an overexposure in which the difference between 'near' and 'far' simply ceases to exist, just as the difference between 'micro' and 'macro' vanished in the scanning of the electron microscope.

The representation of the modern city can no longer depend on the ceremonial opening of gates, nor on the ritual processions and parades lining the streets and avenues with spectators. From here on, urban architecture has to work with the opening of a new 'technological space-time'. In terms of access, telematics replaces the doorway. The sound of gates gives way to the clatter of data banks and the rites of passage of a technical culture whose progress is disguised by the immateriality of its parts and networks. Instead of operating in the space of a constructed social fabric, the intersecting and connecting grid of highway and service systems now occurs in the sequences of an imperceptible organization of time in which the man/machine interface replaces the façades of buildings as the surfaces of property allotments.

Where once the opening of the city gates announced the alternating progression of days and nights, now we awaken to the opening of shutters and televisions. The day has been changed. A new day has been added to the astronomers' solar day, to the flickering day of candles, to the electric light. It is an electronic false-day, and it appears on a calendar of information 'commutations' that has absolutely no relationship whatsoever to real time. Chronological and historical time, time that passes, is replaced by a time that exposes itself instantaneously. On the computer screen, a time period becomes the 'support-surface' of inscription. Literally, or better cinematically, time surfaces. Thanks to the cathode-ray tube, spatial dimensions have become inseparable from their rate of transmission. As a unity of place without any unity of time, the City has disappeared into the heterogeneity of that regime comprised of the temporality of advanced technologies. The urban figure is no longer designated by a dividing line that separates here from there. Instead, it has become a computerized timetable.

Where once one necessarily entered the city by means of a physical gateway, now one passes through an audiovisual protocol in which the methods of audience and surveillance have transformed even the forms of public greeting and daily reception. Within this place of optical illusion, in which the people occupy transportation and transmission time instead of inhabiting space, inertia tends to renovate an old sedentariness, which results in the persistence

Virilio   of urban sites. With the new instantaneous communications media, arrival supplants departure: without necessarily leaving, everything 'arrives'.

Until recently, the city separated its 'intramural' population from those outside the walls. Today, people are divided according to aspects of time. Where once an entire 'downtown' area indicated a long historical period, now only a few monuments will do. Further, the new technological time has no relation to any calendar of events nor to any collective memory. It is pure computer time, and as such helps construct a permanent present, an unbounded, timeless intensity that is destroying the tempo of a progressively degraded society.

What is a monument within this regime? Instead of an intricately wrought portico or a monumental walk punctuated by sumptuous buildings, we now have idleness and monumental waiting for service from a machine. Everyone is busily waiting in front of some communications or telecommunications apparatus, lining up at tollbooths, poring over captains' checklists, sleeping with computer consoles on their nightstands. Finally, the gateway is turned into a conveyance of vehicles and vectors whose disruption creates less a space than a countdown, in which work occupies the centre of time while uncontrolled time of vacations and unemployment form a periphery, the suburbs of time, a clearing away of activities in which each person is exiled to a life of privacy and deprivation.

If, despite the wishes of postmodern architects, the city from here on is deprived of gateway entries, it is because the urban wall has long been breached by an infinitude of openings and ruptured enclosures. While less apparent than those of antiquity, these are equally effective, constraining and segregating. The illusion of the industrial revolution in transportation misled us as to the limitlessness of progress. Industrial time-management has imperceptibly compensated for the loss of rural territories. In the nineteenth century, the city/country attraction emptied agrarian space of its cultural and social substance. At the end of the twentieth century, urban space loses its geopolitical reality to the exclusive benefit of systems of instantaneous deportation whose technological intensity ceaselessly upsets all of our social structures. These systems include the deportation of people in the redeployment of modes of production, the deportation of attention, of the human face-to-face and the urban *vis-à-vis* encounters at the level of human/machine interaction. In effect, all of this participates in a new 'posturban' and transnational kind of concentration, as indicated by a number of recent events.

Despite the rising cost of energy, the American middle classes are evacuating the cities of the East. Following the transformation of inner cities into ghettoes and slums, we now are watching the deterioration of the cities as regional centres. From Washington to Chicago, from Boston to Saint Louis, the major urban centres are shrinking. On the brink of bankruptcy, New York City lost 10 per cent of its population in the last ten years. Meanwhile, Detroit lost 20 per cent of its inhabitants, Cleveland 23 per cent, Saint Louis 27 per cent. Already, whole neighbourhoods have turned into ghost towns.

These harbingers of an imminent 'post-industrial' deurbanization promise an exodus that will affect all of the developed countries. Predicted for the last forty years, this deregulation of the management of space comes from an economic and political illusion about the persistence of sites constructed in the

era of automotive management of time, and in the epoch of the development of   *Virilio*
audiovisual technologies of retinal persistence.

'Each surface is an interface between two environments that is ruled by a
constant activity in the form of an exchange between the two substances placed
in contact with one another.'

This new scientific definition of surface demonstrates the contamination at
work: the 'boundary, or limiting surface' has turned into an osmotic mem-
brane, like a blotting pad. Even if this last definition is more rigorous than
earlier ones, it still signals a change in the notion of limitation. The limitation of
space has become commutation: the radical separation, the necessary crossing,
the transit of a constant activity, the activity of incessant exchanges, the
transfer between two environments and two substances. What used to be the
boundary of a material, its 'terminus', has become an entryway hidden in the
most imperceptible entity. From here on, the appearance of surfaces and
superficies conceals a secret transparency, a thickness without thickness, a
volume without volume, an imperceptible quantity.

If this situation corresponds with the physical reality of the infinitesimally
small, it also fits that of the infinitely large. When what was visibly nothing
becomes 'something', the greatest distance no longer precludes perception. The
greatest geophysical expanse contracts as it becomes more concentrated. In the
interface of the screen, everything is always already there, offered to view in the
immediacy of an instantaneous transmission. In 1980, for example, when Ted
Turner decided to launch Cable News Network as a round-the-clock live news
station, he transformed his subscribers' living space into a kind of global
broadcast studio for world events.

Thanks to satellites, the cathode-ray window brings to each viewer the light
of another day and the presence of the antipodal place. If space is that which
keeps everything from occupying the same place, this abrupt confinement
brings absolutely everything precisely to that 'place', that location that has no
location. The exhaustion of physical, or natural, relief and of temporal
distances telescopes all localization and all position. As with live televised
events, the places become interchangeable at will.

The instantaneity of ubiquity results in the atopia of a singular interface.
After the spatial and temporal distances, *speed distance* obliterates the notion
of physical dimension. Speed suddenly becomes a primal dimension that defies
all temporal and physical measurements. This radical erasure is equivalent to a
momentary inertia in the environment. The old agglomeration disappears in
the intense acceleration of telecommunications, in order to give rise to a new
type of concentration: the concentration of a domiciliation without domiciles,
in which property boundaries, walls and fences no longer signify the permanent
physical obstacle. Instead, they now form an interruption of an emission or of
an electronic shadow zone which repeats the play of daylight and the shadow
of buildings.

A strange topology is hidden in the obviousness of televised images.
Architectural plans are displaced by the sequence plans of an invisible montage.
Where geographical space once was arranged according to the geometry of an
apparatus of rural or urban boundary setting, time is now organized according
to imperceptible fragmentations of the technical time span, in which the
cutting, as of a momentary interruption, replaces the lasting disappearance, the

Virilio   'program guide' replaces the chain link fence, just as the railroads' timetables once replaced the almanacs.

'The camera has become our best inspector,' declared John F. Kennedy, a little before being struck down in a Dallas street. Effectively, the camera allows us to participate in certain political and optical events. Consider, for example, the irruption phenomenon, in which the City allows itself to be seen thoroughly and completely, or the diffraction phenomenon, in which its image reverberates beyond the atmosphere to the farthest reaches of space, while the endoscope and the scanner allow us to see to the farthest reaches of life.

This overexposure attracts our attention to the extent that it offers a world without antipodes and without hidden aspects, a world in which opacity is but a momentary interlude. Note how the illusion of proximity barely lasts. Where once the *polis* inaugurated a political theatre, with its *agora* and its *forum,* now there is only a cathode-ray screen, where the shadows and spectres of a community dance amid their processes of disappearance, where cinematism broadcasts the last appearance of urbanism, the last image of an urbanism without urbanity. This is where tact and contact give way to televisual impact. While tele-conferencing allows long-distance conferences with the advantage derived from the absence of displacement, tele-negotiating inversely allows for the production of distance in discussions, even when the members of the conversation are right next to each other. This is a little like those telephone crazies for whom the receiver induces flights of verbal fancy amid the anonymity of a remote control aggressiveness.

Where does the city without gates begin? Probably inside that fugitive anxiety, that shudder that seizes the minds of those who, just returning from a long vacation, contemplate the imminent encounter with mounds of unwanted mail or with a house that's been broken into and emptied of its contents. It begins with the urge to flee and escape for a second from an oppressive technological environment, to regain one's senses and one's sense of self. While spatial escape may be possible, temporal escape is not. Unless we think of lay-offs as 'escape hatches,' the ultimate form of paid vacation, the forward flight responds to a post-industrial illusion whose ill effects we are just beginning to feel. Already, the theory of 'job sharing' introduced to a new segment of the community – offering each person an alternative in which sharing work-time could easily lead to a whole new sharing of space as well – mirrors the rule of an endless periphery in which the homeland and the colonial settlement would replace the industrial city and its suburbs. Consider, for example, the Community Development Project, which promotes the proliferation of local development projects based on community forces, and which is intended to reincorporate the English inner cities.

Where does the edge of the exo-city begin? Where can we find the gate without a city? Probably in the new American technologies of instantaneous destruction (with explosives) of tall buildings and in the politics of systematic destruction of housing projects suddenly deemed as 'unfit for the new French way of life', as in Venissieux, La Courneuve or Gagny. According to a recent French study, released by the Association for Community Development,

> The destruction of 300,000 residential units over a five-year period
> would cost 10 billion francs per year, while creating 100,000 new

jobs. In addition, at the end of the demolition/reconstruction, the fiscal receipts would be 6 to 10 billion francs above the sum of public moneys invested.

One final question arises here. In a period of economic crisis, will mass destruction of the large cities replace the traditional politics of large public works? If that happens, there will be no essential difference between economic-industrial recession and war.

Architecture or post-architecture? Ultimately, the intellectual debate surrounding modernity seems part of a de-realization phenomenon which simultaneously involves disciplines of expression, modes of representation and modes of communication. The current wave of explosive debates within the media concerning specific political acts and their social communication now also involves the architectural expression, which cannot be removed from the world of communication systems, to the precise extent that it suffers the direct or indirect fall-out of various 'means of communication', such as the automobile or audiovisual systems.

Basically, along with construction techniques, there's always the construction *of* techniques, that collection of spatial and temporal mutations that is constantly reorganizing both the world of everyday experience and the aesthetic representations of contemporary life. Constructed space, then, is more than simply the concrete and material substance of constructed structures, the permanence of elements and the architectonics of urbanistic details. It also exists as the sudden proliferation and the incessant multiplication of special effects which, along with the consciousness of time and of distances, affect the perception of the environment.

This technological deregulation of various milieux is also topological to the exact extent that – instead of constructing a perceptible and visible chaos, such as the processes of degradation or destruction implied in accident, aging and war – it inversely and paradoxically builds an imperceptible order, which is invisible but just as practical as masonry or the public highways system. In all likelihood, the essence of what we insist on calling urbanism is composed/decomposed by these transfer, transit and transmission systems, these transport and transmigration networks whose immaterial configuration reiterates the cadastral organization and the building of monuments.

If there are any monuments today, they are certainly not of the visible order, despite the twists and turns of architectural excess. No longer part of the order of perceptible appearances nor of the aesthetic of the apparition of volumes assembled under the sun, this monumental disproportion now resides within the obscure luminescence of terminals, consoles and other electronic nightstands. Architecture is more than an array of techniques designed to shelter us from the storm. It is an instrument of measure, a sum total of knowledge that, contending with the natural environment, becomes capable of organizing society's time and space. This geodesic capacity to define a unity of time and place for all actions now enters into direct conflict with the structural capacities of the means of mass communication.

Two procedures confront each other. The first is primarily material, constructed of physical elements, walls, thresholds and levels, all precisely located. The other is immaterial, and hence its representations, images and messages afford neither locale nor stability, since they are the vectors of a

Virilio   momentary, instantaneous expression, with all the manipulated meanings and misinformation that presupposes.

The first one is architectonic and urbanistic in that it organizes and constructs durable geographic and political space. The second haphazardly arranges and deranges space-time, the continuum of societies. The point here is not to propose a Manichaean judgment that opposes the physical to the metaphysical, but rather to attempt to catch the status of contemporary, and particularly urban, architecture within the disconcerting concert of advanced technologies. If architectonics developed with the rise of the City and the discovery and colonization of emerging lands, since the conclusion of that conquest, architecture, like the large cities, has rapidly declined. While continuing to invest in internal technical equipment, architecture has become progressively introverted, becoming a kind of machinery gallery, a museum of sciences and technologies, technologies derived from industrial *machinism,* from the transportation revolution and from so-called 'conquest of space'. So it makes perfect sense that when we discuss space technologies today, we are not referring to architecture but rather to the engineering that launches us into outer space.

All of this occurs as if architectonics had been merely a subsidiary technology, surpassed by other technologies that produced accelerated displacement and sidereal projection. In fact, this is a question of the nature of architectural performance, of the telluric function of the constructed realm and the relationships between a certain cultural technology and the earth. The development of the City as the conservatory of classical technologies has already contributed to the proliferation of architecture through its projection into every spatial direction, with the demographic concentration and the extreme vertical densification of the urban milieu, in direct opposition to the agrarian model. The advanced technologies have since continued to prolong this 'advance', through the thoughtless and all-encompassing expansion of the architectonic, especially with the rise of the means of transportation.

Right now, vanguard technologies, derived from the military conquest of space, are already launching homes, and perhaps tomorrow the City itself, into planetary orbit. With inhabited satellites, space shuttles and space stations as floating laboratories of high-tech research and industry, architecture is flying high, with curious repercussions for the fate of post-industrial societies, in which the cultural markers tend to disappear progressively, what with the decline of the arts and the slow regression of the primary technologies.

Is urban architecture becoming an outmoded technology, as happened to extensive agriculture, from which came the debacles of megalopolis? Will architectonics become simply another decadent form of dominating the earth, with results like those of the uncontrolled exploitation of primary resources? Hasn't the decrease in the number of major cities already become the trope for industrial decline and forced unemployment, symbolizing the failure of scientific materialism?

The recourse to History proposed by experts of postmodernity is a cheap trick that allows them to avoid the question of Time, the regime of transhistorical temporality derived from technological eco-systems. If in fact there is a crisis today, it is a crisis of ethical and aesthetic references, the inability to come to terms with events in an environment where the appearances are against us. With the growing imbalance between direct and indirect information that comes of the development of various means of communication, and its tendency to privilege information mediated to the detriment of meaning, it seems that the *reality effect* replaces immediate reality. Lyotard's modern crisis of grand narratives betrays the effect of new technologies, with the accent, from here on, placed on means more than ends.

The grand narratives of theoretical causality were thus displaced by the petty narratives of practical opportunity, and, finally, by the micro-narratives of autonomy. At issue here is no longer the 'crisis of modernity', the progressive deterioration of commonly held ideals, the proto-foundation of the meaning of History, to the benefit of more-or-less restrained narratives connected to the autonomous development of individuals. The problem now is with the narrative itself, with an official discourse or mode of representation, connected until now with the universally recognized capacity to say, describe and inscribe reality. This is the heritage of the Renaissance. Thus, the crisis in the conceptualization of 'narrative' appears as the other side of the crisis of the conceptualization of 'dimension' as geometrical narrative, the discourse of measurement of a reality visibly offered to all.

The crisis of the grand narrative that gives rise to the micro-narrative finally becomes the crisis of the narrative of the grand and the petty.

This marks the advent of a disinformation in which excess and incommensurability are, for 'postmodernity', what the philosophical resolution of problems and the resolution of the pictorial and architectural image were to the birth of the Enlightenment.

The crisis in the conceptualization of dimension becomes the crisis of the whole.

In other words, the substantial, homogeneous space derived from classical Greek geometry gives way to an accidental, heterogeneous space in which sections and fractions become essential once more. Just as the land suffered the mechanization of agriculture, urban topography has continuously paid the price for the atomization and disintegration of surfaces and of all references that tend towards all kinds of transmigrations and transformations. This sudden exploding of whole forms, this destruction of the properties of the individual by industrialization, is felt less in the city's space – despite the dissolution of the suburbs – than in the time – understood as sequential perceptions – of urban appearances. In fact, transparency has long supplanted appearances. Since the beginning of the twentieth century, the classical depth of field has been revitalized by the depth of time of advanced technologies. Both the film and aeronautics industries took off soon after the ground was broken for the grand boulevards. The parades on Haussmann Boulevard gave way to the Lumière brothers' accelerated motion picture inventions; the esplanades of Les Invalides gave way to the invalidation of the city plan. The screen abruptly became the city square, the crossroads of all mass media.

From the aesthetics of the appearance of a *stable* image – present as an aspect of its static nature – to the aesthetics of the disappearance of an *unstable* image – present in its cinematic and cinematographic flight of escape – we have witnessed a transmutation of representations. The emergence of forms as volumes destined to persist as long as their materials would allow has given way to images whose duration is purely retinal. So, more than Venturi's Las

Virilio   Vegas, it is Hollywood that merits urbanist scholarship, for, after the theatre-cities of Antiquity and of the Italian Renaissance, it was Hollywood that was the first Cinecittà, the city of living cinema where stage-sets and reality, tax-plans and scripts, the living and the living dead, mix and merge deliriously.

Here more than anywhere else advanced technologies combined to form a synthetic space-time.

Babylon of filmic de-formation, industrial zone of pretence, Hollywood was built neighbourhood by neighbourhood, block by block, on the twilight of appearances, the success of magicians' tricks, the rise of epic productions like those of D.W. Griffith, all the while waiting for the megalomaniacal urban-izations of Disneyland, Disney World and Epcot Center. When Francis Ford Coppola, in *One From the Heart,* electronically inlaid his actors into a life-size Las Vegas built at the Zoetrope studios in Hollywood (simply because the director wanted the city to adapt to his shooting schedule instead of the other way around), he overpowered Venturi, not by demonstrating the ambiguities of contemporary architecture, but by showing the 'spectral' characters of the city and its denizens.

The utopian 'architecture on paper' of the 1960s took on the video-electronic special effects of people like Harryhausen and Tumbull, just at the precise instant that computer screens started popping up in architectural firms. 'Video doesn't mean I see; it means I fly,' according to Nam June Paik. With this technology, the 'aerial view' no longer involves the theoretical altitudes of scale models. It has become an opto-electronic interface operating in real time, with all that this implies for the redefinition of the image. If aviation – appearing the same year as cinematography – entailed a revision of point of view and a radical mutation of our perception of the world, infographic technologies will likewise force a readjustment of reality and its representations. We already see this in 'Tactical Mapping Systems', a video-disc produced by the United States Defense Department's Agency for Advanced Research Projects. This system offers a continuous view of Aspen, Colorado, by accelerating or decelerating the speed of 54,000 images, changing direction or season as easily as one switches television channels, turning the town into a kind of shooting gallery in which the functions of eyesight and weaponry melt into each other.

If architectonics once measured itself according to geology, according to the tectonics of natural reliefs, with pyramids, towers and other neo-gothic tricks, today it measures itself according to state-of-the-art technologies, whose vertiginous prowess exiles all of us from the terrestrial horizon.

Neo-geological, the 'Monument Valley' of some pseudo-lithic era, today's metropolis is a phantom landscape, the fossil of past societies whose tech-nologies were intimately aligned with the visible transformation of matter, a project from which the sciences have increasingly turned away.

SOURCES

―――――

PART I MODERNISM

Theodor Adorno
'Functionalism Today', trans. Jane Newman and John Smith, *Oppositions*, no. 17, Summer 1979, pp. 30–41.

Georges Bataille
'Architecture', trans. Paul Hegarty. Original text: 'Architecture', *Dictionnaire Critique*, 1929, 2, p. 117.
'Museum', trans. Paul Hegarty. Original text: 'Musée', *Dictionnaire Critique*, 1930, 5, p. 300.
'Slaughterhouse', trans. Paul Hegarty. Original text: 'Abattoir', *Dictionnaire Critique*, 1929, 6, p. 329.

Walter Benjamin
'On Some Motifs in Baudelaire', *Illuminations*, trans. Harry Zohn, London: Fontana, 1973, Sections 5–8, pp. 162–72.
'Paris, Capital of the Nineteenth Century', *Reflections*, trans. Edmund Jephcott, New York, London: Harcourt Brace Jovanovich, 1978, Sections 1, 4, 5, 6; pp. 146–9; 154–62.

Ernst Bloch
'Formative Education, Engineering Form, Ornament', trans. Jane Newman and John Smith, *Oppositions*, no. 17, Summer 1979, pp. 45–51.

Siegfried Kracauer
'The Hotel Lobby' (extract), *Mass Ornament*, trans. Thomas Levin, Cambridge, Mass.: Harvard University Press, 1995.

'On Employment Exchanges: The Construction of a Space', trans. David Frisby. Original text: 'Über Arbeitsnachweise: Konstruktion eines Raumes', *Schriften*, Band 5.2, ed. Inka Mülder-Bach, Frankfurt am Main: Suhrkamp Verlag, 1990, pp. 185–92.

Georg Simmel

'Bridge and Door', trans. Mark Ritter, *Theory, Culture and Society*, vol. 11 (1994), pp. 5–10.

'The Metropolis and Mental Life', trans. Edward Shils, *Social Sciences III Selections and Selected Readings*, vol. 2, 14th ed., Chicago: Univ. of Chicago Press, 1948, reprinted in On *Individuality and Social Forms*, Donald Levine (ed.), Chicago: Univ. of Chicago Press, 1971, pp. 324–39.

PART II PHENOMENOLOGY

Gaston Bachelard

Poetics of Space (extract), trans. Maria Jolas, Boston: Beacon Press, 1969, pp. 3–20.

Martin Heidegger

'Building, Dwelling, Thinking', *Poetry, Language, Thought*, trans. Albert Hofstadter, New York: Harper & Row, 1971, pp. 143–61.

'. . . Poetically Man Dwells . . .', *Poetry, Language, Thought*, pp. 211–29.

'The Origin of the Work of Art' (extracts), *Poetry, Language, Thought*, pp. 41–3, 58–60.

'Art and Space', trans. Charles Siebert, *Man and World*, 1973, Fall 6, pp. 3–8.

Hans-Georg Gadamer

'The Ontological Foundation of the Occasional and the Decorative', *Truth and Method*, London: Sheed and Ward, pp. 127–42.

Henri Lefebvre

The Production of Space, trans. David Nicholson-Smith, London: Blackwell Publishers, 1991, pp. 220–6, 360–3.

Gianni Vattimo

'The End of Modernity, The End of The Project?', trans. David Webb, *Journal of Philosophy and the Visual Arts*, Academy Editions, pp. 74–7.

'Ornament/Monument', *The End of Modernity*, trans. Jon Snyder, Polity, pp. 79–89.

PART III STRUCTURALISM

Roland Barthes

'Semiology and the Urban', *The City and the Sign*, M. Gottdiener and A. Lagopoulos (eds), New York: Columbia University Press, 1986, pp. 88–98 (with minor amendments).

'The Eiffel Tower', *The Eiffel Tower and Other Mythologies*, trans. Richard Howard, New York: Hill & Wang, 1979, pp. 3–17.

Umberto Eco
'Functionalism and Sign: The Semiotics of Architecture', *The City and The Sign*, M. Gottdiener and A. Lagopoulos (eds), New York: Columbia Univ. Press, 1986, pp. 56–85.
'How an Exposition Exposes Itself', *Travels in Hyperreality*, trans. William Weaver, London: Pan Books, 1987, pp. 296–9.

PART IV POSTMODERNISM

Jean Baudrillard
'The Beaubourg-Effect: Implosion and Deterrence', trans. R. Krauss, A Michelson, *October*, 20, pp. 3–13.
'America', *Simulacra and Simulations*, trans. Sheila Faria Glaser, Michigan: Univ. of Michigan Press, 1984, pp. 12–13, 91–2; *America*, trans. Chris Turner, London: Verso, 1988, pp. 2–3, 16–18, 30–1, 59–60, 123–5.

Jürgen Habermas
'Modern and Post-Modern Architecture', trans. Helen Tsoskounglou, *9H*, No. 4, 1982, pp. 9–14.

Fredric Jameson
'The Cultural Logic of Late Capitalism', *Postmodernism, or the Cultural Logic of Late Capitalism*, London: Verso, 1991, pp. 1–6, 38–45.
'The Constraints of Postmodernism' (extract), *The Seeds of Time*, New York: Columbia Univ. Press, 1994, pp. 189–205.
'Is Space Political?', Cynthia Davidson (ed.), *Anyplace*, Cambridge, Mass.: MIT Press, 1995, pp. 192–205.

Jean-François Lyotard
'*Domus* and the Megalopolis', *The Inhuman*, trans. Geoffrey Bennington and Rachel Bowlby, Cambridge: Polity Press, 1991, pp. 191–204.

PART V POSTSTRUCTURALISM

Andrew Benjamin
'Eisenman and the Housing of Tradition', *Art, Mimesis and the Avant-Garde*, London: Routledge, 1991, pp. 107–29.

Hélène Cixous
'Attacks of the Castle', trans. Eric Prenowitz. Previously unpublished.

Gilles Deleuze
'Postscript on the Societies of Control', *October*, 59, 1992, pp. 3–8.

'City/State' (with Félix Guattari), trans. Brian Massumi, *Zone 1/2*, pp. 195–9.

Jacques Derrida
'Point de Folie – maintenant l'architecture', trans. Kate Linker, *AA Files*, No. 12, Summer 1986, pp. 65–75.
'Why Peter Eisenman Writes Such Good Books', trans. Sarah Whiting, *Architecture and Urbanism*, August 1988.
'Architecture Where the Desire May Live', interview with Eva Meyer, *Domus*, vol. 671, 1986, pp. 17–25.

Michel Foucault
'Of Other Spaces: Utopias and Heterotopias', *Lotus*, 48/9, 1985/6, pp. 9–17.
'Space, Knowledge, Power', interview with Paul Rabinow, trans. Christian Hubert, *Skyline,* March 1982.
'Panopticism', *Discipline and Punish*, trans. Alan Sheridan, London: Penguin, 1977, pp. 195–228.

Paul Virilio
'The Overexposed City', *Lost Dimension*, trans. Daniel Moshenberg, New York: Semiotext(e), 1991, pp. 9–27.

SELECTED BIBLIOGRAPHY OF MAJOR WRITINGS

―――――

PART I MODERNISM

Theodor Adorno
The Dialectic of the Enlightenment (1947) (with Max Horkheimer), trans. John Cumming, New York: Continuum, 1972.
Minima Moralia (1951), trans. E. F. N. Jephcott, London: Verso, 1978.
The Jargon of Authenticity (1964), trans. Knut Tarnowski, London: Routledge & Kegan Paul, 1973.
Negative Dialectics (1966), trans. E. B. Ashton, London: Routledge & Kegan Paul, 1973.
Prisms (1967), trans. Samuel and Shierry Weber, Cambridge, Mass: MIT Press, 1981.
Aesthetic Theory (1970), trans. C. Lenhardt, London: Routledge & Kegan Paul, 1984.
The Culture Industry, J. M. Bernstein (ed.), London: Routledge, 1991.

Georges Bataille
The Story of the Eye by Lord Auch (1928), trans. Joachim Neugroschal, Harmonsworth: Penguin Books, 1982.
The Accursed Share (1949), Vol. 1, trans. Robert Hurley, New York: Zone Books, 1988.
Eroticism (1957), trans. Mary Dalwood, London and New York: Marion Boyars, 1987.
Visions of Excess: Selected Writings, 1927–1939, ed. Alan Stoekl, trans. Alan Stoekl, Carl R. Lovitt and Donald M. Leslie, Jr, Minneapolis: University of Minnesota Press, 1985.
Theory of Religion, trans. Robert Hurley, New York: Zone Books, 1989.

Walter Benjamin
Illuminations, trans. Harry Zohn, London: Fontana, 1973.
Reflections, trans. Edmund Jephcott, New York: Schocken Books, 1978.
One-Way Street and Other Writings, trans. Edmund Jephcott, London: Verso, 1985.

Ernst Bloch
The Principle of Hope, trans. Neville Plaice, Stephen Plaice and Paul Knight, 3 vols, Oxford: Basil Blackwell, 1981.
The Utopian Function of Art and Literature, trans. Jack Zipes and Frank Mecklenburg, Cambridge, Mass.: MIT Press, 1988.

Siegfried Kracauer
From Caligari to Hitler, Princeton, 1947.
Theory of Film: The Redemption of Physical Reality, New York, 1960.
History, (completed by Paul Oskar Kristeller), Oxford: Oxford University Press, 1969.
Mass Ornament, trans. Thomas Levin, Cambridge, Mass.: Harvard University Press, 1995.

Georg Simmel
On Individuality and Social Forms, Donald Levine (ed.), Chicago: University of Chicago Press, 1971.
On Women, Sexuality and Love, trans. Guy Oakes, New Haven and London: Yale University Press, 1984.
The Philosophy of Money (1900), trans. Tom Bottomore and David Frisby, London: Routledge, 1990.

General
Adorno, Benjamin, Bloch and Lukacs, *Aesthetics and Politics*, foreword by Fredric Jameson, translation editor: Ronald Taylor, London: Verso, 1980.
Buck-Morss, Susan *The Dialectics of Seeing: Walter Benjamin and the Arcades Project*, Cambridge, Mass.: MIT Press, 1991.
Frisby, David *Fragments of Modernity: Theories of Modernity in the Work of Simmel, Kracauer and Benjamin*, London: Routledge, 1988.
Gilloch, Graeme *Myth and Metropolis: Walter Benjamin and the City*, Cambridge: Polity Press, 1995.

PART II PHENOMENOLOGY

Gaston Bachelard
The Psychoanalysis of Fire (1938), trans. Alan Ross, Boston: Beacon Press, 1964; London: Routledge & Kegan Paul, 1964.
Poetics of Space, trans. Maria Jolas, Boston: Beacon Press, 1969.
Water and Dreams: An Essay on the Imagination of Matter, trans. Edith R. Farrell, Dallas: Pegasus Foundation, Dallas Institute of Humanities and Culture, 1983.

Martin Heidegger
Poetry, Language, Thought, trans. Albert Hofstadter, London: Harper and Row, 1971.
The Question Concerning Technology and Other Essays, trans. William Lovitt, London: Harper and Row, 1977.
Nietzsche, trans. David Farrell Krell, London: Harper and Row, 1987.

The Metaphysical Foundations of Logic, trans. Michael Heim, Bloomington, Indiana: Indiana University Press, 1984.

The Basic Problems of Philology, trans. Albert Hofstadter, Bloomington, Indiana: Indiana University Press, 1982.

Hegel's Phenomenology of Spirit, trans. Parvis Emad and Kenneth Maly, Bloomington, Indiana: Indiana University Press, 1988.

The Concept of Time, trans. William McNeill, Oxford: Blackwell Publishers, 1992.

Basic Writings, David Farrell Krell (ed.), London: Routledge, 1993.

Hans-Georg Gadamer

Hegel's Dialectic, trans. P. Christopher Smith, New Haven: Yale University Press, 1976.

Truth and Method, trans. William Glen-Doepel, London: Sheed and Ward, 1979.

Dialogue and Dialectic, trans. P. Christopher Smith, New Haven: Yale University Press, 1980.

Reason in the Age of Science, trans. Frederick G. Lawrence, Cambridge, Mass.: MIT Press, 1981.

The Idea of the Good in Platonic and Aristotelian Philosophy, trans. P. Christopher Smith, New Haven: Yale University Press, 1986.

The Relevance of the Beautiful and Other Essays, trans. Nicholas Walker, Cambridge: Cambridge University Press, 1986.

Henri Lefebvre

Everyday Life in the Modern World, trans. Sacha Rabinovitch, London: Allen Lane, 1971.

The Critique of Everyday Life, trans. John Moore, London: Verso, 1991.

The Production of Space, trans. David Nicholson-Smith, Oxford: Blackwell Publishers, 1991.

Writings on Cities, trans. and eds Eleonore Kofman and Elizabeth Lebas, Oxford: Blackwell Publishers, 1996.

Gianni Vattimo

The End of Modernity, trans. Jon R. Snyder, Cambridge: Polity Press, 1988.

The Transparent Society, trans. David Webb, Cambridge: Polity Press, 1992.

The Adventure of Difference: Philosophy After Nietzsche and Heidegger, trans. Cyprian Blamires with Thomas Harrison, Cambridge: Polity Press, 1993.

General

Norberg-Schulz, Christian *Genius Loci: Towards a Phenomenology of Architecture*, London: Academy Editions, 1980.

Pérez-Gómez, Alberto *Architecture and the Crisis of Modern Science*, Cambridge, Mass.: MIT Press, 1983.

Romanyshyn, Robert *Technology as Symptom and Dream*, London: Routledge, 1989.

PART III STRUCTURALISM

Roland Barthes
Mythologies (1957), trans. Annette Lavers, St Albans: Paladin, 1973.
The Pleasure of the Text, trans. Richard Miller, New York: Moonday Press, 1975.
The Eiffel Tower and Other Mythologies, trans. Richard Howard, New York: Hill & Wang, 1979.
The Fashion System (1967), trans. Matthew Ward and Richard Howard, New York: Hill & Wang, 1983.
S/Z (1970), trans. Richard Miller, New York: Hill & Wang, 1974.
The Empire of the Sign (1970), trans. Richard Howard, New York: Hill & Wang, 1982.
Image, Music, Text, trans. Stephen Heath, London: Fontana, 1977
The Semiotic Challenge, trans. Richard Howard, Oxford: Basil Blackwell, 1988.
Camera Lucida: Reflections on Photography, trans. Richard Howard, London: Vintage, 1993.

Umberto Eco
A Theory of Semiotics, Bloomington: Indiana University Press, 1976.
The Name of the Rose, trans. William Weaver, New York: Harcourt Brace Jovanovich, 1983.
Semiotics and the Philosophy of Language, London: Macmillan, 1984.
Art and Beauty in the Middle Ages, trans. Hugh Bredin, New Haven and London: Yale University Press, 1986.
Travels in Hyperreality, London: Pan Books, 1987.
The Aesthetics of Thomas Aquinas, trans. Hugh Bredin, London: Radius, 1988.
Foucault's Pendulum, trans. William Weaver, London: Secker and Warburg, 1989.
The Limits of Interpretation, Bloomington, Indiana: Indiana University Press, 1990.
Misreadings, trans. William Weaver, London: Cape, 1993.

General
Baird, George and Jencks, Charles (eds), *Meaning in Architecture*, London, 1969.
Broadbent, Geoffrey, Bunt, Richard and Jencks, Charles (eds), *Signs, Symbols and Architecture*, Chichester: Wiley, 1980.
Gottdiener, M. and Lagopoulos, A. P. (eds), *The City and The Sign: An Introduction to Urban Semiotics*, New York: Columbia University Press, 1986.
Lynch, Kevin *A Theory of Good City Form*, Cambridge, Mass.: MIT Press, 1981.
Rykwert, Joseph *The Idea of a Town*, Cambridge, Mass.: MIT Press, 1976.

PART IV POSTMODERNISM

Jean Baudrillard
The System of Objects (1968), trans. James Benedict, London: Verso, 1996.
For a Critique of the Political Economy of the Sign (1972), trans. Charles Levin, St Louis: Telos, 1981.
The Mirror of Production (1973), trans. Mark Poster, St Louis: Telos, 1975.

Symbolic Exchange and Death (1976), trans. Ian Grant, London: Sage, 1993.
Seduction (1979), trans. Brian Singer, London: MacMillan, 1990.
Fatal Strategies: Crystal Revenge (1983), trans. Philip Beitchman and W. G. J. Niesluchowski, London: Pluto, 1990.
America (1986), trans. Chris Turner, London: Verso, 1989.
Cool Memories (1987), trans. Chris Turner, London: Verso, 1990.
The Transparency of Evil: Essays in Extreme Phenomena (1990), trans. John J. St John, London: Verso, 1993.
Baudrillard Live: Selected Interviews, ed. Mike Gane, London: Routledge, 1993.

Jürgen Habermas
Legitimation Crisis (1973), trans. Thomas McCarthy, Boston: Beacon Press, 1975.
The Theory of Communicative Action, Volume 1. Reason and Rationalization on Society (1981), trans. Thomas McCarthy, Boston: Beacon Press, 1984.
The Theory of Communicative Action, Volume 2. A Critique of Functionalist Reason (1981), trans. Thomas McCarthy, Boston: Beacon Press, 1987.
The Philosophical Discourse of Modernity (1985), trans. Frederick Lawrence, Cambridge: Polity Press, 1987.

Fredric Jameson
Marxism and Form, Princeton: Princeton University Press, 1971.
The Prison-House of Language, Princeton: Princeton University Press, 1972.
The Political Unconscious: Narrative as a Socially Symbolic Act, London: Methuen, 1981.
Late Marxism: Adorno and the Persistence of the Dialectic, London: Verso, 1990.
Signatures of the Visible, London: Routledge, 1990.
Postmodernism, or the Cultural Logic of Late Capitalism, London: Verso, 1991.
The Geopolitical Aesthetic: Cinema and Space in the World System, Bloomington, Indiana, Indiana University Press; London: BFI, 1992.
The Seeds of Time, New York: Columbia University Press, 1994.

Jean-François Lyotard
Libidinal Economy (1974), trans. Iain Hamilton Grant, Bloomington, Indiana: Indiana University Press, 1993.
Just Gaming (with Jean-Loup Thébaud) (1979), trans. Wlad Godzich, Minneapolis: Minnesota University Press; Manchester: Manchester University Press, 1984.
The Postmodern Condition (1988), trans. Geoffrey Bennington and Brian Massumi, Minneapolis: Minnesota University Press; Manchester: Manchester University Press, 1984.
The Differend: Phrases in Dispute (1983), trans. George ven den Abeele, Minneapolis: Minnesota University Press; Manchester: Manchester University Press, 1984.
Heidegger and 'the jews' (1988), trans. Andreas Michel and Mark Roberts, Minneapolis: Minnesota University Press, 1990.
The Inhuman: Reflections on Time (1988), trans. Geoffrey Bennington and Rachel Bowlby, Cambridge: Polity Press, 1991.

General

Foster, Hal (ed.), *The Anti-Aesthetic*, Seattle: Bay Press, 1983.
Harvey, David *The Condition of Post-Modernity*, Oxford: Blackwell, 1989.
Jencks, Charles *The Language of Post-Modern Architecture*, London: Academy, 1977.
Kolb, David *Postmodern Sophistications: Philosophy, Architecture and Tradition*, Chicago: University of Chicago Press, 1990.

PART V POSTSTRUCTURALISM

Andrew Benjamin

Art, Mimesis and the Avant-Garde: Aspects of a Philosophy of Difference, London: Routledge, 1991.
The Plural Event: Descartes, Hegel, Heidegger, London: Routledge, 1993.
Translation and the Nature of Philosophy: A New Theory of Words, London: Routledge, 1993.
Object Painting, London: Academy Editions, 1995.
What is Abstraction?, London: Academy Editions, 1996.

Hélène Cixous

Angst, trans. Jo Levy, London: Calder, 1985.
The Newly Born Woman, (with Catherine Clément), trans. Betsy Wing, Manchester: Manchester University Press, 1986.
Reading with Clarice Lispector, trans. Verena Andermatt Conley, Hemel Hempstead: Harvester Wheatsheaf, 1990.
'Coming to Writing' and Other Essays, trans. Sarah Cornell *et al.*, Cambridge, Mass.: Harvard University Press, 1991.
Readings: The Poetics of Blanchot, Joyce, Kafka, Kleist, Lispector and Tsvetayeva, trans. Verena Andermatt Conley, Hemel Hempstead: Harvester Wheatsheaf, 1992.

Gilles Deleuze

Anti-Oedipus: Capitalism and Schizophrenia (1972) (with Felix Guattari), trans. Robert Hurley, M. Seem and H. R. Lane, New York: Viking Press/A Richard Sever Book, 1977.
Kafka: Towards a Minor Literature (1975) (with Felix Guattari), trans. Dana Polan, Minneapolis: University of Minnesota Press, 1986.
A Thousand Plateaus: Capitalism and Schizophrenia (1980) (with Felix Guattari), trans. Brian Massumi, Minneapolis: University of Minnesota Press, 1987.
The Fold: Leibniz and the Baroque (1988), trans. Tom Conley, Minneapolis: University of Minnesota Press, 1992.
Negotiations, trans. Martin Joughin, New York: Columbia University Press, 1995.

Jacques Derrida

Of Grammatology (1967), trans. Gayatri Spivak, Baltimore and London: Johns Hopkins University Press, 1976.
Writing and Difference (1967), trans. Alan Bass, Chicago: University of Chicago Press,

1978.

Positions (1972), trans. Alan Bass, Chicago: University of Chicago Press, 1982.

The Truth in Painting (1978), trans. Geoff Bennington and Ian McLeod, Chicago: University of Chicago Press, 1987.

Spurs: Nietzsche's Styles (1978), trans. Barbara Harlow, Chicago: University of Chicago Press, 1979.

The Postcard: From Socrates to Freud and Beyond (1980), trans. Alan Bass, Chicago: University of Chicago Press, 1987.

Limited Inc., Evanston, Il.: Northwestern University Press, 1988.

Given Time: Counterfeit Money, trans. Peggy Kamuf, Chicago: University of Chicago Press, 1992.

Memoirs of the Blind: the Self-Portrait and Other Ruins, trans. Pascale-Anne Brault and Michael Naas, Chicago: University of Chicago Press, 1993.

Specters of Marx (1993), trans. Peggy Kamuf, London: Routledge, 1994.

Michel Foucault

Madness and Civilisation: A History of Insanity in the Age of Reason (1961), trans. Richard Howard, New York: Vintage, 1973.

The Birth of the Clinic: An Archaeology of Medical Perception (1963), trans. Alan Sheridan, New York: Vintage, 1975.

The Order of Things: An Archaeology of Human Sciences (1966), New York: Vintage, 1973.

An Archaeology of Knowledge (1969), trans. Alan Sheridan, London: Tavistock, 1974.

Discipline and Punish: The Birth of the Prison (1975), trans. Alan Sheridan, London: Penguin, 1977.

The History of Sexuality, Volume 1: An Introduction (1976), trans. Robert Hurley, London: Allen Lane, 1979.

The History of Sexuality, Volume 2: The Use of Pleasure (1984), trans. Robert Hurley, New York: Pantheon, 1985.

The History of Sexuality, Volume 3: The Care of the Self (1984), trans. Robert Hurley, New York: Pantheon, 1986.

Foucault Reader, Paul Rabinow (ed.), New York: Pantheon, 1984.

Paul Virilio

War and Cinema: The Logistics of Perception, trans. Patrick Camiller, London: Verso, 1989.

Lost Dimension, trans. Daniel Moshenberg, New York: Semiotext(e), 1991.

The Aesthetics of Disappearance, trans. Philip Beitchman, New York: Semiotext(e), 1991.

The Vision Machine, trans. Julie Rose, Bloomington, Indiana: Indiana University Press; London: BFI, 1994.

The Art of the Motor, trans. Julie Rose, Minneapolis: University of Minnesota Press, 1995.

General

Gasché, Rudolph *The Tain of the Mirror: Derrida and the Philosophy of Reflection*, Cambridge, Mass.: Harvard University Press, 1986.

Michelfelder, Diana P. and Palmer, Richard E. (eds), *Dialogue and Deconstruction: The Gadamer-Derrida Encounter*, Albany, New York: SUNY, 1989.

Papadakis, Andreas, Cooke, Catherine and Benjamin, Andrew (eds), *Deconstruction Omnibus Edition*, London: Academy, 1989.

Wigley, Mark *The Architecture of Deconstruction: Derrida's Haunt*, Cambridge, Mass.: MIT Press, 1993.

INDEX